Lonely Planet

This book is, in terms of people involved, research undertaken and expense, the biggest project we've yet tackled at Lonely Planet. It has involved three writer-researchers who spent a total of over a year 'on the road' in India gathering the information for this book. On top of that it has taken a great amount of time in drawing maps and doing additional desk research. As usual we're more than grateful for the many people who sent us in additional information and suggestions and for the advice and assistance offered by other travellers whom we met along the way. The feedback we get from our fellow travellers is probably the nicest aspect of producing our guidebooks.

Lonely Planet started in the early '70s when Tony and Maureen Wheeler made a lengthy overland trip and turned their experiences and the information they had gathered into the first edition of *Across Asia on the Cheap*. Since then Lonely Planet has grown to a list of 20 travel guides, many of them unique, a permanent office in Melbourne, Australia and, most important of all, thousands of 'our' travellers out there on the road.

The Authors (see page 695)

The Other People

As usual many other people have provided many other inputs to this book. In particular the delightful cartoons of Indian life are by Tony Jenkins, cartoonist for the Toronto Globe & Mail in Canada. If you like them please tell us because we think they're terrific and, since Tony has drawn many more travelling cartoons, would very much like to put a travellers' sketch book together. Peter Campbell, a long term Lonely Planet helper and contributor, provided a number of drawings for the book and also some of the colour pictures. The cover, which we really like, is also Peter's work. English traveller Mark Carter dropped into our office in Melbourne one day and soon had us all enthused about tracking down old steam engines in India — he wrote the section on 'gricing'. David Stanley, an inveterate traveller and co-author of the excellent *South Pacific Handbook*, provided us with his meticulous notes from several trips to India. He managed to cover a number of places which none of our writers got to. Finally Davindra Garbyal, an experienced trek leader in the Garwhal Himal region, provided us with the information for trekking in that area.

Other thank yous must go to Jane Siegal for information provided to Geoff in India, to Eileen Mills who helped him put his section together and Jim and Alison Hart for hospitality while he was in Melbourne working on the book. Tony and Maureen would like to thank Ashok Khann, a long term friend who went up to Kashmir with them. Wing Commander R N Bhargava, manager of the Jaipur Inn in Jaipur, provided a great deal of assistance to Tony and Maureen while they were in that city. Iqbal, manager of the houseboats Bambari Palace and New Lucky Kashmir, pulled strings to get them on the over-booked Srinagar-Leh flight for which many thanks. The Rajasthan State Tourist Office were extremely helpful to Tony and Maureen throughout their travels in that state. Indeed they were the most helpful 'official organisation' in all of India and thanks must go to the Director of Tourism in Rajasthan, Mr Rajendra Pal Singh, and to the knowledgeable and helpful tourist officers at Khota (S S Shekhawat), Chittor (S K Saxena) and Jodhpur (Rajendra Singh Shekhawat). Delhi Transport also provided Prakash A Raj with bus travel on one of their tours.

Apart from the Rajasthan Tourist Office and Delhi Transport this book has had no official support whatsoever. All expenses in India, all travel expenditure within India, all air fares to and from India have been paid for just like any member of the public. Indian Airlines being Indian Airlines we actually paid for flights within India which were not taken and they would only provide a list of their office addresses and numbers with the greatest reluctance and bad grace.

Last but not least thanks has to go out to those most important people, 'our travellers'. To all of you who took the time to write to us with information and suggestions about India our grateful thanks. Particularly to Janet & Roger Jeffreys (Aus), Alan Samagalski (Aus), Dave & Sally Hillebrandt (UK), Keith & Sue Sillitoe (Aus), Pauline & Martine Hall (UK), John King (UK), Roger Stoddart (UK), Richard Goransen (C), Ronald & Kathy Ralemen (USA), Kaye Cumming (Aus), Soo Town & Dimitris Pantelidis (Gr), Jean Moir (UK), J Foster (NZ), John Daniels (Aus), Roger Suddaby (UK), Myrtle & Monty Berman, Angus Lindsay (UK), Michael Wall & Lizzie Slater, Tony & Lena Cansdale (Aus).

Aus = Australia, UK = UK, C = Canada, USA = USA, NZ = NZ, Gr = Greece.

And the Next Edition
Travel guides are only kept up to date by travelling. Corrections, suggestions, improvements and additions are all greatly appreciated and the best letters score a free copy of the next edition, or any other Lonely Planet guide if you prefer.

India
a travel survival kit

India — a travel survival kit

Published by
Lonely Planet Publications
PO Box 88, South Yarra
Victoria 3141, Australia

Typeset by
Lonely Planet Publications

Printed by
Colorcraft Ltd,
Hong Kong

Photographs by
Tony Wheeler — 96A, 128AB, 129ABC, 193AB, 224ABC, 225AB, 288BC, 289B, 320ABC,
321AB, 609AB
Peter Campbell — 97ABC, 192AB, 289C, 288A, 289A
Geoff Crowther — 193C, 321C, 576ABC, 577AB, 608ABC, 609C
Mark Carter — 96B

Cartoons by
Tony Jenkins

Cover miniature & other illustrations by
Peter Campbell

Design by
Andrena Millen

First Published
October 1981

Crowther, Geoff.
India — a travel survival kit.

Includes index.
ISBN 0 908086 23 7.

1. India — Description and travel — 1947 - —
Guide-books. I. Raj, Prakash A.,
II. Wheeler, Tony. III. Title.

915.4'0452

Contents

Introduction

India, it is often said, is not a country but a continent. From north to south and east to west the people are different, the languages are different, the customs are different, the country is different. There are few countries on earth with the enormous variety that India has to offer and it's a place which somehow gets into your blood. Love it or hate it you can never ignore India. It's not an easy country to handle and more than a few visitors are only too happy to finally be getting on that aircraft and flying away. Yet a year later they'll be hankering to get back.

It all comes back to that amazing variety — it's as vast as it is crowded, as luxurious as it is squalid, the plains are as flat and featureless as the Himalayas are high and spectacular, the food is as terrible as it can be magnificent, the transport as exhilarating as it can be boring and uncomfortable. Nothing is ever quite the way you expect it to be.

India is far from the easiest country in the world to travel around. It can be hard going, the poverty will get you down, Indian bureaucracy would try the patience of even a Hindu saint and the most experienced travellers find themselves at the end of their tempers at some point in India. Yet it's all worth it.

Very briefly India is a triangle with the top formed by the mighty Himalayan mountain chain. Here you will find the intriguing Tibetan region of Ladakh and the astonishingly beautiful Himalayan areas of Kashmir, Himachal Pradesh, the Garwhal Himal of Uttar Pradesh and the Darjeeling and Sikkim regions. South of this stretch the flat Ganges basin with the colourful and comparatively affluent Punjab to the north-west, the capital city New Delhi and important tourist attractions like Agra (with the Taj Mahal), Khajuraho, Varanasi and the holy Ganges itself. This plain reaches

IN INDIA · LESSON ONE

GOLDEN HANDSHAKE Passing a temple a seedy looking type is all smiles and shoots out a warm handshake; very impolite to refuse, you clasp hands... CAUGHT! A vice grip holds you and quick as you can say 'baksheesh' a religious bracelet is fastened to your wrist. You can pay one rupee or be a boor and tear it off. Henceforth, near temples, keep your hands in your pockets & nod.

the sea at the northern end of the Bay of Bengal where you find teeming Calcutta, a city which seems to sum up all India's enormous problems.

South of this northern plain the Deccan plateau rises. Here you will find cities that tell of the rise and fall of the Hindu and Moslem kingdoms and the modern metropolis that their successors, the British, built at Bombay. India's story is one of many different kingdoms competing with each other and this is never more clear than in places like Bijapur, Mandu, Golconda and other centres of central India. Finally there is the steamy south where Moslem influence only reached fleetingly. Here Hinduism was least altered by outside influences and is at its most exuberant. The temple towns of the south are quite unlike those of the north and superbly colourful.

Basically India is what you make of it and what you want it to be. If you want temples there are temples in profusion and with enough styles and types to confuse anybody. If it's history you want India has plenty of it and the forts, abandoned cities, ruins, battlefields and monuments all have their tales to tell. If you want to simply lie on the beach there are enough of those to satisfy the most avid sun worshipper. If walking and the open air is your thing then head for the trekking routes of the Himalayas, some of them are as wild and deserted as you could ask for. If you simply want to meet the real India you'll come face to face with it all the time — on Indian trains and buses getting there may not always be half the fun but it certainly is half the experience. A visit to India is just that, it's not a place you simply and clinically 'see'. India is a total experience, an assault on all the senses, a place you'll never forget.

Facts about the Country

India is the home for one of the world's 'great' civilisations — its social structures as it exists today can be traced back thousands of years and empires of great size and complexity existed here far earlier than anything comparable in Europe. Yet India as an entity is a comparatively recent invention put together by the British. Even the mightiest of India's ancient civilisations did not encompass all of modern India and today India is still as much a country of diversities as unities. Few people in the Tamil speaking south speak Hindi, the national language, for example. Beyond India's own history and development its role as the birth place for two of the world's great religions is enough to ensure its historical importance.

Indus Valley Civilisation

India's first major civilisation flourished for a thousand years from around 2500 BC along the Indus River valley in what is now Pakistan. Its great cities were Mohenjodaro and Harappa and here a civilisation of great complexity developed. The major city sites were only discovered during this century but subsequently other, lesser, cities have been unearthed at sites like Lothal, near Ahmedabad in India. The Indus Valley cities were ruled by a religious group rather than by kings but the most interesting thing about these cities was their highly developed city engineering. Four thousand years ago they already had a sophisticated drainage system and even organised garbage collection! Despite the extensive excavations conducted at the sites comparatively little is known about the development and eventual demise of this civilisation. Their script has still not been deciphered nor is it known why such an advanced civilisation collapsed so quickly with the invasion of the Aryans.

Early Invasions

The early Aryan invasions were vague and disjointed although the people of north India today are defined as Aryans while those of the south as Dravidians. The Aryans came from the north from around 1500 BC and gradually spread across India from the Punjab and Sind (now in Pakistan) and down the Ganges towards Bengal. Under Darius (521-486 BC) the Punjab and Sind became part of the Persian empire but this was still peripheral to India itself. Alexander the Great reached India, in his epic march from Greece, in 326 BC but his troops refused to march further than the Beas River, the easternmost extent of the Persian empire he had conquered, and he turned back without extending his power into India itself. The most lasting reminder of his appearance in the east was the development of Gandharan art, that strange mixture of Graecian artistic ideals with the new religious beliefs of Buddhism.

The Rise of Religions

Two great religions have had their birth on the sub-continent — Buddhism and Hinduism. The Hindu religion is one of the oldest in the world. Even the priest dominated Indus Valley civilisation bears many similarities to Hinduism. The great Hindu books are all thought to refer to actual historical events. The Vedas, written around 1500 to 1200 BC, tell of the victory of Brahma over Indra, the god of thunder and battle. This probably refers to the revival of Brahmanism (the predecessor of Hinduism from which Hinduism evolved) following the Aryan invasions.

Hinduism has had a series of declines and revivals, most recently during the past century, but the greatest challenge it has faced came from India's other great religion, Buddhism. First formulated around 500 BC Buddhism enjoyed spectacular growth after Ashoka embraced it but it lost touch with the general population and faded as Hinduism revived between 200 and 800 AD. India has also been the birthplace of Jainism, a religion contemporary with Buddhism and bearing many similarities to it, but Jainism has never had a following outside India. The Sikhs are a much more recent creation.

The Mauryas & Ashoka

Two centuries before Alexander made his long march east an Indian kingdom had started to develop in the north of India. It expanded into the vacuum created by Alexander's departure when Chandragupta Maurya's empire came to power in 321 BC. From its capital at the site of present day Patna the Mauryan empire eventually spread right across northern India. Under the Emperor Ashoka, one of the classic figures of Indian history, it reached its peak. In 262 BC Ashoka was converted to Buddhism. Throughout his kingdom Ashoka left pillars and rock carved edicts and these delineate to this day the enormous span of his empire. Ashokan edicts and pillars can be seen in Delhi, in Gujurat, in Orissa, at Sarnath in Bihar and at Sanchi in Madhya Pradesh. He also sent missions abroad and in Sri Lanka his name is revered since he sent his brother forth as a missionary to carry Buddhism to that land. The development of art and sculpture also flourished during his rule and his standard, which topped many of his pillars, is now the seal of the modern state of India. Under Ashoka the Mauryan empire controlled more of India than, probably, any subsequent ruler prior to the British. Yet following his death in 232 BC the empire rapidly disintegrated and finally collapsed in 184 BC.

An Interlude, then the Guptas

A number of empires rose and fell following the collapse of the Mauryas. The successors to Alexander's kingdoms in the north-east expanded their power into the Punjab and this later developed into the Gandharan kingdom. In the south-east and east the Andhras or Telugus expanded inland from the coast while the Mauryan empire was directly replaced by the Sungas who ruled from 184 to 70 BC. During this period many more Buddhist structures were completed and the great cave temples of central India were commenced. This was the period of the lesser vehicle or Hinayana Buddhism where the Buddha could never be directly shown but was alluded to through symbols such as stupas, footprints, trees or elephants. Although this form of Buddhism probably continued until about 400 AD it was already being supplanted by 100 AD by the greater vehicle or Mahayana Buddhism.

In 319 AD Chandragupta II founded the Gupta empire, the first phase of which became known as the Imperial Guptas. His successors extended their power over northern India, first from Patna and later from other capitals in north India, such as Ayodhya. The Imperial Guptas gave way to the later Guptas in 455 AD but the Gupta period continued to 606 AD. The arts flourished during the Gupta period with some of the finest work being done at Ajanta, Ellora, Sanchi and Sarnath and poetry and literature also experiencing a golden age. Towards the end of the Gupta period, however, Buddhism and Jainism both began to decline and Hinduism began to rise in popularity once more. The invasions of the White Huns signalled the end of this period of history although at first they were repelled by the Guptas. They had earlier driven the Gandharas from the north-east region, close to Peshawar, into Kashmir. North India broke up into a number of separate Hindu kingdoms and was not really unified again until the coming of the Moslems.

Meanwhile in the South

A continuing theme of Indian history has been that events in one part of the country do not necessarily effect those in another. The kingdoms that rose and fell in the north of the country generally had no influence or connection with those in the south. While Buddhism, and to a lesser extent Jainism, was displacing Hinduism in the centre and north of India, Hinduism continued to flourish in the south. The south's prosperity was based upon its long established trading links with other civilisations. The Egyptians and later the Romans both traded by sea with the south of India and later strong links were formed with South-East Asia. For a time Buddhism and later Hinduism flourished in the Indonesian islands and the people of the region looked towards India as their cultural mentor. The Ramayana, that most famous of Hindu epics, is even today told and retold in various forms in many south-east Asian countries. Yet outside influences also came to the south of India. In 52 AD St Thomas the Apostle is said to have arrived in Kerala and to this day there is a strong Christian influence in this region.

Great empires that rose in the south included the Cholas, the Pandyas, the Cheras, the Chalukyas and the Pallavas. The Chalukyas ruled mainly over the Deccan region of central India although at times their power extended further north. With a capital at Badami in Karnataka they ruled from 550 to 753 AD before falling to the Rashtrakutas only to rise again in 972 and continued their rule through to 1190. Further south the Pallavas pioneered the form of Dravidian architecture with its exuberant, almost baroque style. They also carried Indian culture to Java in Indonesia, to Thailand and Cambodia. In 850 AD the Cholas rose to power and gradually superseded the Pallavas. They too were great builders as their temple at Tanjore indicates. They also carried their power overseas with raids into Ceylon and a long-running war with the Sumatran based Srivijaya empire. At times they actually controlled part of Sumatra and the Malay peninsula.

The First Moslem Invasions

While the Hindu kingdoms were ruled in the south and Buddhism was rising and falling in the north, Moslem power was creeping towards India from the Middle East. It was in 622 AD that Mohammed fled from Mecca and 630 AD when he marched back in and started Islam's period of rapid expansion. Less than a century later there were raids to the Sind and even Gujarat by Arabs carrying, as Mohammed had recommended, the Koran and the sword. Moslem power first made itself strongly felt on the sub-continent with the raids of Mahmud of Ghazni. Today Ghazni is just a grubby little town between Kabul and Kandahar in Afghanistan but from 1001 Mahmud conducted raids on a virtually annual basis. His army would descend upon India destroying infidel temples and carrying off everything of value that could be moved. In 1033, after his death, one of his successors actually took Varanasi but in 1038 the Seljuk Turks, also expanding eastwards, took Ghazni and the raids into India soon ceased.

These early visits were no more than banditry and it was not until 1192 that Moslem power arrived on a permanent basis. In that year Mohammed of Ghori, who had been expanding his powers across the Punjab, broke into India and took Ajmer. The following year his general Qutb-ud-din took Varanasi and then Delhi and, after Mohammed of Ghori was killed in 1206, he became the first of the

Sultans of Delhi. Within 20 years they had brought the whole of the Ganges basin under their control but the Sultans of Delhi were never consistent in their powers. With each new ruler the kingdom grew or shrunk depending on his personal abilities.

In 1297 Ala-ud-din Khilji pushed the borders south into Gujurat and his general subsequently moved much further south but did not maintain the extension. In 1338 Mohammed Tughlaq decided to move his capital south from Delhi to Daulat-abad, near Aurangabad in Maharashtra, but having marched most of Delhi's population south eventually had to return north. Soon after the Bahmani kingdom arose here and the Delhi Sultanate began to retreat north only to be further weakened when Timur made a devastating raid from Samarkand into India in 1398. From then on the power of this Moslem kingdom steadily contracted, until it was supplanted by another Moslem kingdom, the mighty Moghuls.

Meanwhile in the South (again)
Once again events in the south of India took a different path than the north. Just as the Aryan invasions never reached the south so the Moslem invasions also failed to permanently effect events in the south. Between 1000 and 1300 AD the Hoysala empire, with centres at Belur, Halebid and Somnathpur, was at its peak but fell to a predatory raid by Mohammed Tughlaq in 1328 and then the combined opposition of other Hindu kingdoms. Two other great kingdoms developed in the north of modern day Karnataka — one Moslem and one Hindu. With its beautiful capital at Hampi the Hindu kingdom of Vijayanagar was founded in 1336 and was probably the strongest Hindu kingdom in India, during the time the Moslem Sultans of Delhi were dominating the north of the country. Meanwhile the Bahmani Moslem kingdom also developed but in 1489 it split into five separate kingdoms at Berar, Ahmednagar, Bijapur, Golconda and Ahmedabad. In 1520 Vijayanagar took Bijapur but in 1565 the kingdom's Moslem opponents combined to destroy Vijayanagar in the epic Battle of Talikota. Later the Bahmani kingdoms were to fall to the Moghuls.

The Moghuls
Only Ashoka is as giant a figure in Indian history as the Moghul Emperors. These larger than life individuals ushered in another Indian golden age and spread their control over India to an extent rivalled only by Ashoka and the British. Their rise to power was rapid but the decline was equally quick; there were only six great Moghuls, after Aurangzeb they were emperors in name only. The Moghuls did more than simply rule, however, they also had a passion for building which resulted in some of the great buildings in India, indeed Shah Jahan's magnificent Taj Mahal ranks as one of the greatest buildings in the world. Art and literature also flourished under the Moghuls and the magnificence of their court stunned early European visitors.

The six great Moghuls were:

Babur	1527-1530
Humayun	1530-1556
Akbar	1556-1605
Jehangir	1605-1627
Shah Jahan	1627-1658
Aurangzeb	1658-1707

Babur, a descendant of both Timur and Genghis Khan, marched into the Punjab from his capital at Kabul in Afghanistan and defeated the Sultan of Delhi at Panipat. This initial success did not totally destroy opposition to the Moghuls and in 1540 the Moghul empire came to an abrupt end when Sher Shah defeated Humayun, the second great Moghul. For 15 years he lived in exile until he was able to return and regain his throne. By 1560 Akbar, his son and successor, who had come to the throne aged only 14 was able to claim effective and complete control of his empire.

Akbar was probably the greatest of the Moghuls for he not only combined the military ability required of a ruler in that time but he was also a man of culture, wisdom and with a sense of fairness. He saw, as previous Moslem rulers had not, that the number of Hindus in India was too great to simply subjugate them. Instead he integrated them into his empire and made use of many Hindu advisers, generals and administrators. Akbar also had a deep interest in religions and spent many hours in discussion with religious experts of all persuasions including Christians, and eventually formulated a religion of his own devising which combined the best points of all those he had studied.

Jehangir followed Akbar but devoted much of his reign to expressing his love for Kashmir and eventually died while en route there. His tomb is at Lahore in Pakistan. Shah Jahan, however, stuck much more to Agra and Delhi and during his reign some of the most vivid and permanent reminders of the Moghul's glory were constructed. Best known, of course, is the Taj Mahal but that was only one of many magnificent buildings Shah Jahan constructed. Indeed some say that it was his passion for building that led to his downfall and that his son, Aurangzeb, deposed his father in part to put a halt to his architectural extravagances.

Aurangzeb was the last of the great Moghuls and although he extended the empire's boundaries to their furthest extent he also ensured its downfall by failing to follow the ground rules Akbar had so successfully established. Akbar had combined his flair for magnificence and grandeur with a sense of fairness. He had kept his Hindu subjects 'on side' by including them in the governing process and respecting their beliefs. In contrast Aurangzeb was a penny pincher and a religious zealot. His belief in Islam was deep, austere and puritanical and the result was that he soon lost the trust and respect of his subjects and had to cope with revolts on all sides. In many parts of India there are mosques which Aurangzeb had built on the foundations of temples which had been destroyed due to his fanatical beliefs. With his death in 1707 the Moghul empire rapidly disintegrated. Although there were 'Moghul Emperors' right up to the time of the mutiny, when the British exiled the last emperor and executed his sons, they were emperors in name only. In sharp contrast to the magnificent tombs of his Moghul predecessors, Aurangzeb's tomb is a simple affair at Rauza, near Aurangabad.

The smaller states which followed on from the Moghul empire did in some case continue for some time. In the south the viceroyalty in Hyderabad became one of the British-tolerated princely states and continued right to independence. The Nawabs of Oudh in north India ruled eccentrically, flamboyantly and badly until 1854 when the British 'retired' the last Nawab. In Bengal the Moghul unwisely clashed with the British far earlier and was terminated by the Battle of Plassey in 1757.

The Marathas

Moghul power was not simply supplanted by another, greater power. It fell through a series of factors and to a number of other rulers. Not least of which were the Marathas. Throughout the Moslem period in the north of India there were still strong Hindu powers, most notably the Rajputs. Centred in Rajasthan the Rajputs were a sort of warrior caste, a race of chivalrous princes whose place in Indian history is much like that of the gallant knights of England. The Rajputs opposed every foreign foot that tried to walk into India but they were never united or organised in any fashion and when the Rajputs were not battling foreign oppression they were usually fighting with each other. During the Moghul era they were brought into the emperor's army and some of their best military men were Rajputs.

The Marathas first rose to prominence with Shivaji who took over his father's kingdom and between 1646 and 1680 performed feats of arms and heroism all over central India. Retelling the tales of his larger-than-life exploits is still a popular activity by wandering storytellers in small villages. He is a particular hero in Maharashtra, where many of his wildest exploits took place, but Shivaji is revered as much for his abilities in confronting the Moghuls as for the fact that he was a lower caste Sudra and showed that you did not have to be a Brahmin to be a great leader. At one time Shivaji was even captured by the Moghuls and taken back to Agra but, naturally, he managed to escape and continue his adventures.

Shivaji's son was captured, blinded and executed by Aurangzeb and his grandson was not made of the same sturdy stuff but the Maratha empire continued under the Peshwas, hereditary government ministers who became the real rulers. They gradually took over more and more of the weakening Moghul empire's powers, first by supplying troops and then by actually taking control of Moghul land. When Nadir Shah from Persia sacked Delhi in 1739 the declining Moghuls were even further weakened but the expansion of Maratha power came to an abrupt halt in 1761 at Panipat. There, where Babur had won the battle that established the Moghul empire over 200 years earlier, the Marathas were defeated by Ahmad Shah Durani from Afghanistan. Their expansion to the west halted they nevertheless consolidated their control over central India and their region known as Malwa. Soon, however, they were to fall to India's final great imperial power, the British.

The Expansion of British Power

The British were not the first European power to arrive in India nor were they the last to leave — both those honours go to the Portuguese. In 1498 Vasco da Gama arrived on the coast of modern day Kerala having sailed around the African Cape of Good Hope. Pioneering this route gave the Portuguese a century of uninterrupted monopoly control of Indian trade with Europe and in 1510 they captured Goa, the enclave in India which they controlled right through to 1961, 14 years after the British had left.

It was in 1612 that the British made their first permanent inroad into India when they established a trading post at Surat in Gujarat. In 1600 Queen Elizabeth 1 had granted a charter to a London trading company giving them a monopoly on British trade with India. For 250 years British power was exercised in India not by the government but by the East India Company which developed from this initial charter. British trading posts were established on the other coast at Madras in 1640, at Bombay in 1668 and at Calcutta in 1690. The British and Portuguese were not the only Europeans in India. The Dutch also had trading posts and in 1672 the French established themselves at Pondicherry, an enclave they, like the Portuguese in Goa, would hold even after the British had finally departed.

Naturally Anglo-French enmity spread to India and in 1746 the French took Madras only to hand it back in 1749. In subsequent years there was to be much intrigue between the imperial powers. If the British were involved in a struggle with one local ruler they could be certain the French would be backing him with arms, men or expertise. In 1756 Suraj-ud-daula, the Nawab of Bengal attacked Calcutta and outraged Britain with the 'black hole of Calcutta' incident. A year later Robert Clive retook Calcutta and in the Battle of Plassey defeated Suraj-ud-daula and his French supporters thus not only extending British power but also curtailing French influence.

India at this time was in a state of flux due to the power vacuum created by the disintegration of the Moghul Empire. The Marathas were the only real Indian power to step into this gap and they were more a group of local kingdoms who sometimes co-operated, sometimes did not, than a power in their own right. In the south, where Moghul influence had never been so great, the picture was confused by the strong British-French rivalries with one ruler consistently played off against another. This was never clearer than in the series of Mysore Wars with that nemesis of British power, Tipu Sultan. In the Fourth Mysore War in 1789-99, Tipu was killed at Srirangapatnam and British power took another step forward, French influence another step back. The long running British struggle with the Marathas was finally concluded in 1803 which left only the Punjab outside British control and that too came under British control in 1849 after the two Sikh Wars. Britain also took on the Nepalese whom they defeated but did not annexe and the Burmese whom they did.

The Rise & Fall of British India

By the early 19th century India was effectively under British control. In part this take over had come about because of the vacuum left by the demise of the Moghuls but the British also followed the rules Akbar had laid down so successfully. To them India was principally a place to make money and the Indians' culture, beliefs and religions were left strictly alone. Indeed it was said the British didn't give a damn what religion a person held so long as he made a good cup of tea. Furthermore the British had a disciplined, efficient army and astute political advisers. They followed the policy of divide and rule with great success and negotiated distinctly one sided treaties giving them the right to intervene in local states if they were inefficiently run; 'inefficient' could be and was defined as the British saw fit.

Even under the British India remained a patchwork of states, many of them nominally independent but actually under strong British influence. This policy of maintaining 'princely states' governed by Maharajas, Nawabs or whatever continued right through to independence and was to cause a number of problems at that time. The British interest in trade and profit resulted in expansion of iron and coal mining; the development of tea, coffee and cotton growing; the construction of the vast Indian railways network; massive irrigation projects which revolutionised agriculture and other important and worthwhile developments. In the sphere of government and law Britain gave India a well developed and smoothly functioning government and civil service structure. The fearsome love of bureaucracy which India also inherited from Britain may be a downside of that but overall the country reached independence with a better organised, more efficient and less corrupt administrative system than most ex-colonial countries. Britain also made some much less helpful moves in India. Cheap textiles from the new manufacturing industry of Britain flooded into India virtually crippling the local cottage industries. On one hand the British outlawed sati, the practise of adding the wife to a husband's funeral pyre, but on the other hand they encouraged the system of zamindars. These absentee landlords eased the burden of administration and tax collection for the British but also contributed to an impoverished and landless peasantry in parts of India. A problem which in Bihar and West Bengal is still chronic today. The British also instituted English as the language of administration, in a country with so many different languages it still partially fulfills that function of nationwide communication today. On the other hand many British also kept themselves to some extent at 'arms length' from the Indians.

In 1857, less than a half century after Britain had taken firm control of India, they had their first serious setback. Even today the causes of the 'Indian Mutiny' are hard to unravel — it's even hard to define if it really was the 'War of Independence' by which it is referred to in India or merely a mutiny. The causes were a combination of an administration which had been run down and other more specific causes. The dismissal of local rulers, inefficient and unpopular as they might have been, proved to be a flashpoint in certain areas but the main single cause was, believe it or not, bullets. A rumour, quite possibly true, leaked out that a new type of bullet issued to the troops, many of whom were Moslem, was greased with pig fat. A similar rumour developed that the bullets were actually greased with cow fat. Pigs, of course, are unclean to Moslems and cows are holy to Hindus. The British were slow to deny these rumours and even slower to prove that either they were incorrect or that changes had been made. The result was a loosely co-ordinated mutiny of the Indian battalions of the Bengal Army. Of the 74 battalions seven (one of them Gurkhas) remained loyal, 20 were disarmed and the other 47 mutinied. The mutiny first broke out at Meerut, close to Delhi, and soon spread right across north India. There were massacres and acts of senseless cruelty on both sides, long sieges, decisive victories and protracted struggles but in the end the mutiny died out rather than conclusively finished. It never spread beyond the north of India and although there were brilliant self made leaders on the Indian side there was never any real co-ordination or common aim.

The British made two moves with the conclusion of the mutiny. First they wisely decided not to look for scapegoats or exact official revenge, although revenge and looting had certainly taken place on an unofficial level. Second the East India Company was wound up and administration of the country was belatedly handed over to the British government. The remainder of the century was the peak period for the empire on which 'the sun never set' and in which India was one of its brightest stars. Two parallel developments during the latter part of the 19th century gradually paved the way for the independent India of today. First the British gradually began to hand over power and bring more people into the decision making processes. Democratic systems began to be implemented in India although the British government retained overall control. In the civil service higher and higher posts were opened up for Indians and not simply retained for colonial administrators.

At the same time Hinduism began to go through another wholesale resurgence and adjustment. The Hindu religion is one of the world's oldest religions but once before, when it shrunk before the growth of Buddhism, it had failed to keep in touch with its mass support. Once again it was realised that it had lost touch with the masses and required a complete shake up to turn it away from its role as a religion for the priests and high caste Brahmins. Reformers like Ram Mohan Roy, Ramakrishna and Swami Vivekananda pushed through sweeping changes in Hindu society and paved the way for the Hindu beliefs of today, beliefs which have proved to have an enormous appeal to modern western society.

With the turn of the century opposition to British rule began to take on a new light. The 'Congress' which had been established to give India a degree of self rule now began to push for the real thing. Outside of the Congress more hot blooded individuals pressed for independence by more violent means. Eventually the British mapped out a path towards independence similar to that pursued in Canada or Australia, however WW I not only shelved these plans, the events in Turkey, a Moslem country, alienated many Indian Moslems. After the war the struggle was on in earnest and its leader was Mahatma Gandhi.

Gandhi & Passive Resistance

In 1915 Mohandas Gandhi returned from South Africa, where he had practised as a lawyer and devoted himself to righting the wrongs the country's many Indian settlers had to face. In India he soon turned his abilities to the question of independence, particularly after the massacre at Amritsar in 1919 when a British army contingent opened fire on an unarmed crowd of protestors. Gandhi, who subsequently became known as Mahatma, the 'great soul', adopted a policy of passive resistance or 'satyagraha' to British rule. His central achievement was to change the independence struggle from a middle class one to a village level one. He led movements to refuse to pay the iniquitous salt tax and boycotts of British textiles, and for his efforts made a number of visits to British prisons.

Others involved in the struggle did not follow Gandhi's policy of non-cooperation and non-violence and at times the battle was bitter and bloody. Nevertheless the Congress party and Mahatma Gandhi were in the forefront although it was not until after WW II that a conclusion was finally reached. By then independence was inevitable as the war had dealt a death blow to colonialism and the myth of European superiority. Britain no longer had the power or the desire to maintain a vast empire but within India a major problem had developed. The large Moslem minority had realised than an independent India would also be a Hindu dominated India and that despite Gandhi's fair minded and even handed approach others in the Congress party would not be so willing to share power.

Independence

With the close of WW II it was clear that the European colonial era was over and that independence for India would have to come soon, but how? Congress' refusal to deal with the Moslem league had rebounded on them with the Moslem demand for an independent Pakistan, to be carved out of India and separate from it. The abrupt end of the war with the atomic bombing of Japan and the July 1945 Labour party victory in the British election made the search for a solution to the India problem imperative.

Elections within India revealed the obvious — the country was split on purely religious grounds with the Moslem League, led by Muhammad Ali Jinnah, speaking for the overwhelming majority of Moslems and the Congress Party, led by Jawaharlal Nehru, commanding the Hindu population. Mahatma Gandhi remained the father figure for Congress but without an official role and, as events were to prove, his political influence was slipping.

'I will have India divided, or India destroyed', were Jinnah's words. This direct conflict with the Congress desire for an independent greater-India was the greatest stumbling block to the British granting independence but with each passing day the prospects for inter-communal strife and bloodshed increased. In early 1946 a British mission failed to bring the two sides together and the country slid increasingly towards civil war. A 'Direct Action Day', called by the Moslem League in August 1946, led to a slaughter of Hindus in Calcutta followed by reprisals against Moslems. Attempts to make the two sides see reason had no effect and in February 1947 the British government made a momentous decision. The current viceroy, Lord Wavell, would be replaced by Lord Louis Mountbatten and independence would come by June 1948.

Already the Punjab region of northern India was in a state of chaos and the Bengal region in the west was close to it. The new viceroy made a last ditch attempt to convince the rival factions that a united India was a more sensible proposition but they, Jinnah in particular, remained intransigent and the reluctant decision was made to divide the country. Only Gandhi stood firmly against the division, preferring the possibility of a civil war to the chaos he so rightly expected.

As in so many other parts of the world neatly slicing the country in two proved to be an impossible task. Although there were areas which were clearly Hindu or Moslem there were also parts which had very evenly mixed populations and still others where, however the country was divided, isolated 'islands' of Moslems would remain surrounded by Hindu regions. The complete impossibility of dividing all the Moslems from all the Hindus is illustrated by the fact that after partition India was still the third largest Moslem country in the world — only Indonesia and Pakistan had greater populations of Moslems. Even today India has a greater Moslem population than any of the Arab countries or Turkey or Iran. Worse, the two overwhelmingly Moslem regions were on the exact opposite sides of the country — Pakistan would inevitably have an eastern and western half divided by a hostile India. The instability of this arrangement was self-evident but it took 25 years before the predestined split came and East Pakistan became Bangladesh.

Other problems showed up only after the actual independence. Pakistan was painfully short of the administrators and clerical workers with which India is so well endowed. It was an occupation simply not followed by many Moslems. Many other occupations, such as money lenders, were purely Hindu callings and the unfortunate untouchables did the dirty work not only for their higher caste Hindu brothers but also for the Moslems.

Mountbatten decided to follow a breakneck pace to independence and announced that it would come on 14 August 1947. Historians have wondered ever since if much bloodshed might not have been averted if the impetuous and egotistical Mountbatten had not decided on such a hasty process. Once the decision had been made to divide the country there were countless administrative decisions to be made, the most important being the actual location of the dividing line. Since a locally adjudicated dividing line was certain to bring recriminations from either side an independent British referee was given the odious task of drawing the line, knowing that its effects would be disastrous for countless people. The most difficult decisions had to be made in Bengal and the Punjab. In the former, Calcutta, with its Hindu majority, its port facilities and its jute mills was divided from East Bengal, with a Moslem majority and jute production as its major industry but without a single jute mill for its processing or a suitable port for its export.

The problem was far worse in the Punjab where inter-communal antagonisms were already running at a fever pitch. Here one of the most fertile and affluent regions of the country was populated by roughly equal numbers of Hindus and Moslems but also by the majority of India's militant Sikhs. The Punjab contained all the ingredients for an epic disaster and with the announcement of the division line, only days after the independence, the resulting bloodshed was even worse than expected. All over India huge exchanges of population took place as Moslems moved to Pakistan and Hindus to India but in the Punjab the exchange was complete. The dividing line cut neatly between the Punjab's two major cities — Lahore and Amritsar. Prior to independence Lahore's population of 1.2 million included approximately 500,000 Hindus and 100,000 Sikhs. When the dust had finally settled Lahore had a Hindu & Sikh population of only a thousand.

For months the greatest exodus in human history took place east and west across the Punjab. Trainloads of Moslems, fleeing westward, would be held up and slaughtered by Hindu and Sikh mobs. Hindus and Sikhs fleeing to the east would suffer the same fate. The army force sent to maintain order proved totally inadequate and at times all too ready to join the partisan carnage. By the time the Punjab chaos had run its course over 10 million people had changed sides and even the most conservative estimates calculate that a quarter of a million people had lost their lives. The figure may well have been over a half million. An additional million people changed sides in Bengal.

Nor was the outright divison of the Punjab to be the only excuse for carnage. Throughout the British era India had retained many 'princely states' and incorporating these into independent India and Pakistan proved to be a considerable headache. Guarantees of a substantial measure of independence convinced most of them to opt for inclusion into the new countries but at the time of Independence there were still three holdouts. One was Kashmir, predominantly Moslem but with a Hindu Maharaja. In October the Maharaja had still not opted for India or Pakistan and a ragtag Pathan army crossed the border from Pakistan, intent on racing to Srinigar and annexing Kashmir without provoking a real India-Pakistan conflict. Unfortunately for the Pakistanis the Pathans had been inspired to this little invasion by the promise of plunder and they did so much plundering on the way that India had time to rush troops to Srinigar and prevent the town's capture. The indecisive Maharaja finally opted for India, a brief India-Pakistan war took place, the UN eventually stepped in and Kashmir has remained a central cause of disagreement between the two countries ever since. With its overwhelming Moslem majority and its geographic links to Pakistan it is clearly there where Kashmir belongs. But Kashmir is Kashmir and India has consistently evaded a promised plebiscite. India and Pakistan are divided in this region by a demarcation line and neither side agree to this day on an official border.

The final stages of independence had one final tragedy to by played out. On 30 January, 1948 Gandhi, deeply disheartened by partition and the subsequent bloodshed, was assasinated by a Hindu fanatic.

Independent India

Since independence India has made enormous strides but faced enormous problems. The mere fact that India has not, like so many third world countries, bowed to dictatorships, military rule or foreign invasion is a testament to the basic strength of the country's government and institutions. Economically it has made major steps forward in improving agricultural output and its industries have expanded to the stage where India is one of the world's top 10 industrial powers.

Jawaharlal Nehru, India's first Prime Minister, tried to follow a strict policy of non-alignment although India has maintained generally excellent relations with its former coloniser. A fact which has caused some little annoyance to the critics of imperialism. Despite this non-aligned policy India has moved towards the USSR — partially because of conflicts with China and partially because of US support for arch-enemy Pakistan. Since independence Gandhi's belief in peaceful neutrality has on a number of occasions had to be thrown out of the window. Three times India has clashed with Pakistan (1948, 1965, 1971) over bitter disputes concerning Kashmir or the Bangladesh issue. Border wars have been fought with China and India still disputes the area of Aksai Chin in Ladakh which China seized in 1962.

These outside events have taken the attention from India's often serious internal problems. Like any third world country population growth continues to hold the potential for ultimate disaster. India weathered the first energy crisis of the early 70s remarkably well and no better advertisement could be found for the green revolution but whether this will continue to be enough is an open question.

Indira's India

Politically India's major problem since independence has been the personality cult that has developed with its leaders. There have only been two real Prime Ministers — Nehru and his daughter, Indira Gandhi (no relation to the Mahatma). Having won election in 1966 Indira Gandhi faced serious opposition and unrest in 1975 and countered it by declaring a state of emergency, a situation which in many other countries might quickly have become a dictatorship.

During the 'Emergency' a mixed bag of good and bad policies were followed. Freed of much of the usual parliamentary constraints she was able to control inflation remarkably well, boost the economy and decisively increase efficiency. On the negative side political opponents often found themselves behind bars, India's judicial system was turned into a puppet theatre, the press was fettered and there was more than a hint of personal aggrandisement, as in the disastrous Sanjay Gandhi 'peoples' car' plan. An equally disastrous programme of virtually forced sterilisations, also masterminded by her son Sanjay, caused much anger. Despite murmurings of discontent Indira decided that the people were behind her and in 1977 called a general election to give credence to her emergency powers. Sanjay had counselled against holding the election and his opening proved to be a wise one because Indira and her Congress Party were bundled out of power in favour of the hastily assembled Janata, Peoples' Party.

Janata, however, was a device with only one function, defeating Indira. Once it had won, it had no other cohesive function and its leader, Moraji Desai, seemed more interested in protecting cows, banning alcohol and getting his daily glass of urine than coming to grips with the country's problems. With inflation soaring, unrest rising and the economy stumbling nobody was surprised when Janata fell apart in late 1979 and the 1980 election brought Indira back to power with a larger majority than ever.

Unhappily for India her political touch seems to have faded since the emergency days and she has failed to grapple with the problems that grew so rapidly in the Janata era. The accidental death of her son and potential heir, the none too popular Sanjay, seemed to further sap her vitality. India has been further plagued by communal unrest, violent actions against untouchables, upheaval in the north-west, and numerous cases of police brutality and corruption — all of which you'll read about in the papers while in India. Despite all these problems it's worth remembering two important points about this vast country. Of all the people in the world who live in what we know as democratic societies nearly 50% of them are Indians; as 1977 indicated it's a democratic system with teeth. Furthermore India, despite its population problems and vast poverty, manages to do something neither the USSR or China can manage, feed its own people without importing food. The average Indian may not eat all that well but those old tales of famine and starvation are, hopefully, a thing of the past — at least at the present population levels.

GOVERNMENT

India has a parliamentary system of government with, however, certain similarities to the US government. Basically there are two houses — a lower house known as the Lok Sabha (House of the People) and the upper house known as the Rajya Sabha (Council of States). The lower house has up to 500 members elected on a population basis while the upper has up to 250 members. As in the British House of Commons or the Australian House of Representatives the lower house can be dissolved but the upper house, unlike Britain or Australia, cannot. There are also state governments with legislative assemblies known as Vidhan Sabha. The two national houses and the various state houses elect the Indian President but he or she is really a figurehead while the Prime Minister wields the real power. There is a strict division between the activities handled by the states and by the national government. The police force, education, agriculture and industry are all reserved for the state governments. Certain other areas are jointly administered

Delhi cop in riot gear (at Indira Gandhi election rally)

by the two levels of government. All adult Indians have the vote and the consitution provides for special facilities and assistance for India's Harijan's and for the tribal groups still found in various parts of the country.

POPULATION & PEOPLE

India has a population in 1981 of 687 million. Despite extensive birth control programmes it is still growing far too rapidly for comfort. In the last 20 years it has gone from 439 million at the 1961 census to 547 million at the 1971 census to the present figure. Despite India's many large cities the country is still overwhelmingly rural. It is estimated that only about 100 million of the total population live in cities or towns. With increasing industrialisation the shift from village to city will continue to grow.

The Indian people are not a homogeneous group. It is quite easy to tell the difference visually between the shorter Bengalis of the east, the taller and lighter skinned people of the centre and north, the Kashmiris with their distinctly central Asian appearance, the Tibetan people of Ladakh and the north of Himachal Pradesh, or the dark skinned Tamils of the south. Despite these regional variations the government has managed to successfully establish an 'Indian' ethos and nationalistic feeling.

Although India is overwhelmingly Hindu there are large minorities of other religions. These include 76 million Moslems, making India one of the largest Moslem countries in the world, much larger than any of the Arab Middle East nations. Christians number about 19 million, Sikhs 13 million, Buddhists five million and Jains three million. About 7% of the population is classified as 'tribal'. They are found scattered throughout the country although there are concentrations of them in the north-east corner of the country as well as in Orissa and a number of other states.

Birth Control

India's attempts at birth control have been varied but although there has been success to some extent at slowing the rate of increase the picture is far from a happy one. Today many international experts feel that the solution to the population increase problem in the third world is not to slow the birth rate, which will then bring prosperity in its wake, but to establish a degree of prosperity which will then bring a desire for less children. So long as children are a source of security in old age and so long as male heirs are so avidly desired it will be difficult to successfully bring population pressures under control. In the early '70s India had a birth control blitz with slogans and posters appearing all over the country and the famous 'transistor radio in exchange for sterilisation' campaign. Many of those wall paintings showing the happy two child family are still visible around the country. More sinister was the brief campaign of the emergency era when squads of sterilisers terrorised half the country and people were afraid to go out after dark. That overkill campaign probably put the birth control programme in India back by years and it currently enjoys a very low priority in the government's platform.

Castes

The caste system is one of India's more confusing mysteries — how it came about, how it has managed to survive for so long, how much harm it causes, are all topics of discussion for visitors to India. Its origins are lost in the mists of history but basically it seems to have been developed at first by the Brahmins or priest class in order to make their own superior position more permanent. Later it was probably extended by the invading Aryans who felt themselves superior to the indigenous pre-Aryan Indians. Eventually the caste system became formalised into four distinct classes, each with rules of conduct and behaviour.

At the top of the heap is the Brahmin class who are the priests and the arbiters of what is right and wrong in matters of religion and caste. Beneath them come the Kshatriyas who are soldiers and administrators, then the Vaisyas who are the artisan and commercial class, finally the Sudras are the farmers and peasant class. These four castes are said to have come from Brahma's mouth (the Brahmins), his arms (the Kshatriyas), his thighs (the Vaisyas) and his feet (the Sudras). Beneath these four castes is a fifth group, the untouchables, who literally have no caste. They perform the most menial and degrading jobs and at one time to a high caste Hindu to have an untouchable use the same temple, touch you, even have his shadow cast across you, was to be polluted and involve a rigorous series of rituals to be cleansed.

Today the caste system has been much weakened but it still has considerable power, particularly amongst the less educated people. Gandhi put great effort into bringing the untouchables into society including renaming them the 'Harijans' or 'children of god'. But an untouchable by any other name . . . . . . It must be remembered that being born into a certain caste does not really limit you strictly to one occupation or position in life just as being black in the USA does not mean you are poverty stricken and illiterate. Many Brahmins are poor peasants for example and hundreds of years ago the great Maratha leader Shivaji was a Sudra. None of the later Marathas who controlled much of India after the demise of the Moghuls was a Brahmin. Nevertheless you can generalise that the better off Indians will generally be higher caste and that the 'sweeper' who you see cleaning the toilet in your hotel in a desultory fashion will certainly be a Harijan. In fact when Indian Airlines appointed their first untouchable airline stewardess it was certainly front page news on Indian newspapers.

How do you tell what caste a Hindu is? Well apart from knowing that if his job is a menial one such as cleaning streets or in some way defiling such as working in leather he is a Harijan, there is not really any way you can tell. If you see a man with his shirt off and he has the sacred thread looped round one shoulder he is a Brahmin but then Pharsis also wear a sacred thread. Of course if an Indian is a Sikh or a Moslem he will have no caste. In many ways the caste system today also functions as an enormous unofficial trade union with strict rules to avoid demarcation disputes. Each caste can have many subdivisions so that the servant who polishes the brass cannot, due to his caste, also polish silver. Many of the old caste rules have been considerably relaxed although less educated or more isolated Hindus may still be worried about pollution from having a lower caste person prepare their food. Better educated people probably are not too worried about shaking hands with a caste-less westerner though! Nor does the thought of going abroad, and thus losing caste completely, carry too much weight these days.

The caste system still produces enormous burdens for India, however. During the last couple of years there have been frequent and violent outbreaks of violence towards lower caste Hindus. In isolated rural communities higher caste Hindus have lynched Harijans whom they felt were getting 'uppity' and there are often latent tensions between the castes which can easily spill over into violence. In 1980 in one village a number of Harijans were killed after a riot broke out over a bridegroom not dismounting from his wedding horse when passing a group of higher caste men!

BUREAUCRACY India is an innovator and world leader in the field of red tape, buck passing and lunacy in quadruplicate.

The glass globe paperweight is the orb of real power! The more you have the more bureaucratic clout.

Some desks look like rock gardens...

In 1981 there were a whole series of violent riots in Ahmedabad in Gujarat due to the practice of reserving university places for Harijans, whether or not there were sufficient Harijan applicants for the places. Higher caste Hindus who could not obtain university places despite having good qualifications prompted these outbreaks. It's interesting to compare these problems with the situation in the US where, during the desegregation era many blacks experienced great difficulties in being allowed into 'all white' schools and restaurants. Similarly in the US today there is a degree of protest about the reservation of college positions for disadvantaged minorities. Going far back into western history it's interesting that the medieaval ideal of heaven was developed in part to keep the peasants in their place — behave yourself, work hard, put up with your lot and you'll go to heaven. Probably caste developed in a similar fashion — your life may be pretty miserable but that's your caste, behave yourself and you may be born into a better one next time around.

ECONOMY
India is still a predominantly agricultural country but it is also one of the world's major industrial powers with important iron and steel works and a growing manufacturing industry. Textiles are still the backbone of India's industrial exports, how-

ever. Despite these industrial and manufacturing activities 70% of India's population is engaged in work on the land — much of it inefficient and unproductive. Small landholdings, poor methods and lack of investment all contribute to this record although since independence the agricultural production levels have actually increased at a faster rate than the population. The green revolution, involving new strains and improved use of fertilisers, has had dramatic results in India which has actually managed to produce a food surplus for several years now. India also has nearly 200 million cattle but although some of them serve as work animals and there is some dairy production most of them, due to their religious protection, are totally useless.

GEOGRAPHY

India has a total area of 3,287,782 square km. The north of the country is decisively bordered by the long sweep of the Himalayas, the highest mountains on earth. They run in a south-east to north-west direction right across the north of India and separate it from China. Bhutan in the east and Nepal in the centre actually lie along the Himalayas as does Darjeeling, the northern part of Uttar Pradesh, Himachal Pradesh and Jammu & Kashmir. The Himalayas are not a single mountain range but a series of ranges with beautiful valleys wedged between them. The Kulu Valley in Himachal Pradesh and the Vale of Kashmir in J&K are both Himalayan valleys, as is the Kathmandu Valley in Nepal. Nanda Devi (7819 metres) is the highest mountain in India. Beyond the Himalayas stretches the high, dry and barren Tibetan plateau and in Ladakh a small part of this plateau actually lies within India's boundaries.

The final range of the Himalayas, the Siwalik Hills, ends abruptly in the great northern plains of India. In complete contrast to the soaring mountain peaks the northern plain is oppressively flat and slopes so gradually that all the way from Delhi to the Bay of Bengal it drops only 200 metres. The mighty Ganges River, which has its source in the Himalayas, drains a large part of the northern plain and is the major river of India. The Brahmaputra, flowing down from the north-east of the country, is the other major river of the north. In the north-west the Indus River starts out flowing through Ladakh in India but soon dives off into Pakistani territory and is the most important river of that nation.

South of the northern plains the land rises up into the high plateau known as the Deccan. The Deccan Plateau is bordered on both sides by ranges of hills which parallel the coast to the east and west. The Western Ghats are higher and have a wider coastal strip then the Eastern Ghats. The two ranges meet in the extreme south in the Nilgiri Hills. The southern hill stations are in these hills — Matheran and Mahabaleshwar near Bombay in the Western Ghats, Ooty in the extreme south in the Nilgiri Hills. The major rivers of the south are the Godavari and the Krishna. Both rise on the eastern slope of the Western Ghats, flow right across the Deccan and into the sea on the east coast.

The eastern boundary of India is also made by ranges of hills, foothills of the Himalayas, which separate the country from Burma. In this north-eastern region India bends right around Bangladesh, a low-lying country at the delta of the Ganges, and almost meets the sea to totally surround it. On the western side India is separated from Pakistan by three distinct regions. In the north, in the disputed area of Kashmir, the Himalayas forms the boundary between the two countries. The Himalayas drop down to the plains of the Punjab and then merge into the Great Indian Thar Desert. In the eastern part of Rajasthan this is an area of great natural beauty and extreme barrenness. Finally the Indian state of Gujurat is separated from the Sind in Pakistan by the unusual marshland known as the Rann of Kutch. In the dry season the Rann dries right out leaving isolated salt islands on an expansive plain while in the wet it floods over to become a vast inland sea.

CLIMATE

India is so vast that the climatic conditions in the far north have little relation to that of the extreme south. While the heat is building up to breaking point on the plains the people of Ladakh will still be waiting for the snow to melt on the high passes. Basically India has a three season year — the hot, the wet, the cool.

The Hot The heat starts to build up on the plains of India from around February and by April or May it has become unbearable. In central India temperatures of 45°C and above are commonplace. It's dry and dusty and everything is seen through a haze. From the air the country looks parched and barren but usually all you can see below is a blanket of hazy brown from all the dust in the air. Later in May the first signs of the monsoon are seen, short sharp rainstorms, violent electric storms, duststorms that turn day into night and cover everything with a film of dust. The heat towards the end of the hot season is like a hammer blow, you feel listless and tired and tempers are short. It's said to be the time of year when murders and suicides take place!

The hot season is the time to leave the plains, which are at their worst, and retreat to the hills. Kashmir comes into its own and all the Himalayan hill stations are at their best. The hill stations further south — Mt Abu in Rajasthan, Matheran in Maharashtra, Ooty in Tamil Nadu — are generally not high enough to be really cool but they are better than being down at sea level. By early June the snow on the passes into Ladakh should be all melted and the road will be open. You can also get into Keylong from Manali in Himachal Pradesh. This is the best trekking season in Kashmir and Ladakh.

The Wet When the monsoon finally arrives it's a great relief. It doesn't arrive in one day as the chart on the next page indicates. After a period of advance warning the rain comes in steadily, starting around 1 June in the extreme south and sweeping north to have covered the whole country by early July. The monsoon doesn't really cool things off, at first you simply trade the hot, dry, dusty weather for hot, humid, muddy conditions. Even so it's a great relief, not least for farmers who now have the busiest time of year ahead of them as they prepare their fields for the rice planting. During the monsoon it doesn't simply rain solidly, all day, every day. It certainly rains every day but it tends to come down in buckets for a while then the sun comes out and it's quite pleasant. Some places are at their best during the monsoon — like Rajasthan with its many palaces in lakes. While in Nepal the monsoon is a very bad time to trek, in the north-west Indian Himalayan regions this is a good trekking time. In Nepal the trekking season commences when the monsoon finishes but the regions of Himachal Pradesh, Kashmir and Ladakh in India are further north and the winter is too cold for trekking. Although the monsoon brings life to India it also brings its share of death. Every year there are many destructive floods and thousands of people are made homeless. Rivers rise and sweep away road and railway lines and many flight schedules are disrupted. Travel can definitely be more difficult during the monsoon.

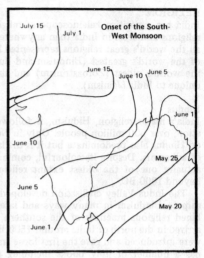

The Cool Finally around October the monsoon finishes and this is probably the best time of year in India. Everything is still green and lush but you don't get rained on daily. The temperatures are delightful, not too hot and not too cool. The air is clear in the Himalayas the mountains are clearly visible, at least early in the day. As the cool rolls on it actually becomes cold at night in the north. Delhi and other northern cities become quite crisp at night in December and January. In the far north it's more than just chilly, it's downright cold. The passes into Ladakh are once more snowed in and nobody wants to be staying on a house-boat on Dal Lake in Kashmir when the lake is frozen over. Snow does bring India's small skiing industry into its own, however, so Kashmir has a winter season too. In the far south, where it never really gets less than hot, the temperatures do become comfortably warm rather than hot. Then around February the temperatures start to climb again and before you know it you're back in the hot weather.

Some Regional Variations As in Sri Lanka the south-east coast is also effected by the north-east monsoon and brings rain from mid-October to the end of December. The usual monsoon is the south-west since it comes from that direction. It's easy to forget just how cold it can get in the far north. Even along the Ganges you'll need a sweater or jacket at night and in Kashmir the snow will be up to your neck. Basically the best time to visit India is November through February except for the northern Himalayan region where April through July is the best time.

RELIGION

India has a positive kaleidoscope of religions, there is probably more diversity of religions and sects in India than anywhere else on earth. Apart from having nearly all the world's great religions represented here, India was also the birthplace of two of the world's greatest (Hinduism and Buddhism), an important home for one of the world's oldest (Zoroastrinism) and also home for an ancient religion which is unique to India (Jainism).

Hindus

India's major religion, Hiduism, is followed by approximately 80% of the population, over 500 million people. Only in Nepal and on the Indonesian island of Bali do Hindus also predominate but it is the largest religion in Asia in terms of number of adherents. Despite its colourful, comic book, almost Disneyland appearance it is actually one of the oldest extant religions with firm roots extending back to beyond 1000 BC.

The Indus Valley civilisation developed a religion which shows a close relationship to Hinduism in many ways and later it further developed through the combined religious practices of the southern Dravidians and the Aryan invaders who arrived in the north of India around 1500 BC. Around 1000 BC the Vedic scriptures were introduced and gave the first loose framework to the religion. Hinduism today has a number of holy books including the Bhagadav Gita which is credited to Krishna, the Mahabharata, the Ramayana, the story of Rama; the Vedas, the Upanishads and the Puranas.

Basically it postulates that we will all go through a series of rebirths or reincarnations that eventually lead to moksha, the spiritual salvation which frees one from the cycle of rebirths. With each rebirth you can move closer or further from eventual moksha, the deciding factor on this is your karma which is literally a law of cause and effect. Bad actions during your life result in bad karma which ends in a lower reincarnation. Conversely if your deeds and actions have been good you will reincarnate on a higher level and be a step closer to eventual freedom from rebirth.

Dharma or the natural law defines the total social, ethical and spiritual harmony of your life. There are three categories of dharma, the first being the eternal harmony which involves the whole universe. The second category is the dharma that controls castes and the relations between castes. The third dharma is the moral code which an individual should follow.

The Hindu religion has three basic practices. They are puja or worship, the cremation of the dead and the rules and regulations of the caste system. There are four main castes defined as the Brahmin or priest caste, the Kshatriyas — soldiers and governors, the Vaisyas are tradespeople and farmers while the Sudras are menial workers and craftspeople. These basic castes are then sub-divided into a great number of lesser divisions. Beneath all the castes are the Harijans or untouchables, the lowest caste-less class for whom all the most menial and degrading tasks are reserved.

Westerners have trouble understanding Hinduism principally because of the vast pantheon of gods involved. In fact you can look upon all these different gods simply as pictorial representations of the many attributes of a god. The one omnipresent god usually has three physical representations. Brahma is the creator, Vishnu is the preserver while Shiva is the destroyer and reproducer. All three gods are usually shown with four arms, but Brahma has the added advantage of four heads to represent his all seeing presence. The four Vedas are supposed to have emanated from his mouths. The gods also have an associated animal known as the god's vehicle on which he or she rides. Each god has a consort who also has certain attributes and abilities. The gods generally have symbols which they hold in their hands. You can often pick out which god is being represented by their vehicles or their symbols. Brahma's consort is Sarasvati, the goddess of learning. She rides upon a white swan and holds the stringed musical instrument known as a veena.

Vishnu, the preserver, is usually shown in one of the physical forms in which he has visited earth. In all Vishnu has paid nine visits and on his tenth he is expected as a Kalki, riding a horse. On his earlier visits he appeared in animal form as in his boar incarnation or his man-lion (Narsingh) incarnation but on visit seven he appeared as Rama, regarded as the personification of the ideal man and the hero of the Ramayana. Rama also managed to provide a number of secondary gods including his helpful ally Hanuman, the Monkey God. Hanuman's faithful nature is illustrated by the representation of Hanuman which is often found guarding fort or palace entrances. Naturally incarnations can also have consorts and Rama's lady was Sita.

On visit eight Vishnu came as Krishna who was brought up with peasants and thus became a great favourite of the working classes. Krishna is renowned for his exploits with the gopis or shepherdesses and his consorts are Radha, the head of the gopis, Rukmani and Satyabhama. Krishna is often blue in colour and plays a flute. Vishnu's final recent incarnation was on visit nine when he came as the Buddha. This was probably a ploy to bring the Buddhist splinter group back into the Hindu fold.

When Vishnu appears as Vishnu, rather than one of his incarnations, he sits on a couch made from the coils of a serpent and in his hands he holds two symbols, the conch shell and the discus. Vishnu's vehicle is the half man-half eagle known as the Garuda. The Garuda is a firm do-gooder and has a deep dislike of snakes, Indonesia's national airline is named after the Garuda. His consort is the beautiful Lakshmi (Laxmi) who came from the sea and is the goddess of wealth and prosperity.

Shiva's creative role is phallically symbolised by his representation as the frequently worshipped lingam. Shiva rides on the bull Nandi and his matted hair is said to have Ganga, the goddess of the river Ganges in it. Shiva is supposed to live in the Himalayas and devote much time to smoking dope. He also has the third eye in the middle of his forehead and carries a trident. Shiva is also known as Nataraja, the cosmic dancer whose dance shook the cosmos and created the world. Shiva's consort is Parvati, the beautiful. She, however, has a dark side when she appears as Durga the terrible. In this role she holds weapons in her 10 hands and rides a tiger. As Kali, the fiercest of the gods, she demands sacrifices and wears a garland of skulls. Kali usually handles the destructive side of Shiva's personality.

Shiva and Parvati have two children. Ganesh is the elephant headed god of prosperity and wisdom and is probably the most popular of all the gods. Ganesh obtained his elephant head due to his father's notorious temper. Coming back from a long trip Shiva discovered Parvati in bed with a young man, not pausing to think that their son might have grown up a little during his absence Shiva lopped his head off! He was then forced by Parvati to bring his son back to life but could only do so by giving him the head of the first living thing he saw — which happened to be an elephant. Ganesh's vehicle is a rat! Shiva and Parvati's other son is Kartikkaya, the god of war.

A variety of lesser gods and goddesses also crowd the scene. Most temples are dedicated to one or other of the gods but curiously there are very few Brahma temples — perhaps just two or three in all of India. Most Hindus profess to be either Vaishnavites (followers of Vishnu) or Shaivites (followers of Shiva). The cow is, of course, the holy animal of Hinduism. Hinduism is not a proselytising religion since you cannot be converted to Hinduism. You're either born a Hindu or you are not, you can never become one. Similarly once you are a Hindu you cannot change your caste — you're born into it and are stuck with it for the rest of that lifetime. Nevertheless Hinduism has a great attraction to many westerners and India's 'export gurus' are many and successful.

A guru is not so much a teacher as a spiritual guide, somebody who by his example or simply by his presence indicates what path you should follow. In a spiritual search one always needs a guru. A sadhu is an individual on a spiritual search. They're an easily recognised group, usually wandering around half-naked, smeared in dust with their hair and beard matted. Sadhus following Shiva will often carry his symbol, the trident. A sadhu is often someone who has decided that his business and family life has reached its natural conclusion and it is time to throw everything aside and go out on a spiritual search. He may previously have been the village postman, or a businessman. Sadhus perform various feats of self-mortification and wander all over India, occasionally coming together in great pilgrimages and other religious gatherings. Many sadhus are, of course, simply beggars following a more sophisticated approach to gathering in the paise but many of them are completely genuine in their search.

Buddhists

Although there are only about five million Buddhists in India the religion is of great importance because it had its birth here and there are many reminders of its historic role. Strictly speaking Buddhism is not a religion, since it is not centred on a god, but is a system of philosophy and a code of morality. Buddhism was founded in northern India about 500 BC when Siddhartha Gautama, born a prince, achieved enlightenment. Gautama Buddha was not the first Buddha but the fourth and is not expected to be the last 'enlightened one'. Buddhists believe that the achievement of enlightenment is the goal of every being so eventually we will all reach Buddhahood.

The Buddha never wrote down his dharma or teachings and a schism later developed so that today there are two major Buddhist schools. The Theravada, Hinayana, 'doctrine of the elders' or 'small vehicle' holds that the path to nirvana, the eventual aim of all Buddhists, is an individual pursuit. In contrast the Mahayana or 'large vehicle' school holds that the combined belief of all followers will eventually be great enough to encompass all mankind and bear it all to salvation. To some the less austere and ascetic Mahayana school is a 'soft option'. Today it is chiefly practised in Viet Nam, Japan and amongst Chinese Buddhists while the Hinayana school is followed in Sri Lanka, Burma and Thailand. There are other, sometimes more esoteric, divisions of Buddhisms such as the Hindu-Tantric Buddhism of Tibet which you can see in Ladakh and other parts of north India.

The Buddha renounced his material life to search for enlightenment but, unlike other prophets, found that starvation did not lead to discovery. Therefore he developed his rule of the 'middle way', moderation in everything. The Buddha taught that all life is suffering but that suffering comes from our sensual desires and the illusion that they are important. By following the 'eight-fold path' these desires will be extinguished and a state of nirvana, where they are extinct and we are free from their delusions, will be reached. Following this process required going through a series of rebirths until the goal is eventually reached and no more rebirths into the world of suffering are necessary. The path that takes you through this cycle of births is karma but this is not simply fate. Karma is a law of cause and effect, your actions in one life determine the role you will play and what you will have to go through in your next life.

In India Buddhism developed rapidly when it was embraced by the great Emperor Ashoka. As his empire extended over much of India so was Buddhism carried forth. He also sent out missions to other lands to preach the Buddha's word and his own son is said to have carried Buddhism to Sri Lanka. Later, however, Buddhism began to contract in India because it had never really taken a hold on the great mass of people. As Hinduism revived Buddhism in India was gradually reabsorbed into the older religion. Today Buddha, to Hindus, is simply another incarnation of Vishnu. At its peak, however, Buddhism was responsible for magnificent structures erected wherever it held sway. The earlier Theravada form of Buddhism did not believe in the representation of the Buddha in human form, his presence was always alluded to in Buddhist art or architecture through symbols such as the Bo tree (under which he was sitting when he attained enlightenment), the elephant which his mother dreamed of before he was born on the wheel of life. Today, however, even Theravada Buddhists produce Buddha images.

Moslems

Moslems, the followers of the Islamic religion, are India's largest religious minority. They number about 75 million in all, over 10% of India's population. This makes India one of the largest Islamic nations in the world. It is the most recent and most widespread of the Asian religions and predominates from the Mediterranean right across to India and is the major religion west of India in Bangladesh, Malaysia and Indonesia.

The religion's founder, the prophet Mohammed, was born in 570 AD in Mecca, now in Saudi Arabia. He had his first revelation from God, Allah, in 610 and this and later visions were compiled into the Moslem holy book, the Koran. As his purpose in life was revealed to him Mohammed began to preach against idolatory that Mecca was then the centre for. Moslems are strictly monotheistic and believe that to search for God through images is a sin. Moslem teachings correspond closely with the old testament of the Bible and Moses and Jesus are both accepted as Moslem prophets although Jesus is not the son of God.

Eventually Mohammed's attacks on local business led to him and his followers being run out of town in 622. They fled to Medina, the 'city of the prophet' and by 630 were strong enough to march back into Mecca and take over. Although Mohammed died in 632 most of Arabia had been converted to Islam within two decades. The Moslem faith was more than just a religion. It also called on its followers to spread the word — if necessary by the sword. In succeeding centuries Islam was to expand over three continents. The Arabs, who first propagated the faith, developed a reputation as being ruthless opponents but reasonable masters so people often found it advisable to surrender to them. In this way the Moslems swept aside the crumbling Byzantine empire, whose people felt no desire to support their distant Christian emperor.

Islam only travelled west for a hundred years before being pushed back at Poitier, in France, in 732, but it continued east for centuries. It regenerated the Persian Empire, which was then declining from its protracted struggles with Byzantium, and in 711, the same year the Arabs landed in Spain, they sent dhows up the Indus River into India. This was more a casual raid than a full scale invasion but in the 11th centuries all of north India fell into Moslem hands. Eventually the Moghul empire controlled most of the sub-continent. From here it was spread by Indian traders on into south-east Asia.

At an early stage Islam suffered a fundamental split that remains to this day. The third Caliph, successor to Mohammed, was murdered and followed by Ali, the prophet's son-in-law in 656. Ali was assassinated in 661 by the Governor of Syria who set himself up as Caliph in preference to the descendants of Ali. Most Moslems today are Sunnites, followers of the succession from the Caliph, while the others are Shias or Shi'ites who follow the descendants of Ali.

Strangely today Islam, which spread out from its initial foundation with such vigour, has become inertial and unchanging. Women in Islamic society may not exactly be second class citizens but they are certainly a second type of citizen. Despite its long period of control over India Islam never managed to make great inroads into Hindu society and the Hindu religion. Converts to Islam were principally made from the lowest castes with the result, at partition, that Pakistan found itself with a shortage of the educated clerical workers and government officials with which India is so liberally endowed. Although it did not make great numbers of converts the visible effects of Moslem influence in India are strong in architecture, art and in food.

Converts to Islam have only to announce that 'There is no God but Allah and Mohammed is his prophet' and they become Moslems. Friday is the Moslem holy day and the main mosque in each town is known as the Jami Masjid or Friday Mosque. The eventual aim of every Moslem is to make the pilgrimage to Mecca and become a haji.

Sikhs

The Sikhs number 13 million and are chiefly found in the Punjab although they are also all over India. They are probably the most visible of the Indian religious groups because of the five symbols introduced by Guru Gobind Singh so that Sikh men could easily recognise each other. They are known as the five kakkars and are: kesha or uncut hair; kangha the wooden or ivory comb; kachha or shorts; kara which is a steel bracelet and kirtipan or the sword. Because of their kesha Sikh men wear their hair tied up in a bun and hidden by a long turban. The wearing of kachha, shorts, and carrying a kirtipan, sword, came about because of the Sikh's military tradition — they didn't want to be tripping over a long dhoti or caught without a weapon. Normally the sword is simply represented by a tiny image set in the comb. The steel bracelet has the useful secondary function of making a good bottle opener. With their beards and turbans and their upright, military bearing the 'noble' Sikh is hard to miss!

The Sikh religion was founded by Guru Nanak who was born in 1469. It was originally intended to bring together the best of the Hindu and Islamic religions. Its basic tenets are similar to that of Hinduism with the important modification that the Sikhs are opposed to caste distinctions and pilgrimages to rivers. They are not, however, opposed to pilgrimages to holy sites. They worship at temples known as Gurdwaras, baptise their children when they are old enough to understand the religion in a ceremony known as pahul and they cremate their dead. The holy book of the Sikhs is the Granth Sahib which contains the works of the ten Sikh gurus together with Hindu and Moslem writings.

In the 16th century Guru Gobind Singh introduced the military overtones into the religion in an attempt to halt the persecution Sikhs were then suffering. From that time all Sikhs have borne the surname Singh or 'Lion'. In all there were 10 gurus, the last one dying in 1708. Sikhs believe in one god and are opposed to idol worship. They practise tolerance and love of others and their belief in hospitality extends to offering shelter to anyone who comes to their gurdwaras. Because of their get-on-with-it attitude to life they are one of the better off groups in India society. They have a well known reputation for mechanical aptitude and specialise in handling machinery of every type from auto-rickshaws to jumbo jets.

Jains

The Jain religion is contemporaneous with Buddhism and bears many similarities to it. It was founded around 500 BC by Mahavira who was the 24th and last of the Jain prophets known as Tirthankars or 'finders of the path'. The Jains now number only about 3½ million and are found all over India but predominantly to the west and south-west. The Jains believe that the universe is infinite and was not created by a deity. They believe in reincarnation and eventual spiritual salvation or moksha through following the path of the Tirthankars. One factor in the search for salvation is ahimsa or reverence for all life and the avoidance of injury to all living things. Due to this belief Jains are strict vegetarians and some monks actually cover their mouths with a piece of cloth in order to avoid the risk of accidentally swallowing an insect.

The Jains are divided into two sects, the Shvetambara and the Digambara. The Digambaras are the more austere sect and their name literally means 'sky clad' since as a sign of their contempt for material possessions, they do not even wear clothes. Not surprisingly Digambaras are chiefly monks who confine their nudity to the monasteries. Jain temples are noted for the large number of similar buildings which are often erected at one place. Their temples also often have many columns, no two of which are ever identical. The Jains tend to be clever and commercially successful and have an influence disproportionate to their actual numbers. Their temples are often extremely well kept. There are many Jains in Rajasthan, Gujurat and Bombay.

Pharsis

This is one of the oldest religions on earth and was founded in Persia by the prophet Zarathustra in the 6th or 7th century BC. He was born in Mazar-i-Sharif in what is now Afghanistan. At one time Zoroastrinism stretched all the way from India to the Mediterranean but today is found only around Shiraz in Iran, Karachi in Pakistan and Bombay in India. The followers of Zoroastrinism are known as Pharsis since they originally fled to India to escape persecution in Persia.

Zoroastrinism was one of the first religions to postulate an omnipotent and invisible god. Their scripture is the Zend-Avesta which describes the continual conflict between the forces of good and evil. Their god is Ahura Mazda, the god of light who is symbolised by fire. Man ensures the victory of good over evil by following the principles of humata or good thoughts, hukta or good words and huvarshta or good deeds. Pharsis worship in fire temples and wear a sadra or sacred shirt and a kasti or sacred thread. When children first wear these sacred items it is done in a ceremony known as Navjote. They keep eternally burning flames in their fire temples but they worship the fire as a symbol of God, not the fire itself. Because Pharsis believe in the purity of elements they will not cremate or bury their dead since it would pollute the fire, earth, air or water. Instead they leave the bodies in 'Towers of Silence' where they are soon cleaned off by vultures.

Although there are only about 85,000 Pharsis, concentrated in Bombay, they are very successful in commerce and industry and have become notable philanthropists. Pharsis have influence far greater than their numbers would indicate and often acted as a channel of communication between India and Pakistan when the two countries were at loggerheads. Because of the strict requirements that a Pharsi must only marry another Pharsi and children must have two Pharsi parents to be Pharsis, their numbers are gradually declining.

Christians & Jews

India also has around 18 million Christians. There have been Christian communities in Kerala as long as Christianity has been in Europe for St Thomas the Apostle is supposed to have arrived here in 54 AD. The Portuguese, who unlike the English were as enthusiastic about spreading their brand of Christianity as making money from trade, left a large Christian community in Goa. Generally though Christianity has not had great success in India, if success is counted in number of converts. Indians who have become Christians have generally been from the lowest castes. There are small Jewish communities in a number of cities but the Jews of Cochin in Kerala are of interest because a group claims to have arrived here in 587 BC.

CULTURE

Painting & Sculpture

Indian art and sculpture is basically religious in its themes and developments and appreciation requires at least some knowledge of its religious background. The earliest Indian artifacts are found in the Indus Valley cities in modern day Pakistan. Pieces are mainly small items of sculpture and it is not until the Mauryan period that India's first major artistic period flowered. This classical school of Buddhist art reached its peak during the reign of Ashoka. The superb sculpture of this period can be seen at its best at Sanchi. The Sungas, who followed the Mauryas, continued their artistic traditions.

When this empire ended the Gandharan period came into its own in the north-west. Close to Peshawar in Pakistan today the Gandharan period combined Buddhism with a strong Greek influence from the descendants of Alexander the Great's invading army. During this period the Buddha began to be represented directly in human form rather than by symbols such as the footprint or the stupa. Meanwhile in India proper another school began to develop at Mathura, between Agra and Delhi. Here the religious influence was also Buddhist but began to be altered by the revival of Brahmanism, the forerunner of Hinduism. It was in this school that the tradition of sculpturing yakshinis, those well endowed heavenly damsels, began to appear.

During the Gupta period from 320 to 600 AD Indian art went through a golden period, and it was during this period that the Buddha images developed to their present day form — even today in Buddhist countries the attitudes, clothing and hand positions have scarcely altered. This was, however, also the end of Buddhist art in India for Hinduism now began to reassert itself. At the same time as the Guptas were bringing Buddhist art to its final zenith in the north a strongly Hindu tradition was developing in the south. Both schools of art produced metal cast sculptures by the lost wax method as well as larger sculptures in stone.

The following thousand years saw a slow but steady development through to the exuberant mediaeval period of Indian Hindu art. This development can be studied at the caves of Ajanta and Ellora where there are some of the oldest wall paintings in India and the sculpture can be traced from the older, stiff and unmoving Buddhist sculptures through to the dynamic and dramatic Hindu figures. These reached their culmination in the period when sculpture became an integral part of architecture and it is impossible to tell where building ends and sculpture begins. Some of the finest examples of this era can be seen in the Hoysala temples of Karnataka, the elaborate sun temple at Konarak and the Chandelas' temples at Khajuraho. In all of these the architecture competes valiantly to match the art work which manages to combine high quality with quite awesome quantity. An interesting common element is the highly detailed erotic scenes. The heavenly maidens of an earlier period have blossomed into scenes, positions and possibilities that leave little to the imagination. Art of this period was not purely a representation of gods and goddesses. Every aspect of human life appeared in the sculptures and obviously in India sex was considered a fairly important aspect!

The arrival of the Moslems with their hatred of other religions and 'idols' caused enormous damage to India's artistic relics. The early invaders' art was chiefly confined to paintings but Indian art went through yet another golden period with the Moghuls. Best known of the art forms they encouraged is the miniature painting tradition. These delightfully detailed and brightly coloured paintings showed the events and activities of the Moghuls in their magnificent palaces. Other paintings included portraits, or studies of wildlife and plants. At the same time there had been a massive revival of folk art and some of these developments also embraced the Moghul miniature concepts but combined them with Indian religious arts. The popular Rajasthan or Mewar schools often included scenes from Krishna's life and escapades — he's always blue. Interestingly this school followed the Persian influenced Moghul school in its miniaturised and highly detailed approach but made no use of the Persian developed sense of perspective, and are generally almost two dimensional. In the north of India, at Jammu, Basohli and Kangra, the Pahari miniatures followed the Moghul school in having a definite sense of perspective but in their often religious themes were closer to the Rajasthan school. The Basohli paintings are very dark and use much gold colouring while the other Pahari paintings are often pale and delicate looking.

The Moghuls greatest achievements were, however, in the architectural field and it is chiefly for their magnificent buildings that they are remembered. After the Moghuls there has not been another major artistic period of purely Indian background. During the British period art became imitative of western trends and ideals. Although there is much British painting in India it is interesting chiefly as an historical record rather than as art in itself.

Music

Indian music is in so many ways so unlike the concept of music in the west that it is very difficult for a westerner to appreciate it without a lengthy introduction and much time spent in listening. The basic difficulty is that harmony, so important to western music, has no place in Indian music. Indian music has two basic elements, the tala and the raga. Tala is the rhythm and is characterised by the number of beats. Teental is a tala of 16 beats. The audience follows the tala by clapping at the appropriate beat which on teental is at 1, 5 and 13. There is no clap at the beat of 9 since that is the khali or 'empty section' and indicated by a wave of the hand.

Just as tala is the rhythm so is raga the melody and just as there are a number of basic talas so there are many set ragas. The classical Indian music group consists of three players who provide the drone, the melody and the rhythm — in other words a background drone, a tala and a raga. The musicians, who are basically soloists — the concept of an orchestra of Indian musicians is impossible since there is not that harmony that a western orchestra provides, each select a tala and raga. The players then zoom off in their chosen directions, as dictated by the tala and the raga selected, and, to the audience's delight, meet every once in a while before once again diverging.

Yehudi Menuhin, who has devoted much time and energy to understanding Indian music, suggests that Indian music is much like Indian society. A group of individuals not working together but every once in a while meeting at some common point and western music is analogous to western democratic societies, a group of individuals (the orchestra) who each surrender part of their freedom to the harmony of the whole. Although Indian classical music has one of the longest continuous histories of any music form the music has not, until quite recently, ever been recorded in any written notation. Furthermore within the basic framework set by the tala and the raga the musicians improvise — providing variations on the basic melody and rhythm.

Best known of the Indian instruments are the sitar and the tabla. The sitar is the large stringed instrument popularised by Ravi Shankar in the west — and which more than a few westerners have discovered is more than just slightly difficult to tune. This is the instrument with which the soloist plays the raga. Other less popular stringed instruments are the sarod (which is plucked) or the sarangi (which is played with a bow). The tabla, a twin drum rather like a western bongo drum, provides the tala. The drone, which runs on two basic notes, is provided by the oboe like shehnai or the tampura.

Dance

Indian dancing all relates back to Shiva's role as Nataraj, the King of Dancers. Lord Shiva's first wife was Sati and when her father, who disliked Shiva, insulted him

Sati committed suicide in a sacrifice by fire that later took her name — Sati. Outraged Shiva killed his father-in-law and danced the Tandava — the Dance of Destruction. Later Sati reincarnated as Parvati, married Shiva again and danced the Lasya. Thus the Tandava became the male form of dance, the Lasya the female form. Dancing at first was a part of the religious temple rituals and the dancers were known as devadasis. Their dances retold stories from Ramayana or the Mahabharata.

Temple dancing is no longer practised but classical Indian dancing is still based on its religious background. Indian dance is divided into nritta — the rhythmic elements, nritya — the combination of rhythm with expression, and natya — the dramatic element. Nritya is usually expressed through eye, hand and facial movements and with nritta makes up the usual dance programmes. To appreciate natya, dance drama, you have to understand and appreciate Indian legends and mythology.

Dance is divided into four basic forms known as Bharat Natya, Kathakali, Kathak and Manipuri. Bharat Natya is further sub-divided into three other classical forms. It is one of the most popular forms of classical dance, originated in the great temples of the south and usually tells of events in Krishna's life. Bharat Natya dancers are always women and, like the sculptures they take their positions from, always dance bent kneed, never standing upright, and use a huge repertoire of hand movements. Orissi, Mohini Attam and Kuchipudi are variations of Bharat Natya which take their names from the places where they originated.

Kathakali, the second major dance form, originated in Kerala and is exclusively danced by men. It tells of epic battles of gods and demons and is as dynamic and dramatic as Bharat Natya is austere and expressive. Kathakali dancing is noted for the elaborate make up and painted masks which the dancers wear. Eyedrops even turn their eyes a bloodshot red!

Manipuri dances come, as the name indicates, from the Manipur region in the north-east. These are a folk dance and the message is made through body and arm movements. The women dancers wear hooped skirts and conical caps which are extremely picturesque.

The final classical dance type is Kathak which originated in the north and at first was very similar to the Bharat Natya school. Persian and Moslem influences later altered the dance from a temple ritual to a courtly entertainment. The dances are performed straight legged and there are intricately choreographed foot movements to be followed. The ankle bells which dancers wear must be adeptly controlled and the costumes and themes are often similar to those in Moghul miniature paintings.

There are many opportunities to see classical Indian dancing while you are in India. The major hotels often put on performances to which outsiders as well as hotel guests are welcome.

FESTIVALS & HOLIDAYS

Due to its religious and regional variations India has a great number of holidays and festivals. Most of them follow the lunar calendar which differs from the western calendar, thus they fall on a different date each year. Apart from the holidays and festivals celebrated nationally there are many local and regional occasions. PH — public holiday.

January   *Sankranti/Pongal* Celebrated predominantly in Andhra Pradesh
                        and amongst the Tamil people of the south this is a harvest festival

Jan (cont)   marking the change of season when the sun is supposed to move
                    to its northern home and the days get longer, the nights shorter.

January 26   *Republic Day* Celebrating the anniversary of India's establishment
                    as a republic in 1950 there are activities in all the state capitals
                    but most spectacularly in New Delhi where there is an enormous-
                    ly colourful military parade. (PH)

February-   *Shivaratri* This day of fasting is dedicated to Lord Shiva. Proces-
   March   sions to the temples are followed by the chanting of mantras and
                    annointing of lingams.

                    Holi This is one of the most exuberant Hindu festivals with
                    people marking the advent of spring by throwing coloured water
                    or powder at one another — don't wear good clothes on this day!
                    On the night before Holi bonfires are built to symbolise the des-
                    truction of the evil demon Holika. (PH)

March-April   *Mahavir Jayanti* This major Jain festival marks the birth of Ma-
                    havira, the 24th and last Jain Tirthankar. (PH)

                    Ramanavami In temples all over India the birth of Rama, an
                    incarnation of Vishnu, is celebrated on this day. (PH)

                    Good Friday This Christian holiday is also celebrated in India.
                    (PH)

May-June   *Buddha Purnima* The Buddha's birth, enlightenment and his
                    reaching of nirvana are all celebrated on this day. The Buddha is
                    supposed to have gone through each of these experiences on the
                    same day but of different years. (PH)

June-July   *Festival of the Cars* Lord Jagannath's great temple chariot makes
                    its stately journey from his temple in Puri, Orissa. Similar, but far
                    less grandiose, festivals take place in other locations.

July-   *Naga Panchami* This festival is dedicated to Ananta, the serpent
   August   upon whose coils Vishnu rested between universes. Offerings are
                    made to snake images and snake charmers do a roaring trade.
                    Snakes are supposed to have power over the monsoon rainfall
                    and keep evil from homes.

                    Janai Purnima After a day long fast high caste Hindus replace
                    the sacred thread which they always wear looped over their left
                    shoulder.

August 15   *Independence Day* The anniversary of India's independence from
                    Britain in 1947. The Prime Minister delivers an address from the
                    ramparts of Delhi's Red Fort. (PH)

August	*Nariel Purnima* A celebration of the official end of the monsoon, observed by sailors and fishermen.

Raksha Bandhan On the same day girls fix amulets known as rakhis to their brothers' wrists to protect them in the coming year. The brothers give their sisters gifts.

Pateti Pharsis celebrate their migration from Persia on this day but one sect of Pharsis sets the date a month earlier. A week later *Khordad Sal* celebrates the birth of Zarathustra.

August-September	*Janmastami* The anniversary of Krishna's birth is celebrated with happy abandon — in tune with Krishna's own mischievious moods. Although it is a national holiday Agra, Bombay and Mathura (his birthplace) are the main centres. (PH)

Ganesh Chaturthi This festival is dedicated to the popular elephant headed god Ganesh. Pune, Madras and Bombay are important centres for its celebration. In Bombay images of the god are carried down into the sea.

Onam Harvest Festival During this Kerala festival the famous snake boat races are held.

September-October	*Dussehra* (Dassehra in the south) This is the most popular of all the Indian festivals and takes place over 10 days. It celebrates Rama's victory over the demon king Ravana and in many places it culminates with the burning of huge images of Ravana and his accomplices in effigy. In Delhi it is known as Ram Lila and there are re-enactments of the Ramayana and fireworks. In Mysore and Ahmedabad there are great processions. In West Bengal the festival is known as Durga Puja since Durga aided Rama in his defeat of Ravana. In Kulu in the north the festival takes place a little later than elsewhere and is a delightful festival when the Kulu Valley shows why it is known as the 'Valley of the Gods'. (PH — two days)

October 2	*Gandhi Jayanti* A solemn celebration of Gandhi's birth date with prayer meetings at the Raj Ghat in Delhi where he was cremated. (PH)

October-November	*Diwali* This is the happiest festival of the Hindu calendar and at night countless oil lamps are lit to show Rama the way home from his period of exile. Today the festival is also dedicated to Lakshmi (particularly in Bombay) and to Kali in Calcutta. In all the festival lasts five days with day one the start of the new business year, day two dedicated to Krishna, the third to Shiva, the fourth to the friendly (but uppity) demon Bali whom Vishnu put in his place. On the fifth day men visit their sisters to have a tika put on their forehead. (PH)

November   *Govardhana Puja* A Hindu festival dedicated to that holiest of
animals, the cow. (PH)

Pushkar Cattle Fair This incredibly colourful cattle fair in Rajasthan includes camel races amongst other events.

Nanak Jayanti The birthday of Guru Nanak, the founder of the
Sikh religion, is celebrated with prayer readings and processions,
particularly in Amritsar and Patna. (PH)

December   *Feast of St Francis Xavier* On December 3 this festival and the
feast of Our Lady of the Immaculate Conception are two of the
most important festivals in Goa.

December 25   *Christmas Day* Also a holiday in India. (PH)

Moslem festivals vary very widely in date from year to year so it is not easy to list
what month they will fall in.

Ramadan The most important Moslem festival is a 30-day dawn
to dusk fast. In Moslem countries this can be a difficult time for
travellers since restaurants are closed and tempers tend to run
short. Fortunately, despite India's large Moslem minority, it
causes no difficulties for visitors.

Id-ul-Fitr This day celebrates the end of Ramadan. (PH)

Id-ul-Zuhar A Moslem festival commemorating Abraham's
attempt to sacrifice his son Ishmael, celebrated with prayers and
feasts. (PH)

Muharram A 10-day festival commemorating the martyrdom of
Mohammed's grandson, Imam Hussain. (PH)

Months of the Year

		Hindi	*English*
Spring	Vasanta	Chait	March-April
		Baisakh	April-May
Hot Season	Grishma	Jeth	May-June
		Asarh	June-July
Rains	Varsha	Sawan	July-August
		Bhadon	August-September
Autumn	Sharada	Asvin	September-October
		Kartik	October-November
Winter	Hemanta	Aghan	November-December
		Pus	December-January
Cold Season	Shishira	Magh	January-February
		Phagun	February-March

Facts for the Visitor

VISAS

If you're from Australia, New Zealand, Great Britain, Canada or Ireland you do not need a visa. If you're from the Scandinavian countries, West Germany or a couple of other places you do not need a visa for a stay of up to 90 days. Otherwise you're going to need a visa which will normally be valid for a 90 day stay. They're available from Indian consular offices and generally take 24 hours to issue and cost about US$2.50. If there is no diplomatic representation in the country the British embassy will be able to advise you.

If your stay in India is going to be more than 90 days a few little hassles pop up. First of all if you are in India on a '90 days without visa' basis you now have to obtain one. If you already have a 90 day visa then you have to extend it. Either activity can be a bit of a hassle — not due to any Indian reluctance to permit people to stay longer but simply due to the usual Indian red tape and bureaucracy. Set aside at least a day for coping with this problem. Whatever your visa situation at 90 days you have to register with the 'Foreigner's Registration Office'. Furthermore if you've been in India more than 90 days you have to get an income tax clearance before you leave. This is relatively simple in that you just have to show a handful of currency exchange forms to indicate that you did spend your own money and weren't working while in India. But as usual it involves a fair bit of form filling and rubber stamping and takes a little time.

All in all it's worth avoiding the 90 day hassles if at all possible. A simple way to do just that is to leave India then come back and start the 90 days again. If you are planning to combine a visit to India with, say, Sri Lanka or Nepal then just make sure you arrive there by day 89.

With your visa you may also get a 'tourist introduction card' and a 'liquor permit'. If you don't have one you can apply for one after you arrive in India from a Government of India Tourist Office. India plays around with the idea of prohibition from time to time and certain states, like Gujarat or Tamil Nadu, are definitely 'dry'. With your All India Liquor Permit you are permitted to purchase alcoholic drinks in those 'dry' states although it is wise to check first if a local state permit is needed — regulations change. The permit is usually valid for three months and can be extended. In the dry states a liquor permit has a blackmarket value and you will probably receive offers to buy your permit. The permit does not allow you to buy unlimited quantities of alcohol but the limits are more than sufficient for most people.

Foreigners' Registration Offices

The main foreigners' registration offices include:

Bombay	Special Branch II, Annexe 2, Office of the Commissioner of Police (Greater Bombay), Dadabhoy Naroji Rd (tel 268111)
Calcutta	237 Acharya Jagdish Bose Rd (tel 443301)
New Delhi	1st floor, Hans Bhavan, Tilak Bridge (tel 272790)
Madras	13 Victoria Crescent Rd, Egmore (tel 88864)

Special Permits

Even with a visa you are not allowed everywhere in India. Certain places require special additional permits. These are covered in the appropriate sections in the main

41

text but briefly they are:

Darjeeling Permits can be obtained from consular offices abroad or from the main Foreigner's Registration Offices in Bombay, Calcutta, Delhi or Madras. They cannot be obtained while en route to Darjeeling from Calcutta or at the border if you are coming through Nepal from Kathmandu. The permits are generally valid for an initial stay of 15 days and are quite easy to obtain. The only exception from the permit system is if you fly to and from Bagdogra, the airport for Darjeeling.

Assam & Meghalaya You require a permit for these remote north-east states and you are also restricted where you may go. The permits can be obtained at the offices in Calcutta.

Andaman & Nicobar Islands For these islands you need a permit from an embassy or consulate abroad or from the Ministry of Home Affairs in New Delhi. The application must be made at least six weeks in advance although they recommend you allow 12 weeks.

Sikkim Similar ground rules apply as for the Andaman and Nicobar Islands. Your initial permit allows a stay of only four days but this is easily extended once in Sikkim. You are restricted as to where you may go in Sikkim.

Bhutan Officially this remote Himalayan region beside Sikkim is still an independent entity although actually India has firm control over foreign policy and most other things in Bhutan. Applications to visit Bhutan must be made through the Director of Tourism, Ministry of Finance, Tachichho Dzong, Thimpu, Bhutan or from the Bhutan Foreign Mission, Chandragupta Marg, New Delhi 110021, India (tel 74075) or from the Bhutanese mission in New York. Before applying you must have the relevant permits for the restricted areas of India you must pass through in order to get to Bhutan. And don't hold your breath — unless you have high up Indian connections or a personal friend in the Bhutanese aristocracy you needn't expect to get a permit. At present permits appear to be issued only to groups and then generally only for tours costing over US$100 per day.

Other Visas

If you're heading to other places around India the visa stories are as follows:

Afghanistan Probably not at the moment if you value your life but there is an embassy in Delhi although it may be easier, cheaper in Pakistan.

Burma The embassy in New Delhi is fast and efficient — 24 hours, Rs 40 — but the usual 'seven days, no longer' rule applies. Note there is no longer a Burmese consulate in Calcutta. There is one in Kathmandu.

Nepal The Nepalese embassy in Calcutta is on Barakamba Rd, quite close to Connaught Place, not out at Chanakyapuri like most other embassies. There is also a consulate in Calcutta. Visas take 24 hours and cost Rs 45. A seven day visa is available on arrival in Nepal but this is more expensive to renew than a regular visa — in as much as you have to exchange $5 per day of extension.

Sri Lanka Most western nationalities do not require a visa to visit Sri Lanka but there are diplomatic offices in New Delhi, Bombay and Madras.

Thailand There are Thai embassies in New Delhi and Calcutta. The visa costs Rs 25 and is issued in 24 hours. Note that if you are flying in and flying out of Thailand within 15 days a visa is not required.

Tax Clearance Certificates

You need one of these if you have stayed in India for more than 90 days and are about to leave. Applies to anyone.

Many travel agencies will offer to do this for you and although this saves time you will be charged Rs 50-100 for the service. You can do it yourself for Rs 10 but you need to set the wheels in motion three days in advance of when you wish to collect. The procedure is as follows:

(1) Locate a Notary Public solicitor and tell him you need an affidavit for tax clearance. He will type this out on special legal paper which costs Rs 2, attach an excise stamp (Rs 3), get you to sign it and charge you a Rs 5 fee.

(2) Take the affidavit to the local Income Tax Office and ask for the Enforcement Directorate. Here you will be asked to produce all the bank receipts you have been given for encashment of travellers' cheques or cash plus all the remaining travellers' cheques and cash you hold. These will be added up and ought to tally with the amount you declared you were carrying on entry (a declaration of this sort is only required if you are carrying US$1000 or more on entry). No need to worry if they don't. You lost them or forgot to ask the bank to endorse your Currency Declaration Form at the time. The Enforcement Directorate will issue you with a 'No Objection Certificate'.

(3) Take the affidavit and the 'No Objection Certificate' to the main income tax office and ask for Form No 31. This form is an application for a Clearance Certificate under Section 230 (1) of the Income Tax Act 1961. Fill in the form and attach the affidavit and 'No Objection Certificate'. Hand in the form and return three days later to collect it.

It is possible to get the Clearance Certificate in less than three days if you have a very good excuse but it will cost you. One of the perks of office for tax officers is backsheesh (bribery). This is why getting the tax certificate through a travel agent is expensive (they take their cut too).

CUSTOMS

The usual bottle of whisky, 200 cigarettes type of duty free regulations apply in India. If you bring in more than US$1000 in cash and/or travellers' cheques you are supposed to fill in a currency declaration form. You're allowed to bring in all sorts of western technological wonders but big ticket items are likely to be entered on a 'Tourist Baggage Re-Export' form to ensure you take them out with you when you go. If you wonder why your battered Instamatic has been singled out to be honoured with a TBRE form perhaps it's because section 3 of customs regulation number 499/15/74 applies to you (our italics):

There is also likelihood of abuse by tourists holding Indian passports and *hippies*. In the case of such tourists therefore, even a camera or transistor radio should be entered on Tourist Baggage Re-Export form before allowing clearance.

MONEY

A$1	=	Rs 9.7	Rs 1	=	A$0.10
US$1	=	Rs 8.5	Rs 1	=	US$0.12
£1	=	Rs 17.8	Rs 1	=	£0.06

The rupee (Rs) is divided into 100 paise (p). There are coins of 1, 2, 3, 5, 10, 20, 25 and 50 paise and notes of Rs 1, 2, 5, 10, 20, 50, 100 and 500. Once upon a time the rupee was divided into 16 annas and you may still hear prices referred to in annas — particularly in markets. Eight annas is half a rupee or 50 paise, four annas is a quarter rupee or 25 paise.

You are not allowed to bring Indian currency into the country or take it out of the country. You are allowed to bring in unlimited amounts of foreign currency or travellers cheques but you are supposed to declare it all on arrival. All money is supposed to be changed at official banks or money changers and you are supposed to be given a currency exchange form for each transaction. In actual practice you can surreptitiously bring rupees into the country with you — they can be bought at a useful discount in places like Singapore or Bangkok. Banks will usually not give you a currency exchange form unless you specifically ask for one. It is worth getting them for several reasons. First of all you will need one for any re-exchange when you depart India. Secondly certain official purchases, such as airline tickets, must be paid for either with foreign currency or your rupees must be accompanied by sufficient exchange forms to account for the ticket price. This is actually a complete waste of time since some little note will be scrawled on the form to the effect that it was sighted when you bought a ticket from A to B. When you buy a ticket from B to C somebody else can quite easily scrawl a similar little note on another corner of the same form! The third reason for saving exchange forms is that if you stay in India longer than 90 days then you have to get an income tax clearance and this requires production of a handful of exchange forms to prove you've been changing money all along and not earning money locally.

In major cities you can change most foreign currencies or travellers' cheques — Australian dollars, Deutschmarks, yen or whatever — but out of town it's best to stick to US dollars or pounds sterling. The pound still has a sentimental appeal in India. Thomas Cook and American Express are both popular travellers' cheques and have a number of branches in India. Many people make the mistake of bringing too many small denomination cheques. Unless you are moving rapidly from country to country you only need a handful of small denominations for end of stay conversions. In between change as much as you feel happy carrying. This applies particularly in India where changing money is such a time consuming bore. Even in major cities it takes a long time. In smaller towns — and that means even quite large places if they have little tourist appeal — changing money can take forever. To change a single travellers' cheque can easily take several hours in some towns. You can also spend a lot of time finding which bank will change money. The answer is to change money as infrequently as possible and try to change it only in big banks in big cities.

There is still a small black market in India but it is so small that it is not worth the effort of searching it out and the risks involved. A particular catch with Indian currency and declaration forms arises if you are buying an airline ticket out of India. You can often get tickets at very useful discounts but these sorts of large purchases must be made with a specific bank exchange form. If you are buying a ticket overseas which costs, say, Rs 8000 officially an agent may be able to offer it to you at Rs 5000. But you must exchange officially Rs 8000 so you get the balance as a Rs 3000 refund from the agent. Since you cannot use your Rs 8000 exchange document to reconvert it (the form specifies it was used to purchase an airline ticket) you're stuck. Two answers — either buy the ticket far enough ahead of your departure that you will use up the money or else have plenty of exchange forms saved up to permit you to re-exchange it on departure.

Credit cards are now widely accepted in India and with American Express or Diners Club you can use your card to obtain more funds locally. With your Amex card you can get travellers' cheques from an Amex office. With your Diners Club

Bank Guards
State Bank of India
Chowk, Varanasi

card you can get cheques from Thomas Cook offices. With their love of forms and carbon paper Indians delight in credit cards. You'll be delighted when you get back and all those bills eventually turn up and you find that superb splash out meal at the Ritz actually cost $8 or something equally ridiculous. Note that the warning above on airline tickets also applies to credit card purchases. You can buy an overseas ticket on your card and end up with several thousand rupees in your pocket too.

When changing money take two precautions in the rupees you are given. First don't take it all in larger denominations. Breaking big notes down is always a problem in India and there is a permanent shortage of small change. So always break big notes (Rs 100 in particular) down as much as possible. Secondly don't accept torn, damaged or dirty notes — when so many are just that it is hard not to but disposing of a damaged note is always difficult. This particularly applies in small towns where money has to be in better condition than in the big cities to be acceptable.

Finally don't run out of money in India. Getting money transferred to India is a time consuming, boring, tricky and unpleasant operation. Even transferred by cable it can take weeks and weeks and by mail it can take forever. Banks have a reputation for not telling people that money has arrived when it actually has — better in their balance than your pocket seems to be the mood. If you must have money sent to you in India specify the bank, the branch and the address you want it sent to and keep your fingers crossed. Preferably send it to a foreign bank since they are much more efficient when it comes to overseas transactions than Indian banks. Overseas banks with branches in India include American Express, Bank of America, Chartered Bank and, particularly, National & Grindlays which has many branches in smaller cities as well as in the major cities where Amex also operate.

Indian money has its own special angles and curiosities. For a start there is never any change. The restaurant may have been crowded all day but when you give them five rupees for a two rupee drink they won't have any change. Actually the shortage of change is not quite as bad as they'd like to make out. Often they do have change but are trying to bluff you into parting with yours rather than vice versa. Solution is to always insist that you haven't got any change, then with luck when you meet up with someone who really doesn't have any you will.

Bus conductors never start trips with change. You pay for a Rs 6.60 fare with a Rs 10 note and your ticket is marked to indicate you're owed Rs 3.40. Don't lose it and don't forget to demand your change at the end of the trip.

Giving you change is also open to game playing. Change is never counted out as it is in the west, you're simply handed a handful. Very often if you stand there looking blank you'll be handed some more. Then some more. Post offices are particularly good at this. You ask for a couple of aerograms, a couple of stamps to America, one for a card to England. Total amount, who knows. Everybody behind you in the queue is jostling to get to the front. You can be certain that first handful of change isn't the total due. Wait.

The quality of change is also important. Notes circulate for far longer than they do in the west and the small notes in particular become very tatty. A note can have holes right through it and be quite acceptable but if it's torn at the top or bottom on the crease line then it's no good and you'll have trouble spending it. The answer to this is to simply accept it philosophically or think of clever uses. Use it for tips, or for official purposes. I'd love to pay the Rs 100 departure tax with 100 totally disreputable Rs 1 notes. Of course you could just take it to a bank but who wants to visit Indian banks more than necessary?

Tony Wheeler

COSTS

Of course it is virtually impossible to say what travelling around India will cost you. It depends on where you stay, what you eat, how you travel and how fast you travel. Two people travelling at exactly the same standard can spend vastly different amounts on a daily basis if one travels twice as fast as the other. A week lying on the beach at Goa watching the waves roll in brings daily costs down very rapidly. From top to bottom: If you stay in luxury hotels, fly everywhere, see a lot of India in a very short trip you can spend a lot of money. India has plenty of hotels at US$50 or more a day. At the other extreme if you scrimp and save, stay in dormitories or the cheapest hotels, always travel second class on trains, learn to exist on dhal and rice, you can see India on less than US$5 for everything. Most travellers will probably be looking for something between those extremes. If you stay in reasonable hotels — the sort of standard the tourist bungalows provide in many states where you have a clean but straightforward room with fan cooling and an attached bathroom. If you eat in regular restaurants but occasionally splash out on a fancy meal when you're in a big town. If you mix your travel, try second class sometimes for short trips, opt for 1st class if you're travelling on a long overnight trip. If you take taxis occasionally rather than always looking for a bus or rickshaw. In that case India could cost you something like US$8 to 15 a day on average. It totally depends on what you're looking for. As everywhere in Asia though remember that you get pretty much what you pay for and many times it's worth paying a little more for the experience it offers. That old fashioned Raj style luxury is part of India's charm and sometimes it's foolish not to lay out the money and enjoy it.

DOCUMENTS

You have to have a passport, it's the most basic travel document. A health certificate while not necessary for India will probably be required for onward travel. Student cards are not the wonder workers they once were — many student concessions have either been eliminated or replaced by 'youth fares' or similar age concessions. Nevertheless a student card still can have many uses so if you can get one then do. Similarly a youth hostel card is not generally required for India's many hostels but you do pay slightly less with one. There is not much opportunity to get behind the wheel in India but if you do intend to drive then get an International Driving Permit from your local national motoring organisation. It's worth having a batch of 'photo booth' photos for visa applications and other uses. If you run out Indian photo studios will do excellent portraits at pleasantly low prices.

TIPPING
In most Asian countries tipping is virtually unknown but India is an exception to that rule although tipping has a rather different role in India than in the west. The term *baksheesh*, which encompasses tipping and a lot more besides, aptly describes the concept in India. You 'tip' not so much for good services but to get things done. A 'tip' to a station porter will ensure you a seat when the train is packed out to the very limit. Judicious baksheesh will open closed doors, find missing letters, perform other small miracles. Tipping is not necessary for taxis nor for cheaper restaurants but if you're going to be using something repeatedly an initial tip will ensure the standards are kept up — if you wonder why the service is slower every time in your hotel restaurant for example. Keep things in perspective though. Demands for baksheesh can quickly become never ending. Ask yourself if it's really necessary or desirable before shelling it out.

CONSULATES & EMBASSIES
Countries with diplomatic relations with India will generally have their consular offices in New Delhi, the capital, although many also have offices in Bombay and/ or Calcutta. See the relevant sections for addresses. Some of the major Indian consular offices overseas include:

Australia	92 Mugga Way, Red Hill, ACT 2603 (tel 062 95 0045)
Burma	545-547 Merchant St, Rangoon (tel 15933, 16381)
Malaysia	Asian Bank Berhad Building, 19 Malacca St, Kuala Lumpur
Nepal	(tel 21728)
Singapore	31 Grange Rd (tel 737 6809)
Sri Lanka	3rd floor, State Bank of India Building, 18-3/1 Sir Baron Jayatilaka Mawatha, Colombo 1 (tel 21604, 22788)
Thailand	139 Pan Lane, Bangkok (tel 35065)
UK	India House, Aldwych, London WC2B 4NA (tel 01 836 8484)
UN	
USA	3 East 64th St, New York, NY 10021
	2107 Massachusetts Ave NW, Washington DC 2008 (tel 265 5050)

INFORMATION
The Government of India Tourist Office maintains a string of tourist offices overseas where you can get brochures, leaflets and some information about India.

The tourist office leaflets and brochures are often very high in their informational quality and worth getting a hold of. On the other hand the overseas offices are not always as useful for obtaining information as those within the country. Some of the overseas offices include:

Australia	Carlton Centre, 55 Elizabeth St, Sydney, NSW 2000 (tel 02 232 1600)
	Elder House, 111 St George's Terrace, Perth, WA 6000 (tel 06 321 6932)
Canada	Suite 1016, Royal Trust Tower (PO Box 342), Toronto Dominion Centre, Toronto 1, Ontario (tel 416 362 3188)
Japan	Pearl building, 9-18 Ginza, 7 Chome, Chuo ku, Tokyo (tel 571 5062/3)
Singapore	Podium Block, 4th floor, Ming Court Hotel, Tanglin Rd, Singapore 10 (tel 235 5737)
Sweden	Sveavagen 9-11 (Box 40016), 103-41 Stockholm 40 (tel 08 215081)
Thailand	Singapore Airlines Building, 3rd floor, 62/5 Thaniya Rd, Bangkok
UK	21 New Bond St, London W1Y ODY (tel 01 493 0769)
USA	30 Rockefeller Plaza, 15 North Mezzanine, New York, NY 10020 (tel 212 586 4901)
	201 North Michigan Ave, Chicago, Illinois 60601 (tel 312 236 6899)
	3550 Wilshire Blvd, Suite 204, Los Angeles, California 90010 (tel 213 380 8855)

Within India the tourist office story is somewhat blurred by the overlap between the national and state tourist offices. As well as the national tourist office each state maintains its own tourist office and this can lead to some confusion. In some cities there will be a state and a national tourist office but sometimes the national office will be much larger than the state one or the state one will be virtually nonexistent. Government of India Tourist Offices include:

Agra	191 The Mall (tel 72377)
Aurangabad	Krishna Vilas Station Rd (tel 2817)
Bombay	123 M Karve Rd (tel 293144)
Calcutta	Embassy 4 Shakespeare Sarani (tel 441402)
Cochin	Willingdon Island (tel 6045)
New Delhi	88 Janpath (tel 320005)
Jaipur	State Hotel (tel 72200)
Jammu	Gulab Bhavan (tel 5121)
Khajuraho	Near Western Group Temples (tel 47)

| Madras | 35 Mount Rd (tel 86240) |
| Varanasi | 15B The Mall (tel 64189) |

The state offices vary widely in their efficiency and usefulness. Some of them are very good, some completely hopeless. In many states the tourist offices also run a chain of Tourist Bungalows which generally offer good accommodation at very reasonable prices. State tourist offices will usually be located in the Tourist Bungalows.

The confusion and overlap between the national and state tourist offices often causes wasteful duplication. Both offices produce a brochure on place A, neither produces anything on place B. More confusion comes in with the division between the Government of India Tourist Office and the Indian Tourism Development Council (ITDC). The latter is more an actual 'doing' organisation than a 'telling' one. The ITDC will actually operate the tour bus on the tour for which the tourist office sells tickets. The ITDC also runs a series of hotels and Travellers' Lodges around the country under the Ashoka name.

GENERAL INFORMATION
Postal & Telephone Services

The Indian postal services and poste restantes are generally excellent. Expected letters almost always are there and letters you send almost invariably get there. American Express, in its major city locations, is an alternative to the poste restante system but the latter is quite OK. Have letters addressed to you with your surname in capitals and underlined, the poste restante, GPO, the city in question. Many 'lost' letters are simply misfiled under Christian names so always check under both your names.

The telephone system in India is hit and miss. Local calls sometimes work, sometimes don't. Trunk calls are even more a matter of chance. Many calls can be dialled direct but if you get through it feels like a pure fluke. It's probably even more flukey if you can actually hear anything. It's more time consuming but more positive putting trunk calls through the operator but again there's no guarantee you'll have a clear line. As for international calls — well sometimes you can get through in 20 minutes, sometimes you won't be able to get through in 24 hours. If you're intending to make an overseas call from the GPO you should come prep-

AGRA - DECEMBER 25th

A call home for Christmas and a telephone clerk who looked much like Santa ared for a long, long wait — bring something to read, something to sit on, food and drink.

Posting a parcel from India
Most people discover how to do this the hard way in which case it demands all morning or all afternoon. If you're not that keen to reach a peak of hitherto unknown frustration then go about it this way:

(1) Take the parcel to a tailor and tell him you'd like it stitched up in cheap linen and the seams sealed with sealing wax. The wax has to be pressed with a seal which cannot be duplicated (if all else fails a non-Indian coin will serve). At some larger post offices this stitching up service is offered outside. For a small parcel it should cost between Rs 4-7.

(2) Go to the post office with your parcel and ask for two customs declaration forms. Fill them in and glue one to the parcel. Write your passport number (or any likely looking number) somewhere on the forms together with 'bona fide tourist'. To avoid excise duty at the delivery end it's best to specify that the contents are a 'gift'. The value of the parcel can be up to Rs 1000. (This concession is for tourists only. Internal parcels cannot exceed Rs 500 in value.)

(3) Get the parcel weighed and ask how much it's going to cost.

(4) Buy the stamps (usually not sold at the parcel counter) and stick them on.

(5) Hand the parcel in at the parcel counter and get a receipt for it.

Even if you do it this way it can still take up to two hours. Any other way and you say goodbye to the whole day.

Time
India is 5½ hours ahead of GMT, 4½ hours behind Australian Eastern Standard Time, 10½ hours ahead of American Eastern Standard Time.

Business Hours
Indian shops, offices and post offices are not early starters. Generally shops are open from 10 am to 5 pm daily and on Saturdays. Some government offices open on alternate Saturdays and some commercial offices are open for Saturday mornings. Post offices are open 10 am to 5 pm on weekdays and on Saturday mornings. Main city offices may be open longer hours, such as 8 am to 6 pm in Delhi. Banks are open for business between 10 am and 2 pm on weekdays and 10 am and 12 noon on Saturdays. The Ashoka Hotel in New Delhi has a bank branch open 24 hours a day for money changing. Sunday is the general closing day.

Electricity
230-240 volts, 50 cycles, alternating current. Electricity is widely available in India but breakdowns and blackouts are not uncommon.

MEDIA
There are a number of daily newspapers in English in India — all of the heavy news variety, there are no tabloids on the sub-continent. The *Times of India* and the *Statesman* are probably the best papers. The former is headquartered in Bombay and the latter in Calcutta but there are many regional editions in both cases. The *Illustrated Weekly of India* makes good reading on long train rides and is readily

available at train and bus station news-stands. The same applies to the fortnightly *India Today*, a news magazine very Time-like in its size, format, approach and layout. The problem with all these Indian publications is that they are so inward looking that you soon become starved for outside news. *Time* and *Newsweek* are readily available throughout India although once you've become used to Indian prices they seem very expensive! There are all sorts of other Indian magazines in English although many are of very limited interest to western visitors — it takes a long time to build up an interest in Indian movie stars and their film-fan magazines! Indian women's magazines, so alike yet so unlike their western counterparts, are definitely worth looking at.

India also has a wide network of radio stations and TV stations are becoming increasingly widespread. The TV programmes are very much intended to be educational rather than sheer entertainment, however.

Sports

India follows a variety of sports including field hockey in which it is one of the world's leaders with a number of Olympic golds to their credit. Soccer has a keen following in a number of big cities but particularly in Calcutta where it is a major sport. India's national sport has to be cricket. There's something about a game with as many idiosyncrasies and peculiarities as cricket which simply has to appeal to the Indian temperament. During the cricket season, if Australia or England are touring India and there is a test match on, you'll see crowds at every street corner in the big cities clamouring to hear what the latest score is from some transistor listener. Test matches with Pakistan, one sign of the thaw in relations between the countries, always have a particularly strong following.

HEALTH

Apart from yellow fever and smallpox vaccinations for people coming from infected areas there are no vaccination requirements for visitors to India. You may consider that some protection is worthwhile, nevertheless, and should consult your doctor as to what he thinks is necessary. Smallpox, it is believed, has now been totally eradicated worldwide. If so then there is no need for vaccination but if you decide to

A national pastime. Test cricket by transistor radio...

go ahead anyway the smallpox vaccination provides protection for three years.

Cholera is a disease of insanitation and usually occurs in epidemics. Protection against cholera is recommended for India and the vaccination is good for six months. A very useful vaccination, although not required but health authorities, is TABT. This provides protection against typhoid, paratyphoid A and B and tetanus. Typhoid and paratyphoid are both diseases of insanitation, spread by contaminated food. Tetanus is usually caused by a cut or skin puncture. All three are prevalent in hot climates. There are a number of medical centres in India where it is possible to get free or low cost cholera and other vaccinations.

Polio is also a disease spread by insanitation and found more frequently in hot climates. A booster every five years is recommended by many doctors. The other vaccination you may wish to consider taking is against infectious hepatitis. This disease is, once again, spread by infected water or food but the degree of protection provided by the gamma globulin injection prescribed against it is still a subject of controversy. Improved procedures are now believed to provide good protection for up to six months.

It is not possible to be vaccinated against malaria but it is absolutely necessary to take precautions against it while you are in India. Malaria is spread by mosquitoes and the disease has a nasty habit of coming back in later years even if you are cured at the time — and it can be fatal. Protection is simple — a daily or weekly tablet depending on which your doctor recommends.

Rabies is also widespread in India — don't be friendly to India's numerous stray dogs and beware of those picturesque monkeys. If you are bitten by a possibly rabid animal you should wash the wound thoroughly and then embark on a 14 day series of injections which will prevent the disease developing. Rabies, once developed, is almost always fatal. New rabies vaccines have been developed which have less side effects than the older animal-derived serums and vaccines.

The usual health problem afflicting visitors to India is far more mundane than rabies, hepatitis or malaria. It's simply Delhi belly, the old upset stomach. Often this can be due simply to a change of diet or a system unused to spicy food. Many times, however, contaminated food or water is the problem. There are two answers to the upset stomach problem. First avoid getting it in the first place by taking care in what you eat and drink. Uncooked foods are always more likely to harbour germs but so are cooked foods once they have been allowed to cool. Try to eat only freshly cooked foods and beware of places where food is left sitting around for long periods, particularly if exposed to flies. The main cause of upset stomaches is probably drinking water — the answer is to either drink hot tea or bottled soft drinks from reputable bottlers. This doesn't always work in the thirsty hot season so if you must drink water try to either have it boiled or carry water purification tablets. These are available from pharmacies in the west or, with more difficulty, in India.

If avoidance fails and you do get a stomach bug the first thing to do is nothing. If you can simply get back to health by yourself you'll probably build up some immunity against it recurring. Stick to hot tea and try not to eat too much. If that fails then try a proprietary, over the counter, stomach upset cure before you bring in the heavy guns. People who take antibiotics at the first sign of an upset stomach are only asking for trouble. Not only does it make another assault more difficult to repel, it also kills off the useful organisms in your digestive tract just as efficiently as it kills off the harmful ones. People whose travels in India are one long series of stomach problems are often the people who overdid the modern medicines. Despite which it is wise to carry a heavy gun in reserve and Lomotil is probably the best general cure for serious problems. In the west it's a prescription drug, ask your doctor for a supply when you get your vaccinations.

During the hot season there are some additional precautions to take to ensure good health. First of all protect yourself from the sun as much as possible — it doesn't burn, due to all the dust haze, so you won't get sunburnt but it certainly does you no good. Secondly keep your liquid intake up. If you find you are urinating very infrequently or your urine turns a deep yellow or orange you're becoming dehydrated. It's very easy to do just that in the hot season. At times like this you have to balance the dangers of drinking the water against the dangers of dehydration. The first is possible, the second is definite so if necessary throw caution to the winds and drink more water. In good restaurants and hotels drinking water is generally OK anyway. During the dry season water is much less like to be polluted. It's during the monsoon that you must be especially careful about drinking water.

Finally some miscellaneous thoughts: make sure your teeth are in good shape before departing — dentists' equipment is not always what we've got used to in the west. Always carry a spare pair of glasses and your prescription in case of loss or breakage. It's relatively easy to get glasses made up in an emergency. Don't walk around in bare feet, that is how you get hookworms or worse. Thongs are useful protectors in hotel showers against athletes' foot or other fungal infections. If a simple stomach upset turns out to be real down-to-earth dysentery the most important thing is not to become dehydrated. Get plenty of liquids. If you get the dreaded hep, rest, good food, no alcohol and generally taking it easy is the cure. Make sure you have a good medical insurance policy, one that covers flying you home in emergencies. If you do need a doctor or other medical help your embassy or consulate or a five-star hotel should be able to recommend someone.

Most important of all don't get overly concerned about your health. Most people survive India with very few problems. During the course of researching this book Tony and Maureen spent three months in India in one stretch, during the hot season, and while Maureen was pregnant, with nothing more than a couple of mild stomach upsets between them.

WHAT TO TAKE & HOW TO TAKE IT

The usual travellers' rule applies — bring as little as possible. It's much better to have to get something you've left behind than find you have too much and need to get rid of it. In the south of India you can count on shirtsleeve weather year round but in the north it can get cool enough to require a sweater or light jacket in the evenings during the winter. In the far north it will get down to freezing and you will need all the warm weather gear you can muster.

Remember that clothes are easily and cheaply purchased in India. You can buy things off the peg or have clothes made to measure in the small tailor shops that are found everywhere in India. In the big cities there are plenty of the Indian fashions that are so popular in the west and the prices often approximate in rupees to what they cost in dollars in the west! One item of clothing to have made as soon as possible is a pair of lightweight pyjama style trousers. You'll find them far cooler and more comfortable than jeans and they'll only cost a few rupees.

Modesty rates highly in India, as in most Asian countries. Although men wearing shorts is accepted as a western eccentricity women should dress more discreetly. A reasonable clothes list would include:

underwear & swimming gear
one pair of jeans, one pair of shorts

a few T-shirts or short sleeved shirts	On the non-clothing side take along
sweater for cold nights	washing gear
one pair of sneakers or shoes	medical & sewing kit
sandals and/or thongs	sunglasses
lightweight jacket or raincoat	padlock
a 'dress up' set of clothes	

Other non-clothing items to consider include an umbrella, invaluable in the monsoon. A sleeping bag can be a hassle to carry but can serve as something to sleep in (and avoid unsavoury looking hotel bedding), a cushion on hard train seats, a seat for long waits on railway platforms, a bed top-cover (since hotels rarely give you one) and, of course, as a sleeping bag. If you're going trekking in the north then a sleeping bag will be absolutely necessary. Note that trekking gear cannot be easily hired in India the way it can be in Nepal. Some travellers find that a plastic sheet is useful for a number of reasons including bed-bug proofing unhealthy looking beds.

Soap, toothpaste and other toiletries are readily available but toilet paper can be difficult to find outside of major centres. A sink plug is worth having since few cheaper hotels have plugs. Women will find tampons are virtually unobtainable in India.

Where to put all this gear — well for budget travellers the backpack is still the best carrying container. Adding a little thief proofing protection by sewing on tabs so you can padlock it shut is worthwhile. An alternative is a large, soft, zip bag with a wide shoulder strap. It's not so easy to carry for distances but it is rather more thief proof and less prone to damage. Some airlines will no longer accept responsibility for damage or theft from backpacks. Suitcases are only for jet-setters!

Miscellaneous Useful Things
It's amazing how many things you wish you had with you when you're in India. One of the most useful for budget travellers is a padlock. In fact a padlock is a virtual necessity. Many cheaper hotels, in fact most of them, have doors locked by a hasp and padlock. You'll find having your own sturdy lock on the door instead of the flimsy thing the hotel supplies does wonders for your peace of mind. Other uses are legion. You can lock a pack onto a railway luggage rack at night for example. It may not make it thief proof but it helps.

A universal sink plug is useful since sinks never have them. Ever tried to wash your underwear in a sink without a plug? A knife (Swiss Army for preference) finds a whole field of uses, in particular for peeling fruit. Some travellers rhapsodise about how useful a miniature electric element to boil water in a cup is.

Toilet paper is a real necessity of course unless you can adapt to the Indian method of a jug of water and your left hand. Since not many trees end up as toilet paper in India the stuff can be very hard to find outside of the big cities and tourist centres. And when you do find it Indian toilet paper is both lousy (either the British masochist style waxed paper stuff or a tube of cardboard cms thick with about a metre and a half of paper wrapped around it) and horrendously expensive. One solution is to come to India with an absurd quantity of this western luxury. That makes more sense than it sounds — toilet paper is extremely light and also extremely bulky. Having your pack half full of paper is one way of ensuring that when it's used up you'll have plenty of space for all those interesting things you'll be buying.

Hot weather survival requires another book of rules in India. First of all a sun hat is essential. Stepping out into the sun in India in the hot season is like using your head as a blacksmith's anvil. You don't just feel the sun, it reaches out and hits you. Secondly a water bottle should always be by your side and thirdly have water purification tablets. In the heat you need water — cups of tea, fruit and soft drinks are just not going to do the job. Purification tabs are not 100% effective but when it gets really hot you're not going to care how effective they are!

INDIAN CLOTHING

Many travellers start wearing Indian clothes while in India — after all much of it is a lot more appropriate to India's climate than jeans and T-shirts. Best known Indian clothing style, and one the wearing of which few western women can carry off properly, is the sari. This supremely graceful attire is simply one length of material, a bit over a metre in width and five to nine metres long (usually around six metres long). It's worn without any pins, buttons or fastenings to hold it in place so in part its graceful appearance is a necessity. The tightly fitted, short blouse worn under a sari is a choli. The final length of the sari, which is draped over the wearer's shoulder, is known as the pallav or palloo.

There are a number of variations in types of saris and styles of wearing them but there are also other styles of women's costume in India. Sikh women wear pyjama like trousers drawn tightly in at the waist and the ankles. Over these trousers, known as salwars, they wear a long, loose tunic known as a kameez. A churidhar is similar to salwars but tighter fitting at the hips. Over this goes a collar-less or mandarin collar kurta — an item of clothing just as popular in the west, where it is worn by men as much as women, as in India.

Although the overwhelming majority of Indian women wear traditional costume many Indian men wear quite conventional western clothing. Indeed a large proportion of India's consumer advertising appears to be devoted to 'suitings & shirtings' — the material for tailor made western-style business suits and shirts. The traditonal lungi originated in the south and today is worn by women as well as men. It's simply a short length of material worn around the thighs rather like a sarong. A dhoti is like a longer lungi but with a length of material pulled up between the legs, effective but a long way from elegant! Pyjama-like trousers, worn by countryfolk, are known as lenga.

There are many religious and regional variations such as the brightly mirrored Rajasthani skirts and their equally colourful tie-dye materials. In Ladakh the women wear superbly picturesque Tibetan costumes with high 'top hats'. Their men wear long dressing gown-like coats. Moslem women, of course, wear much more staid and all-covering attire than their Hindu sisters. More traditional Moslems even wear the all-enveloping tent-like burkha.

Dobi Wallahs

Your clothes will undoubtedly become involved at some point in your travels with the Indian ability to make systems of amazing complexity function smoothly. Travelling in India there's hardly any need for more than one change of clothes. Everyday there will be a knock on your door and the laundry boy will collect all those dusty, sweaty clothes you wore yesterday and every evening those same clothes will re-appear — washed and ironed with more loving care than any washing powder ad-mum ever lavished upon anything. And all for 40 or 50c at the most. But what happened to your clothes between their departure and their like-new return?

Well they certainly did not get anywhere near a washing machine. First of all they're collected and taken to the dobi ghat. A ghat is a place with water, a dobi is a washerman so the dobi ghat is where the dobi plys his trade and washes clothes. In big cities dobi ghats will be huge places with hundred of dobis doing their thing with thousands of articles of clothing.

INDIANS TRYING TO BREAK
STONES WITH WET WASHING...
RANA GHAT - VARANASI

First of all the clothes are separated — all the white shirts are washed together, all the grey trousers, all the red skirts, all the blue jeans. By now, if this was the west, your clothes would either be hopelessly lost or you'd need a computer to keep track of them all. Your clothes are soaked in soapy water for a few hours, following which the dirt is literally beaten out of them. No multi-programmed, miracle of technology can wash as clean as a determined dobi although admittedly after a few visits to the Indian laundry your clothes do begin to look distinctly thinner.

Once clean the clothes are strung out on miles of clothes line to quickly dry in the Indian sun then taken to the ironing sheds where hundreds of ironers wielding primitive irons press your jeans like they've never been pressed before. Not just your jeans — your socks, your T-shirts, ever your underwear will come back with knife edge creases. Then the Indian miracle takes place. Out of the thousands upon thousands of items washed that day somehow your very own brown socks, blue jeans, yellow T-shirt and red underwear all find their way back together and head back for your hotel room. There's a system of marking clothes, known only to the dobis, which is the real reason behind this feat. They say criminals have been tracked down simply by those tell-tale 'dobi marks'.

FILM & CAMERA

Film is available in India but mainly black and white or colour print film and the colour film is not cheap. If you're taking slides then bring it with you, and bring plenty, India is a photogenic country. Black and white film and colour prints can be developed and printed quickly and cheaply in India but colour transparencies will need to be developed overseas. It's up to you whether you send them straight back or carry them back with you at the end of your trip. Film manufacturers warn that once exposed films should be developed as quickly as possible but in practice they seem to last, even in India's summer heat, without deterioration for months.

There are plenty of camera shops who should be able to make minor repairs should you have any camera problems in India. Photography in India presents some special problems. In the dry season the hazy atmosphere makes it difficult to get sharp shots or to get much contrast between what you are photographing and the background. Everything looks washed out and flat even using a polarising filter. In the mountains you should allow for the extreme clarity of the air and light intensity and take care not to over-expose your shots.

Be careful what you photograph. India is touchy about places of military importance — this can include train stations, bridges, airports and any military installations. If in doubt ask. In general most people are happy to be photographed but care should be taken in pointing cameras at Moslem women. Again, if in doubt, ask.

THEFT

Having things stolen is a problem in India, not so much because it's a theft prone country, it isn't but because you can become involved in a lot of hassles getting it replaced. If your passport is stolen you may have a long trip back to an embassy to replace it. Travellers' cheques may be replaceable if stolen but first of all avoid theft. Always lock your room, preferably with your own padlock in cheaper hotels. Never leave those most important valuables (passport, tickets, health certificates, money, travellers' cheques) in your room, they should be with you at all times. Either have a stout leather passport wallet on your belt, or a passport pouch under your shirt, or simply extra internal pockets in your clothing. On trains at night keep your gear near to you, padlocking a bag to a luggage rack can be useful. Never walk around with valuables casually slung over your shoulder. Take extra care in crowded public transport. In Bombay, for example, pickpockets are adept at the razor on the back pocket or shoulder bag technique.

Beware also of your fellow travellers. Unhappily there are more than a few backpackers who make the money go further by helping themselves to other peoples'. At places like Goa be very careful with things on the beach — while you're in the water your camera or money can walk away very fast. If you're unlucky enough to have things stolen some precautions can ease the pain. All travellers cheques are replaceable but it does you little immediate good if you have to go home and apply to your bank to do that. What you want is instant replacement. Furthermore what do you do if you lose your cheques and money and have a day or more to travel to the replacement office? The answer to that is to keep an emergency cash stash in some totally separate place. In that same place you should keep a record of the cheque serial numbers and your passport number. Remember that backpacks are very easy to be rifled through. Don't leave valuables in them, especially for flights. Remember also that something may be of little or no value to a thief but to lose it would be a real heartbreak to you — like film. Finally a good travel insurance policy helps.

PLACES TO STAY

India has a very wide range of accommodation possibilities apart from straight-forward hotels. Some of them include:

Cheap Hotels There are hotels all over India with conditions ranging from extremely drab and dismal (but prices at rock bottom levels) up to quite reasonable standards and at quite reasonable prices. Lazily swishing ceiling fans, mosquito nets on the beds, private toilets and bathrooms are all possibilities even in rooms costing Rs 25 or less a night for a double. A standard term you'll find throughout India is the definition of hotels as 'western' or 'Indian'. It's basically a pretty meaningless differentiation although expensive hotels are always western, cheap ones always Indian. 'Indian' hotels will be more simply and economically furnished but the acid test is likely to be the toilet. 'Western' hotels have to have a sit up style toilet, 'Indian' ones are usually (but not always) the traditional Asian squat style. You can find modern, well equipped, clean places with Indian toilets and dirty, dismal dumps with western toilets so don't be put off them.

Expensive Hotels You won't find 'International Standard' hotels throughout India. The big, air-con, swimming pool places are generally confined to the major tourist centres and the big cities. There are a number of big hotel chains in India. They include the government operated ITDC chain who usually append the name 'Ashoka' to their hotels. There's an Ashoka hotel in virtually every town in India so that test isn't foolproof but the ITDC places include a number of smaller, but higher standard, units in places like Sanchi or Konarak where accommodation possibilities are limited. The Taj Group has some of India's flashiest hotels including the luxurious Taj Mahal Inter-Continental in Bombay, the romantic Rambagh Palace in Jaipur and Lake Palace in Udaipur and other interesting hotels such as the Taj Coromandel in Madras and the Fort Aguada Resort in Goa. The Oberoi chain is of course well known outside India as well as within. Clarks are a small chain with popular hotels in Varanasi and Agra amongst other places. The more expensive hotels in India are not the great bargain they might seem at first. Although labour costs in India are low it takes a lot of people to get anything done. Combine that with high costs for imported equipment and fittings plus the high cost of electricity and power in India and room costs are certainly not low in India compared to other countries' more expensive hotels.

Government Accommodation Back in the days of the Raj a whole string of government run accommodation units were set up with labels like Rest Houses, Dak Bungalows, Circuit Houses, PWD (Public Works Department) Bungalows, Forest Rest Houses and so on. Today most of these are reserved for government officials although in some places they may still be available for tourists, if there is room. In an approximate pecking order the Dak Bungalows are the most basic, they often have no electricity and only basic equipment in out of the way places. Rest Houses are next up and then comes the Circuit Houses which are strictly for travelling VIPs.

Tourist Bungalows These often serve as replacements for the older government run accommodation units. Tourist Bungalows are generally well kept and are often excellent value. They often have dorm beds but rooms are usually doubles only so they're often not much good for solo travellers who want a room rather than a dormitory. The typical tourist bungalow will have rooms at Rs 20 to 40 for a double. The rooms will be well kept, have a fan, double bed, attached bathroom and there may also be more expensive air-conditioned rooms. There will generally be a restaurant or 'dining hall'. There are particularly good Tourist Bungalows in Rajasthan and Orissa although almost every state has some towns where the Tourist Bungalow is definitely the best place to stay.

Railway Retiring Rooms These are just like regular hotels or dormitories except they are at the railway stations. To stay there you are generally supposed to have a railway ticket although a Tourist Introduction Card will often do the trick. The rooms are, of course, excellent if you want to be handy for a train departure although they can be noisy if it is a busy station. They are often very cheap and in some places they are also excellent value. Some stations have retiring rooms of definite Raj pretensions with huge rooms and enough furniture to do up a flat or apartment back home.

Railway Waiting Rooms Emergency accommodation when all else fails or when you just need a few hours shut-eye before your train departs at 2 am. These are a free place to rest your weary head. The trick is to rest it in the comfortable 1st class waiting room and not the depressing and crowded lower class one. Officially you need a 1st class ticket to be allowed to use the 1st class room and its superior facilities. In practice, luck and your Tourist Introduction Card or 2nd class Indrail Pass may work.

Youth Hostels Indian youth hostels are generally very cheap and sometimes in excellent condition with superb facilities. They are, however, often rather inconveniently situated, some distance from the town centres. You are not usually required to be a YHA member, as in other countries, to use the hostels although your YHA card will generally get you a lower rate. Nor do the usual rules about arrival and departure times, lights out times or not using the hostel during the day apply. A list of Government of India hostels includes:

Andhra Pradesh	Hyderabad Youth Hostel, Hyderabad
Goa	Panaji Youth Hostel, Panaji
Gujurat	Gandhinagar Youth Hostel, Sector 16, Gandhinagar
Haryana	Panchkula Youth Hostel, Haryana Tourist Complex, Panchkula, Ambala
Himachal Pradesh	Dalhousie Youth Hostel, Dalhousie
Jammu & Kashmir	Patni Top Youth Hostel, c/o Tourist Office, Kud
Kerala	Trivandrum Youth Hostel, Trivandrum
Madhya Pradesh	Bhopal Youth Hostel, North TT Nagar, Bhopal
Maharashtra	Arrangabad Youth Hostel, Aurangabad
Orissa	Youth Hostel, Chakratirtha Rd, Puri
Punjab	Amritsar Youth Hostel, Mal Mandi, GT Rd, Amritsar
Rajasthan	Jaipur Youth Hostel, SMS Stadium, Jaipur
Tamil Nadu	Madras Youth Hostel, Indira Nagar, Madaras
Uttar Pradesh	Nainital Youth Hostel, Mallitan near Ardwell Camp, The Mall, Nainital
West Bengal	Darjeeling Youth Hostel, 16 Dr Zakir Hussain Rd, Darjeeling

Other There are YMCAs and YWCAs in many big cities — some of these are modern, well equipped, more expensive (but still good value) places. There are also a few Salvation Army Hostels — in particular in Bombay and Calcutta. There are a few camping places around India but travellers with their own vehicles can almost always find hotels with gardens where they can park and camp. Free accommodation is available at some Sikh Temples where there is a tradition of hospitality to visitors. It can be an interesting insight to try it but please don't abuse this hospitality and spoil it for other travellers. At many pilgrimage sites there are dharamsalas offering accommodation to pilgrims and travellers are often welcome to use these. This particularly applies at isolated sites like Ranakpur in Rajasthan.

FOOD

Despite the very fine food that can be prepared in India you'll often find food a great disappointment. In many smaller centres there is simply not a great choice of food and you'll get bored with rice and dahl. When you're in larger cities where the food can be excellent take advantage of it.

Officially Hindus are all vegetarians but in practice that ruling may not always apply. Strict vegetarianism is confined more to the south which has not had the meat eating influence of the Aryan and later Moslem invasions. On the other hand eating meat is not always a great pleasure in India — the quality tends to be low (most chickens seem to die from starvation) and the hygiene is not all that it might be. Beef, from the holy cow, is strictly taboo of course — and leads to interesting Indian dishes like the muttonburger. Pork is equally taboo to the Moslems. All in all whether you're vegetarian or not you'll end up eating a lot more vegetarian food in India.

Railway station restaurants are always a good bet in India. Their food is generally safe and if one more curry will kill you they also have a western menu — at higher prices. Of course no culinary achievement awards are ever going to be made to station restaurants but in general they're not bad. Indian interpretations of western cuisine can be pretty horrific, it's usually best to let them stick to preparing Indian food. Meals served on trains are usually palatable too, and reasonably cheap. At every stop you will be besieged by food and drink sellers. Even in the middle of the night that raucous cry of 'chai, chai' breaks into your sleep. The sheer bedlam of an Indian station when a train is in is a part of India you never forget.

If, after some time in India, you do find the food is getting you down physically or psychologically, there are a couple of escapes. It is very easy for budget travellers to lose weight in India and feel lethargic and drained of energy. The answer is to up your protein intake — eat more eggs which are readily available; buy bananas, mandarin oranges or peanuts, all readily available at stations or in the markets. Another answer, if you're travelling on a budget, is to occasionally splash out on a meal in a fancy hotel or restaurant — compared to what you have been paying it may seem amazingly expensive but try translating the price into what it would be at home.

There are considerable regional variations from north to south, partly because of climatic conditions and partly because of historical influences. In the north, as already mentioned, much more meat is eaten and the cooking is often 'Moghul style' which bears a closer relationship to food of the Middle East and Central Asia. The emphasis is more on spices and less on curry heat. In the north there are also much more grains and breads eaten and less rice. In the south the food is more strictly vegetarian, more rice is eaten and the curries tend to be hotter. Sometimes very hot. Another peculiarity of southern vegetarian food is you do not need eating utensils, it is always eaten with fingers (of the right hand only). Scooping up food that way takes a little practice but you soon become quite adept at it. It is said that eating this way allows you to get the 'feel' of the food, as important to south Indian cuisine as the aroma or the arrangement is for other cooking styles, but it also offers the added protection that you never need worry if the eating utensils have been properly washed.

In the most basic Indian restaurants and eating places the cooking is usually done right out front so you can actually see exactly what is going on and how it is done. Vegetables will be on the simmer all day and tend to be cooked out and mushy to western tastes. In these basic places dhal is usually free but you pay for chappatis, parathas, puris or rice. Sabzi (vegetable stew), dahl and a few chappatis makes a passable meal for less than Rs 2. If you order half plates of the various dishes brewing out front you get half the quantity at half the price and get a little more variety. With chutneys and a small plate of onions, which come free, you can put together a reasonable vegetarian meal for, say, Rs 3, or non-vegetarian for Rs 5. In railway station restaurants and other cheaper restaurants always check the prices and add up your bill. If it's incorrect query it.

At the other end of the price scale there are many restaurants in India's five star hotels that border on the luxurious and by western standards are really absurdly cheap. Paying US$8 to 10 for a meal in India seems exorbitant after you've been there for a while but check what a meal in your friendly local Hilton would cost you. As one traveller put it:

If not on a starvation budget the occasional splurge on a really good meal is very worthwhile in India. Best value are the unlimited 'buffet lunches' which are available at a number of the larger hotels. The *Taj Mahal Inter-Continental* in Bombay is one of the best. A large, opulent dining room complete with orchestra and an astonishing array of every kind of food imaginable. Rs 60, including service, covers all you can eat. The *Oberoi Grand* in Calcutta comes a close second — a much smaller dining room here and perhaps not quite so much variety but the quality is even higher. Where else can you find a tray of steaks to help yourself from? It's slightly more expensive than the Taj but in Madras the *Connemara* is rather cheaper. The food here is not in quite such abundant variety but you can still eat yourself silly. Extras like soft drinks are very expensive in these hotels — drink water or make yourself a milk shake from the ice cream!

Many other international standard hotels, like the *Oberoi Palace* in Srinagar, offer similar deals. For budget travellers it makes a very pleasant change from dhal and rice.

Finally a couple of hints on how to cope with curry. After a while in India you'll get used to even the fiercest curries and you find western food surprisingly bland. If, however, you do find your mouth is on fire don't reach for water. In emergencies that hardly helps at all. Curd (yoghurt) or fruit do the job much more efficiently.

Curry & Spice

Although all Indian food is certainly not curry this is still the basis of Indian cuisine. Curry doesn't have to be hot enough to blow your head off although it certainly can do that if it's made that way. Curry most definitely is not something found in a packet of curry power. The Indian cook has about 25 spices on his or her regular list and it is from these that they produce the curry flavour. Usually the spices are freshly ground in a mortar and pestle known as a *sil-vatta*. Spices are usually blended in certain combinations to produce *masalas*. *Garam masala*, for example, is a red hot combination of cloves and cinnamon with peppercorns.

Popular spices include *saffron*, an expensive spice produced from flowers. This is used to give rice that yellow biriyani colouring and delicate fragrance. *Turmeric* also has a colouring property, acts as a preservative and has a distinctive smell and taste. *Chillies* are ground, dried or added whole to supply that curry heat. They come in red and green varieties but it's the green ones which are hottest. *Ginger* is supposed to be good for the digestion while many masalas contain *coriander* because it is said to cool the body. Strong and sweet *cardamom* is used in many desserts and in rich meat dishes. Other popular spices include *nutmeg, cinnamon, poppy seeds, caraway seeds, cummin, fenugreek, mace, garlic* and *cloves*.

Breads & Grains

Rice is, of course, the basic Indian staple but although it is eaten throughout the country it's only in the south where it is all-important. In the north rice is supplemented by a whole range of breads known as *rotis*. You can also find western style sliced bread in India but it is always horrible, sickly sweet and nearly inedible. The best Indian rice, it is generally agreed, is found in the north where *Basmati* rice grows in the Punjab and Uttar Pradesh.

Indian breads are varied but always delicious. Simplest is the *chappati* which is just flour and water fried up like a thin pancake. If butter or some other oil is added it becomes a *paratha*. If you deep fried it you would have a *poori* in the north or a *loochi* in the east. Made of lentil flour it would be a *dosa* in the south, dosas are actually found all over India and wrapped around curried vegetables you have *masala dosa*, a terrific snack meal. Another type of deep fried bread with a stuffing is the *kachori*. Bake the bread in an oven and you have *nan*. Whatever you do with it Indian rotis taste great.

Use your chappati or paratha to mop up or scoop up your curry. An *idli* is a kind of rice dumpling, often served with a spicy curd sauce or with spiced lentils and chutney. *Papadums* are crispy deep fried wafers often served with thalis or other meals.

Basic Dishes

Curries can be vegetable, meat (usually chicken or lamb) or fish but they are always fried in *ghee*, clarified butter, or vegetable oil. North or south they will be accompanied by rice but in the north the various excellent breads will also come with them. There are various dishes which aren't really curries but are close enough to them for western tastes. *Vindaloos* have a vinegar marinade and tend to be hotter than most curries. *Pork vindaloo* is a favourite dish in Goa. *Kormas*, on the other hand, are rich, substantial dishes prepared by braising. *Doopiaza* literally means 'two onions' and is a type of korma which uses onions at two stages in its preparation.

Probably the most basic of Indian dishes is *dhal*, rather like a thick lentil soup. Dhal is almost always there whether as an accompaniment to a curry or as a very basic meal in itself with chappatis or rice. In many places dhal and rice is just about all there is on the menu so you'll get heartily sick of it before you leave! Other basic dishes include *mattar paneer* — curried cheese; *saag gosht* — meat and spinach; *alur dam* — potato curry; *alu chhole* — spicy-sour chick peas and diced potatoes.

Tandoori & Biriyani

Tandoori food is a northern speciality and refers to the clay oven in which the food is cooked after first being marinaded in a complex mix of herbs and yoghurt. Tandoori food, tandoori chicken is a special favourite, is not as hot as curry dishes and usually tastes terrific. *Biriyani*, and again chicken is a popular biriyani dish, is another northern Moghul dish. Here the chicken or other meat is mixed with a deliciously flavoured, orange coloured rice which is sometimes spiced with nuts or dried fruit. A *pulao* is a simpler version of a biriyani and you will also find it in other Asian countries further west. Those who have the idea that Indian food is always curry and always fiery hot will be surprised by tandoori and biriyani dishes.

Regional Specialities

Rogan Josh is a straightforward curried lamb which is always popular in the north and in Kashmir where it originated. *Gushtaba*, pounded and spiced meat balls cooked in a yoghurt sauce, is another Kashmiri speciality. Still in the north *chicken makhanwala* is a rich dish cooked in a butter sauce. Many coastal areas have excellent seafood including Bombay where the *pomfret*, a flounder like fish is popular; as is Bombay duck which is not a duck at all but another fish dish. *Dhansak* is a Pharsi speciality found in Bombay — lamb or chicken cooked with curried lentils and steamed rice. Further south Goa also has excellent fish and prawns and in Kerala state Cochin is famous for its prawns.

Another indication of the influence of central Asian cooking styles on north Indian food is the popularity of *kebabas*. You'll find them all across north India with a number of local variations and specialities. In Calcutta *kati kebabas* are a local favourite. Another Bengali dish is *dahi maach* — curried fish in yoghurt sauce, flavoured with ginger and turmeric. Further south in Hyderabad you could try *haleen*, pounded wheat with a lightly spiced mutton gravy.

Side Dishes

Indian food generally has a number of side dishes to go alongside the main meal. Probably the most popular is *dahi* — curd or yoghurt. It has the useful ability of instantly cooling an over-heated curry — either blend it into the curry or, if it's too late, you can administer it straight to your mouth. Curd is often used in the cooking as a dessert as well as appearing in the popular drink *lassi*. *Raita* is another popular side dish consisting of curd mixed with cooked or raw vegetables, particularly cucumber (just life Greek zatziki) or tomato.

Sabzi are curried vegetables, *bhartha* is pureed or minced vegetables (particularly in the north), *bhujias* are fresh vegetables. *Mulligatawny* is a soup like dish which is really just a milder, more liquid curry. It's a dish adopted into the English menu by the Raj. *Chutney* is pickled fruit or vegetables and is the standard relish for a curry.

Thali

A *thali* is the all purpose Indian vegetarian dish. Although it is basically a product of South India you will find restaurants serving thalis or 'vegetarian plate meals' all over India. In addition there are some regional variations like the particularly sumptuous Gujurati thalis. It takes its name from the 'thali' dish in which it is served. This consists of a metal plate with a number of small metal bowls known as *katoris* on it. Sometimes the small bowls will be replaced by a simple indentation right in the plate and in more basic places the 'plate' will be a big, fresh banana leaf. A thali consists of a variety of curry vegetable dishes, relishes, a couple of papadums, puris or dosas and a mountain of rice. A fancy thali may have a *pata*, a rolled leaf stuffed with fruit and nuts. There'll probably be a bowl of curd and possibly even a small dessert. Thalis are consistently tasty and good food value but they have two other unbeatable plus points for the budget traveller — they're cheap and they're usually 100% filling. Thalis can be as little as Rs 2.50 and will rarely cost more than Rs 10 at the very most — big hotel apart. A thali is usually 100% filling because they're almost always 'all you can eat'. When your plate starts to get empty they come round, add another mountain of rice and refill the katoris. Thalis are always eaten with fingers although you may get a spoon for the dahi or dahl.

Snacks

Samosa, tasty little curried vegetable snacks, fried up in a pastry triangle, are found all over India. *Bhelpuri* is a popular Bombay snack pedalled all over the city. *Chana* is spiced chick peas *(gram)* served with puris. *Sambhar* is a soup like lentil and vegetable dish with a sour tamarind flavour.

Western Food

Sometimes Indian food simply becomes too much and you want to escape to something familiar and reassuring. It's not always easy but railway station restaurants often have something palatable and close to 'back home'. The Indian food blues are particularly prone to hit you at breakfast time — somehow idlis never really feel like a breakfast. Fortunately that's the meal where you'll find an approximation to the west most easily obtained. All those wonderful Indian varieties of eggs can be obtained — half-fried, omelettes, you name it. Toast and jam can almost always be

found and very often you can get cornflakes and hot milk, although Indian cornflakes would definitely be rejects from Mr Kellogg's production line. The Scots must have visited India too because porridge is often available on the breakfast menu.

That peculiar Raj-era term for a mid-morning snack still lives — *tiffin*. Today tiffin means any sort of light meal or snack. One western dish which Indians seem to have come 100% to terms with is chips (french fries). It's quite amazing how, if they are available they will almost always be excellent.

Desserts & Sweets

Indians have quite a sweet tooth and an amazing selection of desserts and sweets to satisfy it. *Kulfi* is a widely available dessert, a sort of Indian interpretation of ice cream. You can, of course, also get normal ice cream all over India. The major brands are healthy and very good. *Rasgullas* are another very popular Indian dessert, sweet little balls of rose water flavoured cream cheese.

The desserts are basically rice or milk puddings, various interesting things in sweet syrup or else sweet pastries. *Gulub jamuns* are a typical example of the small 'things' in syrup — they're made of flour, yoghurt and ground almonds. *Jalebi* are pancakes in syrup. Milk dishes are usually boiled until the liquid has been removed and then have various ingredients added to make a dessert like *barfi* which has coconut with almond or pistachio flavouring. *Sandesh* is another variety of milk dish, a particular favourite in Calcutta. *Payasam* is a southern sweet made from milk simmered with crushed cashews, cereals and sugar, topped with raisins. *Firnee* is a rice-pudding dessert with almonds, raisins and pistachios.

Many of the Indian sweets come covered in a thin layer of silver, as do some of the desserts. It's just that, silver beaten paper thin. Don't peel it off, it's quite edible. There are countless sweet shops with their goodies all lined up in glass showcases. Prices vary from Rs 5 to 10 for a kg but you can order 50 or 100 gm at a time or simply ask for a rupee's worth. These shops also often sell dahi (curd) which makes a very pleasant dessert as well as being a good curry cooler. Sweets include all sorts of unidentifiable goodies, try them and see. *Halwa* is a translucent, vividly coloured sweet rather like Turkish delight.

Fruit

If your sweet tooth simply isn't sweet enough to cope with too many Indian desserts you'll be able to fall back on India's wide variety of fruit. It varies all the way from tropical delights in the south to apples, apricots and other temperate region fruits in the north. Some local specialities include cherries and strawberries in Kashmir. Apricots are found in Ladakh and in Himachal Pradesh. Apples are found all over this north-western region but particularly in the Kulu Valley of Himachal Pradesh.

Melons are widespread all over India, particularly watermelons which are a fine thirst quencher when you're unhappy about the water and fed up with soft drinks. Try to get the first slice before the flies discover it. Coconuts are even better and in the hot season there'll be coconut stalls on many city street corners. When you've drunk the milk the stall holder will split the coconut open and cut you a slice from the outer covering to scoop the flesh out with.

Mangoes and bananas are also found in many parts of India and also pineapples in Assam and elsewhere. You don't see oranges very often but tangerines are widespread in central India, particularly during the hot season. You can go through an awful lot of them in a day.

Pan

An Indian meal should properly be finished with *pan* — the name given to the collection of spices and condiments chewed with *betel*. Found throughout eastern Asia betel is a mildly intoxicating and addictive nut but by itself it is quite inedible. After a meal you chew a pan as a mild digestive. Pan sellers have a whole collection of little trays, boxes and containers in which they mix up either *sadha* (plain) or *mitha* (sweet) pans. The ingredient may include, apart from the betel nut itself, lime paste (the chemical not the fruit), the powder known as *catachu*, various spices and even a dash of opium in a pricey pan. The whole concoction is folded up in a piece of edible leaf which you pop in your mouth and chew. When finished you simply spit the left-overs out and add another red blotch to the sidewalk. Over a long period of time indulgence in pan will turn your teeth red-black and even addict you to the betel nut. But trying one occasionally won't do you any harm.

Cooking Back Home

There are all sorts of books about Indian cooking should you want to continue the experiment after you leave India. *Indian Cookery* by Dharamjit Singh (Penguin, London, 1970) is a useful paperback introduction to the art.

Drinks

Surprisingly tea is not the all purpose and all important drink it is in Iran and Afghanistan. Worse the Indians, for all the tea they grow, make some of the most hideously over-sweetened, murkily-milky excuse for that fine beverage you ever saw. It may go by the name of *chai*, just like the rest of Asia, but what a let down. Still some people like it and it is cheap. Better tea can be obtained if you ask for tray tea which gives you the tea, the milk and the sugar separately and allows you to combine them as you see fit. Usually tea is 'mixed tea' which means it has been made by putting cold water, milk, sugar and tea all into one pot and bringing the whole concoction to the boil then letting it stew for a long time. The result can be imagined.

Tea is more popular in the north while in the south coffee, which is generally good, is the number one drink. There are Indian Coffee Houses all over the country. You should not drink water unless you know it has been boiled but frankly that is often a difficult thing to do. In the hot season it is simply too dry not to drink water — if you quenched your thirst all the time on Indian soft drinks you'd drop dead from a sugar overdose. Water is generally safer in the dry season than the monsoon (when it really can be dangerous) and adding your own purifying tablets can further improve it. Some travellers report that in the major cities it is 'certainly chlorinated' and can be drunk without ill effect. You can probably count on the water being reasonably safe in big hotels and the better restaurants. Although it is no safer than the water it's made with, lemon squash, *nimbu pani*, is almost always excellent in India.

Soft drinks are a safe substitute for water although they tend to have a high sugar content. Coca Cola got the boot from India a few years back for not co-operating with the government but there are many substitutes with names like Campa Cola, Thums Up, Limca, Fanta, Gold Spot or Double Seven. By Asian standards they are pretty expensive at around Rs 1.50 to 2 for a 190 ml bottle. They're also very sickly sweet if you drink too many of them, as you're virtually forced to do in the hot season. One very pleasant escape is the Kashmiri apple juice drink Apco but unfortunately it's only really available in Kashmir. Apple juice drinks are also available in Himachal Pradesh. Coconut milk, straight from the young coconut, is a popular street side drink. Another escape from soft drinks is soda water — Bisleri Soda is particularly widely available and has the further advantage over soft drinks of coming in a larger bottle. With soda water you can get excellent, and safe, lemon squash sodas.

Alcohol is expensive when available and many places have prohibition unless you have a liquor permit (see visas). A bottle of Indian beer can cost anything from Rs 8 up to Rs 30 in a flashy hotel; Rs 8 to 12 is the usual price range. Indian beers have delightful names like Golden Eagle, Rosy Pelican, Cannon Extra Strong, Kingfisher, Guru or Punjab. They're not too bad if you can find them cold but all tend to be rather gassy. Beer and other Indian interpretations of western alcoholic drinks are known as IMFL — Indian Made Foreign Liquor. Local drinks are known as Country Liquor and include *toddy*, a mildly alcoholic extract from the coconut palm flower, and *feni*, produced from fermented cashew nuts.

Indian Menus

One of the delights of Indian menus is the amazing way writers can have with English. Start the morning, for example, with corn flaks, also useful for shooting down enemy aircraft. Or perhaps corn flex, Indian corn flakes are often so soggy they'll do just that. Even before your corn-whatever you should have some tea and what a variety of types of tea India can offer. You can try bed tea, milk tea, light tea, mixed tea, tray tea, plain tea, half set tea and even (of course) full set tea. Eggs also offer unlimited possibilities. Like half fried eggs, or pouch eggs or (alternatively) egg pooch, or bolid eggs, sliced omelettes, or skerem boil eggs (interesting combination there) or simply aggs. Finally you could finish off breakfast with that popular Scottish dish — pordge.

Soup before a meal — how about French onion soap? Or Scotch brath, mughutoni or perhaps start with a parn coactale. Follow that up with some amazing interpretations of western dishes, like the restaurant that not only had Napoleon spaghetti but also Stalin spaghetti! Perhaps a seezling plator sounds more like it? Or simply bum chicken? A light meal — well why not have a sandwitch? And if you want a drink how about orange squish or that popular Indian soft drink Thumps Up.

Chinese dishes offer a whole new range of possibilities including mashrooms and bamboo sooghts, spring rolos, plane fried rice and park fried rice. Finally for dessert you could try apple pai or treat yourself to leeches & cream!

BOOKS

India is a great place for reading — there's plenty to read about, on those never ending bus or train trips there is plenty of time to read, and when you get to the big cities you'll find plenty of bookshops to get the reading matter from. The suggested books that follow are only a few ideas of interesting books that should be readily available. Of course there are far more books of great interest but now long out of print. In addition there are many beautiful coffee table books on India — ideal for whetting the appetite or for conjuring up the magic of India after your return. India has equally spawned a large number of cookery books — if you want to get into curry and all those spices you'll have no trouble finding plenty of instructions. Indian art has also generated a great number of interesting books of all types.

India is also one of the world's largest publishers of books in English. After the USA and the UK it's up there with Canada or Australia as a major English language publisher. You'll find a great number of interesting books on India by Indian publishers, books which are generally not available in the west. At the other extreme Indian publishers also do cheap reprints of western bestsellers at prices far below western levels. A meaty Leon Uris or Arthur Hailey novel, ideal for an interminable train ride, will often cost less than $2. Compare that with your local bookshop prices. Recently published British and American books also reach Indian bookshops remarkably fast and with very low markups.

Novels

Plenty of authors have taken the opportunity of setting their novels in a continent as colourful as India. Rudyard Kipling with books like *Kim* and *Plain Tales from the Hills* is the Victorian English interpretor of India par excellence. In *A Passage to India* E M Forster perfectly captures that collision of incomprehension between the English in India and the Indians. A very readable book.

Much more recent but again following that curious question of why the English and Indians, so dissimilar in many ways were also so similar in others, is Ruth Prawer Jhabwala *The Heat and The Dust*. The contemporary narrator of the tale also describes the backpacker's India in a flawless fashion.

India's 'big' novel of recent years was the monster tome *Far Pavilions* by M M Kaye. Women's magazine romance in some ways but also some interesting angles on India.

General Books

John Keay's *Into India* (John Murray, London, 1973) is a fine general introduction to travelling in India. One traveller's observations and perceptions of life in India today provide an illuminating idea of what it's really like.

Paul Theroux's best selling railway odyssey *The Great Railway Bazaar* (paperback by Ballantine in the USA, Penguin in the UK) takes you up and down India by train (and across most of the rest of Asia) and turns the whole world into a railway carriage. Engrossing, like most such books, as much for insights into the author as into the people he meets.

Karma Kola by Gita Mehta (Cape, London, 1980) is accurately subtitled 'the marketing of the mystic east'. It amusingly and cynically describes the unavoidable and hilarious collision between India looking to the west for technology and modern methods while the west was descending upon India in search of ancient wisdom.

Ved Mehta has written a number of interesting personal views of India. *Walking the Indian Streets* (Penguin paperback) is a slim and highly readable account of the culture shock he went through on returning to India after a long period abroad. *Portrait of India* is by the same author. Ronald Segal's *The Crisis of India* (Penguin, London, 1965) is written by a South African Indian on the theme that spirituality is not always more important than a full stomach — a counter argument to all the praise of Hinduism and its spirituality.

History

If you want a thorough introduction to Indian history then look for the Pelican two volume *A History of India*. In volume 1 Romila Thapar follows Indian history from about 1000 BC to the coming of the Moghuls in the 16th century AD. Volume 2 by Percival Spear follows the rise and fall of the Moghuls through to India since independence. At times both volumes are a little dry but if you want a reasonably detailed history in a handy paperback format they're worth having.

Christopher Hibbert's *The Great Mutiny — India 1857* (Penguin, London, 1980) is a recently published single volume description of the often lurid events of the Mutiny. This readable paperback is illustrated with contemporary photographs.

Plain Tales from the Raj edited by Charles Allen (Futura paperback, London, 1976) is the delightful book derived from the delightful series of radio programmes of the same name. It consists of a series of interviews with people who took part in British India on both sides of the table. Extremely readable and full of fascinating little insights into life during the Raj era.

Freedom at Midnight is India's best selling book of the past decade. Its authors, Larry Collins and Dominique Lapierre have written other equally popular modern histories but you could hardly ask for a more enthralling series of events than those that led to India's independence in 1947. In the west it is only available in hardback but in India you can find *Freedom at Midnight* in a cheap Bell Books paperback (Vikas Publishing, Delhi, 1976).

Religion

If you want to understand India's religions a little better there are plenty of books about them available in India. The English series of Penguin paperbacks are amongst the best and are generally available in India. In particular *Hinduism* by K M Sen (Penguin, London, 1961) is brief and to the point. If you want to read the Hindu holy books those are also available in translations: *The Upanishads* (Penguin, London, 1965) and *The Bhagavad Gita* (Penguin, London, 1962).

Penguin also have a translation of the Koran and if you want to know more about Buddhism *Buddhism* by Christmas Humphreys (Penguin, London, 1949) is an excellent introduction.

Guides

First published in 1859 the 22nd edition of *A Handbook for Travellers in India, Pakistan, Nepal, Bangladesh & Sri Lanka* (John Murray, London, 1975) is that rarest of animals, a Victorian travel guide. If you've got a deep interest in Indian architecture and can afford the somewhat hefty price then take along a copy of this immensely detailed guidebook. Unfortunately its system of following 'routes', in the manner of all good Victorian guidebooks, makes it somewhat difficult to locate things but the effort is worth it. Along the way you'll find a lot of places where the British army made gallant stands and find more than a few statues of Queen Victoria — most of which have been replaced by statues of Mahatma Gandhi.

There are a great number of regional and local guidebooks published in India. Many of them are excellent value and describe certain sites (the Ajanta and Ellora Caves or Sanchi for example) in much greater detail than is possible in this book. The guides produced by the Archaeological Survey of India are particularly good. Many of the other guides have a most amusing way with English.

Other Lonely Planet Regional Guides

It's pleasant to be able to claim that for more information on India's neighbours and for travel beyond India most of the best guides come from Lonely Planet! If you're heading north to Nepal then look for *Kathmandu & the Kingdom of Nepal* with complete information on the mountain nation. If you're planning on trekking in Nepal or simply want more information on trekking in general then look for *Trekking in the Himalayas*.

For other Indian neighbours there is also, generally, a Lonely Planet guide. *Pakistan — a travel survival kit* was published at the same time as this India guide and is the first guide to the 'unknown land of the Indus'. *Burma — a travel survival kit* is the only English language guide to that thoroughly delightful and totally eccentric country. If your travels take you south to Sri Lanka then you need *Sri Lanka — a travel survival kit* whether you're planning to explore the ancient cities or simply laze on the beaches. Finally if you simply want more information on the north-west of India then look for our comprehensive guide to *Kashmir, Ladakh & Zanskar*.

If you're travelling further than India across Asia to Europe (Iran permitting) then our book is *Across Asia on the Cheap*. If it's further east you want then look for *South-East Asia on a Shoestring*.

Not to be Missed Films

Once you've read all you can about India keep your eyes open for a showing of Louis Malle's two-part film *Phantom India*. Running about seven hours in all this is a fascinating in-depth look at India today. At times it's very self-indulgent but as an overall view it can't be beaten — and it has been banned in India. The Australian ABC TV channel has produced two excellent documentary series on India, one titled *Journey into India*, the other *Journey into the Himalayas*. Both of them, but particularly the former, are worth seeing if you get a chance.

Maps

Bartholomew's map of *India, Pakistan, Nepal, Bangladesh & Sri Lanka* is probably the most useful general map for India. It gives you plenty of detail of small towns and villages to help speed along those long bus or train trips. If it has any fault for the traveller it is that it does not always include places of great interest but small population — thus places like Khajuraho or Ranakpur may not appear. The map is widely available in India as well as overseas.

Locally the Government Map Office produces a series of maps covering all of India. In Delhi their office is opposite the tourist office on Janpath. It's upstairs, above the cafeteria beside the Central Cottage Industries Emporium. The maps are not really all that useful since they will not allow production of anything at a reasonable scale which shows India's sea or land borders.

The Government of India Tourist Office has a number of excellent give-away city maps and also a reasonable all India map. State tourist offices do not have much by the way of maps but the Himachal Pradesh office has three excellent trekking maps which cover the trekking routes in that state.

THINGS TO BUY (AND SELL)

India is packed with beautiful things to buy — you could easily load yourself up to the eyeballs with goodies you pick up around the country. The cardinal rule with purchasing handicrafts is to bargain and bargain hard. You can get a good idea of what is reasonable in quality and in price by visiting the various state emporiums, particularly in New Delhi, and the Central Cottage Industries Emporiums. Here you can inspect items from all over the country at fixed prices which indicate fairly well what you can knock the regular dealers down below. As with handicrafts in any country don't buy until you have developed a little understanding and appreciation. Rushing in and buying the first thing you see will inevitably lead to later disappointment. In touristy places, particularly places like Varanasi, take extreme care with the commission merchants — these guys hang around waiting to pick you up and cart you off to their favourite dealers where whatever you pay will have a hefty margin built in to it to pay their commission. Stories about 'my family's place', 'special deal at my friend's place', are just stories and nothing more.

Carpets It may not surprise you that India produces and exports more hand crafted carpets than Iran but it probably is more of a surprise that some of them are of virtually equal quality. In Kashmir, where India's best carpets are produced, the carpet making techniques and styles were brought in from Persia even before the Moghul era. The art flourished under the Moghuls and today Kashmir is packed with small carpet producers. There are many carpet dealers in Delhi as well as in Kashmir. Persian motifs have been much embellished on Kashmiri carpets which come in a variety of sizes — three by five foot, four by six foot and so on. They are either made of pure wool, wool with a small percentage of silk to give a sheen (known as silk touch) or pure silk. The latter are more for decoration than hard wear. Expect to pay from Rs 5000 for a good quality four by six carpet and don't be surprised if the price is more than twice as high.

Other carpet making areas include Badhoi and Mirzapur in Uttar Pradesh or Warangal and Eluru in Andhra Pradesh. In Kashmir and Rajasthan the coarsely woven woollen numdas are made. These are more primitive and folksy than the fine carpets. Around the Himalayas and Uttar Pradesh daris, flat weave cotton warp and weft rugs are woven. In Kashmir gabbas are applique-like rugs. The many Tibetan refugees in India have brought their craft of making superbly colourful colourful Tibetan rugs with them. A three by five foot Tibetan rug will be less than Rs 1000.

Unless you're an expert it is best to have expert advice or buy from a reputable dealer if you're spending large amounts of money on carpets. Check prices back home too, many western carpet dealers sell at prices you would have difficulty matching even at source.

Papier Mache This is probably the most characteristic Kashmiri craft work. The basic papier mache article is made in a mould then painted and polished in successive layers until the final intricate design is produced. Prices depend upon the complexity and quality of the painted design and the amount of gold leaf used. Items made include bowls, cups, containers, jewel boxes, letter holders, tables, lamps, coasters, trays and so on. A cheap bowl might cost only Rs 10, a large, well made item might approach Rs 1000.

Pottery In Rajasthan interesting white glazed pottery is made with hand-painted blue flower designs. They're attractively simple in their design. Terracotta images of the gods and children's toys are made in Bihar.

Metal Work Copper and brass items are popular throughout India. Candle holders, trays, bowls, tankards, ashtrays are all made in Bombay and other centres. In Rajasthan and Uttar Pradesh the brass is inlaid with exquisite designs in red, green and blue enamel. Bidhri is a craft of Andhra Pradesh and particularly Hyderabad where silver is inlaid into gunmetal. Hookah pipes, lamp bases and jewellery boxes are all made in this manner.

Jewellery Many Indian women put most of their wealth into jewellery so it is no wonder that there is so much of it available. For western tastes the heavy folk-art jewellery of Rajasthan has particular appeal. You'll find it all over the country but in Rajasthan in the greatest profusion of all. In the north you'll also find Tibetan jewellery, even chunkier and more folk-like than the Rajasthan variety.

Leatherwork Of course Indian leatherwork is not made from cow-hide but from buffalo-hide or some other substitute. Chappals, those basic sandals found all over India are the most popular purchase. In craft shops in Delhi you can find well made leather bags, handbags and other items. In Kashmir leather shoes and boots, often of quite good quality, are made, along with coats and jackets of often absymally low quality.

Textiles This is still India's major industry and 40% of the total production is made at the village level where it is known as khadi. Bedspreads, table cloths, cushion covers or material for clothes are all popular purchases. There are an amazing variety of styles, types and techniques around the country. In Gujarat and Rajasthan heavy material is embroidered with tiny mirrors and beads to produce the mirror-work used in everything from dresses to stuffed toys to wall hangings. Tie dye work is also popular in Rajasthan.

In Kashmir embroidered materials are made into shirts and dresses. Fine shawls of pashmina goats' wool also come from Kashmir. Phulkari bedspreads or wall hangings come from the Punjab. Batik is a recent introduction from Indonesia but already widespread, Kalamkari cloth from Andhra Pradesh and Gujarat is an associated but far older craft.

Bronze Figures In the south delightful small images of the gods are made by the age old lost wax process. In this a wax figure is made then a mould formed around it and the wax melted and poured out. The molten metal is poured in and when solidified the mould is broken open. Figures of Shiva as dancing Nataraj are amongst the most popular.

Wood Carving In the south images of the gods are also carved out of sandalwood. Rosewood is used to carve animals, elephants in particular. Carved wooden furniture and other household items, either in natural finish or lacquered, are also made in various locations. In Kashmir intricately carved wooden screens, tables, jewellery boxes, trays and the like are carved from Indian walnut. They follow a similar pattern to that seen on the decorative trim of houseboats. Old temple carvings can be delightful.

Clothes & Saris In Bombay and Delhi in particular you can find many readymades exactly like those you'll find from India in western boutiques. Indeed they're most probably the rejects from some export order or other. The prices are so low you need hardly worry but as usual it's wise to check the quality. Saris, the most Indian of women's outfits, are made in various styles and types of material around the country. In Varanasi they're made of silk, often with gold edging.

Paintings Reproductions of the beautiful old miniatures are painted in many places but beware of paintings claimed to be antique — they're highly unlikely to be so. Also note that quality can vary very widely, low prices often mean low quality and if you buy before you've had a chance to look at a lot of miniatures and develop some appreciation you'll inevitably find you bought unwisely.

Other Marble inlay pieces from Agra are pleasant reminders of the beauty of the Taj, they either come as simple little pieces or larger items like jewellery boxes. Applique work is popular in many places such as Orissa but in the Kutch region of Gujarat interesting stuffed toys are made. Indian musical instruments always have an attraction to travellers although you don't see nearly as many backpackers lugging sitars around as you did 10 years ago. A more sensible Indian music buy might be records or tapes. You can always take back Indian tea, food products like mango pickles or papadums, packs of beedies. Solo male travellers heading on to Thailand might even consider a few packs of India's highly subsidised condoms a wise investment! At the many Bata shoe shops in India western style shoes are cheap and reasonably well made.

Antiques   Articles over 100 years are not allowed to be exported out of India. If you have doubts about some item and consider that it could be defined as an antique you can check with:

Bombay	Superintending Archaeologist, Antiquities, Archaeological Survey of India, Sion Fort
Calcutta	Superintending Archaeologist, Eastern Circle, Archaeological Survey of India, Narayani Building, Brabourne Rd
New Delhi	Director, Antiquities, Archaeological Survey of India, Janpath
Madras	Superintending Archaeologist, Southern Circle, Archaeological 1 Survey of India, Fort St George
Srinagar	Superintending Archaeologist, Frontier Circle, Archaeological Survey of India, Minto Bridge

Things to Sell

All sorts of western technological items are good things to sell in India but note that cameras, tape recorders, typewriters and the like will most probably be entered into your passport to ensure they leave the country with you. Particularly in Calcutta, Delhi and Madras there is a good market for your bottle of duty free whisky. The same applies in Patna if you fly down from Nepal. Pocket calculators and watches are popular things to sell and are less likely to be recorded in your passport. Be very wary of the buying to sell later game — most people buying things in India to sell elsewhere know what they are about and have spent a lot of time testing the market and establishing good relations with suppliers. Buying precious stones in Agra or Jaipur to sell in Nepal is a favourite game which is unlikely to return the average traveller any profit.

LANGUAGE

There is no 'Indian' language which is part of the reason why English is still so widely spoken, over 30 years after the British left. The country is divided up into a great number of local languages and in many cases the state boundaries have been drawn on linguistic lines. In all there are 14 major languages in India and probably over two hundred minor languages and dialects. The scope for misunderstanding can be easily appreciated! The most important Indian language is Hindi, spoken by about 50% of the population. In recent years major efforts have been made to promote Hindi as the national language of India and to gradually phase out English. A stumbling block to this plan is that while Hindi is the predominant language in the north and also related to other northern languages such as Punjabi, Gujurati, Oriya and Bengali it bears little relation to the Dravidian languages of the south and in the south very few people speak Hindi. Tamil is the most important Dravidian language while others include Telugu, Kanada and Malayalam. It is from the south where the most vocal opposition to the adoption of Hindi comes and the strongest support for the retention of English.

For many educated Indians, English is virtually their first language and for a great number of Indians who speak more than one language it will be their second language rather than another Indian language. Thus it is very easy to get around India with English — after all many Indians have to speak English to each other if they wish to communicate. Nevertheless it's always nice to know at least a little of the local language so the following words and phrases are in Hindi.

where is a hotel (tourist office)?		hotal (turist afis) kahan hai?	
how far is........?		..........kitni dur hai?	
how do I get to.........?		.........kojane ke liye kaise jana parega?	

hello, goodbye	namaste	what is your name?	
yes/no	han/nahin		apka shubh nam?
please	meharbani se	what is the time?	kya baja hai?
thank you	shukriya, dhanyawad	come here	yahan ao
how much?	kitne paise?	show me the menu	
this is expensive			mujha minu dikhao
	yeh bahut mehnga hai	the bill please	bill lao

big	bara	night	rat
small	muskarana	week	saptah
today	tambaku	month	mahina
day	din	year	sal
medicine	dawa	rice	inam
ice	baraf	tea	chai
egg	anda	coffee	kafi
fruit	phal	milk	dudh
vegetables	sabzi	sugar	chini
water	pani	butter	makkhan

There are many phrase books and teach yourself books available in India for Hindi and the other major languages, if you want to learn more of the language. Some of them are typically and amusingly Indian. A section on a visit to the doctor in one phrase book included the following useful series of phrases, the first of which is quite unlikely in India:

I suffer from severe constipation
I am feeling a bit out of sorts today
The patient is sinking fast
He has much run down
The patient is in a precarious condition
Cholera has broken out in the city
He is dying by inches

Numbers

A peculiarity of Indian numbers is that whereas we count in tens, hundreds, thousands, millions, billions the Indian numbering system goes tens, hundreds, thousands, hundred thousands, ten millions. A hundred thousand is a lakh and ten million is a crore. These two words are almost always used in place of their English equivalent. Thus you will see ten lakh rather than one million and one crore rather than ten million. Furthermore the numerals are generally written that way too — thus 3,00,000 (three lakh) not 300,000 (three hundred thousand) or 1,05,00,000 (one crore, five lakh) not 10,500,000 (ten million, five hundred thousand). If you say something costs five crore or someone is worth ten lakh it always means 'worth of rupees'.

1	ek	6	chhe	100	sau
2	do	7	sat	1000	hazar
3	tin	8	ath	100,000	lakh
4	char	9	nau	10,000,000	crore
5	panch	10	das		

WHERE TO FIND WHAT

India can offer almost anything you want whether it's beaches, forts, amazing travel experiences, fantastic spectacles or simply a search for yourself. Below are just a few of those possibilities and where to start looking.

Beaches

People don't generally come all the way to India simply to laze on a beach — but there are some superb beaches here if you're in that mood. On the west coast, at the southern end of Kerala there's Kovalam while further north Goa has a whole collection of beautiful beaches complete with the soft white sand, the gentle lapping waves, the swaying palms, just like on the postcards. Over on the east coast you could try the beach at Mahabalipuram in Tamil Nadu. From the Shore Temple the beaches stretch north towards Madras and there are some fine places to stay. In Orissa the great temple of Konarak is only a couple of km away from another superb, and virtually deserted, beach.

Kovalam	Kerala	page 605
Goa		page 505
Mahabalipuram	Tamil Nadu	page 628
Konarak	Orissa	page 438

Faded Touches of the Raj

Although the British have been gone from India for over 30 years there are still many places where you'd hardly know it. Of course much of India's government system, bureaucracy, communications, sport (the Indians are crazy over cricket) and media are British to the core but you'll also find the British touch in more unusual, enjoyable and amusing ways. For example the Fairlawn Hotel in Calcutta where the Raj definitely lives in totally unfaded glory. The imposing Victoria Memorial, also in Calcutta, where they tried to build an imitation British Taj Mahal. The Maharajah's Palace in Mysore, rebuilt after it burnt down earlier this century. Could anything be more British than the Dal Lake houseboats, all chintz, over-stuffed armchairs and understatement? Or the Residency at Lucknow where with stiff upper lip the British held out against those pesky mutineers in 1857. Or relax in true British style for afternoon tea at Gleneary's Tea Rooms in Darjeeling, come to think of it all of Darjeeling is a touch of the Raj.

Fairlawn Hotel	Calcutta	West Bengal	page 277
Victoria Memorial	Calcutta	West Bengal	page 273
Maharajah's Palace	Mysore	Karnataka	page 530
houseboats	Dal Lake	Kashmir	page 184
The Residency	Lucknow	Uttar Pradesh	page 224
Gleneary's Tea Rooms	Darjeeling	West Bengal	page 296

Freak Centres

India has been the ultimate goal of the on-the-road-hippy-dream for years and

India

The States of India

1 Meghalaya
2 Assam
3 Arunachal Pradesh
4 Nagaland
5 Manipur
6 Mizoram
7 Tripura

somehow the '60s still continues in India's kind climate. From the clothes, the attitude and the music, Woodstock lives and the Beatles haven't even broken up yet. Goa has always been a great freak centre, the beaches are an attraction at any time of the year and every full moon is the occasion for a great gathering of the clans — but Christmas is Goa's peak period when half the freaks in India seem to flock to its beaches. In Rajasthan the holy lake of Pushkar has a smaller, but semi-permanent, freak population. Or south at Kovalam the fine beaches attract a steady clientele. The technicolour Tibetan outlook on life (they've got a way with hotels and restaurants too) works well in Kathmandu so why not in India — you'll find Dharamsala and Manali, both in Himachal Pradesh, also have longer term populations of visitors. Varanasi and the holy Ganges also has a freak centre reputation as does Mysore in the south. Hampi, capital of the Vijayanagar kingdom, is very small in terms of number of visitors but definitely on the circuit. Finally Mahabalipuram, south of Madras on the east coast, has temples and beaches too, a sure-fire combination.

Great Places to Stay

India has some superb hotels — it's also got a large number of bug infested filthy dumps and a fair number of 'international class' hotels which are mediocre in standards and service but decidedly first class in price. But it's hard to think of a more enchanting hotel than the *Lake Palace* in Udaipur — it's far more than merely a palace, elegant, whimsical and romantic are all labels that can be applied to it. Or in Kashmir staying on a houseboat is half the fun of going there, they come in all price ranges from the rock bottom 'doonga boats' to 'five star' luxury complete with television. The *Fairlawn Hotel* in Calcutta is Raj style elegance totally untarnished by time, a shame if this one ever fades. In Bombay the elegant *Taj Mahal Inter-Continental Hotel* is probably the best in India — even if you don't stay there its air-conditioned lounge and strategic location is a magnet for everyone from back-packers on up. There are some very fine Tourist Bungalows, run by the state government tourist offices, scattered around India. They're often in fine locations and they're cheap. At the Ajanta Caves the *Fardapur Holiday Camp* (a tourist bungalow in all but name) is absurdly cheap, very comfortable and has a great verandah to sit around on and sip a lukewarm beer. Pushkar has the delightful fortress-like *Sarovar Tourist Bungalow* overlooking the lake. Tanjore also has an excellent tourist bungalow. In Cochin the *Bolghatty Palace Hotel* is an old Dutch Palace built in 1744 and later a British residency — now a cheap hotel. The *Kovalam Beach Hotel* is also superb as are the more expensive hotels on the beaches north of Mahabalipuram. Finally the *Naggar Castel*, high up on the valley side between Kulu and Manali, is a fairytale eagle's nest and so romantic it's ridiculous!

double room

Getting There is Half the Fun

A lot of travel in India can be indescribably dull, boring and uncomfortable. Trains take forever, buses fall apart and shake your fillings loose, even Indian Airlines contrives to make your delay time far longer than your flying time. Despite the hassles there are a fair number of trips where getting there is definitely half the fun. Trains of course are the key to Indian travel and elsewhere in this book you'll find a section on India's unique and wonderful old steam trains. The Darjeeling Toy Train which winds back and forth on its long climb up to the hill station is half the fun of visiting Darjeeling. Other 'toy trains' include the run up to Matheran, just a couple of hours outside of Bombay, and the 'rack train' which makes the climb to Ooty from Mettupalayam in Tamil Nadu. Then there is the delightful backwater trip through the waterways between Allepey and Qulon — not only is it a fascinating trip it's also quite absurdly cheap. Indian buses are generally a refined form of torture but the two day trip between Srinagar in Kashmir and Leh in Ladakh is simply too good to miss. Just to show there are comfortable buses in India you could take the super de-luxe bus between Delhi and Chandigarh which actually shows a movie en route. Finally there could hardly be a more spectacular flight in the world than the Srinagar-Leh route which crosses the full width (and height) of the Himalayas.

Places to be/When to be there

India is a country of festivals and there are a number of places and times simply not to be missed. Starting with the independence day festival in New Delhi each January —elephants, processions and military might with Indian princely splendour. In June-July the great Festival of the Cars at Puri is another superb spectacle as the gigantic temple car of Lord Jagannath makes its annual journey, pulled by thousands of eager devotees. September-October is the time to head for the hills to see the delightful Festival of the Gods in Kulu. That is part of the Dussehra festival which in the south is known as Dassehra and is at its most spectacular in

Mysore. November is the time for the huge and colourful Cattle Festival at Pushkar in Rajasthan. Finally at Christmas where else is there to be in India than Goa?

Deserted Cities

There are a number of places in crowded India where great cities of the past have been deserted and left. Fatehpur Sikri, near Agra, is the most famous since Akbar founded, built and left this impressive centre in less than 20 years. Hampi, the centre of the Vijayanagar Empire is equally impressive. Not too far from there are the ancient centres of Aihole and Badami.

Great Forts

India has more than its share of great forts, many of them now deserted, to tell of its tumultuous history. The Red Fort in Delhi is one of the most impressive but Agra Fort is an equally massive reminder of Moghul power at its height. A short distance south is the huge, impregnable looking Gwalior Fort. The Rajputs in Rajasthan could build forts like nobody else and they've got them in all shapes and sizes and with every imaginable tale to tell. Chittorgarh Fort is tragic, Bundi and Kota Forts are whimsical, Jodhpur Fort huge and high, Amber Fort simply beautiful. Further south there's Mandu, another fort impressive in its size and architecture but with a tragic tale to tell. Further south again at Daulatabad it's a tale of power, ambition and not all that much sense with another immense fort (they went in for large size) which was built and soon deserted. Important forts in the south include Bijapur and Golconda. Naturally the European invaders had their forts too. You can see Portuguese forts in Goa and at Daman. The British too built their share — Fort William in Calcutta is, unfortunately, not open to the public but Fort St George in Madras certainly is and has a fascinating museum.

Gurus & Religion

With India's great importance as a religious centre it's no wonder that so many people embark on some sort of spiritual quest while they're there. There are all sorts of places, all sorts of gurus but one of the best known would have to be Bhagwan. Rajneesh with his orange folk in Pune. Rishikesh has been a guru centre ever since the Beatles went there with the Maharishi Mahesh Yogi, it's still popular today. Vrindaban near Mathura, which is between Delhi and Agra, is the centre for the Hare Krishna movement. Muktananda has his ashram at Ganeshpuri while the Theosophical Society is headquartered in Madras. The Ramakrishna Mission has centres all over India although Calcutta is its headquarters. There are plenty of other centres but one guru you won't find in India is the Divine Light Mission's Muharaj ji, when he's there he stays in a hotel his followers report.

Holy Cities

Yes in amongst all India's holy cities there are seven of them of particular holiness. Some of them, like Varanasi, are obvious while some, like Dwarka, are not so straightforward. Three of them are dedicated to Shiva, three to Vishnu, Kanchipuram covers both gods.

Getting There

FROM THE UK
The official fare from London to Bombay or New Delhi is £439 economy one-way, £556 for a 90-day round trip excursion or £466 for a 120-day excursion. In actual fact you can do considerably better than that through London's many cheap ticket specialists. Check the travel page ads in *The Times* or *Time Out*. Typical fares being quoted ranged from £175 to 200 one-way or £295 to 350 return. The very cheapest fares are likely to be on something like Ariana Afghan Airlines which (surprise, surprise) nobody wants to fly on these days. Iraqi Airlines will be marginally more expensive, then companies like Kuwait Airways, Aeroflot and so on.

FROM HOLLAND
Agents specialising in cheap flights to India quote a variety of fares to India's major cities. To Bombay you can fly with Kuwait Air, Pakistan International Airlines, Bangladesh Biman or Air India at one-way fares varying from f790-880, return f1430-1620. To Delhi you can choose from Kuwait Air, PIA, Air India, Aeroflot or Thai International (from London, Parks or Frankfurt) with fares from f790 to f1040 one-way or f1580-1875 return. To Calcutta it's Air India, Bangladesh Biman, Thai International or Aeroflot and one-way fares range from f826-1290, return f1490-2485. Stopovers are possible on some of the routes and return tickets are generally valid for one year.

FROM THE USA
Air fares from the USA are more complex than anywhere else in the world so it's wise to see a travel agent for the latest information. The regular one-way fare to Delhi is US$999 from New York, US$1248 from Los Angeles. One-way advance purchase fares start from around two-thirds that level, round trip excursion fares are not much more than the one-way economy fare. From the west coast there will also be all sorts of cheap deals to South-East Asia with Korean Airlines, China Airlines and so on. From there you can easily fly to Calcutta from Bangkok.

FROM AUSTRALIA
Australian travellers have been waiting a long time for a reasonable air fare between Australia and India but it is still not here yet. While there are alll sorts of advance purchase fares available between Australia and South-East Asia or between Australia and Europe, to India it's a choice only of regular economy fares or a not very useful excursion ticket. One-way economy fares (double for return) are from Melbourne or Sydney to Bombay or Delhi A$891, to Madras A$807, to Calcutta A$818. The excursion fares are limited to minimum-maximum stays of 14-60 days — too short for a proper visit to a country as vast as India. Again from Melbourne or Sydney the return fare will be to Bombay or Delhi A$1028, to Madras A$931 or to Calcutta A$944.

As usual when the situation is stupid there are alternatives. If you shop around a few travel agents you might be able to better that excursion fare or even find a one-way ticket to Delhi for something under A$550. Similarly a return with a stay of up to six months could be found for under A$1100. If you can't find a co-operative travel agent then consider taking an advance purchase ticket to Singapore or Bangkok and flying on from there to India. Singapore-Madras tickets are available for about A$225, Singapore-Bombay for about A$275. Advance purchase tickets to Singapore vary from A$396-504 one-way or A$568-776 return. Put the two together and you'll get there much cheaper than a regular ticket from Australia. From Bangkok it costs about A$100 to fly to Calcutta. Australia-Bangkok fares vary from A$472-602 one-way or A$676-926 return.

FROM NEW ZEALAND

Here the story is even worse than for Australia. Nothing remotely sensible.

OVERLANDING — FROM EUROPE

The classic way of getting to India has always been overland but sadly the events in Iran and Afghanistan have turned the cross-Asian flow into a trickle. In the old days you travelled through Europe to Greece, crossed from Europe into Asia at Istanbul in Turkey, crossed Turkey by a number of routes to Iran. You then continued to Tehran, possibly made a loop down to see Isfahan and Shiraz, then it was on to Mashed and finally Afghanistan. In that magical country you followed the well beaten track through Herat, Kandahar and Kabul with possibly an excursion further north to the Bamiyan Valley and then Mazar-i-Sharif. From Kabul you crossed the Khyber Pass into Pakistan then followed the Grand Trunk Road through Peshawar to Lahore and eventually into India near Amritsar in the Punjab.

Today Afghanistan is virtually completely off limits and Iran is certainly difficult, even impossible if you are an American. Despite the tensions and uncertainties many overlanders did continue to go through Iran right through the year of the US hostage drama but Iraq has made the situation there even more difficult. Similarly the Iraq situation has also made the alternative route of going down through the Middle East to the Arabian Gulf and then flying or shipping from there to either Pakistan or India much more difficult. In all the Asia overland trip is certainly not the breeze it once was although people continue to do it. For more details see the Lonely Planet guide *Across Asia on the Cheap.*

OVERLAND — THROUGH SOUTH-EAST ASIA

In contrast to the difficulties in central Asia the South-East Asian overland trip is still wide open and as popular as ever. From Australia the first step is to Indonesia, either Bali or Jakarta. Although most people fly from an east coast city or from Perth to Bali there are also flights from Darwin and from Port Hedland in the north of Western Australia. From Bali you head north through Java to Jakarta from where you either ship or fly to Singapore or continue north through Sumatra and then cross across to Penang in Malaysia. After travelling around Malaysia you can ship or fly from Penang to Madras in India or, more popularly, continue north to Thailand and eventually fly out from Bangkok to India, preferably via Burma.

An interesting variation on the straightforward route is to start out from Australia to Papua New Guinea and from there cross to Irian Jaya, then Sulawesi in Indonesia. There are all sorts of travel variations possible in South-East Asia, the region is a delight to travel through, good value for money, the food is generally excellent and healthy and all in all it's an area of the world not to be missed. For full details see the Lonely Planet guide *South-East Asia on a Shoestring.*

TO/FROM MIDDLE EAST & AFRICA

There are many flights between Bombay and the Gulf states. Approximately every 20 days there is a ship operating Bombay-Karachi-Port Qaboos-Dubai-Doha-Bahrain. The trip takes about six days Bombay-Kuwait but about 13 in the opposite direction. The operator is P&O Strath and their agents are:

Bombay	Mackinnon, Mackenzie & Co, 4 Shoorji Vallabdhas Marg
Kuwait	Kuwait Maritime & Mercantile Co, KSC, PO Box 78

Fares from Bombay to Kuwait are approximately US$175 in bunk class, US$222 in cabin class.

There are also plenty of flights between Bombay and East Africa, due to the large Indian population there. The shipping services between Africa and India will now only carry freight, including cars, not passengers.

TO/FROM PAKISTAN

Relations between India and Pakistan have certainly improved if travel connections between the two countries are anything to go by. After the Bangladesh war they were limited to one road crossing point which was open for one morning each week. Connections are still very limited but you now have a choice of road or rail crossing (every day of the week) as well as a variety of direct flights.

Air Pakistan International Airlines and Indian Airlines operate flights Karachi-Bombay (10 times weekly) for US$93, Karachi-Delhi (four times weekly) for US$115, Lahore-Delhi (four times weekly) for US$75.

Land There is a daily direct train between Amritsar in India and Lahore in Pakistan. You have to buy one ticket from Amritsar to the border (Rs 4.75) and another from there to Lahore (Rs 3.10). The border town is Attari. Departing Amritsar at 9.30 am you usually arrive in Lahore by 2 pm, including a couple of hours passing through immigration and customs. Coming the other way you leave Lahore at 2 pm and get to Amritsar at 6 pm. In Pakistan immigration and customs are handled at Lahore station.

From Amritsar you cannot buy a ticket until the morning of departure and there are no seat reservations. So arrive early and push. Money changers offer good rates for Pakistan rupees on the platform but you cannot get Indian rupees coming the opposite way. Overall the crossing is trouble free with no hassles from officials on either side.

The old road crossing is still open but fewer travellers use this since the rail route has opened. This entails taking a bus to the border at Wagah, again between Lahore and Amritsar, walking across the actual border then taking a minibus to near the General Bus Station in Lahore. Prior to partition there were, of course, many more routes but the roads have been cut, the railway lines have been torn up.

TO/FROM BANGLADESH

You can enter or exit Bangladesh from several points although the Calcutta-Dacca route is the most used. Note that if you are departing Bangladesh by land you must make absolutely certain you have the current correct border checkpoint listed on your exit permit. They often don't know what is going on at the Immigration Office in Dacca and you can have a lot of hassles if your exit permit lists an exit point which is not in use. People have taken days to cross the border. A typical tale from one traveller:

I left Bangladesh by land through the north to Siligori and Darjeeling. I crossed the border north of Titalya or, on other maps, Tetulia. The army camp on the Bangladesh side near the frontier is called Banglabanda. The border is closed — by this I mean there is no fronter checkpost, no customs or immigration. The road is blocked off and has grass growing over it, however the Dapartment of Immigration and passports in Dacca are not aware of this so they issued me with a Road Permit authorising me to leave Bangladesh by this route. At first the army near the frontier (at Tetulia) would not let me proceed but eventually the Road Permit impressed them enough to let me walk across the border. No stamps on the passport!

Calcutta It takes several steps but the cost is low and it can be quite interesting. Calcutta to Bangaon takes two to three hours by rail and costs about Rs 4 in 2nd class. It is then about six km and something either side of Rs 5 by rickshaw to the border, followed by a shorter ride on the other side to Benapol. Two bus rides follow from there to Khulna and then Jessore, total time about four hours at a cost of about T12. It is also possible to do it by share taxi. From here you can fly, bus or train to Dacca. The train costs T35 and departs early (very) in the morning. Ditto for the all-day bus ride. Of course you could always fly direct from Calcutta for US$34, at least two flights daily.

Darjeeling Head south to Siliguri first of all then bus via Jalpaiguri to Haldibari (total about 2½ hours) or train direct. The Indian border checkpoint is here but you have got a little travelling yet before you reach Bangladesh. First an hour by bus to Hemkumari, then a two km walk to Chilhat. You are in Bangladesh then but Dacca is still a long way away. The train trip is long and crowded so train first to Saidpur then bus to Bogra and again to Dacca. A couple of days travel.

Shillong This trip is likely to be difficult while the crisis in the north-east continues. From Shillong you bus to Dawki where you leave India after a km walk. Tamabil is the first village in Bangladesh, from where you bus to Sylhet and train to Dacca. The train takes 11 hours and costs from T20 depending on the class. You can also fly Sylhet-Dacca.

TO/FROM SRI LANKA

The transport situation between Sri Lanka and India has improved dramatically since the revived Sri Lankan airline Air Lanka took the air. After its predecessor, Ceylon Air, went bankrupt in spectacular fashion Indian Airlines were the only airline flying the India-Sri Lanka routes and, as a result, were even more hopelessly overbooked than usual. This flowed on to the heavily booked Rameswarum-Talaimannar ferry service which also became hopelessy overbooked. More flights have taken the pressure off the air and sea connections but you should still book as far ahead as possible.

Air The Colombo-Madras services are the most frequent and most popular and cost US$68 one-way but there are also connections between Colombo and Trivandrum (US$45) and Colombo and Tiruchirapalli (US$48).

Sea The ferry service from Rameswaram at the southern end of India to Talaiman-nar in Sri Lanka is usually suspended in November and December due to the monsoon. At other times it operates three times weekly. Fares from Rameswarum are Rs 50 in upper deck, Rs 35 in lower deck. From Talaimannar, in Sri Lankan rupees, it's Rs 97 and Rs 68. Going to Sri Lanka if you are not pausing at Rameswarum, you should take the night train from Madurai which gets you to the port just before dawn. It's only a few minutes walk from the station to the port, say Rs 3 in a horse cart. The doors to the ferry terminal open at 8 am and it's a bit of a stampede to get in and get your tickets. Upper deck tickets are a wise investment — not for the extra comfort but because you get precedence for getting off and therefore have more chance of a berth on the train from Talaimannar.

The Indian bureaucracy takes several hours to get through so it will probably be after 11 am when they start loading passengers on the *Ramanujam*. She was built in 1929 but is in good shape, reasonably clean and has good food. Loading also takes a long time since there are no deep water docking facilities and you have to get out to the ship by lighter. With the inevitable delays it will probably be after dark by the time you've completed the 3½ hour crossing to Sri Lanka. Make sure you have some Sri Lankan currency on you to pay the Rs 10 port charges on arrival. If you're fast off the boat rush to the booking office at the Talaimannar station (which is right at the dock) and try to book a berth on the train. The train is supposed to depart around 10.30 am but usually doesn't leave until the ferry is totally cleared, which may mean after midnight. If you don't get a berth be prepared for a fairly sleepless night and keep a close eye on your gear.

Much the same story applies from Sri Lanka, there is an overnight train from Colombo which gets you to Talaimannar at dawn for the departure to Rameswaram. Try to book ahead, the ferry can get very crowded at certain peak times. Note that Rameswaram is virtually an island connected by a causeway to the mainland. The only way there is by rail but cars can be taken on the train. Cars can also be transported on the ferry but the loading process, involving two lighters tied together, is guaranteed to put grey hairs on any car owner's head.

TO/FROM NEPAL
There are a number of road crossings into Nepal and also a variety of air links with India.

Air You can fly to Kathmandu, the capital of Nepal, from Delhi (US$125), Calcutta (US$84) or Patna (US$36). Note that flying Delhi-Patna and Patna-Kathmandu is much cheaper than flying Delhi-Kathmandu direct. In Delhi you can get a ticket from Student Travel which takes you Delhi-Agra-Khajuraho-Varanasi-Kathmandu-Calcutta-Bangkok and this is excellent value at around US$350.

Land For full details on the land routes into Nepal see the appropriate sections in the book. Most popular is the route where you cross the border from Raxaul to Birgunj and take the daily all day bus up to Kathmandu. See the Patna section in Bihar for details on this trip. Second is the Bhairawa crossing near Lumbini from where buses run to Pokhara. This crossing point is reached via Gorakhpur in Uttar Pradesh. Finally there is the crossing from Darjeeling which then involves a lengthy bus trip along the southern lowlands known as the Terai before you intersect the Birgunj-Kathmandu road. See Darjeeling in West Bengal for details. There are other roads into Nepal from northern Bihar to the east of Birgunj but they are rarely used by travellers.

TO/FROM THE MALDIVES
Although most people fly to Male in the Maldive Islands via Colombo in Sri Lanka there are also direct flights from Trivandrum to Male for US$58.

TO/FROM MALAYSIA

Not many travellers connect between Malaysia and India because it is so much cheaper from Thailand but there are sea and air connections between Penang and Madras. Malaysian Airlines Systems fly Penang-Madras for M$823 although you can generally pick up that ticket from travel agents for less than M$500.

The *Chidambaram*, which crosses between Penang and Madras every two weeks is the most reliable shipping service between South-East Asia and Asia proper. It's used by many travellers who take cars or motorcycles across Asia. A VW Kombi would cost you about US$500 to transport across, a motorcycle about US$150. Plus port charges at both ends. Fares on the *Chidambaram* vary widely depending on the berth and class you travel. A two berth cabin with 'English diet' would be about US$200, a four berth cabin with 'Indian diet' about US$140. More expensive fares also allow you to use the swimming pool and other de-luxe facilities during the four day crossing. In Madras the agent is the Shipping Corporation of India, c/o KPV Shaikh Mohamed Rowther, 41 Linghi Chetty St. In Penang it's R Jumabhoy & Sons, 39 Green Hall.

TO/FROM SINGAPORE

Singapore is a great cheap ticket centre and you can pick up Singapore-Bombay tickets for about S$600, Singapore-Madras for about S$500. The ship *Chidambaram* also operates from Singapore but there is nothing to be gained by taking it from there rather than Penang in Malaysia.

TO/FROM THAILAND

Bangkok is the most popular jumping off point from South-East Asia into Asia proper because of the flights from there to Calcutta or to Rangoon in Burma, Dacca in Bangladesh or Kathmandu in Nepal. The popular Bangkok-Kathmandu flight is about US$250. You can stopover on this route in Burma and make the seven day circuit of that fascinating country. Bangkok-Calcutta is about US$170 but note the bargain ticket available from Delhi through Kathmandu and Calcutta to Bangkok.

TO/FROM BURMA

There are no land crossing points between Burma and India, or any other country for that matter. If you want to visit Burma your only choice is to fly there. Thai International and Burma Airways Corporation both fly Calcutta-Rangoon.

CHEAP TICKETS IN INDIA

Although you can also get cheap tickets in Bombay and Calcutta it is in Delhi where the real wheeling and dealing goes on. There are countless 'bucket shops' around Connaught Place but the Student Travel Information Centre in the Imperial Hotel is one of the best places for tickets out of India. Note that if you purchase any cheap ticket you have to pay the full official fare through a bank — the agent gets you a bank form stating what the fare is, you pay the bank, the bank then pays the agent. You then receive a refund from the agent but it's in rupees. So either buy your ticket far enough ahead that you will use those rupees up or have plenty of bank exchange certificates in hand in order to change the rupees back. This also applies to credit card purchases.

Some typical fares from India would be Delhi-Australia for about Rs 6000, Delhi to various European capitals for around Rs 4000 or a bit less from Bombay. The cheap flights to Europe will be with airlines like LOT, Kuwait Airways or Iraqi Airlines.

AIRPORT TAX

India now has one of the highest airport taxes in the world for international flights. For flights to neighbouring countries (Pakistan, Sri Lanka, Bangladesh, Nepal) it's Rs 50 but to more distant countries it's a hefty Rs 100. India's neighbours are also getting into rip-off airport taxes, it's Rs 100 in Nepal and Sri Lanka although, fortunately, that's a fair bit less than Indian Rs 100 in both cases.

Communications

Communicating in India has special rules, not altogether unlike other places in Asia but totally unlike those that prevail in the west. Any answer rather than a negative one for example — will the bus stop here? Yes. Which could equally mean no, but I'd have to disappoint you by telling you so. Or I've got no idea or I simply can't raise the energy to think about that question. Similarly am I heading in the right direction for the Grand Hotel? Yes, which might mean good grief, you've come so far in the wrong direction already I'd hate to be the one to tell you. The answer is to always word questions so that a commitment must be made. Not 'is this the way' but 'which is the way?'. But then you can fall for the any answer rather than no answer syndrome — down that way and round the corner then straight for a km just might mean 'I've got no idea at all'. Never ask directions just once.

More annoying than fouled up communications are no communications at all. Many Indians, and away from the main tourist centres taxi or auto-rickshaw drivers are particularly prone to this, simply feel that communicating with a foreigner is completely impossible. Hop in an auto-rickshaw and ask for the 'Grand Hotel'. Complete incomprehension. Pronounce 'Grand Hotel' 20 different ways but, despite the fact that the Grand Hotel is the town's number one landmark, it's not getting through. Eventually an English-speaking passer-by is found, 'where do you want to go?', 'Grand Hotel' you tell him, 'Grand Hotel' he says to the auto-rickshaw driver and you're saved.

Even more annoying than that is the pre-cognated communication. He knows better than you do what you want. The fact that you're saying airport quietly, loudly or even screaming it has no bearing on the conviction that what you really want is a hotel and if I can get you into the Hotel Super I'll get a commission on it.

Getting Around

TRAINS

The Indian Railways system is the fourth largest in the world with a route length of over 60,000 km and nine million passengers carried every day. The first step in Indian Railways is to get a timetable. The *Indian Bradshaw*, available for less than Rs 10, is the complete timetable for every service in India. It's more than most people need so unless you have a real passion for train timetables it can be safely ignored — although if you do intend to head off down the narrow gauge lines on the local passenger trains and would like to know the name of every station you'll be stopping at it can be an interesting investment. *Trains at a Glance* is a handier volume available from railway newstands for Rs 1.25. In less than 100 pages it covers all the faster trains on all the main routes and for most travellers will provide more than sufficient detail. There are a number of factors to be considered when coming to grips with Indian railways. First of all getting there may not always be half the fun but it is certainly 90% of the experience. Indian rail travel is quite unlike any other sort of travel in any other place on earth. At times it can be incredibly frustrating, since the trains are not exactly fast, and at times it can be quite uncomfortable. But an experience it certainly is. Money aside if you simply want to get from A to B then fly, if getting from A to B is as much a part of India as what you see at both ends then take the train.

Note that during and shortly after the monsoon rail services in India can be drastically affected by floods and high rivers. This particularly applies in low-lying areas along the Ganges basin or where major rivers run to the sea such as on the north coast region of Andhra Pradesh. The *Trains at a Glance* timetable indicates the km distance between major stations and a table in front shows the equivalent fares for distances from 1 km to 5000 km. With this information it is very easy to calculate the fare between any two stations. The fares quoted in this guide are simply approximations. Travel times vary widely between trains and the times indicated are usually for the faster mail or express services. In any case Indian trains often suffer delays.

Classes There are generally two classes — first and second — but there are a number of subtle variations on this basic distinction. For a start there is 1st class and 1st class air-conditioned. The air-con carriages only operate on certain trains and on certain routes. Then there is second class reserved and second class unreserved. In second class reserved you have a seat assigned to you and you alone. In unreserved the train carries as many people as can be crammed on board. Which usually means there is not a square cm of sitting, standing, squatting or hanging space left. Train travel in India is always more comfortable if you can travel reserved.

Trains What you want is a mail or express train. What you do not want is a passenger train. No Indian train travels very fast but at least the mail and express trains do keep travelling for more of the time. Passenger trains spend a lot of time at a lot of stations which quickly becomes very boring unless you have a keen interest in small town stations.

Gauge What you want nearly as much as a mail or express train is broad gauge. There are three gauges in India, well three types of gauges. In broad gauge the rails are 1.676 metres apart. Metre gauge is, as it says, one metre apart. Narrow gauge is either 0.762 metres or 0.610 metres. Broad gauge has two advantages — first it is much faster and second the carriages are much wider so they're more comfortable. On the narrow gauges you'll spend longer getting there and do it in carriages which are more crowded and uncomfortable. In areas where there are no broad gauge lines it is always worth considering taking a bus which will usually be faster. These areas include Rajasthan and the northern Bihar and Uttar Pradesh areas towards the Nepalese border.

Life on Board It's India for real on board the trains. In 2nd class, unreserved travel can really be a nightmare since they are always hopelessly crowded and not only with people; Indians seem unable to travel without the kitchen sink and everything that goes with it. There's an ongoing campaign to educate people not to carry so much junk but it doesn't seem to have much effect. Combined with the crowds, the noise and the confusion there's the discomfort. Fans and lights always seem to have a habit of failing when trains are stationary for prolonged stops and there's no air moving through the carriage. Toilets are often so dirty as to be unusable and in any case there'll be somebody asleep in it. And worst of all there are the stops. Trains seem to stop often, interminably and for no apparent reason. Often it's because somebody has pulled the emergency stop cable because he's close to home. Still, it's all part of life on the rails.

Railway platform drinking water vendor. Drinking water is available at most platforms from faucets but some people prefer not to leave their seats. This car-side service extends to food, drink, newspapers and holy man's blessings

Costs Fares all operate on a distance basis. The *Trains at a Glance* timetable indicates the distance in km between all the stations and from this it is quite simple to calculate the cost between any two stations. If you have a ticket for at least 320 km you can break your journey at the rate of one day per 160 km so long as you travel at least 160 km to the place you leave the train. This can save a lot of hassling around buying tickets and also, of course, results in a small cost saving. Costs and distances are listed below for mail and express trains, passenger trains are cheaper:

km	air-con	1st class	air-con chair	2nd class
100	Rs 64	Rs 34.00	Rs 19.50	Rs 6.35
200	Rs 92	Rs 52.00	Rs 28.00	Rs 11.55
300	Rs 123	Rs 74.00	Rs 38.00	Rs 16.30
400	Rs 149	Rs 90.00	Rs 46.50	Rs 20.70
500	Rs 192	Rs 106.00	Rs 54.00	Rs 25.30
1000	Rs 360	Rs 184.50	Rs 88.50	Rs 45.50
2000	Rs 563	Rs 319.00	Rs 144.00	Rs 76.65

Reservations The cost of reservations is nominal — it's only the time it takes which hurts! Reservations can be made up to six months in advance and the longer in advance you make them the better. Your reservation ticket will indicate which carriage and berth you have and when the train comes into the station you will find a sheet of paper affixed to each carriage listing the names of the various passengers beside their appropriate berth number. It's Indian rail efficiency at its best.

Sleepers There are second class and first class sleepers. First class sleepers are generally private compartments with two or four sleepers in them, often with a toilet as well. Usually the sleeping berths fold up to make a sitting compartment during the daytime. Sleeping berths are only available between 9 pm and 6 am. The sleeper reservation charge is Rs 2 in first class and Rs 5 in air-conditioned class. The second class sleepers are three tier and on these there is a flat additional charge of Rs 5 for the entire journey over the usual 2nd class cost. For any sleeper reservation you must book at least several days ahead. At busy times, such as on the Delhi-Jammu route for Kashmir during the hot season, you need to plan weeks ahead. There is usually a board up in the station indicating what is available or how long before the next free sleeper comes up on the various routes. You have to fill in a sleeper reservation form so save time by doing this before you get to the front of the queue. They're usually found in boxes around the reservation hall.

Two-Tier v Three-Tier On second class sleepers there are two sorts of sleepers, two-tier and three-tier. Superficially the padded two-tier sleepers seem more comfortable than the hard wooden three-tier ones. During the day the three-tier sleepers are folded up to make seats for six or eight. At night they are folded down, everybody has to bed down at the same time and a guard ensures nobody unreserved gets into the carriage. In the two-tier compartments there are still regular seats down below the padded bunks so people get on and off and it's noisier and more difficult to sleep. In any case the racket and noise from the chai-wallahs and other merchants operating at every station makes sleeping on Indian trains a pretty hit and miss affair.

Getting a Space Despite Everything If you've got to travel on a certain date and it's a long trip you will want a sleeper. If there are none left then it's time to try and break into the quotas. Ask at the tourist office if there is a tourist quota on that train. Ask the stationmaster, usually helpful men who speak English, if he has a station quota or if there is a VIP quota. The latter is often a good last bet because VIPs rarely turn up to use their quotas. If all that fails then you're going to be travelling unreserved and that can be no fun at all. To ease the pain get yourself some expert help. For a few rupees baksheesh you can get a porter, or the tourist officer may find one for you, who will absolutely ensure you get a seat. If it's a train starting from your station the key to success is to be on the train before it arrives in at the station. Your porter will do just that so when it rolls in you simple dawdle on board and take the seat he has warmed for you. If it's a through train then it's every man for himself and you can be certain he'll be better at it than you are — he'll also not be encumbered with baggage or backpacks.

Indrail Passes

The very popular Indrail Passes permitting unlimited travel on Indian trains for the period of their validity are available overseas or from the main railways offices in New Delhi, Bombay, Calcutta or Madras. In India they are available only if paid for in US dollars or pounds sterling. The costs and period of validity, in US dollars, are as follows:

days	air-con		1st class		2nd class	
	adult	child	adult	child	adult	child
7 days	80	40	40	20	15	8
15 days	120	60	60	30	25	13
21 days	160	80	80	40	30	15
30 days	190	95	95	48	40	20
60 days	260	130	135	68	60	30
90 days	300	150	165	83	75	38

Indrail tickets can be bought overseas through travel agents or in India at certain major railway offices. Payment in India must be made in either US dollars or pounds sterling, cash or travellers' cheques. Indrail passes cover all reservation and berth costs at night. They can be extended if you wish to keep on travelling. The offices in India which handle Indrail passes are:

New Delhi	Railway Tourist Guide, Northern Railway Baroda House
New Delhi	Central Reservation Office, Northern Railway, Connaught Place
Bombay	Railway Tourist Guide, Western Railway, Churchgate
Bombay	Railway Tourist Guide, Central Railway, Victoria Terminal
Calcutta	Railway Tourist Guide, Eastern Railway, Fairlie Place
Calcutta	Central Reservation Office, South-Eastern Railway, Esplanade Mansion
Madras	Central Reservation Office, Southern Railway, Madras Central

Is the Indrail Pass worth having? — well yes and no. In purely financial terms they're probably not. While researching this book Tony made 16 rail trips during one fairly intensive 38 day period of travel. He generally made short trips by 2nd class and longer trips by 1st class, overnight trips included a sleeper. The 11 2nd class trips and five 1st class trips cost a total of US$42. Travelling only by 2nd class it would cost only US$18, by 1st class only it would have cost US$66. By comparison a 30 day Indrail Pass is US$40 in 2nd class, US$95 in 1st. So even the 2nd class pass would have been more expensive than a pay-as-you-go mixture of 2nd and 1st. Even if bus trips taken during the period were made, if possible, by rail there would still not have been a financial saving.

At 90 days, however, the pass comes closer to breaking even. Travelling at the same intensity the 2nd class pass would still be much more expensive than paying as you go but the 1st class is virtually on a par. The reason the 1st class pass makes more sense is because it only costs about 2.5 times the cost of a 2nd class pass whereas the actual cost of 1st class is about four times as high. This comparison involves a pretty heavy schedule and if you start travelling less and pausing more your pass will quickly begin to look like bad value. This particularly applies to the very short passes. A seven day 2nd class pass breaks even when you travel 300 km a day for the whole period. At the usual speed of Indian trains that virtually means being on a train all the time. Or two 1600 km trips, say a 36 hour trip Bombay-Calcutta and then back again, all in the same week.

That's the downside of Indrail passes but pure cost isn't all there is to it. First of all you never need to join the interminable queues to buy tickets. You already have your ticket so if you're travelling unreserved you simply hop aboard. If you are travelling reserved then you still have to get a reservation and that's where the second advantage comes in. Train reservations aren't just issued from A to Z and then they're all used up. There is always a tourist quota, a VIP quota, a stationmasters quota and so on. Breaking into that quota is never easy but Indrail pass users report that when the train is 'full' production of their pass often results in another quota making a miraculous appearance. One traveller reported that 'I always went round the back to the Chief Reservations Office instead of queueing up, he usually shook my hand and came back in five minutes with the reservations. Only in Bombay did this method not succeed'. Another traveller reported this series of steps for breaking into the tourist quota:

If the train is fully booked go directly to the area officer or station superintendent and ask for 'special permission' to get a berth on the train. You will have to fill out a form and then be given a note to take to the reservation counter where your berth is allocated. Sometimes you're told that your berth is booked and there is nothing further to do. Always insist that they write the berth number on your ticket (especially if you have a tourist quota berth) because your name may not appear on the train listings. If you do not have proof of your bookings you have no recourse with the conductor.

Your Indrail pass also allows you use of the station waiting rooms, often a peaceful haven in the 1st class variety, and makes it easier to get into the retiring rooms. The retiring room dormitories are often used by Indian travelling salesmen who speak English and know all the best local places to eat. The main virtue of the Indrail Pass, however, is its ability to produce a seat or a sleeper when there isn't one. That can be worth far more than mere money so overall, yes an Indrail Pass can be a good buy but it's convenience and simplicity (both very important features in India) which are the plus points, not just cost saving. In particular, short term passes are not so worthwhile, especially the 2nd class ones. If you're going to Indrail it then go the whole hog and get a 1st class pass.

Gricing

Just what gricing is will become apparent over the next couple of pages. Gricing is usually carried out by a gricer, a term that defies description, but is used loosely to identify one of that strange breed, the railway enthusiast. Somewhere in amongst the temples, villages, gurus and instant karma of India is to be found the largest treasure trove of steam locomotives in the world. Eight and a half thousand of them still at work at chores long given over to the infernal combustion engine in the western world. As steam crumbles to the forces of progress elsewhere in the world, in India where nothing moves too fast, steam remains supreme. Three gricers, all crazy Englishmen, of which I was one, spent five months travelling the length and breadth of India chasing these steam engines. The stations and locomotive sheds became our temples, the locomotives the gods we worshipped and our tributes were not measured in gold or silver, but more in the profits of Kodak and Agfa. I don't expect you to become madly enthused over steam locomotives but it's worth checking a few out while in India, some are real museum pieces and some of you have probably never seen a steam locomotive. It will also give you a feel for what held India together for so long and still does to a certain extent.

The locomotives come in all shapes, sizes and colours and from a variety of countries around the world. Although British built engines predominated at one time, over a third of those now in use were built in India between 1950 and 1972. The railways of India are now formed of nine railway zones but these were derived from a much greater number of former independent and state operations. Names such as the Great Indian Peninsular Railway and the Oudh and Rohilkhand have long since passed into obscurity. This patchwork of companies led to a rather haphazard development of steam locomotives so in 1903 the BESA designs (British Engineering Standards Association) were introduced to attempt some sort of standardisation. A further attempt was made in the 1920s with the IRS design (Indian Railway Standard). Nearly all the BESA and IRS designs were of British construction and when locomotives had to be ordered from foreign manufacturers because of full order books in Britain, angry questions were asked in Parliament. During WW II large numbers of American locomotives were brought in to cope with increased

'Tweed' is probably the oldest regularly working engine in the world, built in Glasgow in 1873 and seen at the Saraya Sugar Mills, Sardarnagar, Gorakhpur.

traffic and these paved the way for the standard post-war designs. Although Britain contributed to these, a large number were home grown and builders from America, Germany, Japan and Eastern Europe competed. Unfortunately the attractive BESA and classic British IRS designs are now rather old and rapidly heading for the scrap-yards.

A good place to get to grips with the Indian steam locomotive is the Rail Transport Museum at Shantipath, New Delhi, near the Chanakyapuri diplomatic enclave. Locomotives from all gauges — broad (5 foot 6 inches), metre and narrow (2 foot & 2 foot 6 inches) — are on show in beautiful external condition. The oldest surviving engine in India, built in 1855, is on show along with a diminutive 2 foot gauge loco from Darjeeling, placed strategically next to a 234 ton Beyer Garratt locomotive. The museum is closed on Mondays. One train to watch out for while in Delhi is the Taj Express which leaves for Agra just after 7 am and is usually worked by an immaculate WP-type locomotive painted blue and white. These bullet nosed passen-ger engines never seem to attain the speeds they look capable of, 100 kph being about top whack. Over seven hundred were built between 1947 and 1967 and all require a crew of four — driver, two firemen and a coolie to break up the large lumps of coal.

Other broad gauge engines to watch out for, if you are on your way to Pakistan, are the HPS class at Amritsar and Jullunder. They can also be seen at Lucknow and Ranaghat (north of Calcutta) and although built in 1950 they look very similar to the 1906 BESA designs which they are based on (look for the classification on the cabside numberplate). At Howrah (Calcutta) and along the east coast route HSM locomotives built between 1913 and 1924 can still be seen shunting and the similar HGS class are scattered throughout the Bengal coalfields. The international train from Amritsar to Lahore is worked by a Pakistan Railways HGS loco. The BESA SGS class look real antiques but are now more numerous in Pakistan, only a few re-maining in India at Sealdah (Calcutta). The IRS designs (XB, XC, XD, XE) are scat-tered all over the country and are starting to be retired. Burdwan and Asansol both have about a dozen or so engines used on shunting and a few are scattered around Kerala for similar duties. The standard design WP and WG are found just about everywhere. If you want a ride on a steam locomotive there's plenty of room on the footplate of these and many crews are quite willing to have you on board for some of the journey.

The metre gauge systeam has been built up since 1973 and while not quite as extensive as broad gauge it is possible to travel from the eastern extremities of Assam to within 80 km of Cape Comirin on the metre gauge. The engines are generally cleaner and more colourful than their broad gauge counterparts. One of the main attractions is the rack railway running from Mettupallaiyum to the hill resort of Ootacamund in the Nilagiri Hills, about 100 km south of Mysore. Smart blue engines built in Switzerland push their trains of blue and white coaches through quite spectacular scenery. When the gradient gets too steep a second pair of cylinders on the locomotive activate a mechanism underneath the locomotive which engages the toothed rail in the middle of the track, giving the engine extra 'push'. Wellington is a good place to watch the train climb one side of the valley, cross it by a bridge, then double back and climb the opposite side.

The old BESA engines have mainly disappeared now, most of the remnants of these designs being on the Western Railway. However the short branch from Mathura to Vrindaban (birthplace of Lord Krishna) is still worked by P class engines, originally designed for the passenger trains of the 1920s. The rather attractive IRS engines of classes YB and YD can be seen at their best between Goa and Hubli, resplendent in their livery of orange and green. The standard post-war types YP (passenger) and YG (goods) are found everywhere, a large number having been built in India. A couple of interesting metre gauge lines run from Jodhpur to the Thar Desert towns of Barmer and Jaisalmer, worked by ten specially built locomotives from America, one of which is kept in its original Jodhpur Railways condition for visiting enthusiasts. One metre gauge line even runs through the Gir Forest Lion Reserve in Gujurat, but the chances of seeing a lion from it are nil.

For a real adventure you can't beat the narrow gauge lines, built to serve more remote areas and connect them with the main lines. Years ago my Mum told me of the little toy train that used to take her to school and I've wanted to see it ever since. Let's hear it for the Darjeeling Himalayan Railway. The diary reads.......

The little tank engine barks its way up steep grades, around tight bends, all at quite a speed. There are loops and reverses, places where you can look down and see where you were half an hour ago. Soon out of Tindhana we stall on a curve, so a following freight train comes and gives us a push, but no go. Then it backs down and takes another run at our train. Wham! and we're on our way again!

Opened in 1880 the railway has been going strong ever since and is arguably the most famous steam railway in the world. The oldest engine, 779 'Mountaineer' was built in 1892 and others of the same design followed until 1927. The bus from Siliguri to Darjeeling takes 3½ hours, the train can take all day but you'd never know what you're missing. If you stand at Batasia loop you may be lucky enough to get a picture of the morning school train from Kurseong with the snow capped Kanchenjunga in the background.

A		
B		

A   film hoardings in Calcutta (WB)
B   toy train to Darjeeling (WB)

A standard broad gauge WP passenger locomotive at Jhansi — specially rolled out for visiting railway enthusiasts to photograph!

The two other spectacular hill railways from Kalka to Simla and from Neral (near Bombay) to Matheran are plagued by diesels although the Matheran line does seen one or two trains a day and is good for panoramic views of the Western Ghats. The first narrow gauge railways in India were built by the Gaekwar of Baroda in 1873 and these lines still exist south of Baroda, based on the town of Dhaboi, which sees 44 steam trains a day. While of no great significance, two lines on the east coast appealed to me. The line from Naupada to Ginupur is worked by eight delightful little engines built at Stoke-on-Trent, the first in 1903 and now painted up to look like something out of Mickey Mouse, have you ever seen a pink steam engine? Further north runs the line from Rupsa to Bangriposi into the land of the Sontal people. Immaculate red and black engines, decorated with paintings of peacocks, operate this line. They were all built by the North British Company of Glasgow between 1906 and 1908.

Finally India boasts perhaps the greatest steam gem of all — 'Tweed', a metre gauge relic built by Dubs of Glasgow in 1873. It is still at work at the Saraya Sugar Mills near Gorakhpur and is probably the oldest steam engine in the world, still in regular use.

A word of warning if you decide to take a few snaps of steam locomotives for the folks back home, the Indians can go a bit overboard when it comes to security on the railways, so either make sure there are no police or other officials, or get a permit from the Indian consular office before you leave home. If it sounds silly the joke's on you when you are facing the guy at New Jalpaiguri station who is threatening to burn your film and smash your camera. Luckily I talked my way out of it — Happy Gricing!

Mark Carter

A   Jantar Mantar in New Delhi (ND)
B   Golden Temple in Amritsar (P)
C   Sikh guard at the Golden Temple (P)

BUS

Travelling around India by train has such an overpowering image — those up and down mail trains, the sights, sounds and smells of the stations, the romantic names and exotic old steam engines — that people forget there is also an extensive and well developed bus system. In many cases this simply extends from the railway system, fanning out from railhead stations, or goes where the railways do not or cannot go, up to Kashmir for an example. There are, however, many places where buses offer a parallel service to the railways and in some cases a better or faster one. In places where the only railways are on the narrower gauges it will often be much faster to take a bus — this includes the routes in northern Bihar and Uttar Pradesh up to the Nepal border. Agra-Jaipur, Delhi-Jaipur and Bombay-Goa are other examples of routes where buses are faster and more convenient than the trains.

Buses vary widely from state to state although you can make the general observation that travel by bus is crowded, cramped, slow and none too comfortable. In some states there is a choice of buses on the main routes — thus in Jammu & Kashmir there are A and B class buses, even de-luxe and air-conditioned buses on the popular Jammu-Srinagar run. There are also a variety of buses in Haryana, particularly on the Delhi-Chandigar route where there is even a bus which shows movies en route! There is generally a state operated bus company in each state but in some states (Orissa, J&K for example) this is backed up by privately operated buses although they may only operate on certain routes. Despite the extra speed buses often offer (and lesser safety) they generally become very uncomfortable rather sooner than trains. If it's a long trip, and particularly one involving overnight travel, you're generally best opting for a train.

There are extensive bus routes in all the major cities. These vary from city to city — in Bombay they're surprisingly good, in Delhi they're surprisingly crowded, in Calcutta they are also very crowded but backed up by a more expensive and marginally less crowded minibus service.

AIR

The Indian domestic airline, Indian Airlines, operates an extensive service throughout the nation and also operates connections to neighbouring countries. Air India also operates a number of domestic services on the Bombay-Delhi, Bombay-Calcutta and Bombay-Madras routes. Indian Airlines has a fleet of A300 Airbuses, Boeing 737s, HS-748s and Fokker F27s. The addition of more Airbuses and 737s in 1980 and 1981 should help to take the strain off the heavily booked Indian Airlines flights, as should another recent heavy fare increase.

Much of the problem with flying Indian Airlines relates not to aircraft shortages but to the lack of an efficient booking system. To say that Indian Airlines is Indian Railways airborne is probably being unfair to Indian Railways — at least the railways equipment and booking system are appropriate to each other. Indian Airlines have multi-million dollar wide-body jet aircraft backed up by a Victorian booking system. Until they finally get their computer system worked out it means, for the traveller, endless wasted hours and continual uncertainty. Without a computer it is virtually impossible to tell how fully booked a given flight is. It's all worked out by 'quotas' from given stations and, of course, demand at one place may far exceed the quotas there while at another place the quota may not be taken up at all. End result is there will actually be space on the flight you have been told is fully booked. It's no wonder that Indian Airlines call their (lengthy) waiting list the 'chance list'.

Air Routes

This chart details the main Indian Airlines' routes and the approximate fare cost in rupees. Note that there are many other lesser routes apart from those shown here.

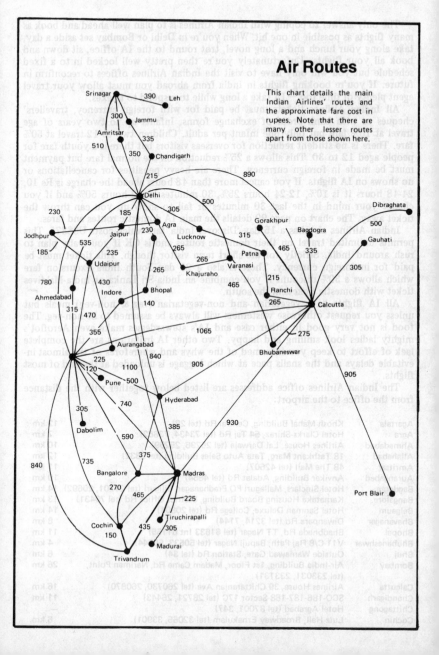

The only answer to coping with Indian Airlines is to plan well ahead and book as many flights as possible in one hit. When you're in Delhi or Bombay set aside a day, take along your lunch and a long novel, trot round to the IA office, sit down and book all your flights. Unfortunately you're then pretty well locked in to a fixed schedule but you will only have to visit the Indian Airlines offices to reconfirm in future. If you're booking flights in India from abroad you must allow your travel agent plenty of time too — IA take a long while to respond to telexes.

All Indian Airlines tickets must be paid for with foreign currency, travellers' cheques or with bank proof of exchange forms. Infants up to two years of age travel at 10% fare but only one infant per adult. Children two to 12 travel at 50% fare. There is no student reduction for overseas visitors but there is a youth fare for people aged 12 to 30. This allows a 25% reduction on the normal fare but payment must be made in foreign currency. There are heavy penalties for cancellations or no shows on IA flights. If you cancel more than 48 hours ahead the charge is Rs 10, 24-48 hours it is 10%, 12-24 hours 25%, 30 minutes to 12 hours 50% and if you change your mind in the last 30 minutes or fail to show up you can throw the ticket away. The chart on page 99 details the main IA domestic routes and fares.

Indian Airlines also has a 15 day 'Discover India' fare which costs US$375. This permits unlimited travel on their domestic routes and is OK if you really plan to rush around India. Strictly for the short term visitor though. This ticket must be paid for in foreign currency. There is also a 21 day South India excursion fare which allows a 30% discount if you combine an India-Sri Lanka or India-Maldives ticket with domestic tickets in the south.

All IA flights have vegetarian and non-vegetarian (veg & non-veg) meals but unless you request otherwise westerners will always be assumed to be non-veg. The food is not very good in either case and IA's stewardesses make even Aeroflot's mighty ladies look smiling and happy. Two other IA irritations are the complete lack of effort to keep you informed of the whys and wherefores of the almost inevitable delays and the snails pace at which luggage is unloaded at the end of most flights.

The Indian Airlines office addresses are listed below together with the distance from the office to the airport:

Agartala	Khosh Mahal Building, Central Rd (tel 28)	12 km
Agra	Hotel Clarks-Shiraz, 54 Taj Rd (tel 73434, 73862)	7 km
Ahmedabad	Airlines House, Lal Darwaja (tel 25296, 25299)	10 km
Allahabad	18 Tashkant Marg, Tata Auto Sales Building (tel 2832)	12 km
Amritsar	48 The Mall (tel 42607)	11 km
Aurangabad	Anvikar Building, Adalat Rd (tel 4864)	10 km
Bagdogra	Hotel Sinclars, Mallaguri PO Pradhanagar, Siliguri (tel 21201, 20692)	14 km
Bangalore	Karnataka Housing Board Building, District Office Rd (tel 79431)	13 km
Belgaum	Hotel Sanman Deluxe, College Rd (tel 20801)	14 km
Bhavanagar	Diwanpara Rd (tel 3214, 7144)	8 km
Bhopal	Bhadbhada Rd, TT Nagar (tel 61633 Int 61155)	11 km
Bhubaneshwar	V11-C/8 Raj Path, Bapuji Nagar (tel 50533, 50544)	4 km
Bhuj	Outside Waniawad Gate, Station Rd (tel 34)	6 km
Bombay	Air-India Building, 1st Floor, Madam Cama Rd, Nariman Point, (tel 233031, 233131)	26 km
Calcutta	Airlines House, 39 Chittaranjan Ave (tel 260730, 260870)	16 km
Chandigarh	SCO-186-187-188 Sector 17C (tel 28721, 26443)	11 km
Chittagong	Hotel Agrabad (tel 87001, 347)	—
Cochin	Luiz Hall, Broadway Ernakulam (tel 32065, 33901)	6 km

Coimbatore	503 Trichy Rd, (tel 22743, 22208)	11 km
Colombo	95 Sir Baron Jayatilaka Mawatha (tel 23136, 29838)	18 km
Cuttuck	Barabati Stadium (tel 21535)	—
Dabolim	Dempo House, Panjim (tel 2890, 3822)	37 km
Dacca	Shareef Mansion, 56-57 Moti Jheel, Commercial Area (tel 280977, 256533)	7 km
Darjeeling	Chowrasta, Nelview Ave (tel 355)	—
Delhi	Kanchanjunga, Barakhamba Rd (tel 40052, 40071)	13 km
	Ashoka Hotel (tel 384340, 376549)	
Dirbrugarh	CIWTC Bungalow, Assam Medical College Rd, Dibrugarh (tel 114, 828)	26 km
Dimapur	Kohima-Imphal Rd (tel 575)	5 km
Faridabad	643 Sector 16A, near Magpai Hotel (tel 81-3074)	—
Gauhati	Paltan Bazar (tel 26655, 23128)	22 km
Gorakhpur	Park Rd (tel 3940)	7 km
Gwalior	Tansen Rd, Parraro (tel 21773)	12 km
Hubli	Hubilikar Building, 519 Koppikar Rd (tel 2985)	—
Hyderabad	Saifabad, opposite Ravindra Bharathi (tel 36902)	9 km
Imphal	Mahatma Gandhi Rd (tel 28)	7 km
Indore	164/1 Rabindranath Tagore Marg (tel 7069)	9 km
Jabalpur	Chadha Travels, Jackson Hotel (tel 22178, 21320)	15 km
Jaipur	Mundhara Bhavan, Ajmer Rd (tel 72940, 67783)	15 km
Jammu	Tourist Reception Centre, Veer Marg (tel 2735, 7088)	7 km
Jamnagar	Indra Mahal, near Bhid Bhanjan Temple (tel 4285)	10 km
Jodhpur	High Court Rd (tel 20909)	5 km
Jorhat	Garhali (tel 11, 891)	6 km
Kabul	PO Box No 3220, Shahar-e-nau (tel 21964, 22527)	7 km
Kanpur	15/69 Civil Lines (tel 63356, 60878)	13 km
Karachi	204 Metropole Hotel, Club Rd (tel 511577)	15 km
Kathmandu	Durbar Marg (tel 11198, 13053)	8 km
Keshod	Rajmahal Plot (tel 344)	3 km
Khajuraho	Khajuraho Hotel (tel 35)	5 km
Lahore	33 Falletia Hotel, Eagerton Rd (tel 55712, 65969)	10 km
Leh	Tushita Travel, Ibex Guest House (tel 76)	8 km
Lilabari	Dhakukhana Rd, North Lakhimpur (tel 66)	8 km
Lucknow	Clarks Avadh, 8 Mahatma Gandhi Marg (tel 48081, 44030)	15 km
Madras	19 Marshalls Rd, Egmore (tel 810066, 812218)	16 km
Madurai	Pandyan Buildings, 7A West Veli St (tel 22795)	12 km
Male	4 Lux Wood, Marine Drive (tel 740)	3 km
Mangalore	Moti Mahal, Falnir Rd (tel 27027)	20 km
Mysore	2 Jhansi Laxmibai Rd (tel 21846)	—
Nagpur	242A Manohar Niwar, Rabindranath Tagore Rd, Civil Lines (tel 33962, 25841)	10 km
Nasik	NDCC Bank Building, Old Agra Rd (tel 2100)	—
Patna	South Gandhi Maidan (tel 22554)	8 km
Porbandar	Harish Mansion, opposite Indian Oil petrol pump (tel 18)	5 km
Port Blair	Middle Point (tel 208)	4 km
Pune	15 Sadhu Vaswani (tel 28179, 24940)	8 km
Raipur	Natraj Hotel, GE Rd (tel 26460)	19 km
Rajkot	near Trikon Baug (tel 14857, 23306)	4 km
Ranchi	4 Welfare Centre, Main Rd (tel 21841, 23350)	7 km
Rourkela	B/25 Sector 3 (tel 5165)	—
Silchar	Red Cross Rd (tel 72)	25 km
Srinagar	Tourist Reception Centre (tel 73538, 73270)	13 km
Tezpur	Jenkin Rd, Assam (tel 83)	18 km

Tiruchirapalli	Southern Railway Employees Co-op Credit Society Building, Dindigul Rd (tel 23116, 26288)	8 km
Tirupati	Room 9 & 10, TT Devasthanam Guest House (tel 2369)	15 km
Trivandrum	Air Centre, Mascot Junction (tel 61627, 60181)	7 km
Udaipur	LIC Building, outside Delhi Gate (tel 3952)	25 km
Vadodara	University Rd, Fateh Ganj (Baroda) (tel 63868, 65677)	6 km
Varanasi	Mint House Motel, Cantonment (tel 64146, 66116)	22 km
Vijayawada	Shriniketan 27-1-26, Eluru Rd, Governorpet (tel 72218)	22 km
Visakhapatnam	10 Hume Sastry Rd, Maharani Pete (tel 4665, 2673)	14 km

DRIVING

There are no car rental systems along the lines of those in the west in India but it is possible to hire chauffeur driven cars quite easily. This tends to be a little expensive, not because of the chauffeur but because of the cost of the cars, fuel and upkeep. All are very expensive in India by western standards. Basically a chauffeur driven car is just a long distance taxi. In some places they run fairly regular services, such as Chandigarh-Manali or Jammu-Srinagar in the north-west. It is also possible to hire jeeps for the two day run from Srinagar to Leh in Ladakh.

Fewer people bring their own vehicles to India since the overland trip became so curtailed because of the Russians in Afghanistan and the current situation in Iraq and Iran. If you do decide to bring a car or motorcycle to India it has to be brought in under a carnet, a customs document guaranteeing you will remove the car at the end of your stay. Failing to do so will be very expensive.

Driving in India is a matter of low speeds and great caution. Indian roads are narrow and crowded. At night there are unlit cars and ox carts and in daytime there are fearless bicycle riders. Day and night there are the crazy truck drivers to contend with. A loud horn definitely helps in India since the normal driving technique is to put your hand firmly on the horn, close your eyes and plough through regardless. Vehicles always have the right of way over pedestrians and bigger vehicles always have the right of way over smaller ones. On the Indian roads might is right.

Because of the extreme congestion driving is often a slow, stop-start process, hard on you, on the car, on your fuel economy. Service is so-so in India, parts and tyres are hard to obtain. All in all driving is no great pleasure.

People driving across India on the overland trip will most likely be starting out either from Calcutta, Madras or Bombay. Madras is the most usual shipping point since there is a regular shipping service between there and Penang in Malaysia. The route from Madras crosses the country to Bombay then heads north to Delhi and on out to Pakistan.

Madras & Bombay

	Route	Sector	Total
Madras-Chittoor	A47	157 km	157 km
Chittoor-Bangalore	A47	174 km	331 km
Bangalore-Chitradurga	A47	202 km	533 km
Chitradurga-Hubli	A47	206 km	739 km
Hubli-Belgaum	A47	94 km	833 km
Belgaum-Kolhapur	A47	103 km	936 km
Kolhapur-Pune	A47	234 km	1170 km
Pune-Bombay	A47	185 km	1355 km
Bombay-Nasik	A47	197 km	1552 km
Nasik-Malegan	A47	106 km	1658 km

Malegan-Indore	A47	310 km	1968 km
Indore-Shivpuri	A47	376 km	2344 km
Shivpuri-Gwalior	A47	113 km	2457 km
Gwalior-Agra	A47	117 km	2574 km
Agra-Delhi	A1	204 km	2778 km
Delhi-Ambala	A1	294 km	3072 km
Ambala-Jullundur	A1	174 km	3246 km
Jullundur-Amritsar	A1	77 km	3323 km
Amritsar-Wagah (border)	A1	26 km	3349 km

From Madras the road crosses a plain then climbs up to Bangalore. Karnataka between Bangalore and Belgaum is heavily cultivated and part of the Deccan plateau. From Belgaum the road leaves the hilly Deccan area and runs down to the coast at Bombay. Leaving Bombay it climbs up over the hill range known as the Western Ghats then traverses a number of hill ranges through Dhulia, Indore and Shivpuri, at times the road is very winding. At Shivpuri you can diverge east and visit Khajuraho, then rejoin the route at Gwalior, adding 422 km to the trip. At Agra the route meets the busy Grand Trunk Road and continues to Delhi then across the flat Punjab region to Amritsar and the border with Pakistan.

Calcutta

	Route	Sector	Total
Calcutta-Asansol	A1	222 km	222 km
Asansol-Varanasi	A1	454 km	676 km
Varanasi-Allahabad	A1	128 km	804 km
Allahabad-Kanpur	A1	192 km	996 km
Kanpur-Agra	A1	288 km	1284 km
Agra-Wagah (border)	A1	775 km	2059 km

From Calcutta the road crosses the heavily populated and fertile West Bengal plain. Traffic all the way is heavy and slow as this route traverses the most densely populated part of India. From Agra the route is the same as from Madras or Bombay.

Indian Vehicles

There is a small, but active, vehicle manufacturing industry in India. Basically it makes two cars, the Fiat 1100 and the Hindustan Ambassador. The Fiat is a licence made copy of the 1100 cc Fiat of the early '60s. It's India's most popular car, particularly since the demise of the licence built Triumph Herald, and is manufactured in Bombay. The Calcutta-made Ambassador is nothing less than an early-50s British Morris Oxford. By modern standards it is big, heavy, slow and thirsty for the amount of space it offers so it is hardly surprising that sales have been steadily declining. Also the manufacturing equipment — the jigs, presses and so on — is now so old and worn that making doors and other body parts fit accurately is very difficult. There is a lot of talk about producing new Indian cars but private car ownership has a very low priority in India. Sanjay Gandhi was involved in a plan to produce an Indian 'peoples' car' and the techniques used to raise finance for this project and to obtain cheap land for the factory were major questions raised in the post-emergency period. Only a handful of the Sanjay mini-cars were ever built.

India's truck and bus industry is a much larger and more thriving business with companies like Tata turning out sturdy trucks which you see all over India.

A single cylinder, 350 cc Enfield India

There is also a thriving motorcycle and motor-scooter industry. The motorcycles include the splendid Enfield India — a replica of the old single cylinder 350 cc British Royal Enfield Bullet. Enthusiasts for the old British singles will be delighted to see these modern-day vintage bikes still being made. Motor-scooters include Indian versions of both the Italian Lambretta and the Vespa. When production ceased in Italy, India bought the manufacturing plant from them lock, stock and barrel. Finally there are also a variety of different model mopeds.

BOATS
Apart from ferries across rivers — of which there are a great number in India — there are not many boat trips to be made in India although a couple are really good. One is the popular trip between Bombay and Goa, since rail connections between the two places are not particularly good this shipping service is very popular. It is suspended during the monsoon, however. Further south the backwater trip in Kerala is an excellent way of not only getting from A to B but also experiencing Kerala as you travel — a not to be missed trip. There is also a three times weekly ferry service between India and Sri Lanka.

HITCH-HIKING
Possible but not always easy. There are not that many private cars streaking across India so you are likely to be on board trucks. You are then stuck with the old 'do they understand what I am doing, should I be paying for this, will the driver expect to be paid/unhappy if I don't offer to pay/unhappy if I do or simply want too much' quandary. But it is possible.

LOCAL TRANSPORT
Although there are comprehensive local bus networks in most major towns unless you have time to familiarise yourself with the routes you're better sticking to taxis, auto-rickshaws and rickshaws. In the big cities the buses are usually so hopelessly

overcrowded that you can only really use them if you get on at the starting point — and get off at the terminus! A basic ground rule applies to any form of transport where the fare is not ticketed or fixed (like a bus or train) or metered. Agree the fare beforehand. If you fail to do that you can expect enormous arguments and hassles when you get to your destination. And agree the fare clearly — if there is more than one of you make sure it covers both of you. If you have baggage make sure there is no extra charge for baggage. If you don't you can be certain there will be more extra charges than you could dream of. In almost all forms of powered transport in India from taxis and auto-rickshaws through to jet aircraft note how a disproportionate number of the operators are Sikhs. In India's chaotic traffic conditions a martial background helps.

Airport Transport   There are official buses, either government operated, Indian Airlines or some local co-operative, to most airports in India. Where there isn't one there will be taxis or auto-rickshaws. There are even some airports close enough to town to get to by cycle-rickshaw! The bus services keep other operators reasonably honest so it is not difficult getting to or from any of India's airports.

Taxis   There are taxis in most towns in India and in most of them, certainly in all the major cities, the taxis will be metered. Getting a metered fare is rather a different situation. First of all the meter may be 'broken'. Threatening to get another taxi will usually fix the meter immediately, except during rush hours. Secondly the meter will certainly be out of date. Fares are adjusted upwards so much faster and more frequently than meters are recalibrated that drivers almost always have 'fare adjustment cards' indicating what you should pay compared to what the meter indicates. This is, of course, wide open to abuse. You have no idea if you're being shown the right card or even if the taxi's meter has actually been recalibrated and you're being shown the card anyway. The only answer is to try and get an idea of what the fare should be before departure (ask information desks at the airport or

A TEMPO

your hotel). You'll soon begin to develop a feel for what the meter says, what the cards say and what the two together should indicate.

Auto-Rickshaw An auto-rickshaw is a noisy three wheel device with a driver up front, a two-stroke motorcycle engine and seats for two passengers behind. They're generally about half the price of a taxi, are usually metered and the same ground rules apply as for taxis. Because of their size they are often faster than taxis for short distance trips and their drivers are often decidedly nuttier, glancing blow collisions are not infrequent. Also known as scooters or motor trishaws.

Tempos Somewhat like a large auto-rickshaw these ungainly looking devices operate rather like mini-buses or share taxis along fixed routes. In Delhi there are three-wheeler vehicles pulled by old Harley Davidson motorcycles which perform the same function.

Cycle-Rickshaw Also known as a trishaw this is effectively a three-wheeler bicycle with a seat for two passengers behind the rider. Although they no longer operate in the big cities you will still find them in all the smaller towns and they're the basic means of transport there. Fares must always be agreed in advance with a trishaw rider. In places like Agra, where there are a lot of them, the riders are as talkative and opinionated as any New York cabbie. Once upon a time there also used to be the old man powered rickshaws but today these only exist in Calcutta.

Other In some places tongas (horse drawn two wheelers) and victorias (horse drawn carriages) still operate. Calcutta has an extensive tramway network and Bombay has suburban trains.

Bicycles India is a country of bicycles and they're an ideal way of getting around the sights in a city or even making longer trips. Bicycle shops in most commercial centres will have bicycles for hire and you can often find them even in quite small villages. They charge from Rs 0.25 to 0.50 an hour or from Rs 2 to 4 per day. In some places they may be unwilling to hire to you since you are a stranger but you can generally get around this by offering some sort of ID card as security. Check the time they put in the log book before you pedal off. If you should be so unfortunate as to get a puncture you'll soon spot men sitting under trees with puncture repair outfits at the ready — less than a rupee to fix it. If you're asking distances you'll often be told in furlongs — eight to a mile, five to a km.

TOURS
At almost any place of tourist interest in India, and a good few places where there's not much tourist interest, there will be tours operated either by the Government of India Tourist office, the state tourist office or the local transport company — sometimes by all three. These tours are usually excellent value particularly in cities or places where the tourist sights are widespread. You probably could not even get around the sights in New Delhi on public transport as cheaply as you could on a half day or day tour of that city. These tours are not strictly for western tourists, you will almost always find yourself far outnumbered by local tourists and in many places not on the very beaten track you will often be the only westerner on the bus. Despite this the tours are usually conducted in English — which is possibly the only common language for the middle class Indian tourists in any case. These

tours are an excellent place for meeting Indians. If they have a drawback it is simply that many of them try to cram far too much into too short a period of time. A one day tour which whisks you from Madras to Kanchipuram, Tirukalikundram, Mahabalipuram and back to Madras is not going to give you time for more than the most fleeting glimpse. If a tour looks simply too hectic you're better doing it yourself at a more appropriate pace or taking the tour simply to find out what places you really want to devote more time to.

Coping with India — Getting Things Done

You soon realise why better off Indians have lots of servants. It's nothing to do with being lazy, it's simply that everything takes so long in India that if you did it all yourself you'd never have had the time to become better off in the first place. Travellers too find that a lot of their time is tied up in interminable queues or trying to find out when things depart or where a room is available. The answer is don't do it — get somebody to do it for you. In India labour is cheap, there'll always be some boy at the hotel who will happily stand in the line for hours to pick up your train ticket — all for a few rupees backsheesh. Similarly those hotel touts who swoop out to meet new arrivals in any reasonable size town really do fill a need if every place in town is full. They'll know exactly where the last free room is and save you a lot of futile marching around. If you want something in India and you don't know where to get it don't waste your time looking — announce loudly 'I want to take a taxi to X tomorrow'. Nine chances out of ten somebody at your hotel will have heard about the empty taxi going back to X and willing to take a passenger for half price. Get somebody else to do the leg work!

Ganga

Yes there's an awful lot of that well known weed in India. Shiva, the most worshipped of gods, is supposed to devote a fair amount of time to smoking dope in his remote Himalayan home so it would be pretty difficult to ignore it. In fact there are government hashish shops in places like Varanasi, Puri and Jaipur but effectively it's illegal unless you happen to be a Hindu sadhu or someone similar who clearly needs it!

If you want to find it you'll have little problem anywhere in India. Goa with its large resident travellers' population, Kashmir and the Kulu Valley, where it grows in profusion, and Varanasi, with its religious connections, are all good places. Discretion is the key word wherever you are. Don't smoke in public and don't leave it lying around in hotel rooms.

The places to avoid it include the airports and a number of railway stations. Often dope searches are simply ways of extracting a little basksheesh but it's still wise not to get involved. Along the popular Delhi-Bombay railway route, at Allahabad, from Patna up to the Nepalese border, are all places where dope searches have been known to take place. In Delhi there are occasional dope raids on the cheaper hotels, particularly around Pahar Ganj.

New Delhi

Population: 4.5 million
Area: 1485 square km
Main languages: Hindi & Urdu

New Delhi is the capital of India and also the third largest city. The city actually consists of two parts. Delhi or 'Old' Delhi was the capital of Moslem India between the 12th and 19th centuries. In Old Delhi you will find many mosques, monuments and forts relating to India's Moslem history. The other Delhi is New Delhi, the imperial city created as a capital of India by the British. It is a spacious open city and contains many embassies and government buildings. New Delhi has a third important factor apart from its historic interest and role as the government centre — it is also a major travel gateway. New Delhi is one of India's busiest entrance points for overseas airlines, is on the overland route across Asia and is also the hub of the north Indian travel network.

History

Delhi has not always been the capital of India but it has played an important role in Indian history ever since the epic Mahabharata, 5000 years ago. Under the emperor Ashoka, over 2000 years ago, Pataliputra, near modern day Patna, was the capital of his kingdom. More recently the Moghul emperors made Agra the capital through the 16th and 17th centuries. Under the British Agra was the capital until the construction of New Delhi in 1911. Of course it is only comparatively recently that India as we know it has been unified as one country. Even at the height of their power the Moghuls did not control the south of India for example. But Delhi has always been an

important city or a capital of the northern region of the sub-continent.

There have been at least eight cities around modern Delhi. The first four were south of modern New Delhi, around the area where the Qutab Minar stands. The earliest known Delhi was known as Indraprastha and was centred near the present day Purana Qila. At the beginning of the 12th century AD the last Hindu kingdom of Delhi was ruled by the Tomar and Chauthan dynasties and was also near the Qutab Minar and Suran Kund, now in Haryana.

This city was followed by Siri which was constructed by Allah-ud-Din near the present day Hauz Khas in the 12th century. The third Delhi was Tughlaqabad which is now entirely in ruins and stood 10 km south-east of the Qutab Minar. The fourth Delhi also dates from the 14th century and was also a creation of the Tughlaqs. Known as Jahanpanah it also stood near the Qutab Minar.

The fifth Delhi, Ferozabad, was sited at Ferozshah Kotla in present day Old Delhi. Its ruins contain an Ashoka pillar, moved here from elsewhere, and traces of a mosque in which Tamarlane prayed during his attack on India.

The Emperor Sher Shah created the

sixth Delhi at Purana Qila, near India Gate in New Delhi today. Sher Shah was an Afghan ruler who defeated the Moghul Humayan and took control of Delhi. The Moghul Emperor Shah Jahan constructed the seventh Delhi and his Shahjahanabad roughly corresponds to Old Delhi today and is still largely preserved. Constructed in the 17th century his Delhi included the Red Fort and the majestic Jami Masjid. Finally the eighth Delhi, New Delhi, was constructed by the British and officially inaugurated in 1911.

Delhi has seen many invaders through the ages. Tamarlane plundered it in the 14th century and in 1739 the Persian Emperor Nadir Shah sacked the city and carted the Kohinoor Diamond and the famous Peacock Throne off to Iran. The British captured it in 1803 but during the Indian mutiny in 1857 Delhi was a centre for resistance to the British. Prior to partition Delhi had a very large Moslem population and Urdu was the main language. Now Punjabis have replaced many of the Moslems and Hindi predominates.

Orientation

Delhi is a relatively easy city to find your way around although it is very spread out. All of Delhi of interest to visitors is on the west bank of the Yamuna River and it divides basically into two parts — old Delhi and New Delhi. Desh Bandhu Gupta Rd and Asaf Ali Rd mark the boundary between the tightly packed streets of the old city and the spaciously planned areas of the new capital.

Old Delhi is the 17th century walled city with city gates, narrow alleys, the enormous Red Fort and Jami Masjid of Shah Jahan, temples, mosques, bazaars and the famous street known as Chadni Chowk. Here you will also find the Old Delhi Railway Station and, a little further north, the Interstate Bus Terminal near Kashmiri Gate. Near New Delhi Railway Station, and acting as a sort of 'buffer zone' between the old and new cities, is Paharganj. There are a number of popular cheap hotels and restaurants in this area.

The 'hub' of New Delhi is the great circle of Connaught Place and the streets that radiate out from it. Here you will find most of the airline offices, banks, travel agents, the various state tourist offices and the national one, more budget accommodation and several of the big hotels. The Regal Cinema, at the south side of the circle, and the Plaza Cinema, at the north, are two important Connaught Place landmarks and very useful for telling taxi or autorickshaw drivers where you want to go. Janpath, running off Connaught Place to the south, is one of the most important streets with the Government of India Tourist Office, the Student Travel Information Centre in the Imperial Hotel and a number of other useful addresses. New Delhi is a planned city of wide, tree lined streets, parks and fountains. It can be further sub-divided into the business and living areas around Connaught Place and the government areas around Raj Path to the south. At one end of Raj Path is the India Gate memorial and at the other end is the Indian Parliament building.

South of the New Delhi government areas are Delhi's more expensive residential areas with names like Defence Colony, Lodi Colony or Friend's Colony. Delhi airport is to the southwest of the city and about half way between the airport and Connaught Place is Chanakyapuri, the diplomatic enclave. Most of Delhi's embassies are concentrated in this modern area and there are also a number of the major hotels here.

Information

The Government of India Tourist Office (tel 43005-8) is at 88 Janpath and is open from 8 am to 7 pm in summer,

Connaught Place

Chelsford Road

Vivekanand Road

Panchkuin Road

1st Class
Railway
Reservation
Office

York Hotel

Marina
Hotel

Plaza
Cinema

K

L

Nirula's

Radial Rd. 3

Volga Restt.

B

C

Radial Rd.

Radial Rd. 6

Alka
Hotel

Wengers
Amex
Thai Int.
P.O.
Brit.
Airways

D

A

M

Bhagat Singh
Marg

G

United
Coffee
House

E

Super
Bazaar

Radial Rd. 2

Radial Rd. 7

State Emporia

Gaylord
Restaurant

Radial Rd. 1

Under-
ground
Bazaar

F

Metro

N

Super
Bazaar

Barakhamba Road

Indian
Airlines

Baba Kharak Singh Marg

Regal
Cinema

Al Arab
Restaurant

Kwality

Radial Rd. 8

Delhi
Transport
Corp.

G.P.O.
+ Poste
Restante

Air
India

Hanuman Road

Ringo
Guest Ho.

Kasturba Gandhi Marg

Parliament Street

Cottage
Industries
Emporium

Tourist Office

Janpath Guest
House

Y.M.C.A.

Jantar
Mantar

Map
Sales
Office

Janpath

Janpath

Y.W.C.A.
International
Guest House

Imperial Hotel,
Student Travel
+ Thos. Cooks

Tolstoy Marg

Haryana, H.P., J & K, Rajasthan +
U.P. Tourist Offices

9 am to 7 pm in winter. The office has a lot of information and brochures on destinations all over India but none of it is on display — you have to know what you want and ask for it. They have a good give-away map of Delhi and New Delhi. The Tourist Office can also assist you in finding accommodation. At the airport there is a tourist counter which is open around the clock for domestic and international arrivals. Here too they can help you find accommodation.

There is also a Delhi Tourism Corporation (tel 46356) which is located in N block, Connaught Place. Most of the state governments have information centres in Delhi. The offices for Andhra Pradesh, Assam, Bihar, Gujurat, Karnataka, Madhya Pradesh, Maharashtra, Orissa, Punjab and West Bengal are all located in the State Emporia Building on Baba Kharak Singh Marg. The offices for Haryana, Himachal Pradesh, Jammu & Kashmir, Rajasthan and Uttar Pradesh are in the Chandralok Building, 36 Janpath.

In the Imperial Hotel the Student Travel Information Centre is the place for obtaining or renewing student cards and they have excellent air ticketing services. When it's time to fly home they're the people to see. There are many other cheap ticket specialists operating around Connaught Place — they leap out and grab you.

Banks & Post Offices There are major offices of all the Indian banks and overseas ones operating in India. As usual some branches will change travellers' cheques, some will not. American Express have their office in A Block Connaught Place and although they are usually crowded their service is very fast. There is a post office at 9A Connaught Place but the GPO and New Delhi's efficient poste restante is in the centre of the traffic circle at the junction of Baba Kharak Singh Marg and Ashoka Rd, some little distance from Connaught Place. Note that poste restante mail addressed simply to 'Delhi' will end up at the inconveniently situated old Delhi post office. Some people also send mail to the Tourist Office on Janpath or the Student Travel Information Centre. Of course Amex have their client mail service.

Bookshops There are a number of excellent bookshops around Connaught Place — a good place to stock up with hefty paperbacks to while away those long train rides or to look for interesting Indian books. Some of the better shops include the New Book Depot in A Block Connaught Place, the English Book Depot and the Piccadilly Book Store.

Libraries & Organisations The US Information Service is at 24 Kasturba Gandhi Marg and is open from 10 am to 6 pm. The British Council's Library is open from 10 am to 7 pm and is in the AIFACS Building, Rafi Marg. Sapru House on Barakhamba Rd is an institution devoted to the study of people of the world and has a good library. The India International Centre beside the Lodi Tombs has lectures each week on art, economics and other contemporary issues by Indian and foreign experts.

Airlines
Addresses of airlines that fly to Delhi include:

Aeoroflot	Kanchenjunga Building, Barakhamba Rd (tel 42843)
Air France	6 Scindia House, Connaught Place (tel 374775)
Air India	Scindia House, Connaught Place (tel 344225)
Alitalia	19 Kasturba Gandhi Marg (tel 351019)
British Airways	1A Connaught Place (tel 343428)
Indian Airlines	Kanchenjunga Building, Barakhamba Rd (tel 40052)
KLM	9A Connaught Place (tel 343998)

Lufthansa	56 Janpath (tel 321142)
Pan Am	Chandralok Building, 36 Janpath (tel 322322)
Nepal Airlines	44 Janpath (tel 321572)
Thai International	12A Connaught Place (tel 343608)
SAS	12A Connaught Place (tel 343638)

Embassies
Addresses of some of the embassies in
Delhi include:

Australia	1/50G Shantipath, Chanakyapuri (tel 690336)
Bangladesh	18 Jorbagh (tel 611512)
Bhutan	Chandra Gupta Marg (tel 699 227)
Burma	3/50F Nyaya Marg, Chankyapuri (tel 619461)
Canada	7/8 Shantipath, Chanakyapuri (tel 619461)
Denmark	2 Golf Links (tel 618354)
Finland	42 Golf Links (tel 611547)
Germany (West)	6-50G Shantipath, Chankyapuri (tel 694361)
Indonesia	50A Chanakyapuri (tel 692392)
Iran	65 Golf Links (tel 699521)
Ireland	13 Jor Bagh (tel 617435)
Japan	4-50G Chankyapuri (tel 694271)
Malaysia	50-M Satya Marg, Chanakyapuri (tel 690314)
Nepal	Barakhamba Rd (tel 381484)
Netherlands	6/50F Shantipath, Chanakyapuri (tel 699271)
New Zealand	39 Golf Links (tel 618281)
Norway	Kautilya Marg, Chanakyapuri (tel 615982)
Pakistan	Shantipath, Chanakyapuri (tel 690301)
Singapore	48 Golf Links (tel 618139)
Sri Lanka	27 Kautilya Marg, Chanakyapuri (tel 370201)
Sweden	Nyaya Marg, Chankyapuri (tel 694225)
Thailand	56N Nyaya Marg, Chankyapuri (tel 615985)
UK	Shantipath, Chankyapuri (tel 690371)

USA	Shantipath, Chankyapuri (tel 690351)
USSR	Shantipath, Chankyapuri (tel 615708)
UN	55 Lodi Estate (tel 690410)

Delhi Architecture
The various periods of Delhi's history
can be traced in the many historic buildings
around the city. These can be
roughly divided into early, middle and
late Pathan periods followed by early,
middle and late Moghul periods.

Early Pathan (1193-1320) The Qutab
Minar complex dates from this period
which was characterised by the combination
of Hindu designs with those of the
Moslem invaders. Domes and arches
were the chief elements they brought in.
Middle Pathan (1320-1414) The Tughlaqabad
buildings date from the beginning
of this period. Later buildings
include the Feroz Shah Kotla mosque,
the Hauz Khas tomb, the Nizam-uddin
mosque and the Khirki mosque.
At first local stone and red sandstone
was used, later giving way to stone and
mortar walls with plaster facing. Characteristic
design elements include sloping
walls and high platforms for the
mosques.
Late Pathan (1414-1556) The Saiyad
and Lodi tombs and the Purana Qila
date from this period. The impressive
domes and coloured marble or tile
decorations are characteristic of this
period.
Moghul (1556-1754) During the early
Moghul period buildings were of red
sandstone with marble details,
Humayun's and Azam Khan's tombs are
typical examples. During the middle
period much more use of marble was
made and buildings had bulbous domes
and towering minarets. The Red Fort,
the Jami Masjid and the Fatehpuri
mosque are all good examples but the
supreme building from this period is, of
course, the Taj Mahal in Agra. In the

later Moghul period the style became over elaborate, good examples of this decadent Moghul period are the Sonehri mosque on Chandni Chowk in old Delhi and the Safdar Jang tomb, probably the last notable Moghul building.

Old Delhi

The old walled city of Shahjahanabad stands to the west of the Red Fort and was at one time surrounded by a sturdy defensive wall, only fragments of which now exist. The Kashmiri Gate at the northern end of the walled city, was the scene for desparate fighting when the British retook Delhi during the Mutiny. West of here, near Sabzi Mandi, is the British erected Mutiny Memorial to the soldiers who lost their lives in the events of the uprising. Near the monument there is another Ashoka Pillar. Like the one in Feroz Kotla it was brought here by Feroz Shah Tughlaq.

The main street of old Delhi is the colourful shopping bazaar known as Chandni Chowk. It's hopelessly congested day and night, a very sharp contrast to the open, spacious streets of New Delhi. At the east (Red Fort) end of Chandni Chowk and north of the Jami Masjid there is a Jain temple with a small marble courtyard surrounded by a colonnade. Next to the Kotwali (police station) is the Sunehri Masjid. In 1739 Nadir Shah, the Persian invader who carried off the Peacock Throne when he sacked Delhi, stood on the roof of the mosque and watched while his soldiers conducted a bloody massacre of the Delhi inhabitants.

The west end of Chandni Chowk is marked by the Fatehpuri Mosque which one of Shah Jahan's wives erected in 1650.

Red Fort

The red sandstone walls of Lal Qila, the Red Fort, extend for two km and vary in height from 18 metres on the

river side to 33 metres on the city side. Shah Jahan commenced construction of the massive fort in 1638 and it was completed in 1648. He never completely moved his capital from Agra to his new city of Shahjahanabad in Delhi because his son Aurangzeb deposed him and imprisoned him in Agra Fort.

The Red Fort dates from the very peak of Moghul power. When the emperors rode out on elephant back into the streets of old Delhi it was a display of pomp and power at its most magnificent. The Moghul period at the top was a short one, however. Aurangzeb was the first and last great Moghul Emperor to rule from here. Today the fort is typically Indian with would-be guides leaping forth to offer their services as soon as you enter. It's still a calm haven of peace if you've just left the frantic streets of old Delhi. The city noise and confusion is light years away from the fort gardens and pavilions. If you look out over the fort wall towards the Yamuna River there will probably be assorted musicians, contortionists, rope climbers, magicians, dancing bears and rope climbers down below. Entry to the fort is Rs 0.50.

Lahore Gate The main gate to the fort takes its name from the fact that it faces towards Lahore, now in Pakistan. You enter the fort here and immediately find yourself in a vaulted arcade now given over to small shops. This was once the Meena Bazaar — the shopping centre for ladies of the court. The arcade of shops leads into the Naubat Khana which used to be a gallery for musicians but is now just an open courtyard.

Diwan-i-Am The 'Hall of Public Audiences' was where the emperor would sit to hear complaints or disputes from his subjects. His alcove in the wall was marble panelled and set with precious stones — many of which were looted following the Mutiny. This elegant hall was restored by Lord Curzon.

Diwan-i-Khas The 'Hall of Private Audiences' was the luxurious chamber where the emperor would hold private meetings. Centrepiece of the hall, until Nadir Shah carted it off to Iran in 1739, was the magnificent Peacock Throne. The solid gold throne had figures of peacocks standing behind it, their beautiful colours coming from countless inlaid precious stones. Between them was the figure of a parrot carved out of a single emerald. This masterpiece in precious metals, sapphires, rubies, emeralds and pearls was broken up and the so-called Peacock Throne displayed in Tehran simply utilises various bits of the original. In 1760 the Marathas removed the silver ceiling from the hall so today it is a pale shadow of its former glory. Inscribed on the walls of the Diwan-i-Khas is that famous Persian couplet:

If there is a paradise on earth
it is this, it is this, it is this

Royal Baths Next to the Diwan-i-Khas are the hamams or baths — three large rooms surmounted by domes and with a fountain in the centre. One of the baths was set up as a sauna!

Moti Masjid Built in 1659 by Aurangzeb the Pearl Mosque is next to the baths. It is made of marble and there is an additional Rs 0.50 admission charge to the mosque (free on Fridays).

Other The Rang Mahal pavilion or 'Painted Palace' took its name from the painted interior which has now gone. The Khas Mahal was the private palace of the emperor and was divided into rooms for worship, sleeping and living. There is a small Museum of Archaelogy in the Mumtaz Mahal. The Delhi Gate to the south of the fort led to the Jami Masjid.

Sound & Light Show Each evening a son et lumiere show recreates events of India's history, particularly those connected with the Red Fort. There are shows in English and Hindi and tickets are available from the ITDC in L Block, Connaught Place (tel 42336, 40982) or at the fort. They cost Rs 2.50 and Rs 5. One of the slogans in the fight for independence was that the tri-coloured Indian flag would replace the Union Jack over the Red Fort.

Jami Masjid

The great mosque of old Delhi is both the largest mosque in India and the final architectural extravagance of Shah Jahan. Commenced in 1644 the mosque was not completed until 1658. The mosque has three great gateways, four angle towers and two minarets which stand 40 metres high and are constructed of alternating vertical strips of red sandstone and white marble. Broad flights of steps lead up to the imposing gateways and for Rs 0.50 you can ascend the minarets. There's also a fine view of the Red Fort from the east side of the mosque. The Jami Masjid has a capacity of 25,000 people.

Raj Ghat

North-east of Feroz Shah Kotla, on the banks of the Yamuna, a simple square platform of black marble marks the spot where Mahatma Gandhi was cremated following his assasination in 1948. A ceremony takes place each Friday, the day he was killed. Jawaharlal Nehru, was also cremated here in 1964. The Raj Ghat is now a beautiful park.

Feroz Shah Kotla

Erected by Feroz Shah Tughlaq in 1354 the ruins of Ferozabad, the fifth city of Delhi, are between the old and new

Delhis. In the fortress-palace is an Ashoka pillar with Ashoka's edicts (and a later inscription) on the 13 metre high column. The ruins of an old mosque and a fine well can also be seen in the area but the ruins were used for the construction of later cities.

Connaught Place

At the northern end of New Delhi, Connaught Place is the business and tourist centre of New Delhi. It's a vast traffic circle with an architecturally uniform series of buildings around the edge — mainly devoted to shops, airline offices and the like. It's spacious but busy and you're continually approached by people willing to provide you with every imaginable necessity from an airline ticket to Timbuktu to having your fortune read.

Jantar Mantar

Only a short stroll down Parliament St from Connaught Place this strange collection of salmon coloured structures is another of Maharaja Jai Singh II's observatories. The ruler from Jaipur constructed this observatory in 1725 and it is dominated by a huge sundial known as the 'Prince of Dials'. Other instruments plot the course of heavenly bodies, the paths of stars and predict eclipses.

Laxmi Narayan Temple

Due west of Connaught Place this garishly coloured modern temple was erected by the industrialist Birla in 1938. It's dedicated to Vishnu and his consort Laxmi, the goddess of wealth.

India Gate

The 42 metre-high stone arch of triumph stands at the eastern end of the Raj Path. It bears the name of 90,000 Indian Army soldiers who died in the campaigns of WW I, the North-West Frontier operations of the same time and the 1919 Afghan fiasco.

Rashtrapati Bhavan

The official residence of the President of India stands on Raisini Hill, at the opposite end of the Raj Path to India Gate. Completed in 1929 the palace-like building has an elegant Moghul garden and occupies 130 hectares. Prior to independence this was the Viceroy's House, the residence of the Viceroy of India. At the time of Mountbatten, India's last Viceroy, the number of servants needed to maintain the 340 rooms of the building and its extensive gardens was enormous. There were 418 gardeners alone, 50 of them boys whose sole job was to chase away birds!

Parliament House

Sansad Bhavan, the Indian Parliament Building, stands at the end of Sansad Marg, Parliament St, just north of the Raj Path. This is one of the key elements in the design of New Delhi. A straight line drawn from the parliament building, down Parliament St, passes through the centre of Connaught Place and extended beyond it intersects the Jami Masjid. The building is a circular colonnaded structure 171 metres in diameter.

Museums

Delhi has a wide range of museums and galleries. Some of the most interesting include:

National Museum Located on Janpath just south of Rajpath the National Museum has a good collection of Indian bronzes, terra cotta and wood sculptures dating back to the Mauryan period (2nd-3rd century BC), exhibits from the Vijayanagar period in south India, miniature and mural paintings and costumes of the various tribal peoples. The museum is definitely worth visiting and is open from 10 am to 5 pm daily but closed on Mondays. Entry fee is Rs 0.25 on Tues-Wed-Thurs, Rs 1 on Friday, free on Sat-Sun. There are film

TAILORED BURLAP OVERCOAT

HORNS PAINTED BLUE & GREEN

Lawn mower, Parliament Buildings, NEW DELHI.

shows most days of the week.

Nehru Museum On Teen Murti Rd near Chanakyapuri the residence of the first Indian prime minister has been converted into a museum and has items and documents related to his life. There is a sound and light show about his life and the independence movement during the tourist season. The museum is open from 10 am to 5 pm daily, closed on Mondays, admission is free.

Rail Transport Museum Located at Chanakyapuri, the diplomatic enclave, the railway museum will be of great interest to anyone who becomes fascinated by India's exotic collection of railway engines. The collection includes an 1855 steam engine still in working order and a large collection of oddities such as the skull of an elephant that charged a mail train in 1894, and lost. The museum is open from 9.30 am to 7.30 pm from 1 May to 15 July and 10.30 am to 5.30 pm for the rest of the year. It is closed on Mondays and admission

is Rs 1 and an additional Rs 5 for taking photographs.

Tibet House This small museum has a fascinating collection of ceremonial items brought out of Tibet when the Dalai Lama fled before the Chinese. Downstairs there is a shop selling a wide range of Tibetan handicrafts. It's at 16 Jorbagh, near the Oberoi Inter-Continental Hotel. It's open 9.30 am to 1 pm and 2.30 to 6 pm April-September and 9 am to 1 pm and 2 to 5 pm the rest of the year. It's closed Sundays and admission is free.

International Dolls Museum Located in Nehru House on Bahadur Shah Zafar Marg the museum displays 6000 dolls from 85 different countries. Over a third of them are from India and an exhibit is being prepared that will show 500 dolls in the costumes worn all over India. The museum is open from 10 am to 6 pm daily, closed Mondays. Admission is Rs 0.50, half price for children.

Crafts Museum Recently relocated to

the Aditi Pavilion at the Exhibition Grounds, Mathura Rd, this museum contains a collection of traditional Indian crafts in textiles, metal, wood and ceramics. The museum is now part of a village life complex where you can visit rural India without ever leaving Delhi. Opening hours are 9.30 am to 4.30 pm, closed Sundays. Admission is free.

Other The Museum of Natural History is opposite the Nepalese Embassy on Barakhamba Rd. It has a modest collection of fossils and a few stuffed animals and birds. Nothing special. There is a National Philatelic Museum at Dak Tar Bhavan, Sardar Patel Square on Parliament St. It's closed on Sundays. At Palam Airport there is an Air Force Museum open from 10 am to 1.30 pm daily except Tuesdays, admission is free.

Purana Qila

Just south-east of India Gate and north of Humayun's Tomb and the Nizamuddin Railway Station is the old fort, Purana Qila. This is the supposed site of Indraprastha the original city of Delhi. The fort has massive walls and three large gateways. Sher Shah, who briefly interrupted the Moghul empire by defeating Humayun, built the fort during his period of rule from 1538 to 1545 before Humayun wrested control of India back. Entering from the south gate the small octagonal red sandstone tower, the Sher Manzil, was later used by Humayun as a library. It was in this tower that he slipped, fell and received injuries from which he died. Just beyond this is the Qila-i-Kuhran Mosque or Mosque of Sher Shah.

Humayun's Tomb

Built in the mid-16th century by Haji Begum, wife of Humayun, the second Moghul emperor, this is an early example of Moghul architecture. The elements in its design — a squat building, light-

ened by high arched entrances, topped by a bulbous dome and surrounded by formal gardens — were to be refined over the years to the magnificence of the Taj Mahal in Agra. This earlier tomb is thus of great interest for its relation to the later Taj. Humayun's wife is also buried in the red and white sandstone, black and yellow marble tomb. Other tombs in the garden include that of Humayun's barber while to the right is the tomb of Isa Khan, a good example of Pathan (Afghan) architecture from the time of the Lodi dynasty. Entry to Humayun's tomb is Rs 0.50 except on Fridays when its free. There's a fine view over the surrounding country from the terrace of Humayun's Tomb.

Zoo

The Delhi Zoo is on the south side of the fort and is open from 8 am to 6 pm in summer, 9 am to 5 pm in winter. Entry fee is Rs 0.50.

Hazrat Nizam-ud-din Aulia

Across the road from Humayun's Tomb is the shrine of the Moslem saint Nizam-ud-din Chisti. He died in 1325 aged 92 and his shrine, with its large tank, is only one of a number of interesting tombs here. They include the later grave of Jahanara, the daughter of Shah Jahan who stayed with him during his imprisonment by Aurangzeb. Mirza Ghalib, a renowned Urdu poet, also has his tomb here as does Azam Khan, a favourite of Humayun and Akbar who was murdered by Adham Khan in Agra. In turn Akbar had Adham Khan terminated and his grave is near the Qutab Minar. The construction of Nizam-ud-din's tank caused a dispute between the saint and the constructor of Tughlaqabad further to the south of Delhi — see Tughlaqabad for details.

Lodi Tombs

About three km to the west and adjoining the Indian International Centre are

New Delhi Area

the Lodi Gardens. In these well-kept gardens there are the tombs of the Sayyid and Lodi rulers. Muhammad Shah's tomb (1450) is a prototype for the later Moghul style tomb of Humayun, a design which would eventually develop into the Taj Mahal. Other tombs include those of his predecessor Mubarak Shah (1433), Ibrahim Lodi (1526) and Sikander Lodi (1517). The Bara Gumbad Mosque is a fine example of its type of plaster decoration.

Safdarjang Tomb

Beside the smaller Safdarjang airport, where Indira Gandhi's son was killed in a light plane accident in 1980, is the Safdarjang Tomb. It was built in 1753-54 by the Nawab of Oudh for his father Safdarjang and is one of the last examples of Moghul architecture before the final remnants of the great empire completely collapsed. The tomb stands on a high terrace in an extensive garden. There are good views from the roof of the tomb which costs Rs 0.50 to enter, free on Fridays.

Moth ki Masjid

South again from the Safdarjang Tomb this mosque is said to be the finest mosque in the Lodi style. It was around this area that Timur defeated the forces of Muhammad Shah Tughlaq in 1398.

Hauz Khas

About midway between Safdarjang and the Qutab Minar this area was once the reservoir for the second city of Delhi, Siri, which lies slightly to the east. Interesting sights here include Feroz Shah's Tomb (1398) and the remains of an ancient college.

Khirki Masjid & Jahanpanah

This interesting mosque with its four open courts dates from 1380. The nearby village of Khirki also takes its name from the mosque. Close to the mosque are the remains of the fourth city of Delhi, Jahanpanah, including the high Bijai Mandal platform and the Begumpur Mosque with its multiplicity of domes.

Tughlaqabad

The massively strong walls of Tughlaqabad, the third city of Delhi, are east of the Qutab Minar. The walled city and fort with its 13 gateways was built by Ghiyas-ud-din Tughlaq and its construction involved a legendary quarrel with the saint Nizam-ud-din. When the Tughlaq ruler took the workers whom Nizam-ud-din wanted for work on his shrine the saint cursed the king with the warning that his city would be inhabited only by Gujars (shepherds). Today that is indeed the situation. The dispute between king and saint did not end with curse and counter-curse. When the king prepared to take vengeance on the saint, Nizam-ud-din calmly told his followers, in a saying that is still current in India today, 'Delhi is a long way off'. Indeed it was for the king was murdered on his way from Delhi in 1325. The fort walls are constructed of massive blocks and outside the south wall of the city is an artificial lake with the king's tomb in its centre. A long causeway connects the tomb to the fort, both of which have walls that slope inward.

Qutab Minar Complex

Situated 15 km south of New Delhi the buildings in this complex date from the onset of Moslem rule in India and are fine examples of early Afghan architecture. The Qutab Minar itself is a soaring tower of victory which was commenced in 1193, immediately after the defeat of the last Hindu kingdom in Delhi. It reaches 73 metres high and tapers from a 15 metre diameter base to just 2.5 metres at the top.

The tower has five distinct storeys, each marked by a projecting balcony. The first three storeys are made of red sandstone, the fourth and fifth of marble and sandstone. Although Qutb-

Alai
Minar

Tomb of
Altamish

iron
pillar

mosque

Court of
Ala-ud-
din

Qutb
Minar

Tomb
of Imam
Zamim

Alai
Darwaza

QUTB MINAR COMPLEX

ud-din commenced construction of the tower he only got to the first storey. His succesors completed it and in 1368 Feroz Shah Tughlaq rebuilt the top storeys and added a cupola. An earthquake brought the cupola down in 1803 and it was replaced, and other modifications made at the same time, in 1829.

Today this impressively ornate tower has a slight tilt but otherwise has worn the centuries remarkably well. Visitors in groups of four can go up the tower to the first storey, from where there is a fine view. It's said that people are only allowed up in groups in order to discourage suicides. Admission is Rs 0.50.

Quwwat-ul-Islam Mosque At the foot of the Qutab Minar stands the first mosque to be built in India, the 'Might

of Islam' mosque. Qutb-ud-din commenced construction of the mosque in 1193 but it has had a number of additions and extensions over the centuries. The original mosque was built on the foundations of a Hindu temple and an inscription over the east gate states that it was built with materials obtained from demolishing '27 idolatrous temples'. Many of the elements in the mosque's construction indicate their Hindu or Jain origins. The original small mosque was surrounded by a cloistered court by Altamish in 1210-30. Ala-ud-din added a court to the east and the magnificent Alai Darwaza gateway in 1300. Points of interest in and around the mosque include:

The Iron Pillar This seven metre high pillar stands in the courtyard of the mosque and has been there since long before the mosque's construction. It was originally erected there in the 5th century AD by the Hindu king Chandra Varman but a six line Sanskript inscription indicates that it was probably brought here from elsewhere. It is thought to date from the Gupta period and may once have been crowned by a Garuda figure, indicating that it may have been in a temple to Vishnu. What those lines of poetry do not tell is how it was made for the iron in the pillar is of quite exceptional purity. Scientists have never discovered how iron of such purity that it has not rusted after 2000 years could be cast with the technology of the time. It is said that if you can encircle the pillar with your hands your wish will be fulfilled.

Alai Minar At the same time as Ala-ud-din made his additions to the mosque he also conceived of a far more ambitious construction programme. He would build a second tower of victory, exactly like the Qutab Minar except it would be twice as high! When he died the tower had reached 27 metres and no one was willing to continue his over-ambitious project. The uncompleted tower stands to the north of the Qutab Minar and the mosque.

Other Ala-ud-din's Alai Darwaza gateway is the main entrance to the whole complex. It was built in 1310 of red sandstone and stands just south-east of the Qutab Minar. The tomb of Imam Zamin stands beside the gateway while the tomb of Altamish, who died in 1235, is by the north-west corner of the mosque.

Around the Qutab

There are a number of other points of interest around this complex. West of the enclosure is the tomb of Adham Khan who, amongst other things, drove Rupmati to suicide following the capture of Mandu (see Mandu). When Akbar became displeased with him he ended up being heaved off a terrace in the Agra Fort. There are some summer palaces in the area and also the tombs of the final kings of Delhi, who succeeded the final Moghuls. An empty space between two of the tombs was intended for the last king of Delhi, who died in exile in Rangoon, Burma, in 1862, following his implication in the 1857 Indian Mutiny.

Tours

Delhi is very spread out so taking a city tour makes a lot of sense. Even by public transport getting from, say, the Red Fort to the Qutab Minar would be comparatively expensive.

There are three organisations which arrange Delhi tours. The ITDC (Indian Tourism Development Corporation) have tours which include guides and a luxury coach — they tend to be overbooked. Their office is in L Bloc, Connaught Place, but their tours also start from the major hotels. Delhi Tourism, a branch of the city government, also arrange similar tours and their office is in N block. Finally the Delhi Transport Corporation has tours which are cheaper than the others. They do not always include guides but are exceptionally good value.

A three hour morning tour costs Rs 8 with the ITDC, Rs 6 with Delhi Transport. Starting at 9 am the morning tour includes the Qutab Minar, Humayun's Tomb, India Gate, the Jantar Mantar and the Laxmi Narayan Temple. The similarly priced afternoon tour covers the Red Fort, Jami Masjid, Raj Ghat, Shantiban and Feroz Shah Kotla. If you take both tours on the same day it costs Rs 15 with the ITDC, Rs 10 with Delhi Transport.

Places to Stay — Top End

Many of the 'tourist class' hotels are at Chanakyapuri, where the foreign embassies are chiefly located. This is about midway between the airport and the New Delhi city centre. Some of the more important hotels include:

Hotel Akbar (tel 370251) is at Chanakyapuri and is an ITDC hotel but rather smaller than the Ashok. Singles/doubles from Rs 275/350.

Ashok Hotel (tel 37010) is at 50B Chanakyapuri and is the 589 room flagship of the ITDC hotel fleet. It offers everything from restaurants, coffee shops, bars, discos, conference rooms and swimming pool to full air-conditioning. Singles/doubles cost Rs 350/450 and up.

Claridges Hotel (tel 370211) is at 12 Aurangzeb Rd, south of the Raj Path in New Delhi. Singles/doubles cost from Rs 300/400.

Hotel Diplomat (tel 373711) is at 9 Sardar Patel Rd, Chanakyapuri and is very small. Singles/doubles cost from Rs 150/250.

Hotel Imperial (tel 311511) is conveniently situated on Janpath near the centre. It's a rather more old-fashioned looking hotel with a very pleasant shopping arcade. Singles/doubles cost Rs 280/360.

Hotel Janpath (tel 350070) is beside the Imperial and is run by the ITDC. Rooms

New Delhi

1 Ashoka Pillar
2 Qudsia Gardens
3 Inter-State Bus Terminal
4 Kashmiri Gate
5 Delhi Station
6 Old Delhi GPO
7 Fatehpuri Mosque
8 Jami Masjid
9 Moti Mahal Restaurant
10 President Hotel
11 New Delhi Station
12 Lakshmi Narayan Temple
13 Connaught Place
14 Delhi Gate
15 Gandhi Memorial
16 Nepalese Embassy
17 YMCA Tourist Hostel
18 YWCA International
   Guest House
19 Baroda House
20 Parliament Building
21 Indian Museum
22 Taj Mahal Hotel
23 Ashoka Hotel
24 Lodi Tombs
25 Oberoi Inter-Continental
26 Nizam-ud-din Station
27 Humayun's Tomb
28 Tibet House
29 Akbar Hotel
30 Rail Transport Museum

cost from Rs 175/275.

Hotel Maurya Sheraton (tel 370271) is on Sardar Patel Marg at Chanakyapuri and has 300 plus rooms with the usual 'international class' features. Singles/doubles cost Rs 600/700.

Hotel Oberoi Inter-Continental (tel 699571) is on Dr Zakir Hussain Rd in the south of New Delhi, near the Purana Qila. There are 350 rooms with the usual luxuries and services and singles/doubles cost Rs 575/650.

The Taj Mahal Hotel is at 1 Man Singh Rd. It's part of the Taj group of hotels and is fairly central yet fairly quiet. Singles/doubles cost from Rs 550/650.

Places to Stay — Middle

There are a number of hotels around Janpath and Connaught Place which fall into the lower and upper part of the middle bracket. Only a couple of doors down from the Tourist Office on Janpath the *Janpath Guest House* (no connection with the Janpath Hotel) is very conveniently situated, clean enough and reasonably well kept but the rooms are claustrophobically small. Still it's pretty good value for New Delhi at Rs 85 for a non air-con double, Rs 140 with air-con.

Hotel Marina on the outer circle of Connaught Place has rooms at Rs 154 with air-con, Rs 110 without. It's fair enough but nothing special. Right on the inner circle the *Hotel Metro* (tel 48905) looks very drab downstairs and at the reception but the rooms are actually quite good. Singles/doubles cost Rs 140/155.

Towards the top of the middle price bracket is the *Alka Hotel* (tel 344328) at 16/90 Connaught Place. Doubles cost Rs 200, all air-con and comfortable — a well kept, pleasantly run hotel. In the southern part of Delhi the *Lodhi Hotel* (tel 619422) is on Lala Rajput Rai Marg and has air-con singles/doubles from around Rs 140/210. There are also some rooms without air-con. Back in the centre *Nirula's Hotel* (tel 44305) is on L

Block, Connaught Place, right beside the Nirula restaurants and snack bars. Singles/doubles range from Rs 150/225; it's quite a small place.

The old fashioned *Hotel Airlines* (tel 517571-73) is directly opposite the New Delhi Railway Station and has singles/doubles from Rs 60/90 or Rs 30 more with air-con. It's rather drab although in an interesting area of Delhi. A good place for a longer stay in Delhi is the *India International Centre* (tel 619431) beside the Lodi tombs in the south of New Delhi. It's a good place to meet people and each week there are lectures on art, economics and other contemporary issues by Indian and foreign experts. The centre, which is also near the Delhi UN offices, has singles from around Rs 100 to 150, depending on whether you become a member or not.

The *YWCA International Guest House* (tel 311561, 383080) 10 Parliament St, has singles/doubles at Rs 75/125 and all rooms have bath and air-con. On Jai Singh Rd the *YMCA Tourist Hotel* (tel 311915) has singles/doubles at Rs 45/80 without air-con, Rs 90/145 with air-con. Dorm beds are also available. Both these Ys are convenient for Connaught Place.

Places to Stay — Bottom End

Delhi is certainly no bargain when it comes to cheap hotels. You can easily pay Rs 30 for the most basic single — a price that elsewhere in India will generally get you a quite reasonable double with attached bathroom. There are basically three areas for cheap accommodation in Delhi. First there are a number of places on or around Janpath near Connaught Place in New Delhi. Near New Delhi Railway Station in Paharganj there are also some places — this is about midway between old and New Delhi. Finally there are a number of rock bottom hotels in old Delhi itself. The last is too far away from the agents, offices, airlines and so on of

New Delhi for most travellers — given Delhi's difficult public transport situation — but it is certainly colourful.

Janpath Area There are a number of cheaper 'lodges' or 'guest houses' near the Indian Government Tourist Office but single rooms can cost Rs 40 or more. For shoestring travellers there are often dormitories however. Some places to try include the well known *Ringo Guest House* (tel 40605) at number 17, round Scindia House behind Air India. It's a touch more expensive than the Janpath Lane guest houses but does have a Rs 10 dormitory. Ditto for the *Sunny Guest House* (tel 46033) at 152 or the *Laguna Guest House* (tel 44869) all in the same block. The rather spartan *Asian Guest House* (tel 44658) at 14 Scindia House is in the same area but a little more expensive again.

Across on Janpath Lane there is *Mrs Colaco's* at number 3. Dorm style from around Rs 10 a bed but it's basic, crowded, noisy and a little hard on the nerves. *Mr S C Jain's Guest House* at 7 Pratap Singh Building is also on Janpath Lane and is similarly priced but also has private rooms from around Rs 35. There is also the *Soni Guest House* on Janpath Lane.

For accommodation information in the Janpath area check with the Tourist Office at 88 Janpath — they can generally recommend something. Or try the helpful Student Travel Information Centre in room 6, Imperial Hotel.

Old Delhi The *Khushdil* and the *Crown Hotels* are at the west end of Chandi Chowk near the Fatehpuri Mosque, an easy walk from old Delhi Station. Both cost from around Rs 15 a single, Rs 25 a double. These old Delhi places are certainly more characterful but you've got to be aware of bed bugs and other nasties in some of the more dive-like places. The *Crown Hotel* used to be the old hippy Mecca in the flower power

days but has now been 'cleaned up'.

Paharganj Area If you walk about a km due west from New Delhi Railway Station you'll come to the Main Bazaar, Paharganj area where there are a number of cheapies and also some good restaurants. The *Vishal Hotel* has dorm beds at Rs 10 (then Rs 8 on following days) and doubles at Rs 25, 35 and 45 with bath — it's recently been 'improved'. The *Vivek Hotel* is a bit cheaper but the *Venus Hotel* is dark, dingy, noisy and cramped — for people with rock bottom standards only. The *Hotel Chankya* has doubles at Rs 25 with bathroom and is clean and run by pleasant people. Ice water dispensers on each floor and there is also a dorm. It's on the road that leads to the right off Main Bazaar Rd, before you get to the Metropolis Restaurant, towards and past the Imperial Theatres on the left. *Hotel Natraj* is right next to the well known Metropolis Restaurant on Chitragupta Rd. Singles cost from Rs 35, make certain of the agreed price when you check in. The rooms have attached baths and fans. The *Hotel Sapna* at 5153 Main Bazaar is pricier. Lots of other places around Paharganj. Or there is the *Skyway Guest House* at 11 Babar Lane, near the Nepalese Embassy.

Other Places Out at Chanakyapuri the *International Youth Centre* (tel 93631) has singles at Rs 30 with attached bath and dorm beds for Rs 8. The rooms are excellent and there is also a cafeteria with good food at pleasantly low prices. It's a very good place to stay if you don't mind the 20 minute bus trip or Rs 6 auto-rickshaw ride to Connaught Place. To get there take a 620 bus from the Plaza in Connaught Place and get off near the Indonesian Embassy. Or take a 662 from the old Delhi Station and get off at the Ashok Hotel. It's right behind the Chinese Embassy on Circular Rd and near the Chanakyapuri Police

Station.

Even further out is the *Ashoka Youth Hostel* at Mehrauli, near the Qutab Minar. It's very cheap at Rs 4 and has cooking facilities but it's a long trip out there. There is also a *Youth Hostel* at 5 Nyaya Marg, Chanokyapuri (tel 376285) — it's a good place to sleep but nothing more. Dorms cost Rs 12 for a bed which includes admittance to the library and a box for your things, bring your own padlock. There's a bank and a travel agency which will arrange trips to Agra, Jaipur, Delhi sightseeing and so on. Good for the embassies too.

If you want to camp there are several possibilities in Delhi. The *Tourist Camp* (tel 278929) is only a km from Connaught Place on Jawaharlal Nehru Marg, across from Irwin Hospital. Fixed tents are available here and it is very popular with overland tours. Campers pay Rs 7 or Rs 8 in the dorm tents. You can check luggage for safety's sake and it's nice to have the grass and gardens to sit in, easy place for washing clothes. Food is expensive and not very good. There are other campsites near Humayun's Tomb (*Delhi State Bharat Scouts Camping Ground*) and at *Qudsia Gardens* near the interstate bus terminal. The latter is very handy for late bus arrivals — Rs 10 for a bunk in a hut, less if you have a tent and it's very clean and friendly. If all else fails there are *Railway Retiring Rooms* at both stations.

Places to Eat

Like places to stay Delhi's many restaurants and snack bars can be divided up both by price range and by location.

Janpath & Connaught Place There has been a real spate of Indian style fast food places opening up around here. Their plus point is that they have quite good food at quite reasonable prices and they're clean and healthy. Their minus is that very few of them have any place

to sit — it's stand, eat and run. They serve Indian (from samosas to dosas) and western (burgers to sandwiches) food. *Nirula's* is probably the most popular and long running of these places and does a wide variety of excellent light snacks both Indian and western. They've also got good cold drinks, milkshakes and ice cream. Next door to the snack bar place on one side is an ice cream parlour and on the other side it's pizzas. Above the ice cream bar there's the fourth part of Nirula's, a sit down restaurant with appetising food including a Rs 20 eat-all-you-like salad smorgasbord. A good, clean place.

Other places around Connaught Place include *Sonali* on Janpath with good Indian chat and masala dosa for only Rs 2.50. The pleasantly relaxed *United Coffee House* on Connaught Place is another good place for a reasonable food in reasonably cool and clean surroundings, *Kolpani* is more or less behind the tourist office at 84A Tolstoy Lane. It's a popular place for breakfast and prices are low. As well as the stand up snack bars 21-flavour ice-cream parlours have also hit Delhi with a vengeance. Nice ice cream though.

There's a good collection of cheap restaurants and food markets in Mohan Singh Place, Irwin Rd, just off Connaught Place. Fresh milk is excellent at *Keventers*, the small milk bar at the corner of Connaught Place and Radial Road Number 3. If you just want a cheap soft drink and somewhere cool to drink it descend into the air-conditioned underground market between Janpath and Parliament St at Connaught Place.

Moving up a price category there are several higher price restaurants worth considering on Parliament St and by the Regal Cinema. The *Kwality Restaurant* on Parliament St is probably the flagship of the chain. It's spotlessly clean and very efficient and the food is excellent. The prices may be higher by Indian standards (ie a really good meal could cost you Rs 50 for two) but you'll probably decide it's worth it. This is also a good place for non-Indian food if you want a break and a good place for breakfast. *Al Arab*, right on the corner, more expensive again but has an interesting Middle Eastern menu with most dishes in the Rs 10 to 20 range and a Rs 22 buffet lunch. Round the corner is *Gaylords* with big mirrors and chandeliers and excellent Indian food. *The Cellar*, also on Connaught Place has pizzas that, for India, are not bad. Good vegetarian food at the *Volga*, it's a little expensive but it's air-conditioned.

Finally there's one Delhi food place that should not be forgotten. *Wenger's* on Connaught Place is a cake shop with an awesome range of little cakes which they'll put in a cardboard box, tie up with a bow and you can self-consciously carry them back to your hotel for private consumption.

Old Delhi & Paharganj The *Mansrover Hotel*, just around the corner from the west end of Chandni Chowk, has a filling fixed price thali for Rs 4. Good cheap Moghul food at the *Karim Hotel* in a small alley just off the south side of the Jami Masjid — Rs 12 for a good meal. The stalls in front of the Jami Masjid are very cheap at about Rs 2-3 a meal. Go for the ones with the big chappatis outside.

In the Paharganj area near New Delhi Station is the long running and ever popular *Metropolis Restaurant*. Food is Chinese and western and a little expensive but it's been a travellers' hangout for years and the food is not bad. The *Khalsa Punjabi Hotel*, on the left side of Main Bazaar Rd towards the station, beyond the Vishal and Venus Hotels, has good food. *Gobind* is a narrow fronted place on the opposite side towards the Metropolis and is good for lassi or expresso coffee. Good breakfast

places down towards the Chankya Hotel where you can get fried eggs, chips and tomatoes for Rs 3.50. Puris and bean and pea curry is a tasty snack from stalls around here. Good cheap food including fantastic porridge at the *Lakshmi Restaurant* at the end of the main bazaar furthest from the New Delhi Station, it's very popular with overlanders. *Cafe Gaylord*, half way down the main bazaar, is also good.

At the other end of the price scale there are two well known tandoori restaurants to consider. The *Tandoor* at the *Hotel President* on Asaf Ali Rd is an excellent place with the usual two waiters per diner service and a sitarist playing in the background. A meal for two might come to Rs 80 to 100 all up but the food is really excellent. The tandoori kitchen can be seen through a glass panel. *Moti Mahal's* on Netaji Subash Marg in Daryaganj in old Delhi is famous for its tandoori dishes including murga musalam but it seems to live more on long reputation than actual ability these days.

Other Places The *YWCA International Guest House's* restaurant has good food or if you are out at Chankyapuri (waiting for a visa perhaps) good and inexpensive Indian food can be had in the *International Youth Centre* near the Indonesian Embassy. The numerous 'international class' hotels have 'international standard' restaurants if you want to splash out.

At the *Haveli Restaurant* in the *Taj Hotel* a classy meal for two might cost around Rs 120. Excellent Chinese food at the *Cafe Chinoise* in the *Oberoi Inter-Continental*. Also at the *Shanghai* in the *Hotel Diplomat* where the prices are lower. *Fujiya* on Malcha Marg in Chanakyapuri has good Japanese and Chinese food. *Bar-e-Kabab* in the *Ashoka* is famous (and expensive) for its tandoori and Moghul dishes. *Gulnar* in the *Hotel Janpath* is cheaper for tandoori food.

Getting to Delhi

Delhi is a major international gateway to India and for details on arriving from overseas see the introduction. It is also a major centre for domestic travel with extensive bus, rail and air connections radiating out from Delhi.

Air Indian Airlines flights depart from Delhi to all the major Indian centres. Some important connections include Bombay (Rs 780, four times daily), Madras (Rs 1100), Calcutta (Rs 895, twice daily), Srinagar (Rs 515), Jaipur (Rs 185), Agra (Rs 150) and Varanasi (Rs 500).

India is not a great place for airfare bargains on domestic flights — Indian Airlines fly too close to 100% capacity to need to worry about the hard sell. But the Student Travel centre does have one interesting ticket worth looking at if your time in India is short and you're travelling east to South-East Asia. This ticket costs about Rs 2500 and takes you Delhi-Agra-Khajuraho-Varanasi-Kathmandu-Calcutta-Bangkok with stopovers everywhere along the way.

The Indian Airlines office in Delhi (tel 40052, 40071) is in the Kanchenjunga Building on Barakhamba Rd. The office occupies a large open area upstairs around the back of the building — you wouldn't know it was there, if you didn't know it was there! Reservations can be made for flights all over India but, as usual with Indian Airlines, it takes rather a long time.

Rail Delhi is an important rail centre and an excellent place to make rail bookings. Baroda House (tel 387889) is just north of India Gate on Kasturba Gandhi Marg. They can make bookings for you here, advise on rail travel in general, and have a tourist quota if you find it impossible to get a reservation. First and air-con class reservations are made at the Northern Railway Reservation Office, State Entry Rd, Connaught Circus. Remember that there are two main stations in Delhi — old Delhi Station and New Delhi Station. The latter is much closer to Connaught Place and if you're departing from old Delhi Station you should allow adequate time to wind your way through the traffic snarls of old Delhi.

There are several tourist special trains operating from Delhi. The Taj Express is ideal for day-tripping to Agra. The train departs from and returns to the New Delhi Station and takes three hours. Fare is Rs 50 in 1st class, Rs 12 in 2nd. The Pink City Express is a direct train from old Delhi Station to Jaipur, departing at 5.55 am and arriving five hours later. Fare is about Rs 75 in 1st class, Rs 16.50 in 2nd.

Some other important connections by mail or express train include:

A   Kashmiri children on the Pahalgam-Aru walk (J&K)
B   a 'supermarket' shikara on Dal Lake in Kashmir (J&K)

		1st class	2nd class
Amritsar	from 8 hours	Rs 98	Rs 23
Bombay	from 29 hours	Rs 270	Rs 65
Calcutta	from 17 hours	Rs 250	Rs 60
Jammu Tawi	from 13 hours	Rs 128	Rs 30
Madras	from 40 hours	Rs 340	Rs 83
Varanasi	from 12 hours	Rs 150	Rs 36

Bus The large Inter-State Bus Terminal is at Kashmiri Gate, north of the old Delhi Railway Station. Buses depart from here for locations all around Delhi — ring 229083 for details. State government bus companies operating from here are:

Haryana Government Roadways (tel 221292), bookings 6 am to 12 noon & 1.30 to 9 pm.

Jammu & Kashmir Government Roadways (tel 224559), bookings 10 am to 5 pm but only on air-con buses.

Rajasthan Roadways (tel 222276), bookings 6 am to 8 pm.

Uttar Pradesh Roadways (tel 226175, 273379), bookings 8 am to 4 pm.

Popular buses include the approximately hourly service to Agra which costs Rs 12. There is also a frequent and fast service to Jaipur for Rs 25. For Chandigarh, from where you can bus or take the narrow gauge train up to Simla, the buses cost Rs 20 but there are also de-luxe buses for Rs 40 and even an air-con bus for Rs 60.

Getting Around

Distances in Delhi are large and the buses are generally hopelessly crowded, which means taxis or auto-rickshaws are the only alternative.

Airport Fortunately airport to city and vice-versa transport is relatively simple. EATS, Ex-Servicemen's Air Link Transport Service, have a regular bus service between the airport and their office in Connaught Place. The fare is Rs 6 and they will drop off or pick up at most of the major hotels en route. A taxi runs about Rs 30 from the airport to Connaught Place. Auto-rickshaws will also run out to the airport although your teeth will be shaking by the time you get there! There is a public bus service to the airport (780) from the Super Bazaar at Connaught Place but it can get very crowded.

Bus Avoid buses during the rush hours when the situation is hopeless and whenever possible try to board (and leave too) at a starting or finishing point — more chance of a seat, less chance of being trampled. The Regal and Plaza Cinemas in Connaught Place are such places. There are some seats reserved for women on the left side of the bus. The Delhi Transport Corporation (DTC) run the buses and you can get a route guide from their office in Scindia House for Rs 0.25. They have an all day

A   flying Srinager-Leh (J&K)
B   Tikse monastery in Ladakh (J&K)
C   Kulu Valley from Nagar Castle (HP)

unlimited travel ticket for Rs 2. Some buses include 504 to the Qutab Minar from the Super Bazaar; the 502 from the Red Fort; 504 will also take you to the Youth Hostel there; 101 runs between the Interstate Bus Terminal and Connaught Place; several buses run between the Regal Cinema bus stand and the Red Fort. A short bus ride (like Connaught Place-Red Fort) will only be about Rs 0.50.

Taxis & Auto-Rickshaws On both the taxis and three-wheeler auto-rickshaws the meters are likely to be out of date and either a fare correction sheet will be produced or you will be asked to pay a percentage over the meter fare. All of them have meters and you should not accept 'meter broken' or 'no longer used' as an excuse. Except during the rush hours or on trips to the airport in the middle of the night an offer to find another vehicle will normally effect an instant repair. Connaught Place to the Red Fort could be, depending on traffic, around Rs 8 by taxi, Rs 4 by auto-rickshaw. There are also old Harley-Davidson auto-rickshaws running fixed routes at fixed prices. From Connaught Place their starting point is by the Plaza Cinema and your Sikh driver will chop his way through the traffic to Old Delhi for about a rupee.

Things to Buy
Good buys in Delhi include silk products, precious stones, leather and woodwork but the most important

thing about Delhi is that here you can find almost anything from almost anywhere in India. If this is your first stop in India, and you intend to buy some thing while you are here, then it's a chance to compare what is available from all over India. If this is your last stop and there was something you missed elsewhere in the country it's a last chance to find it.

Two good places to start are in New Delhi near Connaught Place. The Central Cottage Industries Emporium is on Janpath, right across from the Tourist Office. In this large building you will find items from all over India. Generally they are of good quality and generally they are reasonably priced. Whether it's woodcarvings, brasswork, paintings, clothes, textiles or furniture you'll find it all here. Along Baba Kharak Singh Marg, two streets round from Janpath, are the various State Emporiums run by the state governments. Each displays and sells handicrafts from their state. There are many other shops around Connaught Place and Janpath and the nearby Imperial Hotel, there are a number of stalls and small shops run by Tibetan refugees where they sell carpets, jewellery and many (often instant) antiques.

In old Delhi Chandni Chowk is the famous shopping street. Here you will find carpets and jewellery and in the narrow street called Dariba Kalan perfumes are made as well.

Punjab & Haryana

Haryana
  Population: 10 million
  Area: 44,222 square km
  Capital: Chandigarh
  Main language: Hindi

Punjab
  Population: 15 million
  Area. 50,362 square km
  Capital: Chandigarh
  Main language: Punjabi

The Punjab was probably the part of India which suffered the most destruction and damage at the time of partition yet today it is far and away the most affluent state in India. There's no natural resource or natural advantage that has given the Punjabis this enviable position, it was simply sheer hard work. Prior to partition the Punjab extended across both sides of what is now the Pakistan-India border. Its capital was Lahore, which today is the capital of the Pakistan state of the Punjab. But the population of the Punjab was split between Moslems and Sikhs and by the grim logic of partition that meant slicing the region in two. As millions of Sikhs and Hindus fled eastward and equal numbers of Moslems fled west there were innumerable atrocities and killings on both sides.

The major city in the Punjab is Amritsar, the holy city of the Sikhs, but it is so close to the Pakistan border that it was thought wise to build a safer capital further within the borders of India. At first Simla, the old imperial summer capital, served as capital but Chandigarh, a new planned city, was conceived and built to serve as the capital of the new Punjab. In 1966,

however, the Punjab was to undergo another split. This time it was divided into the predominantly Sikh and Punjabi speaking state of Punjab and the state of Haryana. At the same time some of the northern parts of the Punjab were hived off to Himachal Pradesh. Chandigarh, which now stands on the border of the Punjab and Haryana, remains the capital of both states.

At the time of partition the Punjab was devastated but the Sikh's no-nonsense approach to life has won for the Punjab a position that statistics sum up admirably. The Punjab's per capita income is 50% higher than the all India average (in second place is Haryana). Although Punjabis comprise less than 2½% of the population of India they provide 60% of India's wheat surplus and 50% of its rice surplus. The Punjab provides a third of all the milk produced in India. Punjabis have 5% of India's total bank deposits, they own 10% of India's television sets, their life expectancy is 65 years against the all India average of 47 years. Although the Punjab is predominantly an agricultural state it also has thriving industries including, at Ludhiana, Hero Bicycles who are India's biggest bicycle manumost interesting people in India. See the introductory section on religions for a description of their religion and customs. Apart from anything else the Sikhs are the most instantly recognisable people in India. The requirement that they do not cut their hair (*kesh*) ensures that all Sikh men are bearded and turbaned. For some reason they all look big, bulky men too — you never see a weedy looking Sikh. Sikh women also have a unique costume — the *salvar-kamiz*: wide pyjama style trousers which are fastened at the ankles, topped by a long shirt which almost reaches the

Sikhs, always very dapper...

facturer. The Punjabis also have the highest consumption of alcohol in India — the iron bangle (*kara*) which all Sikh men must wear is an ideal instrument for taking the caps off beer bottles!

From the traveller's point of view neither the Punjab nor Haryana have an enormous amount to offer though. In Haryana the chief attraction is the planned city of Chandigarh while in the Punjab it is the Sikh's golden city of Amritsar. Those cities apart the two states are mainly places of transit. Since they're on the way to the hill stations of Himachal Pradesh and the delights of Kashmir a lot of people do pass through them.

The Sikhs
The Sikhs are the reason for the Punjab's success story and they're amongst the

knees. All Sikh's have the surname Singh, 'lion'.

Curiously, despite their undoubted success the Sikhs have a reputation in India rather like the Irish in the west. The Indians have as many Sikh jokes as the west has Irish jokes. Not many translate very well but they basically follow the same line. Which is strange since the stereotyped Sikh is quite unlike the stereotyped Irishman. Where the Irish joke Irishman is supposed to be all thumbs the Sikhs have a reputation for great dexterity and mechanical ability — Sikhs have always been at home with machines and in India any activity with machines, from driving an auto-rickshaw to piloting a 747, will employ a disproportionate number of Sikhs. Despite which other Indians mock Sikhs as being blunt and straightforward to the point of stupidity!

HARYANA

The state of Haryana has one of the most successful tourist departments in India, which is very interesting when you consider how few tourist attractions the state has. What the clever Haryanans have done is take advantage of their position — if you're going from Delhi to almost any major attraction in the north — Jaipur, Agra, Kashmir, Amritsar — you go through Haryana. So they've built a series of 'service centres' along the main roads. The sort of motel-restaurant-service station complexes which in the west are quite common but in India are all too rare. They're clean and well kept and, if you're after a place to stay, make travelling through Haryana a pleasure. The main Haryana complexes with their distances from Delhi, include:

Badkhal Lake (tel 2202-04, 32 km) restaurants, air-con rooms from Rs 80, camper-huts at Rs 15 & 20, swimming pool, boating.

Sunbird, Surajkund (tel 5357, 18 km) swimming pool and boating, air-con rooms from Rs 80, camper huts at Rs 15 & 20.

Magpie, Faridabad (tel 3473, 30 km) air-con rooms from Rs 50.

Dabchick, Hodal (tel 91, 92 km) elephant rides, boating, children's playground, air-con rooms from Rs 80, camper huts at Rs 20 or Rs 55 with air-con.

Barbet, Sohna (tel 56, 56 km) restaurant, cafe, bath complex, swimming pool, air-con rooms from Rs 95, camper huts at Rs 15 & 30.

Jangle Babbleng Dharuhera (tel 25, Rewari, 70 km) restaurant, cafe, camel riding, air-con rooms from Rs 80, non air-con at Rs 35.

Rosy Pelican, Sultanpur (46 km) restaurant, bird watching facilities, camping site, air-con rooms at Rs 80, camper huts at Rs 15 & 30.

Shama Restaurant (tel 2683, 32 km) restaurant, non air-con rooms at Rs 45.

Mor Pankh (70 km) restaurant, non air-con rooms at Rs 35 & 45.

Uchana, Karnal (tel 2179, 124 km) boating, restaurant, cafe, kebab corner, air-con rooms from Rs 55, camper huts at Rs 20.

Parakeet, Pipli (tel 250, 152 km) restaurant, cafe, camping facilities, air-con rooms from Rs 65, camper huts at Rs 15.

Blue Jay, Samalkha (tel 10, 60 km) restaurant, air-con rooms at Rs 60, non air-con rooms at Rs 35, camper huts at Rs 10 & 25.

Yadavindra Gardens, Pinjore (tel 155, 281 km) at the Moghul gardens, restaurant, open air cafe, dosa shop, mini-zoo, children's games, air-con rooms from Rs 60, camper hut Rs 10.

Panchkula Youth Hostel (270 km) dorm beds at Rs 7.

Skylark, Panipat (tel 3579, 90 km) restaurant, air-con rooms from Rs 70.

Tilyar, Rohtak (tel 3966, 70 km) restaurant, boating, air-con rooms at Rs 65, non air-con rooms at Rs 35.

Myna, Rohtak (tel 2394, 72 km) restaurant, camper huts at Rs 15 & 20.

Flamingo, Hissar (tel 2602, 160 km) restaurant, air-con rooms at Rs 65.

Bulbul, Jind (127 km) restaurant, camper huts at Rs 15.

Kala Teetar, Abubshehr (325 km) restaurant, boating, air-con room from Rs 55.

DELHI TO CHANDIGARH
There are a number of sites of interest along the 260 km route from Delhi to Chandigarh. The road, part of the Grand Trunk Road, is one of the busiest in India with a lot of traffic of all types.

Panipat
Panipat, 92 km north of Delhi, is reputed to be one of the most fly infested places in India — due, it is said, to a Moslem saint who is buried here. He is supposed to have totally rid Panipat of flies but when the people complained that he had done too good a job he gave them all the flies back, times a thousand. It is also the site of three great battles although there is nothing much to be seen of these today. In 1526 Babur defeated Ibrahim Lodi, King of Delhi, at Panipat and thus founded the Moghul empire in India. In 1556 Akbar defeated the Pathans at this same site. Finally in 1761 the Mahrattas, who had succeeded the Moghuls, were defeated here by the Afghan forces of Ahmad Shah Durani.

Gharaunda
The gateways of an old Moghul *sarai* (rest house) stand to the west of this village, 102 km north of Delhi. Shah Jahan built *kos minars*, 'milestones', along the road from Delhi to Lahore and *sarais* at longer intervals. Most of the *kos minars* still stand but there is little left of the various *sarais*.

Karnal & Kurukshetra
Events in the *Mahabharata* are supposed to have occured here, 118 km from Delhi, and also at the tank of Kurukshetra, a little further north. It was at Karnal that Nadir Shah, the Persian who took the Peacock Throne from Delhi, defeated the Moghul Emperor Muhammed Shah in 1739. The Kurukshetra tank has attracted as many as half a million pilgrims at times of eclipses — for at these times the water in the tank is also said to contain water from every other sacred tank in India. Thus its ability to wash away sins is unsurpassed — during the eclipse. Kurukshetra also has an interesting small mosque, the Lal Masjid, and a finely designed tomb.

CHANDIGARH (population 250,000)
When the Punjab was partitioned its capital, Lahore, went to Pakistan. Initially Amritsar became the capital of the Indian Punjab but since it was uncomfortably close to the Pakistan border the decision was made to construct a totally new capital and the French architect Le Corbusier produced the plan. Later the Punjab was split into the two states of the Punjab and Haryana so today Chandigarh serves as the capital of both states. It is directly administered from New Delhi as a union territory. Construction of Chandigarh commenced in the '50s and although to many western visitors it appears to be a rather sterile city and hopelessly sprawling, Indians are very proud of it and Chandigarh's residents feel that it is a good place to live.

Chandigarh is a great disappointment — dismal and dull. Like so many examples of mid-20th century urban planning

1	Secretariat	7	Tourist Office & Bus Station
2	Vidhan Sabha	8	Hotel Mountview
3	High Court	9	YMCA
4	Museum & Art Gallery	10	Aroma Hotel
5	GPO	11	Kwality Restaurant
6	Indian Airlines & Air India	12	Rock Garden

Chandigarh

Sukhna Lake

Railway Station

(read 'pre oil-crisis') it was very much designed with wheeled transport in mind. Plus between buildings there are long, ugly, barren stretches of wasteland. In Le Corbusier's home environment they might be parks or gardens but in India emply ground is obviously doomed. Still the 'rock garden' is an eccentric little amusement.

Information & Orientation
Chandigarh is located on the edge of the Siwalik Hills, the outermost edge of the Himalayas. It is divided into 31 numbered sectors, separated by broad avenues. The bus station and modern shopping centre are in Sector 17. The railway station is inconveniently far out of Chandigarh so buses are much more convenient than trains. The Secretariat and other important government buildings are in Sector 1 to the north. The museum is in Sector 10 and the Rose Garden in Sector 16, next to the bus station. The shopping centre has restaurants, ice cream parlours, book shops and a wide variety of other retail outlets. The tourist office is upstairs in the bus station.

Government Buildings
The Secretariat and the Legislative Assembly Buildings are in Sector 1. Between 10 am and 12 noon you can go to the top of the Secretariat from where there is an excellent view over Chandigarh. Eventually it is intended to build a huge revolving hand to be the centrepiece of the government sector and the symbol of Chandigarh.

Close to the government buildings is a not-to-be-missed attraction, the bizarre Rock Garden (25p admission) — a sort of concrete maze with a lot of rocks and very little garden. A very strange and whimsical fantasy. Close to this is the artificial Sukhna Lake which covers about three square km. You can rent row boats on the lake or just stroll round its two km perimeter.

Museum & Art Gallery
Located in Sector 10 and open daily except Mondays, the art gallery contains a modest collection of Indian stone sculptures dating back to the Gandhara period, together with some miniature paintings and modern art. The adjacent museum has fossils and implements of pre-historic man which have been found in India.

Rose Garden
The Sector 16 Rose Garden is claimed to be the biggest in Asia and contains more than a thousand varieties of roses.

Places to Stay — Top End
The *Oberoi Mount View* in Sector 10 (tel 24729, 26021) is Chandigarh's top hotel. Singles/doubles run from Rs 200/300 and the hotel has all modern facilities. *Hotel Aroma* in Sector 22 (tel 23359) is somewhat cheaper but often rather crowded — as are many of Chandigarh's hotels. Singles cost from Rs 30, doubles from Rs 50. It's about 10 minutes walk from the bus station. There are some rooms with air-conditioning.

Places to Stay — Bottom End
The new *Youth Hostel* is at Panchkula, between Chandigarh and the Pinjore Gardens — a little way out of town but there are many buses and the hostel is good value at Rs 7. It is also possible to get cheaper dormitory style accommodation in the *Panchayat Bhawan* (tel 23698) in Sector 18. This is a government accommodation unit but rather far from the city centre and bus station. There is a *YMCA* (tel 26532) in Sector 11 and three more expensive hotels opposite the railway station — *Jullundur*, *Amar* and *Alankar*.

Places to Eat
There are many restaurants in the modern shopping centre. *Sai Sweets* at

1102 in Sector 22 (about midway between the bus halt and the Aroma Hotel) has expensive (Rs 8) but really excellent thalis and good chat. The *Indian Coffee House*, in the shopping centre, is also a good, economic place to eat.

Getting There
Buses depart from the Interstate Bus Terminal in Delhi (near Kashmir Gate) every hour for the five hour trip to Chandigarh. There is a much wider choice of buses than usual on this route. Apart from the regular buses (Rs 20) there are about six de-luxe buses daily (Rs 40) and three or four air-con buses (Rs 60) which actually show Indian movies en route! Buses are equally frequent from Chandigarh to other centres — to Simla costs Rs 12 (Rs 20 de-luxe), Kulu Rs 25 or Manali Rs 30. It takes about 14 hours to Manali by bus, only nine by taxi. It's five hours to Simla, 12 hours to Kulu, six hours to Amritsar, 10 hours to Dharamsala and seven hours to Pathankot. Buses are more convenient than trains from Chandigarh but railway reservations can be made at the booking agency in sector 22 (tel 29117) and enquiries can be made by phoning 27605. There are daily air connections to Delhi (Rs 150) or to Jammu (Rs 234) and Srinagar (Rs 319).

Getting Around
Chandigarh is much too spread out to get around on foot but a day is certainly sufficient to see all it has to offer. There is an extensive bus network and this is the cheapest way of getting around —

Bus 1 runs by the Aroma Hotel as far as the government buildings in Sector 1. Buses 6, 6A and 6B all run to the railway station. Cycle rickshaws operate on the normal bargaining basis but Chandigarh is a bit big even for them — if you're planning a longer trip across the city consider an auto-rickshaw, they're metered. If you do want to try walking start off at Sector 1 and stroll back through Sector 10 (Museum and Art Gallery) and 16 (Rose Garden) to the bus station and shopping centre in Sector 17.

Things to Buy
Woollen sweaters and shawls from the Punjab are good buys, especially in the Government Emporium. The Chandigarh shopping centre is probably the most extensive in India.

NEAR CHANDIGARH
Pinjore
The Moghul gardens at Pinjore were designed by Fidai Khan, Aurangzeb's foster brother, who also designed the Badshahi Mosque in Lahore, Pakistan. Situated 20 km from Chandigarh the gardens include the Rajasthani-Moghul style Shish Mahal palace. Below it is the Rang Mahal and the cubical Jal Mahal. An otter house and other animals can be seen in the mini-zoo near the gardens. The fountains only operate on weekends.

Places to Stay The rest house here has air-con rooms from Rs 60 and one camper hut at Rs 10.

DELHI TO AMRITSAR
Patiala (population 160,000)
A little south of the road and rail line from Delhi to Amritsar, Patiala was once the capital of an independent Sikh state. There is a museum in the

Moti Bagh and the palaces of the Maharaja in the Baradari Gardens.

Sirhind
This was once a very important town and the capital of the Pathan Sur

dynasty. In 1555 Humayun defeated Sikander Shah here and a year later his son, Akbar, completed the destruction of the Sur dynasty at Panipat. From then until 1709 Sirhind was a rich Moghul city but clashes between the declining Moghul and rising Sikh powers led to the city's sack in 1709 and complete destruction in 1763.

The Pathan style Tomb of Mir Miran and the later Moghul Tomb of Pirbandi Nakshwala, both ornamented with blue tiles, are worth seeing. The mansion or *haveli* of Salabat Beg is probably the largest private home remaining from the Moghul period. South-east of the city is an important Moghul *sarai*.

Ludhiana (population 450,000)
An important textile centre, a great battle of the First Sikh War was fought in Ludhiana. Hero bicycles are manufactured here.

Jullundur (population 325,000)
Only 80 km from Amritsar, this was once the capital of an ancient Hindu kingdom. It survived being sacked by Mahmud of Ghazni nearly a thousand years ago and later became an important Moghul city. The town has a large *sarai* built in 1857.

AMRITSAR (population 500,000)
Travellers heading overland always pass through Amritsar, it's close to the only land crossing open to Pakistan and every traveller crossing Asia inevitably passes through the city. Founded in 1577 by Ram Das, the fourth Guru of the Sikhs, Amritsar is both the centre of the Sikh religion and the major city of the Punjab state — where the majority of Sikhs live. The name Amritsar translates as 'pool of nectar', the name of the sacred pool by which the Sikh's golden temple is built.

The original site for the city was granted by the Moghul emperor Akbar but in 1761 Ahmad Shah Durani sacked the town and destroyed the temple. The temple was rebuilt in 1764 and in 1802 it was roofed with copper gilded plates by Ranjit Singh and became known as the golden temple. During the turmoil of the partition of India in 1948 Amritsar was a flashpoint for the terrible events that shook the Punjab. The region's recovery has been remarkable and today Amritsar even looks better off than other parts of India. You see few beggars on the streets.

Information & Orientation
The old city is south of the main railway station and is surrounded by a circular road which used to contain the massive city walls. There are 18 gates still in existence but only the gate to the north, facing the Ram Bagh gardens, is original. The Golden Temple and the narrow alleys of the bazaar area are in the interior of the old city. The more modern part of Amritsar is north-east of the railway station where you will also find the beautiful gardens known as Ram Bagh, the Mall and the 'posh' Lawrence St. The bus station is a km east of the railway station on the road to Delhi. The Tourist office is opposite the railway station.

The Golden Temple
The holiest shrine of the Sikh religion is in the centre of the old part of town. The temple itself is surrounded by the lake which gave the town its name. A causeway connects the temple in the middle of the pool and a loudspeaker broadcasts a continuous reading of the *Granth Sahib*, in Punjabi. The high priest who reads from the Sikh's holy

Amritsar

Key:-
1. Indian Airlines
2. G.P.O.
3. Punjab Govt. Tourist Office
4. Golden Temple
5. Durgiana Temple
6. Mrs. Bhandari's Guest House
7. Hotel Ritz
8. Kwality Restaurant
9. Youth Hostel
10. Jallianwala Bagh

- - - Main hotel & restaurant area

book sits on the east side of the temple. The original copy of the *Granth Sahib* is kept in the Golden Temple and is occasionally taken out on procession. There is also a temple garden to the south side of the temple enclosure and the Baba Atal Tower stands in this garden. The tall Ramgarhia Minars stand outside the temple enclosure.

Pilgrims and visitors to the Golden Temple must remove their shoes and cover their heads before entering the temple precincts. An English speaking guide is available at the clock tower which marks the temple entrance. The Central Sikh Museum is upstairs in the clock tower.

The Old City

A 15 minute walk from the Golden Temple, through the narrow alleys of the old city, brings you to the Hindu temple known as Durgiani. This small temple, dedicated to the goddess Durga, dates back to the 16th century. A larger temple, built like the Golden Temple in the centre of a lake, is dedicated to the Hindu deities Laxmi and Narayan. There are a number of mosques in the old city including the mosque of Muhammad Jan with three white domes and slender minarets. To the south-west of the city stands the Fort of Govindgarh which was built in 1805-09 by Ranjit Singh who was also responsible for the city walls.

Jalianwala Bagh

This park is just five minutes walk from the Golden Temple and commemorates the death of 2000 Indians at this site who were shot indiscriminately by the British in 1919. This was one of the major events in India's struggles for independence. Bullet marks and the well into which some people jumped to escape can still be seen.

Ram Bagh

This beautiful garden is in the new part of town and also has a museum in the small palace built there by the Sikh Maharajah Ranjit Singh. The museum contains weapons dating back to the Moghul times and some portraits of the ruling houses of the Punjab. It's closed on Wednesdays.

Other

The Govindgarh Fort, built by Ranjit Singh in 1809, is a little south-west of the city centre. Tarn Taran is an important Sikh tank, about 25 km south of Amritsar. There's a temple and tower on the east side of the tank which was also constructed by Ranjit Singh. The temple pre-dates Amritsar. It's said that any leper who can swim across the tank will by miraculously cured.

Places to Stay — Top End

Built by the Punjab state government, the *Amritsar International Hotel* (tel 31991) is a new building near the railway station. Equipped with all modern facilities, such as air-conditioning, singles range from Rs 120. Other more expensive hotels include the air-con *Airlines Hotel* on Cooper Rd (tel 44545) with singles/doubles from Rs 60/70. It too is near the railway station. Or there is the *Astoria* (tel 48979) on Queens Rd and the *Ritz* (tel 44199) at 45 the Mall.

Places to Stay — Middle

Station Link Rd, opposite the railway station, has three moderately priced hotels. *Hotel Skylark* (tel 46738) and *Hotel Chinar* (tel 33455) cost from Rs 40 for a single. *Hotel Palace*, which also houses the state tourist information office, has some cheaper rooms. Close by is the similarly priced *Grand Hotel*.

Near the Mall, in the new area of the city and about a km from the railway station, you'll find the pleasant *Hotel Blue Moon* with singles from Rs 50. In the same area *Hotel Odeon* (tel 43474) is only Rs 30 for a single with attached bath. This is also the area for a number of restaurants, including a *Kwality* branch, opposite the Ram Bagh.

Places to Stay — Bottom End
Tourist Guest House, across from the railway station and near Hotel Airlines, has singles for Rs 20 and is popular with shoestring travellers. If you're on a really tight budget the state government operated *Youth Hostel* is three km out of town on the Delhi road. A dorm bed costs Rs 8 (Rs 6 for members) or you can have a doorless double for Rs 20. The hostel has hot showers and good (but expensive) food, it's one of the better youth hostels in India and also has camping facilities. If you'd really like to come to grips with the Sikh religion you can stay for a few days for free at the guest house of the Golden Temple. Be considerate, don't smoke and don't complain if the standards are not what you expect. Mattresses can be loaned for a returnable Rs 10 deposit. Accommodation is dormitory style. There are many cheap hotels around the temple such as the *Vikas Guest House*; doubles for Rs 25, or the slightly cheaper *Amritsar Majestic Hotel*.

Places to Eat
There are a number of more expensive restaurants in the new part of town such as *Napoli*, *Kwality* and *Crystal*. Near the Kwality restaurant there is an ice cream parlour with 20 flavours of ice cream.

Amritsar also has a number of cheaper and locally popular places such as *Kasar*

de Dhawa near the Durgiana Temple and the telephone exchange in the old town. Parathas and other vegetarian dishes are the speciality here and you can eat well for less than Rs 10. *Kundan di Dhawa* near the railway station and *Mangal de Dhawa* are other popular cheapies. *Sharma Vaishna Dhaba*, near the temple, also has good vegetarian food. The railway restaurant is good.

Getting There
Amritsar is 447 km from Delhi and takes seven hours by mail or express train (Rs 23 in second class, Rs 98 in first). It's rather less comfortable by the bus which takes 10 hours. Amritsar is a jumping off point to other places in north-west India — Pathankot (on the way to Kashmir) is three hours away by bus and Chandigarh is four. Amritsar is regularly connected by air to Delhi (Rs 254) and Srinagar (Rs 215). It is only 30 km from Amritsar to Wagah, the road crossing point into Pakistan. Unless you're in your own vehicle or an overland bus it's easier to take the train service which now operates between Amritsar and Lahore rather than bus to the border, walk across and bus on to Lahore. See the 'Entry & Exits' section for more details.

Things to Buy
Woollen blankets and sweaters are supposed to be cheaper in Amritsar than in other places in India as they are locally manufactured. Katra Jaimal Singh, near the telephone exchange in the old city, is a good shopping area.

PATHANKOT
In the extreme north of the Punjab, 107 km from Amritsar, the town of Pathankot is important, to travellers, purely for its crossroads function. It's the gateway to Jammu in the state of Jammu and Kashmir, which in turn is the jumping off point for the bus trip up to Srinagar. Pathankot is also the bus centre for departures to the Himachal Pradesh hill stations — particularly Dalhousie and Dharamsala. Otherwise it's a dull little place although there's the picturesque Shahpur Kandi Fort, about 13 km north of the town on the River Ravi.

Getting There

The dusty bus station and the railway station are only a hundred or so metres apart. Buses to Jammu take about three hours and costs Rs 5. To Dalhousie it's Rs 8 and about four hours, to Dharamsala Rs 9 and five hours.

Places to Stay

Pathankot has a rest house and cheap hotels like the *Green Hotel* and the *Imperial Hotel*. Reasonable food in the railway station restaurant.

DELHI TO FEROZEPORE

This route takes you through Haryana and the Punjab, further south than the Delhi-Chandigarh and Delhi-Amritsar routes. From Delhi the railway line runs through Rohtak, 70 km out, which was once a border town between the Sikhs and Marathas and the subject of frequent clashes. Bhatinda, 296 km from Delhi, was an important town of the Pathan Sur dynasty. Sirsa, to the south of

Bhatinda, was an ancient city but little remains apart from the city walls. Hansi, south-east of Sirsa, towards Rohtak, was where Colonel Skinner, of the legendary regiment 'Skinner's Horse', died. Faridkot, 350 km from Delhi, was once the capital of a Sikh state of the same name. It has a 700 year old fort. Ferozepore is 382 km from Delhi and the railway line continued to Lahore from here, until partition.

Keeping Your Cool

Sometimes India can simply be too much for anyone to take. It has been called culture shock enough times and in a way that is what it is. Remember that habits and practises which annoy or even revolt you — the continuous hawking and spitting that sometimes seems seems to go on, the practise of making every wall a public urinal, are probably matched by some western practise that an Asian would find just as incomprehensible. Westerners blithely walk into houses without pausing to take their shoes off, they sit on toilet seats, they carry dirty handkerchiefs in their pockets. The habit of fixedly staring at you is one you just have to get

used to. It's simply unembarrased interest and there is nothing you can do about it, staring right back is not going to change anything.

Summon up as much understanding as you can but sometimes pushing and shoving, cutting into queues, continuously trying to get you to do something you don't want to, the inevitable rip-offs all become too much and even the most easy going traveller loses his temper. Treat it as part of life, practise staying cooler next time but if it starts to happen too often perhaps it's time you took a break from India. After all, that's what Nepal and Sri Lanka are there for, isn't it?

Himachal Pradesh

Population: 3.5 million
Area: 55,673 square km
Capital: Simla
Main languages: Hindi, Pahari

The state of Himachal Pradesh came into being in its present form with the partition of the Punjab into Punjab and Haryana in 1966. Himachal Pradesh is essentially a mountain state — it takes in the transition zone from the plains to the high Himalayas and in the trans-Himalayan regions of Lahaul and Spiti actually crosses that mighty barrier to the Tibetan plateau. It's a delightful state for visitors, particularly during the hot season when people flock to its hill stations to escape the searing heat of the plains. High points for the visitor include Simla, the 'summer capital' of British India and still one of India's most important hill stations. The Kulu Valley is simply one of the most beautiful areas on earth — a lush, green valley with the sparkling Beas River running through it and the snow-capped Himalayan peaks forming the background. Then there's Dharamsala, home-in-exile for the Dalai Lama; and a host of other hill stations, lakes, walks and mountains. In the far north of the state the winter snow melts to permit visitors for a few brief summer months to explore the Tibetan culture of Keylong in Lahaul and Spiti.

TREKKING & MOUNTAINEERING
There are a wide variety of trekking possibilities which have, as of yet, been barely exploited. The Himachal Pradesh Tourist Office can supply a booklet titled *Trekkers Guide Himachal Pradesh* which concentrates on treks in the Kulu and Manali area. They also have three excellent large scale maps of Himachal Pradesh which are invaluable for intend-

ing trekkers. The trekking season in Himachal Pradesh runs from mid-May to mid-October. In Manali there is a Department of Mountaineering and Allied Sports (tel 42) which can advise you on trekking possibilities in the state and also on the numerous unscaled peaks.

Equipment and provisions will depend very much on where you trek. In the lower country in the Kulu or Kangra Valleys or around Simla there are many rest houses and villages. On the other hand in Lahaul and Spiti the population is much less dense and conditions much more severe. You will need to be much better equipped in terms of cold weather gear and also food and provisions. Some of the better known treks are detailed in the appropriate sections. There are a great number of Forest Rest Houses, PWD Rest Houses and other semi-official accommodation possibilities along the Himachal Pradesh trekking routes. Enquire at local tourist offices before setting off about using these places.

The HPTD's *Trekking Guide* lists 136 mountains over 5000 metres high. The majority of them are unclimbed, most not even named. It's virgin territory for mountaineers.

WILDLIFE

There are fishing possibilities in many places in Himachal Pradesh and a number of trout hatcheries have been established. The various local tourist offices can advise you on where to fish and how to obtain fishing licences. These are much cheaper than in Kashmir. There are a variety of deer, antelope, mountain goats and sheep which may be seen in the state, some of which are now rather rare. Himalayan black bears and brown bears are found in many parts of the state, the black bear is fairly common but the brown bear is usually only found at higher elevations. Wild boar are found at lower elevations in certain districts. Snow leopards are now very rare and only found at high elevations in the most remote parts of the state. Panthers and leopards are, however, still found in many forested regions. Himachal Pradesh has a variety of pheasants and partridges and many mountain birds.

TEMPLES

Although Himachal Pradesh does not have any particularly renowned temples, at least so far as being touristically well known goes, it does have many quite interesting and architecturally very diverse ones. In the Kangra and Chamba valleys there are a number of 8th to 10th centuries in the Indo-Aryan shikhara style. Pagoda style temples with multi-tiered roofs are found in the Kulu Valley. There are many temples of purely local design, often with interesting wood carvings, particularly in the Chamba region. In the south of the state there are a number of temples with elements of Moghul and Sikh design while in several locations there are cave temples. Finally the Tibetans, who came to the state following the Chinese invasion of their country, have built colourful gompas (monasteries) and temples. The people of Lahaul and Spiti in the north of the state are also of Tibetan extraction and have many interesting gompas.

THINGS TO BUY

The Kulu Valley is full of spinners and weavers, mostly men, and the fine shawls made in Kulu are very popular. These are made from the fleece shed in the summer by mountain goats. The shawls made from pashmina hair from the pashmina goat are the finest. Chamba is well known for its leather chappals (sandals). In the high Himalayas fleecy soft blankets known as gudmas are woven, and traditional rugs and namdas. In the bazaars you can find locally made jewellery and metalwork. Tibetan handicrafts include coral jewellery, Tibetan carpets and religious paraphernalia.

TRANSPORT

Apart from two railway lines which are both narrow gauge and hence rather more 'fun' than 'transport', getting around Himachal Pradesh means taking a bus — unless you can afford a taxi. The two trains run from Kalka, just north of Chandigarh, to Simla and from Pathankot along the Kangra Valley to Jogindarnargar. Himachal Pradesh buses are generally the Indian norm — slow, crowded, uncomfortable and tiring. Things are made a little worse by the mountainous terrain, if you can manage to average 20 kph on a bus trip you're doing well. Taxis are readily available but rather expensive. One way you can make a saving is to find a taxi on a return trip — in that case you can often knock the price down a bit. Ask the people running your hotel, they're often in the know as to who is going where and when.

The HPTDC have a number of deluxe tourist bus services. They often operate overnight.

| Delhi-Simla | Sat, Wed | 11 hrs Rs 57 |
| Simla-Delhi | Sun, Thurs | 11 hrs Rs 57 |

Delhi-Manali	Sat	18 hrs Rs 94
Manali-Delhi	Thurs	18 hrs Rs 94
Chandigarh-Manali	Sun, Thurs	12 hrs Rs 60
Manali-Chandigarh	Mon, Fri	12 hrs Rs 60
Pathankot-Dalhousie	daily	3½ hrs Rs 38

SIMLA (population 60,000)

In the days before independence Simla was the most important British hill station and in the hot season became the 'summer capital' of India. First 'discovered' by the British in 1819 it was not until 1822 that the first permanent house was erected and not until many years later that Simla became the semi-official capital. As the heat built up on the plains each year first the memsahibs, then the sahibs, or at least those who could escape, made their way to the cool mountain air of Simla. The high flown social life of Simla in the summer was legendary and somehow the town still has a British air about it.

Situated at an altitude of 213 metres Simla sprawls along a crescent shaped ridge with its suburbs clinging to the slopes. Along the ridge runs the Mall — from which the British not only banned all vehicles but also, until WW I, all Indians. Today it's a busy scene each evening with throngs of holidaymakers. The Mall is lined with stately English looking houses bearing strangely displaced English names. Simla's English flavour is continued by buildings like Christ Church which dates from 1857, Gorton Castle and the former Viceroyal Lodge on Observatory Hill which dates from 1888. Lajpat Rai Chowk is still better known as Kipling's Scandal Point.

Following independence Simla was initially the capital of the Punjab until the creation of Chandigarh. When the Punjab was broken into the Punjab and Haryana, Simla became the capital of Himachal Pradesh.

Information & Orientation

The ridge along which the Mall runs dips away westward. From the ridge there are good views of the valleys and peaks on both sides. You'll find the Tourist Information Office (tel 3311), the best restaurants and the main shopping centre along the Mall. From the ridge the streets wall away steeply to colourful local bazaars on the hill slopes. The streets are narrow, some of them with verandah-like 'sidewalks'. The bus station is located in the middle of the crowded southern slope. In winter it is warmer on the southern slope than on the cooler northern side where the ice skating ground is located.

Indian Institute of Advanced Study

Situated on a hillock west of Simla this was formerly the palace of the British Viceroy. Many decisions affecting the destiny of the sub-continent were made in this historic building. The huge, fortress-like building has six storeys and a magnificent reception hall and dining hall. Today the building contains a good library.

State Museum

An hour's walk down from the church on the Mall the museum has a modest collection of stone statues from different places in Himachal Pradesh. The Indian miniatures exhibited here include pictures from the Kangra school.

Jakhu Temple

Dedicated to the monkey god, Hanuman, the temple is at an altitude of 2455 metres near the highest point of the

Sanjauli (2256m)

Circular Road

YMCA

Mall Road

Circular Road

Lakkar Bazar

Chota Simla (2134m)

Cart Road

Mall Road

YWCA

Lower Bazar

G.P.O.

Bus Stand

Ravenswood
Holiday Home
Marina Hotel

Himland Hotel

Railway Sta.

The Glen (1829m)

Cart Road

Mall Road

Chadwick Falls (1585m)

Simla

Prospect Hill (2175m)

Mandi
Kalka

Simla ridge. It offers a fine view over the surrounding valleys, out to the snow capped peaks and over Simla itself. The temple is a 45 minute walk from the Mall and appropriately there are many monkeys around the temple.

Walks

Apart from promenading along the Mall and the walk to the Jakhu Temple there are a great number of other interesting walks around Simla. The network of motorable roads, many dating from the British period, offers access to other scenic spots.

The Glen A popular picnic spot four km from Simla at 1830 metres. A stream flows through the forest here and you can reach it via the Cecil Hotel.

Summer Hill Pleasant shady walks in this Simla suburb which is on the Simla-Kalka railway line. It's five km from Simla and at 1983 metres.

Chadwick Falls Reached via Summer Hill, the falls are 67 metres high and are at their best during the monsoon. It's seven km from Simla and at 1586 metres.

Prospect Hill It's a 15 minute climb from Boileauganj to this popular picnic spot. Fine views over the surrounding country and a temple of Kamna Devi. It's five km from Simla and at 2145 metres.

Sankat Mochan Situated seven km from Simla and at 1875 metres you can reach this spot, with its Hanuman temple and fine view of Simla, on foot or by car.

Tara Devi At 1851 metres and seven km from Simla you can reach this hill-top temple by rail and car. There's a PWD Rest House here.

Wildflower Hall On the road to Kufri, 13 km from Simla and at 2593 metres, this was the former residence of Indian commander-in-chief, Lord Kitchener. The present huge mansion, surrounded by pine trees, is not the actual one built

for Kitchener though. From here you have a fine view back to Simla and out to Pir Panjal and Badrinath mountain peaks. There are some recently constructed log huts here at Rs 80 (one bedroom) or Rs 125 with two bedrooms. The huts have bathrooms, kitchens, and living rooms. There's also accommodation in Wildflower Hall itself from around Rs 60. Phone number is Chharabra (Simla) 8/212.

Kufri This is the best known ski resort in Himachal Pradesh and is situated 16 km from Simla at 2501 metres. The skiing season is at its peak in January and February but the snow cover can sometimes be problematical. There is an annual winter sports festival, usually held in the first week of February. If you'd like to try skiing in India equipment can be rented for around Rs 10 per day. The *Indira Rest House* is two km from Kufri.

Mashobra Also accessible by car there are pleasant forest walks around this picnic spot 13 km from Simla at 2149 metres.

Craignano At 2279 metres and 16 km from Simla, Craignano, with its hill-top Rest House, is only three km from Mashobra.

Naldera At 2044 metres Naldera is 23 km from Simla, and has a golf course, Tourist Bungalow and cafeteria.

Fagu There is a very fine view from this spot and a lot of snow in winter. It's 22 km from Simla and at 2510 metres. Fagu also has a potato research centre.

Tours

The HPTDC (Himachal Pradesh Tourism Development Corporation) has a number of conducted tours to places around Simla. Local tours, which are run more frequently in the summer season, cost from Rs 15 and are booked from the tourist office on the Mall. Longer tours include the 64 km trip out to Narkanda where there is a very fine panoramic view of the Himalayas.

Places to Stay
Prices in most places in Simla vary widely between the mid-April to mid-September 'season' and the rest of the year. From June to September accommodation can be difficult to find in Simla at any price.

Simla's two top end hotels are *Oberoi Clarkes* (tel 6091-95) and *Oberoi Cecil* (tel 2073), both on the Mall. Both have singles/doubles at Rs 250/350 including all meals. The Cecil is one of the older and better known hotels in Simla but is only open in May and June. Simla's other 'western style' hotel is the *Himland Hotel* (tel 3595-96) on Circular Rd. All inclusive tariff here runs from Rs 70/100 for singles/doubles.

The state government Tourist Corporation's *Holiday Home* (tel 3971) is on Cart Rd in the eastern part of the city on the southern slope of the ridge. Rooms in the new wing cost from Rs 125 and Rs 160 while in the older annexe they range upwards from around Rs 30 with a shared bath, more with attached bath. Pleasant rooms and good service. The new wing is actually known as the *Hotel Holiday Home* and has a different phone number (tel 6031-32-34).

Other cheaper hotels include the *Ashoka* (tel 2166) with singles from Rs 20 and doubles from Rs 30 to Rs 60. It's a good place if you want to stay on the Mall and enjoy the fine views. The *Grand Hotel* (tel 2121, 2587) is also on the Mall and with prices from Rs 20 it could well be the best value in Simla. The catch is that it is reserved for Government of India officials between mid-April and mid-July. Other hotels along the Mall include the *Marina* (tel 3557) and the *Simla Hotel* (tel 3218).

Cheap hotels around the bus station include the *Vikrant Hotel* (tel 3602) which also has a dorm, or in Ram Bazaar the *Coronation Hotel*. You could also check the *Lord Grey Hotel* (tel 5146) and the *Hotel Tashkent* (tel 2482). There are many other hotels and dharamsalas.

Places to Eat
All the better known restaurants are along the Mall — the best known is probably *Balaji's*. Often crowded it has a pleasant decor and a meal will cost from Rs 15. Upstairs there is another restaurant known as *Fascination*. The *Alfa Restaurant* is also on the Mall. The various *Indian Coffee Houses* along the Mall offer south Indian food and snacks at reasonable prices and they're also a good place to sit, watch the world pass by, and talk.

Getting There
A bus from Chandigarh is the easiest way to get to Simla. The 117 km trip takes four hours and costs Rs 12 in an ordinary bus, Rs 20 in a de-luxe bus. You can reach Chandigarh from Delhi by a variety of buses and by air. By rail to Simla involves a change from broad gauge to narrow gauge at Kalka, a little north of Chandigarh. The narrow gauge trip to Simla takes nearly six hours. Add on two or more hours to change trains at Kalka plus the trip from Delhi and you'll find it much faster by bus. On the other hand the rail trip is great fun! There are buses north from Simla to other hill stations in Himachal Pradesh such as Dharamsala or the Kulu Valley.

Getting Around
Local bus services operate from the Cart Rd bus stand. A bus runs from the bus station to Boileauganj in the west. Apart from that the best way around Simla is to walk. A recently constructed 'tourist lift' takes you to the Mall from the lower part of town, saving a long and tedious climb.

AROUND SIMLA

Kalka

The narrow gauge railway line from Kalka to Simla was built in 1903-04. Although it is cheaper and quicker to go by road the rail trip is fun. Pinjor, 21 km south-east of Kalka, has a Moghul summerhouse and garden which was built by Fidai Khan who built the Badshahi Mosque in Lahore, Pakistan.

Chail

This was once the summer capital of the princely state of Patiala — today the old palace is a luxurious hotel. Chail is 45 km from Simla via Kufri or you can reach it via Kandaghat on the Simla-Kalka road or narrow gauge rail line. Chail, at an altitude of 2250 metres, is built on three hills, one of which is topped by the Chail Palace and one by the ancient Sidh temple. Chail also boasts a temple of quite another religion — cricket, here you will find the highest cricket pitch in the world!

Places to Stay In the *Chail Palace Hotel* (tel Chail 43 & 47) some rooms go down to Rs 100 but the Maharajah and Maharani suites are Rs 250 and Rs 350. Chail also has a number of HPTDC cottages and log huts and the *Himneel Hotel* with singles/doubles at Rs 25/50. There are also a number of local hotels.

Getting There There are direct buses to Chail from Kalka and Simla.

Kasauli

A pleasant little hill station at 1927 metres only a little north of Kalka. It's an interesting 15 km trek from Kalka to Kasauli or you can get there from Dharampur which is on the Kalka-Simla railway line. Only four km from Kasauli is Monkey Point, a picnic spot and lookout with a very fine view over the plains of the south and to the mountains in the north. Sabathu, 38 km from Kasauli, has a 19th century

Gurkha built fortress.

Places to Stay There is a *PWD Rest House* and a number of private guest houses such as the *Alasia*, *Morris* and *Kalyan*. In Dharampur the simple *Mazdoor Dhaba* restaurant near the station has good (and cheap) vegetarian meals and a dormitory upstairs.

Solan

Between Kalka and Simla, on both the railway line and the road, this town is named after the Soloni Devi temple at the southern side of the town. There are pleasant picnic spots and streams around this 1350 metre hill station.

Places to Stay The *HPTDC Tourist Bungalow* has doubles at Rs 40 and dorm beds at Rs 5 plus the *Talk o' Town Cafeteria* — they certainly think up some names!

Narkanda

At 2700 metres, 64 km from Simla, this is a popular spot for viewing the Himalayas, particularly from 3300 metre Hattu peak. From Narkanda you can make trips to Baggi and Khadrala which are on the Hindustan-Tibet road leading to the Tibetan border. Or you can visit the apple growing area around Kotgarh or continue to the Kulu Valley via Luhri.

Places to Stay Narkanda has an old *Rest House* and a *Tourist Bungalow* with doubles at Rs 40 and a dormitory at Rs 10 per bed. Or there's the *PWD Rest House*. Reservations are made through the tourist office in Simla.

Tattapani

There's a direct bus to these popular sulphur hot springs, 51 km from Simla and at only 655 metres. Accommodation is available here in the PWD Rest House.

Chabba

Five km from Basantpur, which is on the road to Tattapani, it's a pleasant walk to this Rest House, 35 km from Simla.

Thanedhar

A centre for apple growing, 82 km from Simla on the route past Narkanda.

Baggi & Khadrala

Also past Narkanda there are Rest Houses in both these places. Baggi is 82 km from Simla and at 2648 metres, Khadrala is 11 km further on and at 2987 metres.

Rohru

Situated 129 km from Simla this is the site for the Rohru Fair which takes place for two days each April. The temple of Devta Shikri is the centre for this colourful fair. The Pabar River, which runs through Rohru, is noted for its trout; there's a trout hatchery 13 km upstream at Chirgaon. Haktoti, a little before Rohru, has an interesting ancient Hindu temple dedicated to the goddess Durga. The temple contains a metre high image of the eight-armed goddess made of copper and bronze.

Places to Stay There's a *Rest House* in Rohru, a small *Forest Rest House* (booked in Rohru) at Chirgaon and log cabins at Seema, eight km upstream towards Chirgaon.

OTHER PLACES IN THE SOUTH

There are a number of other places of interest in the south of the state, where Himachal Pradesh borders with Uttar Pradesh and Haryana. This district is known as Sirmur.

Paonta Sahib

Situated on the Yamuna River, on the border with Uttar Pradesh, Paonta Sahib is a transit point for travellers from the hill stations of northern Uttar Pradesh to Simla and other hill stations in Himachal Pradesh. It is linked with Gobind Singh, 10th of the Sikh's gurus who lived here and at Bhangani, 23 km away, achieved a great military victory when his forces defeated the combined might of 22 hill country kingdoms. His weapons are displayed in the town and his gurdwara still overlooks the river.

Places to Stay There's an *HPTDC Tourist Bungalow*, *Rest Houses* and local hotels.

Renuka

North-west of Paonta Sahib there is a major festival held each November at this lake. The lake also has a small zoo and a wildlife sanctuary with deer and many water birds. There is a tourist inn at the lake.

Nahan

Situated at 932 metres, Nahan is in the Shivalik hills, where the climb to the Himalayan heights commences. There are a number of interesting walks around the town including the trek to Choordhar (3647 metres) from where there are fine views of the plains to the south and the Sutlej river. Saketi, 14 km south of Nahan, has a fossil park with life size fibreglass models of prehistoric animals, whose fossilised skeletons where unearthed here.

Places to Stay There are a number of *Rest Houses* and local hotels.

IN THE SOUTH-WEST

Bhakra-Nangal

The giant Bhakra Dam, one of the largest in the world, provides irrigation water for a vast area of the Punjab and also produces hydro-electric power. The public relations office at the dam arranges permits to inspect this major project.

Bilaspur & Naina Devi

On the shore of the Gobindsagar Lake the interesting Vyas Gufa, Lakshmi Narayan and Radhashyam temples are at this town on the Chandigarh-Mandi route. There are fine views over the lake from Naina Devi.

MANDI

The town of Mandi, on the Beas River, is the gateway to the Kulu Valley. From here you climb up the narrow, spectacular gorge of the river and emerge from this grey and barren stretch into the green and inviting Kulu Valley. At an altitude of only 760 metres it is still quite hot, mainly serves as a travel crossroads as its name, which means 'market', might suggest. Mandi is 202 km north of Chandigarh and 110 km south of Manali. The road from Pathankot and Dharamsala (150 km away) also meet here whether you are going south to Chandigarh or north to the Kulu Valley. The town is famous for its beautiful stone carved temples — Bhutnath, Triloknath, Panchavaktra, Ardhanari and Shyamakli. The Rewabar Lake, a pilgrimage centre for Hindus, Buddhists and Sikhs, is 24 km away.

Places to Stay

Mandi has a *Tourist Lodge* with dorm beds at Rs 5 and a variety of rooms in the lodge and the lodge annexe from Rs 20 to Rs 50. There are also a number of cheap hotels in the town. The *Cafe Shiraz* is run by the state tourist office.

KANGRA VALLEY

The beautiful Kangra valley starts near Mandi, runs north then bends east and extends to Shahpur near Pathankot. To the north the valley is flanked by the Dhauladhar mountain range to whose side Dharamsala clings. There are a number of places of interest along the valley, including the popular hill station

Dharamsala. The main Pathankot-Mandi road runs through the Kangra Valley and there is a narrow gauge railway line from Pathankot as far as Jogindarnagar. The Kangra school of painting developed in this valley.

Baijnath

Only 16 km from Palampur the small town of Baijnath is an important pilgrimage place due to its very old Shiva temple. The temple is said to date originally from 804 AD. There is a PWD Rest House in Baijnath.

Palampur

A pleasant little town surrounded by tea plantations, Palampur is 35 km from Dharamsala and stands at 1260 metres. The main road runs right through Palampur and there are some pleasant walks around the town.

Places to Stay There is an HPTDC *Tourist Bungalow* here. Situated about a km from the bus station it has rooms from Rs 40 to Rs 60.

Kangra

There is little to see in this ancient town, 18 km almost directly south of Dharamsala, but at one time it was a place of considerable importance. The famous temple of Bajreshwari Devi was of such legendary wealth that every invader worth his salt took time to sack it. Mahmud of Ghazni carted off a fabulous fortune in gold, silver and jewels in 1009; in 1360 it was plundered once again by Tughlaq but it was still able to recover and, in Jehangir's reign, was paved in plates of pure silver. The disastrous earthquake which shook the valley in 1905 destroyed the temple which has since been rebuilt. Kangra also has a much ruined fort on a ridge overlooking the Baner and Manjhi rivers. It too was sacked by Mahmud and severely damaged in the 1905 quake. Kangra has a PWD Rest House.

Jawalamukhi

In the Beas valley, 34 km south of Kangra, the temple of Jawalamukhi is famous for its eternally burning flame. It's the most popular pilgrimage site in Himachal Pradesh. Jawalamukhi has a PWD Rest House and there is another pleasant rest house at Nadaun, south of Jawalamukhi on the Beas river.

Chintpurni

Near Bharwain, 80 km south of Dharamsala and across the Beas, this town also has an important temple.

Masrur

Situated three km from Haripur, about 15 km south of Kangra, there are 15 rock-cut temples here. In the Indo-Aryan style and richly carved they are now partly ruined but still show their relationship to the better known, and much larger, temples at Ellora in Maharashtra.

Nurpur

Only 24 km from Pathankot on the main Mandi-Pathankot road, the town acquired its name in 1622 when Jehangir named it after his wife, Nurjahan. Nurpur fort is now in ruins but still has some finely carved reliefs. A ruined Krishna temple, also finely carved, stands within the fort. Nurpur has a PWD Rest House.

TREKS FROM KANGRA VALLEY

From Baijnath you can make an interesting trek to Dharamsala, Chamba or Manali. The first day's trek to Bir Khas can be done by bus. At Bara Bhangal, reached on Day 6, you can choose to go east to Manali or west to Dharamsala or Chamba.

Day 1	Baijnath-Bir Khas	1600 m	26 km
Day 2	Bir Khas-Rajgaunda	2500 m	13 km
Day 3	Rajgaunda-Palachak Deota	2750 m	8 km
Day 4	Palachak Deota-Panardu Got	3700 m	8 km
Day 5	Panardu Got-Thamsar Jot	4750 m	6 km
Day 6	Thamsar Jot-Bara Bhangal	2541 m	14 km

From here you can turn west and in four days reach Chanota which is on the Chamba-Dharamsala trek — see 'Treks from Chamba' for details. The days' walks are:

Day 7	Bara Bhangal-Dhardi	21 km
Day 8	Dhardi-Naya Graun	24 km
Day 9	Naya Graun-Holi	16 km
Day 10	Holi-Chanota	13 km

Alternatively you can turn east and a day's trek will bring you to the Manali Pass treks described under 'Treks from Manali'. There are a number of possible routes down to Manali.

DHARAMSALA (population 12,000)

The hill station of Dharamsala is actually split into several totally separate parts. Close to the snowline the town is built along a spur of the Dhauladhar range and varies in height from 1250 metres at the Civil and Depot Bazaar up through Kotwali Bazaar and Forsyth Ganj to McLeod Ganj at close to 2000 metres. There's quite a temperature variation between the top and bottom.

As in other hill stations there are a wide variety of short and long walks around the station but Dharamsala also has the additional attraction of its strong Tibetan influence. It was here that the Dalai Lama and his followers fled after the Chinese invasion of Tibet. For the serious student of Tibetan culture there's the monastery up at McLeod Ganj and the school of Tibetan studies and its library, one of the best in the world for studying Tibet and its culture, about midway between McLeod Ganj and the lower town.

For the not so serious, McLeod Ganj

Dharamsala

colour and energy; those little Tibetan terriers (yappy but spry) scoot around everywhere; right in the middle of the main street there's a small temple with a giant prayer wheel, and you may even catch a glimpse of the Dalai Lama cruising by in his Mercedes.

Of course Dharamsala was originally a British hill resort and one of the most poignant memorials of that era is the pretty little Church of St John in the Wilderness, only a short distance below McLeod Ganj. It has beautiful stained glass windows and here Lord Elgin, Viceroy of India, was buried after his death in 1863. There are many fine walks and even finer views around Dharamsala. The sheer rock wall of Dhauladhar rises up right behind Mc Leod Ganj. From the road up from the lower town it seems just an arm's length away.

From McLeod Ganj popular walks include the two km stroll to Bhagsu where there is an old temple, a spring, slate quarries and a small waterfall. It's a popular picnic spot and you can continue on beyond here on the ascent to the snowline. Dal Lake is a bit brown and dull, it's about three km from McLeod Ganj, just beyond the Tibetan Children's Village School. A similar distance from McLeod Ganj takes you to the popular picnic spot at Dharamkot where you'll also enjoy a very fine view.

An eight km trek from McLeod Ganj will bring you to Triund at 2827 metres. Situated at the foot of Dhauladhar it's another five km to the snowline at Ilaqa. There is a Forest Rest House for overnight accommodation.

Information & Orientation
The Tourist Office is in the lower town close to the bus stand and the Dauladhar Hotel. It's about 10 km up from the lower part to McLeod Ganj — a 45 minute, Rs 1 plus ride. Walking down, take the steep short cut round to the left of the monastery, by the Dalai Lama's home and down to the cantonment

is a real little freak centre with lots of Tibetan run hotels and restaurants, all the menu favourites, low prices, crowds of western travellers — another Kathmandu in fact. McLeod Ganj is full of by the library. It takes 30 to 40 minutes to walk. Lots of Tibetan handicrafts up in McLeod Ganj, small square Tibetan carpets for Rs 90, bigger five foot by three foot carpets for Rs 750.

Places to Stay — Dharamsala

Dharamsala has two accommodation areas — the lower part of town and the upper part known as McLeod Ganj. In the lower part Dharamsala's de-luxe hotel is the *Dhauladhar* with a Rs 10 dorm or doubles at Rs 40 and Rs 70. There's a restaurant and a pleasant garden patio — ideal for sipping a sunset beer while you look out over the plains below.

As in McLeod Ganj the pick of the cheapies are all Tibetan. There's the very popular and extremely laid back *Rising Moon Hotel & Restaurant*. A long menu, good food, good music and quite amazingly slow service. The hotel side has dorm beds at Rs 5, doubles at Rs 12. Almost directly behind it there's the slightly cheaper *Tibetan Rest House*.

Just left from the fountain you'll find the *Dekyi Palber Hotel & Restaurant* and the *Rose Hotel* — the restaurant for the latter is close to the junction while the hotel is a little further up, then

down off the street to the right. Finally there's the *Simla* opposite the tourist office and the not-so-special *B Mehra* and *Sun & Snow*.

Places to Stay — McLeod Ganj

Most western visitors to Dharamsala stay not in the main part of town but 500 metres (and 10 km by road) higher up the hill at McLeod Ganj. Here the Tibetan community who followed the Dalai Lama into exile have set up a whole series of hotels and restaurants. The accent is very much on cheapness but the hotels are clean and the restaurants surprisingly good. For those heartily sick of dahl and rice they offer a whole range of Tibetan-Chinese dishes plus those western-travellers' menu-favourites such as banana pancakes.

McLeod Ganj is very popular and, due to its popularity, many places are permanently full, but a quick wander will soon turn something up. The Bhagsu Rd from the bus station is the best bet — doubles at Rs 20 (own bathroom) and Rs 15 at the *Tibetan Hotel*. Similar style accommodation at the *Rainbow Hotel* right by the bus stand. Further up the road the *Koko Nor Hotel* and the *Green Guest House* are cheaper

— doubles down to Rs 10-12. Also very popular is the *Om Hotel*, just below the main street, also down towards Rs 10.

For those determined to spend more the Tourist Department has the *Hotel Bhagsu*, a couple of hundred metres out of town, with doubles for Rs 40 or Rs 60. Long stay visitors can find accommodation in locals' houses further out of town for just a few rupees a day.

Foodwise there are lots of little places around McLeod Ganj. The *Om Restaurant* is one of the most popular — a long menu and laid back atmosphere, good music, free plain tea and it's noted for its cakes. The *Tibetan Himalaya Restaurant*, about mid-way between the Hotel Tibet and the Green Guest House, has good pancakes amongst other things.

There are a number of cheaper and rather more basic places such as the *Gakyi Restaurant*. *Friend's Corner* is good for a drink either downstairs or up on the roof.

Getting There

If you're taking an early morning bus it's probably an idea to spend the night down in the lower town — all the buses start from there. Approximate distances, times and fares from Dharamsala to:

	distance	time	fare
to Manali	253	12½ hrs	Rs 24
Kulu	214	10	20
Simla	317	13½	29
Chandigarh	248	9	17
Pathankot	90	3½	8
Delhi	526	14	33

DALHOUSIE

Sprawling over and around five hills Dalhousie was, in the British era, a sort of 'second string' hill station. A place where those who could not aspire to Simla retired to. Founded by Lord Dalhousie there are some pleasant walks around the town. Today Dalhousie also has a busy population of Tibetan refugees — if you take the footpath from Subhash Chowk to Gandhi (GPO) Chowk you'll pass brightly painted pictures which the Tibetans have carved into low relief on the rocks. There is a nice little Tibetan refugee handicrafts shop with carpets in some quite different designs (unusual animals like rabbits and elephants). It's by GPO Chowk.

About two km from GPO Chowk along Ajit Singh Rd, Panchpulla (five bridges) could be quite a nice little spot but it's considerably uglified by the series of horrible concrete steps and seats built over the stream. Along the way there's a very small, and easily missed, fresh water spring known as

Satdhara. Kalatop is 8.5 km from the GPO and offers a fine view over the surrounding country. There's a forest rest house here.

Information & Orientation

The tourist office (tel 36) is by the bus stand but Dalhousie is very scattered. Most shops are clustered around GPO Chowk while the 'town', if Dalhousie can be spoken of as such a thing, is crowded down the hillside close to Subhash Chowk. The houses almost stand on top of one another.

Places to Stay

Dalhousie has plenty of hotels although a fair number of them have a run down, left-by-the-Raj aspect to them. Close to the bus stand the *Mount View Hotel* is an old fashioned place with big doubles at Rs 35 but even a pillow costs extra! And the food in the restaurant is lousy. A little up the hill there's the *Tourist Bungalow*, doubles at Rs 30 but they're often full. A little below the bus stand there's the *Youth Hostel* while up above

Dalhousie

the Mount View there's the *Grand View Hotel* with rooms all the way from Rs 40 to Rs 100 although most are in the Rs 50 and 60 bracket. The *Dalhousie Club* has singles at Rs 19, doubles at Rs 25. All these places, but particularly the Youth Hostel, have fine views out over the mountains in the distance. There is also the *Glory* and *Lall's*, two real cheapies, close to the bus stand.

Other hotels are mainly around Subhash Chowk, up the road from the bus stand, or between the bus stand and GPO Chowk. *Mehar's* has singles at Rs 15-20, doubles at Rs 30-50. The *New Metro* at Subhash Chowk is on top of the restaurant. *Aroma-n-Claire*, beyond Subhash Chowk, has doubles at Rs 70 — it's probably the best hotel in Dalhousie but the food in the restaurant is poor. The *Metro Restaurant* is not bad.

Getting There

Panthankot, 80 km away, is the usual departure point for buses to Dalhousie. The trip takes about four hours and costs Rs 7 to Rs 9 depending on the bus company. Jammu-Pathankot buses cost Rs 5 and take three hours. From Pathankot on to Dharamsala costs Rs 8, there are some straight-through buses from Dalhousie to Dharamsala but although the 'short route' is much more direct on the map it is a bad road and the trip very time consuming. The 8.30 am bus arrives around 5 pm! Only 30 km is unsurfaced.

KHAJJIAR

This grassy 'marg' is 22 km from Dalhousie. Over a km long and nearly a km wide it is ringed by pine trees and with a lake in the middle. There's also a golf course here and a golden domed temple.

Places to Stay

There's a *Tourist Bungalow* with doubles at Rs 30 and Rs 40 or dorm beds at Rs 8, a *Youth Hostel* at Rs 5 and a *PWD*

Rest House.

Getting There

You can walk there in a day or there are buses run by the tourist office (Rs 15 de-luxe, Rs 10 ordinary, return) and regular buses at Rs 3 one way.

CHAMBA

Situated 56 km from Dalhousie, on beyond Khajjiar, Chamba is at 926 metres — quite a bit lower than Dalhousie so it's rather warmer in the summer. Perched on a ledge, high above the river Ravi, it has often been compared to a medieval Italian village and is famed for its many temples. Three of these carved and engraved temples are dedicated to Shiva and three to Vishnu. Chamba also has the Bhuri Singh Museum with an interesting collection relating to the art and culture of this region — particularly the miniature paintings of the Basoli and Kangra schools. The Rang Mahal palace in the upper part of town has been badly fire damaged. Some of its murals are now in the museum.

Chamba has a grassy promenade known as the 'chaugan' — it's only 75 metres wide and less than a km long. The village is a busy local trading centre for villagers from the surrounding hills and each year is the site for the Minjar festival in August with a colourful procession and busy crowds of Gaddi Churachi, Bhatti and Gujjar people. An image of Lord Raghuvira leads the procession and other gods and goddess follow in palanquins.

Chamba is the centre of the Gaddis, traditional shepherds who move their flocks up to the high alpine pastures during the summer and descend to Kangra, Mandi and Bilaspur in the winter. The Gaddis are found only on the high range which divides Chamba from Kangra.

Places to Stay

The *Akhand Chanoi* is the better hotel — singles/doubles at Rs 30/40 and there's also a restaurant. The *Tourist Lodge* (tel 94) has rooms at Rs 15 with bathroom attached, Rs 10 without or Rs 4 in the dorm. The *Janta Hotel* is similarly priced. Meals are available in the *Ravi View Cafe.*

Getting There

Taxis and jeeps can be hired in Dalhousie but they're very expensive. The local bus is Rs 6 or you can walk there in two days, resting overnight in Khajjiar. From Chamba trekkers can make an interesting, but hard going, trek through Bharmour and Triund to Dharamsala. Or via Tisa you can trek all the way into Lahaul or into Kashmir.

TREKS FROM CHAMBA

There are a number of interesting treks from Chamba, both short out-and-back treks and longer treks to places like Dharamsala. Shorter treks include the eight km walk to Sarol, 24 km to Bandal or the 40 km trek to Chhatrari. The temple of Devi Adi Shakti here is dedicated to the goddess of primaeval energy. Chhatrari is on the route to Brahmaur.

Brahmaur (Brahmpura)

Vehicles can cover the whole 65 km from Chamba to Brahmaur although the last 16 km from Kharamukh is either 4-WD or foot. Buses run the first distance. Also known as Shivbhumi this is the heart of the Gaddi's land. There are some very old temples grouped in a compound known as the chaurasi in Brahmaur and accommodation is available in a Forest Rest House.

From Brahmaur it is about 80 km to Dharamsala and takes about six days to walk:

Day 1	Brahmaur-Chanota	22 km
Day 2	Chanota-Kuarsi	13 km
Day 3	Kuarsi-Chatta	13 km
Day 4	Chatta-Lakagot	10 km
Day 5	Lakagot-Triund	6 km
Day 6	Triund-Dharamsala	13 km

The Chatta to Lakagot sector crosses the 4300 metre Indrahas Pass with fine views over the Kangra Valley.

From Brahmaur you can make the 35 km trek to Manimahesh Lake at 3950 metres. This important pilgrimage spot is at the base of the 5575 metre Manimahesh Kailash. Thousands flock here on the 15th day after Janamashtami which falls in August or September each year.

Pangi Valley

Kilar, 167 km north-east of Chamba, is situated in the deep and narrow gorge of the Chenab river. Here you are in the high Himalayas, in the scenic but lightly populated Pangi Valley, between the Pangi and Zanskar Ranges. From Kilar you can trek north-west to Kishtwar in Jammu and Kashmir, or turn east about half way to Kishtwar and cross the Umasi La Pass into the Zanskar Valley, or trek south-east to Keylong and Manali.

THE KULU VALLEY

The fertile Kulu Valley tilts northward from Mandi, at 760 metres, to the Rohtang Pass, at 3915 metres, the gateway to Lahaul and Spiti. In the south the valley is little wider than a precipitous gorge, with the Beas River (pronounced Bee-Ahs) sometimes a sheer 300 metre below the narrow road. Further up the valley widens and the main part of it is 80 km long though rarely more than a couple of km wide. Here there are stone fruit and apple orchards, rice paddies and wheat fields along the valley floor and lower slopes and deodar forests higher up the slopes with snow crowned rocky peaks towering behind. The main towns, Kulu and Manali, are in this fertile section of the valley.

The light complexioned people are friendly, devout, hard working and relatively prosperous. The men wear the distinctive Kulu cap, a pillbox with a flap around the back in which they may stick flowers while the women wear long garments of homespun wool secured with great silver pins, lots of silver jewellery and they are rarely without a large conical shaped basket on their backs, filled with fodder, firewood or even a goat kid.

Other people of the valley are the nomads (Gaddis) who take their flocks of black sheep and white goats up to the mountain pastures in the early summer and retreat before the winter snows. You don't really know what wool smells like until you've travelled in an over-crowded bus of rain-soaked villagers. The valley also has many Tibetan refugees, some running restaurants and hotels in Manali but many others in camps near the rivers, prayer flags fluttering. The Tibetans are great traders, you'll find them in all the bazaars but many work in road gangs, whole families toiling together.

KULU (population 10,000)

At an altitude of 1200 metres Kulu is the district headquarters but it is not the main tourist centre, that honour goes to Manali. Nevertheless there are a number of interesting things to see around Kulu and some fine walks to be made. The town, which sprawls on the western bank of the Beas, is dominated by the grassy maidans at the southern side of town. They're the site for Kulu's fairs and festivals, in particular the colourful Dussehra festival from which the Kulu Valley has gained the name 'valley of the gods'.

Dussehra Festival

The Dussehra Festival, in October after the monsoons, is celebrated all over India but most particularly in Kulu. The festival starts on the 10th day of the rising moon, known as 'Vijay Dashmi' and continues for seven days. Dussehra celebrates Rama's victory over the demon king Ravana but in Kulu the festival does not include the burning of Ravana and his brothers, as in other places around India.

Kulu's festival is a great gathering of the gods from temples all around the valley. Approximately 200 gods are brought from their temples down to Kulu to pay homage to Raghunathji from the temple in Raghunathpura in Kulu. The festival cannot commence until the powerful goddess Hadimba, patron deity of the Kulu rajas, arrives from Manali. Like the other gods she is pulled in her own temple car or 'rath' and Hadimba likes speed and has to be pulled as fast as possible. She not only arrives before all the other gods but also leaves before them. Another curiousity is that the Jamlu god from Manali comes to the festival but does not take part — this god stays on the opposite side of the river from the Dhalpur maidan.

The Raghunathji chariot is brought down, decked with garlands and surrounded by the other important gods. Priests and the descendants of Kulu's rajas circle the 'rath' before the car is pulled to the other side of the maidan. There is great competition to aid in pulling the car since this is a very auspicious thing to do. The procession with the cars and bands takes place on the evening of the first day of the festival. During the following days and nights of the festival there are dances, music, a market and festivities far into the night. On the penultimate day the gods assemble for the 'Devta darbar' with Raghunathji and on the final day the temple car is taken to the riverbank where a small heap of grass is burnt to symbolise Ravana's destruction. Raghunathji is carried back to his main temple in a wooden palanquin.

Temples

Some of the main temples in and around Kulu include:

Raghunathji Temple About a km from Dhalpur in Raghunathpura (or Sultanpur) the temple of the principal god is actually not very interesting. It is only open from 5 pm.

Jagannathi Devi Temple In the village of Bhekhli, three km from Kulu, it's a stiff climb but from the temple there are fine views over the town. Take the path off the main road to Akhara bazaar after crossing the Sarwari bridge.

Vaishno Devi Temple This small cave has an image of the goddess Vaishno and is four km along the Kulu-Manali road.

Bijli Mahadev Temple A jeepable road links Kulu with Bijli Mahadev, eight km away. Situated across the river, high on a projecting bluff, the temple is surmounted by a 20 metre high rod which is said to attract blessings in the form of lightning. At least once a year the image of Shiva in the temple is supposed to be shattered by lightning, then miraculously repaired by the temple pujari.

Bajaura On the main road 15 km south of Kulu, the famous temple of Basheshar Mahadev has fine stone carvings and sculptures. There are large image slabs facing north, west and south. There is a PWD Rest House in Bajaura.

Information & Orientation

The Tourist Information Office (tel 7) is by the maidan at the southern side of town. There's a bus halt area here and all the HPTDC accommodation units and several of the hotels are around the maidan but the main bus station is in the northern area of the town.

Places to Stay

The ITDC *Traveller's Lodge* (tel 79) is to the left of the road just as you enter town from the south. It has six rooms with singles at Rs 100, doubles at Rs 175. Only a little south of the maidan, but a short walk off the main road, is the HPTDC *Tourist Bungalow* (tel 33) — a well run place with doubles at Rs 35 and dorm beds at Rs 10. The Tourist Office is right beside the maidan, opposite the bus halt. Beside it is the generally full *Rest House* and between the two are the *'Aluminium Huts'* — comfortable enough double rooms at Rs 25, but you can do better elsewhere.

Right behind the Tourist Office is the excellent *Bijleshwar Hotel.* It's a new place, very friendly and well run and has doubles with own bathroom for Rs 30. Across the other side of the maidan, towards the river, are the *Sa Ba Guest House* with rooms at Rs 25 and Rs 35 and the *Fancy Guest House* with rooms from Rs 15 to Rs 40 — OK. At the other side of town, by the main bus stand, is the newish *Kulu Lodge* with doubles at Rs 25 or Rs 35 with bath. There are other places around here like the *Kailash Lodge.*

Places to Eat

The *Tourist Bungalow* has the usual sort of dining hall. By the Tourist Office there's the *Tourist Department Cafe* with good snacks and light meals but painfully slow service. Fine if you have plenty of time. In the main street close to the bus halt there's the *Monika Restaurant* and just downhill from the main street is the *Prem Dhaba.*

Getting There

There are direct buses to Kulu from Dharamsala, Simla (235 km), Chandigarh (270 km) or Delhi (512 km). Note that Kulu-Chandigarh buses do not go via Simla. All these direct buses will be continuing to Manali, 42 km further north. A direct bus from Delhi is supposed to take 15 hours but probably takes a good bit more. It costs about Rs 60. Chandigarh-Kulu takes about 12 hours and costs Rs 25. There is an airport at Bhuntar, 10 km south of Kulu, but at present there are no flights operating there. Plenty of taxis make the trip up from the plains but count on around Rs 750 for Simla or Chandigarh to Kulu or Manali. A Kulu-Manali taxi would cost about Rs 120, it's Rs 4 by bus.

KULU TO MANALI

There are a number of interesting things to see along the 42 km between Kulu and Manali. There are actually two Kulu-Manali roads, the direct road runs along the west bank of the Beas while the much rougher and more winding east bank road is not so regularly used, but does take you via Naggar with its delightful rest house.

Raison

Only eight km from Kulu there's a camping place on the grassy meadow beside the river. It's a good base for treks in the vicinity. There are huts at the site which cost Rs 10 and can be booked through the Kulu Tourist Office.

Katrain

At about the mid-point on the Kulu-Manali road this is the widest point in the Kulu Valley and is overlooked by the 3325 metre Baragarh peak. Two km up the road on the left side there is a trout hatchery.

Places to Stay There's a small rest house and a pleasant HPTDC *Tourist Bungalow* with doubles at Rs 30. It's an interesting alternative to staying in Kulu or Manali.

Naggar

High above Katrain, on the east bank of the river, is Naggar with its superb castle rest house. Transport to the castle is a little problematical but the effort is worthwhile for it is a superb place to look around or stay at. At one time Naggar was the capital of the Kulu Valley and the castle was the Raja's headquarters. Around 1660 Sultanpur, now known as Kulu, became the new capital. The quaint old fort is built around a courtyard with verandahs right round the outside and absolutely stupendous views out over the valley. It feels an eon away from any of the hassles India can dish up! Inside the courtyard is a small temple containing a slab of stone with an interesting legend about how it was carried there by wild bees.

There are a number of interesting temples around the castle. The grey sandstone Shiva temple of Gauri Shankar is at the foot of the small bazaar below the castle and dates from the 11th or 12th century. Almost opposite the front of the castle is the curious little Chatar Bhuj temple to Vishnu. Higher up the hill is the pagoda like Tripura Sundri Devi Temple and higher still, on the ridge above Naggar, the Murlidhar Krishna temple. Also up the hill above the castle is Roerich Gallery, a fine old house displaying the art works of Professor Nicholas Roerich, who died in 1947, and his son. Its location is delightful and the views over the valley are very fine.

Places to Stay The *Castle Rest House* has just five double rooms which cost Rs 40. It's deservedly popular and often booked out, the Kulu Tourist Office can

Kulu Valley

make reservations but plan ahead.

Kulu-Manali Transport

Buses run regularly along the main road for Rs 4, the trip takes under two hours. There are only one or two buses daily on the east side of the river and the trip takes a long time, two hours from Manali to Naggar alone. There is a daily tour bus from Manali which costs Rs 15. Cars can get to Naggar by crossing the river at Patlikuhl near Katrain — the bridge is very narrow. Or you can get off the Kulu-Manali bus there and walk up. It's six km up to the castle by road but much less on foot although the path is very steep.

MANALI (population 2500)

Manali, at the top end of the Kulu Valley, is the main resort in the valley. It's beautifully situated, there are many pleasant walks around the town and a large number of hotels and restaurants. It's also very much a 'scene' — at the height of the tourist season it's packed out with Indian and western tourists. Smaller villages around Manali have semi-permanent 'hippy' populations. Manali is famous for its dope which grows wild all around but there have been a number of police busts on the more popular freak hotels so smokers should beware.

Information & Orientation

Manali has one main street where you'll find the bus stop and most of the restaurants. The Tourist Office (tel 25) is further down the street towards the river and opposite the taxi stand. Hotels are scattered all over town, some of them within easy walking distance of the bus stop, some of them, like the Tourist Bungalow, a good long stretch uphill.

Hadimba Devi Temple

The temple of the goddess Hadimba,

Log Huts

Cafe Rohtang

Old Manali Village

Keylong & Leh

Baths

Vashist Village

Hotel Highland

Forest Reserve

John Banon G.H.

Tourist Bungalow

Hadrimba Temple

Moonlight Rest.

Youth Hostel

Hotel Hiltop

P.O.

Taxis

Chandratol Rest.
Tourist Lodge

Tourist Cottage

Adarsh Rest.

Beas Hotel

Grand View Hotel

Mayur Rest.

Tourist Office

Skylark G.H.

Mona Lisa Rest.

Ambika G.H.

Mt. View Rest.

Temple

Mt View G.H.

Bus Stop

Central View G.H.

Aroma Hotel

Kathmandu G.H.

Tibetan Monastery

Manali

ITDC Travellers' Lodge

Mountaineering Institute

Kulu

Nagar

Beas River

who plays such a major part in Kulu's annual festival, is a sombre, wooden temple in a clearing in the dense forest about 2.5 km from the Tourist Office. It's a pleasant stroll up to the temple which was built in 1553. Also known as the Dhungri Temple there is a major festival here in May of each year.

Vashisht Baths

Vashisht village is an extremely picturesque little place, clinging to the steep hillside about six km out of Manali. On foot it's only about 4.5 km since you can follow paths up the hillside while cars have to wind up the road. Worth a wander round to admire the solid architecture, thatched roofs and colourful people. On the way up to the village you'll come upon the Vashisht Hot Baths where a natural sulphur spring is piped into a recently constructed bathhouse. They're open from 7 am to 1 pm and 2 to 7 pm and cost, for 20 minutes soak, Rs 3 (plus Rs 1 per person) in the small baths, Rs 5 (plus Rs 2 per person) in the large de-luxe ones. If you've suffered a long, rough bus trip up to Manali there's no better way to soak away the strain.

Old Manali Village

The current town of Manali is actually a new creation which has superseded the old village, a couple of km away. Follow the trail off the road out of town and you cross the cascading Manaslu stream over a very picturesque bridge and can then climb up to this interesting little village.

Around the Town

Manali is basically a place to get out and walk but there are a few places of interest in the town itself such as the colourful new Tibetan Monastery. It's a pleasant place and also has a carpet making operation; you can buy them and other Tibetan handicrafts here. The Tourist Office will arrange a fishing licence if you want to try your luck with the Beas River trout — you'll need your own gear though.

Tours

There are daily bus tours to the Rohtang Pass (Rs 35) and Naggar Castle (Rs 15).

Places to Stay

Prices in Manali are very variable. In May-June they go sky high, in July-August they drop down a bit and again in September-October. In December-January-February, when there are no tourists at all, the prices are very low. At that time people come down from the hills and can get rooms for Rs 100 to 150 a month which, at the height of the season, can cost that much for a few days! Those same rooms would be up to Rs 15 a day in March-April, then Rs 40 at peak times, even Rs 60 at peak-peaks. When the costs go up Manali's resident freak population tends to head out to the villages around Manali. Even at the height of the season it's possible to rent a house for Rs 100 to 150 a month but conditions are likely to be a little primitive. There may be a stove but you'll need your own cooking utensils and you may have a long walk to get water.

Back in the town there are a number of places run by the HPTDC. They can all be reserved through the tourism development officer, tel 25. The *Tourist Bungalow* is up the hill a little from the town, it's totally covered in ivy and quite a picture. Doubles cost from Rs 40. There are also *Tourist Cottages* and *Log Huts* — these are self-contained, with their own kitchens and living rooms and modern facilities. Nightly costs range from Rs 60 to Rs 200 and more for the flashier Log Huts. The *Janata Lodge* is much simpler, with doubles from Rs 30. There's also the *Beas Hotel*, right beside the Beas River, which costs Rs 5 for dorm beds. All this HPTDC accommodation tends to be fairly heavily booked so plan ahead. The ITDC have an *Ashok Travellers' Lodge* in Manali, a little out of town on the Naggar road. Singles/doubles cost Rs 100/175 including breakfast and dinner. Doubles are really suites with a sitting room and fine views of the snow capped peaks around Manali.

In the private hotel sector your best bet is simply to wander around and have a look at a few, bearing in mind that prices are likely to be quite variable depending on when you're there and how many rooms they happen to have vacant. Some names to start with include the *Skylark Guest House* (doubles Rs 40 to 60), *Kathmandu Guest House* (close to the gompa, Rs 30 to 50), *Mount View Guest House* (similarly priced, pleasant place), *John Banon Guest House* (tel 35, a bit more expensive) and so on. The Tourist Office can supply a more or less complete list of Manali's 40 or so hotels and guest houses, together with their official prices.

Places to Eat

Right beside the bus station is the *Monalisa Restaurant*, a popular little place with excellent food, great music, a varied menu and attentive (uniformed no less) service. It's probably a little expensive for some pockets but if you'd like to eat well in Manali it's highly recommended. There are quite a few other places around Manali — like the *Mount View Restaurant* just down from the bus stop, for good Chinese-Tibetan food. Or the *Adarsh Restaurant* and the *Mayur Restaurant*. The *Chandratal Restaurant* is run by the HPTDC with the standard tourist department menu — not so special. Between the Tourist Office and the bus stop there's a little place with delicious, and cold, bottled apple juice. Following the road out of town you'll come to the *Moonlight Restaurant* — a spartan little place

with good bread and cakes, the local freak centre. The HPTDC's *Cafe Rohtang*, up the hill overlooking the river, has fine views but is rather unfriendly.

Places to Stay around Manali

Vashisht, the picturesque little village just above the hot baths, is probably the main centre for Manali's longer term western residents. There's the *Mount Hotel* and the *Brine Ram Restaurant* by the baths further up the hill, at the start of the village, is *Demroh's Restaurant*, the freak food centre for Vashisht. Very laid back. Other little snack places can be found in the village. There are other villages around Manali with summer populations of westerners — you just have to ask around, talk to people, don't expect to find something on the first day.

Getting There

Chandigarh is the usual departure point for buses to Manali if you're coming up from Delhi. Chandigarh-Manali is 312 km, takes about 14 hours by bus (nine by car) and costs Rs 28. There are also direct buses from Simla (247 km) for Rs 24 and from Dharamsala (253 km) also for Rs 24. It's a long trip to Manali from wherever you start! From Kulu there are frequent buses for Rs 4. Note the introductory details on HPTDC buses in Himachal Pradesh.

AROUND MANALI

Jagatsukh

About 12 km north of Naggar and six km south of Manali on the east bank road, Jagatsukh was another former capital of Kulu State until it was supplanted by Naggar. There are some very old temples in the village, particularly the Shiva temple in shikhara style. Shooru village, nearby, has the old and historically interesting Devi Sharvali temple.

Around Manali

Arjun Gufa, with a legendary cave, is near the village of Prini, five km from Manali. A cold water spring named the Nehru Kund, after Prime Minister Nehru, is six km from Manali on the Keylong road. The Solang Valley is a little north-west of Manali, but before Kothi. The nearest glacier to Manali is here, only 13 km from Manali. You can get there by bus to Palchan village then following the jeep track. Kothi is a pretty little village, 12 km from Manali on the Keylong road. Its rest house is a popular resting place for trekkers heading for the Rohtang Pass. There are very fine views from Kothi and the Beas River flows through a very deep and narrow gorge at this point. The Rahla Falls, 16 km away, are another popular excursion.

The Rohtang Pass to Lahaul is 51 km from Manali and is a favourite day excursion or trekking trip quite apart from its role as the gateway into Lahaul. The view of mountains from the pass crest is very spectacular. In early summer and late autumn the pass can be subject to strong winds and snow blizzards in the afternoon — so try to cross it early.

TREKS FROM MANALI

There are many treks from Manali either round trips or further afield.

Malana Valley

It is less than 30 km from Katrain, on the Kulu-Manali road, across the Chandrakhani Pass to the interesting Malana Valley. The pass is at less than 3600 metres and is open from March to December. Malana can also be reached from the Parbati Valley — either from Manikaran over the 3150 metre Rashoi Pass or from Jari. Jari is connected with the Kulu Valley by a jeepable road and it is only 12 km from Jari to Malana.

There are only about 500 people in Malana and they speak a peculiar dialect with strong Tibetan elements. The 6001 metre peak of Deo Tibba overlooks Malana and from the top of the Chandrakhani Pass you can see snow capped peaks on the border of Spiti to the east. Starting from Naggar it is possible to climb up to the pass summit and return to Naggar on the same day — but it is fairly hard going.

Local legends relate that when Jamlu, the main deity of Malana, first came to Malana he bore a casket containing all the other Kulu gods. At the top of the pass he opened the casket and the breeze carried the gods to their present homes, all over the valley. At the time of the Dussehra festival in Kulu, Jamlu plays a special part. He is a very powerful god with something of the demon in him. He does not have a temple image so, unlike the other Kulu gods, has no temple car to be carried in. Nor does he openly show his allegiance to Ragbhunathji, the paramount Kulu god, like the other Kulu gods. At the time of the festival Jamlu goes down to Kulu, but stays on the east side of the river from where he watches the proceedings. Every few years a major festival is held for Jamlu in the month of Bhadon. In the temple there is a silver elephant with a gold figure on its back which is said to have been a gift from the Emperor Akbar.

It takes three days to trek from Naggar to Malana, spend a day there, then return to Naggar or continue to Jari. A seven day trek Manali to Manali could be:

Day 1	Manali-Rumsu	2060 m	24 km
Day 2	Rumsu-Chandrakhani	3650 m	8 km
Day 3	Chandrakhani-Malana	2100 m	7 km
Day 4	Malana-Kasol	1580 m	8 km
Day 5	Kasol-Jari	1560 m	15 km

Day 6	Jari-Bhuntar	900 m	12 km
Day 7	Buntar-Manali	by bus	

The trek can be extended by continuing from Jari along the east bank of the Beas via Bijli Mahadev, with its famous temple, and Naggar to Manali.

Deo Tibba Trek

This is an easy trek east of Manali to the base of 6001 metre Deo Tibba. The trek offers fine views and pleasant walking through forests and alpine meadows. From Manali you start via Jagatsukh to Khanol and Chhika (not the Chhika north-east of Manali on the way to the Hamta Pass). Seri is at the base of Deo Tibba and from here you can make an excursion to Lake Chandratal.

Day 1	Manali-Khanol	8 km
Day 2	Khanol-Chhika	6 km
Day 3	Chhika-Seri	5 km
Day 4	Seri-Bhanara	14 km
Day 5	Bhanara-Manali	

Chandratal

This circular trek from Manali over the Hamta, Chandratal and Baralacha la passes is one of the finest in Himachal Pradesh and takes 11 days to complete. From Manali you start at Jagatsukh, on the east bank road to Kulu. At the village of Prini you turn north-east and climb up to Chhika — a steep climb at first but later it becomes easier over grassy downs and pleasant meadows. The next day involves a long and wearisome climb over the 4270 metre Hamta Pass, then a quick descent to Chhatru on the Chandra River. The pass is generally open from June to September although it may often be open longer. There are fine views of Deo Tibba (6001 metres) and Indrasan (6221 metres) from the pass. Two days walk takes you through Chhota Dara to Batal where the route branches off north-east to Spiti through the Kunzam Pass. There are magnificent views of the Bara Shigri glacier from here.

Succeeding days take you north over the Chandratal (lake of the moon) pass, the Likhim Gongma (upper) and Likhim Yongma (lower) and the Tokpo Yongma before reaching the Keylong-Leh road at the Baralacha la pass. Three more days walk brings you to Keylong from where you can bus back to Manali. It may be possible to get a bus earlier and shorten the time to Keylong.

Day 1	Manali-Chhika	2960 m	21 km
Day 2	Chhika-Chhatru	3360 m	16 km
Day 3	Chhatru-Chhota Dara	3740 m	16 km
Day 4	Chhota Dara-Batal	3960 m	16 km
Day 5	Batal-Chandratal	4270 m	18 km
Day 6	Chandratal-Likhim Yongma	4320 m	12 km
Day 7	Likhim Yongma-Topko Gongma	4640 m	11 km
Day 8	Topko Gongma-Baralacha la	4885 m	10 km
Day 9	Baralacha la-Patsio	3820 m	19 km
Day 10	Patsio-Jispa	3320 m	14 km
Day 11	Jispa-Keylong	3340 m	21 km

Parbati Valley

The last part of the Malana Valley trek decends the Parbati Valley to its junction with the Kulu Valley. An interesting alternative is to ascend the Parbati Valley to its upper reaches. The Parbati Valley is much wilder and more rugged than the Kulu Valley. From Bhuntar, near the junction of the Beas and Parbati you can visit the Adibrahma temple in Khokhan about a km from Nhuntar or the pagoda shaped temple of Triyugi Narain in Diar village. The first day's walk takes you to Jari, on a hillside high above the Parbati and near where the Malana joins the Parbati.

It's a short trek to Kasol with its pleasantly sited Tourist Hut and Forest Rest House. Good trout fishing here. Manikaran is a very short walk but the river is wild at this point and Manikaran is also famed for its hot springs. The spring close to the river as you enter the village is boiling hot. It's a long walk, rough and stoney at first, to Pulga where again there is a very pleasant Forest Rest House. The pretty little village is 300 metres above the river. This is the usual end point of this trek although hardy and well-equipped trekkers could continue further up the Parbati and cross the Pin Parbati Pass into Spiti. Khirganga, just 10 km upstream from Pulga, has more hot springs. Or you could explore the Tos Nullah which joins the Parbati from the northeast, just upstream from Pulga.

Day 1	Bhuntar-Jari	15 km
Day 2	Jari-Kasol	8 km
Day 3	Kasol-Manikaran	3 km
Day 4	Manikaran-Pulga	16 km

Seraj Valley to Narkanda

The Seraj Valley branches off southeast from the southern end of Kulu Valley and makes an interesting alternative route between the Kulu Valley and Simla. Aut, on the main road between Kulu and Mani, is the starting point and Larji, at the junction of the Sainj and Tirthan rivers is the first stop. There's a PWD Rest House here and good fishing is available during March, April and October — when the Sainj river runs clear. In the lower reaches of the Tirthan valley is Banjar with an interesting group of temples. Continuing south you reach Shoja where there is another PWD Rest House with a scenic setting. From here you can make excursions to the old ruined fort of Raghupur Gahr from where there is a beautiful view, even Simla can be seen on a clear day. Another interesting day trip from Shoja is to the beautiful flower strewn meadow of Dughu Thatch.

From Shoja you cross the 3135 metre Jalori pass. The view of the surrounding mountains from the pass crest is stunning. Khanag, at 2500 metres, is on the other side of the pass and again has a PWD Rest House. Ani, again with a PWD Rest House, is the next stop and

from here you can either continue straight on to the main highway from where buses run to Narkanda and Simla, or turn east to Nirmand with its temple of Devi Ambika. There is a bus service between Ani and Luhri, on the north side of the Sutlej River.

Day 1	Aut-Larji	5 km
Day 2	Larji-Banjar	20 km
Day 3	Banjar-Shoja	13 km
Day 4	Shoja-Khanag	10 km
Day 5	Khanag-Ani	20 km
Day 6	Ani-Luhri	15 km

As an alternative to this route you can branch off at Banjar and follow the Tirthan River to Narakand. Goshaini is the first day's walk from Banjar but you can get that far by bus. It's then a gentle climb to Bathad where there is a PWD Rest House, followed by a very hard climb to the Bashleo pass at 3250 metres, 13 km on. A steep descent takes you to Sarahan, only three km further.

There is another beautifully situated rest house here. From here it is too easy, pleasant walks to Arsu (another PWD Rest House) and then Rampur on the main road.

Day 3	Banjar-Goshaini	13 km
Day 4	Goshaini-Bathad	16 km
Day 5	Bathad-Sarahan	16 km
Day 6	Sarahan-Arsu	13 km
Day 7	Arsu-Rampur	13 km

Solang Valley

There are a number of treks from Manali to the Solang Valley looping back to Manali either from the north or the south. A seven day trek takes you to Beas Kund, the source of the Beas River and across the remains of dying glaciers. The first day takes you to Solang Nullah where there is a mountain hut with rooms for 80 people. There are ski-runs here in the winter. The second day's trek continues to Dhundi where you can see Deo Tibba and Indrasan from this alpine plateau and admire the many alpine flowers. The third day takes you to Beas Kund and back and the next day continues to Shagara Dugh with a good chance of seeing red bears along the way. On the fifth day you reach Marrhi over a small 4000 metre pass with views to the Kulu Valley and the Rohtang Pass. Finally on day six you continue down the Keylong-Manali road to Kothi, via the Rahla water fall, and on the last day return to Manali.

Day 1	Manali- Solang Nullah	2480 m	11 km
Day 2	Solang Nullah- Dhundi	2840 m	8 km
Day 3	Dhundi- Beas Kund & back	3540 m	10 km
Day 4	Dhundi- Shagara Dugh	3600 m	8 km
Day 5	Shagara Dugh- Marrhi	3380 m	10 km
Day 6	Marrhi-Kothi	2500 m	6 km
Day 7	Kothi-Manali		13 km

Manali Pass Treks

These two treks continue on from the Solang Valley trek but loop back to Manali from the south. They are both difficult treks involving long hard ascents over rugged terrain. The first alternative continues from Beas Kund over the Tentu Pass, an arduous and tiring climb, to Phulangot through an uninhabited region. You then cross the Manali Pass to Rani Sui and go via Bhogi Thatch to Kalath, a little south of Manali on the Kulu-Manali road.

Day 3	Dhundi- Beas Kund	3540 m	6 km
Day 4	Beas Kund- Tentu Pass	4996 m	4 km
Day 5	Tentu Pass- camping ground	3856 m	10 km
Day 6	camping ground- Phulangot	4000 m	6 km
Day 7	Phulangot- Manali Pass	4988 m	6 km
Day 8	Manali Pass- Rani Sui	4200 m	8 km
Day 9	Rani Sui- Bhogi Thatch	2800 m	6 km
Day 10	Bhogi Thatch- Kalath	1800 m	12 km

The second alternative is to join the Manalsu Nullah from the Manali Pass and follow this straight back to Manali — up to Day 8 this trek is the same as alternative one.

An easy trek which includes the last two days of alternative one involves going to Rani Sui via Lama Dugh. You leave Manali via the Hadimba Temple and climb through pleasant country to the camp site at Lama Dugh. On the second day you cross the Thanpri Tibba ridge to Rani Sui and then Day 3 and Day 4 are as Day 9 and Day 10 above.

| Day 1 | Manali-
Lama Dugh | 3380 m | 6 km |
| Day 2 | Lama Dugh-
Rani Sui | 4200 m | 5 km |

LAHAUL & SPITI

Only since 1977 have visitors been permitted to cross the Rohtang Pass to Keylong in Lahaul. Only 117 km from Manali this is a Tibetan region, quite unlike the Kulu Valley. The Rohtang Pass has the same 'gateway' nature as the Zoji La pass does between Kashmir and Ladakh. The region is bounded by Ladakh to the north, Kulu to the south and Tibet to the east. All of Spiti and a large chunk of Lahaul is off-limits to visitors. You cannot continue up the jeep road from Keylong to Leh in Ladakh but you can make the long and difficult trek from Keylong to Padum in the Zanskar Valley and from there into Ladakh. See the Lonely Planet guide *Kashmir, Ladakh & Zanskar* for information on treks in this region.

Rohtang Pass

The 3915 metre Rohtang Pass is the only access into Lahaul and it is open only from June to September each year although trekkers can cross the pass a little before it opens for vehicles. During the short season it is open there are regular buses from Manali to Keylong. The tourist office operates a daily Rs 35 bus up to the pass, mainly for tourists to 'see the snow'. It's a very spectacular trip over the pass.

Keylong

The main town in the Lahaul and Spiti region; there are a number of interesting monasteries within easy reach of this oasis-like town. The old Kharding Monastery, formerly the capital of Lahaul, overlooks Keylong, only 3.5 km away. Other monasteries include Shashur (three km), Tayal (six km) and Guru Ghantal (11 km).

Places to Stay There is a *PWD Rest House*, a number of small hotels and the HPTDC sets up tents during the summer season.

Other Places

Gondhla, with its eight storey castle of the Thakur of Gondhla and the historically significant gompa, is a short distance before Keylong on the Manali-Keylong road. You can trek back to Gondhla from Keylong, cutting across the loop the road makes. Between Gondhla and Keylong is Tandi where the Chandrabagha or Chenab River meets the road. Following the Chenab valley to the north-west towards Kilar (see treks from Chamba) will bring you to Triloknath with its six-armed white marble image of Avalokitesvara. Close by is the village of Udaipur with a finely carved wooden temple from the 10th or 11th century which is dedicated to Mrikula Devi.

Spiti

The 4500 metre Kunzam pass connects the Lahaul and Spit valleys. Eventually a road will be completed from Kaza, the principal Spiti village, south-east through Samdoh to meet the Hindustan-Tibet road (see Kinnaur). There are few settlements in this barren, high region. Kaza (or Kaja) is the main village and slightly north-west of this is Kibar (or Kyipur) which is at 4205 metres and reputed to be the highest village in the world. Tabo Kye and Dhankhar are two of the most important gompas.

Climate

As in Ladakh little rain gets over the high Himalayan barrier so Lahaul and Spiti are dry and, for the most part, barren. The air is sharp and clear and the warm summer days are followed by cold, crisp nights. Beware of the burning power of the sun in this region — you can get burnt very quickly even on quite cool days. The heavy winter snow from September to May closes the passes except for a few months of each year.

Culture

The people of Lahaul and Spiti follow a Tibetan form of Tantric Buddhism with a panoply of demons, saints and followers. The monasteries, known as gompas, are colourful places where the monks or lamas lead lives ordered by complicated regulations and rituals. There are many similarities between these people and the Ladakhis, further north. The people of Spiti are almost all Buddhists of Tibetan stock but Lahaul is split roughly 50:50 between Buddhists and Hindus.

Getting There

Although the pass may be open by mid-May a safer date is mid-June. The bus trip takes eight hours and costs Rs 19. It's 475 km from Manali to Leh via Keylong but you need special permission to use this road.

KINNAUR

Most of this region, in the valley of the Sutlej River extending up towards the Tibetan border, is off limits without permission from the Ministry of Foreign Affairs in New Delhi. You can only go as far as the Wangtu Bridge, just beyond Nachar, without a permit.

Rampur

Beyond Narkanda, 140 km from Simla, Rampur is the gateway to the region. It's the site for a major trade fair in the second week of November each year. This was once a major centre for trade between India and Tibet. There are direct buses from Simla to Rampur. Rampur has a PWD Rest House.

Sarahan

The last village in the district before entering Kinnaur, Sarahan is a beautiful little place with the interesting Bhimkali temple which shows a curious blend of Hindu and Buddhist architecture.

Nachar

Situated on the old Hindustan-Tibet road this picturesque village is four km from the Wangtu Bridge, beyond which you need a permit to continue. As in Sarahan the village is on the old road which has been replaced by the nearby new Hindustan-Tibet road. There's a rest house in the orchards.

Tapri & Choltu

Only 15 km further up the valley from Nachar three roads meet at this scenic spot. One is the main road continuing up the valley to Kalpa. The second is the old road, also continuing to Kalpa via Rogi. The third is a small road which crosses the river through Choltu and Kilba to the Sangla Valley. Choltu has a pleasant rest house.

Sangla

The main village in the Sangla Valley is 18 km from Karcham, on the new Hindustan-Tibet road, and can be reached by jeep or on foot. It's a good base for trekking and there's a rest house.

Kalpa

The main town in Kinnaur is close to the foot of 6050 metre high Kinnaur Khailash. This is the legendary winter home of Lord Shiva, during the winter the god is said to retire to his Himalayan home here and indulge his passion for hashish. In the month of Magha, January-February, the gods of Kinnaur are all supposed to meet here for an annual conference with Lord Shiva. Kalpa has a rest house and from here you can continue on the northern side of the river to Puh and Namgia, close to the Tibetan border. Only 14 km from Kalpa the tiny village of Pangli has a small rest house and a fine view of Kinnaur Khailash. Rarang, eight km further on, is another centre for trade to Tibet.

Jammu & Kashmir

Population: 5 million
Area: 222,236 square km
Capital: Srinagar
Main languages: Kashmiri, Dogri

The state of Jammu and Kashmir, J&K for short, is a region of widely varying people and geography. In the south Jammu is a transition zone from the Indian plains to the Himalayas. Correctly the rest of the state is Kashmir but in practice this title is reserved for the beautiful Vale of Kashmir, a large Himalayan valley in the north of the state. Here the people are predominantly Moslem and in many ways look towards Pakistan and central Asia rather than towards India. Finally to the north-east there is the remote Tibetan plateau region known as Ladakh. Only recently opened to foreign tourists, Ladakh is primarily Buddhist and Tibetan in its culture and a very clear contrast to the rest of Kashmir, indeed to the rest of India. Sandwiched between the Kashmir and Ladakh regions is a long narrow valley known as Zanskar. This valley is even more isolated than Ladakh and has still been visited by very few westerners although this will change as a new jeep road into the valley is extended and improved.

Jammu and Kashmir has always been a centre of conflict for independent India. At the time of independence the state should rightfully have gone to Pakistan if a simple religious majority had been the deciding factor. But J&K was not a part of 'British India', it was a 'princely state' and as such the ruler had to decide which way his state would move — to Moslem Pakistan or Hindu India. In other princely states the wrong decision on the prince's part simply resulted in his rule being abruptly terminated but in J&K the Maharaja was allowed to opt for India, despite the overwhelmingly Moslem population. The vacillating Maharaja only made that decision when a Pakistani-prompted invasion was already crossing his borders and the inevitable result was the first Indo-Pakistani conflict. Since that first conflict Kashmir has remained a flashpoint for relations between the two countries. Furthermore Kashmir's role as a sensitive border zone applies not only to Pakistan. In 1962 the Chinese invaded Ladakh prompting India to rapidly reassess their position in this remote and isolated region.

For visitors J&K is one of India's most popular states. Kashmir is simply beautiful and a spell on a houseboat on Dal Lake is one of India's real treats. Kashmir also offers some delightful trekking opportunities and unsurpassed scenery. Ladakh, on the other hand, offers a chance to study a region which, in today's world, is probably even more Tibetan than Tibet. It's one of the most other-worldly parts of India. No special permits are required to visit Kashmir or

Jammu & Kashmir

India-Pakistan cease fire line

India-China cease fire line

PAKISTAN

Drass · Kargil · Mulbekh

Sonamarg · Zoji La Pass

Srinagar · Pahalgam · Nimmu · Leh · Tikse

Gulmarg

KASHMIR · ZANSKAR · LADAKH · Hemis

Anantnag

Kishtwar · Padum

HIMACHAL PRADESH

Jammu

Dalhousie · Keylong

Dharamsala · Manali

Pathankot

Ladakh today but your movements are restricted in that you are not allowed to approach within a certain distance of the border. In Ladakh this means you are not allowed more than a mile north of the Srinagar-Leh road although south of that is quite open.

Kashmir, Ladakh & Zanskar Rolf & Margret Schettler. If you'd like a lot more information about Kashmir and Ladakh, particularly about trekking in Ladakh and Zanskar, then look for this book. It's available from Lonely Planet or in bookshops through our local distributors.

JAMMU (population 160,000)

Jammu is the second largest town in the state but for most travellers it is just a jumping off point for the trip north to Kashmir. Most travellers simply arrive in Jammu one evening and depart the next morning for Kashmir. If you do have time there are a number of interesting attractions in the town. Note that Jammu is still on the plains and in the summer is a sweltering, uncomfortable contrast to the cool heights of Kashmir.

Kashmir, Ladakh & Zanskar

Margret & Rolf Schettler

Jammu

Bus Station

steps

Raghunath Temple

Railway Station + Pathankot

Aroma Hotel

Picnic Hotel

Bus booking office →
Tourist Office

Palace Hotel

Nomdar Hotel

Cosmo +
Notraj Hotels

Standard Hotel

Apsara Hotel

Premier Hotel

Information & Orientation

Jammu is actually two towns — the old town sits on a hilltop overlooking the river. Here you'll find most of the hotels and the Tourist Reception Centre where the Tourist Office is located and from where upper class buses depart for Kashmir. Note that the Tourist Office, typically for Kashmir, closes early in the evening and opens late in the morning, thus preventing most people, who only overnight in Jammu, from using it. Down beside the hill is the bus station for buses to other parts of north India and for the lower class buses to Srinagar. Finally, several km away across the river is the new town of Jammu Tawi where the railway station is located.

Things to See

The Raghunath Temple is in the centre of the city, only a short stroll from the Tourist Reception Centre. This large temple complex was built in 1835. Also centrally located the Rambireswar Temple, dedicated to Lord Shiva, dates from 1883. Situated in the Gandhi Bhavan, by the New Secretariat, the Dogra Art Gallery has an important collection of miniature paintings including many from the locally renowned Basohli and Kangra schools. The gallery is open from 7.30 am to 1 pm in summer and from 11 am to 5 pm in winter but closed on Mondays. Admission is free. On the northern outskirts of town, just off the Srinagar road, is the Amar Mahal Palace, a curious example of French architecture. The palace museum has a family portrait gallery and another important collection of paintings.

Places to Stay

If you're simply passing through Jammu do two things as soon as you arrive — first find a room and second book your bus seat for Srinagar. If you are coming from Srinagar the first step is vital — all the buses tend to arrive at much the same time and the race for accommodation is serious during the tourist season.

The centrally located *Tourist Reception Centre* (tel 5421) on Vir Marg has 128 rooms and is often completely booked out. Rooms vary in price from Rs 30 a double (D block, Indian toilets) to Rs 45 in the new block or Rs 60 with air-con. There is also a very dismal Rs 2 dormitory. In most cases there is a two night limit to your stay — quite enough for Jammu. At the railway station there is a second *Tourist Reception Centre* (tel 8803) with doubles at Rs 25 and dorm beds at Rs 3. The station also has *Retiring Rooms* at Rs 30 a double or Rs 50 with air-con, dorm beds at Rs 6. Note that the railway station is across the Tawi River, several km from the centre. The bus station is close to the centre and has *Retiring Rooms* with doubles at Rs 20 and Rs 3 dorm beds.

Jammu doesn't have a great selection of other hotels. The ITDC *Hotel Jammu Ashok* (tel 5104, 2084) is on the outskirts of town to the north, close to the Amar Mahal Palace. Singles/doubles are Rs 100/140 with air-con, Rs 65/90 without. *Hotel Asia* (tel 6373-75) is in Nehru Market, close to the station or airport but far from the centre. It's similarly priced to the Jammu Ashok. Third of Jammu's 'better' hotels is the *Cosmopolitan* (tel 5520) on Vir Marg, directly opposite the tourist centre. Singles/doubles are priced from around Rs 40/75 up to Rs 100/140 and it's pretty much a dump.

Cheaper hotels are strung along Vir Marg or else close to the bus station. The *Picnic*, down the street beside the tourist centre, has doubles from Rs 35 and is OK, just. Spartan (very) doubles from Rs 15 or 20 at the *Palace Hotel* (tel 6209) or the *Premier Hotel* both on Vir Marg. Down beside the bus station, the address is 'below Gumat' since the street is overshadowed by the hill, you'll find the *Astoria Hotel* (tel 2303) and the *Broadway Hotel* (tel 2636) with doubles at around Rs 50. Across the road are the *Diamond* and the *Mahindra*.

Places to Eat

The usual government tourist centre menu is available at the *Tourist Reception Centre*. Reasonable sort of food. The *Cosmopolitan Hotel's* air-con restaurant is far superior to the hotel — good for a pleasant meal in cool surroundings and a cold beer. A few doors down the *Premier* has Chinese and Kashmiri food.

Getting There

People generally go to Jammu simply to continue on to Srinagar. See details under 'Getting There' for Srinagar. If you're continuing on from Jammu to Srinagar the one important rule to follow is to get your bus ticket as soon

as you arrive. Southbound there are frequent buses from Jammu to Amritsar (Rs 11), Pathankot (Rs 5, three hours) and other cities. Pathankot is the jumping off point for Dharamsala, Dalhousie and the other Himachal Pradesh hill stations.

Getting Around

Jammu has metered taxis, auto-rickshaws and a tempo service between the number of points. From the railway station to the bus station a tempo costs Rs 1.25. The same trip by auto-rickshaw would be Rs 4 to 5. It's only a short distance from the Tourist Reception Centre in the town centre to the bus station, say Rs 2 auto-rickshaw.

JAMMU-SRINAGAR

Although most people simply head straight through from Jammu to Srinagar there are a number of places of interest between the two centres. Some places can also be reached using Jammu as a base. Prior to the completion of the

Jawarhar Tunnel into the Kashmir Valley the trip from Jammu took two days with an overnight stop at Batote.

Akhnoor
This is where the Chenab River meets the plains, 32 km north-west of Jammu. This used to be the route to Srinagar in the Moghul era. Jehangir, who died en route to Kashmir, was temporarily buried at Chingas.

Basohli
Situated fairly close to Dalhousie, which is across the border in Himachal Pradesh, this is the birthplace of the Pahari miniature painting style.

Billawar, Sukrala, Babor & Permandal
All these places have ruined and uncompleted temples of some interest.

Surinsar & Mansar Lakes
East of Jammu these lakes are picturesque and the scene for an annual festival at Mansar.

Vaishno Devi
This important cave temple is dedicated to the three mother goddesses of Hinduism. Thousands of pilgrims visit the cave each year after making a steep 12 km climb from the roadhead at Katra or a shorter and easier climb from a new road.

Riasi
Near this town, 80 km beyond Katra, is the ruined fort of General Zorawar Singh, renowned for his clashes with the Chinese over Ladakh. Near here there is a gurdwara with some interesting old frescoes and another important cave temple.

Ramnagar
The 'palace of colours' has many beautiful Pahari style wall paintings. Buses go here from Jammu or Udhampur. Krimchi, 10 km from Udhampur, has

Hindu temples with fine carving and sculpture.

Kud
This is a popular lunch stop on the Jammu-Srinagar route at 1738 metres. It's also popular in its own right as a hill resort and has a Tourist Bungalow. There's a well known mountain spring, Swami Ki Bauli, 1.5 km from the road.

Batote
Only 12 km further on, and connected to Patnitop and Kud by a number of footpaths, this hill resort at 1560 metres was the overnight stop between Jammu and Srinagar before the tunnel was opened. There is a Tourist Bungalow, tourist huts and several private hotels. As in Kud there is a spring close to the village — Amrit Chasma is only 2.5 km away.

Patnitop
At 2024 metres there are many pleasant walks around this popular hill station. Patnitop is intended to be the nucleus of tourist developments in this area. There are tourist huts, a Rest House and a Youth Hostel in Patnitop.

Sudh Mahadev
Many pilgrims visit the Shiva temple here during the annual July-August Asad Purnima festival which features three days of music, singing and dancing. Five km from Sudh Mahadev is Man Talai where some archaeological discoveries have been made. An eight km walking or jeep track leads to Sudh Mahadev from Kud or Patnitop.

Sanasar
At 2079 metres this beautiful valley is a centre for the Gujjar shepherds each summer. There is a Tourist Bungalow, tourist huts and several private hotels.

Bhadarwah
Every two years a procession of pilgrims

walk from this beautiful high altitude valley to the 4400 metre high Kaplash Lake. A week later the three-day Mela Patt festival takes place in Bhadarwah. There is a rest house in this scenic location.

Kishtwar

Well off the Jammu-Srinagar road there is, however, a trekking route from Kishtwar to Srinagar. You can also trek from Kishtwar into Zanskar. There are many waterfalls around Kishtwar and 19 km from the town is the pilgrimage site of Sarthal Devi.

Jawarhar Tunnel

During the winter months Srinagar was often completely cut off from the rest of India before this tunnel was completed. The 2500 metre long tunnel is 200 km from Jammu and 93 km from Srinagar and has two separate passages. It's rather rough and damp inside. From Banihal, 17 km before the tunnel, you are already entering the Kashmiri region and people speak Kashmiri as well as Dogri. As soon as you emerge from the tunnel you are in the green, lush Vale of Kashmir.

KASHMIR

This is one of the most beautiful regions of India. The Moghul rulers of India were always happy to retreat from the heat of the plains to the cool green heights of Kashmir and indeed Jehangir's last words, when he died while en route to the 'happy valley', was a simple request for 'only Kashmir'. The Moghuls developed the art of their formal garden style to its greatest heights in Kashmir and some of their gardens are beautifully kept even to this day.

One of Kashmir's greatest attractions is undoubtedly the Dale Lake houseboats. During the Raj period Kashmir's ruler would not permit the British (who were as fond of Kashmir's cool climate as the Moghuls) to own land here. So they adopted the superbly British solution of building houseboats — each one a little bit of England, afloat on Dal Lake. A visit to Kashmir, it is so often said, is not complete until you have stayed on a houseboat. Of course Srinagar, Dal Lake and houseboats is not all there is to Kashmir. Around the edges of the valley are Kashmir's delightful hill stations. Places like Pahalgam and Gulmarg are pleasant in their own right and also good bases for trekking trips.

SRINAGAR (population 450,000)
The capital of Kashmir stands on Dal Lake and the Jhelum River and is the transport hub for the valley and also the jumping off point for trips to Ladakh. Srinagar is a crowded, colourful city with a distinctly central Asian flavour. The people indeed look different from the rest of India and when you head south from Srinagar it is always referred to as 'returning to India'.

Information & Orientation

Srinagar is initially a little confusing since Dal Lake, which is so much a part of the city, is such a strange lake. It's actually three lakes, separated by dykes or 'floating gardens' and at times it's hard to tell where lake ends and land begins. On the lake there are houseboats that are definitely firmly attached to the bottom. And houses that look like they could simply float away. Most of the houseboats are at the southern end of the lake although you will also find them on the Jhelum River and north on Nagin Lake. The Jhelum River makes a loop around the main part of town and a canal connecting the river with Dal Lake converts that part of town into an island. Along the south of this 'island' is the Bund, a popular walk. Here you will find the GPO and the handicrafts centre. The large Tourist Reception Centre is just north of the Bund and here the Tourist Office,

Key:-
1 Tourist Reception Centre # buses to Ladakh & Jammu
2 G.P.O.
3 Telegraph Office # local bus stand
4 Local bus stand
5 Museum
6 Youth Hostel
7 Indian Coffee House, Hollywood cafe
8 Ahdous restaurant
9 Capri restaurant
10 Broadway # Nedous Hotels
11 Lhasa Restaurant # Tibetan Guest House
12 Bathing baats
13 Raghunath Temple
14 Pather Masque
15 Shah Hamdam Mosque
16 Zain-ut-Abidin's Tomb
17 Bulbul Shah Masque
18 Government Central Market

Indian Airlines and the J&K Road Transport Corporation are located together with accommodation units and a rather poor restaurant. The Kashmir Tourist Office is very poor.

There are many restaurants, shops, travel agents and hotels in the island part of town. More of the more modern part of Srinagar stretches away south of the Jhelum while the older parts of town are north and north-west of here.

Dal Lake

Much of Dal Lake is a maze of intricate waterways rather than a simple sheet of open water. The lake is divided into Gagribal, Lokut Dal and Bod Dal by a series of causeways. Dal Gate, at the city end of the lake, controls the flow of the lake water into the Jhelum River canal. Within the lake are two islands which are popular picnic spots. Silver Island (Sona Lank) is at the north end of the lake while Gold Island (Rupa Lank) is to the south. Both are also known as Char Chinar because they each have four chinar trees on them. There's a third island, Nehru Park, at the end of the main stretch of the lake side Boulevard but it is a miserable affair. North of here a long causeway juts out into the lake towards Kotar Khana, the 'house of pigeons', which was once a royal summer house.

The waters of Dal Lake are amazingly clear, considering what must be poured into them from the houseboats, and there is always something happening on the lake. Whether you're just lazing on your houseboat balcony watching the shikaras glide by or visiting the Moghul gardens around the lake there's plenty to see and do on Dal Lake. A shikara circuit of the lake is a sybaritic experience not to be missed. A leisurely cruise around will take all day, including visits to the Moghul gardens, and should cost about Rs 50. There's hardly a more leisurely and pleasurable way of getting into the swing of Srinagar. If

your budget is tight you can circuit the lake yourself by bicycle. It's also possible to ride right across the lake on the central causeway.

Jhelum River & Bridges

The Jhelum flows from Verinag, 80 km south of Srinagar, to the Wular Lake to the north. It's wide, swift flowing, muddy and picturesque as it sweeps through Srinagar. The river is famed for its nine old bridges but new bridges have popped up between them. There are a number of interesting mosques and other buildings near the river and a leisurely stroll or bicycle ride through the narrow lanes that run close to the river is very rewarding.

Museum

The Shri Pratap Singh Museum is in Lal Mandi, just south of the river between Zero Bridge and Amira Kadal, the first 'old' bridge. The museum has an interesting collection of exhibits relevant to Kashmir including illustrated titles from Harwan. It's open 10 am to 5 pm, closed on Wednesdays and admission is free.

Shah Hamdan Mosque

Originally built in 1395 the all-wooden mosque was destroyed by fire in 1479 and 1731. The mosque is shaped like a cube with a pyramidal roof rising to a spire. Non-Moslems are not allowed inside.

Pather Masjid

On the opposite bank of the Jhelum is the unused Pather Masjid. This fine stone mosque was built by Nur Jahan in 1623.

Tomb of Zain-ul-Abidin

Back on the east bank between the Zaina Kadal and the Ali Kadal bridges is the slightly decrepit tomb of King Zain-ul-Abidin, the highly regarded son of Sultan Sikander. Built on the foundations of an earlier temple the tomb shows a clear Persian influence in its domed construction and glazed tiles.

Jami Masjid

This impressive wooden mosque is notable for the 300-plus pillars supporting the roof, each made of a single deodar tree trunk. The present mosque, with its green and peaceful inner courtyard was rebuilt to the original design after a fire in 1674. It has had a chequered history. First built in 1385 by Sultan Sikander it was enlarged by Zain-ul-Abidin in 1402 then destroyed by fire in 1479. Rebuilt in 1503 another fire destroyed it during Jehangir's reign. Again it was rebuilt only to burn down once more before its most recent rebuild.

Shankaracharya Hill

Rising up behind the Boulevard, beside Dal Lake, the hill was once known as Takht-i-Sulaiman, the Throne of Solomon. A temple is said to have first been built here by Ashoka's son around 200 BC but the present Hindu temple dates from Jehangir's time. It's a pleasant stroll to the top from where you have a fine view over Dal Lake — the Srinagar TV tower is also here. Alternatively there's a road right to the top.

Chasma Shahi

Smallest of the Moghul gardens at Srinagar the Chasma Shahi are well up the hillside, above the Nehru Memorial Park. The gardens were laid out in 1632 but have been recently extended. These are the only gardens with an admission charge.

Pari Mahal

Just above the Chasma Shahi is this fine old Sufi college. The ruined, arched terraces have recently been turned into a very pleasant and well kept garden with fine views over Dal Lake. From the Pari Mahal you can descend straight down the hill to the road that runs back to the Oberoi Palace Hotel.

Nishat Bagh

Sandwiched between the lake and the mountains the Nishat gardens have a superb view across the lake to the Pir Panjal mountains. Designed in 1633 by Nur Jahan's brother Asaf Khan this is the largest of the Moghul gardens and follows the traditional pattern of a central channel running down a series of terraces.

Shalimar Bagh

Set some distance back from the lake but reached by a small canal, the Shalimar gardens were built for Nur Jahan, 'light of the world', by her husband Jehangir in 1616. During the Moghul period the topmost of the four terraces was reserved for the emperor and the ladies of the court. During the May to October tourist season a nightly son et lumiere (sound and light show) is put on in these beautiful gardens. The English performance is at 9 pm and tickets cost Rs 3 or 7.50.

Hazratbal Mosque

This shiny new mosque is on the northwest shore of Dal Lake. The mosque enshrines a hair of the prophet but to non-believers it will be most interesting simply for its stunningly beautiful setting on the shores of the lake with the snow capped peaks as a backdrop.

Nasim Bagh

Just beyond the mosque these gardens were built by Akbar in 1586 but today this oldest Moghul garden is used by an engineering college and is not maintained as a garden.

Nagin Lake

The 'jewel in the ring' is held to be the most beautiful of the Dal Lakes and is ringed by trees. There are a number of houseboats on this quieter, cleaner lake.

Ideal if you want to get away from it all.

Hari Parbat Fort
Clearly visible on top of the Sharika hill, to the west of Dal Lake, this fort was originally built between 1592 and 1598 during the rule of Akbar but most of the present construction dates from the 18th century. Visits to the fort are only possible with written permission from the Director of Tourism so for most visitors the fort will remain just a pleasant backdrop. At the southern gate to the fort there is a shrine to the sixth Sikh Guru.

Pandrathan Temple
This small but beautifully proportioned Shiva temple dates from 900 AD and is in the military cantonment area on the Jammu road out of Srinagar.

Harwan
At the northern end of Dal Lake archaeologists have discovered an unusual ornamented brick pavement near here. Examples of these bricks can be seen in the Srinagar museum. The water supply for Srinagar is pumped from here and piped along the causeway across the lake.

Places to Stay in Srinagar
The best advice on finding accommodation in Srinagar is to avoid the heavy handed tourist centre who will do their best to steer you into houseboats you may not be interested in. They heavy everybody arriving in Srinagar — whether by air or by bus — but you can easily ignore them and do your own thing. Although houseboats are a prime attraction of a stay in Srinagar there are also plenty of hotels in all price categories.

Places to Stay — Houseboats
There is no greater escape from the noise and hassle of Srinagar, a typically noisy Asian city, than the houseboats. As soon as you get out on the lake traffic, pollution and hassles just fade away. Houseboats are superbly relaxing. Basically most houseboats are the same. You have a small verandah at one and where you can sit and watch the world pass by. Behind this is a living room, usually furnished in British '30s style. Then there is a dining room and beyond that two or three bedrooms, each with attached bathroom. Officially houseboats come in five categories each with an officially approved price, including all meals:

	single/double
de-luxe or 5-star	Rs 170/250
A class	Rs 115/170
B class	Rs 80/130
C class	Rs 50/90
D class or 'donga boat'	Rs 35/45
D class 'lodging only' for whole boat	Rs 30

In practice those 'official prices' are a bit meaningless. For a start there is a wide variance between boats — some are 5-star and others **5-STAR**! A good C class boat can be better than a poor A class boat. Also most houseboats are managed in groups of three or more. You can be sure the food is not going to differ materially from the best boat in the group to the worst. Plus, of course, there is competition. With so many houseboats (there are hundreds of them) a little negotiation is inevitable.

To find a houseboat go down to the shikara ghats along the lakeside and announce you want a houseboat. Either there will be somebody there with a boat available or you can hire a kid with a shikara to paddle you around the boats to ask. Generally you can get away with paying at least the price level for the category below each boat — for an A class boat pay B class prices. If you decide to miss a meal, say lunch, each day that can generally be negotiated into a lower price. Make certain shikara trips to shore are included and if not remember it's only Rs 0.50 from ghat to boat. This is Kashmir so pin down as many details as possible. Check what breakfast is going to be for example — exactly how many eggs? Check they'll supply a bucket of hot water for washing each morning — Kashmir can be chilly.

It's virtually impossible to recommend a particular boat. There are so many, they all only have a few rooms and there are so many variable factors. A pleasant shikara man — who runs you back and forth between boat and shore, makes tea, supplies hot water and so on — can make a nondescript boat into a pleasant one. A pleasant boat can be ruined by a poor cook. Or simply having some pleasant fellow houseboaters to chat with in the evening can make all the difference. Even on the best boats the food can get rather monotonous but there are plenty of 'supermarket' boats cruising by if you need soft drinks, chocolate, toilet paper, hashish or any other of life's necessities.

Places to Stay — Top End

On dry land the *Oberoi Palace Hotel* (tel 2231-34 & 5641-42) is the ex-palace of the Maharaja of Kashmir and is Srinagar's top establishment. It's several km around the boulevard from Dal Gate and singles/doubles run from Rs 360/520. The actual building is rather uninspired, particularly if you've seen the sumptuous palace hotels of Rajasthan, but the gardens in front provide superb views over the lake. The more modern and more central *Broadway Hotel* (tel 5611) is popular and has an excellent restaurant. Singles/doubles cost Rs 200/320.

Next door is the rather run down and decrepit looking *Nedou's Hotel* (tel 73015-16) also on Hotel Rd. Singles/doubles cost Rs 150/200. There are a number of more expensive hotels along the Boulevard, looking out on to Dal Lake.

Places to Stay — Bottom End

There are cheap hotels scattered all around Srinagar although those in the Lal Chowk area tend to be rather noisy. The best bargains in cheap hotels are actually to be found on Dal Lake. Scattered amongst the houseboats there are a number of small hotels actually on (semi) dry land. They're cheap and also quiet but prices are very variable, depending on season and demand. Real cheapies can go as low as Rs 5 or 10 per person. Check the *Latif Guest House* or the *Hotel Sundowna* — the latter has rooms as low as Rs 15, fairly spartan but quite OK and good food. Right next door there's the *Hotel Savoy* with rooms from Rs 25 up to Rs 40 or 50. Again the food is good. A little up market from these places — and further up the channel towards Dal Gate — is *Hotel Heaven Canal* with doubles from Rs 50 to 80.

On solid ground, but still cheap, there's the friendly *Tibetan Guest House* above the Lhasa Restaurant, just off the Boulevard. *Zero Inn,* by Zero Bridge, is also reasonably quiet but rather more expensive at Rs 50 or more a double. Kashmir is not a cheap place for accommodation by Indian standards.

The J&K tourist office operates four accommodation units in Srinagar. At the *Tourist Reception Centre* there are retiring rooms, rooms and suites with prices from Rs 60 to 80. Maximum stay is two days but they are generally full during the season. They have two hotels (*Lalla Rukh* and *Budshah*) but both are in noisy Lal Chowk. Finally there are the *Tourist Huts* near the Chasma Shahi gardens. They come complete with kitchens and cooking equipment but you really need your own transport to get out to them. Cost is around Rs 200 a night for a double.

The *Srinagar Youth Hostel* is across

the river from the town centre, near the museum. Nightly charges are just Rs 2 and reservations must be made through the Education Department. Just beyond the Nagin Lake causeway, only a short distance before the Hazratbal Mosque there's a campsite, a good place if you have your own vehicle.

Places to Eat

Because so many people eat on board their houseboats Srinagar is not a very exciting place for eating out. Surprisingly nobody has yet come up with a floating restaurant — a logical follow on to all those houseboats.

The *Oberoi Palace Hotel* does a very superior buffet dinner at Rs 50 and at lunch-time you can dine, or simply have a snack, on their sweeping lawn. A la carte, most dishes are in the Rs 15 to Rs 25 bracket. The *Broadway* also has a buffet (Rs 40) in their pleasantly carpet-decorated restaurant. Food here (on the non-buffet nights) is quite reasonably priced and you can sample quite possibly the best kahwa tea in Srinagar — an expensive treat.

Ahdoo's, which fronts on to the Bund and backs on to Residency Rd, has been said to have some of the best Kashmiri food in Srinagar but generally fails to live up to its reputation. Most dishes are under Rs 10. Across the road the *Grand* has a similar menu. Others in this area include the *Capri Bar & Restaurant* and the *Premier*.

Just off the Boulevard the Tibetan run *Lhasa Restaurant* does quite good Chinese-Tibetan food. A complete meal for two will cost Rs 40 to Rs 50. Further back towards Dal Gate, on the Boulevard, there's the *Shamyana* with good vegetarian food and reasonable prices.

Right in the central area the *Indian Coffee House* is a good place for a coffee and a chat — the food line here is rather limited: quite good vegetable cutlets and rather so-so masala dosas.

Right across the road the *Hollywood Cafe* has much, much better food than its plain appearance would suggest. Seekh kebab or kanti roast make an excellent lunch here and their french fries are superb by any standards. Plus good cakes or snacks at other times of day.

Ice cream is not bad at *Dimples*, either in the centre (opposite the Hollywood) or by Zero Bridge. The latter is known as the *Little Hut* and also has good milkshakes. There's a good selection of Indian sweets at *Shakti Sweets* also by the Hollywood. The cafe at the Tourist Reception Centre is terrible but you can get early morning snacks from the stalls which set up opposite the TRC for the early bus departures.

Getting There

Flights Indian Airlines fly to Srinagar from New Delhi (Rs 515), Chandigarh (Rs 435), Amritsar (Rs 300), Jammu (Rs 150) and there are flights operating from Srinagar to Leh and back. Flights are more frequent during the summer tourist season, at that time there will probably be a Delhi-Chandigarh-Jammu-Srinagar flight and a Jammu-Srinagar flight by HS-748 each day. A 737 will also fly Delhi-Amritsar-Srinagar and there will probably be another direct 737 and an Airbus. Flight time from Delhi on the direct flights is about an hour and ten minutes. As usual in India you should book your flight as early as possible.

At Srinagar airport, which is about 13 km out of the city, there is a fairly chaotic scene as the Tourist Office tries to register every incoming foreigner and insists that you book any accommodation through the Tourist Reception Centre. It's the first place where J&K Tourism do their best to make themselves unpopular. There's an airport bus to the Tourist Reception Centre in Srinagar which costs Rs 4.

By taxi it costs Rs 30.

In Srinagar the Indian Airlines office is at the Tourist Reception Centre (tel 73538 & 73270) and is open from 10 am to 5 pm. It's also at the Tourist Reception Centre in Jammu (tel 2735 & 7088).

Train & Bus It's 880 km from Delhi to Srinagar although almost everybody coming up from Delhi, or other Indian cities, by land will come through Jammu (591 km from Delhi) from where the buses run daily to Srinagar. By train there are about four services a day from Delhi or New Delhi to Jammu Tawi, across the river from Jammu. The trip takes nine to 13 hours, usually overnight, and costs about Rs 33 in 2nd class, Rs 120 in 1st class. There are also buses from Delhi but people making the trip by road will most probably be coming via Chandigarh, Amritsar or the Himachal Pradesh hill stations.

Buses leave Jammu early in the morning (between 6.30 and 7 am) for the 10 to 12 hour trip to Srinagar in the Kashmir Valley. Bus fares are Rs 20 (B class), Rs 30 (A class), Rs 55 (super de-luxe) and Rs 90 (air-con). B class buses seat two and three, A class two and two, super de-luxe two and two in individual seats with headrests. Although there are many buses (a veritable armada leaves Jammu each morning) you should book a seat as soon as you arrive in Jammu. The same applies from Srinagar as the day before departure all seats may be sold out. There are also taxis operating between the two cities at Rs 110 per seat or Rs 440 for the whole taxi.

For information about booking trains from Jammu while in Srinagar enquire at the railways office in the Tourist Reception Centre or at N D Radha Kishen & Sons, Railway Out Agency, Badshah Chowk, Srinagar (tel 2146). Bus bookings are made at the Tourist Reception Centre (tel 2698), allow plenty of time as the booking system is archaic.

Getting Around
There is a wide choice of transport available either on the lake or out and around it, plus a variety of tours. The tour buses are generally much more comfortable than the usual run of over-crowded local buses and, since many of them offer one-way fares, they can be used for getting out to hill stations in the valley. The best known Kashmiri transport is, of course, the shikara:

Shikaras These are the graceful, long boats which crowd the Srinagar lakes. They're used for getting back and forth from the houseboats or for longer tours. Officially there is a standard fare for every trip around the lake and these are prominently posted at the main landings (ghats); in practice the fares can be quite variable. To be shuttled across to your houseboat should cost Rs 2 in a covered ('full spring seats') shikara but the kids who are always out for a little pocket money will happily paddle you across for 50p or less in a basic, open shikara. Of course late at night, particularly if it is raining, the tables are turned and getting back to your house-boat at a reasonable price may require a little ingenuity! If you hire a shikara by the day or for a longer trip, count on about Rs 7 or Rs 8 per hour.

Try paddling a shikara yourself sometime — it's nowhere near as easy as it looks. You'll spend lots of time going round in circles. If your houseboat hasn't got one to spare some children passing by will find you a boat for Rs 4 or Rs 5 per day.

Taxis & Auto-rickshaws There are stands for these at the Tourist Reception Centre and other strategic locations in town. Srinagar's taxi-wallahs are extremely reluctant to use their meters so you'll have to bargain hard. Count on about Rs 5 for a taxi from the Tourist Reception Centre to Dal Gate (Rs 3 by auto-rickshaw) or Rs 30 to the airport. For longer trips the official fares are all posted by the stands.

Pahalgam	daily	Rs 20 round trip, Rs 10 one way
Daksum	daily	Rs 20 round trip, Rs 10 one way
Gulmarg	daily	Rs 21 round trip, Rs 12.50 one way
Aharbal	Tues, Thur, Sun	Rs 16
Verinag	Wed, Sun	Rs 16
Wular Lake	Mon, Wed, Fri	Rs 16.50
Yusmarg	Tues, Thur, Sun	Rs 13.50 round trip, Rs 7.50 one way
Sonamarg	daily	Rs 18.50 round trip, Rs 10 one way
Moghul Gardens	twice daily	Rs 11

KMDA tours include Pahalgam (Rs 16 round trip, Rs 12 one way), Aharbal (Rs 12), Verinag (Rs 10), Wular Lake (Rs 9.50), Sonamarg (Rs 13) and Moghul Gardens and Shankaracharya Hill (Rs 6).

Bicycles Seeing Srinagar by bicycle is a surprisingly pleasant way of getting around — economical too. You can hire bikes for Rs 4 per day from bicycle shops. There are several along the Boulevard close to Dal Gate. Pleasant trips to be made include:

Round Dal Lake — an all day trip going by the Moghul gardens. It's particularly pleasant around the north of the lake where the villages are still relatively untouched.

Across the lake — you can ride across the lake on the causeway, a nice trip

Buses The Jammu & Kashmir Road Transport Corporation buses go from the Tourist Reception Centre while private buses operate from a variety of stands in Srinagar. Certain major long distance routes are reserved for the J&K buses (Jammu, Leh, etc) but others are open for competition and there will be a great number of buses operating.

Tours The J&K Road Transport Corporation operate a number of daily tours from the Tourist Reception Centre. Private bus companies, particularly KMDA (Kashmir Motor Drivers' Association) also have a number of tours. The J&K RTC tours are:

since there are no problems with vehicle traffic and there is plenty of opportunity to observe the lake life without being in a boat.

Nagin Lake — you can ride out to the Hazratbal Mosque via Nagin Lake and then make a complete loop around the lake on the way back. This trip can easily be combined with a trip along the Jhelum, taking in the various mosques close to the river. The streets here are very narrow so vehicles keep away and bike riding is pleasant.

Things to Buy

Kashmir is famous for its many handicrafts and selling them is an activity pursued with amazing energy. You can visit workshops to see many of them being made. Popular buys include carpets, papier mache articles, leather and furs, wood carvings, shawls and embroidery, honey, tailor made clothing, pleasantly coarse-knitted sweaters and cardigans, that expensive spice saffron and many other items. There are a whole string of Government Handicraft Emporiums scattered around Srinagar but the main one is housed in the fine old British Residency building by the Bund. The flashiest shops are along the Boulevard by Dal Lake. The Bund also has some interesting shops including *Suffering Moses* with high quality goods. Shikaras patrol Dal Lake like sharks, all loaded down with goodies.

KASHMIR VALLEY

When lazing around on your houseboat begins to pall it's time to head off around the valley. There are a number of interesting places in the Kashmir Valley for day trips from Srinagar as well as several popular hill stations which serve as good bases for short or long treks into the surrounding mountains. Pahalgam and Gulmarg are the two main Kashmiri hill resorts.

SRINAGAR-PAHALGAM

The route to Pahalgam passes through a number of interesting places including, if you take the bus tour to Pahalgam, enough Moghul gardens to leave you thoroughly saturated. Only 16 km out of Srinagar is Pampore, centre of Kashmir's saffron industry. Saffron is highly prized for its flavouring and colourful properties and is consequently rather expensive. Sangram, 35 km out, is a centre for production of (would you believe) cricket bats. They're lined up by the road in their thousands.

At Avantipur there are two ruined Hindu temples which were built between 855 and 883 AD. The Avantiswami Temple, the larger of the two, is dedicated to Vishnu and still has some fine relief sculptures and columns of an almost Grecian appearance. The smaller temple to Shiva is about a km before the main temple but also close to the main road. At Anantnag the road forks, the Pahalgam road turning north from here.

Just beyond the Pahalgam turn off is Achabal, a Moghul garden laid out in 1620 by Shah Jahan's daughter Jahanara. This carefully designed garden was said to be a favourite retreat of Nur Jahan. Kokarnag, further on is certain to give you garden overload but is famous for its rose gardens. Back on the Pahalgam route Mattan has a fish filled spring which is an important pilgrimage spot. Above Mattan on a plateau is the huge ruined temple of Martand. Not actually on or even close to the Pahalgam route is Verinag in the extreme south of the Kashmir Valley. The spring here is said to be the actual source of the Jhelum River. Jehangir built an octagonal stone basin at the spring in 1612 and Shah Jahan laid out a garden around it in 1620.

PAHALGAM

About 95 km from Srinagar and at 2130 metres the night time temperatures here are warmer than in Gulmarg which is higher up. The beautiful Lidder River flows right through the town which is at the junction of the Sheshnag and Lidder Rivers and surrounded by soaring, fir covered mountains with snow capped peaks rising behind them. This is an ideal base for short day treks or for the longer treks to the Kolahoi Glacier or the Amarnath Cave — see Kashmir Trekking. Pahalgam is also famous for its many shepherds, they're a common sight, driving their flocks of sheep along the paths all around town.

Information

The rather useless tourist office is just around the corner from the bus halt. Fishing permits have to be obtained in Srinagar but trekking supplies can be bought here.

Pahalgam Walks

Mamaleswara Only a km or so down-stream and on the opposite bank of the Lidder this small Shiva temple with its square, stone tank is thought to date back at least to the 12th century.

Baisaran There are excellent views over the town and the Lidder Valley from this meadow, five km from Pahalgam. A further 11 km takes you to the Tulian Lake at 3353 metres. It is ice covered for much of the year.

Aru The pleasant little village of Aru makes a very interesting day walk, following the Lidder River for 11 km upstream. Unfortunately the main track also takes cars. This is actually the first stage of the Kolahoi Glacier trek.

Places to Stay

There are many hotels along the main street of Pahalgam including the expensive *Pahalgam Hotel* (tel 26) which costs Rs 375 for a double with all meals or the *Woodstock* (tel 27). There is also a *Government Tourist Bungalow* and *Government Tourist Huts* and during the summer season the tourist office operates a number of tent sites with ready set up and furnished tents.

Most budget travellers head across the river to one of the lodges on the other bank. The riverside *Windrush* (not to be confused with another Windrush on the town side) is the most popular. Rooms here vary from as low as Rs 10 in the off-season to Rs 40 or more for a double during the season. The food is fairly good, breakfast, on the verandah overlooking the river, is excellent and there's a superb pot-bellied stove which everyone sits around at night. Plenty of paperbacks in the library too.

Up the hill, a little beyond the Windrush, is the rather cheaper and more basic *Bente's Hotel* while before the Windrush, but also slightly uphill, is the more expensive *Aksa Lodge*. It's rather more luxurious (even hot water) with doubles from Rs 50 to over Rs 100 but not so friendly. The location is superb.

Getting There

Local buses cost Rs 4.50 and take 2½ to four hours, there are six to 10 departures a day. J&K Road Transport have tour buses which cost Rs 10 one way or Rs 20 return. The KMDA tour buses take a long time since they make many stops on the way. Taxis cost over Rs 200 return although you can sometimes find a taxi going back from Pahalgam empty and willing to bargain. If you want to get a return ticket on one of the more comfortable J&K tour buses you have to catch them when they come in around noon in order to get tickets. Get someone from your hotel to do it for you. Ponies can easily be hired in Pahalgam for trekking trips. The fixed costs to popular destinations are all clearly posted.

GULMARG

The large meadow of Gulmarg is 52 km from Srinagar and at 2730 metres. The name means 'meadow of flowers' and in spring it's just that. This is also an excellent trekking base and in winter is also India's premier skiing resort.

Gulmarg Walks

Outer Circular Walk A circular road, 11 km in length, runs right round Gulmarg through pleasant pine forests with excellent views over the Kashmir Valley. Nanga Parbat is visible to the north and Haramukh and Sunset Peak to the south-east.

Khilanmarg This smaller valley is about a six km walk from the Gulmarg bus stop and car park. The meadow, carpeted with flowers in the spring, is the site for Gulmarg's winter ski-runs and offers a fine view of the surrounding peaks and over the Kashmir Valley. During the early spring, as the snow melts, it can be a very muddy hour's climb up the hill.

Alpather Beyond Khilanmarg, 13 km from Gulmarg at the foot of the 4511 metre Apharwat peak, this lake is frozen until mid-June and even later in the year you can see lumps of ice floating in its cold waters. The walk from Gulmarg follows a well graded pony track over the 3810 metre Apharwat Ridge, separating it from Khilanmarg, and then up the valley to the lake at 3843 metres.

Ningle Nallah Flowing from the melting snow and ice on Apharwat and the Alpather Lake, this pretty mountain stream is 10 km from Gulmarg. The stream continues down into the valley below and joins the Jhelum River near Sopore. The walking path crosses the Ningle Nallah by a bridge and continues on to the Lienmarg, another grassy meadow and a good spot for camping.

Ferozpore Nallah Reached from the Tangmarg road, or from the outer circular walk, this mountain stream meets the Bahan River at a popular picnic spot known as 'waters meet'. The stream is reputed to be particularly good for trout fishing; it's about five km from Gulmarg. You can continue on from here to Tosamaidan, a three day, 50 km walk to one of Kashmir's most beautiful margs.

Ziarat of Baba Reshi This Moslem shrine is on the slopes below Gulmarg and can be reached from either Gulmarg or Tangmarg. The Ziarat, or tomb, is of a well known Moslem saint who died here in 1480. Before renouncing worldly ways he was a courtier of the Kashmir king Zain-ul-Abidin.

Places to Stay

Gulmarg has a couple of up-market hotels and a number at the other end of the scale. *Nedou's* (tel 28) is open only from May to October and costs from Rs 250 for a double, room only. *Hotel Highland Park* (tel 30 & 34) is a bit more expensive but even if you're a shoestring traveller it's worth a visit for a cup of tea or coffee in the beautiful gardens (or even a beer in a crested silver tankard!). It's a rather fine establishment.

The cheaper hotels include the *City View* and *Mount View* at around Rs 20 a double — OK but spartan, you really need a fire in the spring or autumn and wood is extra. It's worth remembering how much colder Gulmarg is than Srinagar. The *New Punjabi Hotel*, opposite the Gundwara, is also very cheap. *Kingsley's* (tel 55) is a big, rambling old place with doubles from around Rs 100. It also has a fairly good, but slightly pricey, restaurant.

Getting There

There are a variety of buses running from Srinagar to Gulmarg, many of them on day tours. On a day tour you have only a few hours at the hill resort, just long enough for one of the shorter day walks. The de-luxe tour buses cost Rs 21 return or Rs 11 one-way and leave at 9 am from the Tourist Reception Centre. Ordinary buses leave hourly and cost Rs 10 return or Rs 6 one-way. Until recently the road from Srinagar only ran as far as Tangmarg, seven km distance or 500 metres altitude below Gulmarg. The last stretch then had to be completed on foot or by pony. A road has now been completed over the last stretch although there are still buses operating that terminate at Tangmarg. The winding road from Tangmarg is 13 km in length, nearly twice as far as the more direct pony track. A riding pony costs Rs 12 from Tangmarg up to Gulmarg. Ponies, either riding or pack ponies, can also be hired from Gulmarg to other sites around the valley. Khilanmarg, for example, costs Rs 20 return. Other rates are prominently posted at the car park.

SOUTH OF SRINAGAR

Interesting places in the south-west of the valley include Yusmarg, which is reputed to have the best spring flowers in Kashmir and is a good base for treks further afield. Chari Sharif is on the road to Yusmarg and has the shrine or Ziarat of Kashmir's patron saint. Aharbal was a popular resting place for the Moghul emperors when they made the long trip north from Delhi.

SINDH VALLEY

This is a scenic area north of Srinagar through which the road to Ladakh passes. The Zoji La pass marks the boundary from the Sindh Valley into Ladakh. From Srinagar you pass the Dachigam wildlife reserve, once a royal game park. Anchar Lake is close to Srinagar but rarely visited and has a wide variety of water birds. There is a Moghul garden built by Nur Jahan at Manasbal Lake. The Wular Lake is possibly the largest freshwater lake in Asia and the Jhelum River flows into it. Sonamarg, at 2740 metres, is the last major point in Kashmir and an excellent base for trekking. Its name means 'Meadow of Gold', which could derive from the spring flowers or from the strategic trading position it once enjoyed. There are Tourist Huts, a Rest House and some small hotels here. The tiny village of Baltal is the last place in Kashmir, right at the foot of the Zoji La. In June only you can walk to the Amarnath Cave from here. Prior to that the snow is too deep, after that the slush is too deep! The Zoji La is the watershed between Kashmir and Ladakh — on one side you have the green, lush scenery of Kashmir while on the other side everything is barren and dry.

TREKS IN KASHMIR

There are a variety of treks both within Kashmir and from Kashmir to Ladakh or Zanskar. The short Pahalgam-Kolahoi Glacier trek is particularly popular and

A   Taj Mahal, Agra at sunset (UP)
B   bathing ghats on the Ganges at Varanasi (UP)

the Pahalgam-Amarnath Cave trek is popular not only for the natural scenery but for the great religious festival that takes place here. Porters are not used in Kashmir anywhere near as much as in Nepal. Instead ponies are used to carry the gear.

Pahalgam-Kolahoi Glacier

This short trek takes only four days Pahalgam to Pahalgam but it can be extended before returning to Pahalgam or continued up into the Sindh Valley. The first day from Pahalgam takes you to Aru along the bank of the Lidder River. This is also a very popular day trek from Pahalgam since Aru is a pretty little village. The second day's walk takes you to Lidderwat where there is a very pleasant campsite where the stream from the glacier meets the stream from the Tarsar Lake. On the third day you trek up to the lake and back to Lidderwat. The glacier, climbing from 3400 metres up to 4000 metres descends from the 5485 metre Kolahoi mountain. On day 4 you can either walk straight back to Pahalgam in one day or the trek can be extended another day by walking Lidderwat-Tarsar Lake-Lidderwat.

Instead of returning to Pahalgam three days further trek will take you to Kulan near Sonamarg in the Sindh Valley. It's only 16 km from Kulan to Sonamarg which you can walk or travel by bus.

| Day 1 | Pahalgam-Aru | 12 km |
| Day 2 | Aru-Lidderwat | 12 km |

Day 3	Lidderwat-glacier-Lidderwat	13 km
Day 4	Lidderwat-Pahalgam	24 km
or		
Day 4	Lidderwat-Sekiwas	10 km
Day 5	Sekiwas-Khemsar	11 km
Day 6	Khemsar-Kulan	10 km

Pahalgam-Amarnath Cave

At the full moon in the month of July-August thousands of Hindu pilgrims make the 'yatra' to the Shri Amarnath Cave where a natural ice lingam, the symbol of Lord Shiva, appears. Although at the time of the yatra it's less a trek than a long queue the spirit of this immense pilgrimage is quite amazing. Unfortunately, for the pilgrims, the ice lingam does not always appear and some unlucky pilgrims make the trek for nothing. The first day's walk out of Pahalgam is jeepable and from Amarnath it is possible to continue north to Baltal, near Srinagar although that is quite a hard trek.

Day 1	Pahalgam-Chandanwari	13 km
Day 2	Chandanwari-Sheshnag	12 km
Day 3	Sheshnag-Panchtarni	11 km
Day 4	Panchtarni-Amarnath	8 km

Sonamarg-Wangat

This 81 km trek takes five days and reaches a maximum altitude of 4191 metres. It starts from Sonamarg, reached by bus from Srinagar, then climbs to Nichinai, crosses a mountain chain and drops down to the pleasant campsite at Krishansar. Another pass has to be crossed on the third and fourth day when you reach the Gangabal Lake. From here it's a steep descent

A	Howrah bridge in Calcutta (WB)
B	Burmese pagoda in Eden Gardens, Calcutta (WB)
C	young monks in Darjeeling (WB)

Kashmir Valley

trail
road
river

to Wangat from where you can easily bus back to Srinagar.

Day 1	Sonamarg-Nichinai	15 km
Day 2	Nichinai-Krishansar	13 km
Day 3	Krishansar-Dubta Pani	17 km
Day 4	Dubta Pani-Gangabal Lake	17 km
Day 5	Gangabal Lake-Wangat	19 km

Gangabal Trek

This trek also goes to Gangabal but approaches it from the other side. The trek commences from Erin, north of Wular Lake and takes five days in all. On the fourth day you need ropes and ice-axes to cross the glacier between the Kundsar and Gangabal Lake. The final day's trek also ends at Wangat. At Narannag, just before Wangat, there is an interesting old temple.

Day 1	Erin-Chuntimula-Poshpathri	11 km
Day 2	Poshpathri-Sarbal	11 km
Day 3	Sarbal-Kundsar Lake	9 km
Day 4	Kundsar Lake-Gangabal Lake	11 km
Day 5	Gangabal-Wangat	19 km

Konsarnag Trek

This short trek in the south of the Kashmir valley ascends into the Pir Panjal mountains. The first day's trek is a short walk only taking about three hours. With an early start from Srinagar you can bus to Ahrabal and complete the first walk in the same day. The Konsarnag Lake is a beautiful deep blue stretch of water at 3700 metres.

| Day 1 | Ahrabal-Kungwattan | 9 km |
| Day 2 | Kungwattan-Mahinag | |

| Day 3 | Mahinag-Konsarnag-Kungwattan | |
| Day 4 | Kungwattan-Ahrabal | |

Daksum-Kishtwar

Starting from the south of the Kashmir valley at Daksum this trek is an interesting route to Jammu although you can also trek from Kishtwar into the Zanskar Valley or to Himachal Pradesh. Daksum is 100 km from Srinagar and takes about three hours by road. The maximum altitude is reached on the first day's trek to the Sinthan pass. On the last day it is only a short walk to Dadpath from where buses depart at 10 am and 4 pm to Kishtwar.

Day 1	Daksum-Sinthan Pass	16 km
Day 2	Sinthan Pass-Chatru	8 km
Day 3	Chatru-Mughal Maidan	9 km
Day 4	Mughal Maidan-Dadpath	8 km

Pahalgam-Pannikar

This is quite a hard trek into the Suru Valley which leads to Zanskar. The first two days of the trek follow the Amarnath Cave route. The following days cross the Gulol Gali pass then climb up to the Lonvilad Gali, over the Chalong Glacier and down to Pannikar. From Pannikar you can take the road north to Kargil or east into the Zanskar Valley.

Day 1 & 2	— As Amarnath Cave	
Day 3	Sheshnag-Rangmarg	8 km
Day 4	Rangmarg-Hampet	6 km
Day 5 & 6	— Hampet-Lonvilad Gali	22 km
Day 7	Lonvilad Gali	
Day 8	Chalong Glacier-Pannikar	15 km

LADAKH

'Little Tibet', 'the moonland' and 'the last Shangri La' are all names that have been applied to Ladakh and all with a bit of truth. Ladakh is a miniature version of Tibet — it is situated geographically in Tibet which is a high altitude plateau north of the Himalayas. The people are Tibetan in their culture and religion and there are also many Tibetan refugees. The Himalayas are a very effective barrier to rain — few clouds creep across their awesome height and as a result Ladakh is barren beyond belief. Only where rivers, running from far-away glaciers or melting snow, carry water to habitation do you find plant life — hence the moonland label since Ladakh is as dry as the Sahara. Finally Ladakh could well be a last Shangri La. Only in the mid-70s was it opened to outside visitors. Its strategic isolation is matched by its physical isolation — only from June to September is the road into Ladakh from Kashmir not covered by snow and only since 1979 has there been an airline flight into Ladakh and that flight is one of the most spectacular in the world. If you're in Kashmir don't fail to make the trip to Ladakh. It's an other-wordly place — strange gompas perched on soaring hilltops, shattered looking landscapes splashed with small but brilliant patches of green, ancient palaces clinging to sheer rock walls. But most of all there are the delightful Ladakhis — friendly as only Tibetan people can be and immensely colourful.

General Advice

A sleeping bag is very useful in Ladakh even if you're not trekking or camping. The nights can get very cold and visiting many of the gompas by public transport will require an overnight stop. Be prepared for dramatic temperature changes and for the extreme burning power of the sun in Ladakh's thin air (Leh is at 3500 metres). A cloud across the sun will change the air temperature

from T-shirt to sweater level in seconds. Without a hat and/or sunscreen you'll have sunburn and a peeling nose in hours. Acclimatise to Ladakh's altitude slowly — don't go scrambling up mountainsides as soon as you arrive. A spell in Kashmir is good half-way acclimatisation but people who fly straight from Delhi to Ladakh may feel very uncomfortable for a few days. Note that outside Leh it is not easy to change money and that in the tourist season there is often a severe shortage of small change. One very important word to learn for Ladakh is the all purpose and frequently used greeting 'jullay'. Finally remember that this is a sensitive border region disputed by India, Pakistan and China. You are not allowed more than a mile north of the Srinagar-Leh road.

Religion

At Kargil, on the Srinagar-Leh road, the Islamic influence dies out and you are in a Buddhist region. They follow the Tibetan Tantric Buddhism with much emphasis on magic and demons. All around Ladakh are gompas, the Bud-

to Gulmarg

to Jammu

to Zan
Valle

Gandarbal (19)

Srinagar

Kangan (38)

Sumbal (54)

Sonamarg (84)

Baltal (97)

Zoji La (110)

Machoi (113)

Drass (147)

Kharbu (180)

Kargil (20

dhist monasteries where the religion is carried on. They're fascinating places to visit although they have become very commercially minded since Ladakh's tourist boom commenced. There's a good side to this though, prior to tourists the gompas were gradually becoming more and more run down and neglected. Today many of them are being refurbished and repaired with the profits from visiting westerners! The monks are quite happy to have visitors wander around the gompas, sit in on ceremonies, try the appalling taste of butter tea (bring your own cup) and take photographs.

SRINAGAR-LEH

It's 434 km from the Vale of Kashmir to Ladakh and the road is surfaced most of the way. It follows the Indus River for much of the distance. Buses run along this road daily during the summer season (see Getting There) and take two days with an overnight stop at Kargil. Sonamarg is the last major place in Kashmir, shortly after Sonamarg you climb up over the Zoji La Pass (3529 metres) and enter the Ladakh region.

Zoji La

This is one of the few unsurfaced stretches on the route and it is also the first pass to snow over in the winter and the last pass to be cleared in the summer. It is not, however, the highest pass along the route. The other passes get less snow because they are across the Himalayas and in the mountain rain shadow.

Drass

This is the first village after the pass and the place from where road crews work to clear the road up to the pass for the start of the summer season. In winter Drass is noted for its heavy snowfalls and extreme cold.

Kargil

This was once an important trading post but now it is simply an overnight halt on the way to Leh or the point where you turn south for the Zanskar valley. The people of Kargil are chiefly Moslem and noted for their extreme orthodoxy. Already you are in a region where irrigation is vitally important.

Mulbekh (244) [Namika La (259) Bodh Kharbu (274) Fatu La (295) Lamayuru (310) Khalsi (337) Nurla (348) Saspul (372) Nimmu (398) Spitok (421) Leh (434)

Srinagar-Leh
km from Srinagar

to Manali

Places to Stay *Hotel D'Zojila* is 2.5 km from the town and has doubles from around Rs 75. *Suru View*, behind the bus station, is cheaper at around Rs 40. Cheaper hotels include the reasonable *Argalia* which costs Rs 15 a double but is uncomfortably close to the town's diesel generator, fortunately it shuts down at 10 pm. The similarly priced *Yak Tail* is rather dirty. Along the Srinagar-Leh route there are also *Rest Houses* at Drass, Bodh Kharbu and Mulbekh.

Shergol

Between Kargil and Shergol you cross the dividing line between the Moslem and Buddhist areas. The small village of Shergol has a tiny gompa perched half-way up the eastern slope of the mountain.

Mulbekh

There are two gompas on the hillside above the village of Mulbekh. As in other villages it is wise to enquire if the gompa is open before making the ascent. If not somebody from the village may have keys and will accompany you to the gompas. Just beyond Mulbekh is a huge Chamba statue, an image of a future Buddha, cut into the rock face beside the road. It's one of the most interesting stops along the road to Leh. Those with time to spare can make a short trek from Mulbekh to the village of Gel.

Lamayuru

From Mulbekh the road crosses the 3718 metre Namika La, passes through the large military encampment of Bodh Kharbu and then crosses the 4094 metre Fatu La, the highest pass on the route. Lamayuru is the first of the typical Ladakhi gompas perched on a hilltop with its village at the foot of the hill. In its heyday the gompa had five buildings and as many as 400 monks but today there is only one, tended by 20 or 30 monks.

Rizong

On beyond Khalsi, and a few km of the road, is the nunnery of Julichen and the monastery of Rizong. If you stay here overnight men must stay in the monastery, women in the nunnery.

Alchi

Just before Saspul this gompa is unusual in that it is built on lowland, not perched on a hilltop. It is noted for its massive Buddha statues and lavish woodcarvings and artwork. There are many chortens around the village.

Lekir & Basgo

Shortly after Saspul a steep road turns off to the Lekir Gompa which also has a monastery school. Closer to Leh there is a badly damaged fort at Basgo. Basgo Gompa has interesting Buddha figures but its wall paintings have suffered much water damage.

LEH (population 8500)

Centuries ago this was an important stop on the old caravan silk route from China. Today it's merely a military base and tourist centre but wandering the winding back streets of town is still fascinating. It's situated about 10 km north-east of the Indus in a fertile side valley.

Information & Orientation

Leh is small enough to make finding your way round very easy. There's one main street with the Leh Palace rising up right at the end of it. The bus station and jeep halt is on the airport side of the town. The airport, with it's steeply sloping runway, is several km out of town near the Spitok Gompa. The Tourist Office is in the Dak Bungalow and Indian Airlines is right next door.

Leh Palace

Looking for all the world like a mini-version of the Potala in Lhasa, Tibet, the palace was also built in the 16th century. It is now deserted and badly damaged, a legacy of Ladakh's wars with Kashmir in the last century, the main reason for making the climb up to the palace is for the superb views from the roof. The Zanskar mountains, across the Indus River, look close enough to touch. The palace is still the property of the Ladakhi royal family although they now reside at nearby Stok. It's open 6 to 9 am and after 5 pm.

Leh Gompa

High above the palace and also over-looking the ruins of the older palace the Red Gompa was built in 1430. It contains a fine three-storey high seated Buddha image. It's open 7 to 9 am and 5 to 7 pm. The gompa above is in a very ruined condition but the views down on Leh are superb.

Sankar Gompa

It's an easy stroll to the Sankar Gompa, a couple of km up the valley from the town centre. This interesting little gompa is only open from 6 to 8 am and 6 to 7 pm but it has electric lighting so an evening visit is worthwhile. Upstairs there is an impressive representation of Avalokitesvara complete with 1000 arms and 1000 heads.

Places to Stay

There are an amazing number of hotels and guest houses in Ladakh, many of which only open during the tourist season. Prices are very variable — soaring in the peak season, plummeting at other times. The cheaper guest houses are generally just rooms rented out in private homes.

Leh's top bracket hotels generally quote rates inclusive of all meals — frankly Leh is rather short of restaurants. They include. the *Shambala Hotel*, recently taken over by the Oberoi chain and some distance out of town, the *Kang-Lha-Chhen* and the *Lha-Ri-Mo*. Singles/doubles range up from Rs 250/300.

In the middle category the *Khangri Hotel* is close to the Tourist Office and uncomfortably close to the diesel electricity generator for Leh — which fortunately shuts down at 11 pm. Doubles are Rs 70 to 100, as at the side-by-side *Glacier View* and *Karakorum*, both of which have pleasant gardens, an attraction shared by many of Leh's hotels. The *Hotel Yak Tail* is in this same category. Moving down to Rs 40-50 for a double the *Dreamland* is very popular and close to the centre.

Down in the rock bottom bracket doubles can be found under Rs 30 (less off-season) and dorm beds at Rs 5. Bed bugs are sometimes provided at no extra cost so take care. The *Palace View Kidar Hotel*, close to the polo ground is a very popular rock bottom choice as is the *Antelope Guest House* on the main street. Others include the *Old Ladakh Guest House* or the *Moonland Guest House*. There are many, many cheapies.

Places to Eat

Dreamland Restaurant, near the Tourist Office, Indian Airlines office and Dreamland Hotel is the best in town. Clean, friendly and reasonably priced — most dishes at Rs 5 to 10. Tibetan kothay, various chow meins and other noodle dishes top the bill (a pleasant change from rice and more rice). Nice jasmine tea too. The *Khangri Restaurant*, almost next door, is good but neither as good or as cheap. The *New Gaytime* (great name) is new and seems reasonably

Leh

good. Good tea, not so good snacks at the *Mini Cafe* by Indian Airlines. Some of the other small cafes around town are remarkably insanitary looking — a sure ticket to stomach troubles. For breakfast buy freshly baked central Asian style bread from the little bakeries in the back streets by the mosque. Ideal with honey from Srinagar.

Try the locally made beer, chang, while you're in Ladakh and at least sample the butter tea. The variety of locally grown vegetables and fruit in Leh is limited. It's worth bringing a few menu brighteners, like bars of chocolate or cans of apple juice, from Srinagar.

Getting There

Air Indian Airlines only started flying to Leh in 1979 and has two flights a week costing Rs 393. The flight is very short (only half an hour) and extremely spectacular (you cross right over the Himalayas) but also very problematic. Flights can only be made into Leh in the morning and only when weather conditions are good. If it's possible the conditions could deteriorate after arrival and the aircraft could not leave, the flight will be cancelled. End result is a lot of cancellations, a lot of flights that actually leave Srinagar but are not able to land at Leh (since conditions can change very rapidly) and a lot of frustrated passengers. At difficult times of year such as when the season is about

to start but the road is still closed the flights can be heavily overbooked. The answer is to book well ahead but be prepared for disappointment. If you're unable to get on a flight from Srinagar ask your houseboat owner for help — every Kashmiri has 'connections'.

Road The road should be open from the beginning of June through to October but in practise the opening date can be variable — sometimes mid-May, sometimes mid-June. The trip takes two days, leaving at 7.30 am each morning and arriving at 5 pm each evening. The overnight halt is made at Kargil. There are A class buses for Rs 52 and B class buses for Rs 36. Jeeps, which take up to six passengers, will cost something like Rs 1500 but will permit additional stops and diversions along the interesting route. Before the road officially opens it is possible to cross the Zoji La on foot or by pony although if there is still a lot of snow the Beacon Patrol will only let you through if you're properly equipped. The pass is generally physically cleared of snow before the road is repaired and ready for vehicles and there is generally transport running along the roads on both sides of the pass before the through buses start to operate. Locals cross the pass regularly on foot in these pre-season times so it is easy to tag along with a larger group or find a guide. But it can

1	Police	13	Palace View Guest House
2	State Bank	14	Dreamland Hotel & Restaurant
3	Hotel Glacier View	15	Hotel Khangir & Restaurant
4	Hotel Karakoram	16	Indian Airlines
5	Hotel Shangrila	17	Apsara Guest House
6	Himalayan Hotel	18	Moonland Guest House
7	Khan Lodge	19	New Gay Time Restaurant
8	Hotel Khar Dungla	20	Barmar Restaurant
9	Ali Shah's Postcards	21	Palace View (Kidar) Hotel
10	Hilltop & Mumtaz Restaurants	22	Tibet Hotel
11	Antelope Guest House	23	Leh Motel
12	Hotel La Ri Mo		

be hard work!

Getting Around

There's a bus service to Leh airport from the Indian Airlines office for Rs 2. A jeep would cost Rs 25. There is a resasonably extensive bus network around Leh although the buses are decidedly ramshackle. Jeeps can also be hired — count on around Rs 3 or 4 per km or Rs 250 to 300 for a day. Between a half dozen people this can be a reasonable way of getting to most of the gompas around Leh.

Some bus costs from Leh include: *Kargil* — Rs 20 to 22, daily in summer, Sunday and Thursday in winter. *Choglamsar & Bridge* — 70p, fairly frequently each day. *Hemis* — Rs 6.50, departs 10 or 11 am from Leh, the bus goes to Sakti but you have to hop off at Karu and cross the Karu bridge, and walk six km up to the gompa. The bus returns from Sakti at 2 or 2.30 pm in the afternoon so you can't get to Hemis and back by bus on the same day. *Spitok* — 70p, twice daily. *Shey* — Rs 1.15, three times daily. The bus continues on to *Tikse* (Rs 1.50 from Leh)

which is only a couple of km further out, you could easily bus to Shey, walk on to Tikse then bus back to Leh — or vice versa. Note that Shey Gompa is only open (officially) from 7 to 9 am. *Stok* — twice daily. *Phyang* (Fiang) — Rs 2.75, daily. *Khalsi* — Rs 7, alternate days. *Matho* — Rs 2.55, daily. *Chochot* (other bank of the Indus, between Stok and Stakna) — Rs 2 daily.

Things to Buy

After a number of greedy tourists spirited important antiquities out of Ladakh the government sensibly clamped down on the sale of important older items. You must be able to prove anything you buy is less than 100 years old. Baggage is checked on departure from Leh airport. Things you might buy include chang and tea vessels, cups and butter churns, knitted carpets with Tibetan motifs, Tibetan jewellery or, for just a few rupees, a simple prayerflag. Prices in Ladakh are generally quite high — you might find exactly the same Tibetan inspired item on sale at far lower prices in Kashmir, Dharamsala or Nepal.

AROUND LEH

Spitok Gompa

On a hilltop above the Indus and beside the end of the airport runway, the Spitok Gompa is 10 km from Leh. The temple (Gonkhang) is about a thousand years old and there are fine views over the Indus from the gompa. Entry fee to the gompa is Rs 10.

Phyang

About 16 km from Leh, on the road back towards Srinagar, the gompa has 50 monks and entry fee is Rs 10. There is an interesting little village below the gompa.

Beacon Highway

You are not allowed to visit the Nubra

Valley without special permission but if you could it would involve taking what is probably the highest road in the world. It crosses a pass at 5606 metres! The road is only open in September and October — it takes the whole summer for the snow and ice to melt for that brief time.

Choglamsar

The Tibetan refugee camp here has become an important centre for the study of Tibetan literature and history and Buddhist philosophy. Don't indulge the kids who demand 'bon-bons' — it turns them into beggars. Near here a bridge crosses the Indus to Stok and a rougher road along the other bank of the river to Hemis.

Indus Valley near Leh

to Changtang
Upshi
7.5 km
Hemis Gompa
Karu
18 km
Matho
5.5 km
Stagna
Tuchik
Indus
Nang
RANGE
Tikse
Stagmo
9 km
5 km
Shey
7 km from the Leh-Hemis Road
Shushot
5 km
Stok
Sabu
2 km
1 km
Palam
Choglamsar Tibetan Refugee Camp
ZANSKAR
9 km
the Khardungla-Pass 5602, 45 km into the Nubra Valley, is 100 km
8 km
Sankar, Leh
Pharka (Dakum Khochey)
to Phyang (17 km) & Srinigar
Spitok
to Skiu, Padum (Markha Trek)

Shey

This was the old summer palace of the kings of Ladakh and was built about 550 years ago. It's now in ruins but the palace gompa has a 12 metre high seated Buddha image. Entry fee is Rs 5 and the gompa is open 7 to 9 am and 5 to 6 pm, at other times ask for the monk Tashi in the village below, he will know where to find the key.

Tikse Gompa

The Tikse Gompa is visible from Shey and is about 17 km from Leh. Its new found tourist wealth is being put to good use in extensive restoration work. The monastery is very picturesque and superbly sited on a hilltop overlooking the village and the Indus. Beside the car park is the small Zan-La temple. The gompa has an important collection of Tibetan style books in its library and some excellent artwork. This is an excellent gompa to watch the religious ceremonies either around 6.30 am or noon. They are preceded by long mournful sounds from the horns on the roof. Entry fee is Rs 10.

Hemis Gompa

One of the largest and most important gompas in Ladakh, Hemis is 45 km from Leh on the other side of the Indus. It's quite easy to get there by car or jeep but on public transport you will have to spend the night at the monastery as it is not possible to bus out there, walk the six km up from the river to the gompa, see it, walk back down and get back in one day. The Hemis Gompa is famous for its Hemis Festival which usually falls in the second half of June or in early July. It is not only one of the largest and most spectacular of the gompa festivals it is also virtually the only one which takes place in the summer tourist season. It is possible the business minded monks of other gompas may switch their festivals to more lucrative dates however. The festival takes two days and features elaborate mask dances and crowds of eager spectators. The gompa has an excellent library, particularly well preserved wall paintings and good Buddha figures. If instead of turning right at Karu to climb up to Hemis you had turned left you would have reached the Chemre Gompa, five km off the road and the Trak Tok Gompa, 10 km further on. Both lie in the restricted zone but tourists are allowed to visit these two gompas.

Matho Gompa

The left bank road on the Indus is not in as good condition as the more used right bank road but you can return from Hemis on this road and there are several interesting places to visit. Matho is five km from Stagna, in a side valley. There is an important festival held here where

the monks are possessed by spirits and go into a trance. Stagna, on the road, has a gompa too.

Stok Palace

Close to the Choglamsar bridge a road turns off the left bank road to the palace of Stok. The last king of Ladakh died in 1974 but his widow, the Rani of Stok, still lives in this 200 year old palace. It is expected that her eldest son will become king when he reaches an appropriately auspicious age.

Pharka Gompa

This small cave gompa is almost directly opposite the Spitok Gompa on the Stok side of the Indus. You can reach it by crossing the Choglamsar bridge but the last kms must be made on foot.

ZANSKAR

The long narrow Zanskar valley is even more recently opened than Ladakh. A jeep road is gradually being extended down the valley from Kargil towards Padum, the capital, and this will eventually open Zanskar up to more outside influence. Meanwhile it remains an area for trekkers and some of the treks are definitely hard going. You can make a number of interesting treks either down the valley or out of it to Ladakh, Kashmir or to Himachal Pradesh.

Padum

The 'capital' of Zanskar has a population of less than a thousand of whom about 300 are Sunnite Moslems. There are a few shops in Padum and a tourist office! There are a number of interesting shorter treks that can be made from Padum. Accommodation in Padum can usually be arranged in private houses for Rs 10 to Rs 20 per person.

Zangla & Karsha Gompa

This is an interesting four day trek around Padum. The first day takes you to Thonde on the riverbank with a monastery high above it. Since horses cannot cross the rope bridge from Padum this is the first place on this side of the river where they can be hired for treks further afield to places like Lamayuru. The second day takes you from Thonde to Zangla where the king of Zanskar has his castle. On day three you back track towards Thonde, cross the river and continue to Karsha, the most important gompa in Zanskar. On the final day you can cross the river directly by ferry or continue down to the wooden Tungri Bridge and double back to Padum.

Tugri & Zongkhul Gompa

This four day trek around Padum takes you to the Sani and Zonkhul Gompas by following the route up towards the Muni La then cutting across to the base of the Umasi La.

TREKKING IN LADAKH & ZANSKAR

Trekking in Ladakh and Zanskar can be hard going and you should be equipped for every eventuality. Srinagar is the best place to purchase stores but you will not find trekking gear like you do in Kathmandu in Nepal. Treks into Zanskar are principally down the valley from the north (from Kargil) or up the valley from the south (from Manali in Himachal Pradesh).

Drass-Sanku

This is a short three day trek into the Suru Valley joining the Kargil-Padum road at Sanku. It's simply an alternative route to the road down from Kargil.

Kargil-Padum

The seven day trek to Padum from Kargil on the Srinagar-Ladakh road can be shortened by four days if you can get a ride all the way from Kargil to the Pensi La. When the bridges are completed the route will be open from early June to late-October. The first day's travel is mainly on a surfaced road by bus as far as Sanku. Beyond Parkutse you pass close to Kun and Nun. The Rangdum Gompa is the first gompa reached in Zanskar, the road is still reasonably good to this point. Beyond the gompa you have to cross the 4401 metre Pensi La into Zanskar proper. On the last day's walk from Phe to Padum you cross the river and pass by the Sani Gompa, one of the most important in Zanskar.

Day 1	Kargil-Namsuru
Day 2	Namsuru-Pannikar-Parkutse
Day 3	Parkutse-Parkachik-Yuldo-Rangdum Gompa
Day 4	Rangdum Gompa-Pensi La
Day 5	Pensi La-Abran
Day 6	Abran-Phe
Day 7	Phe-Padum

Manali-Padum

This 10 day trek can be very hard going at its southern end. You first have to bus across the Rothang Pass from Manali to Keylong and on to Darcha where the trek starts. On the second day you cross the Baralacha La, a double pass where even the lower side is higher than Europe's highest mountain and twice the height of Australia's highest! At the end of Day 6 you can continue north to Padum or turn back south and cross the Shingo La back to Darcha in two days. You are not, however, allowed to take the alternative route if you're heading north. On Day 7 you make a detour to the spectacular Phuctal Gompa. Continuing all the way north to Kargil on this route would take, with a few days for shorter treks around Padum, something like 20 days.

Day 1	Darcha-Mane Bar
Day 2	Mane Bar-Sarai Kilang
Day 3	Sarai Kilang-Debni
Day 4	Debni-Chumik Marpo
Day 5	Chumik Marpo-Shingsan
Day 6	Shingsan-Kargiakh
Day 7	Purni-Phuctal Gompa
Day 8	Phuctal Gompa-Katge Lato
Day 9	Katge Lato-Reru
Day 10	Reru-Padum

Padum-Lamayuru

There are a number of alternatives for this trek from Padum into Ladakh, intersecting the road at Lamayuru, about half way from Kargil to Leh. The trek starts out from Padum to Thonde, as on the short trek to the Zangla and Karsha gompas. On Day 3 the difficult ascent to the 4500 metre Shingo La pass has to be made but on Day 4 the Nerag La, at 4900 metres, is even more difficult and a local guide is a necessity. Photosar is a small village from where it is only two days' walk to Lamayuru. There is an alternative route, taking a day longer, from Photosar. The alternative route from Padum starts out on the opposite side of the Zanskar River and takes you to the Lingshot

Gompa before joining up with the first route at Day 5.

Day 1	Padum-Thonde
Day 2	Thonde-Honia
Day 3	Honia-Shingo La-Kharmapu
Day 4	Kharmapu-Nerag La
Day 5	Nerag La-Nerag
Day 6	Nerag-Yulching-Singi La-Photosar
Day 7	Photosar-Shirshi La-Hanupatta
Day 8	Hanupatta-Wanla-Shilla-Prikiti La-Lamayuru

or

Day 1	Padum-Pishu
Day 2-4	Pishu-Lingshot Gompa
Day 5	Lingshot Gompa-Yulching

Padum-Kishtwar

This trek into the southern part of Kashmir is not especially difficult although it crosses the 5234 metre Umasi La, which can only be done in fine weather. You cannot use horses on this route but must take porters. On the second day you reach the Zongkhul Gompa which can also be visited on a short trek from Padum. Day 3 is a long climb and long descent over the snow covered Umasi La. On Day 4 your Zanskari porters will not continue further and you must hire local porters or a pony. The last few days are hard

work with many ascents and descents but the road from Kishtwar, already extending to Galar, is gradually being lengthened.

Day 1	Padum-Ating
Day 2	Ating-Ratrat
Day 3	Ratrat-Umasi La-Bhuswas
Day 4	Bhuswar-Matsel
Day 5	Matsel-Atholi
Day 6	Atholi-Shasho
Day 7	Shasho-Galar-Kishtwar

Other Treks

Padum-Nimmu follows the Padum-Lamayuru route for most of its length then turns off eastwards to join the Srinagar-Leh road at Nimmu. Padum-Leh by the Markha Valley is a hard but rewarding trek which goes via Zangla before turning east over the Charcha La and the Ruberung La to the Markha Gompa and eventually reaching Hemis near Leh. This trek can only be made in late-August. Earlier than that the rivers which must be crossed are too high from melting snow and after that it is too cold. You can trek from Padum to the Phuctal Gompa by an alternative route to that described in Padum-Manali but the trail is poor and very little used.

Uttar Pradesh

Population: 98 million
Area: 294,413 square km
Capital: Lucknow
Main language: Hindi

In terms of population this is the largest state in India. In terms of variety, and of problems, it's also India larger than life. This is one of the great historical and religious centres of India. The Ganges River, which forms the backbone of Uttar Pradesh, is the holy river of Hinduism and there are a number of towns along the river of great importance for pilgrimages — in particular Rishikesh and Hardwar where the river emerges from the Himalayas and starts across the plains, and Varanasi, the most holy city of all. Buddhism also has its great shrine in the state for it was at Sarnath, just outside Varanasi, that the Buddha first preached his message of the middle way.

Historically the state has also been a centre stage for great events. Over two thousand years ago this was a part of Ashoka's great Buddhist empire. More recently it was part of the Moghul Empire and for some years Agra was its capital. Today, of course, Agra is famed for that most perfect of Moghul master-pieces, the Taj Mahal. More recently still it was in Uttar Pradesh that the Mutiny broke out in 1857 (at Meerut) and some of its most dramatic (Lucknow) and unfortunate (Kanpur) events took place here.

Geographically and socially the state also has great variations. Most of it consists of the great Ganges plain, an area of awesome flatness which suffers great floods during every monsoon. The people of this region are predominantly backward farming peasants who scratch a bare existence from the overcrowded land. Yet the north-west corner of the state is a part of the soaring Himalayas with excellent treks, beautiful scenery and even India's highest mountain. It's a state of strong contrasts.

MATHURA (population 150,000)

On the Delhi-Agra road, 57 km north of Agra, Mathura is a site of great age. According to legend this is the place where Lord Krishna was born 3500 years ago. Today Mathura is an important pilgrimage place for followers of this popular incarnation of Vishnu. There are many places in and around Mathura with connections with the Krishna legend.

Mathura, or Muttra as it has also been known, is mentioned by Ptolemy and by the Chinese visitors Fa Hian (in India 401-410 AD) and by the later Hiuen Tsang (634 AD). By that time the 20 Buddhist monasteries with 3000 monks, for this was a great Buddhist centre, had dropped to only 2000. By the time Mahmud of Ghazni arrived on his rape, burn, pillage trip from Afghanistan in 1017 Buddhism had totally disappeared. Sikandar Lodi did further damage to the shrines of Mathura in 1500 but the town rebounded during the tolerant reigns of Akbar and Jehangir, only for fanatical Aurangzeb to do another demolition job. He destroyed the Kesava Deo temple, which had been built on the site of one of the most important Buddhist monasteries, and built a mosque in its place.

Things to See

The Jami Masjid was built by Aurangzeb's governor, Abd-in-Nabir Khan, in 1661 on the site of the Kesava Deo temple. This is the place where Lord Krishna is supposed to have been born in prison. At one time the foundations of the old temple were still visible behind the mosque but they have now been covered over with modern buildings. The modern Kesava temple has been rebuilt behind the Katra. The 300 metre wide Yamuna River, which flows through Mathura, is lined with bathing ghats and is full of large turtles. On the banks of the river the Sati Burj is a four storey tower built in 1570 to commemorate the sati of the builder's mother. Aurangzeb knocked down the upper storeys which have been rebuilt. The ruined Kans Qila fort on the riverbank was built by Raja Man Singh of Amber and Jai Singh of Jaipur also built one of his observatories here but it has since disappeared. Vishram Ghat is the most important bathing ghat where Lord Krishna is said to have rested after killing a tyrant king. Mathura is so full of Krishna reminders (even the Hare Krishnas have their Indian HQ near here) that you can even see the Potara-Kund, near the Katra Kesava, where baby Krishna's nappies (diapers to Americans) are supposed to have been washed.

The Government Museum in Dampier Nagar has sculptures, terra cotta work, coins and bronze objects dating from the 5th century AD. The standing Buddha image, found in excavations at Mathura, is particularly renowned. The museum is open daily except Mondays from 10.30 am to 4.30 pm from 1 July to 15 April and 7.30 am to 12.30 pm the rest of the year. Admission is free. In the city the Dwarkadheesh Temple is a modern Krishna temple while the Gita Mandir, also modern, is on the Mathura-Vrindaban road.

Around Mathura

Mahaban, 11 km south-east of Mathura, is another place from the Krishna legend. The Palace of Nanda, he was Krishna's foster-father, is said to contain his actual cradle. Gokul, a km away, is where Krishna was secretly raised. Hordes of pilgrims flock here during the birthday festival of Lord Krishna, each July-August. At Goverdhan, 26 km from Mathura, Lord Krishna is said to

have protected the inhabitants from Indra's wrath, in the form of rain, by holding the hilltops over them for seven days, neatly balanced on the tip of his finger. Krishna's favourite gopi or milkmaid is said to have come from Barsana, 47 km from Mathura.

Vrindaban, 10 km north of Mathura, is the place where Krishna sported with his milkmaids and even stole their clothes while they were bathing in the river. No wonder he's so popular. The large Red Temple or Gobind Deo (Divine Cowherd, in other words Krishna) was built in 1590 and is one of the most advanced Hindu temples in the north of India. It even has a vaulted ceiling, in contrast to the utilitarian ceilings found in most temples. There are other temples in Vrindaban including the temples of Gopi Nath, Jugal Kishor (1027), Radha Ballabh (1626) and Madan Mohan.

Places to Stay

Mathura has a number of fairly basic hotels and many dharamsalas. The *Agra Hotel* (tel 213) on Bengali Ghat has singles/doubles from Rs 20/25. The *Kwality Hotel*, near the bus stand, (tel 272) is similarly priced. There are also *Railway Retiring Rooms* at the Mathura Junction station. The *Kisan Bhavan*, near the museum, has rooms at Rs 4 a head. There's an *International Guest House* for Krishna freaks at Vrindaban, where the Hare Krishna movement has its HQ.

Getting There

Mathura is on the Delhi-Agra road and railway routes. It's 57 km north of Agra, 141 km south of Delhi.

AGRA (population 700,000)

At the time of the Moghuls, in the 16th and 17th centuries, Agra was the capital of India and its superb monuments date from that era. In particular Agra has its magnificent fort and the building which many people have

visited India solely to see — the Taj Mahal. Situated on the banks of the Yamuna River, with its crowded alleys and its predatory rickshaw riders, Agra is much like any other north Indian city, once you're away from these imposing reminders of Moghul splendour. There's an excellent train service making this eminently practicable. Actually Agra is worth more than a day, particularly if you also intend to visit, as you should, the deserted city of Fatehpur Sikri. In any case the Taj deserves more than a single visit if you are going to appreciate how its appearance changes under different light.

Agra became the capital of Sikandar Lodi in 1501 but it soon passed on to the Moghuls and both Babur and Humayun made some early Moghul constructions here. It was under Akbar that Agra first aspired to its heights of magnificence. From 1570 to 1585 Akbar ruled from nearby Fatehpur Sikri. When he abandoned that city he moved to Lahore (now in Pakistan) but returned to Agra in 1599 and remained there until his death in 1605. Jehangir, with his passion for Kashmir, did not spend a great deal of time at Agra but Shah Jahan is the name inevitably connected with Agra. He built the Jami Masjid, most of the palace buildings inside the Agra Fort and, of course, the Taj Mahal. Between 1638 and 1650, however, he built the Red Fort and Jami Masjid in Delhi and would probably have moved the capital there had he not been deposed and imprisoned by his son, Aurangzeb, in 1658. Aurangzeb did transfer the capital there.

In 1761 Agra fell to the Jats who did much damage to the city and its monuments, even going so far as to pillage the Taj Mahal. In turn it was taken by the Marathas in 1770 and passed through several more changes before the British took control in 1803. There was much fighting around the fort during the Mutiny in 1857.

Information & Orientation
Agra is situated on the west bank of the Yamuna River, 204 km south of Delhi. The old part of the town is north

of the fort where the Kinari Bazaar, the main market place, is located in a narrow street. The cantonment area to the south is the modern part of town, known as Sadar Bazaar. Here you will find the Government of India Tourist Office (tel 72377) at 191 The Mall. The GPO and poste restante is also on The Mall and in this area you will find handicraft shops, restaurants and many moderately priced hotels. De-luxe buses for Delhi and Jaipur also operate from here.

There are also some lower priced hotels and the Tourist Bungalow near the Raja Mandi railway station but this area is rather inconveniently located. It's far from both the Taj and the main hotel and restaurant area. The 'tourist class' hotels are mainly in the spacious areas of Taj Ganj, south of the Taj itself. Immediately south of the Taj there is a tightly packed area of narrow alleys where you can also find some popular rock-bottom hotels.

Agra's main railway station is Agra Cantonment and it is here that trains from New Delhi arrive. The main bus station for cities in Rajasthan and for Fatehpur Sikri is Idgah. The Fort Bus Station has buses going to Mathura. Indian Airlines (tel 73434) is in the Hotel Clarks Shiraz. Agra airport is seven km out of town.

Taj Mahal
If there's a building which evokes a country — like the Eiffel Tower does for France, the Sydney Opera House for Australia — then it has to be the Taj Mahal for India. So much so that the Indian tourist office has centred an advertising campaign around the theme that there's more to India than just the Taj.

This most famous Moghul monument was constructed by the Emperor Shah Jahan in memory of his wife Mumtaz Mahal, the 'lady of the Taj'. It has been described as the most extravagant monument ever built for love for the emperor was heartbroken when Mumtaz, to whom he had been married for 17 years, died in 1629, in childbirth, after producing 14 children. Construction of the Taj commenced in 1632 and was not completed until 1653. Workers were recruited not only from all over India but also from Central Asia and in total 20,000 people worked on the building. Experts were even brought from as far as away as Europe — the Frenchman Austin de Bordeaux and the Italian Veroneo of Venice had a hand in its decoration.

The most unusual story about the Taj is that there might well have been two of them. Shah Jahan, it is said, had intended to build a second Taj as his own tomb, and this second Taj would have been in black marble, a negative image of the white Taj of Mumtaz Mahal. Before he could embark on this second masterpiece Aurangzeb deposed and imprisoned his father. Shah Jahan spent the rest of his life in the Agra Fort, looking out along the river to the final resting place of his favourite wife.

The Taj Mahal stands on a raised marble platform with tall white minarets at each corner of the platform. The central structure has four smaller domes surrounding the huge, bulbous, central dome. The tombs of Mumtaz Mahal and Shah Jahan are in a basement room, above them in the main chamber are false tombs, a common practise in Indian mausoleums of this type. Light is admitted into the central chamber by finely cut marble screens. The echo in this high chamber, under the soaring marble dome, is superb and there is always somebody there to demonstrate it. Although the Taj is amazingly graceful from almost any angle it's the close up detail which is really astounding. Semi-precious stones are inlaid into the marble in beautiful patterns and with superb craftsmanship in a process known as *pietra dura*. The

precision and care which went into the Taj Mahal's design and construction is just as impressive whether you view it from across the river or from arm's length.

The building, which stands right beside the Yamuna River, is in a large and formally laid out garden. Twin red sandstone mosques frame the building when viewed from the river. You enter the Taj grounds through a high red sanstone gateway inscribed with verses from the Koran in Arabic. Paths lead to the Taj, divided by a long watercourse, in which the Taj would be beautifully reflected if there were water in it more often! As is so often repeated the Taj is worth more than a single visit. It's one building under the light of dawn, another at sunset. Still another under moonlight. Full moons bring people flocking to Agra in their thousands. Admission to the Taj costs Rs 2 except on Fridays when it is free. Catch is that on Fridays it can be impossibly crowded and noisy, not very conducive to calm enjoyment of this most serene of buildings. Opening hours are from sunrise to 10 pm but on full moon nights and the four nights around the full moon it stays open until midnight. A bus from Sadar to the Taj costs Rs 0.50.

A final sad note about the Taj — scientists fear that after centuries of undiminished glory the modern world may finally be shortening its life. Industrial pollution, particularly a proposed chemical plant, could cause irreparable damage to the marble before the turn of the century. Not that man hasn't damaged it in the past — in 1764 silver doors at the entrance were ripped off and carted away and raiders have also made off with the gold sheets that once lined the subterranean vault.

Agra Fort
Construction of the massive Agra Fort commenced with the Emperor in 1565

and additions were made right through to the time of his grandson, Shah Jahan. While in Akbar's time the fort was principally a military structure by the time of Shah Jahan the emphasis had shifted and the fort has become partially a palace. There are many fascinating buildings inside the massive walls, 20 metres high with a moat over 10 metres wide, which stretch for 2.5 km. The fort on the banks of the Yamuna River and only the Amar Singh Gate to the south is open. Inside the fort it is really a city within the city. The fort is open from sunrise to sunset and admission is Rs 2 except on Fridays when it is free. There's an entertaining sound & light show at the fort.

AGRA FORT

1 Jami Masjid	9 Mina Mosque
2 Northern Tower	10 Grape Garden
3 Delhi Gate	11 Octagonal Tower
4 Elephant Gate	12 Khas Mahal
5 Ladies' Bazaar	13 Jehangir's Palace
6 Moti Masjid	14 Diwan-i-Khas
7 Nagina Masjid	15 Shish Mahal
8 Diwan-i-Am	16 Amar Singh's Gate

Motif Masjid The 'Pearl Mosque' was built by Shah Jahan between 1646 and 1653. The marble mosque is considered to be perfectly proportioned and a Persian inscription inside the building compares it to a precious pearl. The mosque's courtyard is surrounded by arcaded cloisters and a marble tank stands in the centre.

Diwan-i-Am The 'Hall of Public Audiences' was also built by Shah Jahan and replaced an earlier wooden structure. Shah Jahan's predecessors also had a hand in the hall's construction but the throne room, with its typical inlaid marble work, is indisputably from Shah Jahan. Here he sat to meet officials or listen to petitioners. Beside the Diwan-i-Am is the small Nagina Masjid or 'Gem Mosque' and the 'ladies' bazaar' where merchants would come to display and sell goods to the ladies of the Moghul court.

Diwan-i-Khas The 'Hall of Private Audiences' was also built by Shah Jahan, in 1636-37. Here the emperor would meet important dignitaries or foreign ambassadors. The hall consists of two rooms, connected by three arches.

Octagonal Tower The Musamman Burj or Octagonal Tower stands close to the Diwan-i-Khas and the small, private Mina Masjid. Also known as the Saman Burj, this tower was built by Shah Jahan for Mumtaz Mahal and is another of his finely designed and executed buildings. It was here, with its views along the Yamuna to the Taj, that Shah Jahan died in 1666, after seven years' imprisonment. Unfortunately the tower has been much damaged over the years.

Jehangir's Palace Akbar is believed to have built this palace for his son, it is the largest private residence in the fort.

This was one of the first constructions within the fort where the emphasis started to change from purely military to the fort's later role as a luxurious palace. It is also interesting for its blend of Hindu and central Asian architectural styles — a contrast to the unique Moghul style which had developed by the time of Shah Jahan.

Other Shah Jahan's Khas Mahal is a beautiful white marble structure used as a private palace. The rooms underneath it were intended as a cool retreat in the summer heat. The Shish Mahal or 'Mirror Palace' was supposed to have been the harem dressing room and its walls are inlaid with tiny mirrors. The Anguri Bagh or 'Grape Garden' probably never had any grapevines but was simply a small, formal Moghul garden. It stood in front of the Khas Mahal. The Delhi Gate and Hathi Pol or 'Elephant Gate' are now closed. In front of the Jehangir Palace is the Hauz-i-Jehangri, a huge 'bath' carved out of a single block of stone — by whom and for what purpose is a subject of conjecture. The Amar Singh Gate takes its name from a Maharaja of Jodhpur who was killed by the gate, along with his followers, after a brawl in the Diwan-i-am in 1644! Justice tended to be summary in those days, there is a shaft leading down to the river into which those who made themselves unpopular with the great Moghuls could be summarily hurled.

Itmad-ud-daulah

There are a number of interesting sights on the opposite bank of the Yamuna and north of the fort. You cross the river on a narrow two level bridge carrying pedestrians, bicycles, rickshaws and bullock carts. The first place of interest along the riverside is the Itmad-ud-daulah — the tomb of Mirza Ghiyas Beg. This Persian gentleman's beautiful daughter married the Emperor Jehangir and became known as Nur Jahan, the

'light of the world'. In turn her daughter was Mumtaz Mahal, the lady of the Taj. The tomb was constructed between Nur Jahan between 1622 and 1628 and is very similar to the tomb she also constructed for her husband Jehangir near Lahore in Pakistan. The tomb is of particular interest since many of its design elements foreshadow the Taj, construction of which commenced only a few years later. The Itmad-ud-daulah was the first Moghul structure totally constructed of marble and the first to make extensive use of the *pietra dura* inlay work of marble which is so much a part of the Taj. The mausoleum is small and squat compared to the soaring Taj but the smaller, more human scale, somehow makes it more attractive and the beautifully patterned surface of the tomb is superb. There are also extremely fine marble lattice-work passages admitting light to the interior. It's well worth a visit. The Itmad-ud-daulah is open sunrise to sunset and admission is Rs 2, free on Fridays.

China-ka-Rauza

The 'china tomb' is a km north of the Itmad-ud-daulah. The squat, square tomb, surmounted by a single huge dome, was constructed in his own lifetime by Afzal Khan who died in Lahore in 1639. He was a high official in the court of Shah Jahan. The exterior was covered in brightly coloured enamelled tiles and the whole building clearly displayed its Persian influence. Today it is much decayed and neglected and the remaining tilework only hints at the building's former glory.

Ram Bagh

Laid out by the Emperor Babur, first of the Moghuls, in 1528 this is the earliest Moghul garden. It is said that Babur was temporarily buried here before being permanently interred at Kabul in Afghanistan. The Ram Bagh is two to three km further north of the China-

ka-Rauza on the riverside and is open from sunrise to sunset, admission is free.

Jami Masjid

Across the railway tracks from the Delhi Gate of Agra Fort the Jami Masjid was built by Shah Jahan in 1648. An inscription over the main gate indicates that it was built in the name of Jahanara, Shah Jahan's daughter, who was imprisoned with Shah Jahan by Aurangzeb. Large though it is the mosque is not as impressive as Shah Jahan's Jami Masjid in Delhi.

Akbar's Mausoleum

At Sikandra, 10 km north of Agra, is the tomb of Akbar. The tomb is situated in the centre of a large garden and four identical red sandstone gates lead to the tomb complex. Akbar commenced the construction of his tomb himself but it was completed by his son, Jehangir, in 1613. The tomb is a combination of Moslem and Hindu architectural styles. The building, with three-storey minarets at each corner, is built of red sandstone with white marble polygonal patterns inlaid. Like Humayun's Tomb in New Delhi it is an interesting place to visit to study the gradual evolution in design that culminated in the Taj Mahal. Akbar's Mausoleum is open from sunrise to sunset and entry is Rs 2, except on Fridays when it is free.

Sikandra is named after Sultan Sikandar Lodi, the Delhi ruler who was in power from 1488-1517, immediately preceding the rise of Moghul power on the sub-continent. The Baradi Palace, in the mausoleum gardens, was built by Sikandar Lodi. Across the road from the mausoleum is the Delhi Gate and between Sikandra and Agra are several tombs and two *kos minars* 'milestones'.

Other

The Kinari Bazaar or old market place is an interesting place to wander around. It's in the old part of Agra, near the fort, and the narrow alleys of the market start near the Jami Masjid. Girls beckon to single men from upstairs balconies of the Malka Bazaar in the old city.

Tours

The ITDC have Agra tours operating from Delhi for around Rs 120 for a day tour or Rs 300 with a night stopover and meals included. The latter includes Fatehpur Sikri as well as the main sights in Agra itself. If your time is very limited these may be worth considering. If you're day-tripping from Delhi to Agra the Agra city tours operated by the UP State Road Transport Corporation commence from the railway station and tickets are sold on the tourist Taj Express from Delhi. This tour lasts from 10.30 am to 6.30 pm and covers the Taj, the fort and Fatehpur Sikri. Passengers are picked up half an hour earlier at the Tourist Office, 191 The Mall. At the Cantonment Station tickets can be bought near the Platform 1 enquiry window. Costs start from Rs 15 on an

1	Agra Fort Railway Station	11	Kwality Restaurant
2	Agra Cantonment Railway Station	12	Agra Caterers
3	Idgah Bus Station	13	Tourist Rest House
4	Tourist Office	14	Saraj Restaurant
5	GPO	15	Taj Mahal
6	Hotel Clarks Shiraz & Indian Airways	16	Ram Bagh
		17	Chini Ka Rauza
7	Tourist Bungalow	18	Itmad-ud-Daulah's Tomb
8	Lauries Hotel	19	Highway Inn
9	Jaggi Hotel	20	Rock Bottom Hotels
10	Holiday Inn & Mayur Tourist Complex		

ordinary bus, Rs 22 de-luxe, and go up with drinks or meals included. They are reduced by Rs 3.50 on Fridays. The ITDC also organise Agra tours — a Rs 12 morning tour covers the Taj, the fort and the tomb of Itmad-ud-daulah while a Rs 18 afternoon tour goes to Sikandra and Fatehpur Sikri.

Places to Stay — Top End

Agra's tourist class hotels are generally situated in the open areas south of the Taj. *Hotel Moghul Sheraton* (tel 64701) has elegant, fort-like architecture and offers everything from camel or elephant rides to an in-house astrologer who will tell your fortune for Rs 50. There are 200 rooms with singles/doubles ranging from Rs 350/450. The older *Hotel Clarks Shiraz* (tel 72421) is a long standing Agra landmark. It too is fully air-conditioned, has a swimming pool and the Indian Airlines office is also located here. Singles/doubles cost Rs 250/350. The *Taj Mahal* (tel 64171) used to be a part of the Holiday Inn chain until early '81 when it was dropped. Singles and doubles are similarly priced to Clarks Shiraz.

South-east of the Taj the *Hotel Mumtaz Ashok* (tel 64771) is one of the ITDC chain. It's a smaller hotel with just 40 rooms, all air-conditioned, singles/doubles at Rs 150/225. In the same area the *Mayur Tourist Complex* (tel 64841) is also a smaller hotel with air-con rooms at Rs 100/140, non aircon rooms for Rs 80/100. Hotels that bridge the top to bottom brackets also include *Hotel Lauries* (tel 77047) on Mahatma Gandhi Rd. Singles/doubles cost Rs 80/140 with air-con, less without.

Places to Stay — Bottom End

The Sadar area, close to the Cantonment Railway Station, the Tourist Office and the GPO and only a Rs 2 or 3 rickshaw ride from the Taj, is a good place for reasonably cheap accommodation. There are also many good restaurants in this same vicinity. If you're after rock bottom prices then head for the maze of small streets immediately to the south of the Taj.

The very popular *Tourist Rest House* in on Kachahari Rd, conveniently close to the tourist office and the GPO. This pleasant, quiet and well kept hotel has singles from Rs 10 to Rs 30, doubles from Rs 20 to Rs 40 for the 'better' rooms — with private bathrooms. Food isn't so special though.

Hotel Jaggi (tel 72370) on Taj Rd is also in Sadar Bazaar and has singles/doubles for Rs 20/30 and has a popular restaurant. In the same area, approached through a narrow alley, is *Hotel Jai Hind* with rooms from around Rs 20. *Agra Caterers* (tel 72271) on the Mall has rooms with attached bathroom, reasonable value for money.

Agra's *Tourist Bungalow* (tel 72123) is a long way from everywhere in the Raja Mandi area and not as pleasant as most Tourist Bungalows. Doubles cost Rs 25 although there is also a Rs 5 dormitory. The Agra Fort station *Retiring Rooms* are good.

Major Bakshi Sardar Singh, a retired army officer, takes guests in his own home at 33/83 Ajma Rd (tel 76828). Clean, friendly, conveniently situated and superb food — a double with bathroom costs Rs 45.

The *Highway Inn*, 1.5 km south of the Taj, has excellent camping facilities for Rs 5 with your own tent. They also have tents, a dormitory and rooms as well as a restaurant, spring drinking water, laundry facilities and bicycles for hire. Camping facilities are also available at Hotel Lauries, the Mayur Tourist Complex and the Tourist Bungalow.

A labyrinth of winding, narrow streets runs back from the Taj. Follow the road straight back from the main entrance and you'll find the *Hotel Shah Jahan* with doubles at Rs 15 and 20. It's fairly clean and habitable and has a quite amazing menu. Some passing traveller has put a lot of effort into this wild fantasy but the food is surprisingly good. Excellent breakfasts here. Continue into the maze and right by the tonga stand (ask) you'll find the *Hotel Mumtaz Mahal.* Doubles from just Rs 10, singles Rs 5, dorm beds only Rs 3. Again it's a reasonable place considering the rock bottom prices and it's popular with many travellers. Other similarly cheap places to stay in the vicinity include the *Vijay Hotel* at the East Gate (Rs 10 and free tea). The *Agra Hotel* costs from Rs 30 with a good restaurant and views of the Taj — quiet and friendly. *Hotel Akbar International* (tel 63532) is near the ex-Holiday Inn (five minutes walk from the Taj) and has rooms from Rs 10 all the way to Rs 100.

Places to Eat

The de-luxe hotels all have excellent food — for a major splurge *Clarks Shiraz* is worth considering. In the Sadar area the *Kwality Restaurant* is on Taj Rd, it's air-conditioned and excellent, has a good selection of Indian and Chinese dishes. The nearby *Gaylords* is not quite so good.

On a tighter budget *Hotel Jai Hind* and *Hotel Jaggi* both have reasonably good food although Jaggi's gets mixed reports. Still in the Sadar area is the excellent, and very popular with travellers, *Sarang Restaurant* on Gwalior Rd. It's a pleasantly run place and a complete meal for two will cost you Rs 20 to 30 from start to finish. Good Chinese food here too.

Agra has a local speciality, the sweet dish called *petha.*

Getting There

Air Agra is on the touristically popular daily flight route Delhi-Agra-Khajuraho-Varanasi-Kathmandu and return. It's only a 30 minute flight from Delhi to Agra. Fares from Agra are Delhi Rs 150, Khajuraho Rs 265, Varanasi Rs 385. There is also a daily Delhi-Agra-Jaipur route, Agra-Jaipur costs Rs 186.

Trains Agra is on the main Delhi-Bombay broad gauge railway line so there are plenty of trains coming through. There is a daily express train from Delhi to Agra known as the Taj Express which costs Rs 55 in 1st class, Rs 12.50 in 2nd. The Taj Express departs New Delhi Railway Station at 7 am daily and arrives in Agra three hours later. The return train departs Agra at 7 pm and arrives in Delhi at 10 pm — ideal for a day trip to Agra. Guided tours of Agra and Fatehpur Sikri depart from the railway station as soon as the train arrives. Lucknow is about nine hours away by train.

Bus There are de-luxe buses from Delhi to Agra which cost Rs 20 and take four hours. A similar de-luxe bus between Agra and Jaipur takes six hours and costs Rs 25. This is much faster than a train to Jaipur, which will take nine or 10 hours! Recently a new bus service, operating only in the tourist season, has been commenced between Agra and Khajuraho. The 395 km trip takes about eight to 10 hours and costs Rs 25. The bus departs at 5.30 am. Most regular buses leave from the Idgah Bus Station, there are regular buses to Delhi about every hour, Rs 12.

Getting Around

Agra is very spread out, walking is really not on — even if you could. It's virtually impossible to walk because Agra's hordes of rickshaw-wallahs pursue would-be pedestrians with unbelievable energy and persuasive ability. Beware of rickshaw guys who take you from A to B via a few marble shops, jewellery shops and so on. Just great when you want to catch a train. A simple solution to Agra's transport problem is to hire a rickshaw for the day. You can easily negotiate an all-in daily rate (Rs 10 or less) for which your rickshaw-wallah will not only take you everywhere he'll wait outside while you sightsee or even have a meal. Agra is so touristy that many of them speak excellent English and like western cabbies are great sources of amusing information — like how much they can screw out of fat-cat tourists for a little pedal down to the Taj and back to the air-conditioning. Otherwise Rs 2 or 3 will take you from pretty well anywhere in Agra to anywhere else. If, however, you really don't want to be pedalled around, Agra is sufficiently traffic free to make pedalling yourself an easy proposition. There are plenty of bicycle hire places around.

Things to Buy
Agra is well known for leather goods,

jewellery and marble items inlaid like the *pietra dura* work on the Taj. The Sadar area and around the Taj itself are the main tourist shop areas although the prices here are likely to be more expensive. Around Pratapur there are many jewellery shops but if you're heading to Jaipur you'll find precious stones are cheaper there. Subhas Emporium in Sadar is a good place for marble. Beware of rickshaw-wallahs taking you to shops — they'll inevitably be raking off a commission at your expense.

FATEHPUR SIKRI
Between 1570 and 1586, during the reign of the Emperor Akbar, the capital of the Moghul Empire was situated here, 40 km west of Agra. Then, as suddenly and dramatically as this new city had been built, it was abandoned. Today it's a perfectly preserved Moghul city at the height of the empire's splendour. And an attraction no visitor to Agra should miss.

The legend relates that Akbar was without a male heir and made a pilgrimage to this spot to see the saint Shaikh Salim Chisti. He foretold the birth of Akbar's son, later the Emperor Jehangir, and in gratitude Akbar named his son Salim. Furthermore Akbar transferred his capital to Sikri and built a new and splendid city. Later, however, the city was simply abandoned due, it is said, to difficulties with the water supply.

Akbar was known to be very tolerant towards other religions although he was Moslem and he spent much time discussing and studying them in Fatehpur Sikri. He also developed a new religion called 'Deen Ilahi' which attempted to synthesise elments from all the major religions. Akbar's famous courtiers such as Birbal, Raja Todarmal and Abu Fazal had their houses near his palace in the city.

Information & Orientation
The deserted city lies along the top of a ridge while the modern village with its bus stand and railway station is down on the southern side. Fatehpur Sikri is open from sunrise to sunset and entry is Rs 2, free on Fridays. The Jami Masjid is outside the city enclosure.

Jami Masjid or Dargah Mosque
Fatehpur Sikri's mosque is said to be a copy of the mosque at Mecca and is a very beautiful building containing elements of Persian and Hindu design. The main entrance is through the 54 metre high Buland Darwaza, the Gate of Victory. The impressive gateway is reached by an equally impressive flight of steps. An inscription inside the archway includes the useful thought that 'The world is a bridge, pass over it, but build no house upon it. He who hopes for an hour may hope for eternity'. Just outside the gateway is a deep well and when there are sufficient tourists assembled local daredevils leap from the top of the entrance into the water.

Inside the mosque is the tomb or dargah of Shaikh Salim Chisti, surrounded by marble lattice screens. Just as Akbar came to the saint, four centuries ago, looking for a son so do childless women visit his tomb today. The

Fatehpur Sikri

- ⨯—⨯ Wire Fence

saint's grandson, Islam Khan, also has his tomb within the mosque. Abul Fazi and Faizi, adviser and poet to Akbar, had their homes just outside the mosque.

Palace of Jodh Bai
North-east of this mosque is this palace, named after Jehangir's wife although it was probably more used by Akbar's wife, who was a Hindu. Here again the architecture is a blend of styles with Hindu columns and Moslem cupolas. The 'Palace of the Winds' is a projecting room with walls entirely made of stone lattice work. The ladies of the court probably sat in here to keep a quiet eye on events below.

Bhirbal Bhavan
Built either by or for Raja Birbal, Akbar's favourite courtier, this small palace is extremely elegant in its design and execution. Victor Hugo, the Victorian-era French author, commented that it was either a very small palace or a very large jewellery box. Birbal, who was a Hindu and noted for his wit and wisdom, unfortunately proved to be a hopeless soldier and lost his life, and most of his army near Peshawar in 1586. Enormous stables adjoin the Jodh Bai Palace with nearly 200 enclosures for horses and camels. Some stone rings for the halters are still in place.

Karawan Sarai & Hiran Minar
The Karawan Sarai or 'caravanserai' was a large courtyard surrounded by the hostels used by visiting merchants. The Hiran Minar or 'Deer Minaret' is said to have been erected over the grave of Akbar's favourite elephant. Stone elephant tusks protrude from the 21 metre high tower and Akbar is said to have shot at deer and other game which were driven in front of him, from the top. The flat expanse of land stretching

away from the tower was once a lake and occasionally floods even today.

Miriam's House

Close to the Jodh Bai Palace, this house was used by Jehangir's mother and at one time was gilded throughout — giving it the name the 'Golden House'.

Panch Mahal

The amusing little 'Five Storey Palace' was probably once used by the ladies of the court and originally had stone screens on the sides. These have now been removed making the open colonnades inside visible. Each of the five storeys is stepped back from the previous one until at the top there is only a tiny kiosk, its dome supported by four columns. The lowest floor has 56 columns, no two of which are exactly alike.

Ankh Michauli

The name of this building translates as something like 'hide and seek' and the emperor is supposed to have amused himself by playing that game with ladies of the harem! The building was more probably used for storing records although it has some curious struts with stone monsters carved into them. By one corner is a small canopied enclosure where Akbar's Hindu guru may have sat to instruct him.

Diwan-i-Khas

The exterior of the Hall of Private Audiences is plain but its interior design is quite unique. A stone column in the centre of the building supports a flat-topped 'throne'. From the four corners of the room stone bridges lead across to this throne and it is thought that Akbar would sit in the middle while his four principal ministers would sit at the four corners.

Diwan-i-Am

Just inside the gates at the north-east end of the deserted city is the Hall of Public Audiences. This consists of a large open courtyard surrounded by cloisters. Beside the Diwan-i-Am is the Pachchisi courtyard, blocked out like a gigantic gamesboard. It is said that Akbar played chess here, using slave girls as the pieces.

Other

Musicians would play from the Norbat Khana, at one time the main entrance to the city, as processions passed by beneath. The entrance road then passed between the mint and treasury before reaching the Diwan-i-Am. The Khwabgah was Akbar's own sleeping quarters, in front of the Daftar Khana or record office. Beside that is the tiny, but elaborately carved Rumi Sultana or 'Turkish Queen's House'. Near the Karawan Sarai badly defaced elephants still guard the Hathi Pol or Elephant Gate. There is also a Hakim or doctor's house and a fine Hammam or Turkish Bath beside it. Outside the Dargah Mosque are the remains of the small stone-cutters' mosque. Shaikh Salim Chisti's cave was supposedly at this site and the mosque predates Akbar's imperial city.

Getting There

The tour buses only stop for an hour or so at Fatehpur Sikri. If you want to spend longer it is worth taking a regular bus from the Idgah Bus Station. The trip takes a bit over an hour, along the way you pass milestones, known as kos minars, about every three km. There's also a train service there but it's very slow.

BETWEEN DELHI & KANPUR

Aligarh (population 280,000)
Formerly known as Koil this was the site of an important fort as far back as 1194. During the upheavals following the death of Aurangzeb and the collapse

of the Moghul empire the region was scrapped over by the Afghans, the Jats, the Marathas and the Rohillas — first one coming out on top, then another. In 1776 the fort's name was changed to Aligarh (the high fort) but in 1803, despite French support for then ruler Scindia, it fell to the British. The fort is three km north of the town and its present form dates from 1524. The ancient City of Koil has traces of Buddhist and Hindu temples of great antiquity.

Sankasya

Reached via Farrukhabad and Pakhna, from where it is 11 km, there is an Ashokan elephant capital here. A mound, topped by a ruined stupa, marks the spot where Buddha descended from heaven to earth after preaching to his mother.

Kanauj

Only a few dismal ruins indicate that this was once a mighty Hindu city, which quickly fell into disrepair after Mahmud of Ghazni's raids. This was the place where Humayun was defeated by Sher Shah in 1540 after which he

temporarily had to leave India.

Etawah

This town rose to some importance during the Moghul period only to go through the usual series of rapid changes during the turmoil that followed the Moghuls. The Jami Masjid shows similarities to the mosques of Jaunpur and there are bathing ghats on the riverbank, below the ruined fort.

Bareilly (population 360,000)

Former capital of the region known as Rohilkand, Bareilly came under British control when the Rohillas, an Afghan tribe became too involved with the Marathas and the Nawab of Oudh.

Rampur (population 180,000)

This was a former Rohilla state capital. The State Library has an important collection of old manuscripts and is housed in a fine building in the old fort. There is a large Jami Masjid nearby and interesting bazaars around the walls of the palace. The library contains a fine collection of old miniatures, some of great importance, but these are normally only on view for scholars.

KANPUR (population 1,400,000)

Sometimes called 'the Manchester of India' this important industrial town attracts very few tourists although it is not a great distance south of Lucknow. During the 1857 Mutiny some of the more tragic events took place here, at that time known as Cawnpore. Sir Hugh Wheeler defended a part of the Cantonment for most of the month of June but with supplies virtually exhausted and having suffered considerable losses he surrendered only to have his party massacred. All Souls Memorial Church, built in 1875, has some rather moving reminders of the tragic events at Kanpur. It's two km from the station. Kanpur has a large and modern zoo.

Places to Stay

Hotel Meghdoot (tel 51141) at 17/3B Mhatma Ghandhi Marg is air-conditioned and has restaurants, shops and so on. Singles/doubles cost from Rs 125/180. The Yatrik Hotel (tel 60345-456) is at 65/58A Circular Road and has air-con rooms at Rs 60/80 or air-cooled rooms at Rs 35/60 for singles/doubles. There are other cheaper hotels in Kanpur.

Getting There

Kanpur can be reached daily by air from Delhi (Rs 221) and Calcutta (Rs 475). It's on the main Delhi-Calcutta railway line, some express trains take less than five hours Delhi-Kanpur.

LUCKNOW (population 900,000)

The capital of Uttar Pradesh, Lucknow rose to prominence as the capital of the Nawabs of Oudh. These rulers controlled a region of north-central India for about a century after the decline of the Moghul Empire and most of the interesting monuments in Lucknow date from this period from the mid-18th century. The Nawabs were:

Sa'adat Khan Burhan-ul-mulk	1724-1739
Safdar Jang	1739-1753
Shuja-ud-daula	1753-1775
Asaf-ud-daula	1775-1797
Sa'adat Ali Khan	1798-1814
Ghazi-ud-din Haidar	1814-1827
Nasir-ud-din Haidar	1827-1837
Muhammad Ali Shah	1837-1842
Amjad Ali Shah	1842-1847
Wajid Ali Shah	1847-1856

It was not until Asaf-ud-daula that the capital of Oudh was moved to Lucknow. Safdar Jang, lived and ruled from Delhi and his tomb is a familiar landmark near the Safdarjang airport. After Sa'adat Ali Khan the rest of the Oudh Nawabs were a uniformly hopeless lot and Wajid Ali Shah was so extravagant, lazy and indolent that to this day his name is regarded by many in India as synonymous with lavishness. In 1856 the British, as was their wont, pensioned him off for incompetence and exiled him to Calcutta for the rest of his life. This was one of the sparks that lit the Indian Mutiny. Lucknow became the scene for some of the most dramatic events of the Mutiny as the British residents of Lucknow held out in the Residency for 87 harrowing days only to be besieged again for a further two months after being relieved.

The Nawabs were Shi'ite Moslems and Lucknow remains the principal Indian Shi'ite city — unlike other major Moslem cities in India like Delhi and Agra where the Moslems are mainly Sunnites. Shi'ites predominate in Iran but in most other Islamic nations the Sunnites form the majority.

Information & Orientation

Lucknow is rather spread out and it is quite a distance between the various places of interest. Lucknow is an interesting place but sadly neglected by tourists and the mausoleums of the Nawabs were jerry built, have generally deteriorated rather badly and are somewhat over-rated.

The historic monuments are mainly in the north-eastern part of the old city around the chowk area. The main shopping area with its narrow alleys is Aminabad while the modern area with wide avenues and large shops is the fashionable Hazratganj. The major bus station, for Gorakhpur and Varanasi buses, is in Kaiserbagh. The main railway station, in the south of the city, is called Charbagh. The Tourist office is at 21 Vidhan Sabha Marg.

Great Imambara

The Bara or Great Imambara was built

Lucknow

Faizabad
Aliganj

Sultanpur

Airport
Kanpur

Chowk

Mankameshwar Mandir Rd.

Gomti R.

Vishwa Vidyalaya

Gomti Marg.

Hospital Rd.

J. Narain Rd.

Nabi Ullah Rd.

Nadan Mahal Rd.

Murtoza Hussain Rd.

Aminabad Road

Aishbagh Road

Subhash Marg

Guru Govind Singh Marg

Buddho Road

Shivaji Marg

Station Rd.

Cantonment Rd.

Bisheshwar Nath Rd.

Shah Najaf Rd.

Sapru Marg

Ram Tirth Marg

Haider Canal

La Martinier Marg

Kalidas Marg

Vikramaditya Marg

Vivekanand Marg

Mohatma Gandhi Marg

Hazratganj

Sapho Marg

in 1784 by Asaf-ud-Daula as a famine relief project. The central hall of the Imambara, containing its builder's 'pretentious' tomb, is 50 metres long and 15 metres high, it is one of the largest vaulted galleries in the world. Beneath it there are many underground passages which have now been blocked up. An external stairway leads to an upper floor laid out as an amazing labyrinth known as the bhulbhulaiya. A guide, to ensure you're not lost forever, costs not more than Rs 5. There's a fine view over the city and the Aurangzeb Mosque from the top. There is a mosque with two tall minarets in the courtyard of the Imambara. To the right of this, in a row of cloisters, is a 'bottomless' well. The Imambara is open from 6 am to 5 pm and admission is Rs 1.50.

Rumi Darwaza
Beside the Bara Imambara and also built by Asaf-ud-Daula, this huge and finely designed gate is a replica of one in Istanbul.

Husainabad Imambara
Also known as the Chhota or 'small' Imambara, it was built by Muhammad Ali Shah in 1837 to serve as his own mausoleum. The large courtyard encloses a raised rectangular tank with small imitations of the Taj Mahal on each side. One of them is the tomb of Muhammad Ali Shah's daughter, the other that of her husband. The main building of the Imambara is topped with numerous domes, the main one is golden, and minarets, while inside are the tombs of Ali Shah and his mother. Paying Rs 2 to the guide will also permit you to see the Nawab's silver covered throne. The watchtower opposite the Imambara is known as Satkhanda or the 'seven-storey tower' but it actually only has four storeys since construction was abandoned at that level when Ali Shah died in 1840. The Imambara is open from 6 am to 5 pm, it's six km from the Tourist Bungalow.

Clock Tower
Opposite the Husainabad Imambara is the 67 metre high clock tower and the Husainabad Tank. The clock tower was built between 1880 and 1887.

Picture Gallery
Also facing the Husainabad Tank is a baradari or summer house, also built by Ali Shah. Now restored it houses portraits of the various Nawabs of Oudh. It is open from 8 am to 5 pm and admission is Rs 0.75.

Jami Masjid
West of the Husainabad Imambara is the great Jami Masjid mosque. One of Lucknow's few buildings of real architectural merit it has two minarets and three domes. Construction was commenced by Muhammad Ali Shah but completed after his death. This is one of the few mosques in India which is not open to non-Moslems.

Residency
Built in 1800 for the British Resident this extensive building was to become the stage for the most dramatic events

A   Palace of the Winds, Jaipur (R)
B   haveli door, Jaisalmer (R)
C   wall painting, Udaipur Palace (R)

of the 1857 mutiny — the Sieges of Lucknow. The British inhabitants of Lucknow all took refuge in the Residency with the outbreak of the mutiny. The commander, Sir Henry Lawrence, expected to be able to hold out for as long as 15 days before relief arrived. It was 87 days later when a small force under Sir Henry Havelock broke through the besiegers to the remaining half-starved defenders. The story was still not over for once Havelock and his troops were within Residency the seige was recommenced and continued from 25 September until 17 November when Sir Colin Campbell broke through to the Residency for the second time.

Today the Residency is maintained in exactly the condition it was in at the time of the final relief. The shattered walls are still scarred by cannon shots and the cemetery at the nearby ruined church has the graves of 2000 men, women and children including that of Sir Henry Lawrence who died during the first siege. The area around the Residency is maintained as well kept lawns and gardens but at the time of the siege the surrounding buildings were only separated from the Residency by narrow streets and lanes. The besiegers frequently attempted to dig tunnels into the Residency.

From 1857 right up to the day India became independent in 1947 a Union Jack was flown night and day from one of the Residency's towers. Times have changed, today there is Martyr's Memorial to the martyrs of India's independence struggle directly opposite the Residency. It was opened in 1957,

the 100th anniversary of the mutiny. There are no set opening hours for the Residency but the 'model room', where a model of the positions during the siege is on display, only opens from 8 am to 5 pm. Admission is Rs 2 except on Fridays when it is free.

Lakshman Tila
This high ground on the right bank of the River Gumti was the original site of the town which became known as Lucknow in the 15th century. Aurangzeb's Mosque now stands on this site.

Shah Najaf Imambara
Close to the Tourist Bungalow this mausoleum takes its name from Najaf, the town 190 km south-west of Baghdad in Iraq where Hazrat Ali, the Shi'ite Moslem leader, is buried. The Imambara is the tomb of Ghazi-ud-din Haidar Khan who died in 1827. His wives are also buried here. This was the scene for desperate fighting in November 1857 during the second relief of Lucknow. The domed exterior is comparatively plain but inside there are chandeliers and at one time the dome was said to be covered with gold. Many precious items from the mausoleum were looted following the mutiny. The Imambara is open from 6 am to 5 pm.

Martiniere School
Outside of the town is this strange school built by the Frenchman Major-General Claude Martin. Taken prisoner at Pondicherry in 1761 he joined the East India Company's army, then in 1776 entered service with the Nawab

A   intricately carved ceiling dome of the temple at Ranakpur (R)
B   fort entrance at Bundi (R)
C   sati hand prints at the fort gate, Jodhpur (R)

of Oudh while at the same time maintaining his East India Company connections. He quickly made a very substantial fortune from his dual occupations of soldiering and businessman and started to build a palatial home which he named Constantia. He designed much of the building himself and his architectural abilities were to say the least a little mixed — Gothic gargoyles were piled merrily atop Corinthian columns to produce a finished product which a British Marquess sarcastically pronounced took its ideas from a wedding cake. Martin died in 1800, before his stately home could be completed, but left the money and the directions that it should become a school. 'Kim', the boy hero of Kipling's story of the same name, went to this school and there are similar establishments, also financed from Martin's fortune, in Calcutta and Lyons, France. The building is two km from the Tourist Bungalow and is fronted by an artificial lake with a 38 metre high column in its centre.

Other

Near the Kaisarbagh, with the palace of the last Nawab, there are the stone tombs of Sa'adat Ali and his wife. There is also a summer house in this garden. There are two museums, both closed on Mondays, and a children's museum. The Archaeological Museum (admission 15p) is in the Kaiserbagh. The State Museum (open 10.30 am to 4.30 pm, admission 15p) is in the Banarsi Bagh. The Zoo, founded in 1921, is also here and has a large collection of snakes. Admission is Rs 0.60 and it is open from 5 am to 7 pm. Sikandarbagh, scene of pitched battles in November 1857, is now the home of the National Botanical Research Institute. The gardens are open from 6 am to 5 pm. General Havelock, who led the first relief of Lucknow has his grave and memorial in the Alambagh. Nadan Mahal is the tomb of the first governor

of Oudh appointed by Akbar. It is one of the earliest buildings in Lucknow, dating from around 1600. Other buildings nearby include the small Sola Khamba pavilion and the tomb of Ibrahim Chisti.

Tours

There are state government operated tours starting from the Tourist Bungalow at 8 am or the railway station a little later each day. They cost Rs 10 and cover a number of Lucknow's spread out sights.

Places to Stay — Top End

Hotel Clarks Avadh (tel 40131) at 8 Mahatma Gandhi Marg is Lucknow's best hotel. It has everything from central air-conditioning to restaurants and a 24 hour coffee shop. Singles/doubles cost Rs 200/300. Also in the Hazratganj area is the rather old-fashioned looking *Hotel Carlton* (tel 44021-24) on Shah Najaf Rd. Singles/doubles here cost Rs 100/190 or without air-con they are Rs 60/100.

Places to Stay — Bottom End

The state government *Tourist Bungalow* (tel 32257) at 6 Sapru Marg in Hazratganj is good value at Rs 25 a double or Rs 40 air-cooled, Rs 60 air-con. The rooms are well furnished and have attached bathrooms. There is also a Rs 5 dorm. Get there on a 4 bus from the station.

The popular *Hotel Capoore* (tel 43958) is also in Hazratganj and costs Rs 30 a singles, Rs 40 a double. Near the botanical gardens the *Avadh Lodge* (tel 43821) at 1 Ram Mohan Rai Marg cost Rs 40/60 for singles/doubles. Like the Tourist Bungalow it has facilities for camping if you're travelling with your own vehicle.

There are *Railway Retiring Rooms* for both the Northern Railway and the North-Eastern Railway at the Charbagh Station. The Northern rooms start from a Rs 10 dormitory and go up to Rs 35 doubles or Rs 50 with air-con. The North-Eastern rooms are cheaper, dorm beds at Rs 5, non air-con doubles at Rs 20.

Places to Eat
Hotel Carlton has the best, and most expensive, restaurant in Lucknow. Good Indian and western food is available at the *Kwality*, *Seem* and *Royal Cafe* restaurants. In the same area you can get good South Indian vegetarian food at low prices. *'Chaudhary's Place* is very popular for Indian sweets and the snacks known as chat.

Getting There
Air Lucknow is on a daily route Delhi-Lucknow-Patna-Ranchi-Calcutta. From Delhi the fare is Rs 305, from Calcutta it is Rs 622. The Indian Airlines office (tel 44030, 48081) is at Hotel Clarks Avadh. Amausi Airport is 14 km out of Lucknow.

Train By express train Lucknow is eight hours from Varanasi, nine hours from Agra and only seven hours from Delhi if you travel on the Gomti Express. There is only a narrow gauge line between Lucknow and Gorakhpur, for the Nepal border, so this trip takes eight hours by train. Both the narrow gauge North-Eastern railway lines and the broad gauge Northern railway lines run through the main railway station.

For Northern railway enquiries ring 51234 or 51333. First class bookings are made on 51833, 2nd class on 51488. North-Eastern railway enquiries are made on 51433 and all reservations are made on 51383.

Bus Charbagh bus station, by the railway station, can be phoned on 50988. Kaiserbagh bus station number is 42503. Buses to Delhi, Agra, Allahabad, Varanasi, Kanpur, Gorakhpur and so on all operate from Kaiserbagh.

To Nepal From the border at Sunauli, from where you enter Nepal to Pokhara, it is a 12 hour bus ride to Lucknow.

Getting Around
Local transport is not very frequent but a tempo will take you from the GPO to chowk, quite near the Great Imambara, for Rs 0.75. There are also buses from chowk to the railway station. Or you could take a rickshaw from Hazratganj to Aminabad and then a bus to chowk. The two Imambaras and the Jami Masjid are all around the chowk area while Shah Najaf is in Hazratganj and the Residency is about midway between the two.

Things to Buy
Lucknow is famed for its hand woven embroidery known as chican. It's made into saris for women and kurtas for men. Prices are lower in Aminabad but you have to bargain.

ALLAHABAD (population 600,000)
The city of Allahabad is 135 km west of Varanasi at the confluence of two of India's most important rivers — the Ganges and the Yamuna (Jumna). This meeting point of the rivers, the 'sangam', naturally has great sin-washing powers and is an important pilgrimage site. It is even more holy since the invisible or imaginary Saraswati River is also supposed to join the Ganges and the Yamuna at this point. Allahabad also has an historic fort built by Akbar which overlooks the confluence of the rivers and contains an Ashoka pillar. The Nehru family home, Anand Bhawan, is in Allahabad and is open for inspection. Not many western visitors pause in Allahabad but it can be an interesting and worthwhile stop. Allahabad is built on a very ancient site since it was known in Aryan times as Prayag and

Brahma himself is said to have performed a sacrifice here. The Chinese pilgrim Hiuen Tsang described visiting the city in 643 AD and it acquired its present name in 1584, under Akbar. Later Allahabad was taken by the Marathas, sacked by the Pathans and finally ceded to the British in 1801 by the Nawab of Oudh. It was in Allahabad that the East India Company officially handed over control of India to the British Government in 1858, following the Mutiny.

Information & Orientation

Allahabad is less congested and more modern than its sister city, touristy Varanasi. Civil Lines, with its modern shopping centre, has broad tree-lined avenues and the main bus station is located here. The older part of town is near the Yamuna River. There are three railway stations — the main one is Allahabad Junction and is situated in the central part of the city, just south of the Civil Lines area. Trains for Varanasi, however, go from the city station, about three km away. Most hotels are midway between the two stations. The Tourist Office (tel 52722) is at the Tourist Bungalow on Mahatma Gandhi Rd.

Sangam

The confluence of the rivers is the scene for a great annual bathing festival which takes place between mid-January and mid-February of each year. The festival, known as Magh Mela, lasts from 15 days to a month and attracts thousands of pilgrims who come for a dip in the holy rivers. Every 12th year the Magh Mela is known as the Kumbh Mela and the thousands grow to over a million pilgrims! A huge temporary township springs up on the vacant land

on the Allahabad side of the river and elaborate precautions have to be taken for the pilgrims' safety — in the early '50s 350 people were killed in a stampede to the water. The Kumbh Mela alternates between Nasik, Ujjain and Hardwar every three years and will next return to Allahabad in 1989. At the confluence the Ganges is about two km wide — it's a shallower, muddier river than the clearer, deeper Yamuna. Don't pay more than Rs 5 for a boat trip out on the rivers, it's a bit of a tourist trap.

The Fort

Built by Akbar in 1583 the fort, which stands at the confluence on the Yamuna side, has massive walls and pillars and three magnificent gateways flanked by high towers. The fort is made from huge bricks and is at its most impressive when viewed from the river. Apart from one Moghul building there are no constructions remaining within the fort — which is just as well since foreigners are not allowed inside. Officially passes can be obtained from the Security Officer (tel 51370) but it appears you're simply told no.

Ashoka Pillar

Unfortunately you are not allowed to see the Ashoka pillar in front of the gateway inside the fort. The 10.6 metre high, polished sandstone shaft dates from 232 BC and was found lying on the ground in the fort in 1837 and set up at its present location. Inscribed on the column are Ashoka's edicts and a later inscription eulogising the victories of Samudragupta (326-375 AD). This is the only record of the events in this Gupta ruler's life. There is also a later inscription by Jehangir.

1	Allahabad Junction Railway Station	5	YMCA
2	Allahabad City Railway Station	6	Museum
3	Tourist Office & Tourist Bungalow	7	Anand Bhawan
4	GPO	8	Fort

The Undying Tree

A small door in the east wall of the fort, near the river, leads to the 'undying banyan tree' — one place in the fort you are allowed to visit. This tree is mentioned by Hiuen Tsang who tells of pilgrims sacrificing their lives by leaping to their deaths from the tree in order to seek salvation. The tree is also known as Akshai Veta.

Anand Bhawan

The Nehru family home was donated to the Indian government by Indira Gandhi in 1970. Situated in the eastern part of town, near the Ganges, the exhibits in the house show how this well-off family became involved in the struggle for Indian independence and later produced three generations of astute politicians — Motilal Nehru, Jawaharlal Nehru and Indira Gandhi. The two storey mansion has a large garden and the house contains many personal items connected with the life of three generations of the Nehru family. Opening hours are 9.30 am to 12 noon and 1.30 to 5 pm, closed Mondays. The exhibits would be of much more interest if they were labelled in English as well as Hindi.

Khusru Bagh

This garden, close to the railway station, contains the tomb of Prince Khusru, son of Jehangir, who was executed by his own father. Nearby are the tombs of his sister and of his Rajput mother.

Allahabad Museum

Located on Kamla Nehru Rd the museum has a fine collection of Rajasthani miniatures and terra cotta figures. Entry fee is Rs 0.20 and the museum is open from 6.30 am to 12.30 pm from 15 April to 15 July and from 10 am to 6.30 pm in other months. The Museum is closed on Wednesdays. To the north of Alfred Park is the Municipal Museum

and opposite that is a lovely Children's Park.

Other

The Bharadwaja Ashram is mentioned in the Ramayana, the Allahabad University now occupies its site. The Nag Basuki Temple on the banks of the Ganges and the subterranean Patalpuri Temple are other important shrines.

Places to Stay

Barnett's Hotel (tel 2231) is at 14 Mahatma Gandhi Marg and has singles/doubles at Rs 80/120 with air-con, Rs 75/100 without. It is fairly centrally located and all rooms in this small hotel have attached bathrooms. The *Tourist Bungalow* (tel 53640) is at 35 Mahatma Gandhi Marg and is probably the best place to stay in Allahabad. Rooms cost Rs 30 for a double, Rs 50 if air-cooled and Rs 75 if air-conditioned. It is a Rs 1 rickshaw ride from the main railway station. There is also a Rs 5 dormitory. In the rock bottom bracket the *Central Hotel*, near the clock tower in the centre of the old part of town, has rooms down to Rs 10. There are many other hotels around town and *Railway Retiring Rooms* at the station (tel 2278) with doubles at Rs 30 and dorm beds at Rs 5.

Places to Eat

You can get meals in the *Tourist Bungalow. Lucky Sweet Mart* has good Indian sweets.

Getting There

Air Allahabad is on the route Delhi-Kanpur - Allahabad - Varanasi - Calcutta which is operated four days a week. Fares are Rs 420 from Delhi, Rs 570 from Calcutta.

Rail Allahabad is on the main Delhi-Calcutta railway route and takes about 10 hours from Delhi or four hours from Varanasi. From Delhi fares are approximately Rs 135 in 1st class, Rs 33 in second. Allahabad is a good place to travel to Khajuraho from. If you spend the night here you can catch a morning train to Satna from where buses go to Khajuraho. If you're a backpacker beware of the police at Allahabad Railway Station — they conduct frequent drug searches.

AROUND ALLAHABAD
Bhita
On the opposite side of the Yamuna, 18 km south-west of Allahabad, are the excavated remains of this fortified city. Archaeological digs in 1910-11 revealed successive layers dating from the Gupta period (320-455 AD) right back to the Mauryan period (321-184 BC) and even earlier. There is a museum with stone and metal seals, coins from various kingdoms of the time, terra cotta statues and figures and various utensils and personal possessions.

Garwha
The ruined temples in this walled enclosure are about 50 km from Allahabad. Garwha is eight km from Shankargarh and the final three km has to be completed on foot. The major temple has 16 beautifully carved stone pillars and inscriptions reveal that the temples date back to the Gupta period at the very least. Some of the better sculptures from Garwha are now shown in the State Museum in Lucknow.

Kausambi
This ancient Buddhist centre is 63 km from Allahabad and used to be known as Kosam. At one time this was the capital of King Udaya, a contemporary of the Buddha. A huge fortress measuring over six km around is near the village and the broken remains of an Ashoka pillar, minus any pre-Gupta period inscriptions, can be seen inside the fort. A bus runs right to the fort at Kausambi.

BETWEEN LUCKNOW & VARANASI
Bahraich & Saheth-Maheth
The nephew of that scourge of India, Mahmud of Ghazni, was killed in Bahraich in 1033. There is a shrine to him about three km from the town. At Saheth-Maheth the Buddha performed the miracle of sitting on a thousand petalled lotus and multiplying himself a million times. The town is also known as Sravasti and can be reached from Gorakhpur on the Naugarh-Gonda loop line. Gainjohwa is the nearest station and there are extensive ruins and a few modern Buddhist temples.

Faizabad (population 120,000)
This was once the capital of Oudh but rapidly declined after the death of Bahu Begam. Her mausoleum is said to be the finest of its type in Uttar Pradesh. Her husband, who preceded her as ruler, also has a fine mausoleum. There are pleasant gardens in Guptar Park, where the temple from which Rama is supposed to have disappeared, stands. Faizabad station has good food.

Ayodhya
Only six km from Faizabad, Ayodhya is the home town of Ramayana hero Ram Chandra. There are numerous picturesque temples and ghats — since the town is on the Gogra (Ghaghara) River. This was also a great Buddhist centre at one time and, as usual, Hiuen Tsang dropped by to list how many monasteries there were and how many

monks in residence.

Places to Stay There is a rather primitive *Tourist Bungalow* near the station, it has rooms and a Rs 4 dormitory.

Jaunpur (population 85,000)

Founded by Firoz Shah Tughlaq in 1360 this town later became the capital of the independent Moslem Sharqui Kingdom. Eventually it fell to Sikandar Lodi and then the Moghuls prior to the arrival of the Moslems it had a great number of Hindu, Buddhist and Jain temples, shrines and monasteries. Many of these have been utilised by the Moslems to construct Jaunpur's architecturally unique mosques.

The more important mosques include the 1408 Atala Masjid, built on the site of a Hindu temple dedicated to Atala Devi. The massively constructed Jami Masjid was built between 1438 and 1478 during the Sharqi period. There are a half dozen other mosques worth of note — the Jaunpur mosques

are notable for their use of Jain and Hindu building materials, for their two storey arcades and large gateways and for their unusual minarets. The tombs of the Sharqi sultans are north of the Jami Masjid. Other important constructions include Feroz Shah's 1360 fort and the stone Akbari Bridge which was built between 1564 and 1568.

Places to Stay Jaunpur has some cheap hotels and the *Marwari Dharamsala*, near the fort, where you can get a private room for just Rs 2.50.

Getting There Buses and taxis are available from Varanasi, 58 km away.

Chunar

The fort here overlooks the Ganges and was captured by Humayun in 1537 but taken by Sher Shah soon after and not recovered by the Moghuls until 1575 when Akbar took it. Chunar is 37 km from Varanasi and can be reached by bus.

GORAKHPUR (population 250,000)

This is a town travellers making for Pokhara in Nepal usually pass through. Lumbini, just across the border in Nepal, is the birthplace of Buddha. Kushinagar, about five km east of Gorakhpur, is supposed to be the site of the Buddha's death and cremation. There are a number of Buddhist buildings of various ages here and large seated and reclining Buddha images. The loop line from Gorakhpur to Gonda can be used to visit Lumbini, just across the border in Nepal, or Saheth-Maheth (Sravasti) in India.

Places to Stay

The *Standard Hotel*, opposite the railway station, costs Rs 25 a double. The *Kailash Hotel* is Rs 10 a single with

attached bathroom.

TO LUMBINI

Lumbini is the birthplace of Buddha and also close to the 'backdoor' entrance into Nepal for Pokhara. All those going to Lumbini, even pilgrims just crossing the border for a few hours, require a Nepali visa. This can be obtained at the border check point for Rs 60 Nepalese. Buses run from Naugarh station on the Gonda-Gorakhpur loop line as far as the border at Kakarhwa from where you take a rickshaw (Rs 5) for the last few km to Lumbini. There is a check post in Naugarh (India) where you must report before proceeding in either direction. Naugarh has a *Mahabodhi Society Rest House* where you can stay for a donation.

VARANASI (population 650,000)

Varanasi, the 'eternal city' is one of the most important pilgrimage sites in India and also a major tourist attraction. Situated on the banks of the sacred Ganges, Varanasi has been a centre of learning and civilisation for over two thousand years. It was at Sarnath only 10 km from Varanasi, that the Buddha first preached his message of enlightenment 25 centuries ago. Later the city became a great Hindu centre but was looted a number of times by Moslem invaders from the 11th century on. These destructive visits climaxed with the Moghul Emperor Aurangzeb who destroyed almost all of the temples and converted the most famous one into a mosque.

Varanasi has also been known as Kashi and Benares but its present name is the restoration of an ancient name meaning the city between two rivers — the Varauana and Asi. For the pious Hindu the city has always had a special place. Besides being a pilgrimage centre it is considered especially auspicious to die here, ensuring an instant routing to heaven. To this day Varanasi is a centre of learning, especially Sanskrit, and students flock here from all over India. Ironically Varanasi is in the centre of the most backward areas of India — a largely agrarian, rural and overpopulated area that has developed little since independence. On the other hand Varanasi has become a symbol of the Hindu renaissance and has a special role in the development of Hindu — the national language of India.

Information & Orientation

The old city of Varanasi is situated along the west bank of the Ganges and extends back from the riverbank ghats in a winding collection of narrow alleys. They're too narrow for anything but walking and tall houses overhang the picturesque, though hardly clean, lanes.

It's a fascinating area to wander around. The town extends from Raj Ghat, near the bridge, to Asi Ghat, near the University. Areas known as Chowk, Lahurabir and Godaulia are situated just outside the old city area along the river.

One of the best ways to get oriented in Varanasi is to remember the positions of the ghats, particularly important ghats like Dasaswamadh Ghat. The Cantonment area around the railway station is entirely new and major hotels like Clarks and Benares are situated across the tracks. Here you will also find the Government of India Tourist Office (tel 64189) at 15B The Mall. The broad, tree lined avenues of the Cantonment are a great contrast to the crowds of people, bicycles and rickshaws in the old part of town.

The Indian Airlines Office (tel 64146, 66116) is in the Mint House Motel, opposite Nadesar Palace in the Cantonment. Babatpur Airport is a lengthy 22 km out of the city. Railway reservations at the Cantonment Station are made on 64920. The bus station is also in the Cantonment.

The Ghats

Varanasi's principal attraction is the long string of bathing ghats which line the west bank of the Ganges. Ghats are the steps which lead down to the river, from which pilgrims make their sin cleansing dip in the river and on which, at the two 'burning ghats', bodies are cremated. The best time to visit the ghats is at dawn, then pilgrims will be there for their early morning dip, the city will be coming alive, the light will be magical and Varanasi will seem a quite amazingly exotic place.

There are over 100 ghats in all, of which Dasawamadh Ghat is probably the most convenient starting point. A trip from there to Manikarnika Ghat makes an interesting short introduction to the river and will cost about Rs 3 to

Key to Sarnath:-
① Burmese Monastery
② Ashoka Column
③ Dhamekh Stupa
④ Mulgandha Kuti-Vihar
⑤ Archeology Museum
⑥ Chaukhandi Stupa
⑦ Main Shrine
⑧ Dharmarajika Stupa

Varanasi

→ Patna Calcutta

→ Mirzapur

Ram Nagar Rd

Key:-
1. Cantt. Railway Station
2. City Railway Station
3. Kashi Railway Station
4. Tourist Office ≠ Hotel de Paris
5. Indian Airlines
6. G.P.O.
7. Chowk Police Station
8. Clark's Hotel
9. Tourist Bungalow
10. Modern Lodge
11. Central Lodge ≠ Banaras Lodge
12. Vijayanagaram Palace
13. Durga Temple ≠ Satyanarayan Tulsi Manas Temple
14. Siva Temple
15. Nandeshwar Palace
16. Chai Baba's

Gai Ghat
Panchganga Ghat
Ram Ghat
Manikarnika Ghat
Lalita Ghat
Mir Ghat
Dasashwamedh Ghat
Rana Ghat
Kedar Ghat
Harishchandra Ghat
Hanuman Ghat
Shivala Ghat
Anandmayee Ghat
Tulsidas Ghat
Asi Ghat

Ram Nagar Fort Palace
Ferry
Hanuman Ghat
Nagwa Ghat

Madanpura Road
Godaulia
Sonarpura Rd
Asi Road
Durgakund Rd
Chintamani Rd
Luxa Road
Aurangabad Road
Sheopurwa Rd
Raja Motichand Road
Durgakund Rd

Mirg
Harishchandra Road
Panch Koshi Road

→ Allahabad

5 if you hire a boat. An alternative is to hire a boat between a group of people for a longer trip — your hotel may be able to help.

Look out for the people on the ghats, the women bathing discreetly in their saris, the young men going through contortionist yoga exercises, the Brahmin priests offering blessings (for a price) and the ever present beggars giving others an opportunity to do their karma some good. Look for the lingams which mark each ghat, for Varanasi is the city of Shiva. Look for the buildings and temples around the ghats, often tilting precariously or in some cases actually sliding down into the river. Each monsoon causes great damage to the riverbank buildings of Varanasi. Look for the burning ghats where bodies are cremated after making their final journey to the holy Ganges swathed in white cloth and carried on a bamboo stretcher — or even the roof of a taxi. Manikarnika and the less used Harischandra Ghat are the main burning ghats.

The Asi Ghat, the furthest ghat upstream, is one of the five special ghats which pilgrims are supposed to bathe from in order and on the same day. The order is Asi then Dasaswamadh, Barnasangam, Panchganga and finally Manikarnika. Much of the Tulsi Ghat has fallen down towards the river. The Bachhraj Ghat is Jain and there are three riverbank Jain temples. Many of the ghats are owned by Maharajas or other princely rulers — such as the very fine Shivala or Kali Ghat owned by the Maharaja of Varanasi. The Dandi Ghat is the ghat of ascetics known as Dandi Panths and near that is the very popular Hanuman Ghat.

The Harischandra or Smashan Ghat is a secondary burning ghat. Bodies are cremated by outcastes known as chandal. Above the Kedar Ghat is a shrine popular with Bengalis and south Indians. Mansarowar Ghat was built by Man Singh of Amber and named after the Tibetan lake at the foot of Mt Kailash, Shiva's Himalayan home. Someswar or 'Lord of the Moon' Ghat is said to be able to heal diseases. The Munshi Ghat is very picturesque while Ahalya Bai's Ghat is named after the Maratha woman ruler of Indore.

The Dasaswamadh Ghat's name indicates that Brahma sacrificed (madh), ten (das) horses (aswa) here. It's one of the most important ghats and also conveniently central. Note its statues and the shrine of Sitala, goddess of smallpox. Raja Man Singh's Man Mandir Ghat was built in 1600 but has been poorly restored in the last century. Note the fine stone balcony on the northern corner of the ghat. Raja Jai Singh of Jaipur also erected one of his unusual observatories on this ghat in 1710. It is not as fine as the Jai Singh observatory in Delhi or Jaipur but its setting is unique.

The Mir Ghat leads to the Nepalese Temple with its erotic sculptures. Between here and the Jalsain Ghat the Golden Temple stands back from the river. The Jalsain Ghat, where cremations are made, virtually adjoins one of the most sacred of the ghats, the Manikarnika Ghat. Above the steps is a tank known as the Manikarnika Well, Parvati is said to have dropped her earring here and Shiva dug the tank out to recover it, filling the depression with his sweat! The Charanpaduka is a slab of stone between the well and the ghat which bears footprints made by Vishnu. Privileged VIPs are allowed to be cremated at the Charanpaduka. There is also a temple to Ganesh on the ghat.

Dattatreya Ghat bears the footprint of the Brahmin saint of that name in a small temple near the ghat. Scindia's Ghat was originally built in 1830 but was so huge and magnificent a structure that it collapsed into the river and had to be rebuilt. The Ram Ghat was built by the Raja of Jaipur. As its name

A pilgrim couple at the banks of the Ganges...

indicates five rivers are supposed to meet at the Panchganga Ghat. Above the ghat is Aurangzeb's smaller mosque, also known as the Alamgir Mosque, built over a Vishnu temple. The Gai Ghat has a figure of a cow made of stone upon it. The Trilochan Ghat has two turrets emerging from the river and water between them is especially holy. Raj Ghat was the ferry pier until the road and rail bridge was completed here.

Golden Temple

Dedicated to Vishveswara (Vishwanath), Shiva as Lord of the Universe, the Golden Temple is across the road from its original position. Aurangzeb destroyed the original temple and built a mosque over it — traces of the 1600 temple can be seen behind his mosque. The present temple was built in 1776 by Ahalya Bai of Indore and the gold

plating on the towers was provided by Maharaja Ranjit Singh of Lahore. Next to the temple is the well known as Gyan Kupor the 'well of knowledge'. Much esteemed by the faithful this well is said to contain the Shiva lingam removed from the original temple and hidden to protect it from Aurangzeb. Non-Hindus are not allowed into the temple but can view it from upstairs in a house across the street. Near the temple, which is interesting to visit in the evening, are narrow alleys filled with an incredible number of shops.

Great Mosque of Aurangzeb

Constructed using columns from the Biseswar Temple which Aurangzeb razed, his great mosque has minarets towering 71 metres above the Ganges. Armed guards protect the mosque.

Durga Temple

The Durga Temple is commonly known as the Monkey Temple due to the many monkeys that have made it their home. It was built in the 18th century by a Bengali Maharani and is stained red with ochre. The small temple is built in north Indian Nagara style with a multi-tiered shikara. Durga is the 'terrible' form of Shiva's consort Parvati so at festivals there are often sacrifices of goats. Although this is one of the best known temples in Varanasi it is, like the other Hindu temples, closed to non-believers. However, you can look down inside the temple from a walkway at the top. Next to the temple is a tank with stagnant water where, as usual, pilgrims bathe.

Tulsi Manas Temple

Right next to the Durga Temple is this modern, marble shikara style temple. Built in 1964 the walls of the temple are engraved with verses and scenes from the Ram Charita Manas, the Hindu version of the Ranayana. This tells of the history and deeds of Lord Rama, an incarnation of Vishnu, and its mediaeval author, Tulsi Das, lived here while writing this epic Hindi version. He died in 1623. Non-Hindus are allowed into this temple.

Benares Hindu University

A further 20 minutes walk from the Durga Temple, or a Rs 1 rickshaw ride, is the Benares Hindu University, constructed at the beginning of the century. The large university covers an area of five square km and you can get there by bus from Godaulia or by a rickshaw for about Rs 3. The university was founded by Pandit Malviya as a centre of education in Indian art, culture and music and for the study of Sanskrit. The Bharat Kala Bhawan or BHU at the university has a fine collection of miniature paintings. It's open 11 am to 4 pm (8 am to 12 noon in summer) and closed on Sundays.

New Vishwanath Temple

It's about a 30 minute walk from the gates of the university to the new Vishwanath Temple, planned by Pandit Malviya and built by the wealthy Birla family of industrialists. A great nationalist, Pandit Malviya wished to see Hinduism revived without its caste distinctions and prejudices — accordingly this temple, unlike so many in Varanasi, is open to all, irrespective of caste or religion. The interior has a Shiva lingam and verses from Hindu scriptures are inscribed on the walls. The temple is supposed to be a replica of the original Vishwanath Temple, destroyed by Aurangzeb.

Alamgir Mosque

Locally known as Beni Madhav Ka Darera this was originally a Vishnu temple erected by the Maratha chieftan Beni Madhav Rao Scindia. Aurangzeb destroyed it and erected the mosque in its place but it is a curious Hindu-Moslem mixture with the bottom part entirely Hindu.

Bharat Mata Temple

Dedicated to 'Mother India' this temple has a marble relief map of India instead of the usual images of gods and goddesses. It was opened by Mahatma Gandhi and non-Hindus are allowed inside. The temple is about 1.5 km south of the Cantonment station.

Ramnagar Fort

On the other side of the river this 17th century fort is the home of the Maharaja of Benares. Tours or a ferry across the river will take you to the fort with its interesting museum. The museum contains old silver and brocade palanquins for the ladies of the court, elephant howdahs made of silver, old brocades, a replica of the royal bed and an armoury of swords and old guns. The fort is open from 10 am to 12 noon and 1 to 5 pm and entry to the museum costs Rs 1.

Tours

Varanasi tours are quite good value — costing around Rs 10 each for morning and afternoon tours or Rs 20 for both. They start from the Tourist Bungalow or the major hotels in the Cantonment area in the morning and from the Government of India Tourist Office on The Mall in the afternoon. Telephone 63233 for booking details. The morning tour leaves at 6 am and takes you down the Ganges by the ghats, around the various temples and out to the university. The morning tour finishes at 12.15 pm and the afternoon tour commences at 2.30 pm and runs to 6.25 pm — definitely a full day. The afternoon tour takes you out to Sarnath and to the Ramnagar Fort. In summer all times are half an hour earlier.

Places to Stay — Top End

Varanasi has three major 'tourist class' hotels — all in the new Cantonment area near the railway station. *Hotel Clarks Varanasi* (tel 62021) is the oldest, dating back to the British era, and is somewhat Victorian in appearance. Air-conditioned singles/doubles are Rs 150/230 and there is a swimming pool, shops and other facilities.

Hotel Varanasi Ashok (tel 52251) is entirely new and centrally air-conditioned although somewhat smaller in size. Rooms are similarly priced to Clarks. *Hotel de Paris* (tel 64461) is also on The Mall and has singles/doubles from Rs 120/180 or slightly less without air-conditioning. These hotels are all about a Rs 3 rickshaw ride from the town centre.

Other more expensive hotels include the *Diamond Hotel* (tel 55561) at Bhelupur and the *Ajaya Hotel* (tel 53440) at Lahurabir, midway between the station and the old town. Ajaya has rooms from as low as Rs 20 up towards Rs 100 with air-con. *Hotel International* (tel 67140) is similar and also OK.

Places to Stay – Bottom End

The *Tourist Bungalow* (tel 63186) is only a five minute walk from the station and is a popular low-budget place. Rickshaws may be unwilling to take you there from the station because they don't get a commission as with many of the cheap hotels. Most rooms are doubles at Rs 25 but there are some singles at Rs 12, all with private bathrooms. There's also a Rs 5 mixed dorm with big lockers. The management is helpful and there's a reasonably good restaurant.

The *Tourist Dak Bungalow* (tel 64461) on The Mall is also very popular with overlanders and has camping facilities. Singles here cost Rs 25, doubles Rs 50, if you're camping with your own vehicle that is Rs 5 a day. There are *Railway Retiring Rooms* at the Cantonment Station with singles/doubles for Rs 15/30.

Still in the Cantonment area the *Mint House Motel* (tel 67124) at Nadesar is an old mansion converted into a hotel. Singles/doubles are Rs 20/30. Near the Varuna Bridge *Hotel Overlanders* has doubles for Rs 25 and also camping facilities. *Hotel Amar* (tel 64044) is near the railway station and just before the Tourist Bungalow. Clean, good room service and doubles are Rs 25, often with your own (fully functioning) shower. *Hotel Relax*, in the same area, charges Rs 12 for a single.

Hotel Sunite at 712/16 B1 Bagh Baulia, Ram Kotora, is just off Kabir Chaura, the main street between the station and the old city. Doubles cost Rs 20 to 30 and there are clean showers. In the city centre, near Dasaswamadh Ghat and Gadaulia, *Benares Lodge* (tel 52739) and *Central Hotel* (tel 62776) cost about Rs 20 for singles – they're well known places. Staying close to the river does have the advantage over the Cantonment places in that it tends to be cooler during the hot season. *Tandon House Lodge* is right on the river at Gai Ghat. Small clean rooms at just Rs 15 a double. *Yogi Lodge*, near the ghats and the Golden Temple is popular with people on a really rock bottom budget. Doubles are Rs 15, dorm beds Rs 5 and it also has a restaurant. Some of these places simply charge whatever they feel you're foolish enough to pay but this one is pretty good.

The more expensive *Hotel India* (tel 66388) costs Rs 50 a double with bath – it's clean and comfortable. Close to the river *Hotel KMM* (tel 62636) is around Rs 20 a double, rooms have private bathrooms and there's a reasonable restaurant. *Sri Vankateswar Lodge* (tel 66800) on Dasaswamadh Ghat Rd is only 100 metres from the river – around Rs 15 a double in this popular cheapie.

Most rock bottom of all at Varanasi are houseboats on the river – great if you like mosquitoes.

Places to Eat

The popular *Tourist Bungalow* has a good menu with reasonable prices. The waiters tend to bully you for a tip so leave 10 or 20 paise if you want to enjoy cheap eating again! As usual the railway station restaurant is the cheapest place for eggs and breakfast and they also make good 'pot tea'. Varanasi's station restaurant actually has a good reputation for all types of food. Near the railway station the *Nar-Indra Hotel* has a restaurant which is not only cheap but clean too, often difficult to find that combination here.

The Chinese *Mandarin Restaurant* near the Tourist Bungalow is pretty good although, as usual, it's distinctly Indian-Chinese. *Winfa Restaurant* in Lahurabir, behind the cinema, is possibly Varanasi's best Chinese restaurant. Around Rs 10 for a meal. There is also a good, but reasonably expensive, *Kwality Restaurant* in Lahurabir.

In Dasaswamadh, in the alleys between the ghats and Godaulia, there are many small restaurants with good thalis for about Rs 3. Most of them do not even have a name. There is also the *KCM* health food place in Godaulia, across the street from the cinema.

Varanasi is well known for its excellent sweets and *Madhur Jalpan Grih*, on the same side of the street as the cinema in Godaulia, is an excellent place to try them. *Basant Behar* in Lahurabir is also very good. Varanasi is also supposed to have very high quality pan.

Getting There
Air Varanasi is on a number of Indian Airlines routes including the popular daily tourist service Delhi-Agra-Khajuraho-Varanasi-Kathmandu. Three times weekly there is a Delhi-Kanpur-Allahabad-Varanasi-Calcutta service. Fares to or from Varanasi include Delhi Rs 500, Allahabad Rs 120, Khajuraho Rs 265, Bhubaneswar Rs 465 and Calcutta Rs 465.

Trains There are not a great number of trains running directly between Delhi and Varanasi or Calcutta and Varanasi although most Delhi-Calcutta trains do pass through Moghulserai, two hours south of Varanasi by bus. Express trains

Cop — DIRECTING TRAFFIC
VARANASI

between Delhi and Varanasi take 13 to 16 hours and cost Rs 150 in 1st class, Rs 36 in 2nd. From Calcutta it takes about 12 hours to Varanasi and the fare is about Rs 145 in 1st, Rs 34 in 2nd.

The Upper India Express is a direct Delhi-Varanasi train. It leaves Delhi at 8 pm and arrives in Varanasi at around 1 pm the next day. This is also a good train in the opposite direction as it departs Varanasi around 6 pm and reaches New Delhi at 10 am. Patna and Allahabad are about six and four hours away by train respectively.

Bus The bus station is next to the main railway station. If you are heading for Nepal the bus may be better than rail since there are only metre gauge trains from here to the border. Buses leave almost hourly to Gorakhpur, five hours away. A tourist bus operates from there to Sunauli on the Nepal border in only three hours. There are also direct buses operating Varanasi-Sunauli very early in the morning and costing Rs 20.

Getting Around

Godaulia (also spelt Godowlia and Gadaulia) is the mid-town bus stop just an easy walk from the ghats. It's a very useful city landmark. Lanka is the bus stop closest to Benares Hindu University. Between the railway station and Godaulia a bus costs about Rs 0.25 but unless you can get on at the starting point Varanasi buses tend to be very crowded. A bus from Godaulia to Sarnath, 10 km away, costs Rs 1.75.

Rickshaws are still comparatively cheap in Varanasi, between the railway station and Godaulia, near Dasaswamadh Ghat, is about Rs 1 to 1.50. There are a number of places to rent bicycles around Lanka — all day rates are Rs 5 for a new bike, Rs 2 for an old one.

Things to Buy

Varanasi is famous all over India for silk brocades and beautiful Benares saris. However, there are lots of rip-off merchants and commission men at work. Invitations to 'come to my home for tea' will inevitably mean to somebody's silk showroom where you will be pressured into buying things. The same process applies to sitars — yes Ravi Shankar does live here (or nearby) but don't believe that every sitar maker is his personal friend!

SARNATH

Only 10 km away from Varanasi, that most holy of Hindu cities, is Sarnath, one of the major Buddhist centres. Having achieved enlightenment at Bodh Gaya it was Sarnath where the Buddha came to preach his message of the middle way to final nirvana. Later Ashoka, the great Buddhist emperor, erected magnificent stupas and other buildings here. Sarnath was at its peak when those indefatigable Chinese travellers Fa Hian and Hiuen Tsang visited the site. In 640, when the latter made his call, Sarnath had 1500 priests, a stupa nearly 100 metres high, Ashoka's mighty stone pillar and many other wonders. Soon after Buddhism went into decline and by the time the destructive Moslem invasions of India had commenced Sarnath was little more than a shell. The invaders destroyed and desecrated the buildings, even Akbar built a monument to his father, Humayun, over one stupa, and time did the rest. It was not until 1836 when British archaeologists commenced excavations that Sarnath regained some of its past glory. Sarnath was known as the 'deer park'.

Dhamekh Stupa

Believed to date from around 500 AD, this stupa was probably rebuilt a number of times over earlier constructions. The geometrical and floral patterns on the stupa are typical of the Gupta period but excavations into the stupa have revealed brickwork from the Mauryan period around 200 BC.

Dharmarajika Stupa

This large stupa has been comprehensively excavated by 19th century treasure seekers. Near it is the building known as the 'main shrine' where Ashoka is said to have meditated.

Ashoka Pillar

Standing in front of the main shrine is the remains of Ashoka's Pillar. At one time this stood over 20 metres high but today the capital has been removed and can be seen in the Sarnath museum. An edict issued by Ashoka is engraved on the remaining portion of the column. The capital is the Ashokan symbol of four back-to-back lions which has now been adopted as the state symbol of modern India. On the lower portion of the column are representations of a lion, an elephant, a horse and a bull. The lion is supposed to represent bravery, the elephant symbolises the dream Buddha's mother had before his birth and the horse recalls that Buddha left his home on horseback in search of enlightenment.

Museum

Sarnath's excellent Archaeological Museum has the capital from the Ashokan pillar together with many other relics found on the site. These include many figures and sculptures from the various periods of Sarnath — Mauryan, Kushana, Gupta and later. They include the earliest Buddha image found at Sarnath, Buddha figures in various positions dating back to the 5th and 6th centuries and many images of Hindu gods such as Saraswati, Ganesh and Vishnu from the 9th to 12th centuries.

Other

There is a modern Maha Bodhi Society temple known as the Mulgandha Kuti-Vihar. It has a series of frescoes in the interior, painted by a Japanese artist. A Bo tree growing here is a transplant from the tree in Auradhapura in Sri Lanka, which in turn is said to be an offspring of the original tree under which the Buddha attained enlighteenment. The brick remnants of the monastery or vihara can still be seen and amongst the mango trees you can see a deer park off to one side.

Places to Stay

Sarnath has a *Tourist Bungalow* (tel 8485) with rooms at Rs 25 or dorm beds at Rs 5.

Getting There

You can visit Sarnath on a tour from Varanasi or get there by bus for Rs 1.50.

NORTH FROM DELHI

Meerut (population 400,000)
Only 67 km north-east of Delhi this was the place where the 1857 Mutiny first broke out. There's little to remember that event by today although the cemetery near St John's Church has the graves of, amongst others, Sir Ochterlony whose monument dominates the Maidan in Calcutta. The Suraj Khund is the most interesting Hindu temple in Meerut.

Saharanpur (population 250,000)
Situated 178 km north of Delhi the large botanical gardens here, known as the Company Bagh, are over 150 years old.

NORTHERN UTTAR PRADESH

The northern part of Uttar Pradesh, a rough rectangle bordered by Himachal Pradesh to the north-west, China to the north-east and Nepal to the north-east, is an area of hills, mountains and lakes. There are a number of popular hill stations such as Naina Tal and Almora, important pilgrimage centres like Hardwar and Rishikesh, where the holy Ganges leaves its Himalayan birthplace and joins the plains for its long trip to the sea. And, of course, there are many trekking routes — most of them little known and even less used.

Toll Taxes

If you're travelling up to the Uttar Pradesh hill stations (Naini Tal, Almosa, Raniket, Mussoorie) somebody will jump on the bus just as you approach the towns to charge you a Rs 1 or 2 toll tax. In Himachal Pradesh these toll taxes are included in the bus fare.

DEHRA DUN (population 250,000)

Also spelt Dehra Doon this is the gateway to places in the Garwhal Himal such as Badrinath and Joshimath. Dehra Dun is in the centre of a forest area and has a forest research institute. The town is situated in an inter-montane valley in the Siwaliks, the southernmost and lowest of the Himalayan ranges. The high range just to the north contains the hill station Mussoorie, 22 km away.

Information & Orientation

The Tourist Office (tel 3217) is close to the bus stands and the railway station. The clock tower is the 'hub' of the town and most of the hotels are situated on the road from the railway station to the tower. There are two main bus stations — the one nearer the railway station is for buses to the hills and the one nearer the clock tower is for other destinations.

Things to See & Tours

There are a number of pleasant picnic spots around the town plus the Forestry Research Institute. The institute is the biggest research centre for forestry and forest products in India and also has a botanical garden. Popular picnic spots, with their distance from the town, include Sahastradhara (14 km) with natural sulphur springs. The Takeshwar Temple (6 km) is a Shiva temple while just beyond Anarwala village (7 km) is the 'robbers' cave'. Laxman Sidh is another temple, located on the Dehra Dun-Rishikesh road. Tapovan

Dehra Dun

(6 km) is two km off the Dehra Dun-Raipur road and has an ashram. A sightseeing tour from the Tourist Office costs Rs 10 and goes to the institute and some of the picnic spots.

Places to Stay

Hotel Madhuban (tel 4094-97) on Rajpur Rd has air-con rooms at Rs 110/160, non air-con at Rs 60/75. *Hotel Meedo* (tel 7088), near the railway station, is a new building with good rooms — singles cost Rs 22. In the same area the *Hotel Prince* is similarly priced. Opposite the hospital there's the slightly better *Hotel Relax* with singles starting from Rs 30 to 40.

Places to Eat

Vaishno Restaurant, opposite the Jain dharamsala, near the station, has a Rs 4 thali including the dessert known as khir. Good Indian dishes at *Moti Mahal*. *Kumar Sweets* has an excellent selection of sweets including their speciality, kesar ka halwa.

Getting There

Dehra Dun is connected with major north Indian cities by rail. There is a de-luxe bus service operating between Delhi and Dehra Dun. The trip takes six hours and costs Rs 30.

MUSSOORIE (population 20,000)

At an altitude of 2000 metres and 22 km beyond Dehra Dun, Mussoorie is a popular hill resort in the hot weather. It's situated on a horseshoe shaped hill and much fruit is grown here. There is a ropeway up to Gun Hill and Municipal Gardens to the west of the town.

Places to Stay

There are a number of more expensive hotels including the *Savoy Hotel* (tel 601-02-04) with all inclusive prices from Rs 175/330 for singles/doubles. Or the *Roselynn Estate Hotel* (tel 201) where doubles range from around Rs 60 to Rs 200 depending on the standard of the room and the time of the year. At the other end of the scale the *Mullingar Hotel*, at the top of Landour Bazaar, is not only the cheapest place around it's also good value.

Getting There

Frequent buses operate between the railhead at Dehra Dun and Mussoorie. There is a road from Mussoorie to Simla direct but foreigners are not allowed to take it without a permit.

HARDWAR (population 85,000)

Hardwar is at the base of the Siwalik Hills, where the Ganges River, coming down from the high Himalayas, passes through a gorge and starts its slow progress across the plains to the Bay of Bengal. It is a town of great pilgrimage importance due to this propitious location and has many ashrams and itinerant sadhus. If you wish to study Hinduism you may find Rishikesh, 24 km further north, a more pleasant place. Despite its religious sanctity Hardwar is really just another noisy, north Indian city. Every 12 years the Kumbh Mela comes to Hardwar and draws as many as half a million pilgrims. It takes place every three years at Allahabad, Nasik, Ujjain and here.

Information & Orientation

The main street of Hardwar is narrow and long although the suburban area is quite spread out. The bus stand and railway station are side by side, the Tourist Office (tel 19) is a little north of them.

Hardwar

Key:-
① Tourist Office
② General Post Office

N

Rishikesh

Har Ki
Paudi Ghat

Vilwakeshwar
Mahadeo Temple

Bus
Station

Railway
Station

Tourist
Bungalow

Ganga Canal

Roorkee

Things to See

Although Hardwar is a very old town mentioned by the Chinese scholar-traveller Hiuen Tsang its many temples are of comparatively recent origin and of little architectural interest although they do have many idols and illustrated scenes from the Hindu epics. Har-ki-pairi is the most important bathing ghat as it is supposed to be at the precise spot where the Ganges leaves the mountains and enters the plains. Consequently it's power to wash away sins at this spot is superlative. There is supposed to be a footprint of Vishnu in a stone at this ghat. The *Daksha Mahadev Temple*, four km downstream, is Hardwar's most important temple. According to the legend Daksha was the father of Sati, Shiva's first wife. Daksha performed a sacrifice here but neglected to invite Shiva and Sati was so angry at this disrespect to her husband that she managed to spontaneously self-immolate! Other temples and buildings of lesser interest include the Sapt Rishi Ashram, where the Ganges divides up into a number of smaller streams, and the Parmath Ashram, six km towards Rishikesh, with fine images of the Goddess Durga. The Mansa Devi Temple is three km from the Tourist Office, while Beauty Point, in the same direction, offers fine views over the town. Chandi Devi and a number of other temples are reached by a three km walk. 'Hardwar is a far nicer place to visit than Varanasi', reported one traveller, 'there aren't the 'no entry' signs on the temples or the hard-sell salesmen. It's smaller and easier to get around, more beautiful'.

Places to Stay

Hardwar and Rishikesh are so close that it is quite easy to stay in the latter and day trip to Hardwar. If you want to stay in Hardwar the UP state government *Tourist Bungalow* costs Rs 25 a double, Rs 5 in the dorm, but is a little inconveniently situated across the river from the main part of town. Near the Tourist Office is the *Hotel Gurudev* on Station Rd which costs Rs 20 for a single. There are many cheaper hotels and also *Railway Retiring Rooms.*

Places to Eat
Chotewala, near the Tourist Office, does full thalis for Rs 5.

Getting There
Hardwar is 222 km from Delhi, 52 km from Dehra Dun and 24 km from Rishikesh. There are direct buses from all these places. By train it is 14 hours from Lucknow or seven hours from Delhi.

RISHIKESH (population 22,000)
Surrounded by hills on three sides, Rishikesh is a quieter and more easy going place than Hardwar although at an altitude of 356 metres it is only 63 metres higher. Like Hardwar there are many ashrams and sadhus and this is an excellent place to study Hinduism. Back in the '60s Rishikesh gained instant, and fleeting, fame as the place where the Beatles came to be with their guru, the Maharishi Mahesh Yogi. Rishikesh is also the jumping off point for treks to Himalayan pilgrimage centres like Badrinath, Kedarnath and Gangotri.

Information & Orientation
The Tourist Office (tel 209) is on Railway Station Rd. The bus stand is round the corner from it on Agarwal Rd.

Things to see
The most interesting ghats and temples in Rishikesh are across the river on the left (east) bank but are connected by a free launch system. The Lakshman Jhula suspension bridge is further upstream. Interesting temples include the Parmarth Temple with many images from Hindu mythology. The Lakshman Temple is by the bridge, three km from the town centre. Neel Khanth Mahadev is 12 km further on, fine views on the way up to the temple at 1700 metres.

Meditation
Studying Hinduism has, naturally, become somewhat commercialised at Rishikesh. The Divine Life Society, founded by Swami Shivanand, is an authentic place. It's on the Tourist Bungalow side of the river. You can stay there for short term study or for longer three month courses. Or simply drop by for the evening lecture at 'Satsanga'. At Ved Niketan an Indian sadhu gives lectures in English to those interested. And, of course, there's the Maharishi Mahesh Yogi's Transcendental Meditation Centre.

Places to Stay
The *Tourist Bungalow* (tel 372) is the best place in town and has rooms with attached bath for Rs 15/25 for singles/doubles. Food is also available here and there's a pleasant garden for relaxing in. The Tourist Bungalow is three km from the bus and railway station. *Hotel Indralok* is next to the station and costs Rs 20 for a single with attached bath. It's a new hotel with a good dining hall. Other hotels include the *Hotel Menka* (tel 285) also near the bus stand and the *Janta Tourist Lodge* on Dehra Dun Rd. As at Hardwar there are many dharamsalas offering free accommodation to pilgrims.

Getting There
There is a branch railway line from Hardwar up to Rishikesh and regular direct buses.

Key :-
1. Bus Station
2. Tourist Office
3. G.P.O.
4. Hotel Menka
5. Tourist Bungalow
6. Forest Rest House
7. Mahesh Yogi Ashram

Rishikesh

River Chandrabhaga

Dehradun Road

Badrinath Rd.

Narendra Nagar Road

Laxman Jhoola Bridge

Parmarth Temple

River Ganga

Railway Station

Station Road

Agarwal Road

Tilak Rd.

Ghat Rd.

Main Bazar

Someshwar Mandir Marg

College Rd.

Hardwar Laxman Jhoola Marg

I.D.P.L. Road

Virbhadra Road

Triveni Ghat

River Ganga

CORBETT NATIONAL PARK

On the banks of the Ram Ganga River in the foothills of the Himalayas, this park is famous for its wide variety of wildlife. The park is particularly renowned for its tigers but also has elephants, several types of deer, panthers and sambars. The river has crocodiles and there is much birdlife. The park was established in 1935 and later renamed after Jim Corbett, who spent many years in this area and wrote the book *The Man-Eaters of Kumaon*.

Dhikala is the main accommodation centre in the park, 51 km from Ramnagar, the nearest railhead to the park. Most tours into the park are operated from Dhikala although there are also three day package tours operated from New Delhi. Entry to the park costs Rs 25 for three days, then Rs 5 per day.

Places to Stay

At Dhikala there are *Cabins* (Rs 100 per day without air-conditioning), *New* and *Old Forest Rest Houses* (Rs 60 per day), *Tourist Hutments* (Rs 30), *Swiss Cottage Tents* (Rs 7.50) and camping facilities

(Rs 2.50 per person). There are also *Forest Rest Houses* at Sarapduli, Bijrani, Gairal, Kanda and Sultan.

ALMORA (population 23,000)
This picturesque hill station was taken from Nepal following the 1815 Gurkha War. It's at an altitude of 1650 metres and many travellers live in cottages in the hills around the town. There is a good walk from Almora up to the Kasar Devi temple which has excellent views.

Places to Stay
There are a number of hotels and the popular *Tourist Cottage* with doubles for Rs 15.

NAINI TAL (population 28,000)
In this lake dotted area of the Kumaon Hills the pretty hill town of Naini Tal was once the summer capital of Uttar Pradesh. There are many interesting walks and lakes around the town — which itself is divided into two parts,

upper and lower lake (Tal). Climb up to China Peak in the early morning for the fine view over Naina Tal and the snow-clad Himalayas off in the distance.

Places to Stay
Most places here are rather expensive — including the *Grand Hotel* on The Mall, the *Royal Hotel* and the *Swiss Hotel* — all with rooms from around Rs 100. There is a *Youth Hostel* (Rs 6 in the dorm) at the west end of the town, about three km from the bus stand. *Sharma Vaishnow Restaurant* in the Malli Tal Bazaar offers all-you-can-eat vegetarian meals for Rs 4.

RANIKHET
North of Naini Tal and only a short distance west of Almora this hill station offers excellent views of the snow-capped Himalayas. Only eight km away, Chaubattia is famous for its fruits.

TREKKING IN THE GARWHAL HIMAL
Although the Garwhal Himal is little known as a trekking region it boasts a number of famous peaks, including Trisul and India's highest mountain, Nanda Devi. There are also many important pilgrimage sites such as Badrinath and Kedarnath or Gaumukh, the actual source of the Ganges. The trekking routes pass through rich, green forests and across beautiful meadows that are carpeted with flowers in summer. Glistening glaciers complement the soaring Himalayan peaks and there are many excellent state government operated tourist bungalows along the routes to simplify the question of shelter.

The best times to trek in the Garwhal Himal are May-June and September-October. Some places, like the Valley of Flowers and the high altitude bugyals (meadows) are at their best during the July-August rainy period. The Mount-

aineering Division, located at the Tourist Bungalow in Rishikesh, can provide more information on trekking in the Garwhal Himal.

Kedarnath
Like Badrinath this is a Hindu pilgrimage spot of great importance. The temple of Lord Kedar (Shiva) is surrounded by snow-capped peaks but although the shrine is said to date back to the 8th century, very little is known about it. To get to Kedarnath you can either make the short, direct trek from Sonprayag, 205 km from Rishikesh, or you can follow the longer and more arduous yatra route from Gangotri. Along the way you pass through beautiful scenery and see many colourful mountain villages. The trek starts from Mela, 20 km beyond Uttarkashi towards Lanka and Gangotri.

Day 1	Mala-Belak Khal	15 km
Day 2	Belak Khal-Budakedar	14 km
Day 3	Budakedar-Ghuttu	16 km
Day 4	Ghuttu-Panwali Khanta	12 km
Day 5	Panwali Khanta-Maggu	8 km
Day 6	Maggu-Sonprayag	9 km
Day 7	Sonprayag-Kedarnath	20 km*
Day 8	Kedarnath-Sonprayag	20 km*

* the first six km of Sonprayag-Kedarnath can be made by taxi.

Gangotri & Gaumukh

This trek to the source of the holy Ganges can be made from either Mussoorie or Rishikesh. Lanka, reached via Uttarkashi-Bukhi-Dabrani is the end of the vehicle road. It's 212 km from Mussoorie to Lanka, 247 km from Rishikesh. The tiny village of Gangotri stands at 3140 metres. The temple of the Goddess Ganga is on the right bank of the Bhagirathi River — which eventually becomes the holy Ganges. Gaumukh is the actual source of the river, at the base of the Bhagirathi peaks. At 4225 metres the Gangotri Glacier is nearly 24 km long and two to four km wide. The glacier ends at Gaumukh, where the Bhagirathi River finally appears. The glacier has gradually retreated over the centuries but during the Vedic era it is supposed to have reached down to Gangotri. Beyond Gaumukh places like Nandanvan and Tapovan are great pilgrimage centres where sadhus often retreat to meditate in remote caves.

Day 1	Lanka-Gangotri	11 km
Day 2	Gangotri-Chirbasa	12 km
Day 3	Chirbasa-Gaumukh	7 km
Day 4	Gaumukh-Chirbasa	7 km
Day 5	Chirbasa-Gangotri	12 km
Day 6	Gangotri-Lanka	11 km

Nanda Devi Sanctuary

Some of the most outstanding peaks in the Central Himalaya are clustered between the glaciers of Gangotri and Milan. Nanda Devi is the most important peak with its camel humped summit; it is the highest mountain in India at 7818 metres. The Nanda Devi Sanctuary is surrounded by almost 70 white peaks, like some sort of natural fortress. The sanctuary has a perimeter of nearly 120 km and an area of 640 square km. It's dotted with meadows and waterfalls and is the base camp and starting point for mountaineering assaults on the Nanda Devi.

The seven day trek from Lata, the roadhead 15 km from Joshimath, to Tilchaunni is at times difficult and tedious. The scenic grandeur you walk through will often compensate for weary bodies and frayed nerves. The first six km from Lata to Lata Kharak is a tiring uphill struggle of 1524 metres but one is well rewarded by glorious views of Ronti, Nanda Ghunti and Bethartoli across the Rishi Ganga. The broad, open grassy ridge of Lata Kharak is covered with flowers in the summer but it is always windy and cold. From here there are fine views of the northern face of Bethartoli Himal and the Trisul Massif to the south. Another long uphill trek crosses the 4253 metre Dharansi Pass takes you to Dharansi. On approaching the pass you get your first glimpse of Dunagiri (7068 metres) and immediately after crossing it Nanda Devi can be seen.

From Dharansi the trail winds its way across the Malatuni Pass (4238 metres), where the western face of Hanuman (6076 metres) can be seen, then descends almost 750 metres through grass and snow slopes and dense forest to a stream. After crossing the stream you finally arrive at the hospitable meadows of Dibrugheta where a camp can be made by the river. In summer the grass is carpeted with flowers. From here to Deodi the track rises steeply at first then makes a long traverse across several ridges before you cross a bridge over the Rishi Ganga and arrive at Deodi. From Deodi it is an eight km trek through juniper and rhododendron forests to Ramani. Nanda Devi comes ever closer as you approach Tilchaunni.

Day 1	Joshimath-Lata	15 km*
	Lata-Lata Kharak	6 km
Day 2	Lata Kharak-Dharansi	10 km
Day 3	Dharansi-Deodi	13 km
Day 4	Deodi-Ramani	8 km
Day 5	Ramani-Bhujgara	6 km
Day 6	Bhujgara-Tilchaunni	8 km
Day 7	Tilchaunni-Nanda Devi base camp	5 km
Day 8	Nanda Devi base camp-Bhujgara	6 km
Day 9	Bhujgara-Ramani	14 km
Day 10	Ramani-Dibrugheta	17 km
Day 11	Dibrugheta-Dharansi	4 km
Day 12	Dharansi-Joshimath	31 km**

* by bus
** last 15 km by bus

Yamunotri & Dodital

Yamunotri is the source of the Yamuna River — it emerges from a frozen lake of ice and glaciers on the Kalinda Parvat at an altitude of 4421 metres. There is a temple of the goddess Yamunotri on the left bank of the river and just below the temple there are several hot springs where the water emerges at boiling point. Two more days walk brings you to Dodital where a dense forest of oak, pine, deodar and rhododendron surrounds a dazzling body of water. The lake is filled with fish and many colourful birds can be seen around it. Dodital is at 4024 metres and is fed by natural springs in its depths.

Day 1	Mussoorie-Hanumanchatti	81 km*
Day 2	Hanumanchatti-Jankichatti	7 km
Day 3	Jankichatti-Yamunotri-Jankichatti	14 km
Day 4	Jankichatti-Basard	14 km
Day 5	Basard-Dodital	16 km
Day 6	Dodital-Agro	15 km
Day 7	Agro-Kalyani-Gangori-Uttarkashi	17 km

* 75 km by bus, 6 km by taxi

Kuari Pass

There are two routes from Joshimath to the Kuari Pass. One route goes through Auli and Gorson, Tali and Chitrakhanta

and this is more rewarding than the other route via Mrig to Tugasi and Khulara then Gailgarh to Kuari. From Auli the path trails its way through rich green forests, with the mountains always in view. The camping grounds are an absolute delight — undulating slopes, carpeted in grass and set in beautiful natural surroundings. From Tali to Chitrakhanta there is only a narrow goat track which horses and mules cannot use.

At 4268 metres Kuari, reached by a narrow pass, offers a superb panorama of the Himalayas to the north-east and the vast stretches of verdant valleys to the south-east. Nanda Devi, Dunagiri, Bethatoli, Hathi Parvat and Devastan are some of the peaks which can be seen. On a clear day it is possible to sight the Nanda Devi Sanctuary. Gailgarh, just five km from Kuari, is a little gem in wonderful surroundings. Six km south-east of Gailgarh is the snow-capped 5183 metre peak of Pangarchulia. It can be easily scaled with only normal trekking gear and from its summit Badrinath and other snow-covered peaks can be seen.

Delisera, six km east of Gailgarh, is a little hamlet at 3354 metres. In the local dialect 'sera' means 'the rice fields' and the terraced slopes around here are thought to date back countless years. In late June the entire land is a tapestry of flowers. Bore Kund, six km north-east of Gailgarh, is a lovely lake which is reputed to be very deep.

Day 1	Joshimath-Gorson	15 km*
Day 2	Gorson-Chitrakantha	9 km
Day 3	Chitrakantha-Kuari	8 km
Day 4	Kuari-Donabetti	7 km
Day 5	Donabetti-Panna	8 km
Day 6	Panna-Son Kharak	14 km
Day 7	Son Kharak-Rammani	6 km
Day 8	Ramani-Ghat	14 km
	Ghat-Nandprayag	29 km**

* first eight km by taxi
** by taxi

Khatling Glacier

The first four days of this trek follow the yatra route to Kedarnath, before the trail branches off north-east to the glacier. It then retraces the route to Ghuttu and continues south-west to Ghamsali from where buses run to Tehri and Rishikesh. The Khatling Glacier is a lateral glacier from the centre of which the Bhilangana River emerges. The rich pasturelands here make ideal camping sites — the summer rains make the flat land on the glacial moraines into excellent pastures. The glaciers are associated with the giant hanging glaciers of Ratangian, Jogin and Phating. Around the glacier are the snow capped peaks of the Jogin ground (6466 metres), spectacular Sphetic Prishtwan (6905 metres), Kirti Stambh (6402 metres) and Barte Kanta (6579 metres).

The yatra route is tiring, with its constant ascents and descents, but colourful. There are many rippling streams to be crossed by improvised log bridges. Gangi, the last village before the glacier, is still very much cut off from the outside world. The people here are so isolated that they have been forced to frequently intermarry within their own community and as a result many people are sterile.

Day	1-3	as Kedarnath Trek	
Day	4	Ghuttu-Reeh	10 km
Day	5	Reeh-Gangi	10 km
Day	6	Gangi-Khansoli	15 km
Day	7	Khansoli-Khatling	11 km
Day	8	Khatling-Naumuthi	9 km
Day	9	Naumuthi-Kalyani	12 km
Day	10	Kalyani-Reeh	15 km
Day	11	Reeh-Dhapardhar	15 km
Day	12	Dhapardhar-Gamsali	25 km
		Gamsali-Tehri	31 km (bus)
Day	13	Tehri-Rishikesh	72 km (bus)

The Khatling Glacier trek can also be made from the Kearnath side. In that case the first three days of the trek are like Days 6, 5 and 4 of the Kedarnath Trek. On Day 3 you reach Ghuttu and then the route is the same as from the Gangotri side.

Valley of Flowers & Hemkund

The beautiful 'Valley of Flowers' and the holy Hemkund lake can be reached in one short trek from Govind Ghat. In addition you can also visit the pilgrimage centre of Badrinath, now accessible by road, on the same trip. From Rishikesh it is 252 km by bus to Joshimath and a further 44 km to Badrinath. You then have to backtrack 30 km to Govind Ghat for the start of the trek.

Badrinath Surrounded by snow-capped peaks Badrinath has been a Hindu pilgrimage centre since time immemorial. There are many temples, ashrams and dharamsalas here. The most important temple, on the left bank of the Alakananda shows clear Buddhist influence in its architecture, indicating that in an earlier period this must also have been a Buddhist centre.

The mountaineer Frank Smythe is believed to be the discoverer of the Valley of the Flowers. Between mid-June and mid-September the valley is an enchanting sight with a bewildering variety of flowers fluttering in the gentle breezes. As a backdrop snow clad mountains stand in bold relief against the skyline. The valley is nearly 10 km long, two km wide, and is divided by the Pushpawati stream, into which several tiny streams and waterfalls merge. The huge Ghoradhungi mountain blocks one end of the valley.

From the valley you can backtrack to Ghangariya then follow the Laxma Ganga to the lake of Hemkund. In the Sikh holy book, the Garanth Sahib, the Sikh Guru Govind Singh recounts that in a previous life he had meditated on the shores of a lake surrounded by seven snow-capped mountains. Hemkund Sahib, Sikh pilgrims have decided, is that holy lake. From Govind Ghat it is a gentle incline to the Valley of

Flowers but the trek from the pretty hamlet of Ghangariya to Hemkund is rather steeper.

Day 1	Govind Ghat-Changariya	14 km
Day 2	Ghangariya-Valley of Flowers	6 km
Day 3	Valley of Flowers-Ghangariya	16 km
	Hemkund-Ghangariya	

Roopkund Lake

At an altitude of 4778 metres, below the 7122 metre high Trisul massif, the Roopkund Lake is sometimes referred to as the 'mystery lake', because of skeletons of humans and horses which have been found here. Every 12 years thousands of devout pilgrims make an arduous trek when following the Raj Jay Yatra from Nauti village, near Karanprayag. The pilgrims are said to be lead by a mysterious four horned ram which takes them from there through Roopkund to the Shrine of Nanda Devi, where it disappears. A golden idol of the goddess Nanda Devi is carried by the pilgrims in a silver palanquin.

The trek commences from Gwaldom, accessible by bus from Rishikesh. It passes through delightful alpine pastureland and snow fields and offers magnificent views of peaks in the Garwhal Himalaya such as Trisul and Nanda Ghunti.

Day 1	Rishikesh-Gwaldom	240 km (bus)
Day 2	Gwaldom-Debal	10 km
Day 3	Debal-Mandoli	15 km
Day 4	Mandoli-Wan	14 km
Day 5	Wan-Badni Bugyal	8 km
Day 6	Badni Bugyal-Baggubasa	8 km
Day 7	Baggubasa-Roopkund-Baggubasa	8 km
Day 8	Baggubasa-Wan	16 km
Day 9	Wan-Kannual	9 km
Day 10	Kannual-Sheetal	9 km

Day 11	Sheetal-Ghat	14 km
	Ghat-Nandprayag	30 km (taxi)
Day 12	Nandprayag-Rishikesh	192 km (bus)

Pindari Glacier

The magnificent Pindari Glacier is the most easily accessible in the region. It owes its existence to the snow sliding down from Nanda Khat and other lofty peaks. The glacier, three km long and nearly half a km wide, is at an altitude of 3353 metres. Close to the glacier there is an undulating meadow and to the east a moraine projects into the glacier.

The trek offers views of the soaring peaks all the way and passes through pine forests, glades of ferns and wildflowers and past tumbling waterfalls. From mid-May to mid-June there are many wildflowers while from mid-September to mid-October the air is exceptionally clear and it has not yet got too cold. Starting from Rishikesh you go by bus to Kapkot before actually starting to walk. There is an excellent view of the glacier from Purkiya and some trekkers stop here. On the return trek you can travel by road from Bajnath to Almora and Naini Tal rather than return to Rishikesh. There are PWD Inspection Bungalows at most of the night stops.

Day 1	Rishikesh-Gwaldon	240 km (bus)
Day 2	Gwaldon-Kapkot	76 km (bus)
Day 3	Kapkot-Loharkhet	13 km
Day 4	Loharkhet-Khati	18 km
Day 5	Khati-Purkiya	14 km
Day 6	Purkiya-Pindari	5 km
Day 7	Pindari-Khati	19 km
Day 8	Khati-Loharkhet	18 km
Day 9	Loharkhet-Bajnath	47 km (bus)
Day 10	Bajnath-Kausani-Almora	
		71 km (bus)

Bihar

Population: 62 million
Area: 173,876 square km
Capital: Patna
Main language: Hindi

The northern state of Bihar is one of the most backward and depressed in India. Its tightly packed population scratches a bare living from rice growing. For visitors Bihar is usually little more than a place to be crossed, with perhaps a pause in Patna if they are heading for Nepal by land. Yet 25 centuries ago this was the capital of the greatest empire in India for Ashoka ruled his kingdom from Pataliputra, where Patna is today. Furthermore Bihar was a great religious centre for Jains, Hindus and, most important, Buddhists. It was at Bodhgaya that the

Buddha sat under the Bo tree and attained enlightenment and a descendant of that original tree still flourishes there today. Nearby Nalanda was a world famous university for the study of Buddhism in the 5th century AD while Rajgir was associated with both the Buddha and with the Jain apostle Mahavira.

PATNA (population 550,000)

For many centuries Patna, whose ancient name was Pataliputra, was the capital of a huge empire which ruled a large part of ancient India. Today it is the capital of the rather backward state of Bihar. The city sprawls along the bank of the Ganges, which at this point is very wide; between Varanasi and Patna three major tributaries join the Ganges and the river triples in width. The only way to cross the Ganges at Patna is by ferry but a bridge is now under construction and is expected to be completed in the early '80s.

Information & Orientation

The city stretches for 15 km along the south bank of the Ganges. The main railway station, airline offices, the ferry to cross the river and the airport are all

at the western end of the town while the older and more traditional parts of Patna are to the east. The 'hub' of new Patna is at Gandhi Maidan. The main market area is Ashok Raj Path which starts from Gandhi Maidan. Two important roads near the railway station, Frazer Rd and Exhibition Rd, have recently changed their names to M Haque Path and Braj Kishore Path respectively.

Golghar

Overlooking the Maidan the huge bee-hive shaped Golghar was built in 1786 as a granary to store surpluses against possible famines. It stands about 25 metres high and steps wind around the outside to the top from where you have a fine view over Patna and the Ganges. Inside there is a superb echo. The

254

Golghar was built by Captain John Garstin at the instigation of the British administrator Warren Hastings following a terrible famine in 1770 but it has scarcely been used since that time.

Patna City Museum

The excellent museum contains metal and stone sculptures dating back to the Maurya (3rd century BC) and the Gupta periods, terra cotta figures and archaeological finds from sites in Bihar such as Nalanda. There are also original Chinese and Tibetan scrolls and paintings. The museum is closed on Mondays.

Kumrahar

Pataliputra, Ashoka's capital in the 3rd

Key:-
1. Tourist Office
2. Ferry Jetty (Ferry to Pal
3. G.P.O.
4. Indian Airlines
5. Dak Bungalow
6. Patna Museum
7. Golghar
8. Kumrahar Excavations
9. Har Mandir
- - - Main hotel area

century BC, has been excavated at the small village of Kumrahar, south of Patna. It was earlier the capital of Chandragupta (321-297 BC), Bindusara (297-274 BC) before Ashoka ruled from here between 274 and 237 BC. The main points of interest are the assembly hall with its large pillars which date back to the Mauryan period and the remnants of the brick Buddhist monastery known as Anand Bihar. North-west of Kumrahar is Bhikna Pahari where Ashoka built a retreat for his brother Mahinda. Kumrahar is six km from central Patna but the excavations are fairly esoteric and likely to be of interest only to those with a keen interest in archaeology and India's ancient history.

Har Mandir

At the eastern end of the city, in the Chowk area of old Patna, stands one of the holiest Sikh shrines. Built by Ranjit Singh it marks the place where Govind Singh, the 10th and last of the Sikh gurus, was born in 1660. On the bottom floor of this dome-shaped structure there are holy Sikh scriptures and an exhibition of photos about the Sikh religion together with personal belongings of the Guru including his shoes and cradle. You must cover your head as you enter the shrine. A tempo from Gandhi Maidan to the Chowk area will cost only Rs 2. Celebrations to mark the Guru's birth are held here in December-January of each year.

Patna

Khudabaksh Oriental Library

Founded· in 1900 this library has a renowned collection of rare Arabic and Persian manuscripts, of Moghul and Rajput paintings and oddities like the Koran inscribed in a book only an inch wide. The library also contains the only books rescued from the sack of the Moorish University of Cordoba in Spain.

Other

Gulzarbagh, to the east of the city, was the site of the East India Company's opium wharehouse. Today the building houses a Bihar government printing works. The Sher Shahi, built by the Afghan ruler Sher Shah in 1545 is the oldest mosque in Patna and a heavy,

domed structure. Other mosques include the squat Pathar ki Masjid and the riverbank Madrassa. Jalan's Quila houses a collection of antiques. A km west of the Har Mandir is the old cemetery which may still bear some reminders of the British days.

Tours

Patna Tours & Travels, which has an office near the railway station, operates daily sightseeing tours around the city during the tourist season. A half day tours costs Rs 15. The Bihar tourist office and the same travel agency also arrange day trips around the historic sites of south Bihar, such as Nalanda and Rajgir, for Rs 25.

Places to Stay — Top End

Hotel Pataliputra (tel 23467) at Beer Chand Patel Path has rooms with and without air-conditioning. Prices range from Rs 125/175 with, Rs 50/80 without, for singles/doubles. *Hotel Maurya Clarks* (tel 22036-67) is on South Gandhi Maidan and is Patha's top hotel. All rooms are air-con, the usual mod-cons are available and singles/doubles cost Rs 175/260. The third top end hotel is the *Hotel Republic* (tel 22028) in Lawlys Building, Exhibition Rd. Singles/doubles run from Rs 60/80 without air-con, more expensive with.

Places to Stay — Bottom End

There are a number of reasonable hotels around the railway station and airline office area. Most travellers passing through Patna pause just for a day on their way to Kathmandu and these places are quite adequate. The *Hotel Rajasthan* (tel 25102) is near Nepal Airlines. Singles run from Rs 18-22, doubles Rs 22-50. Between the station and Gandhi Maidan the *Hotel Rajdhani* (tel 23784) has singles at Rs 20 a night. The *Hotel Palace* (tel 26364) has singles at Rs 26. If you're on a tight budget there is the *Hotel Park* and *Hotel Grand*.

Places to Eat

The rather expensive *Ashok Restaurant* near the railway station is good. *Hotel Rajasthan* has a clean restaurant with a good selection of Indian dishes. Masala dosas cost only Rs 1 at the *Udipi Coffee House*.

Getting There

Train There are a number of trains daily between Delhi and Patna. The Assam Mail starts from Delhi at 9.40 am and reaches Patna at 3 am the next day. Other express and mail trains take a similar amount of time. From Delhi to Patna fares are around Rs 185 in 1st Class, Rs 46 in 2nd. Calcutta-Patna takes about 12 hours and the fares are around Rs 110 in 1st class, Rs 27 in 2nd.

Air There is a daily flight Delhi-Lucknow - Patna - Ranchi - Calcutta and vice versa. Delhi-Patna costs Rs 586 and Calcutta-Patna costs Rs 343.

Getting Around — Across the River

There is no bridge over the Ganges at Patna although one is under construction and due for completion in the early '80s. To get across you must take the ferry steamer which departs from Mahendra Ghat early in the morning, at 9 am and 1 pm, and late in the evening. Mahendra Ghat is near Gandhi Maidan or a Rs 2 rickshaw ride from Patna station. The ferry crossing takes about an hour and costs Rs 2.50. The ferry crosses to Palaza Ghat near Sonpur on the other side.

PATNA-NEPAL

Patna is very popular as a jumping off point for Nepal whether you are travelling by land or air. On the way to Raxaul, the Indian border town to Nepal, you can pause at a number of towns.

Sonepur

Just across the river from Patna, and close to Paleza Ghat where the ferry docks, is Sonepur. A month long cattle fair is held here each October-November, culminating at the full moon night of Kartika Purnima. At one time even elephants were bought and sold at this fair.

Vaisali

Only 44 km north of Patna this was the birthplace of Mahavira, one of the Jain Tirthankars. Over two thousand years ago this was the capital of a republic but very little of the city remains suspected to lie here have been excavated although an Ashoka pillar, topped by his lion symbol, has been unearthed. It was one of a series of Ashoka's pillars erected along the route between Pataliputra (Patna) and Nepal.

Vaisali is not on the direct Patna-Muzaffarpur route but you can easily divert to make the route Patna-Hajipur-Lalganj-Vaisali-Muzaffarpur, all by bus.

Places to Stay There is a *Youth Hostel* and a *Tourist Rest House* here. The dorm costs Rs 4. The local speciality at Vaisali is chura, a mixture of rice and curd.

Muzaffarpur (population 140,000)

Apart from being a bus and train changing point on the way to the Nepal border Muzaffarpur is of no real interest. This is a poverty ridden and agriculturally backward area.

Places to Stay *Hotel Deepak* has reasonable food and very spartan rooms at just Rs 8.

Motihari & Raxaul

North of Muzaffarpur the area becomes even more backward and depressed. Motihari is a small provincial town which is also the district headquarters. Raxaul is right on the border and is virtually a twin town with Birgunj, just across the border. The border is not closed at night.

Places to Stay *Hotel Kaveri* in Raxaul costs Rs 10 per night for a single and is a reasonable place to stop, unless you want to cross and stay in Birgunj.

Patna-Nepal Routes

Air Delhi-Kathmandu by air costs US$111 but Patna-Kathmandu is only US$31. Thus there is a considerable saving to be made by travelling Delhi-

Gandhi

thing at an intersection - MUZAFFARPUR

Patna by land and flying Patna-Kathmandu. Even the Delhi-Patna air-fare is only around US$55 so flying Delhi-Patna-Kathmandu is over US$20 cheaper than flying Delhi-Kathmandu direct. There are daily flights each way between Patna and Kathmandu with Indian Airlines and Royal Nepal Airlines Corporation.

Land By land you can get from Patna to Raxaul, on the India-Nepal border, either by bus or train. From Birgunj, just across the border, it's an all day bus trip up to Kathmandu, most buses depart early in the morning but there are a few leaving later and stopping overnight along the route.

By bus or train you first have to cross the river from Patna. By train you have to change in three places — Muzaffarpur-Motihari-Sagauli-Raxaul. This is a narrow gauge train and quite slow so you can count on the trip taking all day. You then overnight in Raxaul or Birgunj and take the bus to Kathmandu the next morning. There is one direct night train operating Palaza Ghat-Raxaul but you arrive too late for the morning buses so either way you'll have to overnight on the way.

It's much faster by bus since this only involves one change at Muzaffarpur. A government bus or minibus will take you from Palaza Ghat to Muzaffarpur in two hours. In Muzaffarpur buses for Raxaul can be found near the railway station for Rs 8, there is also a de-luxe bus which costs Rs 14 and can do the trip in just three hours.

PATNA-VARANASI
Sasaram

At the junction of the Grand Trunk Rd with the road to Patna there are some fine Moslem tombs in this town, particularly that of the Afghan ruler Sher Shah who died in 1545. The dome of his tomb, visible from the railway line, rises 46 metres above the water level of the surrounding tank. The tomb of his father and the unfinished tomb of his son are also in Sasaram. There are more Moslem tombs at Maner. At Dehri, 17 km from Sasaram, the railway and the Grand Trunk Rd crosses the River Son on a three km long bridge. The 'impregnable' hill fort of Rohtas is 38 km from here.

PATNA-GAYA

Nalanda

This was a great Buddhist centre over a thousand years ago until the monastery school and library were sacked and burnt by Moslems. When Hieun Tsang, the Chinese scholar and traveller stayed here for five years in the early 7th century AD there were 10,000 monks and students in residence. The remains are still extensive and include the Great Stupa with steps and terraces and with a few still intact votive stupas around it. An archaeological museum houses sculptures and other remains found on the site and an international centre for the study of Buddhism was established here in 1951. There are Burmese, Japanese and Jain rest houses at Nalanda. Buses connect Nalanda with Rajgir, Gaya and Patna; the latter is 90 km away.

Rajgir

Little remains of the Buddhist ruins at Rajgir, 19 km south of Nalanda towards Gaya. The first Buddhist council was held here after the Buddha attained nirvana. During the Buddha's life this was the capital of this part of India and he spent 12 years here. Buy one of the small, locally available guidebooks to the sites. They're Rs 1 to Rs 2.50. There is a Japanese stupa on a nearby hill and three km away there are hot sulphur springs.

Places to Stay The *Tourist Bungalow Number 2* is convenient and has a dormitory. There's also a *Rest House* and *Youth Hostel* in Rajgir. The Burmese Temple has a coffee house within the grounds which specialises in South Indian food. It's clean and popular and handy for the Tourist Bungalow.

Pawapuri

The Jain Thirtankar Mahavira attained nirvana here, 25 km from Nalanda. It is an important Jain pilgrimage spot.

GAYA (population 200,000)

Just as nearby Bodhgaya is a major centre for Buddhist pilgrims so is Gaya a centre for Hindu pilgrims. Gaya is second only to Varanasi in its sanctity and pilgrims believe that offering *pindas* (funeral cakes) here will free their ancestors from bondage to the earth. They must also perform a lengthy circuit of the holy places around Gaya. Gaya is 80 km south of Patna.

Vishnupad Temple

In the crowded central part of the old town the sikhara style temple was constructed in 1787 by Queen Ahalya Bai of Indore. The temple is situated on the banks of the Falgu river but although you can view the exterior of the temple and the picturesque bathing ghats, non-Hindus are not allowed into the temple interior. During the monsoon the river carries a great deal of water but it dries up completely during the winter.

A 30 metre high octagonal tower surmounts the temple. Inside, the 40 cm long 'footprint' of Vishnu is imprinted in solid rock and surrounded by a silver plated basin.

Other

A temple of the Sun God stands north of the Vishnupad temple. A flight of 1000 stone steps leads to the top of the Brahmajuni Hill, a km south-west. There is a good view over Gaya from the top of the hill. At the base of the hill is the Akshyabat or immortal banyan tree which pilgrims visit to complete the cycle of rituals for their ancestors which they commenced in Varanasi. Situated 20 km north of Gaya the Barabar caves are very ancient, dating back to 200 BC. Two of the caves have inscriptions from Ashoka himself. These are the 'Marabar' caves of E M Forster's *Passage to India*.

BODHGAYA

There are four holy places associated with the Buddha — Lumbini, in Nepal, where he was born; Sarnath, near Varanasi, where he first preached his message; Kushinagar, near Gorakhpur, where he died; and Bodhgaya, where he attained enlightenment. A Bo tree growing at Bodhgaya is said to be a direct descendant of the original tree under which the Buddha sat, meditated and achieved enlightenment.

Buddhists from all over the world flock to Bodhgaya, along with many westerners who come here to learn about Buddhism or meditation. Bodhgaya is small and quiet but if you are not planning a longer study stay a day is quite sufficient to see everything.

Bodhi Tree

The sacred Bo tree growing here is said to be a direct descendant of the original tree under which the Buddha sat. Although that tree has died a sapling from the original tree was carried to Sri Lanka by Mahinda, the Emperor Ashoka's son, when he brought Buddhism to that island. That tree now

Places to Stay

There are *Railway Retiring Rooms* at Gaya station and a few other places to stay around the station — spartan but OK for a short pause.

Getting There

It takes eight hours by train from Calcutta (Rs 106 1st class, Rs 25 2nd class) or six hours from Varanasi (Rs 47 1st class, Rs 10 2nd class). Patna to Gaya takes three to five hours by a slower train.

Getting Around

A rickshaw from the station through the narrow alleys to the Vishnupad temple will cost about Rs 2.

flourishes at Anuradhapura in Sri Lanka and in turn a sapling from that tree was carried back to Bodhgaya where it grows today. A red sandstone slab under the tree is said to be the Vajrasan, or diamond throne, on which the Buddha sat.

Mahabodhi Temple

A pyramidal spire 50 metres high tops the Mahabodhi temple inside of which is a large gilded image of the Buddha. You enter the temple courtyard through the east gateway with a typical Buddhist *torana* gateway. The temple is said to stand on the site of a temple originally erected by Ashoka in the 3rd century BC. Although the current temple was restored in 1882 and earlier in the 11th century it is said to be basically the same as a temple standing here in the 7th century, or even earlier. The Chinese pilgrim Hiuen Tsang describes visiting this earlier temple in 635 AD.

The stone railing around the temple, parts of which still stand, was originally thought to date from Ashoka but is now considered to be from the Sunga period around 184-72 BC. The carved and sculptured railing has been restored although parts of it now stand in the museum in Calcutta and the Victoria & Albert Museum in London. Stone stupas, erected by visiting pilgrims, dot the temple courtyard. The Buddha is said to have bathed in the nearby lotus pond.

Monasteries

The Tibetan monastery has an interesting wheel of law while the Japanese monastery has a very beautiful image of the Buddha brought from Japan. There is also a Burmese monastery; the Burmese attempted a restoration of the Mahabodhi in 1306-09. Since Hindus regard the Buddha as an incarnation of Vishnu Bodhgaya is also sacred to Hindu pilgrims.

Places to Stay

The *Ashoka Tourist Lodge* has singles/doubles at Rs 35/70 including breakfast. It's the best place available and all rooms have bathrooms. There's also a *Tourist Bungalow* with doubles at Rs

writer in Bihar Province....

25 or dorm beds at Rs 10 and a *Youth Hostel*.

If you're planning a longer stay and/ or don't mind roughing it a little it is possible to stay at the monasteries. The Burmese monastery has clean rooms and the management is helpful. Since there are few Burmese visitors these days you can usually find space to stay. The monastery has a garden and a library with English books. The Japanese monastery is also clean and comfortable but during the tourist season it can be packed with Japanese tour groups. Your stay there is limited to three days.

Simple vegetarian meals are available at the *Kalyan Hotel* near the Mahabodhi Temple for Rs 2.

Getting There
Bodhgaya is 13 km from Gaya and buses, minibuses and rickshaws make the trip. They start from the Kacheri in the city centre at Gaya, a Rs 1 rickshaw ride from the station. Buses depart every hour but it is advisable to only travel during the daytime. At night it's better to stay in Gaya.

SOUTHERN BIHAR
Parasnath
Just inside the Bihar state boundary from Bengal, and only a little north of the Grand Trunk Road, this is the major Jain pilgrimage centre in the east of India. Like so many other pilgrimage centres it's perched on top of a steep hill reached by a stiff climb on foot. The 24 temples, representing the 24 Jain Tirthankars, stand at 1366 metres altitude. Parasnath, the 23rd Tirthankar, achieved nirvana at this spot, 100 years after his birth in Varanasi.

Hazaribagh
South of Gaya the hill resort of Hazaribagh is in the Damodar valley. There's a wildlife sanctuary here and accommodation is available in a *Tourist Lodge*

or a *Forest Rest House*. Hazaribagh is a quiet little place 67 km from the railway junction at Hazaribagh Road.

Ranchi
At the other end of the Damodar valley, 93 km away, is Bihar's other hill resort. Ranchi is nearly as quiet as smaller Hazaribagh. At the foot of Ranchi Hill is an artificial lake flanked by two temples. Jagannathpur village, 10 km south-west, has the Jagannath Temple, a smaller copy of the great Jagannath Temple at Puri which also celebrates its own, smaller, festival of the cars. The high Hundru falls are 43 km north-east of Ranchi; there are other falls in the area. The isolated but beautiful resort of Neterahat is 150 km away, close to the border with Madhya Pradesh.

Calcutta

Population: 8 million
Main language: Bengali

Calcutta is capital of West Bengal

Calcutta is the largest city in India and by now may be ahead of London as the largest city in the British Commonwealth. It's an often ugly and desperate place that to many people sums up the worst of India yet it's also one of the more fascinating centres in India and has some scenes of rare beauty. At the beginning of this century Calcutta was the capital of British India but, unlike Delhi, Calcutta is not an ancient city with a long history and many impressive relics of its past. If fact Calcutta is really a British invention dating only 300 years.

In 1686 the British abandoned Hooghly, their trading post 38 km up the Hooghly river from present day Calcutta, and moved down river to three small villages — Sutanati, Govindpur and Kalikata. Calcutta takes its name from the last of those three tiny settlements. Job Charnock, an English merchant who later married a Brahmin's widow whom he dissuaded from becoming a sati, was the leader of the British merchants who made this move. At first the post was not a great success and was abandoned on a number of occasions but in 1696 a fort was laid out near present day BBD Bag (Dalhousie Square) and in 1698 Aurangzeb's grandson gave the British official permission to occupy the villages.

Calcutta then grew steadily until 1756 when Suraj-ud-daula, the Nawab of Murshidabad, attacked the town. Most of the British inhabitants escaped but those captured were packed into an underground cellar where, during the night most of them suffocated in what became known as 'the black hole of Calcutta'. Early in 1757 the British, under Clive, retook Calcutta and made peace with the Nawab. Later the same year, however, Suraj-ud-daula, sided with the French and in the Battle of Plassey, a turning point in British Indian history, was killed. A much stronger fort was built in Calcutta and the town became the capital of British India. Much of Culcutta's most enduring development took place between 1780 and 1820. Later in the 19th century, however, Bengal became a spark point in the struggle for Indian independence and this was a major reason for the decision to transfer the capital to New Delhi in 1911. Loss of political power did not alter Calcutta's economic control and the city continued to prosper until after WW II.

Partition affected Calcutta more than any other major Indian city. Bengal and the Punjab were the two areas of India which were both mixed in their Hindu-Moslem populations and positioned so that the dividing line would have to be drawn through them. The result in Bengal was that Calcutta, the jute producing and export centre of India, became a city without a hinterland

Key:-
1. B.B.D. Bagh
2. Tourist Office
3. Indian Museum
4. Victoria Monument
5. Sister Teresa's Mission
6. Kali Temple
7. Nakhoda Mosque
8. Sitambara Jain Temple
9. Digambara Jain Temple
10. Nepalese Consulate
⋯ Budget & Midrange Hotel Area
(Sudder St. & Chowringhee Lane)

while across the border in East Pakistan (Bangladesh today) the jute (a plant fibre used in making sacking and mats) was grown without anywhere to process or export it. Furthermore West Bengal and Calcutta were disrupted by tens of thousands of refugees fleeing from East Bengal, although fortunately without the communal violence and bloodshed that partition brought to the Punjab.

The massive influx of refugees, combined with India's own post war population explosion, led to Calcutta becoming an international urban horror story. The mere word Calcutta was enough to conjure up visions of squalor, starvation, disease and death. The work of Mother Teresa's Calcutta mission also focussed worldwide attention on Calcutta's festering problems. In 1971 the India-Pakistan conflict and the creation of Bangladesh led to another flood of refugees and Calcutta's already chaotic condition further deteriorated. Economically Calcutta suffered further setbacks, the port has been silting up making navigation from Calcutta down to the sea steadily more difficult and limiting the size of ship which can use the port. The Farakka Barrage, 250 km north of Calcutta, is designed to improve the river flow through Calcutta but has been a subject of considerable dispute between India and Bangladesh since it will also effect the flow of the Ganges through the latter country.

Furthermore Calcutta has been plagued by chronic labour unrest and resulting declines in productivity. The situation is summed up in Calcutta's hopeless power generation system. Electrical power in Calcutta has become such an on-again, off-again condition that virtually every hotel, restaurant, shop or small business has to have some sort of stand-by power generator or battery lighting system. The workers are blamed, the technicians are blamed, the power plants are blamed, the coal miners are blamed, even Indian railways

are blamed for not delivering the coal on time but it's widely pointed out that Bombay certainly doesn't suffer the frequency and extent of power cuts that are simply a way of life in Calcutta. The Marxist government of West Bengal has come in for much criticism for the chaos currently existing in Calcutta but, it is also pointed out, their seeming neglect and mismanagement of the city is combined with a considerable improvement in the rural situation. Threats of flood or famine in the countryside no longer send hordes of refugees streaming into the city as in the past.

Despite all these problems Calcutta is a city with a soul and one which many Calcutta residents are inordinately fond of. The Bengalis, so ready to raise arms against the British in the struggle for independence, are also the poets and artists of India. The contrast between the Bombay and Calcutta movie industries more or less sums it up. While Bombay, the Hollywood of India, churns out movies of amazing tinsel banality the smaller number of moviemakers in Calcutta make non-commercial gems that stand up to anything produced for sophisticated western movie-goers. It carries through to Calcutta in other ways too, amongst the squalor and confusion Calcutta has places and times of sheer magic — flower sellers beside the misty, ethereal Hooghly River; the majestic sweep of the Maidan; the arrogant bulk of the Victoria Memorial; the superb collection exhibited in the Indian Museum — it's all part of this amazing city.

Information & Orientation

Calcutta sprawls north-south along the Hooghly River which divides it from Howrah, on the west bank. If you arrive from anywhere west of Calcutta by rail you'll come into the immense Howrah station and have to cross the Hooghly Bridge into Calcutta proper. Some of

PARAKEET LEAPS FROM BAMBOO CAGE AND SELECTS YOUR FORTUNE CARD

YOUR FUTURE IS FOR THE BIRDS!

Fortune teller on a Calcutta sidewalk

Calcutta's worse slums sprawl away behind the station on the Howrah side. For visitors the more relevant parts of Calcutta are south of the bridge in the areas around BBD Bag and Chowringhee. BBD Bag, as Dalhousie Square has been renamed, is the site of the GPO, the West Bengal Tourist Office and close to the American Express Office and various railway booking offices. South of BBD Bag is the open expanse of the Maidan along the river, and away from the river the area known as Chowringhee. Most of the cheap and middle range hotels are concentrated in Chowringhee together with many of the airline offices, restaurants, travel agencies and the Indian Museum. At the southern end of Chowringhee you'll find the Government of India Tourist Office on Shakespeare Sarani and nearby the Birla Planetarium and the Victoria Memorial.

There are a number of landmarks in Calcutta and a couple of important streets to remember. The Octherlony Monument at the northern end of the Maidan is one of the most visible — it's a tall column rising from the flat expanse of the Maidan. Sudder St runs right off Chowringhee and is the core of the Calcutta travellers' scene. Most of the popular cheap hotels are along Sudder St so it is well known to any taxi or rickshaw wallah and the airport bus runs right by it. Furthermore the Indian Museum is right on the corner of Sudder St and Chowringhee. Further down Chowringhee, which runs alongside the Maidan all the way, is Park St with a great number of more expensive restaurants and the Thai International office — an important address for people heading on to South-East Asia. On again is Shakespeare Sarani.

Like many Indian cities getting around Calcutta is slightly confused by the habit of renaming city streets, particularly those with Raj day connotations. As usual this renaming has been done in a half hearted fashion, many streets still have the old names up, some maps show old names, others new, taxi-wallahas inevitably only now the old names. It's going to be a long time before Chowringhee Rd becomes Jawaharlal Nehru Rd! Other renamed roads include Ballyganj Store Rd (now Gurusday Rd), Bowbazar St (Bepin Behary Ganguly), Buckland Rd (Bankim Ch Rd), Harrington St (Ho Chi Minh Sarani!), Harrison Rd (Mahatma Gandhi Rd), Kyd St (Dr M Ishaque Rd), Lansdowne Rd (Sarat Bose Rd), Lower Chitpur Rd (Rabindra Sarani), Lower Circular Rd (Acharya Jagadish Bose Rd), Machuabazar St (Madan Mohan St & Keshab Sen St), Mirzapore St (Suryya Sen St), Theatre Rd (Shakespeare Sarani), Wellesley St (Rafi Ahmed Kidwai Rd) and Wellington St (Nirmal Chunder St).

The Calcutta GPO is on BBD Bag (Dalhousie Square) and is large and has an efficient poste restante. American Express is nearby at 21 Old Court House St (tel 236281). The Government of India Tourist Office (tel 441402, 443521) is at 4 Shakespeare Sarani. There is also a counter at Calcutta airport but it never appears to be open when flights come in. The West Bengal Tourist Bureau is at 3/2 BBD Bag (tel 235917) — the opposite side to the post office. They too have a counter at the airport.

Calcutta is famous for its culture — films, poetry, art and dance all have their devotees here. There are dances on at the Oberoi Grand Hotel every night at 7 pm, reduced entrance charge with a student card. At Rabindra Sadan on Cathedral Rd (tel 44 9936) there is a dance-drama performance, Bengali poetry readings or similar on most nights.

Embassies & Consulates Some of the useful address in Calcutta include:

Bangladesh	9 Circus Ave (tel 445208, 445524)
Bhutan	48 Tivoli Court, Pramothesh Barua Sarani (tel 441301)
West Germany	1 Hastings Park Rd (tel 459141)
Nepal	19 Sterndale Rd (tel 454293)
Netherlands	18A Brabourne Rd (tel 225864)
Thailand	18B Mandeville Gardens (tel 460836)
UK	1 Ho Chi Minh Sarani (tel 445171)
USA	5/1 Ho Chi Minh Sarani (tel 443611)

Airline Offices Most airline offices are located around Chowringhee. There you will find Thai International and Bangladesh Biman both on Park St and British Airway and Royal Nepal Airlines both at the corner of Chowringhee and Middleton St. Pan American is between Middleton St and Ho Chi Minh Sarani on Chowringhee. Air India is further down Chowringhee, just beyond Shakespeare Sarani. Burma Airways is on Esplanade Row East, just north of the Maidan tram terminus. Indian Airlines (tel 263390, 260730) is at 39 Chittaranjan Ave.

Botanical Garden
On the west bank of the Hooghly, south of Howrah, are the extensive Botanical Gardens. They stretch for over a km along the river front and occupy 109 hectares. The gardens were originally founded in 1786 and initially administered by Colonel Kyd. It was from these gardens that the tea now grown in Assam and Darjeeling was first developed. Prime attraction in the gardens is the 200 year old Banyan, claimed to be the largest in the world. It covers an area of ground nearly 400 metres in circumference and continues to flourish despite having its central trunk removed in 1925, due to fungus damage. The gardens are at Sibpur and can be

BBD Bag (Dalhousie Square)

Hooghly River

Strand Road

South Subhash Road

Clive Row

Old China Bazar St.

Zakaria St.

Biplabi R. Bose Sarani Rd.

Brabourne Rd.

Ezra St.

Fairlie Place

India Exch. Pl.

E. Railways Booking Office (2nd Class & Tourist Quota)

Lyons Range

Writers Building

Rabindra

New C.I.T. Road

G.P.O.

Kalighat St.

E. Railways Booking Office (1st Class)

B.B.D. Bagh

Lal Bazar St.

Shipping Corp. of India

Bipin Behari Ganguly St.

Hare St.

Church Ln.

West Bengal Tourist Office

Weston St.

K. Sankar Roy Rd.

St. John's Church

Old Court House St.

Ganesh

Mango Ln.

Indian Airlines

High Court

Town Hall

West Council House St.

Amex

Gt. Eastern Hotel

Bentinck St.

Chandra

Princep

Avenue

Raj Bhavan

Waterloo St.

Amber Restaurant

Esplanade West

S.E. Railways Booking Office

Dacre's Ln.

Chittaranjan

St.

Chauk St.

Avenue

Eden Gardens

Esplanade

Burma Airways

Tipu Sultan's Mosque

Lenin Sarani

Chandni

Hospital St.

Tram Terminus

Cottage Industries Emporium

Ochterlony Monument

Bus Terminus

S. N. Banerji Road

Red Road

Nanak Sarani

Dufferin Rd.

J. Nehru Road (Chowringhee)

Oberoi Grand

Market

reached by crossing the bridge — total distance 19 km from Chowringhee. More directly you may be able to get a ferry across the river from Chandpal or Takta Ghat or from the Matia Bruz Ghat further south. The gardens are open from sunrise to sunset. A 55 or 56 bus will take you to the gardens. The trip takes about an hour.

Indian Museum

Conveniently situated on the corner of Sudder St and Chowringhee the Indian Museum was built in 1875 and is probably the best museum in India and one of the best in Asia. It's so convenient to the many hotels around Sudder St that if you're staying there you should not fail to drop in, if only for a few minutes. Its widely varied collection includes oddities such as a whole roomful of meteorites. Other exhibits include the usual fossils, stuffed animals, skeletons and so on including a number of unique fossil skeletons of pre-historic animals. These include giant crocodiles and an amazingly big tortoise. The art collection includes many fine pieces from Orissan and other temples and a superb collection of Buddhist Gandharan art. This interesting meeting point between Greek artistry and Buddhist ideals was centred around the North-West Frontier Province, now in Pakistan, and produced Buddha images and other sculpture of extreme beauty. Almost anywhere you have been in India you will find some reminder of it in the Indian Museum, it's well worth a visit.

The museum is open from 10 am to 5 pm daily except Mondays. Between December and February it closes half an hour earlier. Entry fee is Rs 0.50 except on Fridays when it is free.

Octherlony Monument

Now officially renamed the Sahib Minar this 48 metre high column towers over the northern end of the Maidan. It was erected in 1828 and named after Sir David Ochterlony who was credited with winning the Nepal War (1814-16). There's a fine view from the top of the column but permission to ascend it must be obtained from the Deputy Commissioner of Police, Police HQ, Lal Bazaar. The column is a curious combination of Turkish, Egyptian and Syrian architectural elements.

Rabindra Sarobar & Ramakrishna Mission

In the south of the city Rabindra Sarobar is a park and picnic spot with a central lake. Beside the park is the recently opened Ramakrishna Mission Institute of Culture with a library, reading rooms and lecture halls.

Maidan & Fort William

After the events of 1756 the British decided there would be no repetition and set out to replace the original Fort William, near Dalhousie Square, with a massive and impregnable new fort. First they cleared out the inhabitants of the village of Govindpur and in 1758 laid the foundations of a fort which, when completed in 1781, would cost them the awesome total, for those days, of £2 million. Around the fort a huge expanse of jungle was cut down to give the cannons a clear line of fire but, as usual, the fort has never fired a shot in anger. You can walk around the fort's massive walls with deep fortifications and trenches fronting them but visitors are only allowed inside with special permission since the fort is still in use today.

The area cleared around Fort William became the Maidan, the 'lungs' of modern Calcutta. This huge green expanse stretches three km north to south and is over a km wide. It is bounded by Strand Rd along the river to the west and by Chowringhee Rd, lined with shops, hotels and eating places, to the east. The stream known as Tolly's Nulla forms its southern boundary and here you will also find a race-course and the Victoria Memorial. In the north-west corner is Eden Gardens while Raj Bhavan overlooks it from the north.

Within the gardens there are cricket and football fields, tennis courts, ponds and trees. Cows graze there, political discussions are held there, people stroll across it or come there for early morning yoga sessions. And of course it's used, like any area of open land in India, as a public toilet.

Eden Gardens

In the north-west corner of the Maidan are the small and pleasantly laid out Eden Gardens. A tiny Burmese pagoda was brought here from Prome in Burma in 1856, it's set in a small lake and is extraordinarily picturesque. The gardens were named after Lord Auckland, the former Governor General's, sisters. The Calcutta cricket grounds are also within the gardens.

Across from the gardens there is a pleasant walk along the banks of the Hooghly. Ferries run across the river from several ghats and there are plenty of boatmen around offering to take you out on the water for half an hour.

Victoria Memorial

At the southern end of the Maidan stands the most solid reminder of British Calcutta, in fact probably the most solid reminder of British India. The Victoria Memorial is a huge white marble museum, a strange combination of classical European architecture with Moghul influences or, as some have put it, an unhappy British attempt to build a better Taj Mahal. The idea behind the memorial was conceived by Lord Curzon, the money for its construction raised from 'voluntary contributions by the princes and peoples of India', the Prince of Wales (later King George V) laid the foundation stone in 1906 and it was opened by another Prince of

Wales (later the Duke of Windsor) in 1921.

Whether you're interested in the British Raj period or not the memorial is an attraction not to be missed, it tells the story of the Empire in India at it's peak, just when it was about to embark on its downhill slide. The imposing statue of Queen Victoria, at her bulky and least-amused best, fronts the memorial and sets the mood for all the displays inside.

Inside you'll find portraits, statues and busts of almost all the main partic-ipants in British-Indian history — British, Indian and other nationalities. Scenes from military conflicts and events of the mutiny are illustrated. There are some superb watercolours of Indian landscapes and buildings made by travel-ling Victorian artists. A Calcutta exhibit includes many early pictures of the city and a model of Fort William. Of course there are many fine Indian and Persian miniatures and rare manuscripts and books. Queen Victoria appears again inside, much younger and slimmer than her statue outside. There's also a piano she played as a young girl and other memorabilia. There's a huge painting of King Edward VII entering Jaipur in a regal procession in 1876. French guns captured at the Battle of Plassey are on exhibit and the black stone throne of the Nawab whom Clive defeated in that battle. To top it all there is a good view over the Maidan from the balcony over the entrance.

A Brief Guide to the Victoria Memorial is available in the building for Rs 1.50. The memorial is open from 10 am to 5 pm but closed on Mondays. Entry costs Rs 0.50.

St Paul's Cathedral

Built between 1839 and 1847, St Paul's Cathedral is one of the most important churches in India. It stands just to the east of the Victorial Memorial at the southern end of the Maidan. The steeple

CALCUTTA - IN THE MAIDAN
Committing nuisance...

fell during an earthquake in 1897 and following further damage in an 1934 quake it was redesigned and rebuilt.

Birla Planetarium
This planetarium, near the Tourist Office, is one of the largest in the world and well worth the Rs 3.50 admission. It's open from 12.30 to 6.30 pm daily, to 8 pm on Saturdays and from 10 am to 8 pm on Sundays. There are programmes in English several times daily.

Kali Temple
Also known as Kalighat this temple is believed to be about 200 years old and to be the actual temple from which Kalikat (anglicised to Calcutta) takes its name. According to legend when Shiva's wife's corpse was cut up one of her fingers fell here, since when it has been an important pilgrimage site. The temple is about two km directly south of St Paul's Cathedral.

Zoo
South of the Maidan, Calcutta's 16 hectare zoo was opened in 1876. Some of the animals are displayed in near natural conditions. The zoo is open from sunrise to sunset and admission is Rs 0.50.

Howrah Bridge
Until 1943 the Hooghly was crossed by a pontoon bridge which had to be opened to let river traffic through. There had been considerable opposition to construction of a bridge due to fears that it would effect the river currents and cause silting problems. This problem was eventually avoided by building a bridge that crosses the river in a single 450 metre span with no piers at all within the river. The cantilevered bridge

is similar in size to the Sydney Harbour Bridge and if anything even uglier! It carries a flow of traffic which Sydney could never dream of — it's intriguing to stand at one end of the bridge at morning rush hour time and watch the procession of double decker buses come across. They heel over like yachts due to the weight of passengers hanging on to the sides. In between there are countless rickshaws, lumbering bullock carts, hordes of bicycles and even the odd car. The bridge is also known as Rabindra Setu.

Dalhousie Square — BBD Bag

When Calcutta was the centre of administration for British India this was the centre of power. On the north side of the square stands the huge 'Writers Building' which dates from 1880. In those days clerical workers were known as 'writers' and the East India Company's 'writers' have been replaced by modern day ones employed by the West Bengal state government. That's where all the quintuplicate forms, carbon copies and red ink comes from. Also on Dalhousie Square is a rather more useful place — the Calcutta GPO — and on the other side of the square is the West Bengal Tourist Development Corporation's office.

Until it was abandoned in 1757 the original Fort Williams used to stand where the post office now does. It stretches from there down to the river, which has also changed its course since that time. Brass markers indicate where the fort walls used to be by the post office. Calcutta's famous black hole actually stood at the north-east corner of the post office but since independence all indications of its position have been removed. The black hole was actually a tiny guardroom in the fort and 146 people were forced into the room on that fateful night when the city fell to Suraj-ud-daula. Next morning only 23 were still alive.

St John's Church

A little south of Dalhousie Square is the Church of St John which dates from 1787. The graveyard here has a number of interesting monuments including the octagonal mausoleum of Job Charnock, founder of Calcutta, who died in 1692. Admiral Watson, who supported Clive in retaking Calcutta from Suraj-ud-daula is also buried here.

Other British Buildings

The Victoria Memorial is the most imposing reminder of the British presence in Calcutta but the city's commercial wealth resulted in quite a few other interesting buildings. Raj Bhavan, the old British Government House, is now occupied by the Governor of West Bengal and entry is restricted. The Marquess Wellesley built it between 1799 and 1805 and it is modelled on Lord Curzon's home Kedleston Hall in Derbyshire, England which was only completed a couple of years before it. It stands at the north end of the Maidan and there are many rare works of art and other interesting items inside including Tipu Sultan's throne.

Next to it is the Doric style Town Hall and next to that the High Court which was copied from the Staadhaus at Ypres and completed in 1872. It has a tower 55 metres high. Just south of the zoo in Alipur is the National Library, the biggest library in India, which is housed in the former residence of the Lieutenant Governor of Bengal, Belvedere House.

Other Museums

Calcutta has a number of other interesting museums apart from the magnificent Indian Museum and the Victoria Memorial. In Calcutta University the Asutosh Museum has a collection of art objects with a particular emphasis on Bengali folk art. Admission is free and it is open from

10.30 am to 4.30 pm on weekdays, 10.30 am to 3 pm on Saturdays. At 19A Gurusday Rd there is the Birla Industrial & Technological Museum which is open from 10 am to 5 pm daily. Admission is free except on Sundays when it costs Rs 0.25. Those philanthropic Birlas have also provided the Birla Academy of Art & Culture at 109-109 Southern Ave. That is open from 3 to 6 pm daily except Mondays and admission is Rs 0.25. It has a good collection of sculptures and modern art.

On Cathedral Rd, beside the cathedral, there is a permanent exhibition at the Academy of Fine Arts which is open from 3 to 8 pm daily except Mondays. Entry is free. The Nehru Children's Museum is at 94/1 Jawaharlal Nehru Rd and is open from 1 to 8 pm daily except Mondays. Admission is Rs 0.50 for adults, Rs 0.25 for children.

On Muktaram Babu St, a narrow lane in north Calcutta, is the Marble Palace, an incongruous one man collection of statues and paintings including works of Rubens and Sir Joshua Reynolds. It's open from 10 am to 4 pm except on Mondays and Thursdays and entry is free with a permit from the Government of India Tourist Office. Nearby is the rambling old Tagore House, a centre for Indian dance, drama, music and other arts. This was where Rabindranath Tagore, India's greatest modern poet, was born and died. It's just off Rabindra Sarani.

Sitambara Jain Temple
In the north-east of the city this temple was built in 1867 and dedicated to Sheetalnathji, the 10th of the 24 Jain Tirthankars. The temple is an ornate mass of mirrors, coloured stones and glass mosaics and overlooks a garden. It is open from 6 am to 12 noon and 3 to 7 pm daily.

Nakhoda Mosque
North of BBD Bag is Calcutta's principal Moslem place of worship. The huge Nakhoda Mosque is said to be able to accommodate 10,000 people and was modelled on Akbar's tomb at Sikandra near Agra. The red sandstone mosque has two 46 metre high minarets and a brightly painted onion-shaped dome.

Belur Math
North of the city on the west bank is the headquarters of the Ramakrishna Mission, Belur Math. Ramakrishna, an Indian philosopher, preached the unity of all religions and, following his death in 1886, his follower Swami Vivekananda founded the Ramakrishna Mission in 1897 and there are now branches all over India. Belur Math, the movement's international headquarters, was founded in 1899. It is supposed to represent a church, a mosque and a temple, depending on how you look at it. Belur Math is open from 6.30 am to 12 noon and from 3.30 to 7.30 pm daily. Admission is free.

Dakshineshwar Kali Temple
Across the river from Belur Math is this Kali temple where Ramakrishna was a priest when he reached his spiritual vision of the unity of all religions. The Kali temple was built in 1847.

Barrackpore
There is a memorial to Gandhi called Gandhi Ghat at this point, 25 km north of Calcutta on the banks of the Hooghly.

Serampore
Across the river from Barrackpore, 25 km from Calcutta, this was a Danish centre until the Danish holdings in India were transferred to the East India Company in 1845. The old Danish Church and the Danish cemetery still stand. The missionaries Ward, Marshman and Carey operated from here in the

early 1800s. Mahesh, three km from Serampore, has a large and very old Jagannath temple. In June-July of each year the Mahesh Yatra car festival takes place here and is second in size only to the great festival at Jagannath.

Tours

The India Tourism Development Corporation (tel 443124) at 4 Shakespeare Sarani and the West Bengal Tourist Bureau (tel 238271) at 3/2 BBD Bag both have daily tours of Calcutta except on Sundays. The morning tour from 8 am to 12.30 pm costs Rs 12 and includes the area around BBD Bag in the city including Eden Gardens, Raj Bhavan, out to the Jain temple plus the further out sites like Belur Math, the Dakshineshwar Temple and the Botanical Gardens. The afternoon tour operates from 1.30 to 5.15 pm and costs the same but you can get a combined ticket for Rs 18 if you take both tours on the same day. The afternoon tour covers the Indian Museum, Victoria Memorial and the Zoo. The morning tour is better value since it covers the further out sights while on the afternoon tour you could esaily get around yourself and have more time.

On Saturdays, Sundays and holidays there are launch trips on the Hooghly for Rs 7 to 12 depending on the duration of the trip. Note that the tourist offices often cancel tours on short notice — check the day before if the tour will be operating.

Places to Stay — Top End

Calcutta does not have a great number of top class hotels. Out at the airport the *ITDC Airport Ashoka* (tel 440933 & 575111) is new and convenient for passengers in transit. Singles/doubles (all aircon) are Rs 225/300.

Most of the other hotels are centrally located. At 15 Chowringhee the *Oberoi Grand* (tel 230181) is pretty plain externally but pleasantly grand inside and costs from Rs 495/595 for singles/doubles. The *Park Hotel* (tel 248301) at 17 Park St is a more modern hotel at Rs 350/450.

Other more expensive hotels include the *Great Eastern Hotel* (tel 232311) at 1-3 Old Court House St. Once again it's back to the Raj era and costs Rs 150/235 with air-con, Rs 125/175 without. The *Hotel Hindustan International* (tel 442394) is at 235/1 Acharya J C Bose Rd and costs from Rs 290/425 for singles/doubles. The *Hotel Rutt Deen* (tel 443884) is at 21B Loudon St and costs Rs 200/300.

Places to Stay — Middle

It's said often enough that 'getting there is half the fun', well at the *Fairlawn Hotel* (tel 244460) at 13A Sudder St, staying there is half the fun. It's a piece of Calcutta that definitely should not be missed because here the Raj doesn't just live, it's simply never ended. The terribly English couple who still, 30+ years after independence, run it look like they've been time-warped from Brighton in the '50s and their establishment is spotless, packed with memorabilia and a positive delight. The bearer bears your gear upstairs on his head, meal times are announced with a gong (and a hissed 'Sahib, Memsahib, dinner is ready' if you dare to be late) and in mid-afternoon there's tea and biscuits. At Rs 175/265 for an air-con room with all meals it's an experience not to be missed. There are also some non air-con rooms.

Everything else pales but there are a few other places such as the *Lytton Hotel* (tel 232760 & 233937) at 14 Sudder St with air-con singles/doubles at Rs 100/150. Or round at 2 Chowinghee Place the *Carlton Hotel* (tel 233009 & 238853) at Rs 90/125 with air-con, Rs 70/100 without.

Places to Stay — Bottom End

Sudder St, running off Chowringhee beside the Indian Museum, is Calcutta's cheap accommodation centre. Here you will find most of Calcutta's cheaper accommodation and eating places. At 2 Sudder St the *Salvation Army Red Shield Guest House* (tel 242895) has 15 rooms and eight dorm beds. It's Rs 12.60 in the dormitory, Rs 32 for a double. The rooms tend to be small and breakfast, included in the price, is fairly basic, but it's clean, well kept and so popular that it is usually full.

Down Sudder St a bit, Stuart Lane turns off to the right and here you'll find two of Calcutta's most popular rock bottom establishments. The *Modern Lodge* (tel 244960) is at number 1, the *Hotel Paragon* at number 2. Dorm beds at around Rs 8, singles/doubles at Rs 15/25 — often one will be a few rupees cheaper than the other but there is not much in it. They're OK, clean sheets and toilets, reasonable food. There are other cheap hotels around Sudder St but many are strictly for emergency use only. 'Avoid them like the plague, you stand a good chance of getting it', reported one traveller.

There are also a number of places which are up a notch, in price at least. At 6/2/3 Sudder St the *Astoria Hotel* (tel 241359) has singles/doubles at Rs 70/85 including 'bed tea' and breakfast. At 5/1 Sudder St *Hotel White Hall* (tel 243311) has singles/doubles from Rs 25/35. Round on Kyd St, virtually on the corner with Free School St, the *Neelam Hotel* has singles/doubles from Rs 35/55 — it's rather drab.

Calcutta has a selection of Ys. The *YMCA* (tel 233504) is at 25 Chowringhee and takes men only from Rs 44 single, Rs 58 double — a big, gloomy building. There is a second, similarly priced *YMCA* (tel 240260) at 42 Surendra Nath Banerjee Rd. The *YWCA* (tel 240260) is also similarly priced at 1 Middleton Row — ladies only here.

The *Youth Hostel* (tel 672869) is at 10 J B Ananda Dutta Lane in Howrah. It's small and homely, take a 52 or 58 bus from Howrah Station to Shamasri Cinema or a 63 to Khirertala.

If you're transitting Calcutta by air there are *Airport Rest Rooms* (tel 572-611) at the airport. Singles are Rs 20, doubles Rs 30-45 and there's a reservations desk in the terminal. Finally Howrah Station has *Railway Retiring Rooms* at Rs 6/10 for singles/doubles or Rs 5 in a dorm.

Places to Eat

Amber at 11 Waterloo St, behind the Great Eastern Hotel, occupies three floors and is one of Calcutta's better restaurants for Indian and western food. There are a number of places along Park St, in fact it's virtually solid restaurants along part of the street. There's a good *Kwality* at 17 Park St, beside the Park Hotel. On that side of the street there are half a dozen other places, some with un-Calcutta names like *Blue Fox* and *Moulin Rouge*! On the other side of the road there's a *Magnolia* (ice cream), *Gupta* (has thalis), a *Snack Bar*, *Silver Grill* and *Flury's* for quick snacks and take-aways.

At the *Fairlawn Hotel* on Sudder St food is English style but surprisingly good. If you're staying there all meals are included in the room cost. If you're not, and would like to experience that old-style service, meals can probably be arranged.

There are a few cheap restaurants around Sudder St and along Free School St although Calcutta is certainly not over-endowed with cheap restaurants. The *Sikh Restaurant*, across from the Salvation Army Hostel, is a long-standing popular place for the travellers. Down on Free School St the *New India Restaurant* is fairly cheap and the food isn't bad although it looks pretty drab during the day. *Cafe 48* is also not bad. A recent rave for *Supersnax* at 55A Free

School St at the corner of Ripon St (just inside and to the left of the bakery on the corner): 'run by a retired army colonel, very friendly, unusual, wholesome dishes'.

A local speciality in Calcutta is moghul paratha.

Getting There

Air Calcutta is connected by air with all the major centres and in particular it's the jumping off point for flights to the north-east region, to Darjeeling and to Port Blair in the Andaman Islands. Some fares include Madras Rs 930, flights daily; Bombay Rs 1065, flights daily; Delhi Rs 895, two flights daily; Bhubaneswar Rs 280; Varanasi Rs 465; Patna Rs 340; Bagdogra (for Darjeeling) Rs 335; Gauhati Rs 305; Port Blair Rs 905.

Rail Calcutta has two major railway stations. Howrah on the west bank of the Hooghly handles most trains into the city but if you're going north to Darjeeling or the north-east region then the trains will be from Sealdah Station on the Calcutta side. The Eastern Railway Booking Office (tel 224356) is at 6 Fairlie Place for 2nd class and tourist quota bookings. For 1st class it's on the Strand Rd. The South-Eastern Railway Booking Office (tel 239530, 235074) is at Esplanade Mansions.

To Delhi trains takes from 17 hours and costs approximately Rs 60 in 2nd class, Rs 250 in 1st. To Varanasi they take from 12 hours and costs Rs 34 in 2nd class, Rs 145 in 1st. For Darjeeling it takes about 12 hours from Calcutta (Sealdah Station) to New Jalpaiguri or Siliguri from where you take a bus or the toy train up to the hill station. Fare from Calcutta is Rs 40 in 2nd, Rs 143 in 1st. It's a long way from Calcutta to Bombay, a 1968 km trip taking 36 hours even on the fast mail train. Fares are Rs 77 in 2nd class, Rs 320 in 1st class. The trip to Madras

is nearly as long — 33 hours to cover 1662 km at a cost of about Rs 68 in 2nd class, Rs 280 in 1st. During and soon after the monsoon the railway line can be cut by the Godavari and Krishna Rivers in north Andhra Pradesh. If this is the case the Calcutta-Madras service will make a long loop inland and the trip will take rather longer. The normal service runs down the coast all the way, passing through Bhubaneswar in Orissa en route.

Bus The bus services from Calcutta are not so good an alternative as they are from a number of other Indian cities. It's generally better to travel from Calcutta by rail although there are a number of useful routes to other towns in West Bengal.

Ship See the Andaman & Nicobar Islands section for details on the shipping services from Calcutta.

Getting Around

Airport There's an airport bus which costs Rs 10 and runs by the Indian Airlines office and down Chowringhee past Sudder St. If you're departing Calcutta via Thai International it departs from the Thai office on Park St. A taxi costs about Rs 30 so between four that is as cheap as the bus and since so many people leave India from Calcutta on the same (Thai International) flights it is quite easy to get a group together for a taxi. There is a public mini bus from BBD Bag to the airport for Rs 2. If your endurance knows no limits you can get to the airport from Howrah Station in an 11A then a 30B bus. Incidentally Calcutta's airport takes its name, Dum Dum Airport, from the fact that this was where the explosive dum dum bullet, banned after the Boer War, was once made.

Buses Calcutta's bus system is absolutely hopelessly crowded. It's an edifying sight to watch the double deckers come across Howrah Bridge during the rush hour. Fares from Rs 0.20. Take a 5 or

6 between Howrah Station and Sudder St, ask for the Indian Museum. There is also a secondary private minibus service which is rather faster and slightly more expensive. You need to be a midget to ride in these buses though. Beware of pickpockets in any Calcutta public transport.

Trams Calcutta also has a public tram service but they're like sardine tins. Take a 12A from Howrah to the Indian Museum. On Sunday it is possible to buy a day ticket from the terminus for Rs 1. They're quiet, well quiet by Calcutta standards, on that day.

Underground Calcutta may eventually have an underground railway system. It's being built at minimum cost and in maximum time almost totally by hand. Calcutta's soggy soil makes digging holes by hand no fun at all and after each monsoon it takes half the time to the next monsoon simply to drain out what has already been dug. Meanwhile it simply causes Calcutta's chaotic traffic to be even worse.

Taxis Calcutta's taxi drivers are renowned for their passions for strikes which causes the buses to be even worse than usual. The real taxi fare is probably 300% of the metered fare by the time this book is ready.

Rickshaws Calcutta is the last holdout of the man-powered rickshaw. The rickshaw-wallahs would not accept the new fangled bicycle rickshaws when they were introduced elsewhere in India. After all, who could afford a bicycle? You may find it morally impossible to have a man trotting around pulling you in a carriage but they are useful for carting heavy baggage. And Calcutta's citizens are quite happy to use them.

Things to Buy

Calcutta has the usual government emporiums and quite a good Central Cottage Industries Emporium at 7 Chowringhee. New Market, formerly Hogg Market, is Calcutta's premier shopping bargain though. Here you can find a little of almost everything and it is always worth an hour or so wandering around. A particular bargain, if you're flying straight home from Calcutta, is caneware. Ridiculously cheap compared to prices in the west and, of course, very light if rather bulky. The market is also a place to sell as well as buy. Watches and cameras are always in demand and you can also change money at a small premium over the bank rate. If nobody approaches you the uniformed porters will know where to find what you want. One traveller noted 'selling whisky and cigarettes in the market was difficult, eventually got Rs 180 for a litre bottle of whisky, Rs 125 for a carton of cigarettes. Goodies bought from Singapore be noted in your passport'.

West Bengal

Population: 49 million
Area: 87,853 square km
Capital: Calcutta
Main language: Bengali

At the time of partition Bengal was split into East Bengal and West Bengal. East Bengal became the eastern wing of Pakistan and later, with the disintegration of that country, Bangladesh. West Bengal became a state of India with its largest city, Calcutta, as its capital. The state is long and narrow, running from the delta of the Ganges river system at the Bay of Bengal in the south to the heights of the Himalayas at Darjeeling in the north. There is not a great deal of interest in the state apart from these two extremes — Calcutta, all noise, confusion and squalor at one end and Darjeeling, serene and peaceful at the other. Nevertheless the intrepid traveller will find a number of places to consider visiting, either south of Calcutta on the Bay of Negal or north along the route to Darjeeling.

SOUTH OF CALCUTTA
Down the Hooghly

The Hooghly River is a very difficult river to navigate due to the constantly shifting shoals and sandbanks. Hooghly River pilots have to continuously stay in touch with the river to keep track of the frequent changes in its course. When the Hooghly Bridge was constructed it was feared that it would cause severe alterations to the river's flow patterns. The tide rises and falls 3.5 metres at Calcutta and there is a bore, which reaches two metres in height, at the time of the rising tide. Because of the navigational difficulties and the silting up which the Hooghly is experiencing, Calcutta is losing its importance as a port.

Falta, 43 km downriver, was the site of a Dutch factory and the British retreated here in 1756 when Calcutta was captured by Suraj-ud-daula. It was also from here that Clive recaptured Calcutta. A little below Falta the Damodar joins the Hooghly. The Rupnarain also joins the Hooghly and a little up this river is Tamluk, an important Buddhist centre over a thousand years ago. The James and Mary shoal, the most dangerous on the Hooghly, is just above the point where the Rupnarain river enters. It takes its name from a ship which was wrecked here in 1694.

Diamond Harbour

A resort 51 km south of Calcutta by road, Diamond Harbour is at the point where the Hooghly turns south and flows into the open sea. Launches run from here to Sagar Island.

Places to Stay Accommodation in the *Sagarika Tourist Lodge* (doubles from Rs 50) can be booked through the West

WEST BENGAL

Bengal Tourism Corporation in Calcutta.

Haldia
The new port of Haldia is 96 km south of Calcutta and on the west bank of the Hooghly. The port was constructed to try to regain the shipping lost from Calcutta due to the port's silting problems. There are regular buses between Calcutta and Haldia.

Sagar Island
At the mouth of the Hooghly this island is considered to be the point where the Ganges joins the sea and a great three day bathing festival takes place here early each January. A lighthouse marks the south-west tip of the island but navigation is still difficult for a further 65 km south.

Digha
Close to the border with Orissa, 243 km south-east of Calcutta on the Bay of Bengal, Digha is a beach resort with a six km long beach. There are daily buses between Calcutta and Digha operated by the CSTC. The trip takes about six hours.

Places to Stay There is a *Tourist Lodge* with doubles at Rs 30 and meals also available. Digha has a wide range of other accommodation including a *Tourist Cottage*, the *Saikatabas* and the *Hotel Sea Hawk*. These can all be booked through the West Bengal Tourist Development Corporation in Calcutta (tel 235917). Digha also has a number of private hotels and boarding houses.

Bakkhali
Also known as Fraserganj this is another beach resort, 132 km from Calcutta and on the east side of the Hooghly. Accommodation here can again be reserved through the West Bengal Tourist Corporation. From here you can get boats across to the small island of Jambu Dwip to the south-west.

Sunderbans
Spreading across the border into Bangladesh the Sunderbans is the forest at the delta where the Ganges meet the sea. Royal Bengal tigers can still be seen here, particularly on Lothian Island and Chamta Block. There are many other animals including deer, wild boar, monkeys, snakes and crocodiles.

trading post although it was taken by the British during conflicts with the French.

Hooghly

This historic town is 41 km north of Calcutta and very close to two other interesting sites — Chinsura and Bandel. Hooghly was an important trading port long before Calcutta rose to prominence. In 1537 the Portuguese set up a factory here; prior to that time Satgaon, 10 km further north, had been the main port of Bengal but it was abandoned due to the river silting up. There are still a few traces of Satgaon's former grandeur including a ruined mosque.

The Portuguese were kicked out of Hooghly in 1632 by Shah Jahan, after a lengthy seige, but allowed to return a year later. The British East India Company also established a factory here in 1651. The Imambara, built in 1836, with its gateway flanked by lofty minarets, is the main sight in the city. Across the road from it is an older Imambara, dating from 1776-77.

Chinsura

Only a km or so south of Hooghly, Chinsura was exchanged by the Dutch with the British for the Indonesian Island of Sumatra in 1825. The Dutch Church is octagonal and dates from 1678, there is a Dutch cemetery with many old tombs a km to the west.

Bandel

Only a couple of km north of Hooghly, Bandel is 43 km north of Calcutta. A Portuguese Church and monastery was built here in 1599 but destroyed by Shah Jahan in 1640. It was later rebuilt.

Getting There Get off the train at Naihati and take the hourly shuttle service across the river.

Bansberia

A further four km north of Bandel, Bansberia has the Vasudev temple with

NORTH OF CALCUTTA
Chandernagore

This was another of the French enclaves in India which were handed over at the same time as Pondicherry in 1951. On the banks of the Hooghly, 39 km north of Calcutta, there are still a number of buildings dating from the French era. The first French settlers arrived here in 1673 and it later became an important interesting terracotta wall carvings and also the Hanseswari Temple.

Jairambati & Kamarpukur

Ramakrishna was born in Kamarpukur, 143 km north-west of Calcutta, and there is a Ramakrishna Mission Ashram here. Ramakrishna was a 19th century Hindu saint who did much to rejuvenate Hinduism when it was going through a period of decline during the British rule. Jairambati, five km away, is another important point for Ramakrishna devotees.

Shantiniketan

Near Bolpur, the Vivabharati University is located here. The brilliant and prolific poet, writer and nationalist Rabindranath Tagore (1861-1941) founded a school here in 1901. It later developed into a university with an emphasis on man's relation with nature — many classes are conducted in the open air. Tagore went on to win the Nobel prize in 1913 and is credited with introducing India's historical and cultural greatness to the modern world. Despite his work for India's independence he was knighted by the British.

Places to Stay There's a small *University Guest House* and *Railway Retiring Rooms* at Bolpur station.

Nabadwip & Mayapur

Nabadwip is an ancient centre of Sanskrit culture, 114 km north of Calcutta. There are many temples here and across the river at Mayapur; both are important pilgrimage centres.

Plassey

In 1757 Clive defeated Suraj-ud-daula and his French supporters here, a turning point in British influence in India. Plassey is 172 km north of Calcutta.

Murshidabad (population 18,000)

This was once an important trading town between inland India and the port

of Calcutta, 221 km south. Today it's a quiet town in central Bengal, a chance to see typical rural Bengali life, but this was once the home of Suraj-ud-daula, the local sultan who put Calcutta's British residents into that infamous 'Black Hole'. A year later the British defeated his forces at Plassey and nominated a more reliable successor.

They built him a large Italian style palace, the Nizamat Kila, which was completed in 1837 and it still stands right beside the Bhagirathi River (closed Fridays). Cross the river by small boat to see Suraj's tomb at Khusbagh, the 'Garden of Happiness', where the Nawabs are buried. Opposite is the Moti Jhil or 'Pearl Lake', a fine place to view the sunsets. There are a number of other interesting buildings and ruins and this is a notable silk producing area.

Places to Stay Near the palace in Murshidabad is the *Hotel Historical* which has rooms at Rs 10. If it's full you can sleep on the roof. Meals cost Rs 3. The *Tourist Lodge* in Berhampore is cleaner and more reliable but it's 12 km away by bus. Rooms can be booked through the West Bengal Tourism Corporation in Calcutta and doubles run from Rs 30 or there is a Rs 5 dorm.

Getting There There are seven trains daily from Sealdah Station in Calcutta and the trip takes six hours.

English Bazaar (population 70,000)

Near this town, north of the Ganges on the route to Darjeeling, there are the interesting remains of several ancient Bengali capital cities.

Gaur

Seven km south of English Bazaar this was the capital of Bengal in the pre-Moslem days. The large city stood at the junction of the Ganges and Mahananda rivers and was once extensively fortified. There are still many remains of the fortifications, mosques and towers.

Old Malda

At the junction of the Kalindri and Mahananda rivers, this was once an important place as the port for the former Moslem capital of Pandua. An English factory was established here in 1656 but moved to English Bazaar in 1771.

PERMITS

Before you can visit Darjeeling, Kalimpong or Sikkim special permits are required. Only in the case of Darjeeling are certain exceptions made to this rule (see below). All these places are located in what the Indian Government refers to as 'sensitive border regions' and the rationale behind the permit requirements is to keep track on who goes there. Anyone having the slightest familiarity with Indian bureaucracy will know what a farce this is. As far as Darjeeling and Kalimpong are concerned it's merely a formality but it keeps plenty of people employed pushing pens and wielding rubber stamps. Anywhere else in the world it would be called 'Job Creation'. With Sikkim obtaining a permit is more involved and you must plan ahead.

Darjeeling

The only exception to the permit rule is if you travel by air from Calcutta to Bagdogra (the nearest airport to Darjeeling), return the same way, and your stay in Darjeeling does not exceed 15 days from the date of arrival at Bagdogra. If you do this you can have your passport endorsed at Bagdogra airport checkpost for a visit to Darjeeling.

If you intend to go there by bus or train then you must obtain a permit. You can get these from any of the following places:
Indian Embassies, Consulates and High

Pandua

Gaur one alternated with Pandua as the seat of power. Many of Pandua's now ruined buildings were constructed from material taken from Gaur, which accounts for its strange blend of architectural styles. Pandua is 11 km from Old Malda and 18 km from English Bazaar.

Commissions outside India.
Ministry of Home Affairs, Government of India, North Block, New Delhi.
Home Political Department, Writers' Building, BBD Bagh, Calcutta. The office is on the first floor — ask for Mr Gautama.
Any Foreigners Registration Office in India. In Calcutta the office is at 237 Acharya J C Bose Rd.

There is one form to complete, no photographs are required and the permit is issued free of charge within 24 hours within India. Permits allow for a stay of seven days, extendable in Darjeeling at the Foreigners Registration Office, Laden La Rd (tel 2261). No photographs are required and no fee charged for extensions and they are issued while you wait.

If you're planning on trekking to Sandakphu and/or Phalut a separate special permit is required obtainable, again, from the Foreigners Registration Office in Darjeeling. If you flew into Bagdogra airport then you are exempted from this requirement on condition that you report your intentions to the Foreigners' Registration Office, Darjeeling, 24 hours before leaving.

Kalimpong

A permit for Darjeeling does not automatically entitle you to visit Kalimpong. To go there you must obtain a seperate endorsement on your Darjeeling permit. Ask for it at the same time you apply for the Darjeeling permit or get one from the Foreigners Registration Office in Darjeeling. A three day visit is normally allowed. If you want longer, get authorisation before you go.

Sikkim

There are no exceptions to the permit requirements for Sikkim regardless of your mode of transport. You need to apply at least six weeks in advance of your proposed visit either to an Indian Embassy/Consulate/High Commission outside India or to the Deputy Secretary, Ministry of Home Affairs (F-1), North Block, New Delhi 110001. There are three forms to complete, three photographs are required and you have to state the exact days on which you want to visit. No fee is charged for the permit. If you apply via an Embassy/Consulate/High Commission you will receive a letter some four to six weeks

after you applied which states that 'the Government of India has no objection to your visit' and that you can pick up your permit from the Deputy Commissioner's Office, Darjeeling (situated at the junction of Cutchery Rd and Cart Rd next to the Loreto Convent). The initial permitted length of stay varies between two and four days but is extendable in Gangtok at the Foreigners Regional Registration Office. Extensions are a mere formality and issued on the spot — just tell them where you want to go and how much time you require. No photographs are required and no fee charged for extensions. Your permit will be collected on leaving Sikkim at the Rangpo checkpost.

Note that you can go trekking as far as Dzongri in western Sikkim without further involvement with bureaucracy but the area north of Phodang in eastern Sikkim is a restricted area. You will need further permission to go there.

DARJEELING (population 50,000)

Straddling a ridge at 2123 metres and surrounded by tea plantations on all sides, Darjeeling has been a very popular hill station since the British established it as a rest and recreation centre for its troops in the mid-1800s. These days foreign travellers and Indian nationals come here to escape from the heat, humidity and hassle of the North Indian plain and some indication of its popularity can be gleaned from the fact that there are almost 60 hotels alone recognised by the West Bengal Tourist Development Corporation apart from scores of others which don't come up to its requirements. Here you will find yourself surrounded by mountain people from all over the eastern Himalayas who have come here to work, trade or, in the case of the Tibetans, as refugees. Outside of

the monsoon season (June-September) the views over the mountains to the snowy peaks of Kanchenjunga and down to the swollen rivers in the valley bottoms are magnificent. It's a fascinating place where you can see Buddhist monasteries, visit a tea plantation and see how it's processed, go for a ride on the chair lift which takes you down 2050 metres over eight km to the valley bottom, spend days hunting for bargains in colourful markets and handicraft shops, or go trekking to high altitude spots near the border with Sikkim. Like most places in the Himalayas, half the fun is in getting there and Darjeeling has the unique attraction of the famous 'toy train'. This miniature train which loops and switchbacks its way up the steep mountainsides from New Jalpaiguri to Darjeeling has been a favourite with travellers for many years.

Until the beginning of the 18th century the whole of the area between the present borders of Sikkim and the plains of Bengal, including Darjeeling and Kalimpong, belonged to the Rajas of Sikkim. In 1706 they lost Kalimpong to the Bhutanese and control of the remainder was wrested from them by the Gurkhas who invaded Sikkim in 1780 following consolidation of the latter's rule in Nepal. These annexations by the Gurkhas, however, brought them into conflict with the British East India Company. A series of wars were fought between the two parties eventually leading to the defeat of the Gurkhas and the ceding of all the land they had taken from the Sikkimese to the East India Company. Part of this territory was restored to the Rajas of Sikkim and the country's sovereignty guaranteed by the British in return for British control over any disputes which arose with neighbouring states. One such dispute which arose in 1828 led to the despatch of two British officers to this area and it was during their fact-finding tour that they spent some time at Darjeeling (then called Dorje Ling = 'Place of Thunderbolts'). The officers were quick to appreciate Darjeeling's value as a site for a sanatorium, hill station and as the key to a pass into Nepal and Tibet. The officers' observations were reported to the authorities in Calcutta and a pretext eventually found to pressure the Raja into granting the site to the British in return for an annual stipend of Rs 3000 (raised to Rs 6000 in 1846).

This transfer, however, rankled with the Tibetans who regarded Sikkim as a vassal state and Darjeeling's rapid development as a trading centre and tea growing area in a key position along the trade route leading from Sikkim to the plains of India began to make a considerable impact on the fortunes of the lamas and leading merchants of Sikkim. Tensions arose and in 1849 two British travellers, Sir Joseph Hooker and Dr Campbell, who were visiting Sikkim with the permission of the Raja and the British Government were arrested. Various demands were made as a condition of their release but the Sikkimese eventually released both prisoners unconditionally about a month later. In reprisal for the arrests, however, the British annexed the whole of the land between the present borders of Sikkim and the Bengal plains and withdrew the annual Rs 6000 stipend from the Raja. The latter was restored to his son and raised to Rs 9000 in 1868 and raised again to Rs 12,000 in 1874. The annexations brought about a significant change in Darjeeling's status. Previously it had been an enclave within Sikkimese territory and to reach it the British had to pass through a country ruled by an independent Raja. After the take-over, Darjeeling became continuous with British territory further south and Sikkim was cut off from access to the plains except through British territory. This was eventually to lead to the invasion of Sikkim by the Tibetans and the British military expedition to Lhasa.

When the British first arrived in

A & B   Temple sculptures, Khajuraho (MP)
C   Taj-ul-Masjid, Bhopal (MP)

Darjeeling it was almost completely under forest and virtually uninhabited though it had once been a sizeable village before the wars with Bhutan and Nepal. Development was rapid and by 1840 a road had been constructed, numerous houses and a sanatorium built and a hotel opened. By 1857 it had a population of some 10,000. Most of the increase in the population was accounted for by the recruitment of labourers from Nepal who were brought in to work the tea plantations which had been established in the early 1840s by the British following the smuggling of tea seeds from China. Even today, the vast majority of people speak Nepali as a first language and the name Darjeeling continues to be synonymous with tea. Although it's from here that some of the world's finest tea originates, the tea industry is presently in dire straights. The quality of the soil is deteriorating and most of the tea trees are more than 100 years old. Very little replanting has been done and if it is to survive it seems likely that massive government aid will be necessary.

Until the late 1800s, all supplies for Darjeeling and all exports from the town had to be moved by bullock cart along the road which connects it to Siliguri. This road, which is still known as the Hill Cart Road, was so called because its gradient is such that even bullock carts could climb it. Naturally, this form of transportation was slow and, even by the standards of the time, expensive. Rice which sold in Siliguri for Rs 98 a ton fetched Rs 240 a ton

by the time it reached Darjeeling. The problem was eventually overcome when an astute officer of the Eastern Bengal Railway, Franklin Prestage, came up with a scheme for constructing a miniature railway — the famous 'Toy Train'. Construction of this railway started in 1879 and was completed by 1881 at a cost of Rs 1,700,000 including the initial rolling stock though improvements were made to it from time to time, one of the most important being the Batasia loop on the final descent into Darjeeling.

Although the Buddhists, with their monasteries at Ghoom and Darjeeling, are perhaps the most conspicuous religious group they constitute only a minority of the population — about 14%. The majority of the inhabitants profess Hinduism reflecting their origins in the northern Indian states and Nepal. Christians and Moslems comprise little more than 3% each of the district's total population though there are numerous churches scattered around Darjeeling.

The best time to visit Darjeeling is between April and mid-June and between September and November. During the monsoon months (June to September) clouds obscure the mountains and the rain is often so heavy that whole sections of the road from the plains are washed away though the town is rarely cut off for more than a few days at a time. The average temperatures range from a maximum of 15°C to a minimum of 8.5°C in summer and from a maximum of 6°C to a minimum of 1.5°C in winter. If you go there during the monsoon an umbrella is

A   A Devi Jagadamba & Kandariya Mahadev Temples, Khajuraho (MP)
B   B Temple of the Sun, Konarak (O)

more or less essential — cheaply bought in the market.

Orientation

Darjeeling is strung out over a ridge facing west and spills down the hillside in a complicated series of interconnecting roads and flights of steps which it will take you at least several days to become familiar with. The main road is the Cart Rd running along the lower part of the town and along which are located the railway station and the bus and taxi stand. The most important route connecting this road with Chowrasta at the top of the ridge is Laden La Rd/Nehru Rd. Along these two roads are situated a fair number of the budget hotels and cheap restaurants, the GPO, the bus terminals for Sikkim and Kathmandu, the Foreigners Registration Office, the State Bank of India, curio shops, photographic supply shops and the Tourist Office. At the Chowrasta end of Nehru Rd and on Gandhi Rd above Laden La Rd are located many of the mid-range hotels and restaurants. The bulk of the top-range hotels are clustered around Observatory Hill beyond Chowrasta. There are others along Dr Zakir Hussain Rd and A J C

Bose Rd. The Youth Hostel is situated on the very top of the ride above Dr Zakir Hussain Rd.

Services & Useful Addresses

The Tourist Office is located on the 1st Floor at the back of the Ambassador Hotel, Chowrasta. (The address is officially 1 Nehru Rd, tel 2050). Very little literature is available except maps of Darjeeling backed by a brief description of places of interest which cost Rs 1.50. Don't come here for information about the treks to Sandakphu and Phalut or you'll regret it once you're on your way. Indian Airlines (tel 2355), is at 1 Nehru Rd, Chowrasta (underneath the Ambassador Hotel).

The Foreigners Registration Office, Laden La Rd is probably one of the most popular, though somewhat involuntary, meeting places for travellers. Darjeeling Permit extensions take a few minutes. No photographs are required and there's no fee. Permits for Kalimpong take only 10 minutes or so. There's one form to fill in, no photographs and the permit is issued free of charge. They normally allow for a three-day stay. Remember that if you're going to Sikkim the validity of your Darjeeling

1	Railway Station & Tourist Reception Centre	14	Timber Lodge
2	Bus Stand (Kalimpong, Siliguri, etc)	15	Hotels Kadambari & Nirvana
		16	Tibetan Restaurants (eg Solti)
3	Buses to Gangtok (Sikkim Nationalised Transport)	17	Chowrasta Restaurant
		18	State Bank of India
4	Buses to Kathmandu	19	Market
5	Taxi Stand	20	Ropeway (Chairlift)
6	Tourist Office & Indian Airlines	21	Himalayan Mountaineering Institute & Zoo
7	Foreigners Registration Office	22	Tibetan Refugee Centre
8	Deputy Commissioner's Office	23	Raj Bhavan
9	GPO	24	Botanical Gardens
10	Darjeeling Tourist Lodge	25	Tiger Hill
11	Youth Hostel	26	Monastery
12	Sailabash Tourist Lodge	27	Ghoom Monastery
13	Several Mid-range Hotels	28	Happy Valley Tea Estate

permit may need extending to cover you for the return journey.

The State Bank of India on Laden La Rd is the usual place to change money but it's one of the most inefficient and slowest bank branches I've ever come across. It's also unbelievably decrepit. I wouldn't bank a pair of sweaty old socks here let alone money. Be prepared for a long session changing money, snails would leave this lot standing!

The best place to hire trekking gear from is the youth hostel but note that you must leave a deposit or valuables to cover the value of the articles which you borrow (deposits returnable less hire charges on returns of the equipment). Typical charges are: sleeping bag (Rs 4.50 a day); rucksack (Rs 2 a day); air pillow (Rs 0.25 a day); air mattress (Rs 1.50 a day); bed roll (Rs 2.50 a day); two-person tent (Rs 6 a day); aluminium camp cot (Rs 4 a day). The Youth Hostel also keeps a book where trekkers write comments and suggestions about the routes. It's well worth reading through this book if you're thinking of going trekking. The only trouble is, the entries are written in many different languages and, in many ways, you need to have been on the trek to make head or tail of what is being said. It's high time someone put all the information together in a coherent form and illustrated it with maps. Whatever you do, don't bother asking the Tourist Office for information about trekking.

Viewpoints

Tiger Hill The highest spot in the area at 2590 metres, Tiger Hill is situated near Ghoom, about 11 km from Darjeeling. The hill is famous for its magnificent dawn views over Kanchenjunga and other eastern Himalayan peaks. On a clear day even Mt Everest is visible. Accommodation is available here at a Tourist Lodge.

Senchal Lake Close to Tiger Hill is Senchal Lake which supplies Darjeeling with its domestic water. It's a particularly scenic area and popular as a picnic spot with Indian holidaymakers. Entrance to the lake costs Rs 0.50.

Religious Centres

Ghoom Buddhist Monastery This is probably the most famous monastery in Darjeeling and is located about eight km from town just below the Hill Cart Rd and railway near Ghoom. It enshrines an image of the Maitreya Buddha (the coming Buddha). Foreigners are allowed to enter the shrine and take photographs. A small donation is customary and the monks here are very friendly. There is another monastery nearby in Ghoom itself.

Aloobari Monastery Located nearer Darjeeling, on Tenzing Norgay Rd, this monastery is still in the process of construction. Visitors are welcome and the monks often have Tibetan and Sikkimese handicrafts and religious objects (usually hand bells) for sale.

Dhirdham Temple The most conspicuous Hindu temple in Darjeeling, it is located just below the railway station and built along the lines of the famous Pashupatinath temple in Kathmandu.

Museums, Parks & Gardens

Himalayan Mountaineering Institute Located on Jawahar Rd West about two km from the town, the institute is the only one of its kind and exists to train mountaineers. It also has a museum containing an interesting collection of mountaineering equipment, specimens of Himalayan flora and fauna (though not one of the Abominable Snowman!) and a relief model of the Himalayas. It is open from 9 am to 5 pm during summer and 9 am to 4 pm during winter except between 1 pm and 2 pm. Except during the tourist season it is closed on Tuesdays. The entrance fee is Rs 0.50.

Zoological Park Adjacent to the Himalayan Mountaineering Institute, the park has a collection of high-alititude fauna including the Siberian Tiger, Himalayan Black Bear, deer, panda and a bird collection. The entrance fee is Rs 0.50.

Botanical Gardens Located below the bus and taxi stand near the Market these gardens contain a representative collection of Himalayan plants, flowers and orchids. The hot houses are well worth a visit. The Gardens are open between 6 am and 5 pm, entrance is free.

Handicraft Centres
Tibetan Refugee Self-Help Centre The centre was established in October 1959 to help rehabilitate Tibetan refugees who had fled from Tibet with the Dalai Lama following the Chinese invasion. Religious importance is attached to this place as the 13th Dalai Lama (the present is the 14th) stayed here during his visit to India in 1919-22. The centre produces superb carpets, woollens, wood carvings and leather work and has various Tibetan curios for sale (coins, banknotes, jewellery, etc). You can wander at leisure through the various workshops and watch the work in progress. The weaving and dying shops and the wood carving shop are particularly interesting and the people who work there very friendly. Their prices, however, are on a par with those in the curio shops of Chowrasta and Nehru Rd. It's an interesting place to visit apart from the workshops and the views en route are magnificent.

Curio Shops The majority of these are located on Chowrasta and along Nehru Rd. All things Himalayan are sold here — thankas, brass statues, religious objects, jewellery, wood carvings, woven fabrics, carpets, etc — but if you're looking for bargains you have to shop judiciously and be prepared to spend plenty of time looking through various shops. Thankas in particular are nowhere near the quality which was usual 10 years ago. They may look impressive at first sight but on closer inspection you will find that little care has been taken over the finer detail. The brocade surroundings (said to originate from China) are often of much finer quality. Wood carvings tend to be excellent value for money. Most of the shops accept international credit cards. In addition to the curio shops themselves there is the market off the Cart Rd next to the bus and taxi stands. Here you can find excellent and relatively cheap patterned woollen sweaters. If you need an umbrella these can be bought here for around Rs 12. Made out of bamboo, they are collectors' items themselves!

Bengal 'Manjusha' Emporium Located on the Cart Rd about two km from town on the way to Ghoom and opposite the Ava Art Gallery, this emporium sells Himalayan handicrafts, silk and handloom products from West Bengal. It's open on all working days from 8 am to 5 pm.

Tea Plantations
Tea is, of course, Darjeeling's most famous export. From its 78 gardens are produced 10.5 million kgs annually — 2% of India's total. It employs over 46,000 people in the area. The most convenient garden to visit is the Happy Valley Tea Estate only two km from the centre of town where tea is still produced by the 'orthodox' method as opposed to the 'Curling, Tearing and Crushing' (CTC) method adopted in the plains. The process is a fascinating one to observe and you should set aside

a half day to visit the estate.

After picking, the fresh, green leaves are placed 15 to 25 cm deep in a 'withering trough' where the moisture content is reduced from 70-80% to 30-40% using high velocity fans. When this is complete the withered leaves are rolled and pressed so as to break the cell walls and express their juices onto the surface of the leaves. Normally two rollings at different pressures are undertaken and in between rolls the leaves sifted to seperate the coarse from the fine. Next the leaves, coated with their juices, are allowed to ferment on racks in a high-humidity room, a process which develops their characteristic aroma and flavour. This fermentation must be controlled carefully since either over- or under-fermentation will ruin the tea. The process is stopped by feeding the fermenting leaves onto a conveyor belt which passes through a chamber into which is forced dry air at 115-120°C and which reduces the moisture content further to around 2-3%. The last process is the sorting of the tea into grades. In their order of value they are: Golden Flowery Orange Pekoe (unbroken leaves), Golden Broken Orange Pekoe, Orange Fannings and Dust (the latter three all consisting of broken leaves).

In the last few years modern agricultural practices have been brought to the tea estates to maintain and improve their viability. They were one of the first agricultural enterprises to use clonal plants in their replanting schemes though very little of this has been done and, as was mentioned earlier, most of the tea trees are at least 100 years old. The fact that most of them are getting towards the end of their useful or even natural lives is causing grave concern to the growers and government assistance has already started in an attempt to save the gardens from extinction. This is important not just because of the value of the tea exported but because of the large numbers of people in this area who would be made redundant if the gardens were to close.

The Happy Valley Estate is open daily from 8 am to 12 noon and between 1 pm and 4.30 pm except on Mondays and Sunday afternoons.

The Passenger Ropeway

Located at North Point, about three km from town, this was the first passenger ropeway to be constructed in India. It is eight km long and connects Darjeeling with Singla Bazar on the Little Ranjit River at the bottom of the valley. This is a superb excursion though not one for vertigo sufferers. The return fare costs Rs 16. Before you go there ring 2731 to enquire about the availability of chairs.

Places to Stay — Top End

The top-range hotels includes the *Oberoi Mt Everest*, Gandhi Rd (tel 2616/2236) where rooms cost Rs 250 a single and Rs 350-400 a double with full board. There is a bar and foreign money can be exchanged here. *Windamere Hotel*, Bhanu Sarani (The Mall) (tel 2396) costs Rs 150 a single and Rs 200 a double with full board. Same facilities as the Oberoi.

Central Hotel, Robertson Rd (tel 2033) costs Rs 88 a single and Rs 160-190 a double including full board. *New Elgin Hotel*, H D Lama Rd (tel 2182) costs Rs 70-85 a single and Rs 140-150 a double. Bed and breakfast rates are Rs 25-30 extra. *Pine Ridge Hotel*, 19 Nehru Rd (tel 2094) costs Rs 95-105 a double. Meals are extra and they have no single rooms. *Hotel Bellevue*, Nehru Rd (tel 2129) costs Rs 110-150 a double. Meals are extra.

Places to Stay — Middle

The *Tourist Lodge*, Bhanu Sarani (The Mall) (tel 2611-13) is managed by the West Bengal Tourist Department. Rooms here cost Rs 75-150 a double (there are no singles) but note that full board is compulsory and the charge for meals is Rs 30 a day plus 10% service charge. It's not a particularly inviting building but many tourists stay here.

Ambassador Hotel, IB Chowrasta (tel 2781) costs Rs 34-46 a double. *Capital Hotel*, 1A Gandhi Rd (tel 2860) costs Rs 50-55 a double. *Kundu's Hotel*, 2A Rockville Rd (tel 2867) costs Rs 40-55 a double. Note there is another Kundu's Hotel at 1 Gandhi Rd (tel 2146) which has rooms for Rs 55-60 a double.

Meghdoot Hotel, 4 Laden La Rd (tel 2975) costs Rs 30-55 a single and Rs 55-110 a double. *Mayfair Hotel*, 6 Gandhi Rd costs Rs 25-36 a double. *Rex Hotel*, 1A Gandhi Rd (tel 2571) costs Rs 40 a single and Rs 65 a double.

Places to Stay — Bottom End

Hotel Kadambari, situated below the railway station, has concrete box rooms with attached 'bathroom' (buckets of hot water delivered) and toilet, clean sheets and blankets for Rs 20 a triple. It's clean and run by very friendly staff. Lounge and dining room on the top floor with excellent views across the valley.

Hotel Nirvana, located next door to the Hotel Kadambari, is similar in quality and facilities to the Kadambari. Rooms cost Rs 25 a triple for back rooms and Rs 30 a triple for the front rooms. Friendly people. *Timber Lodge* is at the back of Laden La Rd — to get there take the stone steps on the left hand side of the restaurants opposite the top end of the GPO and take the first turning on the right. The place is very popular with budget travellers though definitely on the decrepit side of rustic. The manager is very pleasant and eager to please but there's no hot water available. Rooms here cost Rs 6 a single and Rs 12 a double. *Shamrock Hotel* is located 100 metres further along the dirt track from the Timber

Lodge. Rooms here cost Rs 10 a double (downstairs) and Rs 15 a double (upstairs). Communal facilities and no hot water. The *Youth Hostel*, above Dr Zakir Hussain Rd (tel 2290), is very popular with trekkers and other budget travellers. Costs Rs 12 a double and Rs 6 in the dormitory (or Rs 5 in the low season). Clean and well-maintained building with a friendly manager. Meals can be provided and there are cooking facilities. Excellent views across the mountains. A book is kept here with trekkers' comments about the route to Sandakphu and Phalut and if you're thinking of doing the trek you'd be well advised to spend an hour or two reading through it (there are sections in every language under the sun!). The Hostel is theoretically open only to YHA members and students. Trekking gear is available for hire.

At Tiger Hill near Ghoom there is the *Tourist Lodge* where you can stay if you want to watch the sunrise over Kanchenjunga. Rooms here cost Rs 30 a single and Rs 35 a double or Rs 8.50 in the dormitory. All the rates are with full board. Advance booking is advisable — either ring the Lodge direct (tel 2813) or contact the Tourist Office at the junction of Nehru Rd and Chowrasta.

The above is only a limited selection of the scores of hotels and lodges available in Darjeeling. You will find plenty of others along virtually any road you choose. The object of this list is to see you through the first couple of days. After that you may well find others that are far more appealing than the above and decide to move.

Places to Eat

Most of the cheaper restaurants are located along Laden La Rd, Nehru Rd and Cart Rd. Many of them are Tibetan restaurants and popular with budget travellers but there's little to choose between them. Some of the better ones include *Himalaya Restaurant*, Laden La

Rd, opposite the State Bank of India. A good Tibetan restaurant which serves porridge, omelettes and other Tibetan food. Porridge, omelette and tea costs Rs 5. Friendly management and run by an old man who chants mantras all morning!

Chowrasta Restaurant, Chowrasta, is an open-air restaurant which serves excellent South Indian food (vegetarian only). Masala dosa for Rs 2 and special dosa for Rs 3. A good place to sit and drink tea in the afternoons and enjoy the views. *Solti Restaurant* is on Laden La Rd, opposite the top end of the GPO and below the Timber Lodge. They offer Tibetan, Chinese and 'European' food. The omelettes, chips and pancakes are excellent (Rs 2.80 for onion and tomato omelette and Rs 2 for pancakes) but avoid the chicken like the plague unless you're bent on being buried with botulism.

Glenary's Restaurant is near the junction of Laden La Rd and Nehru Rd. An excellent mid-range cafe with surprisingly reasonable prices. Come here for a minor splurge and to get a glimpse of the ghost of the Raj — the waiters all wear white uniforms with cummerbunds and frilly turbans!

Getting There

Flights The nearest airport to Darjeeling is at Bagdogra down on the plains near Siliguri, about 90 km from Darjeeling. From Bagdogra you can get to Darjeeling either by rail or road. There are daily flights by Indian Airlines to Bagdogra from Calcutta at 12 noon and from Bagdogra to Calcutta at 1.30 pm. The fare is Rs 335 and the journey takes 55 minutes. Indian Airline office in the Darjeeling area are at Siliguri (tel 21201), Kalimpong (tel 241), Darjeeling (tel 2355) and Bagdogra Airport (tel 20366).

If you fly into and out of Bagdogra then you are exempted from the permit requirements for Darjeeling. On arrival at Bagdogra your passport will automatically be endorsed for a 15 day visit to Darjeeling. Flying into and out of Bagdogra does not exempt you from the permit requirements for Sikkim. If you're intending to go there you must apply for one of these in advance.

Trains The quickest way to get from Calcutta to Darjeeling (or vice versa) is to take the daily 'Darjeeling Mail' from Sealdah Station, Calcutta to New Jalpaiguri and then a bus or taxi from there to Darjeeling. But the most interesting way of doing the last stage of the journey from New Jalpaiguri to Darjeeling is to take the 'Toy Train' even though this will add three hours to the journey. The train times to and from New Jalpaiguri are as follows: Depart Calcutta (Sealdah Station) 7 pm. Arrive New Jalpaiguri 6.30 am next day. Depart New Jalpaiguri 7.15 pm. Arrive Calcutta (Sealdah Station) 7.15 am next day. The fares are Rs 143 in 1st Class and Rs 39.50 in 2nd Class. Second Class sleeping berths can be booked at Eastern Railways Booking Office, Fairlie Place, Calcutta; New Jalpaiguri Station between 8.30 am and 10.30 am and between 2.30 pm and 4.30 pm; Darjeeling Railway Station. Note if you intend to go by 2nd Class rail all the way between Calcutta and Darjeeling (or vice versa) you can book a ticket all the way for Rs 44. If you're booking in Darjeeling a sleeping berth can be booked for you on the night mail train from New Jalpaiguri.

Another train which might be of use to you along the main line if you're heading west is the Siliguri-Mughal Salai train. Mughal Salai is only a few km from Varanasi (Benares). This train departs Siliguri daily at 6.30 pm and takes 23 hours to Mughal Salai. The fare is Rs 45 in 2nd Class including the journey on the 'Toy Train' from Darjeeling to Siliguri.

The Toy Train The journey to Darjeeling from New Jalpaiguri or Siliguri by this miniature railway is a superb experience and one which shouldn't be missed even though it does take three hours longer than the buses.

The idea for a railway to Darjeeling was put forward by Franklin Prestage, an agent working for the Eastern Bengal Railway, in 1870. The scheme was accepted and construction begun in 1879. It was completed in 1881 and in 1885 a further km extension was added to take the line into the market area (now in disuse). Later on, in 1914, it was further extended south towards Kishanganj close to the Nepalese border to cope with the transport of jute and, in 1915, from Siliguri to 15 km beyond Sevok on the way to Kalimpong. The initial cost of the original section to Darjeeling was Rs 1,700,000 including rolling stock. The whole line is an ingenious feat of engineering and includes four complete loops and five switchbacks some of which were added after the initial construction had been completed to ease the line's gradient at certain points. Altogether, there are 132 unmanned level crossings!

Officially there are three departures in either direction daily but in practice there can be more and the departures from New Jalpaiguri don't necessarily follow the official timetable (though they do from Darjeeling). From New Jalpaiguri they depart at approximately 7.30 am, 8.30 am, 2.15 pm and 4.30 pm. From Darjeeling they depart at 7 am, 10.30 am and 5 pm. The fares are Rs 45.50 in 1st Class and Rs 7 in 2nd Class and the journey takes 7 hours. Meals are available on the train.

Your permit for Darjeeling will be checked at New Jalpaiguri Station both on entering and leaving. There is also a Tourist Reception Office at the station.

Buses Most of the buses from Darjeeling depart from the Bazar Bus Stand (Cart Rd). Most jeeps and taxis depart from the Motor Stand, Robertson Rd/Laden La Rd. There are many different companies operating buses, jeeps and taxis. Take your pick.

Calcutta-Siliguri (and vice versa). Daily departures in either direction at 8 pm arriving at 7 am the following morning by 'Rocket Service'. The fare is Rs 48.50 and bookings can be made with North Bengal State Transport Corporation at Esplanade Bus Stand, Calcutta (tel 23 1854); Bazar Taxi Stand, Darjeeling, or at Siliguri Bus Stand (tel 20531). This company also runs buses from Siliguri to Patna and vice versa. The buses leave Siliguri daily at 11 am and arrive in Patna at 10 pm. The fare is Rs 24.

New Jalpaiguri/Siliguri-Darjeeling (and vice versa). There are numerous buses, jeeps and taxis in either direction daily between 6 am and 10 pm. The journey takes 3½ to four hours (sometimes less) and costs Rs 6.60-14 from Siliguri and Rs 8.50-16 from New Jalpaiguri depending on the quality of the bus and whether you go by bus, jeep or taxi (the cost in order of cheapness is: bus, jeep, taxi).

Bagdogra-Darjeeling (and vice versa). Minibuses and jeeps connect the airport with Darjeeling. The fare is Rs 22-25 and the journey takes three hours approximately.

Darjeeling-Kalimpong Many buses, jeeps and taxis in either direction daily from 6 am to 10 pm. Buses depart from the Bazar Motor Stand. Jeeps and taxis depart either from the Bazar Motor Stand or from the Robertson Rd/Laden La Rd taxi stand. The fare is Rs 10-13 and the journey takes 2½ hours. The Kalimpong Motor Transport Syndicate, for example, at the Bazar Motor Stand runs jeeps for Rs 12 in the back seats and Rs 13 in the front seats. Your permit for Kalimpong will be checked by military at Teesta bridge. The road as far as Teesta is pretty rough in parts but from there to Kalimpong it's in good shape.

Darjeeling-Gangtok If you don't want to go by taxi or jeep there is only one bus line to Gangtok. This is run by Sikkim Nationalised Transport (SNT) whose office in Darjeeling is located in the first building below the GPO on Laden La Rd (it's unmarked). There is one minibus daily in either direction and as there are few seats available, early booking is essential. The bus departs at 8 am, takes five hours and costs Rs 30.50. Your permit will be inspected before you cross the bridge at Rangpo and at Rangpo itself you will have to visit the Police Station to fill in the visitors' book. On the way out your permit will be collected at Rangpo.

Darjeeling-Kathmandu There are at least three companies which operate buses to Kathmandu. The details are as follows:

'Indiana' buses. The office is opposite the GPO on Laden La Rd. Their bus departs once daily from *Siliguri* at 4.30 pm. It arrives at the border at 5.15 pm. You stay there the night and then depart at 5 am the next morning arriving in Kathmandu the same day at 5 pm. The fare is Rs 56.

'Kankai' buses. The office is situated opposite the top side of the GPO on the left hand side down a very narrow alley between the cafes — there is an advertising board on the street outside. Their buses depart Darjeel-

ing once daily at 12 noon. You stay overnight on the border and continue on to Kathmandu the following day arriving there at 6 pm. The fare is Rs 69.

'Shabnam Travel' buses. The office is situated between the Himalaya Restaurant and the Foreigners Registration Office on Laden La Rd. Their buses depart Darjeeling once daily at 12 noon. You stay overnight at the border and then leave for Kathmandu at 6 am the next morning arriving there at about 6 pm. The fare is Rs 82 which includes the price of the hotel at the border.

The two cheaper buses work as follows: Bus to Siliguri; jeep to Kakaivita (border); bus to Kathmandu. Hotels are available at the border town from Rs 3 upwards. There is no Nepalese Consulate in Darjeeling, the nearest one is in Calcutta. Seven day visas are available at the border and can be extended in Kathmandu.

One traveller's experience of the Darjeeling-Kathmandu trip during the monsoon: 'took us three days to do the trip due to landslides and bridges being destroyed. Got some incredible shots of us wading through thigh-deep water in swirling, full flowing rivers to get across and hopefully find another bus to the next disaster. Never again!'

TREKS IN THE DARJEELING REGION

The best months to trek in this region are April, May, October and November. There may be occasional showers during April and May but, in a way, this is the best time to go as this is the season when many shrubs are in flower, particularly the rhododendrons. There may also be occasional rains during the first half of October if the monsoon is pro-

longed. November is generally dry and visibility excellent during the first half of December though it's usually rather cold by then. After the middle of December there are occasional snow falls.

In planning what clothes to take with you bear in mind that you will be passing through valley bottoms as low as 300 metres and over mountain ridges as high as 4000 metres so you'll need clothing for low, tropical climates and

Darjeeling Treks

high mountain passes. No matter what time of the year you go it's a good idea to take a light raincoat which can be folded up and put inside your rucksack since the weather may be unpredictable, particularly at high altitudes.

Trek 1
Darjeeling - Manaybhanjang - Tonglu - Sandakphu - Phalut and return (118 km to Sandakphu and 160 km to Phalut return).

This is the most popular of the treks and the best one for those with limited time at their disposal. It offers excellent views of Kanchenjunga and of Everest and passes through superb tropical countryside.

On the first day either walk or take a jeep or taxi to Manaybhanjang, 26 km

from Darjeeling. The first day's walk to Tonglu is a fairly steep climb of 11 km via a succession of zig-zags all the way up to the bungalow. Tonglu looks directly on Darjeeling and commands an excellent view of Kanchenjunga.

The next day's walk to Sandakphu covers 22 km and initially passes through bamboo thickets with many ascents and descents until Kalapokhri is reached. About five hours should be allowed be allowed for this part of the trek. The last part up to Sandakphu bungalow involves a steep climb and should take about three hours. On a clear day you can see both Kanchenjunga and Everest from Sandakphu — the latter is only 144 km from Sandakphu as the crow flies. You can either continue on to Phalut from Sandakphu or return to Darjeeling. If you decide to continue the trek starts with a steep descent and then levels out for the next 13 km or so finishing up with a steep zig-zag ascent to Phalut bungalow. Phalut is at the trijunction of Nepal, Sikkim and West Bengal and the views from here are similar to those from Sandakphu.

It's possible to return to Manaybhanjang from Phalut in one day if you start out early enough (allow about eight hours continuous walking) or you can return in two days at a more leisurely pace by breaking the journey at Tonglu.

Trek 2
Darjeeling - Manaybhanjang - Tonglu - Sandakphu - Phalut - Ramam - Rimbik - Jhepi - Darjeeling via Bijanbari (153 km in total).

The first part of this trek up to Phalut follows the same route as in Trek 1. Leaving Phalut there is a steep descent along a forest bridle path for about 11 km to the Ramam River which is crossed by a bridge. A further three km brings you to Ramam Youth Hostel, 14 km from Phalut. This part of the journey takes you through dense forests of rhododendrons, silver firs, chestnuts, oaks, magnolias and hemlocks. On the next day's walk to Rimbik the road stays more or less level for nine km, crosses the Shirikhola River, and then rises steeply for a km before levelling out again in the vicinity of Rimbik Forest Bungalow and the Youth Hostel. If you need supplies there is a small bazaar at Rimbik.

The next day's walk begins with a fairly steep descent over about eight km to the bridge across the Lodoma River. After this the path levels out and passes through cultivated land until it reaches Jhepi Bungalow, 17 km from Rimbik.

From Jhepi the road climbs some 150 metres over two km to a spur on which Kaijali sits and then drops down to Bijanbari six km further on. You can either take a jeep from here to Darjeeling 36 km away, or walk there via Pulbazar and Singtam.

Trek 3
Darjeeling - Manaybhanjang - Tonglu - Sandakphu - Phalut - Ramam - Rimbik - Palmajua - Batasi - Manaybhanjang - Darjeeling (178 km in total).

This trek initially follows the same route as Trek 2 as far as Rimbik. From Rimbik to Palmajua is about 14 km facing Kanchenjunga all the way. A further 11 km takes you to Batasi along a track which ascends steadily to Deoraly and then descends, gradually at first and steeply towards the end, to Batasi. The next day's walk takes you over the final 14 km to Manaybhanjang from where you can either take a jeep or walk to Darjeeling.

Accommodation along the trekking routes
There are an adequate number of bungalows and youth hostels along the trekking routes though, if possible, advance reservation should be made for the bungalows before you leave Darjeeling. This isn't necessary with the youth hostels. The bungalows are fairly well furnished and have cooking equipment, sheets and blankets. Firewood can be bought from the chowkidar. The youth hostels provide, as you might expect, somewhat more basic accommodation and usually only have mattresses and blankets though some do have basic cooking equipment. Bungalows and youth hostels are located in the following places:

Place	accommodation	charge	altitude (metres)
Manaybhanjang	Youth Hostel	Rs 0.50	2134
Jorepokhri	Dak Bungalow	Rs 3.50	2256

Tonglu	Youth Hostel	Rs 0.50	3070
	Dak Bungalow	Rs 3.50	
Sandakphu	Youth Hostel	Rs 0.50	3636
	Dak Bungalow	Rs 3.50	
Phalut	Dak Bungalow	Rs 3.50	3600
Ramam	Youth Hostel	Rs 0.50	2560
Rimbik	Youth Hostel	Rs 0.50	2286
Jhepi	Dak Bungalow	Rs 2.00	1624
Bijanbari	Inspection Bungalow	Rs 3-5	762
Palmajua	Forest Bungalow	Rs 3.00	2210
Batasi	Firest Bungalow	Rs 3.00	2098

Reservations for the Dak Bungalows should be made with the Deputy Commissioner, Darjeeling Improvement Fund Department, Darjeeling, except in the case of the Bungalow at Jhepi which can be reserved through the District Land Revenue Officer, Darjeeling. Reservations for the Inspection Bungalows should be made with the Divisional Engineer, State Electricity Board, Siliguri. Reservations for the Forest Bungalows should be made with the Divisional Manager, West Bengal Forest Development Corporation, Darjeeling.

Rice, dal, eggs, chicken, onions and potatoes can be bought at most places en route though they're likely to be more expensive than in Darjeeling. In addition there are small chai shops en route at Sandakphu, Meghma, Garibas, Rimbik, Jhepi, Lodoma and Bijanbari. If you would be happy with this kind of diet then you need carry no food with you. If not, then take your own supplies from Darjeeling.

Before you go on any of these treks you're advised to browse through the book at the Darjeeling Youth Hostel where trekkers write their comments about the routes.

KALIMPONG

Kalimpong is a quiet, little bazaar town set amongst the rolling foothills and deep valleys of the Himalayas at at altitude of 1250 metres. It was once part of the lands belonging to the Rajas of Sikkim until the beginning of the 18th century when it was taken from them by the Bhutanese. In the 19th century it passed into the hands of the British and thus became part of West Bengal. Though its name conjures up images of a really fascinating Himalayan outpost, it doesn't have a great deal of interest other than the two Bhuddhist monasteries and the fine views over the surrounding countryside. The most interesting part of Kalimpong is the journey there from Darjeeling via the Teesta Riverbridge. If you have no permit for Sikkim then it's worth visiting just for the journey but if you do have a permit then you could by-pass Kalimpong without missing a great deal. The market here is over-rated.

Information & Orientation

Though it's a much smaller town than Darjeeling, Kalimpong has a similar kind of lay-out straddling a ridge and consisting of a series of interconnected streets and flights of steps. Life centres around the Motor Stand and Chowrasta and it's here that most of the cheap cafes and budget hotels are located though very few of the latter can be recommended since they're all pretty dilapidated affairs. The nearest decent

Kalimpong

K.D. Pradhan Road

Tirpai Hill

Church

School

Rishi Road

School

Mani Rd.

D.S. Gurung Road

R.C. Mintri

Bus Stand

Sports Ground

Thakur Bari Temple

Main Road

Ongden Road

Darjeeling Gangtok Siliguri

Tharpo Choling Monastery

Bhutanese Monastery

Market

Key :-
1. Buses to Gangtok
2. Post Office & State Bank of India
3. Chowrasta
4. Shangri-La Tourist Lodge
5. Himalayan Hotel
6. Sherpa Lodge
7. Gompu's Hotel & Restaurant
8. Crown Lodge
9. Lodge Mayal Lyang
10. Kalimpong Hotel
11. Hotel Maharaja (Restaurant)

hotels are the Crown Lodge below the Motor Stand and the Himalayan Hotel and Shangri La Tourist Lodge out beyond the junction of Main Rd and the road from Darjeeling. There are other fairly decent hotels out on Rishi Rd but they're quite a walk from town. The Tharpo Choling Monastery on Tirpai Hill and the Bhutanese Monastery are both a long, but pleasant, walk from town.

There is no Tourist Office in Kalimpong. There is a Railway Out-Agency Booking Office on the Motor Stand where you can make reservations.

Places to Stay — Top End
Luxury Tourist Lodge (tel 384) is run by the West Bengal Tourist Bureau and

is the most expensive hotel in town. Rooms here cost Rs 50 a single and Rs 125 a double both with their own bathroom.

Places to Stay — Middle
Himalayan Hotel (tel 248) is located on the right hand side up the hill just past the Post Office. Rooms here cost Rs 25 a single including breakfast or Rs 50 a single and Rs 100 a double with full board. *Shangri La Tourist Lodge* (tel 230) is located in its own grounds off the road leading to Darjeeling. Rooms here cost Rs 35 a double or Rs 8 in the dormitory. It's popular with travellers.

Crown Lodge is a few metres down a side street off Ongden Rd and visible from the Motor Stand. Rooms here cost Rs 20 — double bed, fan, clean sheets and own bathroom. It's very clean and rooms are pleasantly furnished and decorated (the wiring is the most immaculate I've seen anywhere in India!). The management are very friendly and morning tea is included in the room charges. Recommended.

Sherpa Lodge overlooks the playing field. Rooms here cost Rs 25 a single. It's of a similar quality to the Crown Lodge. The *Kalimpong Hotel* is another mid-range hotel located on Rishi Rd but it's quite a long walk from town.

Places to Stay — Bottom End
There are quite a number of these on the far side of the Motor Stand but the majority of them look like the ceiling would fall on your head if you raised your voice and can't really be recommended. They're certainly cheap but before you try them ask at *Gompu's Hotel & Restaurant* on Chowrasta. They have a few rooms above the restaurant with good views of the street life outside. They'll ask Rs 20 a double initially but will settle for less if you eat there (it's a good restaurant).

Places to Eat
Gompu's Restaurant, Chowrasta is a pleasant restaurant with friendly staff. They serve Tibetan food (Rs 5-8 on average per dish) and western breakfast materials (omelettes Rs 4; toast Rs 0.75 a slice). Good food.

Hotel Maharaja, R C Mintri Rd has excellent South Indian vegetarian food. A masala dosa will cost you Rs 1.50. *Nizam Restaurant* is a tiny and very friendly chai shop between the Crown Lodge and the Motor Stand. Simple food available. There are plenty of other cafes along Main Rd.

Tharpa Choling Monastery
This monastery belongs to the Yellow Hat sect (Sakya-pa) which was founded in Tibet in the 14th century and is the one which the Dalai Lama belongs to. This particular monastery was founded in 1937 though it looks like it has been on the decline for centuries. It's worth a visit if only for the walk.

Bhutanese Monastery (Thongsa Gompa)
This is the oldest monastery in the area and was founded in 1692. Unlike the Tharpo Choling Monastery it obviously has some enthusiastic benefactors as it's looking very prosperous and has been newly repainted and restored.

Flower Nurseries
Kalimpong is an important orchid-growing area and flowers are exported from here to many cities in northern India. The Sri Ganesh Moni Pradhan Nursery, the Standard Nursery and the Sri L B Pradhan Nursery are among the most important in the area.

The Market
Though of some interest, the market here is over-rated. It's worth a look if you've come to Kalimpong anyway but it's not worth making a special journey to Kalimpong just to see it. There's nothing for sale here than you can't find in either Darjeeling or Gangtok.

Getting Around — Buses, Jeeps & Taxis
Kalimpong-Darjeeling Frequent departures daily in either direction by bus, jeep and taxi. The journey takes about three hours and costs Rs 10-13 depending on what form of transport you take. All the transport leaves from the Motor Stand.

Kalimpong-Siliguri Frequent departures daily in either direction by bus, jeep and taxi. Costs Rs 8.50.

Kalimpong-Gangtok (Sikkim) There are several bus companies which do this run, the main one being Sikkim Nationalised Transport which has two buses daily at 8.30 am and 2 pm costing Rs 12. The journey takes four hours. 'Jayshree' (sometimes spelt 'Joy Shree') also have one bus daily at 2.30 pm which costs Rs 12. Both these companies have offices on the Motor Stand. The companies are fond of calling their buses 'luxury' which is a joke and should be treated as such. The other company which runs buses to Sikkim is Mintri Transport Ltd who have an office on Main St in the same building as Indian Airlines. Their bus leaves daily

at 9.30 am and costs Rs 10.50.
Kalimpong-Bagdogra Mintri Transport Ltd operate one bus daily to Bagdogra at 8.30 am.

If you're one of those rare and lucky people who have managed to get hold of a Bhutanese visa then transport is available from Kalimpong to Phuntsholing on the Bhutanese border.

Siliguri — Places to Stay
If you want to pause in Siliguri the *Airviw Hotel*, directly opposite the bus station, has singles/doubles at Rs 10/16. It's a typical huge Indian hotel with

loads of rooms. Good food can be found at only slightly above normal prices at places like the *Saliya* and other classier hotels further down Hill Cart Rd.

Coping with India — Beggars
Two problems which face most travellers in India are beggars and getting things done. During the emergency a determined effort was made to stamp out begging — beggars were rounded up, trucked a long way out of town and left to make their own way back. Despite various official statements about how people don't need to beg India is a country with only limited social services and a place where being down and out is no fun at all. Beggars are a way of life and after all giving is good for the giver as well as the receiver. For the traveller it's worth remembering a few ground rules and then doing whatever you feel best. First of all beggars in the tourist areas are there because that's where the money is and they're taking a professional outlook on extracting it

from you. The real poverty in India is not in the cities but out in the country where tourists never get. Secondly if you start handing it out to all and sundry outside your hotel entrance you'll soon find a lot more alls and a lot more sundries waiting for you. Thirdly however much you handed out you're only going to be adding a drop to the ocean. Nevertheless cold hard reality doesn't rule out how you and your conscience are going to feel. So if you want to do something but keep things within bounds you can always decide I'm going to hand out so much per day and then stop, I'm only going to hand out to particularly desperate cases, or, and probably most sensibly, I'm not going to give a damn thing but I'll make a donation to one of the aid organisations which work in India.

Sikkim

Population: 250,000
Area: 7214 square km
Capital: Gangtok
Main language: Nepali

Until fairly recently Sikkim ('New House') was an independent Himalayan kingdom though in treaty relations with the Indian government which allowed the latter to control Sikkim's foreign affairs and defence. In 1975, however, following a period of political crises and riots in the capital, Gangtok, India annexed the country and Sikkim became the 22nd Indian state. The move was far from universally popular at the time though tensions have now cooled and the central government has been spending relatively large amounts of money to subsidise road building, electrification, water supply, and agricultural and industrial development. India's motivation for much of this activity was undoubtedly its fear of Chinese military designs in the Himalayan region and even today you'll see a lot of military activity going on along the route from Darjeeling to Gangtok.

For many years, Sikkim was regarded as one of the last 'Shangri Las' in the Himalayan region because of its remoteness, its spectacular mountain terrain, varied flora and fauna and its ancient Buddhist monasteries. It was never easy to get there and even now a special permit must be obtained from the central government before a visit can be made. It's likely that this requirement will continue for the foreseeable future but it's becoming more and more a formality as tourism is promoted. Foreign visitors are now permitted to trek up into the remote Dzongri region of western Sikkim without further permission being required but, for the present, much of eastern Sikkim alongside the Tibetan border remains out of bounds.

The country was originally peopled by the Lepchas, a tribal people who are thought to have migrated from the hills of Assam around the 13th century. The Lepchas were forest foragers and small patch cultivators who worshipped nature spirits and were a pacific people in temperament. They still make up some 18% of the total population of Sikkim though their ability to lead their traditional life style has been severely limited due to immigration from Tibet and, more recently, from Nepal.

The Tibetans started to emigrate into Sikkim during the 15th and 16th centuries due to religious strife between the various Lamaist sects at that time. In Tibet itself the yellow hat sect — the Sakya-pa to which the Dalai Lama belongs — gradually gained the upper hand whereas in Sikkim the red hat sect — Nying-ma-pa — remained in control and was, until the country became a part of India, the official state religion. Though the Lepchas originally retreated to the more remote regions in the face of the waves of Tibetan immigrants a blood brother-

Sikkim

TIBET

NEPAL

▲ Kanchenjunga

Yumthang

Lachen

Lachung

Chungthang

River

Dzongri

Tista

Mangan

Gyangtse
Shigatse

Bakhim

Dikchu

Phodang

Yuksam

Brang

Natu La
Pass

Pemayangtse

Keozing
(Sosing)

Rumtek

Gangtok

Gezing

Dentam

Pakyong

Singtam

Rangli

Namchi

Rangpo

Rhenok

BHUTAN

Naya Bazar

Sakyong

WEST BENGAL

Tista R.

Kalimpong
Darjeeling

present, much of eastern Sikkim along-side the Tibetan border remains out of bounds.

The country was originally peopled by the Lepchas, a tribal people who are thought to have migrated from the hills of Assam around the 13th century. The Lepchas were forest dwellers and small-patch cultivators who worshipped nature spirits. As were a peaceful people, in temperament they still are in some parts. The tribal population of Sikkim about this ability to find that the jungle had been severely depleted of game by migrant hunters. Tensions between Bhutya and Lepcha led to conflict, but during the early days of the Buddhist monasteries, strict wars were between the two leaders. A broth-erhood was eventually engineered be-tween their leader, Thekong Tek, and the Bhutyas leader, Khye-Bumsa, and the heavy hand of spiritual and temporal authority imposed on the anarchistic

Lepchas. The union generated a good deal of suspicion between the two groups particularly when the Lepchas were persuaded to bring all their literature and totems to a ceremony where it was destroyed by the Tibetans. Having imposed their control over the Lepchas, the Dalai Lama in Lhasa appointed Penchoo Namgyal as the first king of Sikkim in 1641. At this time the country included the whole of the area bounded by the present state plus a part of eastern Nepal, the Chumbi Valley (Tibet), the Ha Valley (Bhutan) and the Terai foothills from the present border down to the plains of India including Darjeeling and Kalimpong.

Between 1717 and 1734, during the reign of the fourth king, a series of wars were fought with the Bhutanese which resulted in the loss of much territory in the southern foothills including Kalimpong, then a very important bazaar town on the trade route leading from Tibet to India. More territory was lost after 1780 following the Gurkha invasion from Nepal though the invaders were eventually checked by a Chinese army with Bhutanese and Lepcha assistance. Unable to advance into Tibet, the Gurkhas turned south and came into conflict with the British East India Company. A series of wars were fought between the two parties ending in the treaty of 1817 whereby the borders of Nepal were delineated and the Gurkhas ceded to the British all the Sikkimese territory they had taken. A substantial part of this territory was returned to the Raja of Sikkim in return for control by the British of all disputes between Sikkim and its neighbours. The country thus became a buffer state between Nepal, Tibet and Bhutan.

In 1835, the British, seeking a hill station as a rest and recreation centre for its troops and officials, persuaded and ·pressured the Raja into ceding the Darjeeling area in return for an annual stipend. The Tibetans objected to this transfer of territory as they continued to regard Sikkim as a vassal state and Darjeeling's rapid growth as a trade centre began to make a considerable impact on the fortunes of the leading lamas and merchants of Sikkim. Tensions rose and in 1849 a high ranking British official and a botanist, who were exploring the Lachen region with the permission both of the Sikkimese Raja and the British government, were arrested. Following threats of intervention, the two prisoners were unconditionally released a month later but the British annexed the whole of the area between the present Sikkimese border and the Indian plains and withdrew the Raja's stipend (the latter was eventually restored to his son).

Further British interference in the affairs of this area led to the declaration of a protectorate over Sikkim in 1861 and the delineation of its borders. The Tibetans, however, continued to regard all these actions as illegal and in 1886 invaded Sikkim to reassert their authority. They were thrown back by the British and a military expedition sent to Lhasa in 1888 as a punitive measure. The powers of the Sikkim Raja were further reduced and high-handed treatment by British officials prompted him to flee to Lhasa in 1892 though he was eventually persuaded to return.

Being keen to develop the area, the British encouraged immigration from Nepal, as they had done in Darjeeling, and a considerable amount of land was brought under rice and cardamom cultivation. As a result of this influx of labour, which was still going on right up until the 1960s, the Nepalese constitute some 75% of the population of Sikkim. The subject became a heated topic of discussion in the late '60s and the Raja was constrained to prohibit further immigration. Further steps were taken to placate those of non-Nepalese origin in the form of new laws regarding the rights of citizenship but these inflamed the opposition political parties. The Raja's American-born wife was also active in stirring up a resentment against the Nepalese and matters eventually reached a head with demonstrations in

Gangtok and the flight of the Raja to India. Though India had inherited the treaties with Sikkim from the British at independence they were in no mood to be seen propping up the regime of an autocratic Raja in Sikkim while doing their best to sweep away the last traces of princely rule in India itself. Their response to this instability in a very sensitive border region with China was to pension off the Raja and annex the country. Though there was much resentment over this action at the time and international protests, the political situation has cooled down and Sikkim is now governed by its own democratic congress with representatives in the central government in New Delhi.

The current population make-up of Sikkim consists of approximately 18% Lepcha, 75% Nepalese and the rest Butyas and Indians from various northern states. About 60% of the population are Hindus and 28% Buddhist although the two religions exist, as in many parts of Nepal, in a syncretic form. The ancient Buddhist monasteries, of which there are a great many, are one of the principal attractions of any visit to Sikkim.

GANGTOK (population 14,000)

Gangtok, the capital of Sikkim, occupies the west side of a long ridge flanking the Ranipool River. Scenically, it has a very spectacular setting and excellent views of the entire Kanchenjunga range can be obtained from many points in the vicinity. On the other hand, it's not, as many people expect it to be, a smaller version of Kathmandu overflowing with ancient temples, palaces, monasteries and narrow, colourful bazaars. Gangtok only became the capital in the mid-1800s, the previous ones being sited at Yoksam and Rabdantse. It has undergone rapid modernisation in recent years.

Information & Orientation

To the north is Raj Bhavan, the former British and later Indian Residency, and above it the Tourist Lodge and Enchen Monastery. Lower down along the ridge is the palace of the former Raja (known as the Chogyal) and the large and impressive Royal Chapel (the Tsuk-La-Khang). The chapel, but not the palace, is open to visitors. Nearby is the huge Secretariat complex, built in traditional style, which was damaged during a recent earthquake. On a continuation of this ridge but much lower is the Namgyal Institute of Tibetology established in 1958 and, like the Secretariat building, built in the traditional style. The library here can be visited and a collection of objects relating to Tibetan Buddhism, including some unique and very beautiful silk embroidered thankas, is on permanent display. An orchid sanctuary surrounds the Institute which itself is enclosed in a peaceful forest. Not too far beyond the Institute is a large white stupa and adjoining it a Buddhist monastery and school for young lamas. Inside the temple here are huge images of Guru Padma Sambhava, the Indian teacher of Buddhism in Tibet, and his manifestation, Guru Snang-Sid Zilnon.

All the other main facilities — hotels, cafes, bazaars, bus stand, post office, tourist information centre and the Foreigners Registration Office — are located either on or very near to the main road from Darjeeling. The Tourist Office is very well equipped and staffed with friendly and exceptionally helpful people. Just below the office is a display of some of the main crafts produced by the Cottages Industries Emporium located much higher up on the main road.

Extending Your Permit

You might think that after all the effort and waiting that was required to get your permit

Gangtok

Phodang
Lachen

P.W.D.
Bungalow

Cottage
Industries
Emporium

G.P.O.

Enchey
Monastery

Nor-Khill
Hotel

Bus Station

Post
Office

Foreigners
Registration
Office

Tourist
Office

Shere Punjab
Hotel

Hotel Orchid

Main Bazar

Palace

Hotel
Tashi Delek

Tsuklakhang
(Royal Chapel)

Lall
Market

National Highway

Secretariat
Complex

Deer Park

Institute of
Tibetology & Orchid Sanctuary

Rumtek
Rangpo
Darjeeling

Chörten

for Sikkim (see Darjeeling) that extensions would be difficult to come by. Not so! In fact, it's remarkably uncomplicated. You merely go along to the Foreigners Registration Office on the National Highway, tell them where you want to go and so how much time you require, and they do it for you on the spot. No waiting, no photographs required and no forms to fill in. Remember that if you're thinking of visiting all four of the most famous monasteries in Sikkim — Rumtek, Pemayangtse, Tashidingand, Phodang — you'll need *at least* one week and probably a little longer. The main reason for this is the times of the buses to these places which prevent you from returning on the same day.

Tsuk-La-Khang

The Royal Chapel is the principal place of worship and assembly of the Budhists and the repository of a large collection of Buddhist scriptures. It's a beautiful and impressive building whose interior is covered with murals and lavishly decorated altars holding images of the Buddha, Bodhisatvas and Tantric deities. There are also a great many fine wood carvings. It's open every day to visitors but no photography is allowed inside. The chapel is the site of many important festivals, the most interesting being the one to the God of Kanchenjunga (around mid-September) and another in celebration of the New Year when the famous Black Hat dance is performed, demonstrating the triumph of good over evil.

Institute of Tibetology Orchid Sanctuary & Chorten

This institute is the only one of its kind in the world and was established to promote research on the language and traditions of Tibet as well as into Mahayana Buddhism. It has one of the world's largest collection of books and

rare manuscripts on the subject of Mahayana Buddhism plus many religious works of art and a collection of astonishingly beautiful and incredibly finely executed silk embroidered thankas. The director of the institute is a very friendly man who will spend time showing you around if you care to approach him. The institute is open to the public from 10 am to 4 pm Monday through Saturday. It is closed Sundays and every second Saturday. There is no entrance fee.

Adjoining the institute is the Orchid Sanctuary where most of the 454 species of orchid found in Sikkim can be seen, depending on the season. The best season to visit is between April and May, July and August, and October and November.

About a km beyond the institute stands a huge chorten whose gold apex is visible from many points in Gangtok. Next to it is a monastery for young lamas whose shrine contains huge images of Guru Padma Sambhava.

Institute of Cottage Industries
(Cottage Industries Emporium)

Located high up on the main road above the town, this multicraft institute specialises in producing hand-woven carpets, blankets, shawls, Lepcha weaves, patterned decorative paper and 'Choktse' tables exquisitely carved in relief. It's open for visiting between 9 am and 12.30 pm and 1 and 3.30 pm daily except Sundays and every second Saturday. In addition to the shop here, there is a smaller display of craftwork on the ground floor of the Tourist Office which is well worth a visit.

Deer Park

This is a popular viewpoint right on the edge of the ridge next to the Secretariat building. In it are, as you might expect, deer and an image of the Buddha which is a replica of that standing at Sarnath in India.

Enchey Monastery

Situated next to the Tourist Lodge, about three km from the centre of town, is the 200-year old Enchey Monastery. It's well worth a visit particularly if you're in Gangtok during December when annual religious dances are performed here.

Lall Market

If you've been to Kathmandu or Darjeeling then this market will come as a disappointment. It has none of their colour, magic or range of products and is of marginal interest only.

Tours

The Department of Tourism offers tours of the various points of interest in Gangtok and of Rumtek Monastery daily from February to May and from October to December. For reservations on these tours, contact the Department of Tourism, Gangtok Bazaar (tel 292).

Gangtok city tour This tour includes visits to Tashi View Point, the Deer Park, Enchey Monastery, the Royal Chapel, Secretariat, Cottage Industries Institute, the Institute of Tibetology and the nearby chorten and orchid sanctuary. The tour runs from 9.30 am to 12.30 pm and costs Rs 15.

Rumtek Monastery This tour takes you on a visit to the monastery. It starts at 1.30 pm and ends at 4.30 pm.

Places to Stay — Top End

Nor-Khill Hotel (tel 386/618) costs Rs 185 a single and Rs 260 a double plus 10% service charges. The tariff includes full meals. *Hotel Tashi Delek* (tel 311/458) operates on American plan (full board) and costs Rs 160 a single and Rs 260 a double. Bed and breakfast only costs Rs 100 a single and Rs 190 a double.

Places to Stay — Middle

Tourist Lodge (tel 292/664) costs Rs 30 a single and Rs 40 a double. The hotel is managed by the Government of Sikkim Tourist Department. Transport is available from the Tourist Office above the Bus Stand.

Hotel Orchid (tel 381) costs Rs 40 a double without own bathroom, Rs 50 a double and Rs 75 a triple with own bathroom in the tourist season. In the low season rooms cost Rs 20 a double without own bathroom, Rs 30 a double and Rs 45 a triple with own bathroom. If you occupy a double room on your own during the off season then the charge is Rs 15 a double with own bathroom. The place is clean, has attractive rooms with excellent views of Kanchenjunga, hot water when the electricity is on (there are frequent power cuts in Gangtok) and a restaurant and bar on the top floor. The restaurant serves excellent food (chicken curry Rs 7; vegetables Rs 3; fried dhal Rs 1.50

including rice). Beers cost Rs 8 and tots of Sikkimese spirits Rs 2. The staff are friendly and the place is secure. Avoid getting a room on the top floor at the back — someone has economised on glazing and facilities are communal though the prices are the same. *Green Hotel* (tel 254) is located a little way up the main bazaar from the Tourist Office on the same side of the road. Rooms here cost Rs 15 a single with common bath (Rs 10 in the off season) and Rs 20-50 a double with own bathroom (Rs 12-35 in the off-season). Attached restaurant. *Karma Hotel* costs Rs 35 a single and Rs 40-50 a double both with attached bathroom. There is no reduction during the off-season. *New Hotel Quality* (tel 619) costs Rs 25 a single and Rs 40 a double both with attached bathroom. There are no reductions during the off season. *Deeki Hotel* costs Rs 25 a single with common bathroom and Rs 35 a double with own bathroom. (Doubles cost Rs 25 with own bathroom in the off season).

Places to Stay — Bottom End

Shere Punjab is located just below the Hotel Orchid. Rooms here cost Rs 12 a single with common bathroom and Rs 20 a double with own bathroom. *Doma Hotel* costs Rs 8 a single and Rs 20 a double both with common bathrooms. The *PWD Bungalow* is located high up on the National Highway beyond the Cottage Industries Emporium. There are only two rooms available here so book in advance if possible. The double-bedded rooms cost Rs 10 per bed. Reservations from the Executive Engineer, CPWD North, Sikkim Highway, Gangtok.

Places to Eat

There are very few good restaurants in Gangtok which are not attached to hotels and you'll probably find that most of the time you eat at your own hotel. The restaurant at the *Hotel Orchid* is popular with middle-class local people

and open to non-residents. Their food is excellent. Other than this there are a number of simple vegetarian cafes around the bus stand and along the main bazaar where you can obtain basic food at very low prices (Rs 2-3 on average). About half a km uphill from the bus stand on the National Highway, where a road branches off to the left and leads to the stadium and Nor-Khill Hotel, there is a cafe which serves snacks and tea or coffee but which also sells cheese. If you have a yen for some of this wonderful stuff then come here. Try thungba from a chang shop in the market — a large bamboo mug full of millet to which you add hot water to get fresh chang.

Getting There

There is no airport in Gangtok and no rail connection. The nearest airport is at Bagdogra and the nearest railheads at Ghoom (on the 'Toy Train' line from Siliguri to Darjeeling) or Siliguri (on the main line). Bus transport is nationalised so the only buses available are those operated by Sikkim Nationalised Transport (SNT). There is a fee for reservations of Rs 0.50, except on the Gangtok-Siliguri and Gangtok-Kalimpong routes.

Gangtok-Siliguri Buses three times daily at 7 am, 8.30 am and 1 pm. From Siliguri to Gangtok the buses depart at 7 am, 9.30 am and 1 pm. The journey takes about five hours (the fastest bus is the first one in the morning) and costs Rs 15.

Other companies which cover this route are: Aspara (Agents: Janata Auto Agency, New Market, Gangtok and near the Armadeep Hotel, Siliguri). They have one bus daily in either direction at 1.30 pm from Gangtok and 7.30 am from Siliguri. Sikkim Beauty (Agents: M/S Punchshed, New Market, Gangtok, and near the Armadeep Hotel, Siliguri) also have one bus daily in either direction at 2 pm from Gangtok and 8.30 am from Siliguri. North Bengal Transport's daily bus in either direction departs at 12.30 pm from Gangtok and 6 am from Siliguri. The journey takes five hours.

Gangtok-Bagdogra SNT bus once daily in either direction at 8 am from Gangtok and from Bagdogra after arrival of the plane. The journey takes five hours.

Gangtok-Darjeeling SNT bus once daily in either direction at 8.30 am. The journey takes five six hours and costs Rs 30. Note that this bus is heavily oversubscribed and so it's advisable to book in advance. SNT use what is probably their best mini-bus for this trip. If you need to get to Darjeeling but the bus is booked out then take a bus first to Kalimpong and then another bus from there.

Gangtok-Kalimpong SNT buses twice daily in either direction at 8.30 am and 1.30 pm. The journey takes four hours and costs Rs 11.50. Other companies which cover this route are: Sangam Transport with one bus daily in either direction at 2 pm from Gangtok and 7 am from Kalimpong. The journey takes four to five hours. Tista-Rangit Transport have one bus daily in either direction at 9 am from Gangtok and 3 pm from Kalimpong. The journey takes about four hours.

Internal Sikkimese buses

To Rumtek Two buses daily in either direction at 10 am and 4.30 pm from Gangtok and 7.30 am and 1 pm from Rumtek. The journey takes about two hours and costs Rs 4.50. Note that the last bus from Gangtok and the first from Rumtek take longer because they're crowded with local people and so there

are many stops. In addition you have to get off the bus at the Ranipool River and walk across the bridge as it's structurally weak and won't take the weight of a fully-laden bus. In fact, it looks like it would plummet into the river if you raised your voice!

To Phodang One bus daily in either direction at 4.15 pm from Gangtok and 7.30 am from Phodang. The journey takes about 3½ hours and costs Rs 5.25. Note that because of the timing of the buses, if you want to see anything of Phodang and the other monasteries in the area a visit here will occupy the best part of three days. This could well mean extending your permit.

To Gezing (sometimes spelt Geyshing) One bus daily in either direction at 9.30 am from Gangtok and 7.30 am from Gezing. The journey takes about seven to eight hours and costs Rs 18. This is the bus you need to take if you're heading for Pemayangtse and Dzongri. Pemayangtse is about six km from Gezing but basic accommodation is available in Gezing if the bus is late. It's clear that a trip to Pemayangtse will, like a trip to Phodang, take at least three days. Make sure your permit covers you for this period.

In addition to SNT buses, jeeps and Ambassador taxis are available to the above places though they work out quite expensive. The charges are: Gangtok-Rumtek: Rs 135 return per car. The return journey takes a half day. Gangtok-Phodang: Rs 190 return per car. Journey time as for Rumtek. Gangtok-Pemayangtse: Rs 600-700 depending on the route taken. The trip takes two days.

AROUND GANGTOK
Rumtek Monastery

Rumtek is visible from Gangtok on the other side of the Ranipool valley at about the same elevation yet it's 24 km away by road. The monastery is the seat of the Gyalwa Karmapa, the head of the Kagyu-pa sect of Tibetan Buddhism.

The sect was founded in the 11th century by Lama Marpa who was the disciple of the Indian guru, Naropa. It later split into several sub-sects of which the most important are Duk-pa, Kagyupa and Karma-pa. The teachings of the sect are orally transmitted to the disciples. The main monastery here is a recent structure which was built by the Gyalwa Karmapa strictly according to the traditional architectural designs on which the monastery he came from in Tibet was constructed. Visitors are welcome at the monastery and there's no objection to you sitting in on the prayer and chanting sessions. They'll even bring you a cup of salted butter tea when it's served to the monks. Mural work is still being done and if you're interested in the Tibetan style of religious painting then Rumtek is a must for you. It's a very interesting place and well worth a visit. The old monastery can still be seen just beyond the new structure though it's not obvious as it's hidden by trees.

If you follow the tarmac road beyond Rumtek for two or three km there is another interesting, but smaller, monastery off to the left through a gate.

Places to Stay If you wish to stay at Rumtek for the night there is a lodge opposite the monastery with about 20 rooms available. Most of them have two to three single beds in them. It's basic but clean and blankets and candles are provided (there's no electricity most of the time) and it's beautifully quiet and peaceful. The price of the rooms is negotiable but you shouldn't have to pay more than Rs 5 for a bed. Just below the lodge is a small chai shop which serves eggs and fresh bread in the morning (two fried eggs, bread and tea cost Rs 3.50) and chow-chow in the evening. Friendly people.

Pemayangtse Monastery & Tashiding Monasteries

Pemayangtse Monastery, situated at a height of 2085 metres, is the second oldest monastery in Sikkim and belongs to the Nyingma-pa sect. This Tantric sect was established by the Indian teacher Padma Sambhava in the 8th century. All monasteries of this sect are characterised by a prominent image of this teacher together with two female consorts. The followers of the sect wear red caps and the monastery here is the head of all others in Sikkim. Pemayangtse is about six km from the bus terminus at Gezing but Tashiding is a full day's hike from Pemayangtse up along a ridge. The hike starts with a 1½ hour walk to a river which is crossed and then a further two hours' walk to Tashiding village, going up hill all the way. The monastery itself is further up the hill near the summit but hidden by pine trees. Sangacholing monastery is also in the vicinity.

Places to Stay For accommodation there is a choice of at least four basic lodges at Gezing for around Rs 10 a room — any number of people can share a room. Food is also available there and a typical meal of rice, dahl and eggs would cost about Rs 5. If you want something slightly better there is the *PWD Rest House* about two km up the hill from Gezing towards Pemayangtse. It's excellent value at Rs 10 per room but prior booking is necessary from the CPWD in Gangtok between 9.30 am and 4.30 pm. The chowkidar here cooks excellent meals for a further charge.

At Tashiding there is a *Forestry Department Bungalow* where you can stay for Rs 10 per room but you must bring your own blankets and sheets. To stay here you need authorisation from

Key:

═══ Metalled Road
╌╌╌ Unmetalled Road
▬ ▬ ▬ Track
⌒⌒⌒ Glaciers
〰 Rivers
▪ Villages & Towns
☆ Monasteries

TREKKING ROUTES IN
WEST SIKKIM

Pemayangtse-Dzongri-
Kanchenjunga Base Camp

the Tourist Office in Gangtok or the Forestry Department in Gezing. The monastery is some 15 minutes' walk from the village. Good meals are available in the village chai shop and if you go there to eat you'll have the whole village for company!

If you're looking for luxury accommodation then there is the *Pemayangtse Tourist Lodge* (tel 73). Rooms here with full board cost Rs 145 a single and Rs 200 a double. For reservations contact the Tourist Office in Gangtok.

Phodang Monastery

This is the farthest you are permitted to go in eastern Sikkim without further entanglement with bureaucracy. Phodang Monastery at Thumlong, 40 km north of Gangtok, has recently been rebuilt but just above it is Labrang Gompa where the original construction is still intact. Labrang is accessible only by bridle path and you should allow about half an hour to get there from Phodang. If you're allowed to go further up the road to Mangan and Singhik a clear, unobstructed view of Kanchenjunga can be had.

TREKKING IN SIKKIM

Trekking is now being allowed up to Dzongri in western Sikkim but you need a further endorsement on your permit to do this at present. Though the regulations are elastic up to a point depending on how you put yourself across, officially you're allowed to trek up to Dzongri for up to 10 days so long as you're accommpanied by a travel agent recognised by the Indian Tourist Development Corporation and a liaison officer or guide provided by the government of Sikkim, that you travel by air from Calcutta to Bagdogra, and that you follow one of either of the following routes: Nayan Bazar-Pemayangtse-Yaksum-Dzongri or Rangpo-Gangtok-Yaksum-Dzongri. In other words, you have little choice than to go with an organised tour at present unless you have political clout in the Sikkimese bureaucracy. The travel agents which organise these treks are: Yak & Yeti Travels, Gangtok; Snow Lion Treks, Gangtok, and Sikkim Himalayan Adventure, Gangtok. The best time to go trekking is from mid-February to late May and from October to December. Trekking gear can be hired at the agencies in Gangtok.

North-East Frontier

state	capital	area (square km)	population
Assam	Gauhati	79,500	19,200,000
Manipur	Imphal	22,300	1,400,000
Meghalaya	Shillong	22,400	1,300,000
Nagaland	Kohima	16,500	700,000
Tripura	Agartala	10,400	2,000,000
Arunachal Pradesh	Itanagar	83,600	500,000
Mizoram	Aizawi	21,000	400,000

The north-east region is the most varied and at the same time the least visited part of India. Prior to independence the whole region was known as Assam Province but it was finally split into five separate states and two Union Territories — Mizoram and Arunachal Pradesh. In many ways the north-east is quite unlike the rest of India. It is the chief tribal area of India with a great number of tribes who speak many different languages and dialects — in Arunachal Pradesh alone over 50 distinct languages are spoken! In many ways these tribal people are similar to the hill tribes found right across the sweep of country at the eastern end of the Himalayas which extends from India through Burma and Thailand into Laos. Also the north-east has a high percentage of Christians, particularly in the more isolated areas where the population is predominantly hill tribespeople.

For a number of reasons India has always been touchy about the north-east and this attitude has increased dramatically in 1980-81, making a visit to the north-east a tricky proposition at present. For a start the north-east is a sensitive border zone where India meets with Bhutan, China, Burma and Bangladesh. Equally important the region is physically remote from the main Indian land mass — only the narrow Siliguri corridor connects it to the rest of India and prior to independence the usual route to Assam would have been through Bangladesh. Today, reaching the north-east by train involves a long journey by metre gauge rail. Roads have been dramatically improved but there are still very few of them compared to the rest of India. For these reasons the Indian government has been sensitive

317

about visitors and only permitted them to go to Assam and Meghalaya; the other five regions, all bordering with China or Burma, were for all practical purposes off-limits. Even a visit to Assam and Meghalaya required a special permit although this was readily available, at least for certain distinct tourist attractions.

Dramatic events in 1980 and 1981 have virtually shut the region off completely. The north-east has developed into the most troubled part of India and the central government has experienced great difficulty in asserting its authority there. Strikes, riots, violence and terrorism have all been part of the story and at times even the Indian Airlines' flights to the north-east have had to be suspended. There are a number of reasons for this unrest including a feeling of neglect by the central government — poor transport links and lack of infrastructure development are main complaints. This feeling has become increasingly strong with the rising price of oil since Assam pumps a substantial part of India's small, but important, oil output. Very little of this oil wealth finds its way back to improve Assam's industrial development and the whole region remains overwhelmingly agricultural. Neglect may be a major issue but the number one complaint has been about 'foreigners'. The cycle of events in Bangladesh, just to the south-east of the region, combined with that tightly packed country's undiminished birthrate has pushed thousands of Bengalis over the lightly policed borders into the north-east region. This influx of 'foreigners' has resulted, in some cases. in the indigenous population actually becoming outnumbered. Demands that 'foreigners' be repatriated has been a major part of the unrest. Of course such a wholesale repatriation is an impossibility, particularly since many of these Bengali 'foreigners' have been resident in the region

for generations — legally or not. Nevertheless the strife in the region continues undiminished and while it does visits to the north-east are far from easy.

Permits

Normally permits are required for the two accessible states of the region — Assam and Meghalaya. These would usually be granted with the minimum of formality. You can approach these states either through Bangladesh, by looping north of Bangladesh through the Siliguri corridor or by air.

Assam Permits for Assam actually only permitted you to visit Gauhati (the capital) and the game reserves at Manas and Kaziranga. Permits can be applied for at Indian consular offices overseas. In India the Foreigners's Registration Office, Hans Bhavan (near Tilak Bridge), Bahadur Shah, Zafar Marg, New Delhi 110002 or the Trade Adviser, Government of Assam, 8 Russel St, Calcutta 700071 issued them. Normally the permit allows a maximum stay of 15 days but this could be extended in Assam. If you fly to Gauhati and follow a specified route to Kaziranga and back you are allowed to visit Assam without a permit. For places in Assam apart from Gauhati, Manas and Kaziranga permission must be requested from the Home Ministry, Government of India, North Block, New Delhi at least six weeks in advance. In Calcutta you apply to the Trade Adviser 'sufficiently in advance'.

Meghalaya The Meghalaya Information Centre in Calcutta is right next to the Assam office at 9 Russel St and they issue permits with equal ease for a seven day visit. Shillong, the capital of Meghalaya, is approached via Gauhati or through Bangladesh. As in Assam permits are usually extendable after you arrive.

Indian Airlines routes in the north-east
(fares in Rs)

Dibrugarh
Tezpur Liabari 75
225 105 57 120
500 105 105 Jorhat
Gauhati 185
185 Dimapur
305 140
465 185 Silchar
350 75 Imphal
Calcutta 150
225 Agartala

ASSAM

The largest and most easily accessible of the north-east states, Assam is a major tea producing area (60% of India's tea comes from here) and also produces a large proportion of India's oil. The main attractions for the visitor are the Manas and Kaziranga wildlife reserves which are home for India's rare one-horned rhinoceros.

GAUHATI (population 140,000)

Capital of the state, Gauhati is on the banks of the Brahmaputra River. It has many ancient Hindu temples but its main importance is as a gateway to the north-east and a jumping off point for visits to the wildlife reserves.

Information

The Tourist Office (tel 24475) is on Station Rd.

Temples

Umananda Temple is a Shiva temple on Peacock Island in the middle of the river. There's a pleasant ferry across the river. The Navagrah Temple is the 'Temple of the Nine Planets'. In ancient times this was a centre for the study of astronomy and astrology. It is situated on the Chitrachal Hill, near the city. Gauhati's best known temple is the Kamakshya on the Nilachal Hill, 10 km from the city. It attracts pilgrims from all over India, especially during the Ambuchi festival in August. The temple is the centre for Shakti (energy) worship and Tantric Hinduism due to the fact that when Shiva was sorrowfully carrying away his first wife's (Sati's) corpse her yoni fell here! The temple was rebuilt in 1665 after being destroyed by Moslem invaders. In the centre of Gauhati the Janardhan Temple has an image of the Buddha, indicating how Buddhism was assimilated back into Hinduism.

A | Ferry at Daman (Gu)
B | Unloading the fish at dawn, Sasoon Dock, Bombay (M)
C | Buddha statue in Ellora Caves (M)

Other

The Assam State Zoo has tigers, lions, panthers and, of course, Assam's famous rhinos — plus African two-horned ones for comparison purposes. It's open from 6 am to 6 pm in summer, 7 am to 5 pm in winter, and admission is Rs 0.50. There is an Assam State Museum with exhibits pertaining to Assam and its history. The musuem is open from 9.30 am to 3.30 pm daily except on Sundays when it closes at 12.30 pm and Monday when it is shut. Entry is free. There is also an Assam Forest Museum open 10 am to 4 pm daily except Saturdays when it closes at 1 pm and Sundays when it is shut. The Assam Government Cottage Industries Museum is open the same hours on the same days and entry is also free.

Tours

There are government operated tours to Kaziranga from Saturday at 12 noon to Sunday at 5 pm for Rs 120. Manas tours operate at the same times and for the same price.

Places to Stay

The *Hotel Belle Vue* (tel 24225) is on Mahatma Gandhi Rd and costs Rs 100/150 for air-con singles/doubles, Rs 80/120 without air-con. *Hotel North-Eastern* (tel 25314) is on G N Bordoloi Rd and costs Rs 75/120 including breakfast. *Hotel Nova* (tel 23258) in Fancy Bazaar is cheaper at Rs 80/100 with air-con, Rs 30/50 without.

Cheaper hotels include the *Hotel Ambassador* (tel 25587) in Paltan Bazaar with singles/doubles at Rs 20/35. The *Hotel Alka* (tel 24205) in Fancy Bazaar and the *Happy Lodge* (tel 23409) in Paltan Bazaar are similarly priced.

There's a government *Tourist Bungalow* (tel 24475) on Station Rd with accommodation at Rs 12 per person. There are *Railway Retiring Rooms* (tel 26688) with dormitory accommodation at Rs 4 or doubles and triples at Rs 6 per person.

Getting There

See the chart on the previous page for details of air routes to the north-east — these all run from Calcutta. There are also buses and a number of train services. A change from broad gauge to narrow gauge is necessary to reach the north-east from other parts of India. From Calcutta it's 991 km to Gauhati and takes about 24 hours with fares of Rs 184 in 1st class, Rs 45 in 2nd. It's a further 19 hours to Dibrugarh, 1552 km from Calcutta with fares of Rs 268 in 1st class, Rs 64 in 2nd. New Delhi is over 1900 km and nearly 40 hours away even on the fastest train. There are also a number of services from Lucknow which is 1400 km away.

AROUND GAUHATI

Hajo

On the north bank of the Brahmaputra, 24 km from Gauhati, Hajo is an important pilgrimage centre for Buddhists and Moslems. Some Buddhists believe that it was here that the Buddha attained nirvana and they flock to the Hayagriba

A Colva Beach, Goa
B Rice fields near Pandua, Goa
C A mini-sadhu in Pondicherry (TN)

Gauhati

Key:-
1 Railway Station & Bus Station
2 Indian Airlines
3 Tourist Office
4 G.P.O.
5 Tourist Lodge
6 Kalpana Hotel
7 Nova Hotel
8 North Eastern Hotel
9 Ambassador Hotel
10 Stadium Guest House
11 Belle View Hotel

Madhab temple. For Moslems the Pao Mecca mosque is considered to have one quarter (pao) the sanctity of the great mosque at Mecca.

Sualkashi

Also across the river from Gauhati, 20 km away, this is a famous silk weaving centre where the Endi, Muga and Pat silks of Assam are made in small household weaving centre. There is a regular ferry service across the river and a bus service several times daily.

Other

Bashistha Ashram is 12 km south of Gauhati and the rishi or sage Basistha once lived here. It's also a popular picnic spot. The beautiful natural lagoon at Chandubi is 64 km from Gauhati. Darranga, 80 km way on the Bhutan border, is a great winter trading area for the Bhutia mountain folk. Barpeta, with a monastery and the shrine of a Vaishnavaite reformer, is 145 km north-west of Gauhati.

WILDLIFE PARKS

Assam is famous for its rare one-horned Great Indian Rhinoceros — when Marco Polo saw them he thought he had found the legendary unicorn! Kaziranga and Manas are the two well known parks in Assam although there are also smaller parks at Orang and Sonai.

Kaziranga

North-east of Gauhati, Kaziranga wildlife reserve is on the banks of the Brahmaputra River and is famous as the last major home of 'Rhinoceros Unicornis'. The 430 square km park is thought to have a rhino population approaching a thousand but in 1904 they were on the verge of extinction here. The park became a game sanctuary in 1926 and by 1966 the numbers had risen to about 400.

The park also has wild buffaloes, deer, elephants, tigers, bears and a wide variety of water birds including the pelicans which breed here. One of the standard ways of observing the wildlife is from elephant back and the rhinos are said to have become quite used to elephants toting camera-packing tourists.

Information The park is at its best from February to May. There is a Tourist Information Centre (tel 23) at Kaziranga but you're supposed to give 10 days notice for booking accommodation or transport. They have a minibus and a jeep and also organise those elephant rides into the long grass. There's a Rs 5 entry charge to the park and an additional Rs 5 charge for a still camera, higher charges for telephoto lens (!) or movie cameras.

Places to Stay There is a wide variety of accommodation around the park:

Kaziranga Forest Lodge — singles/doubles Rs 75/120 with air-con, Rs 60/90 without.

Tourist Bungalow No 1 — Rs 22/44.

Tourist Bungalow No 2 — Rs 12/24.

PWD Inspection Bungalow, Kaziranga — Rs 5 per person.

Forest Inspection Bungalow, Beguri — Rs 35 a double but bedding and mosquito nets are not included.

Forest Inspection Bungalow, Arimarh — actually within the the park, Rs 30 a double, no electricity.

Forest Inspection Bungalow, Kohora — Rs 35 a double.

Soil Conservation Inspection Bungalow — Rs 40 a double.

Getting There There are flights from Calcutta via Gauhati to Jorhat which is 84 km from the park. By rail Furketing is the most convenient station, 72 km away, from where buses run to Kaziranga. Gauhati is 233 km away on Highway 37. There are state transport buses from Gauhati.

Jorhat

A little beyond Kaziranga this is the gateway to the north-eastern part of Assam. Sibsagar, 55 km away, has the huge Jay Sagar tank and many temples in the environs. This was the old capital of the Ahom kingdom. There's a small *Tourist Bungalow* by the tank.

Manas

In the foothills of the Himalayas, north-west of Gauhati, Manas wildlife sanctuary is right on the border with Bhutan. Three rivers run through the sanctuary which has a wide variety of bird and animal life. The rare pygmy hog and the golden langur (monkey) are amongst the most notable animals here although you may also see rhinos.

Information Manas is best between January and March, there is excellent fishing in November-December. Mothangiri is the main town in the park but the Tourist Information Centre (tel 49) is at Barpeta Road. Park entry charges and camera charges are the same as Kaziranga. Boats can be hired for excursions or fishing trips on the Manas River.

Places to Stay *Manas Tourist Lodge* has rooms in the Upper Bungalow for Rs 7 per bed, Rs 12 per room on the ground floor or Rs 8 per bed, Rs 15 per room on the 1st floor. At the Lower Bungalow it's Rs 6 per bed, Rs 10 per room. You can also camp for Rs 3 if you have a tent. The *Forest Bungalow* costs Rs 5 per room including bedding and mosquito nets but no electricity. There is a *Rest House* at the Barpeta Road Tourist Centre with doubles at Rs 30.

Getting There Gauhati, 176 km away, is the nearest airport. Barpeta Road, 40 km from Mothangiri, is the nearest railway station. Transport from here to Mothangiri must be arranged in advance.

MEGHALAYA

Created in 1971 the state is the home for Khasia, Jaintia and Garo tribespeople. The hill station of Shillong is the state capital while Cherrapunji, 58 km away, is said to be the wettest place on earth with an average annual rainfall of 1150 cm, nearly 40 feet! In one year 2300 cm (75 feet) of rain fell. It's no wonder the name means 'abode of clouds'.

SHILLONG (population 16,000)

A pleasant hill station but other than observing the tiny red light district behind the Delhi Hotel there's not much to do here apart from pass through. The people around Shillong, the Khasias, are matrilineal, passing down property and wealth through the female rather than the male line.

Places to Stay

There's a good *Tourist Bungalow* near the polo grounds but the *Pinewood* is Shillong's premier hotel. Cheap accommodation can be found in the Basar Bazaar where there is also a tourist office. Good food at the *Lhasa Restaurant*.

Getting There

A good road runs the 100 km from Gauhati in Assam to Shillong. Cherrapunji is 58 km south of Shillong, if it's not raining the views from here over Bangladesh are superb. Permission is required from the Commissioner of Police to visit the area but it is given quite readily. Coming from Bangladesh you cross the border at Dawki from where it's a 1½ km walk to the town and then a 3½ hour trip to Shillong.

OTHER STATES & TERRITORIES

The other north-eastern regions are generally hard to get permission to visit even at the best of times. All of them border either with China or Burma. The following information is for interest only.

Arunachal Pradesh

The furthest north-east of the regions this was known as the North-East Frontier Agency under the British. Arunachal Pradesh borders with Bhutan, China and Burma and is a mountainous, remote and predominantly tribal area. The old 'Stillwell Road' used to run from Ledo in the south of Arunachal Pradesh to Myitkyinya in the north-east of Burma. Built in 1944 by General 'Vinegar Joe' Stillwell it must rate as one of the most expensive roads in the world. The 430 km cost US$137 way back then and after just a few months use has hardly been used since. All road routes into Burma are closed.

Nagaland

South of Arunachal Pradesh and north of Manipur, the remote and hilly state of Nagaland is bordered by Burma. Kohima, the capital of Nagaland, was the furthest point Japanese troops advanced into India during WW II.

Manipur

South of Nagaland and north of Mizoram, Manipur also borders with Burma. The state is inhabited by over two dozen different tribes, many of them Christians. The state is famous for its Manipuri dances and its handloomed textiles. Imphal (population 110,000) is the capital, surrounded by wooded hills and lakes and with the golden Shri Govindaji temple. During WW II a road was built from Imphal to Tamu on the Burma border but, as with the Stillwell road further north, this route into Burma is also closed.

Mizoram

This finger like extension in the extreme south-east of the region pokes down between Burma and Bangladesh. The name means hill people's land — Mizo (man of the hill) and ram (land). It's a picturesque place where the population is both predominantly tribal and overwhelmingly Christian.

Tripura

The tiny state of Tripura is almost totally surrounded by Bangladesh. It's a wooded and lush region with many beautiful waterfalls. Agartala is the capital near where is the lake palace of Nirmahal. Here too the population is largely tribal.

Transport in the Region

The only railway to these states and territories terminates at Ledo but the roads have been much improved of late. Indian Airlines operates a comprehensive service to the region from Calcutta.

Rajasthan

Population: 29 million
Area: 342,214 square km
Capital: Jaipur
Main language: Rajasthani

Rajasthan, the 'Land of Kings', is India at its exotic and colourful best. This is the home of the Rajputs, a group of warrior clans who have controlled this part of India for a thousand years with a code of chivalry and honour akin to that of the mediaeval European knights. The Rajputs were never a united force, like the Marathas of central India; when they were not warring against outsiders they were generally squabbling amongst themselves. Thus they were never a real opposition to the Moghuls but their bravery and sense of honour were unparalled.

The Rajput warriors would fight on against all odds and, when no hope was left, the women and children would commit suicide by marching into a funeral pyre in a ritual known as *jauhar*. Meanwhile the men would don the saffron robes of rejoicing worn at weddings and ride forth to certain death. Over and again this grim tale would unfold as stronger forces attacked the Rajputs. In Chittorgarh's long history three times the women consigned themselves to the flames while the men rode out to martyrdom. It's hardly surpising that Akbar persuaded Rajputs to lead his army or that Aurangzeb clashed unsuccessfully with them.

Under the British Rajasthan continued as a collection of princely states under the collective name of Rajputana, each with its own Maharaja. Independent India combined them with Ajmer to make Rajasthan. Huge, often battle scarred, forts dominate almost every town in Rajasthan. They're a clear reminder of the state's warlike past. And what forts they are — battlements, turrets, massive walls and inside palaces of amazing luxury and whimsical charm. They're redolent of that impossibly romantic Rajput sense of honour and bravery above all.

Rajasthan's exotic atmosphere extends to far more than just splendid forts for the Rajasthanis themselves are a brilliant splash of colour. The men top their outfit with a huge, pastel coloured turban and almost without exception sport fierce 'soup-strainer' moustaches. The bright, mirrored skirts of the women are equally colourful. They complement it with chunky jewellery worn from head toe — Rajasthani jewellery is a favourite purchase for visitors to the state.

Geographically Rajasthan is a somewhat dry and inhospitable place but it's very varied. A line drawn south-west to north-east divides the state into the hilly and rugged south-east region and the barren north-east Thar Desert which extends across the border into Pakistan. Apart from historic cities, colourful people and superb scenery Rajasthan also has some popular travellers centres —

Rajasthan

peaceful Pushkar with its holy lake and the exotic desert city of Jaisalmer, like some fantasy from the Thousand and One Nights. It's a fascinating state.

Art & Architecture

Rajasthan has a school of miniature painting, derived from the Moghul style but with some clear differences — in particular the palace and hunting scenes are complemented by religious themes, particularly relating to the Krishna legends. This art carried through to the elegant palaces the Rajputs built when they were freed of confrontation with the Moghuls. Many of them are liberally covered with colourful frescoes.

Most of Rajasthan's early architecture was damaged or destroyed by the first waves of Moslem invasions. Fragments remaining from that period include the Adhai-din-ka-jhonpra mosque in Ajmer, which is basically a converted Hindu temple of great elegance, or the ruined temples at Osian, near Jodhpur. There are many buildings from the 10th to 15th century including the superb Jain temples at Ranakpur, Mt Abu and Jaisalmer. Most of the great forts date, in their present form, from the Moghul period.

Festivals

Rajasthan has the usual Indian festivals, some celebrated with especial local fervour, and also a number of special festivals of its own. The harvest festival of Gangaur is particularly important and Teej, celebrating the start of the monsoon, is also very popular in Rajasthan, where the monsoon rains fill the many lakes and tanks and the state is at its most beautiful. Rajasthan also has many fairs, best known of which is the immense and colourful Pushkar cattle fair.

Palaces, Tourist Bungalows & Prohibition

Rajasthan is famous for its delightful palace hotels — in these harder times many of Rajasthan's Maharajas have had to turn their palaces into hotels to make ends meet. Two of the best are the beautiful Lake Palace Hotel in Udaipur and the Rambagh Palace in Jaipur. At a rather more day-to-day level the state has an excellent series of government operated Tourist Bungalows in almost every big town. They're often the best value in town, have a restaurant and, usually, the local tourist office. For the real shoestringers they also often offer dormitory accommodation. Finally, Rajasthan operates a half-hearted prohibition, you'll need a permit to get a beer.

JAIPUR (population 650,000)

The capital of the state of Rajasthan is popularly known as the 'pink city' from the pink coloured sandstone with which the buildings in its old, walled city are constructed. In contrast to the cities in the Ganges plain Jaipur's avenues are broad and there is a harmony which is quite remarkable. The town is situated in a desert-like landscape, surrounded by barren hills. Rajasthan is a sparsely populated state and Jaipur seems less crowded and more relaxed than its large size and population would indicate.

Jaipur owes its name, its foundation and its careful planning to the great warrior-astronomer Maharajah Jai Singh II (1699-1744). His predecessors had enjoyed good relations with the Moghuls but in 1727, with Moghul power on the wane, Jai Singh decided the time was ripe to move down from his hill side fortress at nearby Amber to a new site on the plains. He laid out the city with its surrounding walls and six rectangular blocks by principles of town planning laid down in the *Shilpa-Shastra*, an ancient Hindu treatise on architecture. In 1728 he constructed the remarkable observatory which is still one of Jaipur's central attractions.

Orientation

The walled 'pink city' is situated in the north-east of Jaipur while the new parts have spread away to the south and west.

1	Central Bus Station	13	Niros Restaurant
2	GPO	14	LMB Restaurant
3	State Govt Tourist Office	15	Rajasthan Handicraft Emporium
4	Indian Airlines	16	Museum
5	Youth Hostel	17	Govt of Rajasthan Tourist Office
6	Achrol Lodge	18	Nehru Bazaar
7	Gangaur Tourist Bungalow	19	City Palace & Museum
8	Teej Tourist Bungalow	20	Jantar Mantar
9	Jaipur Ashok Hotel	21	Hawa Mahal
10	Jaipur Inn	22	Vidyadharji ka Bagh
11	Rambagh Palace Hotel	23	Sisodia Rani Palace & Gardens
12	Man Singh Hotel		

Jaipur

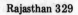

The main shopping centre in the old city is Johari Bazaar or the jeweller's market. Unlike other shopping centres in narrow alleys in India and Asia this one is broad and open. Mirza Ismail Rd (M I Rd) is the main street of the new part of Jaipur and the modern shopping centre. Most of the hotels and restaurants frequented by budget travellers are located around the railway station and bus stand to the south-west. Jaipur's tourist attractions are mainly concentrated in the old city. The state tourist office is in the Teej Tourist Bungalow while the Government of India tourist office is in the Rajasthan State Hotel.

Old City

The old city is encircled by a crenollated wall with seven gates — the major gates are Chandpol, Sanganeri and Ajmeri. The broad (over 30 metres wide) avenues of the pink city divide it up into neat rectangles. It's an extremely colourful city — in the evening light the pink and orange buildings have a magical glow which the brightly clothed Rajasthanis complement. The strange looking camel drawn carts are part of the passing scene in Jaipur and black faced monkeys peer out from some of the buildings. The Iswari Minar Swarga Sul, the 'minaret piercing heaven', near the Tripolia Gate, was built to overlook the city.

Palace of the Winds

Built in 1799 the Hawa Mahal or Palace of the Winds is Jaipur's central landmark although it is actually little more than a facade. The five storey building looks out over the main street of the old city. It's pink sandstone windows are semi-octagonal in shape and delicately honeycombed. It was originally built to enable ladies of the royal household to watch the everyday life and processions of the city. You can climb to the top of the Hawa Mahal and get an excellent view over the city. The palace was originally built by Maharaja Sawaj Pratap Singh and is part of the City Palace complex.

City Palace

In the heart of the old city the City Palace occupies a large area divided into a series of courtyards, gardens and buildings. The outer wall was built by Jai Singh but other additions are much later, some right up to the start of this century. Today the palace is a blend of Rajasthani and Moghul architecture, the former Maharaja still lives in part of the palace.

The centre of the palace is the seven storey Chandra Mahal with fine views over the gardens and the city. Today the ground and first floor of the Chandra Mahal forms the Maharaja Sawai Man Singh II Museum. The apartments are maintained in luxurious order and the museum has an extensive collection of art, carpets, enamelware and old weapons. The paintings include miniatures in the Rajasthani, Moghul and Persian schools. The armoury has a collection of guns and swords dating back to the 15th century plus many of the ingenious and tricky weapons which the warrior Rajputs were famous for. The textile section contains dresses and costumes of the former Maharajas and Maharanis of Jaipur.

Other points of interest in the palace include the Diwan-i-Am or Hall of Public Audiences with its intricate decorations and manuscripts in Persian and Sanskrit, the Diwan-i-Khas or Hall of Private Audiences with a marble paved gallery. There is also a clock tower and the newer Mubarak Mahal.

Outside the buildings you may see a large silver vessel which a former Maharaja used to take drinking water with him to England. Being a devout Hindu he could not drink the English water! The palace and museum are open daily except on holidays and entry is Rs 4 (Rs 1 for students). Hours are 9.30 am to 4.45 pm.

Observatory

Across from the City Palace is the observatory or Jantra Mantra which Jai Singh built from 1728. In all he built five of these curious complexes. Jai Singh's passion for astronomy was even more notable than his prowess as a warrior and before commencing construction he sent scholars abroad to study foreign observatories. Of the five he built the Jaipur observatory is the largest and best preserved — it was restored in 1901. The others are in Delhi (the oldest, dating from 1724), in Varanasi, Ujjain and there was one in Muttra but has now disappeared. At first glance the observatory appears to be just a curious collection of abstract sculptures but in fact each construction has a specific purpose such as measuring the positions of stars, altitudes and azimuths, or to calculate eclipses. The most striking instrument is the sundial with its 30 metre high gnomon. This casts a shadow which moves up to four metres an hour! Admission to the observatory is 30p, free on Mondays, open 9 am to 5 pm.

Central Museum

Situated in the Ram Niwas Gardens, south of the old city, the museum is housed in the architecturally impressive Albert Hall. The upper floor contains portraits of the Jaipur Maharajahs and many other miniatures and works of art. The ground floor has a collection of costumes and woodwork from different parts of Rajasthan and a description of the people and life in the rural areas of the state. The collection, which started in 1833, is also notable for its brassware, jewellery and pottery. Entry to the museum is 10p, free on Mondays. It is open daily except Fridays from 10 am to 5 pm.

Other

The Ram Niwas Gardens also has a zoo with birds, animals and a crocodile breeding farm. Entry is 20p. Jaipur has a Modern Art Gallery and by phoning 62227 you can visit the Kripal Kumbh at B-18/A Shiv Marg where Jaipur's famous blue pottery is made. There are also some interesting excursions out of the city including one to the ancient capital at Amber.

Tours

The Rajasthan Tourist Office operates a daily Rs 10 tour which starts from the Teej Tourist Bungalow (tel 74260) or the Railway Station (tel 69714). The tour lasts from 8 am to 1 pm or from 1 to 6.30 pm and visits the Hawa Mahal, the City Palace, the observatory and Amber. There is a similar tour operated in the mornings by the ITDC from the Rajasthan State Hotel (tel 65451).

Places to Stay — Top End

Jaipur is a major tourist centre and conveniently close to Delhi so it has a wide variety of hotels in all categories. The *Rambagh Palace* (tel 75141) on Bhawani Singh Marg, was the palace of the Maharajahs of Jaipur after the City Palace. Situated to the south of the town it is a charming old building, fully air-conditioned and with a luxurious indoor swimming pool. Singles/doubles cost Rs 280/350. The Polo Bar is one of the hotel's main attractions. Polo is still a big deal in Jaipur, the previous Maharajah died while playing!

Welcomhotel Mansingh (tel 72161-2-3) is on Sanasar Chandra, close to the railway and bus stations. It is part of the Welcomhotel group, it looks like a huge red sandstone palace and costs Rs 225/300. The *Hotel Jaipur Ashok* (tel 75171) is also centrally located in Bani Park. Part of the ITDC chain it costs Rs 150/250. *Hotel Clarks Amer* (tel 82216) is on Jawahar Lal Nehru Marg and costs Rs 200/300.

Places to Stay — Middle

The *Rajasthan State Hotel* (tel 74040) is on M I Rd near the railway station and is also the site for the Government of India tourist office. Singles/doubles costs Rs 100/150 with air-con. *Hotel Imperial* (tel 78651) in the main shopping centre midway between the railway station and the City Palace is cheaper with doubles from Rs 60 (non air-con) and Rs 100 (air-con). The *Achrol Lodge and Tourist Camp* (tel 72254) at Civil Lines costs Rs 60 to 70 for a double but also has good camping facilities.

There are two tourist bungalows, both close to the railway station. The *Gangaur Tourist Bungalow* (tel 74373) is on M I Rd and costs Rs 60/100 with air-con, Rs 50/70 without. The *Teej Tourist Bungalow* (tel 74260) in Bani Park is cheaper at Rs 60/80 with air-con, Rs 30/40 without. It also has a Rs 8 dormitory. Because of the wide variety of accommodation alternatives available in Jaipur the tourist bungalows are not the great bargains they are elsewhere in Rajasthan.

Places to Stay — Bottom End

The *Jaipur Inn* (tel 66057) in Bani Park is Jaipur's most popular location for budget travellers. It's clean, well run, helpful and friendly and there's good food available. A dorm bed costs Rs 5 or there are doubles from Rs 15 to 25 — all with common bathroom facilities. There's an extra charge of Rs 1 for a mattress and Rs 1 for sheets. You can also camp here and it's a good meeting place.

Other popular cheapies include the *Evergreen Guest House*, opposite the GPO, with doubles from Rs 15. Clean, friendly, a small garden and a 'delightfully pushy young Moslem proprietor'. There's also the *Everhappy Guest House* nearby. *Hotel Rajdhani* (tel 61276) near the railway station charges Rs 20 to 30 for singles. There are also *Railway Retiring Rooms* at the station with singles, doubles and dormitory accommodation.

Places to Eat

Niro's, on M I Rd, is one of Jaipur's best and most expensive restaurants — pleasant decor, soft music, chicken specialities and about Rs 25 for a meal. *LMB*, in Johari Bazaar, is well known for its vegetarian food — try the excellent sweet dish known as 'rasmalai'. There is also a *Kwality* on MI Rd.

For a real splurge have lunch at the *Rambagh Palace Hotel*. It's a real experience, there's a set menu (the menu itself is leather bound) for Rs 45 and that covers as much as you can eat.

The *Madras Hotel* near the station serves, as you might expect, masala dosa and other south Indian dishes. Basic, all-you-can eat thalis are available at *Krishna Bhojnalaya* at the top of the stairs between 63 and 64 Johri Bazaar.

The *Circuit House*, between the Evergreen Paying Guest House and the railway station, is a good place for breakfast. For Rs 6 you get cornflakes, two eggs, toast and coffee — good value. Along the road from there to the right there are several nice places to eat. Jaipur has a number of good Chinese restaurants.

Getting There

Air There are direct flights from Jaipur to Delhi (Rs 185), Agra (Rs 185), Jodhpur (Rs 225), Udaipur (Rs 235) and Bombay (Rs 665). The Indian Airlines office (tel 72940) is on Ajmer Rd. The airport is 15 km out of town.

Rail The train services from Jaipur are generally not as fast as buses because they are on metre gauge. The Pink City Express leaves old Delhi Railway Station at 6 am and reaches Jaipur at 11 am. The Jaipur-Delhi services leaves at 5 pm and arrives at 10 pm. Fares are Rs 75 in 1st class, Rs 16.50 in 2nd. An overnight train leaves Delhi in the late evening and arrives in Jaipur at around dawn. All Jaipur trains leave from the old Delhi station. The Chetak Express continues through Jaipur to Ajmer and

Udaipur.

Bus From Delhi or Agra de-luxe buses operated by the Rajasthan State Transport take five hours to Jaipur. The 306 km trip costs Rs 26 from Delhi. There are also ITDC de-luxe buses from Agra for Rs 35, they stop for one hour at Fatehpur Sikri en route. These buses start from the Tourist Office in Agra.

Tours ITDC operate a one day conducted tour to Jaipur from Delhi. The tours depart from the Hotel Janpath, Ashok or Akbar or the ITDC office in L Block, Connaught Place and cost Rs 150 per person.

Getting Around

Jaipur has taxis (unmetered), auto-rickshaws and a city bus service which also operates out to Amber. A cycle rickshaw from the station to the Jaipur Inn will cost Rs 1 or 2, from there to the city Rs 3 or 4. You can hire bicycles from near the railway station.

Things to Buy

Jaipur is well known for precious stones which seem to be cheaper here than anywhere else in India. Try to find the narrow street called Gopalji ka rasta, off Johari Bazaar and don't forget to bargain! Shops around the City Palace and the Hawa Mahal are likely to be more expensive although they do have many interesting items including miniatures and clothes. Marble statues, jewellery and textile prints are other Jaipur specialities. The Rajasthan Government Emporium in M I Rd is reasonably priced, they also have a branch in Amber.

AMBER

Situated on the Jaipur-Delhi road, 11 km out of Jaipur, Amber was the ancient capital of Jaipur state before the move was made to Jaipur. The fortress-palace was constructed from 1592 by Raja Man Singh the Rajput commander of Akbar's army. It was later extended and completed by the Jai Singhs before the shift to Jaipur on the plains below. The fort is a superb example of Rajput architecture, stunningly situated on a hillside overlooking a lake which reflects its terraces and ramparts.

From the road you can climb up to the fort in 10 minutes but it's a popular activity to ride up on elephant back — count on Rs 50. Within the palace you can get cold drinks, should the climb have been' a hot one, before exploring the palace.

An imposing stairway leads to the Diwan-i-Am or Hall of Public Audiences with a double row of columns and latticed galleries above. Steps to the right lead to the small Kali temple. There is also the white marble Sila Devi Temple.

The Maharaja's apartments are on the higher terrace — you enter through a gateway decorated with mosaics and sculptures. The Jai Mandir or Hall of Victory is noted for its inlaid panels and glittering mirror ceiling. Opposite the Jai Mandir is the Sukh Niwas or Hall of Pleasure with an ivory inlaid sandalwood door and a channel running right through the room which at one time carried cooling water. From the Jas Mandir you can enjoy the fine views from the palace ramparts over the lake below.

Amber palace is open from 9 am to 5 pm and entry costs Rs 4.

AROUND JAIPUR

There are a number of other attractions around Jaipur including several on the road between Jaipur and Amber. Jaipur tours usually stop at some of these sites on the way to or from Amber.

Gaitor

The cenotaphs of the royal family are at Gaitor, 6.5 km from Jaipur on the road to Amber. The white marble cenotaph of Maharajah Jai Singh II is the most impressive and is decorated with carved peacocks. Next to it is the cenotaph of his son. Opposite the cenotaphs is the Jal Mahal water palace in the middle of a lake and reached by a causeway.

Galta

If you leave the city by the Surya Gate it's a 2.5 km climb to the temple of the Sun God at Galta, 100 metres above the city to the east and with fine views over the surrounding plain. A deep temple-filled gorge stands behind the temple.

Tiger Fort

The Nahargarh Fort looks out over the city from a sheer ridge 6.5 km away. It's reached by a jeepable road from Amber through the hills. The fort was initially built in 1734 and extended in 1868.

Sisodia Rani Palace & Gardens

Eight km from the city on the Agra road, the palace was built for the second wife of Maharajah Jai Singh, the Sisodia Princess. The outer walls of the palace are illustrated with murals of hunting scenes and the Krishna legend, and the palace is surrounded by terraced gardens.

Vidyadhar's Garden

Nestled in a narrow valley, this beautiful garden was built in honour of Jai Singh's chief architect and town planner.

Sanganer

Situated 16 km south of Jaipur this small town is entered through the ruins of two 'Tripolias' or triple-gateways. The town has a ruined palace and a group of Jain temples with fine carvings. Entry to the temples is restricted. The town is noted for hand made paper and block printing.

BHARATPUR

This small town is best known for its bird sanctuary — a must if you are interested in bird watching. Bharatpur also has an 18th century fort with a small museum. It is 55 km from Agra and 180 km from Delhi via Mathura.

Bird Sanctuary

No less than 328 kinds of birds have been sighted at the sanctuary, 117 of which are migrants, which come from as far away as Siberia or China. It takes about a week to fly from Siberia to India! The sanctuary was the duck shooting preserve of the Maharajas of Bharatpur when this was a princely state. Shooting has not been permitted since 1964 and today there are 80 types of ducks seen in the sanctuary. October to February is the best time to visit the sanctuary. There is an entry fee per car or bus plus charges for photography or for taking boats onto the

waters. The sanctuary covers 52 square km of low lying marshland.

Lohagarh Fort

The 'Iron Fort' was built in the early 18th century and took its name from its supposedly impregnable defences. Maharajah Suraj Mal, the fort's constructor and the founder of Bharatpur, built two towers within the ramparts, the Jawahar Burj and the Fateh Burj, to commemorate his victories over the Moghuls and the British. The fort is open from 9 am to 5 pm daily and admission is free. The museum is closed Fridays, it has sculptures, inscriptions and works of art from the region.

Places to Stay

There is an ITDC operated *Ashok Forest Lodge* (tel 2322, 2864) in the sanctuary, near the entrance. Singles/doubles cost from Rs 60/80 or Rs 70/100 with aircon. There is also the cheaper *Sarus*

Tourist Bungalow (tel 2169) on the Agra road.

Getting There
It is only three hours by train from Delhi to Bharatpur. There are tongas and cycle rickshaws for getting around the town and the Rajasthan Tourist office has a mini bus (see the tourist officer in the Tourist Bungalow).

DEEG
This small town, 35 km from Bharatpur or Mathura, contains the summer palace of the Maharajah of Bharatpur. Built two centuries ago it seems like a 'modest' palace for a 'modest' Maharajah but in 1762 the Maharajah of Bharatpur had the temerity to attack the Red Fort! Some of the booty he carried off included an entire marble building which can still be seen. Deeg has palaces and gardens laid out with foundations in the Moghul style. The palace is open from 8 am to noon and 1 to 7 pm and admission is free.

SARISKA WILDLIFE SANCTUARY
Situated 107 km from Jaipur and 200 km from Delhi, the sanctuary is in a valley surrounded by barren mountains. The sanctuary, which covers 480 square km, has blue bulls (nigaio), sambhar, spotted deer, wild boar and, above all, tigers. The sanctuary can be visited year round except during July/August when the animals move to higher ground. The best time to see the wildlife is in the evening or at night; night outings are arranged at a cost of Rs 15 per person.

The *Tiger Den Tourist Bungalow* at the sanctuary is good but rather expensive at Rs 40/60 for singles/doubles. There is also a cheaper *Forest Rest House.* Sariska is 35 km from Alwar which is a convenient town from which to approach the sanctuary.

AJMER (population 280,000)
South of Jaipur, Ajmer is a green oasis on the shore of the Ana Sagar Lake and hemmed in by barren hills. Ajmer always had great strategic importance and in its time it was sacked by Mahmud of Ghazni on one of his periodic forays from Afghanistan. Later it became a favourite residence of the great Moghuls. Sir Thomas Roe met with Jehangir in Ajmer in 1616 — one of the first contacts between the Moghuls and the British. Later the city was taken by the Scindias then handed over to the British in 1818 — it was thus one of the few places in Rajasthan which was controlled directly by the British rather than being part of a 'princely state'. Ajmer is a major pilgrimage place for Moslems during the fast of Ramadan. Today it is an easy going and quite interesting town although for many travellers it is just a stepping stone to nearby Pushkar.

Information
The Tourist Office is in the Tourist Bungalow (tel 20430).

Orientation
The bus stand is on the Jaipur side of town and close to the Tourist Bungalow while the railway station, and most of the other hotels, are on the other side of town. The lake is more or less between the two but slightly to the north.

Ana Sagar Lake
This artificial lake was created in the 12th century by damming the River Luni. On its bank is a fine park, the Dault Bagh, with a series of marble pavilions which were erected by Shah Jahan in 1637. It's a popular site for an evening stroll. Because the lake tends to

Key:-
1. G.P.O.
2. Akbar's Fort (Museum)
3. Jain Temple
4. Darghwa
★ Hotels

Ajmer

Ana Sagar

Pushkar

Dault Bagh

Foy Sagar

Adhaidin ka Jhopra

Lohagal Road

Jaipur

Tourist Bungalow

Jaipur Road

Bus Stand

Kuchery Rd.

Railway Station

Circular Road

Srinagar Road

Jaipur

Beawar Road

Taragarh Fort

Bundi Kota Udaipur

dry up if the monsoon is poor the city's water supply is taken from the Foy Sagar Lake, five km further up the valley. Good views from the hill beside the Dault Bagh.

Dargah

In the old part of town, at the foot of a barren hill, this is one of India's most important places of pilgrimage for Mos-

lems. The Dargah is the tomb of a Sufi saint who came to Ajmer in 1192. Construction of the shrine was completed by Humayun and the gate added by the Nizam of Hyderabad. Akbar used to make the pilgrimage to the Dargah from Agra once a year.

As you enter the courtyard, removing your shoes at the gateway, there is a mosque constructed by Akbar on the right. The large iron cauldrons are for offerings which are customarily shared amongst families connected with the shrine's upkeep. On an inner court there is another mosque built by Shah Jahan. Constructed of white marble it has 11 arches and a Persian inscription running the full length of the building.

The saint's tomb is in the centre of the second court with a marble dome and inside the actual tomb is surrounded by a silver platform. The shrine doors have horseshoes nailed on them, offerings from successful horse dealers!

Adhai-din-ka-jhonpra

Continue on beyond the Dargah and on the very outskirts of town you'll come to the ruins of this mosque which, according to legend, was built in 2½ days — as its name indicates. It was originally a Jain college built in 1153 but in 1192 Muhammad Ghori took Ajmer and converted it into a mosque by adding a seven-arched wall in front of the pillared hall. Although the mosque is now much damaged it is a particularly fine piece of architecture — the pillars are all different and the arched 'screen', with its damaged minarets, is noteworthy. If you continue beyond the mosque for three km you'll reach, after a steep climb, the Taragarh or Star Fort with an excellent view over the city.

Akbar's Palace

Back in the city, and quite near the railway station, this imposing fort was built by Akbar in 1570 and today houses the Ajmer museum. The collection has some fine sculpture and a collection of Moghul and Rajput armour. The museum is closed on Fridays.

Nasiyan Temple

The 'Red Temple' is a Jain temple built in the last century with a double storey hall containing gilt wooden figures from the Jain mythology. The series of large models depict the Jain concept of the ancient world. Admission is Rs 0.10, it's certainly worth a visit.

Places to Stay

Although there are a number of hotels along the road opposite the railway station the *Khadim Tourist Bungalow* (tel 20490) is the best place to stay. It's only a few minutes walk from the bus stand, from the railway station it's just Rs 1 or 2 by trishaw. Singles/doubles cost Rs 20/25 (ordinary), Rs 30/40 (deluxe) and Rs 50/60 (air-con). There is also a dorm for Rs 5.50. A nice setting and good rooms.

The Welcom group is planning a new hotel, the *Ajaymeru*, to be built near the lake. The string of hotels by the railway station vary from dismal to OK. *Nagpal Tourist Hotel* (tel 21603) costs Rs 18/28 for singles/doubles or the *Hotel Ratan* (tel 21238) is Rs 13/22 — both with attached bathrooms. *Hotel Anand* (tel 20098) offers 'homely comforts and modern living' in its Rs 15/25 rooms; the *Hotel Malwa* is similar. There are a number of cheaper, more basic hotels, also in the main bazaar.

Places to Eat

The *Tourist Bungalow* has the usual dining room, there's a vegetarian restaurant downstairs in the Hotel Ratan. The more expensive *Honeydew* and *Elite Restaurants* flank the KEM (King Edward Memorial) Rest House near the railway station.

Getting There & Around

There are buses every half hour from Jaipur to Ajmer, the 138 km trip takes 2½ to three hours. Some buses go straight through non-stop, the trip costs Rs 10. From Ajmer you can continue on to Jodhpur (198 km, 15 buses daily), Udaipur (302 km via Chittorgarh, eight buses daily), Chittorgarh (190 km, eight buses), Kota (200 km via Bundi, seven buses). There are also buses to Abu Road, Agra, Delhi and Ujjain.

PUSHKAR

Like Goa or Dharamsala, Pushkar is one of those travellers' centres where people go for a little rest and recuperation from the hardships of life on the Indian road. It's a delightful little village, only 11 km from Ajmer but separated from it by Nag Pahar, the 'Snake Mountain', and right on the edge of the desert. The town clings to the side of the beautiful Pushkar Lake with many bathing ghats, for Pushkar is also an important pilgrimage centre for Hindus. It's a really nice, laid back place but in October-November each year it comes alive with the huge Pushkar Cattle Fair.

Cattle Fair

At the full moon of Kartik Poornima each year up to 200,000 people flock to Pushkar, bringing with them 50,000 cattle for several days of pilgrimage, horse dealing, camel racing and colour festivities. The Rajasthan Tourist Office has promoted it as an international attraction by adding Rajasthan dance programmes and other cultural events and putting up a huge tent city for foreign visitors. It's one of India's biggest and most colourful festivals. The fair will take place:

1981	8-11 November
1982	27-30 November
1983	16-20 November
1984	4-8 November

Temples

Pushkar is packed with temples although many were destroyed by Aurangzeb. The most famous is that of Brahma, which is said to be the only temple to Brahma in India. It's marked by a red

Ajmer is compact enough to get around on foot and by trishaw. Buses to Pushkar go from outside the railway station.

spire and over the entrance gateway is the 'hans' or goose symbol of Brahma who is said to have personally chosen Pushkar as its site. The Rangji temple is also important.

Places to Stay & Eat

The *Sarovar Tourist Bungalow* (tel 40) is on the opposite side of the lake from the Brahma Temple. It's an exotic looking old palace once owned by the Maharajah of Jaipur. Built around a courtyard there are five very pleasant de-luxe rooms overlooking the lake for Rs 20/25 (single/double), other rooms are Rs 18/20, dorm beds are Rs 5.50 or you can camp for Rs 2. A catch — the Tourist Bungalow is full all the time, you just have to hang around in Pushkar until a room comes vacant.

There are plenty of small hotels and guest houses around town like the *Krishna Hotel* for Rs 10 a double — friendly little place with a restaurant downstairs. If you wander around looking hopeful a kid will grab you! Also plenty of small food stalls. The *Sun Set Cafe* by the Tourist Bungalow, right by the water, is popular. This is also a good place to go swimming and the sunset views over the lake are spectacular.

During the Cattle Fair, which attracts several thousand foreign visitors, the tourist office tent city costs Rs 100 per day including food or Rs 25 in a dormitory tent.

Getting There

Buses run frequently from Ajmer, outside the railway station, for Rs 1.50. It's quite a spectacular climb up and over the hills but the bus is likely to be too crowded to offer much of a view. The private minibuses are like little old hot rods.

Things to Buy

Like any good freak centre there are lots of travellers' clothes tailors in town. During the Cattle Fair there are many artisans selling locally made jewellery and other items.

KISHANGARH

Noted for its school of painting which is still produced today, this small town is 27 km from Ajmer.

KOTA (population 240,000)

Kota was the capital of an independent state of the same name which was intergrated into Rajasthan after independence. Today Kota is the industrial centre of Rajasthan (mainly chemicals) due principally to the hydroelectric power plants on the Chambal River. There is also an atomic power plant near Kota.

Information

The Tourist Officer is at the Chambal Tourist Bungalow.

Orientation

Kota is strung out along the east bank of the Chambal River. The railway station is well to the north, the tourist bungalow and bus stand in the middle and the Chambal Garden, the Fort and the Kota Barrage to the south.

Fort

The Kota Fort has two museums, the government museum (open 10 am to 5 pm, daily except Friday) is only of mild interest but the Rao Madho Singh Museum (open 11 am to 5 pm, daily except Friday) is superb. It is entered by a gateway topped by rampant elephants like the fort at Bundi. Inside, having paid your Rs 1 entry fee, you'll find exhibits of weapons, clothing and more fine murals like those at Bundi. Indeed until 1572 Kota was part of the state of Bundi.

Chambal Gardens

The gardens, south of the fort at Amar Niwas, are a popular picnic spot and have a pond well stocked with garwhal crocodiles. The pond also has some flamingoes who appear remarkably unbothered by their companions. At Bhitariya Kund, upstream from the Chambal Gardens, there is a popular swimming spot in the surprisingly clear waters of the Chambal River. The Kota Barrage acts as a control over the river's waters and feeds an irrigation canal system. It's also used to cross the river when the 'Irish' bridge from Bundi is flooded. A little upstream from Kota the Chambal runs through a spectacular gorge.

Jag Mandir

Near the tourist bungalow this large tank has a building on a small island in the centre. Beside the tourist bungalow there is a curious collection of somewhat neglected, but imposingly large, royal tombs.

Close to Kota

There are a number of interesting sites around Kota. At Baroli, 40 km from Kota, on the way to Pratap Sagar, there is one of the oldest temple complexes in Rajasthan. Many sculptures from these 9th century temples are displayed in the Kota government museum. The Pratap Sagar Dam is the Chambal's second dam. At Jhaira Patan, 60 km from Kota on the Jhalawar road, are the ruins of an old Surya or sun temple. Ramgarh, 64 km from Kota on a jeepable road, has some notable temples. Only eight km out of Kota there's a bridge built by Colonel Tod, a notable British 'Political Agent' of the Raj days and the author of the *Annals and Antiquities of Rajasthan.*

Places to Stay

The *Brij Raj Bhawan Palace Hotel* (tel 3071) is mainly used by Kota's not too frequent tourist groups. The palace is not too special, lots of hunting pictures decorated the walls including one of the local Maharajah hunting moose in Canada. The *Chambal Tourist Bungalow* (tel 6527) is conveniently close to the bus stand. There are singles/doubles at Rs 20/25, 30/40 and 50/60 with air-con. Plus dorm beds for Rs 5.50. Another pleasant tourist bungalow. There are a number of other hotels in Kota including the *Payal Hotel* (tel 5401) at Nayapura and the *Navrang Hotel* (tel 3294) at Civil Lines. There are also *Railway Retiring Rooms* at the station.

Getting There & Getting Around

Kota is connected by buses to Bundi, Ajmer (Rs 15), Chittorgarh (Rs 16, six hours), Udaipur (Rs 22) and other centres in Rajasthan. The Chittorgarh and Udaipur buses only depart at very inconvenient times. Kota is a junction town on the Bombay-Delhi broad gauge line. Around town there are trishaws, auto-rickshaws, buses and tempos. The tempos run a regular service between the railway station, bus stand and main part of town.

BUNDI (population 35,000)

Bundi is a picturesque little town, well off the beaten tourist track, 142 km to the south-east of Ajmer and only 39 km west of Kota. The town is beautifully sited in a narrow valley, brooded over by the gloomy Taragarh Fort. The road into Bundi comes in along the other side of the valley so you have a good view over the town and across to the fort as you arrive. A word of warning — Bundi is almost too unspoilt. So few tourist pass through that most things are kept under lock and key. If you want to see the famous palace murals you must either make enquiries beforehand to ensure the keys are there or else be prepared to 'persuade' the chowkidar to let you into whatever is open.

Orientation

The bus station is at the Kota, eastern end of town. Since accommodation in Bundi is limited you can best see Bundi by stopping, looking around and then continuing on rather than planning to stay overnight. Simply walk into the town and you'll see the Taragarh Fort and palace up the hill on your right. The town is surrounded by a walled fortification with four gateways.

Taragarh Fort
The Star Fort was built in 1372 and is reached by a steep road up the hillside to its enormous gateway topped by rampant elephants. Inside the palace is the Chitrashala or picture gallery with the walls covered in murals of hunting, historical and religious scenes painted in the Bundi style. There's a fine view over Bundi from the fort ramparts. Directly below are the Ratan Daulat or horse stables.

Naval Sagar
Also visible from the fort is the square artificial lake of Naval Sagar. In the centre is a temple to Varuna, the Aryan God of Water.

Other
Bundi's other attractions are all out of town and difficult to reach without transport. The modern palace is at Phool Sagar with its beautiful articial tank and gardens several km out of town on the Ajmer side. Shikar Burj is a small hunting lodge and picnic spot near Bundi. Cenotaphs of Bundi's rulers are near here at Khshar Bagh. Another small palace, the Sukh Niwas, is located at the Jait Sagar tank.

Places to Stay
Bundi's accommodation is of the 'government-officials-only-tourists-not-welcome' variety. There's a *Circuit House* (Rs 15) and a much less luxurious *Dak Bungalow* (Rs 3) near the bus stand.

Getting There & Around
It takes about five hours by bus from Ajmer to Bundi and costs Rs 12. From Bundi it's only an hour or so to Kota and costs Rs 4. Buses also to Chittorgarh and Udaipur from Bundi. Around town you've got a choice of walking or taking a tonga.

CHITTORGARH (population 30,000)
The hilltop fortress of Chittorgarh sums up the whole romantic, doomed ideal of Rajput chivalry. Three times in its long history Chittor was sacked by a stronger enemy and on each occasion the end came in textbook Rajput fashion. The men donned the saffron bridal robes of martyrdom and rode out from the fort to certain death. Meanwhile the women built a huge funeral pyre and marched in to the flames in the form of ritual suicide known as *jauhar.*

Chittor's first defeat took place in 1303 when Ala-ud-din Khilji, the Pathan King of Delhi, besieged the fort in order to capture the beautiful Padmini who was married to Bhim Singh, uncle of the Rana. When defeat was inevitable the Rajput noblewomen, including Padmini, committed *jauhar* and Bhim Singh led the orange-clad noblemen out to their deaths.

In 1535 it was Bahadur Shah, the Sultan of Gujurat, who besieged the fort and once again it was *jauhur* for the women and the orange robes for the men. It is said that 13,000 Rajput women and 32,000 Rajput warriors died.

It was only 33 years later, in 1568, that the final 'Sack of Chittor' took place and on this occasion it was the Moghul Emperor Akbar who took the town. Once again the fort was defended heroically but once again the odds were overwhelming and the women performed *jauhar*, the fort gates were flung open and 8000 orange-robed warriors rode out to their deaths. Maharana Udai Singh fled to Udaipur and re-established his capital there. In 1616 Jehangir returned Chittor to the Rajputs but they did not move the capital back from Udaipur.

Today the fort of Chittor is a virtually deserted ruin but impressive reminders of its heyday still stand and perhaps

Chittorgarh

Key:-
1. Tourist Office & Jantar Rest House
2. Tourist Bungalow
3. Rawat Bagh Singh Memorial
4. Chhattris of Jaimal & Kalla
5. Tower of Fame & Mahavir Temple
6. Fateh Prakash Palace
7. Archaeological Museum & Office
8. Palace of Rana Kumbha
9. Kumbha-Shyam & Meera Temples
10. Tower of Victory
11. Mahasatee Sthal & Samiddheshwar Temples
12. Gomukh Reservoir
13. Temple of Neelkanth Mahadev
14. Padmini Palace

you can catch a whiff of that romantic heroism in the air.

Information

The Tourist Office (tel 9) is in the *Janta Tourist Rest House* near the railway station.

Orientation

The fort stands on a 700 acre site on top of a 180 metre high hill which rises abruptly from the surrounding plain. Until 1568 the town of Chittor was also on the hilltop, within the fort walls, but today the modern town, known as Lower Town, sprawls to the west of the hill. The bazaar and older part of the town is close to the base of the hill. A river separates it from the bus stand, railway line and the modern part of the town.

The Fort

Bhim, one of the Pandava heroes of the Mahabharata, is credited with the fort's original construction and all of Chittor's attractions are within the fort. A zigzag ascent over a km long leads through seven gateways to the main gate on the western side, the Ram Pol. On the ascent you pass two chattris, memorials marking spots where Jaimal and Kalla, heroes of the 1568 siege, fell during the struggle against Akbar. Another chattri, further up the hill, marks the spot where Patta fell. The main gate on the eastern side of the fort is the Suraj Pol. Within the fort there is a circular road around the ruins and a deer park at the southern end.

Palace of Rana Kumbha

Entering the fort and turning right you come almost immediately to the ruins of this palace. The palace contains elephant and horse stables and a Shiva temple. One of the jauhars is said to have been performed in one of the palace's vaulted cellars. Across from the palace is the archaeological office and

museum and the treasury building or Nau Lakha Bhandar.

Fateh Prakash Palace

Just beyond the Rana Kumbha Palace, this much more modern palace (Maharana Fateh Singh died in 1930), houses an interesting museum with statues found in various buildings in the fort.

Tower of Victory

Continuing anti-clockwise around the fort you come to the Tower of Victory or Jaya Stambh. Erected by Rana Kumba to commemorate his victory over Mahmud Khilji of Malwa in 1440, the tower was constructed between 1458 and 1468. It rises 37 metres in nine storeys and, for 50p, you can climb the broad stairs to the top. Hindu sculptures adorn the outside of the tower but the dome was damaged by lightning and repaired during the last century. Close to the tower is the Mahasati, an area where the ranas were cremated during Chittorgarh's period as the Mewar capital. There are many sati stones here. The Sammidheshwar Temple stands in the same area.

Gaumukh Reservoir

Walk down beyond the temple and at the very edge of the cliff is this deep tank. A spring feeds the tank from a carved cow's mouth in the cliff side — from which the reservoir get its name. The opening here leads to the cave in which Padmini and her compatriots are supposed to have committed jauhar.

Padmini's Palace

Continuing south you come to Padmini's Palace, beside a large pool with a pavilion in its centre. Legends relate that Padmini stood in this pavilion and that Ala-ud-din was permitted to see her reflection in a mirror in the palace. This glimpse was the spark that convinced him to destroy Chittor in order to possess her. The bronze gates in this pavilion were carried off by Akbar and can now be seen in the fort at Agra. Continuing round the circular road you pass the deer park, the Bhimlat Tank, the Suraj Pol Gate, the Neelkanth Mahadev Jain temple and reach the Tower of Fame.

Tower of Fame

Chittor's other famous tower, the Kirti Stambha or Tower of Fame, is older (probably built around the 12th century) and smaller (it stands 22 metres high) than the Tower of Victory. Built by a Jain merchant it is dedicated to Adinath, the first Jain Tirthankaras, and is decorated with nude figures of the various Tirthankaras — thus indicating that it is a Digambara or 'sky-clad' monument. A narrow stairway leads through the seven storeys to the top.

Other Buildings

Close to the Fateh Prakash Museum is the Meera Temple, built in the ornate Indo-Aryan style during the reign of Rana Kumbha and associated with the mystic-poetess Meerabai. The larger temple in this same compound is the Kumbha Shyam Temple or Temple of Vriji. The Jain, but Hindu influenced Singa Chowri Temple is also nearby. Across from Padmini's Palace is the Kalika Mata Temple, an 8th century Surya or Sun God temple which was later converted to a temple to the Goddess Kali. At the northern tip of the fort is another gate, the Lokhota Bari, while at the southern end there is a small opening from which criminals and traitors were hurled into the abyss.

Tours

There is a daily Rs 8 tour which takes in all the main sites on the fort. The tour operates from the Tourist Office and Tourist Bungalow from 8 am to 1 pm daily and also from 3 pm to 6 pm during the cooler winter months.

Places to Stay

Accommodation possibilities in Chittor are limited. The *Panna Tourist Bungalow* (tel 273) is close to the railway station and the Udaipur road. It's a fairly modern building with singles/doubles at Rs 20/25 or Rs 45/55 with air-con and a dormitory with beds at Rs 5.50. Closer to the railway station is the *Janta Tourist Rest House* (Avas Grika) (tel 9) where the Tourist Office is also located. Dormitory beds cost Rs 5.50 or there are spartan doubles at Rs 11 or Rs 16.50 with bath. Also close to the railway station is the very basic, and not so special, *Hotel Savaria* where doubles cost Rs 15. There are other similar hotels and there are also *Railway Retiring Rooms* at Rs 10/18.50 for singles/doubles. The Tourist Bungalow has a dining hall.

Getting There & Getting Around

Chittor is on the bus and rail routes. It's 182 km from Ajmer or 115 km from Udaipur by road. Bus fare to Udaipur is Rs 9, it takes three hours. Bundi is 156 km away. It's six km from the railway station to the fort and the fort itself sprawls quite a bit — so if you're not taking a tour you'll need transport. There are tongas or unmetered auto-rickshaws for hire or you can rent a bicycle.

AROUND CHITTORGARH
Menal

On the Bundi-Chittorgarh road, 48 km from Bundi, Menal is a complex of Shiva temples built during the Gupta period. Bijolia, 16 km from Menal, was once a complex of a hundred temples but today only three are left standing. One has a huge figure of Ganesh. A diversion between Menal and Bijolia takes you to Mandalgarh the third fort of Mewar built by Rana Khumbha — the others are the great fort of Chittorgarh and the fort at Kumbalgarh.

Nagri

One of the oldest towns in Rajasthan, Nagri is 14 km north of Chittor and Hindu and Buddhist remains from the Mauryan to the Gupta periods have been found here.

UDAIPUR (population 225,000)

The lake city of Udaipur is a cool oasis in the dry heart of Rajasthan. It's probably the most romantic city in a state where every city has some romantic or exotic tale to tell. Udaipur has several palaces two of which should not be missed. The Lake Palace, now converted into a luxury hotel, is simply delightful — if you can afford to stay there don't miss the opportunity. Even if you can't it's worth the expense of the boat trip out there to have a look around. The huge City Palace on the lake side has been converted into a musuem and is well worth a visit. Udaipur also has gardens, fountains, museums and temples and there are a number of interesting excursions around Udaipur.

The Maharana of Udaipur is the highest ranking of the Rajput rulers and head of the 'Solar' Rajput clan. Udaipur is also known as the 'City of Sunrise' and the Maharana's standard bears an image of the sun. Udaipur was founded in 1567 by Maharana Udai Singh, following the third sack of Chittor.

Information & Orientation

The old city, bounded by the remains of a city wall, sprawls away on the east side of Lake Pichola. The railway station and bus station are both just outside the city wall to the south-east. The Tourist Office (tel 3509) and the Tourist Bungalow are also outside the city walls, to the north-east and only a km or so from the bus stand. There are also tourist information counters at the railway station and airport. The GPO is directly north of the old city, behind the movie theatre at Chetak Circle.

Pichola Lake

The beautiful Pichola Lake was enlarged by Maharana Udai Singh after he founded the city. He built a masonry dam known as the Badi Pol and the lake now stretches for four km in length by three km wide. The City Palace extends for a considerable distance along the east bank of the lake while south of the palace a pleasant garden runs down to the lake side. North of the palace it is very interesting to wander along the lake side where there are some beautiful scenes of bathing and dobhi ghats. Out in the lake there are two islands — Jagniwas and Jag Mandir.

Islands

Jagniwas is the Lake Palace island, about 1.5 hectares in size. The palace was built by Maharana Jagat Singh II in 1754 and covers the whole island. Today it has been converted into a luxury hotel with courtyards, fountains, gardens and a swimming pool. It's a quite delightful place and even if you can't dream of staying there it's worth the trip out to have a look around. A launch crosses to the island from Bhansi Ghat, just south of the Palace Museum. The trip out and back, including coffee or tea and biscuits in the hotel, costs Rs 10.

The other island palace, Jag Mandir, may also eventually become a hotel. It was commenced by Maharana Karan Singh but takes its name from Maharana Jagat Singh (1628-1652) who made a number of additions to it. It is said that the Moghul Emperor Shah Jahan derived some of his ideas for the Taj Mahal from this palace, after he stayed here in 1623-24, while leading a revolt

Udaipur

1	Railway Station	9	Rose Garden
2	Long Distance Bus Terminal	10	Samor Garden
3	Tourist Office & Tourist Bungalow	11	Chetak Circle
4	GPO	12	Jagdish Temple
5	Keerti Hotel	13	Lok Kala Mandal Museum (Folk
6	Lake View Hotel		Museum)
7	State Hotel	14	Lake boat moorings
8	Indian Airlines	15	Hotel Hill Top
		16	Saheliyon ki Bari

against his father, Jehangir. Looking across the lake from the southern end, with the city and its great palace rising up behind the island palaces, is a scene of rare beauty.

City Palace & Museum

The huge City Palace towers over the lake, it's the largest palace complex in Rajasthan. The palace is actually a conglomeration of buildings added by various Maharanas but it manages to retain a surprising uniformity of design. It was originally commenced by Maharana Udai Singh, the city's founder. The palace is surmounted by balconies, towers and cupolas and there are fine views over the lake and the city from the upper terraces. The palace is entered from the northern end through the Bari Pol of 1600 and the triple Tripolia Gate of 1725 with its eight carved marble arches. It was once a custom for Maharanas to be weighed under the gate and their weight in gold or silver to be distributed to the populace.

The main part of the palace is now preserved as a museum with a large and very varied collection. The museum includes the Mor Chowk with its beautiful mosaics of peacocks, the favourite Rajasthani bird. The Manak or Ruby Mahal has glass and porcelain figures. Krishna Vilas has a remarkable collection of miniatures. In the Bari Mahal there is a fine central garden. More paintings can be seen in the Zanana Mahal. The Moti Mahal has beautiful mirror work, the Chini Mahal is covered in ornamented tiles. Other exhibits even include the

princely Rolls-Royces.

The City Palace Museum is entered through the Ganesh Deori to the Rai Angam or Royal Courtyard. The museum is open from 9.30 am to 4.30 pm and entry is Rs 2.50.

Jagdish Temple

Only 150 metres north of the entrance to the City Palace this fine Indo-Aryan temple was built by Maharana Jagat Singh in 1651 and enshrines a black stone image of Vishnu as Jagannath, Lord of the Universe. A brass image of the Garuda is in a shrine in front of the temple and the steps up to the temple are flanked by elephants.

Lake Fateh Sagar

North of Lake Pichola this lake was originally built in 1678 by Maharana Jai Singh but heavy rains destroyed the dam and it was reconstructed by Maharana Fateh Singh. There is a pleasant lake side drive that winds along the east bank of the lake and a number of hills and parks overlook it. Nehru Park is a popular garden island with a restaurant in the middle of the lake. You can 'get to it for Rs 1 by a boat service from the bottom of Moti Magri Hill.

Pratap Samak

Atop the Moti Magri or 'Pearl Hill' overlooking Fateh Sagar Lake is a statue of Rajput hero Maharana Pratap who frequently defied the Moghuls astride his charger Chetak. The path to the top goes through elegant gardens including a Japanese rock garden. The park is open from 9 am to 6 pm and admission is Rs 1.

Bhartiya Lok Kala Museum

This small museum and foundation for the preservation of folk arts has an interesting collection including dresses, dolls, masks, musical instruments, paintings and, the high point of the exhibits, puppets. There are regular puppet shows in the museum. Opening hours are 9 am to 6 pm and admission is Rs 1.

Saheliyon ki Bari

In the north of the city the 'Garden of the Maids of Honour' is a small ornamental garden with fountains, kiosks, marble elephants and a delightful lotus pool. It's open 9 am to 6 pm and entry is Rs 0.50, Rs 2 to have the fountains turned on.

Ahar Museum

East of Udaipur there are the remains of an ancient city with a small museum and the cenotaphs of the Maharanas of Mewar.

Other

Patel or Sukhadia Circle is north of the city — in the centre is a huge fountain, illuminated at night. Sajjan Niwas Gardens have pleasant lawns, a zoo and a children's train ride. Beside it is the Rose Garden or Gulab Bagh.

Tours

There's a daily tour, starting from the Tourist Bungalow, from 8.30 am to 1.30 pm each day. It costs Rs 12 and takes in all the main city sights. A Rs 25 afternoon tour from 2 to 7 pm goes out to Eklingi, Haldighati and Nathdwara.

Places to Stay — Top End

Udaipur's top hotel is also one of the most delightful hotels in India. It's the luxurious Lake Palace Hotel (tel 3241-45) in the middle of Pichola Lake.

Singles/doubles are Rs 300/400 and it's the very image of what a Maharaja's palace should be like with the additional touch that it occupies its own little island. Even if you can't stay here it's worth taking the boat trip out to see how the other half lives.

The Oberoi Shikarbadi (tel 3200) is out of town on the Ahmedabad Rd and has singles/doubles at Rs 225/280. Between Pichola and Fateh Sagar Lakes there are two upper notch hotels side by side. The ITDC operated Laxmi Vilas Palace Hotel (tel 4411) has rooms at Rs 100/150 with air-con, Rs 60/90 without. Right beside it is the Rajasthan State Hotel (Anand Bhavan, tel 3257) with air-con rooms at Rs 90/125.

A number of hotels span the top to bottom bracket. Lake End Hotel (tel 3841) is by Fateh Sagar Lake and has rooms at Rs 75/100 with air-con, Rs 60/80 without. Hotel Hill Top (tel 3708) also overlooks Fateh Sagar from 5 Amba Mata Marg. Rooms cost Rs 40/60 with bath and at that price it's excellent value with good food and service and fine views over the lake.

Places to Stay — Bottom End

The Kajri Tourist Bungalow (tel 3509) is conveniently situated but it's not one of the better tourist bungalow in Rajasthan. The Tourist Office is also situated here, at the traffic circle on Ashoka Rd, and there is also a restaurant. Singles/doubles start from Rs 20/30 without bath, Rs 30/40 with bath, Rs 45/55 air-cooled or Rs 60/70 air-con. There is also a Rs 8 dormitory.

The Keerti Hotel (tel 3639) on Sarsvati Marg is very popular with travellers. There are rooms at all sorts of prices from Rs 10/15 for the most basic singles and doubles up to de-luxe rooms at Rs 30 or Rs 55 with air-con. There is also a Rs 4 dormitory. Near the bus stand there are a whole string of hotels, all with low prices and most of them offering reasonable accommodation. Apsara Hotel (tel

3400), *Mamta Hotel* (tel 3927), *Sonika Hotel* (tel 5353) all on City Station Rd, and *Alka Hotel* (tel 3611) on Shastri Circle all have rooms from Rs 10/15 for singles/doubles.

Round on Lake Palace Rd by the Sajjan Niwas Gardens and near the zoo, the *Rang Niwas Hotel* (tel 3891) is a relaxed, pleasant place built around a green courtyard. Singles cost from Rs 15 to 35, doubles from Rs 30 to 45. Udaipur also has *Railway Retiring Rooms* at Rs 7/12 or Rs 3.50 in the dormitory.

Finally there's one delightful place situated just outside Udaipur. The *Pratap Country Inn* is operated by the same people as the Keerti so go there first and they'll arrange transport out there for you. It's at Titadha village, about six km out of the city. City buses run there every hour for Rs 0.60. They have tents and rooms at prices from as low as Rs 10 to as high as Rs 70 and a Rs 5 dormitory. There's a swimming pool, free horse riding, camels, slightly expensive food, beautiful surroundings and a very laid back atmosphere.

Places to Eat

Udaipur is not over-endowed with good places to eat although you can get good Chinese food here. The *Tourist Bungalow* has a restaurant with the usual menu and variable results — sometimes the food is surprisingly good, sometimes it is not. There are a number of places by Chetak Circle including a so-so *Kwality*, the *Chetak Restaurant* and *Berry's Restaurant*. A number of vegetarian places around Suraj Pol include the *Jagdish Hindu Lodge* and the *Krishna Gujrati Lodge*.

Getting There

Air Udaipur is connected by Indian Airlines with Delhi via Jaipur, Jodhpur, Aurangabad and Bombay. Air fares are Delhi Rs 390, Jaipur Rs 235, Jodhpur Rs 185, Aurangabad Rs 430, Bombay Rs 585. Dabok Airport is 24 km out of the city, the Indian Airlines office (tel 3952) is at Delhi Gate.

Rail The daily Chetak Express between Delhi and Udaipur takes nearly 21 hours. Fares are Rs 148 in 1st class, Rs 36 in 2nd. The train goes via Jaipur and Ajmer. There is also a daily express between Udaipur and Ahmedabad taking nine to 10 hours.

Bus There are frequent buses from Udaipur to other regional centre such as Ahmedabad (about six times daily), Mt Abu (twice), Ajmer (once), Jodhpur (once), Bundi-Kota (three times),.Jaipur (seven buses daily), Chittorgarh (approximately hourly). The three hour trip to Chittor costs Rs 8.50.

Getting Around

There's a reasonably OK city bus service, taxis are unmetered, auto-rickshaws are metered but won't use them. Udaipur is small enough and slow enough to make getting around on a bicycle quite enjoyable. You can hire bicycles all over town (quite a few places just by the Tourist Bungalow) at a cost of around Rs 0.30 per hour, Rs 2.50 per day.

AROUND UDAIPUR

Eklingi (22 km)

This interesting little village with a number of ancient temples is only a short bus ride north of Udaipur. In the village itself there is a Shiva temple which was originally built in 734 AD although its present form dates from the rule of Maharana Raimal who ruled from 1473 to 1509. The walled complex includes an elaborately pillared hall under a large pyramidal roof. There is a four-faced Shiva image of black marble. The temple is only open during

Around Udaipur

rather odd hours — 4.45-7.30 am, 10.30 am-1.30 pm, 5.30-7.45 pm.

At Nagada, about a km off the road and a km before Eklingi, there are three old temples. The Jain temple of Adbudji is fairly well ruined but its architecture is interesting and this is a very old temple. Nearby is the Sas Bahu or 'Mother and Daughter-in-Law' group. It's quite a little complex with some very fine and intricate architecture and carvings, including some erotic figures.

You can get out to these temples most conveniently by hiring a bicycle in Eklingi itself. There are buses from Udaipur to Eklingi every half hour to an hour and the cost is Rs 2. There is a small Rs 5 guest house in the village.

Haldighati (40 km)

This is where Maharana Pratap valiantly defied the superior Moghul forces of Akbar in 1576. The site is only a battle-field and the only thing to see is the chhatri to his horse, Chetak, a few km away.

Nathdwara (48 km)

The important 18th century Vishnu temple of Sri Nathji stands here. It's a popular pilgrimage site but non-Hindus are not allowed inside. The black stone Vishnu image was brought here from Mathura in 1669 to protect it from Aurangzeb's destructive impulses. According to a legend when an attempt was later made to move the image its wagon sunk into the ground up to the axles — indicating that the image would prefer to stay where it was!

Kankroli & Rajsamand Lake (65 km)

At Kankroli, Dwarkadhish (an incarnation of Vishnu) is similar to Nathdwara and, like that temple, is open for extremely erratic hours. Near here there is a lake created by the dam constructed by Maharana Raj Singh in 1660. There are many ornamental arches and chhatris along the huge bund. Raj Singh tangled with Aurangzeb on a number of occasions.

Kumbhalgarh Fort (84 km)

This is the most important fort in the Mewar region after Chittorgarh and was built by Maharana Kumbha in the 15th century. The seven great gates of the Badal Mahal lead to the Cloud Palace. The fort, with its many temples and palaces, was renovated in the last century.

Jagat (58 km)

The 10th century Ambika Mata Temple here is not as good as some tourist literature would indicate. It is not in very special condition.

Jaisamand Lake (48 km)

This is the second largest artificial lake in Asia and was built by Maharana Jai Singh in the 17th century. There are beautiful marble chhatris around the embankment, each with an elephant in front. The summer palaces of Udaipur queens are also located here and nearby is a wildlife sanctuary.

Rikhabdeo (65 km)

The Jain temple to Adinath is on the Ahmedabad road. Major offering are made every day in this architecturally elegant temple, parts of which date back to the 14th century.

Ranakpur (98 km)

One of the most important, and biggest, Jain temples in India the extremely beautiful Ranakpur complex is situated in the remote and peaceful Aravalli Valley. The main temple in the complex is the Chaumukha or 'Four-Faced' temple, dedicated to Adinath. This huge, beautifully crafted and well kept marble temple was built in 1439. It has 29 halls, supported by 1444 pillars, no two of which are alike. Within the complex there are two other Jain temples to Neminath and Parasnath and, a little distance away, a Sun Temple. A km away from the main complex is the Amba Mata Temple.

The temple is open to non-Jains from noon to 5 pm. There is a dharamsala within the complex where you can stay for a donation. If you arrive at meal time you can get a good thali in the dining hall just inside the main entrance to the complex on your left, again for a donation. Ranakpur is 39 km from Palna (or Falna) Junction on the Ajmer-Mt Abu rail and road routes. From Udaipur there are half a dozen buses a day to Ranakpur and you can continue on from here to Jodhpur or Mt Abu on the same day — but the trip to Ranakpur can be a real time consuming bore. The Rs 6 trip can take five to six hours, an average of well under 20 kph!

MT ABU (population 12,000)

Rajasthan's only hill station spreads out along a 1200 metre high plateau in the south of the state. It's a pleasant hot season retreat from the plains but you won't find many western travellers here — visitors are predominantly Indians, inlcuding many honeymooners. Mt Abu is a popular hill station for Gujurat as well as Rajasthan. There is more than simply lower temperatures to attract visitors up here — Mt Abu has a number of important temples, particularly the superb Dilwara group of Jain Temples.

Information & Orientation

Mt Abu stretches along a plateau about 22 km long by six km wide. It is 27 km from Abu Road, the railway station for Mt Abu. The main part of the town extends along the road in from Abu Road, down to the Nakki Lake. Coming in by bus you pass first the Tourist Bungalow, up a hill to your right, then a string of hotels before you arrive at the bus stand, opposite which is the Tourist Office (tel 51). Continuing from here you pass more hotels and restaurants, the small market to your right, and eventually arrive at the lake front. The GPO is on Raj Bhavan Rd, opposite the Art Gallery and Museum.

Nakki Lake

Virtually in the centre of Mt Abu the small lake takes its name from the legend that it was scooped out by a god, using only his nails or 'nakk'. It's a short and easy stroll around the lake — look for the strange rock formations around it. Best known is Toad Rock which looks just like a toad about to hop

Key:-
1. Tourist Office
2. Market
3. Art Gallery & State Museum
4. Hotel Bikaner Palace
5. Jaipur House Hotel
6. Youth Hostel
7. Hotel Saraswati
8. Hotel Hill Tone
9. Tourist Guest House
10. Tourist Bungalow

11. M.K. Cold Drinks
12. Nina Sheeba Restaurant
13. Abu Restaurant
14. Bus Station
15. Rajasthan Emporium

Guru Shikhar

Dilwara Jain Temple

Adhar Devi Temple

Ganesh Temple

The Crags

Honeymoon Point (Andra Point)

Subhash Rd

Nakki Lake

Raghunath Temple

Rajendra Rd

Pilgrim Rd

Sunset Point Rd

Sunset Point

Mt Abu

Hanuman Temple & Gaumukh

Toll Gate

Abu Road

into it. Others, like Nun Rock, Nandi Rock or Camel Rock, require rather more imagination to picture them. You can hire boats and row (or be rowed) out on the lake. The 14th century Raghunath Temple stands beside the lake.

Viewpoints

There are various viewpoints around the town, best known of which is Sunset Point. Hordes stroll out here every evening to catch the setting sun and there are food stalls and all the usual entertainments. Other popular points include Honeymoon Point, which also offers a view of the sunset, the Crags and Robert's Spur.

Museum & Art Gallery

The small museum is on Raj Bhavan Rd and is open from 10 am to 5 pm daily, except Fridays. Admission is free. There is also a Rajasthan Emporium further back towards the market.

Adhar Devi Temple

Three km out of the town, there are 200 steep steps to climb to this Durga temple in a natural cleft in the rock. You have to stoop down to get through the low entrance into the temple. Good views over Mt Abu from up here.

Dilwara Temples (5 km)

These Jain temples are Mt Abu's main attraction and amongst the finest examples of Jain architecture in India. The complex includes two temples where the art of marble carving has been carried to unsurpassed heights. The older of these temples is the Vimal Vasahi which is dedicated to the first Tirthankar, Adinath, and was built in 1031. The central shrine has an image of Adinath while around the courtyard are 52 identical cells, each with a Buddha-like cross-legged image. The entrance to the courtyard is formed by 48 elegantly carved pillars. In front of the temple stands the 'House of Elephants' with figures of elephants marching in procession to the temple entrance.

The later Tejpal temple is dedicated to Neminath, the 22nd Tirthankar, and

was built in 1230 by the brothers Tejpal and Vastupal. Like Vimal they were ministers in the government of the ruler of Gujurat. Although the Tejpal temple is important as an extremely old and complete example of a Jain temple its most notable feature is the fantastic intricacy and delicacy of the marble carving. In places the carving is so fine that the marble becomes almost transparent. In particular the lotus flower which hangs from the centre of the dome is an incredible piece of work. It's difficult to believe that this huge lace-like filigree actually started as a solid block of marble.

There are three other temples in the enclosure but they all pale beside the Tejpal and Vimal Vasahi. The complex is open from 12 noon to 6 pm and there is a Rs 5 camera charge. Note that no leather at all is permitted in the complex — apart from removing shoes or sandals you must take off belts and even camera cases if they are leather.

Achalgarh (11 km)

The Shiva temple of Achaleshwar Mahadeva has a number of interesting features including a toe of Shiva, a brass Nandi, and, where the Shiva lingam would be, a deep hole said to extend all the way to the underworld. Outside, by the car park, is a tank beside which are three stone buffaloes and the figure of a king shooting them with a bow and arrows. A legend states that the tank was once filled with ghee but demons, in the form of buffaloes, came down and drank it each night — until the king shot them. A path leads up the hillside to a group of colourful Jain temples with fine views out over the plains.

Guru Shikhar (15 km)

At the end of the plateau is 1721 metre Guru Shikhar, the highest point in Rajasthan. There is now a road almost up to the summit. On the top there is the Atri Rishi Temple and there are good views all around.

Gaumukh Temple (8 km)

Down on the Abu Road side of Mt Abu a small stream flows from the mouth of a marble cow, giving the shrine its name. There is also a marble figure of the bull Nandi, Shiva's vehicle. The tank here, Agni Kund, is said to be the site for the sacrificial fire made by the sage Vasishta from which four of the great Rajput clans were born. An image of Vasishta is flanked by figures of Rama and Krishna.

Tours

There are daily tours from the bus stand costing Rs 10. They run from 8 am to 1 pm and 2 to 7 pm and visit the Dilwara Temples, Achalgarh, Guru Shikhar, Adhar Devi and other places. In the season they tend to be heavily booked so plan ahead.

Places to Stay

Mt Abu has a quite amazing number of hotels at all sorts of prices. The *Mount Hotel* (tel 55) is a little inconveniently situated but very pleasant. Singles/doubles cost Rs 100/150. The centrally located *Hotel Hill Tone* (tel 137) has singles/doubles at Rs 75/125 and an intriguing sign outside announcing that they have honeymoon suites: 'cave and bamboo type'!

A bit further back from the bus stand, and up a steepish path, the *Shikkar Tourist Bungalow* (tel 69) is the biggest place in Mt Abu. Rooms vary widely in price and also from the high season to low season. Off season singles can start at Rs 10 but in season they can go as high as Rs 30 or with air-con Rs 50. Doubles start from Rs 15 in the off-season, and go up to Rs 40, Rs 60 with air-con. Dorm beds are Rs 8 in season. The Tourist Bungalow also has a restaurant and bar.

Amongst the lower price places there is the pleasant *Tourist Guest House* (tel 160) at the foot of the driveway to the Tourist Bungalow. Built around a courtyard this clean, well run place has doubles at Rs 20 with bath and mosquito nets, Rs 15 without bath. Off-season rates are lower. *Saraswati Lodge* (tel 7) is a clean, bright place with similar prices to the Tourist Guest House.

Other similarly priced cheapies include the *Bharati Hotel* (tel 61) just before the market and the *Navjivan Hotel* (tel 53) and *Hotel Tourist* (tel 53 also) directly across the road from the Bharati. Good vegetarian food at these three places too. The *Youth Hostel* is also central and has dorm beds at Rs 5.

Places to Eat

Mt Abu also has a wide selection of eating places although there are no real standouts. The *Tourist Bungalow* has the usual Tourist Bungalow menu in its restaurant and it becomes (as usual) fairly boring after a couple of meals. The Hotel Hill Tone has the flashier *Madhuban Restaurant* but it looks better than the food is. On the other hand the *Nina Sheeba Restaurant*, on the Sunset Point road, has fairly reasonable Chinese food.

Good Gujurati thalis for Rs 5 are available at the *Tourist Navjivan-Bharati Hotel* trio between the bus stand and the market. At the corner of the road down to the lake *MK Cold Drinks* has excellent ice cream and also does thalis. The *Bharti Restaurant* across the road also does Gujurati thalis and from here down to the lake there are a number of small snack places including a *Havmor Icecream*. This is a popular place for an evening stroll. On the lake itself there's a large concrete 'boat' restaurant, the *Jal Mahal*, but it's OK for a cup of tea or coffee, nothing more.

Watch out for Mt Abu's own soft

drink, the ginger Rim Zim. It tastes absolutely appalling.

Getting There
Abu Road, the railhead for Mt Abu, is a small place with the bus station right by the railway station. There are regular buses making the 27 km climb up to Mt Abu. It takes about an hour and costs Rs 3 or Rs 3.50 by 'express' bus. A taxi will cost Rs 50. There's a toll gate as you enter Mt Abu where bus passengers are charged Rs 1.50. People arriving by taxi or other forms of transport are charged Rs 2.50.

There's an extensive bus schedule from Mt Abu and to many destinations you will find it faster and more convenient to go straight there by bus rather than going down to Abu Road and waiting for a train. For example there are four buses daily to Ahmedabad, the trip takes about seven hours and costs Rs 18. To Udaipur it takes seven to 11 hours, depending on the route taken, and costs Rs 18 to 28.

Getting Around
There are buses from the bus stand to the various sites in Mt Abu but it takes a little planning to get out and back without too much hanging around. Some buses go just to Dilwara (Rs 0.90) others out to Achalgarh (Rs 1.10) so it's a matter of deciding which to go to first depending on the schedule. There are also plenty of taxis with posted fares to anywhere you care to mention. Mt Abu's unique form of transport is large 'baby prams' in which you can sit and be wheeled around! They're all seemingly operated by 'Abu Enterprises' but are mainly used by parents who dump their children in them.

Things to Buy
The Rajasthan Emporium is on Raj Bhavan Rd but there are also quite a few shops on the road down to the lake front. Jewellery shops have a good selection of Rajasthani jewellery. Note that here, as in most of India, jewellery is usually sold by weight.

JODHPUR (population 400,000)
The largest city in Rajasthan after Jaipur, Jodhpur stands at the edge of the Thar Desert. The massive fort, topping a sheer rocky hill which rises right in the middle of the town, totally dominates the city. Jodhpur was founded in 1459 by Rao Jodha, a chief of the Rajput clan known as the Rathores. His descendants ruled not only Jodhpur but also other Rajput princely states. The Rathore kingdom was once known as Marwar, the 'Land of Death'.

The old city of Jodhpur is surrounded by a wall 10 km long which was built about a century after the city was founded. From the fort you can clearly see where the old city ends and the new city begins. The old city is a fascinating jumble of winding streets of great interest to wander around. Eight gates lead out from the walled city. It's one of the most interesting cities in India and, yes, it was from here that those baggy/tight horse riding trousers, jodhpurs, took their name.

Orientation & Information
The Tourist Office, railway stations and bus stand are all outside the old city. High Court Rd runs from the Raika Bagh railway station, directly across from the bus stand, round by the Umaid Gardens, the Tourist Bungalow and Tourist Office, and round beside the city wall towards the main station and the GPO. The GPO is right by the main station, the Tourist Office (tel 21900) is at the Tourist Bungalow. You can use the subterranean swimming pool at the Umaid Bhawan Palace Hotel (tel 22316) for Rs 10.

Key:-
1. G.P.O.
2. Main Railway Station
3. Raika Bagh Railway Station
4. Bus Terminus

5. Tourist Office & Bungalow
6. Market & Clock Tower
7. Jaswant Thada
8. Fort Meherangarh
9. Raika Bagh Palace
10. Umaid Bhawan Palace

Jodhpur

Meherangarh Fort

The 'Magestic Fort' is just that, sprawled across the 125 metre high hill this is the most impressive and formidable fort in fort-studded Rajasthan. A winding road leads up to the fort entrance from the city below. The first gate is still scarred by cannon balls — indicating that this was a fort that earned its keep. The gates include the Jayapol, built by Maharaja Man Singh in 1806 following his victory over the armies of Jaipur and Bikaner, and the Fatehpol or Victory Gate, erected by Maharaja Ajit Singh

in 1707 to commemorate his defeat of the Moghuls. The final gate is the Lohapol or Iron Gate beside which there are 15 handprints, the sati marks of widows of the Maharajas — six of them alone are widows of Maharaja Man Singh who threw themselves upon his funeral pyre in 1843.

Inside the fort, which is still run by the Maharaja of Jodhpur, there are a whole series of courtyards and palaces. The palace apartments have evocative names like the Moti Mahal or Pearl Palace, the Sukh Mahal or Pleasure

Palace, the Phool Mahal or Flower Palace. They house a fantastic collection of the trappings of Indian royalty There's an amazing collection of elephant howdahs, used when the Maharajas rode on elephant back in glittering processions through their capitals. Miniature paintings of a variety of schools hang on the walls, there's a superb collection of folk music instruments; the inevitable Rajput armoury, palanquins, furniture and costumes. One room even has a collection of, often humorous, baby cradles! The palace apartments are beautifully decorated and painted and have delicately carved, red sandstone, latticework windows.

At the southern end of the fort there's a collection of old cannons on the ramparts, looking out over the sheer drop down to the old town below. There's no guardrail and you can clearly hear voices and shouts carrying up from the houses far below you — it's very magical. Note the many blue houses — painted that colour to distinguish them as belonging to Brahmins. The Chamunda Temple, to Durga, stands at this end of the fort.

The fort is open from 9 am to 5 pm and admission is Rs 5 for the complete museum including a guide to open the locked doors. Rs 3 gets you into the unlocked part of the fort. There's an additional Rs 10 charge to use a camera (Rs 15 with a flash). A couple of musicians will usually stand just inside the entrance and strike up a merry Rajasthani number to herald your arrival — it helps to set the mood for a visit to this superb fort.

Jaswant Thada
Part way down from the fort, just off the fort road, is this white marble memorial to Maharaja Jaswant Singh II. The cenotaph was built in 1899 and the royal crematorium and three later cenotaphs are near to it. Inside there is a collection of portraits of the various Jodhpur rulers.

Clock Tower & Markets
The clock tower is a popular landmark in the old city. The colourful Sardar Market is close to the tower and narrow alleys lead from here to bazaars for textiles, silver and handicrafts. See the note in Places to Eat about Makhania Lassi in the cafe in the gateway to the market.

Umaid Gardens & Museum
The Tourist Bungalow is on the edge of this garden on High Court Rd. The Government Museum is within the gardens and has a variety of exhibits including paintings, portraits of the Jodhpur rulers, manuscripts, an armoury and local arts and crafts. The museum is open from 10 am to 5 pm and admission is Rs 0.30.

Umaid Bhawan Palace
Maharaja Umaid Singh, who died in 1947, lived at first in the Raika Bagh Palace but in 1928 commenced construction of the Umaid Bhawan Palace on the outskirts of town. Constructed of marble and red sandstone this immense palace was designed by the president of the British Royal Institute of Architects and not finally completed until 1943. It is also known as the Chhittar Palace because of the local Chhittar sandstone used. Probably the most surprising thing about this grandiose palace is that it was built so close to independence. Surely the Maharaja, or even more to the point his British advisers, could see that the upheavals of independence were just around the corner and that Maharajas, princely states and grand extravagances would all soon be a thing of the past? Today most of the palace has been turned into a hotel but it's a gloomy, sepulchral place — devoid of that zany, whimsical charm that the Udaipur and Jaipur

IN RAJASTHAN...

palace have in such abundance. Even the basement swimming pool is a dark, clinical sort of place. The palace is open 9 am to 5 pm and admission is Rs 2.

Tours

There are daily tours starting from the Tourist Bungalow from 8.30 am to 1 pm and 2 pm to 6.30 pm. Cost is Rs 10 and they cover the Umaid Bhawan Palace, Meherangarh Fort, Jaswant Thada, Mandore Gardens and the museum.

Places to Stay

The *Umaid Bhawan Palace Hotel* (tel 22316) is Jodhpur's premier hotel. It's fairly small, just 45 rooms, but has all the palatial luxuries from a theatre to squash and tennis courts, that underground swimming pool and a bar. Singles/doubles cost Rs 210/310. The *Ajit Bhawan Palace* (tel 20409) on Airport Rd is sometimes used for groups.

The *Ghoomar Tourist Bungalow* (tel 21900) is on High Court Rd by the Umaid Gardens. Singles/doubles cost Rs 30/40 or Rs 50/60 with air-con, dorm beds are Rs 8. The Tourist Office is also located here and the Indian Airlines desk. There are *Railway Retiring Rooms* (tel 22741) with singles/doubles at Rs 7/15 near the main railway station.

There are a string of cheaper hotels near the railway station with rooms in the Rs 10 to 20 bracket. Best of them is probably the *Adarsh Niwas Hotel* (tel 23936) which also has a very good restaurant. Others include the *Agarwal Lodge* (tel 20837), the *Charli Bikaner* (tel 23985), the *Alpana Hotel* (tel 24504), *Raghunath Das Dharamshala* (tel 20386) and the *Shanti Bhawan Lodge* (tel 21689). The *Arun Hotel* (tel 20238) is at Sojati Gate.

Places to Eat

Very good non-vegetarian food at the *Kalinga Restaurant* in the Adarsh

Niwas Hotel near the railway station. *Pankaj* at Jalori Gate has good vegetarian food or you could try the *Coffee House* at Sojati Gate. There is also a restaurant at the *Tourist Bungalow.* While you're in Jodhpur try Makhania Lassi, a delicious thick cream variety of that ultra-refreshing drink. You can find it at *Agra Sweet Home,* right opposite the Sojati Gate, but also at the place in the gateway to the central market. It's so popular here that they claim to sell 1500 glasses a day, at Rs 2 each! Other popular specialities in Jodhpur include the baclava like dessert known as mawa kachori and mawa ladoo, another popular dessert.

Getting There

Air Air services to Jodhpur have recently been recommenced by Indian Airlines. There are flights from Udaipur (Rs 185) and Jaipur (Rs 225). The Indian Airlines office (tel 20909) is in the Tourist Bungalow.

Bus There are bus services operated by Rajasthan State Roadways from the bus stand at Raika Bagh to other major centres in Rajasthan. Some road distances from Jodhpur include Barmer 220 km, Bikarer 240 km, Jaipur 340 km, Jaisalmer 290 km, Abu 264 km, Ranakpur 175 km, Udaipur 275 km. There is a daily bus to Jaisalmer at 1

pm, the trip takes seven hours. Jodhpur-Mt Abu takes 10 hours.

Rail From Delhi it takes about 16 hours by train to Jodhpur and costs Rs 132 in 1st class, Rs 32 in 2nd class. Not many people would make that trip straight through, it's 10 or 11 hours Jaipur-Jodhpur at a cost of Rs 75 in 1st class, Rs 16.50 in 2nd. There are overnight trains to Bikaner and overnight and day trains to Jaisalmer — see the relevant sections for details.

Getting Around

Jodhpur has unmetered taxis and metered (but not very metered) auto-rickshaws as well as tongas. You'd have difficulty getting through the narrow lanes of the old city in anything wider than an auto-rickshaw. There are regular city buses to places around Jodhpur like Mandore, Balsamand and Mahamandir.

Things to Buy

The usual Rajasthani handicrafts are available in Jodhpur but this is a good place to look for antiques. There are many little shops in the convoluted streets of the old town but Abani Handicrafts, next door to the Tourist Bungalow, has a large and varied collection. They also have a branch in the palace hotel.

AROUND JODHPUR

Mahamandir (2 km)

The 'Great Temple' is a small walled town north-east of the city. It is built around a 100-pillared Shiva temple but is not of great interest.

Balsamand Lake & Palace (7 km)

Originally constructed in 1159 this lake and garden is to the north of the city. A palace, built in 1936, stands on the lake side and this is a popular excursion spot. The gardens are open 8 am to 6 pm and entry is Rs 1. The larger Pratap

Sagar Lake and Kailana Lake, (where there is also a garden) west of Jodhpur, provide the city's water supply.

Mandore (9 km)

Further north this was the capital of Marwar prior to the foundation of Jodhpur. Today it is a popular local attraction due to its extensive gardens with high rock terraces. The gardens also contain the cenotaphs of Jodhpur rulers including Maharaja Jaswant Singh and, largest and finest of all, the soaring temple shaped memorial to Maharaja Ajit Singh.

The 'Hall of Heroes' contains 15 figures carved out of a rock wall. The brightly painted figures represent Hindu deities or local heroes on horse back. The Shrine of 33 Crore (330 million) Gods has painted figures of gods, spirits and divinities. There are regular buses to Mandore from Jodhpur.

Other

Sardar Samand Lake is a wildlife centre 55 km from Jodhpur. The route passes through a number of colourful villages and there is a summer palace of the Maharaja here — accommodation can be arranged. Dhawa or Doli is another

wildlife sanctuary with many antelopes, 45 km from Jodhpur on the road to Barmer. Osian is an ancient Thar Desert town 58 km out. The ruins of 16 Jain and Brahmanical temples from the 8th to 11th century stand here and the town is inhabited by hundreds of peacocks. The architecturally interesting temples are in a beautiful area of small hills and sand dunes. At Soyala, 74 km out on the Nagaur road, there is an interesting Shiva temple. Nagaur is 135 km from Jodhpur and has an historic fort and palace — it's an interesting site in an otherwise dull stretch of desert.

JAISALMER (population 20,000)

Jaisalmer is one of Rajasthan's, indeed India's, most exotic and unusual towns. It's so remote and isolated that few people have even heard of it. Yet travellers who make the effort to get there are never disappointed in this mediaeval looking place, something right out of tales of the Arabian Nights. A 'living museum' and the 'golden city' are just two descriptions which have been applied to the desert outpost. Centuries ago its strategic position on the camel train routes between India and central Asia brought great wealth to Jaisalmer. The merchants and townspeople build magnificent houses and mansions — all exquisitely carved from a golden-yellow sandstone. From the humblest shop to the palace and the temples in the fort the whole town glows in the same golden colour. Even today new buildings must be designed to blend in with the old.

The rise of shipping trade and the port of Bombay pushed Jaisalmer into decline. After WW II partition, and the cutting off of the trade routes through to Pakistan, seemingly sealed the town's fate and water shortages could have pronounced the death sentence. But the

'65 and '71 Indo-Pakistan wars revealed Jaisalmer's strategic importance, paved roads and a railways linked it to the rest of Rajasthan, even electricity finally reached out to the remote town. Today military bases are the pillar of the town's economy but increasing numbers of travellers are waking up to the fascination of this exotic place.

Orientation & Information

Finding your way around Jaisalmer is not really necessary — it's a place you simply wander around and get lost in. Within the old city walls the streets are a tangled maze but it's small enough not to matter. You simply head off in what seems like the right direction and eventually you'll get there. The old city is completely surrounded by a lofty fort wall and within this a hill rises with more fortified walls. The Jain temples and the old palace are on this hilltop. The central market area is directly below the hill while the bank, the new palace and several other shops and offices are near the Amar Sagar Gate to the west. Just outside the gate is the bus stand while the railway station is outside the city walls at the other side. The Tourist Office is at the

Jaisalmer

Tourist Bungalow, just beyond the bus stop on the west side of the old city.

Havelis

The beautiful mansions built by Jaisalmer's wealthy merchants are known as havelis and several of these fine sandstone buildings are still in beautiful condition. Patwon ki Haveli is the most elaborate and magnificent of all the Jaisalmer havelis. It stands in a narrow lane and one of its apartments is painted with beautiful murals — unfortunately at present the building is closed up and not lived in. Salim Singh ki Haveli was built about 300 years ago and is still partially lived in. Salim Singh was the prime minister when Jaisalmer was the capital of a princely state and his mansion has a beautifully arched roof with superb carved brackets in the form of peacocks. The mansion is just below the hill and, it is said, once had two additional wooden storeys in an attempt

to make it as high as the Maharaja's palace. The Maharaja had the upper storeys torn down! The late 19th century Nathmal ki Haveli was also a prime minister's house. The left and right wings of the building were carved by brothers and are very similar but not identical. Yellow sandstone elephants guard the building and the front door alone is a work of art.

Gadi Sagar Tank

This tank, south of the city walls, was once the water supply of the city and there are many small temples and shrines around the tank. In winter a wide variety of water birds flock here. The beautiful arched gateway across the road down to the tank is said to have been built by a famous prostitute. When she offered to pay to have this gateway constructed the Maharaja refused permission since he would have to pass under it on going down to the tank and that, he felt, would be unseemly. While he was away she built the gate anyway — and added a Krishna temple on top of it so the king could not subsequently tear it down.

Fort

Built in 1156 by Rawal Jaisal the fort crowns the 80 metre high Trikuta hill. About a quarter of the old city's population resides within the fort walls which have 99 bastions around the circumference. There is a very fine view over the old city from the fort walls. Jaisalmer's seven storey palace stands just within the first gate of the fort. There are carved balconies and cupolas and the Satiyon ki Sidhiyan where women became satis.

Jain Temples

This group of fine Jain temples were built in the 12th to 15th century within the fort walls. They are beautifully carved and dedicated to Rikhabdevji and Sambhavnathji. The Gyan Bhandar, a library containing some extremely old manuscripts, is within the temple complex. The temples are only open in the morning until 12 noon. There is also a Shiva and a Ganesh temple within the fort.

Places to Stay

The *Moomal Tourist Bungalow* (tel 92) is just outside the city walls to the west. It's very close to the bus halt but quite a distance from the railway station which is clear the other side of the walled town. Singles/doubles cost Rs 30/40 here or Rs 50/60 with air-conditioning, there's also a Rs 8 dormitory. It's a modern building with a restaurant and bar and it's quite comfortable.

Jaisalmer's other upper bracket hotel is the *Jaisal Castle Hotel* (tel 62) which is situated right on the ramparts of the fort, by the Jain temples. Singles/doubles, all with attached bathrooms, are Rs 30/40 and there's also a restaurant in this pleasantly run place. The

operators also organise camel safaris out into the desert around Jaisalmer. The hotel is in a traditional old Jaisalmer house with large rooms, all with attached bath. Sunsets from the roof of the hotel are superb, the hotel is 'out of this world' according to one visitor. A new hotel, the *Rawal Jaisal*, is being bult near Kadi Bundar, north of the town.

There is quite a travelling community in Jaisalmer these days and a number of cheap hotels have sprung up to cater for them. Right in the central market area there's the *Sunil Bhatia Rest House* with singles/doubles at Rs 5/10. Continue on a hundred or so metres towards the Amar Sagar Gate and a small sign will direct you to the right to the *Rama Guest House*. Others in this same Rs 10-20 price bracket include the *Tourist Hotel* on the south side of the city behind the municipality, the small *Sunray Hotel* behind the Bank of India building right by the Amar Sagar Gate and the new palace, or the *Golden Rest*. They are all as basic as their prices would indicate but OK. Local musicians sometimes visit the lodges, stay overnight and can be persuaded to do an encore the next morning, on the flat roof.

Places to Eat

There are a number of cold drink and food places around the market area and near the Golden Rest. The small (and basic) *Gaylord Restaurant* is across from the Bank of India. Near here, by Mahendra Travel, there is also the small *Ghoonghat Restuarant*. The *Tourist Bungalow* has a restaurant (with slightly higher prices) as does the *Jaisal Castle Hotel*.

Getting There

Jaisalmer is 290 km from Jodhpur via Pokarana, Dechu and Balesar or 330 km from Bikaner via Pokaran and Phalodi. There are two buses daily to Bikaner, a 10 hour trip, and one bus daily to Jodhpur. It is easier to get to Jodhpur by train, there is a day train and a night train in each direction and the trip takes about 10 hours. Fares are Rs 74 in 1st class, Rs 16.50 in 2nd. Note the comments in the introductory section on Gricing about the unique engines used on this run. The Maharaja of Jodhpur's personal railway carriage can be hired by groups to make the trip in real royal luxury. The carriage takes 20 people and it costs Rs 11,000 (including meals) to have the carriage hooked on to the regular train.

Getting Around
Unmetered taxis and jeeps are available, about Rs 10 from the railway station to the Tourist Bungalow. Around the city the tourist office's jeep can be hired for sightseeing for Rs 20 for up to 10 km locally, Rs 1.50 a km for more than 10 km out of the city. You can also hire bicycles in Jaisalmer and ride out to nearby places. For camel hire and camel safaris contact Jaisal tours (tel 97) or Mahendra Travel.

Things to Buy
Jaisalmer is famous for embroidery, Rajasthani mirror work, rugs, blankets, old stone work and antiques. At Kadi Bundar, north of the city, tie dye and other fabrics are made.

Festivals
The recently commenced Desert Festival is intended to take place in January-February of each year. Camel races and dances, folk music, desert ballads, puppeteers — they're all part of the activity. At the full moon night of Purnima a sound and light drama is performed at Sam.

AROUND JAISALMER
There are some fascinating places in the area around Jaisalmer although it soon fades out into a barren sand-duned desert which stretches across the lonely border into Pakistan. The most interesting way of exploring the desert around the town is on a camel safari — check with Jaisal Tours at the Jaisal Castle Hotel about the camel safaris they organise. These are arranged principally for group tours but other arrangements can be made at a cost of around Rs 150 per day depending on what you want to do. The usual tours take four days and three nights in a circuit around Jaisalmer via Mool Sagar, the Sam sand dunes and back via Lodruva passing through Hindu, Moslem, Rajput, tribal and abandoned villages. You can also do longer seven day safaris to Pokran or 11 days to Bikaner. October to February is the best time for camel safaris.

Amar Sagar (6 km)
North-west of Jaisalmer this used to be a very pleasant formal garden but it has now fallen into ruins. The lake here dries up several months into the dry season. A beautifully carved Jain temple is being painstakingly restored by craftsmen brought in from Agra. Commenced in the late '70s this monumental task is expected to take many years.

Lodruva (15 km)
Further out beyond Amar Sagar are the deserted ruins of this ancient capital. The Jain temples, which were rebuilt in the late '70s, are the only reminders of the magnificence of the city at its peak. The temples have ornate carved arches at the entrance and a Kalputra, the 'divine tree', within. In the temple there's a hole from which a snake is said to come every evening to drink an offering of milk. Only the 'lucky' can see it. At the same time as they rebuilt the temples, Jain benefactors had the road out from Jaisalmer sealed, but immediately beyond Lodruva it deteriorates into a desert track.

Around Jaisalmer

Mool Sagar (9 km)
Directly west of Jaisalmer this is another pleasant small garden and tank. Continuing in this direction you reach

the Sam sand dunes, about 40 km from the town. This is the nearest point to Jaisalmer for the real Sahara like desert.

Bada Bagh & Cenotaphs
North of the town Bada Bagh is a fertile oasis with a huge old dam, much of Jaisalmer's vegetables and fruit is grown here and carried into the town by colourfully dressed women each day. Above the gardens are royal cenotaphs with beautifully carved ceilings and equestrian statues of the former rulers. This is a popular place to come in the early evening to watch the setting sun turn Jaisalmer a beautiful golden brown.

Other
Three km off the road to Barmer, at a point 14 km from Jaisalmer, the 180 million year old fossils of old trees can be seen. A desert national park is intended to be established in the Thar Desert near the road to Barmer.

POKRAN
The junction where the Jaisalmer-Bikaner and Jaisalmer-Jodhpur roads split is the site for another magnificent Rajasthan fortress. The yellow sandstone fort rises from the yellow desert sands and shelters a tangle of narrow streets with balconied houses decorated with parrots, elephants and Rajasthan's inevitable peacocks. The usually quiet town springs to life at its annual cattle fair.

BARMER
This desert town is a centre for wood carving, carpets, embroidery, block printing and other handicrafts. Barmer is 153 km from Jaisalmer and 220 km from Jodhpur. At Kiradu, 35 km west of Barmer, there are 11th century Kathiawar-style temples with Gupta elements in their design.

BIKANER (population 200,000)
This desert town in the north of the state was founded in 1488 by Rao Bikaji, a descendant of the founder of Jodhpur, Jodhaji. Like many other Rajasthan cities it is surrounded by a high, battlemented wall and, like its smaller sister to the south, Jaisalmer,

it was once an important staging post on the great caravan trade routes. The city is chiefly interesting for its superb large fort but it is also noted for the fine camels bred here and there is a government camel breeding farm near the city. The Gang Canal, built between 1925 and 1927, has irrigated a great area of previously arid land around Bikaner.

Information & Orientation

The city is encircled by a seven km long city wall with five entrance gates, built in the 18th century. The fort and palace, built of Bikaner's same reddish-pink sandstone, is within the city walls. The GPO is at the collectorate, the city post office is inside Kot Gate. The Tourist Office is located at the Tourist Bungalow.

Junagarh Fort

Constructed between 1588 and 1593 by Raja Rai Singh, a general in the Moghul Emperor Akbar's army, the fort has a 986 metre long wall with 37 bastions and two entrances. The Suraj Pol or Sun Gate is the main entrance to the fort. The palaces within the fort are at the southern side — they're a picturesque ensemble of courtyards, balconies, kiosks, towers and windows. Amongst the places of interest are the Chandra Mahal or Moon Palace with paintings, mirrors and carved marble panels. The Phool Mahal or Flower Palace has inset mirrors work and more paintings. The Sheesh Mahal or Glass Palace is also decorated with glass and mirrors. The Karn Mahal was built to commemorate a notable victory over

Bikaner, Rajasthan

A SIDEWALK HOT MILK VENDOR ON A GRAND SCALE. HOT MILK, SUGAR & CURD MIXED UP WITH A FLOURISH FOR 75 PAISA (9¢) A GLASSFULL. ENTERTAINMENT FREE.

the Moghul Aurangzeb. Other palaces include the Rang Mahal, Bijai Mahal and Anup Mahal. The Durga Niwas is a beautifully painted courtyard, the Ganga Niwas, another large courtyard, has a finely carved red sandstone front. Har Mandir is the royal temple, dedicated to Lord Shiva. The fort is open from 9.30 am to 5 pm, closed on Wednesdays, and admission is Rs 2. There is a museum, library of Persian and Sanskrit manuscripts and armoury in a corner of the fort.

Lalgarh Palace
The 'Red Fort' was built by Maharaja Ganga Singh (1881-1942) in memory of his father Maharaja Lal Singh. The Bikaner royal family still live in part of the palace which is made of red sandstone and has beautiful lattice work. There is a collection of old photographs and the usual exhibition of half of India's wildlife, shot and stuffed, inside. Entry to the palace costs Rs 1 and it is open from 9 am to 6 pm.

Ganga Golden Jubilee Museum
Said to be one of the best musems in Rajasthan it contains pre-Harrapan, Gupta and Kushan pieces and a wide collection of terracottas, pottery, paintings, particularly miniatures of the Bikaner school, and weapons. It is open from 10 am to 5 pm but closed on Fridays. Entry is Rs 0.25, the museum is near the Circuit House.

Places to Stay
Unusually, accommodation is often fully booked in Bikaner — you may have to search around. The *Lalgarh Palace Hotel* (tel 312) has singles/doubles at Rs 200/275 including meals. The new *Dhola-Maru Tourist Bungalow* is on Pooran Singh Circle and has singles/doubles at Rs 30/40. There are *Railway Retiring Rooms* at the station and nearby there is a *Dak Bungalow* (tel 151) with doubles at less than Rs 10. If that fails there are a string of similarly low-priced hotels near the station. The *Delight Hotel*, the *Deluxe Hotel* (tel 192), the *Green Hotel* (tel 296) and the *Roopan Hotel* (tel 373). There's a dharamsala opposite and two km away there is a *Circuit House* with rooms at Rs 12.

Places to Eat
Chhotu Motu Joshi Restaurant is just down from the Green Hotel towards the station and has good and cheap vegetarian food and terrifically cold lassi. There is also the *Ambar Restaurant* on Station Rd.

Getting There
Bus On the edge of the Thar Desert, Bikaner is connected by rail and road with the rest of Rajasthan. There is a national highway to Jaipur (320 km) and to Jaisalmer (330 km). Jodhpur is 240 km away. There are regular bus services.
Rail There are day and night trains from Delhi to Bikaner and the 468 trip takes 11 or 12 hours. Fares are Rs 102 in 1st class, 24 in 2nd. There is a daily overnight train to and from Jodhpur and the 277 km trip takes eight hours and costs Rs 69 in 1st, Rs 14.50 in 2nd. The 379 km trip between Jaipur and Bikaner takes 10 to 11 hours and again there is an overnight train with fares of Rs 86 in 1st class, Rs 19.50 in 2nd class.

Getting Around
Taxis are unmetered, Bikaner also has auto-rickshaws and tongas.

AROUND BIKANER
Bhand Sagar Temple (5 km)
The 16th century Jain temple to the 23rd Tirthankar, Parasvanath, is the most important of the complex but others include the Chintamani Temple

of 1505 and the Adinath Temple. There is a fine view of the city wall and surrounding countryside from the park behind the temple.

Devi Kund (8 km)
This is the site of the royal chhatris or cenotaphs of many of the Bika dynasty rulers. The white marble chhatri of Maharaja Surat Singh is amongst the most imposing.

Camel Breeding Farm (10 km)
This government-managed camel breeding station is probably unique in Asia. There are hundreds of camels here and rides are available. The British army had a camel corps drawn from from Bikaner during WW I.

Gajner Wildlife Sanctuary (32 km)
A number of animals can be seen in this reserve on the Jaisalmer road. In winter imperial sand grouse migrate here. The old royal summer palace stands on the bank of the lake and is sometimes used as a hotel.

Karni Mata Temple (33 km)
At Deshnok on the Jodhpur road this temple is dedicated to the mystic Karni Mata. The huge silver gates to the temple and the marble carvings were donated by Maharaja Ganga Singh and a golden umbrella tops the temple but the main interest here is the rats. The temple is infested with holy rats which are fed and cared for in the belief that they will reincarnate as mystics or holy men.

The Indian passion for labelling and logging things is never better illustrated than in the Rajasthan Tourist Bungalows where every movable item, and a good few that aren't, is coded and numbered. And doubtless listed in some giant register somewhere. In one room I spotted this notation: TBGL-Ju-TP Stand 8 (R No 8), that is to say Tourist Bungalow Jodhpur — Toilet Paper Stand 8 (in room number 8)!

Tony Wheeler

After a short time in Rajasthan you soon realise why the peacock is the state bird. They're everywhere. Peacocks stroll parks and gardens, sit on top of roofs, wander around hotels. If it's not real ones then there are mosaic ones in palaces, painted ones on walls, glass ones in windows. And they're every bit as colourful as Rajasthan itself.

Gujurat

Population: 29 million
Area: 195,984 square km
Capital: Gandhinagar
Main language: Gujarati

The west coast state of Gujurat is not one of India's busiest destinations. Although it is quite easy to slot Gujarat in between Bombay and the cities of Rajasthan few people pause to explore this interesting state. Yet Gujarat has a long and varied history and a great number of interesting places to visit. If you want to go right beyond history into the realm of legend then the Temple of Somnath was actually there to witness the creation of the universe! And along the south coast are the sites where many of the great events in Lord Krishna's life took place.

On more firm historic footing Lothal was the site of a Harappan or Indus Valley Civilisation city over 4000 years ago. The main sites from this very ancient culture are now in Pakistan but it is thought Lothal may have survived the great cities of the Sind by as much as 500 years. Gujarat also featured in the exploits of the great Buddhist Emperor Ashoka and one of his rock edicts can be seen near Junagadh.

Later Gujarat was to suffer Moslem incursions from Mahmud of Ghazni on through the Moghuls and was to be a battlefield between the Moghuls and the Mahrattas. It was an early contact point with the west and at Surat the first British commercial outpost was established. The Portuguese enclaves of Daman and Diu survived within the borders of Gujarat right up to 1961. More recently Gujarat had a close tie with the life of the father of modern India, Mahatma Gandhi. It was in Gujarat that the Mahatma was born and spent his early years and it was to Ahmedabad, the great city of Gujarat, that he returned to wage his long struggle with the British for independence.

Gujarat has always been a centre for the Jains and some of its most interesting sights are Jain temple centres like those at Palitana and Girnar. The Jains are an influential and energetic group and as a result Gujarat is one of the wealthier states of India with a number of important industries, particularly textiles. Apart from the Jain temples other major attractions of Gujarat include the last Asian lions in the Gir Forest and the fascinating Indo-Saracenic architecture of Ahmedabad.

Geographically Gujarat can be divided into three areas. The mainland region includes the major cities of Ahmedabad, Surat and Baroda. The Gulf of Cambay divides the mainland strip from the flat, often barren, plain of the Kathiawar Peninsula, also known as Saurashtra. This was never incorporated into British India but survived the more than 200 princely states right up to independence. In 1956 they were all amalgamated into the state of Bombay but in 1956 this was in turn split, on linguistic grounds, into Maharashtra and Gujarat. Finally the Gulf of Kutch divides Saurashtra from Kutch which is virtually an island cut off from the rest of Gujarat, to the east, and Pakistan, to the north, by the low-lying 'Ranns' of Kutch.

GUJURATI FOOD

The strict Jain vegetarianism has contributed to Gujarat's distinct regional cuisine. Throughout the state you'll find the Gujurati variation of the thali — it's the traditional all-you-can-eat vegetarian meal with an even greater variety of dishes than usual. But with the drawback, if you're not sweet-toothed, that it can be overpoweringly sweet. Popular dishes include *kadhi*, a savoury curry of yoghurt and fried puffs, flavoured with spices and finely chopped vegetables. *Undhyoo* is a

winter speciality of potatoes, sweet potatoes, broad beans and aubergines roasted in an earthenware pot which is buried 'undhyoo', upside down, under a fire. In Surat there's a local variation on this which is more spicy and curry hot. *Sev Ganthia* is a crunchy fried chickpea flour snack which you buy from *farsan* stalls.

In winter, in Surat, you can try *paunk*, a curious combination of roasted cereals, or *jowar* garlic chutney and sugar. Then there's *khaman dhokla*, a salty, steamed chickpea flour cake. Or *doodhpak* which is a sweetened, thickened milk-based dessert with nuts. *Srikhand* is a dessert made from yoghurt spiced with saffron, cardomon, nuts and candied fruit. *Gharis* are another rich sweet made of milk, clarified butter and dried fruits — it's another speciality of Surat. In summer *am rasis* is a popular

Gujarat

mango juice drink.

THINGS TO BUY

With its busy modern textile works it's not surprising that Gujurat has a number of interesting buys in this line. At the top end of this field there are the extremely fine, and often extremely expensive, Patola silk saris still made by a handful of master craftsmen in Patan. From Surat comes the zari or gold thread embroidery work. Surat is also a centre for silk saris. At a more mundane, but still beautiful, level there are the block prints of Ahmedabad where you will also find hand painted cloths in the traditional black, red, maroon and ochre colours. Look for

them at Madhupura Rani-no-Hajiro on Mirzapur Rd, near the Ahmedabad GPO.

Jamnagar is famous for its tie-dye work which you'll find in the bazaar shops in Jamnagar and other centres in Saurashtra. Brightly coloured peasant embroideries and bead work are also found in Saurashtra, along with woollen shawls, blankets and rugs while brass covered wooden chests are manufactured in Bhavnagar. In Kutch embroidered stuffed toys are made. Finally in Ahmedabad there are antique shops with wooden carvings such as window frames, shutters or doorways from old houses. In Ahmedabad you'll find most Gujurati handicrafts displayed at Handloom House or Gurjari, both on Ashram Rd.

FESTIVALS & FAIRS

Gujurat has a busy calendar of events. Some of the main ones include:

January — Makar Sankranti An end of winter festival celebrated with kite flying contests.

January/February — Muharram Tazias, large replicas of the tombs of two Moslem martyrs are paraded in the evening, particularly in Surat, Junagadh and Ahmedabad.

September/October — Navaratri Nine nights of music and dancing celebrate this festival of the mother Goddess Amba. The Dandiya Ras, which Lord Krishna danced with his milkmaids or gopis, is featured. Champaner celebrates this festival with particular fervour.

October — Dussehra The 10th day of Navaratri culminates in the celebration of Rama's victory over the evil Ravana in the Ramayana.

October/November — Sharad Purnima Song and dance celebrates the end of the monsoon on the full moon night of the month of Sharad.

Gujurat has many fairs in temple towns and also in small villages. They're a chance to see religious festivals and

celebrations and also, in the villages, a shop window on to local handicrafts. Ambaji, a village 177 km north of Ahmedabad, celebrates four major festivals in the year. At the Bhavnath Fair, at the foot of Mount Girnar in the month of Magha (January/February) you have a fine chance to hear local folk music and see folk dances. The tribal Adivasi people have a major festival at Dangs near Surat — it's known as the Dangs Durbar. Lord Krishna's birthday or Janmashtamia falls in August and his temple at Dwarka is the place to be. Along the coast at Porbandar the Madhavrai Fair is held in the month of Chaitra (March/April) and celebrates Lord Krishna's elopement with Rukmini. In the same month there is a major festival at the foot of Pavagadh Hill by Champaner, near Baroda. Mahakali is the Goddess it honours. Somnath has a large fair at the full moon of Kartika Purnima in November/December. Lord Shiva, the three-eyed one or Trinetreshwar, has an important festival in his honour in Bhadrapada (August/September) in Ternetar village — a chance to see colourful local tribal costumes.

AHMEDABAD (population 1,750,000)
The principal city of Gujurat, Ahmed-abad is also one of the major industrial cities of India, it has been called the 'Manchester of the East' due to its many textile industries. Over the centuries Ahmedabad has had a number of periods of grandeur followed by decline. It was originally founded in 1411 by Ahmed Shah and in the 1600s was thought to be one of the finest cities in India. Sir Thomas Roe, the noted English ambas-sador, judged it, in 1615, to be: 'a goodly city as large as London' but in the 1700s it went through a period of decline. Its industrial strength once again raised the city up and from 1915 it became famous as the site for Gandhi's ashram and from where he launched his famous march to break the Salt Law.

Today this comparatively little vis-ited city has a number of attractions for travellers. Gandhi's Ashram at Sabarmati can be visited and there is a small museum. In the city there are some of the finest examples of Islamic archi-tecture in India and a number of other interesting buildings both religious and secular. Ahmedabad is one of the best places to study the blend of Hindu and Islamic architectural styles known as the Indo-Saracenic. The new capital of Gujurat, Gandhinagar, is 23 km from Ahmedabad. Visitors in the hot season should bear in mind the Moghul emper-or Jehangir's derisive title for Ahmed-abad: Gardabad, 'the city of dust'.

Orientation
The city sprawls across the Sabarmati River. Two main roads run back from the river to the railway station, about a km away. They are Relief Rd (Tilak Rd) and Gandhi Rd. The city walls are now virtually all demolished but some of the gates remain. The airport is off to the north-east of the city. The Gandhi Ashram is on the west bank of the Sabarmati River, to the north of the city.

Bhadra & Teen Darwaza
The ancient citadel, the Bhadra, was built by Ahmed Shah in 1411 and later named after the Goddess Bhadra, an incarnation of Kali. It is now used for government offices and is of no partic-ular interest. There is a post office in the former Palace of Azam Khan within the citadel. In front of the citadel stands the triple gateway or Teen Darwaza, from which sultans would watch processions from the palace to the Jami Masjid.

Jami Masjid
The Friday Mosque is beside Gandhi Rd, a short distance down from Teen Darwaza. This large mosque was built in 1424 by Ahmed Shah, the city's founder. There are 260 columns sup-porting the roof with its 15 cupolas but in the great earthquake of 1819 the two 'shaking' minarets lost half their height and another tremor in 1957 completed the demolition. In this early Ahmedabad mosque much of the building was made from items salvaged from demolished Hindu and Jain tem-ples. It is said that a large black slab by the main arch is actually the base of a Jain idol, buried upside down for the Moslem faithful to tread on!

Tombs of Ahmed Shah & His Queens
The Tomb of Ahmed Shah stands just outside the east gate of the Jami Masjid. His son and grandson, who did not long survive him, also have their cenotaphs in this tomb with its perfor-ated stone windows. Women are not allowed into the central chamber. Across the street is the tomb of his queens on a raised platform — it's now really a mar-ket and in very poor shape compared to Ahmed Shah's tomb.

Ahmedabad

River
Sabarmati

City Rd.

Civil Hospital Rd.

Balvantrai Rd.

Dudheshwar Rd.

Sahid Haribhai Rd.

Gandhi Br.

Kasturba G. Road

Sant S. Das Rd.

K. Vaghela Rd.

Vidyagauri Marg

Dr. Tankaria Rd.

Dr. Ambedkar Rd.

Railway Station

Nehru Br.

Sri R.C. Road

Relief Road

M. Gandhi Rd.

R. Jani Marg

Ellis Br.

Sardar Patel Rd.

Vive Kanand Rd.

M. Davanand Rd.

Pritamrai Rd.

M.B. Kadri Marg

Jamalpur Rd.

Sardar Br.

Jagganathji Rd.

Zoo

Sewage Farm Rd.

Bhakta V. Dhola Marg

Bhulabhai Park Rd.

Kankaria Lake

0   Scale   ½ km

1	Tourist Office	15	Dada Hari's Well
2	Local Bus Terminal	17	Hathee Singh Temple
3	GPO	18	Rani Rupmati Mosque
4	ITDC Hotel	19	Siddi Saiyad Mosque
5	Hotel Sabar	20	Azam Khan's Mosque
6	Cama Hotel	21	Swami Temple
7	Ritz & Ambassador Hotels	22	Jami Masjid & Market
8	Gulmarg & Esquire Hotels	23	Shaking Minarets
9	Chetak, Capri, Metropole & Plaza	24	Rani Sipri Mosque
	Hotels & Kwality Restaurant	25	Indian Airlines
10	Hotel Ashiana	26	Chetna Restaurant
11	Gokul Hotel	27	Bhadra
12	Hotel Moti Mahal	28	Teen Darwaza
13	Long Distance Bus Station	☆	Havmor Ice-Cream Bar
14	Mata Bhawani's Well	★	Gandhi Cold Drinks Bar

Sidi Saiyad's Mosque

This small mosque once formed part of the city wall, it is close to the river end of Relief Rd. Constructed by Sidi Saiyid, a slave of Ahmed Shah, it is noted for its beautiful carved stone windows in which the branches of a tree are intricately intertwined to form the complete window.

Ahmed Shah's Mosque

Dating from 1414 this was one of the earliest mosques in the city and was probably built on the site of a Hindu temple, using parts of that temple in its construction. It is located in the south-west of the Bhadra and the front of the mosque is now a garden.

Rani Rupmati's Mosque

A little north of the centre this mosque was built between 1430 and 1440 and named after the Sultan's Hindu wife. The minarets were partially brought down by the disastrous earthquake of 1819. Note how the dome is elevated to allow light in around its base. The mosque, as so many of Ahmedabad's early mosques, displays elements of Hindu and Islamic design.

Rani Sipri's Mosque

A little south-east of the centre this small mosque was built in 1514 and is also known as the Masjid-e-Nagira or 'jewel of a mosque' due to its extremely graceful and well executed design. Its slender, delicate minarets are again a blend of Hindu and Islamic styles. The mosque is said to have been built by a wife of Sultan Mehmood Begada after he executed their son for some minor misdemeanour.

Sidi Bashir Mosque — shaking minarets

A little south of the railway station, outside the Sarangpur Gate, the Sidi Bashir Mosque is famed for its shaking minarets or 'Jhulta Minar'. When one minaret is shaken the other rocks in sympathy, this was said to be a protection against earthquake damage. Unfortunately this mosque is generally closed and the opening hours posted outside appear to bear no relation to reality. The Raj Babi Mosque also had shaking minarets, one of which was dismantled by an inquisitive Englishman in an unsuccessful attempt to find out how it worked. Within the railway station area, a little to the north, are minarets lacking a mosque which was destroyed in a battle between the Moghuls and Mahrattas in 1753.

Hathee Singh Temple

Just outside the Delhi Gate, to the north of the old city, this is a Jain temple in typical style and, as so often with Jain temples, made of white marble. Built in 1848 the temple is dedicated to Dharamanath, the 15th Jina or Jain apostle.

Step Well of Dada Hari

Step wells or Baolis are a strange construction unique to Gujurat and this is one of the best. The curious well has a series of steps leading down to lower and lower platforms, eventually terminating with a small octagonal well. Built in 1499 the depths of the well are cool, even on the hottest day, and it must have been quite beautiful in its prime. Today it is completely neglected but it's an eerie, interesting place with galleries above the well and a small portico at ground level. Behind the well is the equally neglected Mosque and Tomb (Rauza) of Dada Hari. The mosque has a tree-motif like the windows of Sidi Saiyad's Mosque.

There is a second step well, that of Mat Bhawani, a couple of hundred metres north of Dada Hari's. Ask children to show you the way. It's thought to be several hundred years older and is much less ornate and is now used as a crude Hindu temple.

Kankaria Lake

South-east of the city this artificial lake was constructed in 1451 and has 34 sides, each 60 metres long. It is now a local picnic spot but was once frequented by the Emperor Jehangir and his Empress Nur Jahan. The zoo and children's park by the lake are outstanding. The Ghattamendal pavilion in the centre houses an aquarium.

Other Mosques & Temples

It's very easy to get mosque-ed out in Ahmedabad. If your enthusiasm for mosques is limited then don't go further than Sidi Saiyad's and the Jami Masjid. If you have real endurance then you could continue on to Dastur Khan's Mosque, near the Rani Sipri Mosque, Or Haibat Khan's Mosque, Saiyid Alam's Mosque, Shuja'at Khan's Mosque, Shaikh Hasan Muhammed Chisti's Mosque and Muhafiz Khan's Mosque.

Then for a complete change you could plunge into the narrow streets of the old part of town and seek out the brightly painted Swami Narayan Temple. Enclosed in a large courtyard it dates from 1850. To the south of this Hindu temple are the nine tombs known as the Nau Gaz Pir or 'Nine Yard Saints'.

Around the Town

Ahmedabad can be quite an interesting place to wander around. The bazaar streets are narrow, crowded and colourful with many houses having ornately carved wooden fronts. There are Jain bird-feeding places known as 'parabdis' in many streets. Children catch pigeons then release them just for fun. The older parts of the city are divided into totally separate areas known as 'pols'. It's easy to get lost! Across the river there are many more modern buildings including the Ahmedabad Mill Owner's Association building and the museum both designed by Le Corbusier who also had a hand in the new capital of Gandhinagar. There's little evidence of the British period in Ahmedabad, unlike so many large cities. The chief landmarks of that era are the tall smokestacks that ring this industrial city. On the sandy bed of the Sabarmati River traditional block printed fabrics are still stretched out to dry, despite the 70-plus large textile mills. The river dries up to a mere trickle in the hot season.

Other places of interest in and around the town include the ruined tomb of Darya Khan (1453) north-west of the Hathee Singh Temple. It has a particularly large dome. Near it is the Chhota Shahi Bagh and across the railway line is the Shahi Bagh. Ladies of the harem used to live in the chhota (small) garden. In Saraspur, east of the railway line, the

Temple of Chintaman is a Jain temple originally constructed in 1638 but converted by Aurangzeb into a mosque.

Museums

Ahmedabad has a number of museums including the Calico Museum of Textiles (tel 5100) which has a display of antique and modern textiles including rare tapestries, wall hangings and costumes and displays of old weaving machines. It is open 8.30 to 10.30 am from April to June and from July to March it is open 11 am to 12 noon and 3 to 5 pm. Admission is free. The N C Mehta Museum of Miniatures (tel 78369) is at Sanskar Kendra, Paldi and has an excellent exhibit of the various schools of Indian miniature paintings. It is open 9 to 11 am and 4 to 7 pm, daily except Mondays. The building was designed by Le Corbusier.

There is also the Shreyas Folk Museum with exhibits of the folk arts and crafts of Gujarat, the National Institute of Design, the Tribal Research and Training Institute Museum and a Philatelic Museum. The Institute of Indology on the university campus (tel 78295) has an important collection of illustrated manuscripts and miniatures and one of the finest collections relating to Jainism in India. It is open from 11.30 am to 5.30 pm weekdays, 11.20 am to 2.30 pm on Saturdays, closed Sundays. Admission is free.

Sabarmati Ashram

Situated six km from the centre of town, on the west bank of the Sabarmati River, this was Gandhi's headquarters during his long struggle for Indian independence. His ashram was founded in 1918 and still makes handicrafts, hand-made paper and spinning wheels. Gandhi's spartan living quarters are preserved as a small museum and there is a pictorial exhibit of the major events in his life. On Sundays, Tuesdays, Thursdays and Saturday evenings there is a son et lumiere show in English at 8.15 pm. There is a small admission fee for this performance.

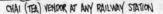

CHAI (TEA) VENDOR AT ANY RAILWAY STATION

Tours

There are tours operated from the Lal Darwaza bus stand each day which cost Rs 8. The Tourism Corporation of Gujarat have a Rs 25 tour each Sunday which departs at 8 am and returns at 2.15 pm and includes the Gandhi Ashram, the Adalaj Vav step-well and the Calico Museum of Textiles and Shreyas Folk Museum. They also have longer (four or five days) tours around north Gujarat, south Gujarat and Saurashtra.

Places to Stay — Top End

The *Cama Hotel* (tel 25281-85) is on Khanpur Rd, centrally located and pleasantly situated overlooking the river. Singles/doubles, air-con, are Rs 175/350. It's got a good restaurant (excellent breakfast) and is probably the best top end place in Ahmedabad. Out of town at the Kandla Highway Crossing on Narol Rd is the *Hotel Ahmedabad International* (tel 87282) with rooms at slightly lower rates.

There are a number of other upper notch places close to the Cama Hotel and the river. The *Ritz Hotel* (tel 24373-75) is pleasantly secluded in a garden well back from the road. Singles/doubles are Rs 85/130, all with attached bath and air-conditioning. Almost next door to it is the *Hotel Ambassador*.

Moving away from the river there is the *Hotel Capri* (tel 24643-44) on Relief Rd almost next door to the Kwality Restaurant. Singles/doubles cost Rs 60/100 without air-con, Rs 90/140 with it. Opposite Piramshah Roza, near the Regal Cinema on Pankore Nama, is the 'Indian-modern' *Gokul Hotel* (tel 38 2770-80) with singles/doubles at Rs 100/150, all with air-conditioning. The *Hotel Kingsway* near the Relief Cinema (tel 26806-07) spans the middle to upper bracket with singles from Rs 50-80 and doubles at Rs 80-120. There are rooms with and without air-conditioning. Or there's the *Hotel Capital* at

Chandanwadi, Mirzapur (tel 26396-97) where again there are air-con and non air-con rooms and prices range from around Rs 40 to Rs 120.

Across the river on Ashram Rd is the *Hotel Nataraj* (tel 44 8647-48) with singles/doubles at Rs 150/175. Again all rooms are air-con. On the same road is the new *Hotel Karnavati Ashok* (tel 76351) with singles/doubles from Rs 160/250 and up. Note that top end places may charge a 10% luxury tax on top of a 10% service tax.

Places to Stay — the bottom end

If you don't mind being out of town a bit there's the modern *Gandhi Ashram Guest House* at the Sabarmati Ashram, close to the river. There are just nine rooms (so it's wise to book ahead) each with attached bath and balcony. Singles/doubles are Rs 25/50, phone 86 7652 or contact the tourist office, 44 9683.

Other cheap hotels are scattered, mainly around the centre. There's nothing very special or any great bargains to be found. Right behind the big Capri Hotel and the Kwality Restaurant on Relief Rd is the *Plaza Hotel* where singles/doubles with attached bathroom are Rs 25/40. Habitable but little more. Close by in these small alleys off Relief Rd are the *Chetak Hotel* (Rs 30/50) and the *Metropole Hotel* (Rs 35/60).

The *Hotel Ashiana* is also central, doubles cost Rs 25 without bath, Rs 35 with, it's very basic. The *Hotel Sabar* is just beyond the Cama, but back from the river and has doubles at Rs 40 to Rs 75 with air-con. Good food too in this quieter location. Behind the Bhadra citadel, right next to the Ahmed Khan Mosque, is the *Hotel Natraj* with singles/doubles at Rs 25/35. It's a modern building, close to the centre but fairly quiet — it's also close to the Lal Darwaja bus station.

For emergencies more than anything there's the *Alankar Hotel* at Kapasia Bazaar near the railway station. There are many other hotels (like the *Hotel Moti Mahal*) close to the railway station and railway retiring rooms at Rs 15 single, Rs 20 double. Or the *Hotel Gulmarg* and *Hotel Esquire* both in Lal Darwaza, near the river end of Relief Rd. Both relatively expensive and the Gulmarg is also rather drear.

Places to Eat
A number of hotels, like the *Cama Hotel*, have pleasant dining rooms, often with air-con, a near necessity in the hot weather. On Relief Rd there's a *Kwality Restaurant*, it's one of the better class Kwalitys with an extensive English-Chinese-Indian menu. Further down the road, on the opposite side, is a *Havmor* ice cream parlour where, apart from good quality ice cream, you can also get snacks and cold, flavoured milk. There are a number of clean milk bars where you can get bottles of (curiously) flavoured milk. Very close to the Teen Darwaza Gate is the tiny *Gandhi Cold Drinks Bar* with more good ice cream and cold drinks.

Ahmedabad is, of course, a good place to sample a Gujurati thali, see the Gujurat food section. One of the best thali specialities in Ahmedabad is the *Chetna Restaurant* on Relief Rd where you may have to queue to get in for its Rs 8, all-you-can-eat thali. It can be a little hard to locate since the sign is not in English but it almost adjoins Krishna Talkies (well their sign is not in English either) and is directly across the road from the Oriental Building. Other good places for a thali include the *Hotel Sabar* where the thali costs about Rs 10 and for Rs 3 you can follow it up with fruit salad for dessert. More expensive at the flashy *Gokul Hotel* where a thali costs Rs 12 and dessert is Rs 4.

Getting There
Ahmedabad is not on the main broad gauge line between Delhi and Bombay although there is a broad gauge line running south to Bombay and a metre gauge line runs north to Delhi via the major towns of Rajasthan. Delhi-Ahmedabad is 939 km and takes nearly 24 hours except for the twice weekly Sarvodhya Express which only takes 17 hours but this train takes the broad gauge line from Delhi via Kota and Ratlam to Baroda then turns north to Ahmedabad. Fares between Delhi and Ahmedabad are approximately Rs 47 second class, Rs 180 first class.

There are plenty of daily trains between Ahmedabad and Bombay, the 491 km trip takes 10 to 15 hours with the fastest mail trains making the trip in around nine hours. Fares are around Rs 27 second class, Rs 104 first class. The Delhi trains taking the metre gauge line north will get you to Abu Road in about five hours (186 km), to Ajmer in 12 hours (491 km), and to Jaipur in 15 hours (626 km).

Indian Airlines have a daily Delhi-Ahmedabad flight which takes one hour 15 minutes and costs Rs 390. There are two daily flights Bombay-Ahmedabad which take 50 minutes to one hour 35 minutes depending on the aircraft. Fare is Rs 228.

Getting Around
There are the usual buses and taxis around Ahmedabad and hordes of reckless auto-rickshaw drivers. In Ahmedabad's frantic traffic conditions venturing out in an auto-rickshaw is a nerve shattering experience. On the plus side the auto-rickshaw wallahs use their meters 100% and without argument. Admittedly the meters are now reading less than one third of the correct fare but they do use them.

OUTSIDE OF AHMEDABAD
Sarkhej

Only eight km out of Ahmedabad the suburb of Sarkhej is noted for its elegant group of buildings. They're possibly the finest group of buildings in Ahmedabad. The architecture here is interesting in that the style is almost purely Hindu, with little evidence of the Saracenic influence felt so strongly in Ahmedabad. The buildings include the Mausoleum of Azam and Mu'azzam — built in 1457 they are the brothers who were responsible for Sarkhej's architecture. As you enter Sarkhej you pass the Mausoleum of Mahmud Begara and, beside the tank and connected to his tomb, that of his queen, Rajabai (1460). Also by the tank is the tomb of Ahmad Khattu Gaj Buksh, a renowned Moslem saint and spiritual adviser of Ahmed Shah. The saint is said to have died in 1445 at the age of 111. Next to this is the fine mosque — 'the perfection of elegant simplicity'. Like the other buildings it is notable for the complete absence of arches, a distinct feature of Moslem architecture. Also around the tank is the palace with pavilions and a harem. The Dutch established a factory in Sarkhej in 1620 due to the indigo grown here.

Batwa

South-east of Ahmedabad, the suburb of Batwa has tombs of a noted Moslem saint (himself the son of another saint) and the saint's son. Batwa also has an important mosque.

Adalaj Vav

Situated 19 km north of Ahmedabad this is one of the finest of the Gujarati step wells or baolis. Built by Queen Rudabai in 1499 it provided a cool and secluded retreat during the hot summer months.

Cambay

The old sea port of Ahmedabad is sit-uated to the south-west, at the northern end of the Gulf of Cambay. At the height of Moslem power in Gujarat the entire region was known as Cambay and when, in 1583, the first ambassadors arrived from England they bore letters from Queen Elizabeth addressed to Akbar, the 'King of Cambay'. The Dutch and Portuguese had established factories in the port before the British arrived but the rise of Surat eclipsed Cambay and when its port silted up the city's decline was inevitable.

Nal Sarovar

From November to February this 116 square km lake is home for vast flocks of indigenous and migratory birds. Particularly early in the morning and in the evening you may see ducks, geese, pelicans and flamingos. There is a Holiday Home with accommodation near the lake, it has to be booked through the tourist office in Ahmedabad.

Lothal

About 80 km south of Ahmedabad, towards Bhavnagar, this site is of great interest to archaeologists as the city which stood here, 4500 years ago, was clearly closely related to the Indus Valley cities of Moenjodaro and Harappa — both in Pakistan. It has the same neatly laid out street pattern, the same carefully assembled brickwork and the same scientific drainage system. The name Lothal actually means 'mound of the dead' in Gujurati, just as Moenjodaro does in Sindhi. At its peak this was probably one of the most important ports on the sub-continent and trade was possibly carried on with the civilisations of Mesopotamia, Egypt and Persia.

Getting There Lothal is a day trip from Ahmedabad. You can reach it by rail, disembarking at Bhurkhi on the Ahmedabad-Bhavnagar railway line, from where you can walk or take a bus. Or you can bus there straight from Ahmedabad.

Places to Stay Cheap accommodation is available at the *Tourist Centre*.

Modhera

The ruined Sun Temple of Modhera was built by King Bhimdev I (1026-27) and bears some relationship to the later, and far better known, Sun Temple of Konorak in the state of Orissa. Like that temple it was designed so that the sun shone on the image of Surya, the Sun God, at dawn at the time of the equinoxes. The main hall and shrine is reached through a pillared porch. The exterior of this fine temple is intricately and delicately carved. As at Somnath it was Mahmud of Ghazni who did the ruining.

Getting There Modhera is 106 km north-west of Ahmedabad. There are buses direct to Modhera or you can take the train to Mehsana from where buses make the 40 km trip to Modhera.

Unjha

A little north of Mehsana, the station for visits to the Modhera Temple, the town of Unjha is interesting for the marriage customs of the Kadwakanbis who live in this region. Marriages occur only once every 11 years and on that day every unmarried girl over 40 days old must be wed — if no husband can be found a proxy wedding takes place and the bride immediately becomes a 'widow' and later remarries when a suitable husband shows up. Further north again is Sidhpur with the very fragmented ruins of an ancient temple. This region was once an important centre for growing opium poppies.

Patan

Situated about 120 km north-west of Ahmedabad, this was an ancient Hindu capital before being sacked by Mahmud of Ghazni in 1024. Now a pale shadow of its former glory it still has over 100 Jain temples and is a centre for the manufacture of beautifully designed Patola silk saris. There's another step well here.

Getting There Patan is 25 km north-west of the Mehsana railway station which also serves as a jumping off point for Modhera.

GANDHINAGAR (population 25,000)

The old state of Bombay was split into Maharashtra and Gujurat in 1960 and a new capital was planned for the state of Gujurat. Situated on the west bank of the Sabarmati, 32 km north-east of Ahmedabad, Gandhinagar is named after Mahatma Gandhi, who was born in Gujurat. It is India's second planned city, after Chandigarh, and like that city is laid out into numbered sectors. Construction of the city commenced in 1965 and the secretariat was moved there in 1970.

Places to Stay

Gandhinagar has an excellent *youth hostel* which costs Rs 5 in sector 16 and in sector 11 there is the *Pathik Ashram* government rest house. Other rest houses and guest houses are located at Pethapur and opposite Sachivalaya. The Tourist Information Centre is also at Sachivalaya (tel 2211/479-82). Buses from Ahmedabad cost Rs 1.25.

BARODA (population 500,000)

Also known as Vadodara this was the capital of the princely Gaekwad state prior to independence. Today it is a pleasant medium-sized city with some interesting museums and art galleries and a fine park. A good place for a short pause.

Orientation & Information

The railway station, bus stand and a cluster of cheaper hotels are all off to one side of the city. The tourist office is in a small, upstairs office across from the station to the left. A road runs straight out from the station, across the river by the Sayaji Bagh and into the main part of town.

Sayaji Bagh & Baroda Museum

This extensive park is a popular spot for an evening stroll and also has a small zoo. A mini-railway encircles the park. Within the park is the Baroda Museum and Art Gallery which is open 9.30 am to 4.45 pm daily, except Saturday when it opens at 10 am. Admission is 20p. The museum has a varied collection while the gallery has Moghul miniatures and also a collection of European masters. Also within the park grounds is the

relatively new planetarium where there is an English language performance at 6 pm each evening, admission is Rs 2.

Maharajah Fateh Singh Museum

A little south of the centre this royal art collection includes European works by Raphael, Titian and Murillo and exhibits of Graeco-Roman, Chinese and Japanese art as well as Indian exhibits. The museum is open 9 am to 12 noon and 3-6 pm from July to March, 4-7 pm April to June. It is closed on Mondays and admission is 75p. The museum in in the Palace grounds.

Other

The flamboyant Lakshmi Vilas Palace has a large collection of armour and sculptures but is not normally open to the public. The Naulakhi Well, a fine 'baoli' or step well, is 50 metres north of the palace. These interesting multi-level wells are unique to Gujurat. Others you may visit are the Dada Hari well in Ahmedabad and the Adalaj well just outside that city. The Railway Staff College now occupies the Pratap Vilas Palace; there are a number of other palaces in the city. The Gaekwad rulers' family vault, the Kirti Mandir, is decorated with murals by Indian artist Nandial Bose. The centre of town is built around a large artificial tank swarming with fish — vendors sell fish food to throw to them.

Tours

From the railway station, book at the tourist office opposite, there is a daily tour from Tuesdays to Saturdays departing at 2 pm and returning at 6 pm. Tour cost is Rs 5.

Places to Stay

The *Utsav Hotel* (tel 51415) on Professor Manekra Rd, near the centre, is centrally air-conditioned and has singles/doubles at Rs 100/150. It also has the Tana Restaurant. Other top end hotels include the *Express Hotel* on R C Dutt Rd (tel 67051-54) with air-con singles/doubles from Rs 125/175.

In the cheaper category there are a lot of places within walking distance of the railway station. If you head straight out from the station and take the second road right you'll find the *Laxmi Lodge* where doubles cost Rs 30. The pleasant and well kept *Apsara* is Rs 40 for small, but comfortable, doubles with attached bathroom. Across the road and a little further down is the big *Ambassador*

where singles are Rs 40 and doubles Rs 60. Finally right on the corner is the *Chandan Mahal* at Rs 50 with bath, Rs 40 without. There are other cheap hotels along this road (like the *Garden Hindu Hotel* back on the corner) or on the next street (the *Baroda Guest House*) but they're not so good.

The *Municipal Corporation Guest House*, or Pravashi Gruh, is directly opposite the railway station and has singles at Rs 20 to 25, doubles at Rs 30, 36 and 50. It's conveniently situated but rather drab and grey.

Places to Eat

The *Ambassador Hotel* is popular for its excellent Rs 6 thalis. Along the main road from the station towards the gardens and river there's a reasonable *Kwality*, good lunch-time snacks on its verandah, and a *Havmor*. The railway station has quite a good restaurant.

Getting There

Baroda is 112 km south of Ahmedabad and 419 km north of Bombay. It's on the main Bombay-Ahmedabad railway line so there are plenty of trains running through or you can go by bus. Rail fare to Bombay is Rs 23 second class, Rs 95 first class. To Ahmedabad it is Rs 8 second class, Rs 37 first class. Between Baroda and Ahmedabad you pass through Anand, a small town noted for its dairy production. At the station hordes of sellers besiege passing trains selling 75p bottles of *cold* milk. There is a daily one hour 25 minute freight connection with Bombay costing Rs 189.

BROACH (BHARUCH)

(population 100,000)

This very old town was mentioned in historical records nearly 2000 years ago. In the 1600s English and Dutch factories were established here. The fort over-looks the wide Narbada (or Narmada) River from its hilltop location and at its base is the Jami Masjid which was constructed from a Jain temple. On the riverbank, outside the city to the east, is the Temple of Bhrigu Rishi, from which the city took its name of Bhrigu-kachba, later shortened to Bharoch. Near Broach the town of Suklatirtha has a holiday home and at the nearby island of Kabirwad, in the river, there is a gigantic banyan tree which covers a hectare.

AROUND BARODA
Champaner
North-east of Baroda, 47 km along the main broad gauge railway line to Delhi, Champaner was taken by Sultan Mahmud Begara in 1484. The Jami Masjid in this city is one of the finest mosques in Gujurat and is similar in style to the Jami Masjid of Ahmedabad. The hill of Pavagadh, with its ruined fort, rises beside Champaner, in three stages. In 1553 the Moghuls, led by Humayan himself who scaled the fort walls with the use of iron spikes driven into the rocks, took the fort and its city. Parts of the massive fort walls still stand. There are

SURAT (population 500,000)
Standing on the banks of the River Tapti this was once one of the major ports and trading towns of western India and 200 years ago had a population greater than it does today and was far more important than Bombay. In the 12th century Parsis first settled in Surat; they had earlier been centred 100 km south in Sanjan, where they had fled from Persia five centuries before. In 1573 the city fell to Akbar after a prolonged siege and soon became an important Moghul trading port and also the departure point for Moslem pilgrims bound for Mecca.

Surat soon became a wealthy city and in 1612 the British established a trading factory in Surat followed by the Dutch in 1616 and the French in 1664. Portuguese power on the west

two important festivals held here each year. The name Pavagodh means 'quarter of a hill' and is said to indicate that the hill is actually a chunk of the Himalayan mountainside which the monkey God Hanuman carted off to Lanka in an episode of the Ramayana.

Places to Stay Champaner has a Holiday Home with singles and doubles and dormitories.

Dabhoi Fort
The 13th century fort of Dabhoi is 29 km south-east of Baroda. It is a fine example of Hindu military architecture and noted for the design of its four gateways — particularly the Hira or Diamond Gate.

Dakor
Equidistant from Baroda and Ahmedabad the temple of Ranchodrai in this town is sacred to Lord Krishna and is a major centre for the Sharad Purnima festival in October or November.

coast had been severely curtailed by a crashing naval defeat at the hands of the British in 1615. This was the first British settlement in India. In 1664 Moghul power and prestige suffered a severe blow when the Mahratta leader Shivaji sacked the town. In a classic display of British stiff upper lip Sir George Oxenden, sent a message to Shivaji, from the strongly defended English Factory, that he should 'save the labour of his servants running to and fro on messages and come himself with all his army'. Perhaps Shivaji took him seriously because the English Factory was not attacked.

Although the English Factory later transferred its 'Presidency' to Bombay, Surat continued to prosper and in 1720 a dock was built followed by two British shipyards. In 1759, by which time

Moghul power was long past its prime, the British virtually took full control over the ruler of the city and by 1800 the city was in British hands. Today Surat is no longer of any importance as a port but it is an important manufacturing town with a major textile industry.

Orientation

An eight km long wall encircled Surat on its land side while the Tapti River forms the other side. Until the sack of the city by Shivaji the walls were made of mud but they were then reconstructed in brick. The railway station, with many cheaper hotels in its immediate vicinity, is connected to the old fort beside the river by one of Surat's few wide roads.

Castle

Built in 1546 the castle is beside the Tapti Bridge on the river bank. It is of no great interest today since most of it is given over to offices but there is a good view over the city and river from the bastions. Ask for the Tapti Bridge if you want to get to it.

Factories

Without a guide you would have difficulty finding the remains of the factories and in any case there is little to indicate their former importance. They are near the IP Missin High School. The English Factory is about midway from the castle to the Kataragama Gate out of the old city. Standing close to the river the Portuguese Factory, French Lodge and Persian Factory were also close by. From the river bank you can see the Tapti Bridge to your left and across the river to your right you'll see the mosque studded suburb of Rander. There's a small temple to Hanuman by the river.

Cemeteries

Just beyond the Kataragama Gate, to the right of the main road, is the now very run down, overrun and neglected English Cemetery. Note how many of the tombstones are for children under five years of age. As you enter the cemetery the huge mausoleum to the right is of Sir George Oxenden who died in 1669. The structure is actually a tomb within a tomb since his brother was buried here 10 years earlier then a larger mausoleum constructed over that tomb. Another large tomb next to it is said to be that of Gerald Aungier, the next President of the English Factory. Like any scrap of waste ground in India the English Cemetery has become a public toilet and the imposing mausoleums are in a sorry state. Backtrack towards the city and about half a km after the Kataragama Gate, and a hundred or so metres off the road to the left (to the right if you're coming out from the centre) is the Dutch Cemetery. The mausoleum of Baron Adriaan van Reede, who died in 1691, is a massive structure and at one time was decorated with frescoes and wood carvings. Note the inscription on the wall where 'Souratta' rates capital letters while lesser 'bombai' is in lower case. Adjoining the Dutch Cemetery is the Armenian Cemetery.

Other

Surat has a number of mosques and Jain, Hindu and Parsi temples. Cotton, silk and the manufacture of bangles are important industries in Surat. The nearby town of Rander, five km across the Hope Bridge, was built on the site of a very ancient Hindu city after it had been taken by the Moslems in 1225. Swally (Suvali) was the old port for Surat, situated 19 km to the west. It was off Swally, in 1615, that Portuguese colonial aspirations in India were ended by the British navy.

Places to Stay

Surat's numero uno hotel is a km or two away from the railway station on top of the textile market. The *Tex Palazza Hotel* (tel 20301-10) is on the Ring Rd and has rooms from Rs 50/100 singles/ doubles without air-con to Rs 75/125 with air-con. Breakfast is an extra Rs 10 per person.

There are lots of hotels near the railway station but no standouts. They're all within reasonable walking distance. In the basic cheapie bracket the *Subras* has dorm beds at Rs 6 and cell-like singles/doubles at Rs 12/20 with common bath and Rs 16/30 with attached bath. The next door *Rupali* is Rs 4 (dorm), Rs 10 (single) and Rs 25 (double with bath) but it's a grubby little place.

The *Central* is slightly higher class as is the pleasant enough *Hotel Dreamland* (singles Rs 25, doubles Rs 45-55) — the Rs 10 difference gets you a carpet on the floor! Close by are two basic cheapies — the *Hotel Ashoka* and the *Simla Guest House* — the latter has doubles at Rs 20, fair value and reasonably clean.

Just a bit further down is the *Hotel Anisha* with singles from Rs 20 to Rs 65 and doubles from Rs 30 to Rs 80 with

common bath, attached bath or air-con. Again in reasonable order but expensive for what it is. The *Satkar* would be better value if it was better kept and less grubby — doubles at Rs 30 or Rs 40 with common bath and Rs 65 with bath and air-con. It's on the sixth floor and rooms are quite reasonable. Surat bottom end hotels offer no real bargains.

Places to Eat

The *Tex Palazzo Hotel* also boasts India's first revolving restaurant and like so many revolving restaurants around the world the food takes a distant second place to the view. At least it's not outrageously expensive — say Rs 30 for a complete meal including dessert and tea or coffee. But the splendours of Surat unfold below you through windows nearly as grubby and dirty as those on the average Indian bus! In fact it's rather the way you'd imagine an Indian revolving restaurant to be. The ride to the top costs Rs 1.

Back at ground level you can get a Gujurati thali for Rs 7 in the same hotel. You pay a similar price in the good air-con restaurant upstairs in the otherwise rather grotty *Subrasa Hotel* near the railway station. Downstairs the thalis are cheaper but you pay extra for second helpings.

AROUND SURAT

There are a number of beaches near Surat. Only 16 km out, Dumas is a popular health resort. Hajira is 28 km from the city, Ubhrat is 42 km out while Tithal is 108 km away and only five km from Valsad on the Bombay-Baroda rail line. Navsari, 29 km south of Surat, has been a headquarters for the Parsi community since the earliest days of their settlement in India. Udvada, which is only 10 km north of Vapi, the station for Daman, has the oldest Parsi sacred fire in India. It is said that the fire was brought from Persia to Diu, on the opposite coast of the Gulf of Cambay, in 700 AD. Sanjan, in the extreme south of the state, is the small port where they first landed. A pillar marks the spot.

DAMAN

Right in the south of Gujurat the tiny enclave of Daman was, along with Diu, taken from the Portuguese at the same time as Goa. It is still, officially, governed from Goa along with Diu. Its main function in Gujurat seems to be as a place to get a drink since Gujurat is completely 'dry'. Lots of 'Finest scotch whisky — Made in India'! The streets of Daman are lined with bars!

The Portuguese seized Daman, which totals 380 square km in area, in 1531 and were officially ceded the region by Bahadur Shah of Gujurat in 1559. There is still some Portuguese flavour to the town with a fine old fort and a number of churches and other imposing Portuguese buildings. The town is split in two by the Damao Ganga River. A ferry shuttles back and forth for 10p and a bridge is under slow construction. The northern part of the town, with the hotels, restaurants, bars and so on is known as 'little' Daman while the southern part, with government buildings and churches, all enclosed within an imposing wall, is known as 'big' Daman. Although Daman is, like Goa, beside the sea, its beaches bear no relation to those glowing, golden stretches further south. Daman's beaches are grey, drab, dirty and dismal — quite apart from their function as the local toilet.

Places to Stay

The *PWD Rest House* is very well kept and rooms at Rs 6 are a great bargain, but it is often full up. Right across the road is the *Brighton Hotel* which is a reasonable second best with rooms from Rs 15 to Rs 20 but this too is often full. A little further back up the road from the beach the *Sovereign Hotel* is big and also well kept with rooms at a variety of prices from Rs 15, Rs 20 and up. Some of them are rather cubicle like but there is also a popular upstairs restaurant — a good place for a beer on the verandah. Back beyond the taxi stand the *Hotel Tourist* is a dump to avoid — a newish building but totally neglected and miserable at Rs 12 per person. Daman has lots of bars but not a great variety of places to eat.

Getting There

Vapi Station on the main railway line is the jumping off point for Daman. Vapi is about 170 km from Bombay and 90 km from Surat. Take care, not all trains stop at Vapi so be very certain yours will be halting there or you'll sail straight by (as we did — Tony). From Vapi it's 10 or so km into Daman and there are plenty of share taxis at Rs 2 per person. Or buses at less than Rs 1.

SAPUTARA

In the south-east corner of the state this cool hill resort stands at 1000 metres and is a popular base for excursions to the Mahal Bardipara forest wildlife sanctuary 60 kms away or to the Gira waterfalls, 52 km distant. Saputara

means 'abode of serpents' and there is a sacred snake image on the banks of the river Sarpagana.

Places to Stay

Saputara has a variety of *Holiday Homes* and *Tourist Bungalows*.

SAURASHTRA

The often bleak plains of the Kathiawar Peninsula are inhabited by colourful and friendly, but reserved, people. It's a pleasant area to travel around and there is an extensive network of metre gauge railway lines to make that travel much easier. The peninsula took its name from the Kathi tribespeople who used to roam the area stealing whatever was not locked into the many village forts or *kots* at night. You may notice, around Kathiawar, long lines of memorial stones known as *palias* — men are usually shown riding on large horses while women ride on wheels, which shows that they were in carriages.

The Bhavnagar lock gate keeps ships afloat during low tides in the city's port.

Places to Stay

Bhavnagar has two better hotels, both with air-con rooms. They are the *Apollo Hotel* (tel 5251-52) opposite the Central Bus Stand and the *Hotel Takte-Khurshid* (tel 6881) on Waghawadi Rd, near Takhteshwara. Other basic hotels include the *Evergreen Guest House* (tel 4605), the *Kashmir Hotel* near the Pathik Ashram and the *Geeta Lodging & Boarding* (tel 3985). Bhavnagar also has the *Pathik Ashram* with rooms from around Rs 15 and railway retiring rooms. The *Mahavir Lodge*, near the station, has good thalis for Rs 4.

Getting There

Bhavnagar is 244 km by road from Ahmedabad or about 270 km by rail. The rail trip takes about seven hours and costs Rs 16 second class, Rs 70 first class. There are also buses connecting Bhavnagar with Ahmedabad and other centres in the region. There's a daily flight connection with Bombay which costs Rs 169.

BHAVNAGAR (population 250,000)

Founded as a port in 1723, Bhavnagar is still an important trading post for the cotton goods manufactured in Gujurat. The Gandhi Smriti is a library, small museum, gallery and memorial to the founder of India. Bhavnagar also has the Gaurishankar Lake, a popular picnic spot, and the Takhteshwar Temple with fine views from its hilltop location.

PALITANA

Situated 56 km from Bhavnagar, the town of Palitana is merely a gateway to Shatrunjaya, the 'place of victory'. From the town you have a two km walk, ascending 600 metres to the hilltop where, over a period of 900

years, 863 temples have been constructed. The hilltop is dedicated entirely to the Gods, at dusk even the priests depart from the temples and leave them deserted.

Almost all the temples are Jain and this hill, one of the holiest pilgrimage places for Jains, is another indication of the merit Jains believe is derived from constructing temples. The hilltops are bounded by a sturdy wall and the temples are grouped into nine enclosures or *tuks* — each with a central major temple and many minor ones clustered around. Some of the earliest temples were built here in the 11th century but in the 14th and 15th centuries those spoilsport Moslems knocked them down so the current temples date from the 1500s down to the present time.

The hilltop affords a very fine view in all directions, on a clear day you can see the Gulf of Cambay beyond Bhavnagar. The most notable of the temples is that to Shri Adishwara, the first Jain Tirthankar. Note the frieze of dragons around the temple. Adjacent to this temple is the Moslem shrine of Angar Pir, women wanting children make offers of miniature cradles at this shrine. Built in 1618 by a wealthy Jain merchant the Chaumukh, or 'four faced' shrine, has images of Adinath facing out in the four cardinal directions. Other important temples are those to Kumar Pal, Sampriti Raj and Vimal Shah. The marble temples are so thick on the hill summit that it looks like some giant, glistening white wedding cake from a distance. The temples are open 7 am to 7 pm. Temple jewels are shown at 9 am and 3 pm.

Valabhipur

North of Palitana this ancient city was once the capital of this part of India. Extensive ruins have been located and archaeological finds exhibited in a museum but there's little to see apart from scattered stones.

Places to Stay

Palitana has the Gujurat Tourism Corporation's *Hotel Sumeru* on Station Rd. There are rooms at Rs 25 single, Rs 40 double and also a dormitory at Rs 8. Vegetarian food is available in the restaurant. There is also the *Readymoney Guest House*.

DIU

Like Daman this tiny ex-Portuguese enclave is not governed as part of Gujurat but is treated as part of the Goa-Daman-Diu group. Diu is an island, about 11 km long by three km wide, separated from the coast by a narrow channel. You reach Diu through the town of Una. The island has a beautiful, if tiny, bazaar and a huge fort, constructed by the Portuguese in 1536, at the eastern end. Diu was once an opium exporting centre. Like Goa and Daman it was taken by India in 1961. You can hire bicycles to get around this restful little place.

Places to Stay

There's a *PWD Rest House* at Rs 6 a single (good vegetarian meals at Rs 4).

JUNAGADH (population 100,000)

Few travellers make the trip out to Junagadh but it's an interesting town in itself and is situated right at the base of the temple studded Girnar Hill. Junagadh is also the jumping off point for visits to the Gir Forest, last home of the Asian lion.

The city takes its name from the fort which enclosed the old city. The Ashokan edicts, dating from 250 BC, near the town indicate the great antiquity of this site. At the time of partition the Nawab of Junagadh opted to take his tiny state into Pakistan but the inhabitants were predominantly Hindu and the Nawab soon found himself in exile.

Uparkot

The old fort, from which the city derived its name, stands on the eastern side of Junagadh. It is very old and has been rebuilt and extended many times in its history. In places the fort walls are 20 metres high and the fort is entered by an ornate triple gateway. Inside there is a mosque, the Jami Masjid, built from a demolished Hindu temple. Other points of interest in the fort include the Tomb of Nuri Shah and two fine wells known as the Adi Chadi and the Naughan. The Adi Chadi was named after two slave girls who fetched water from it. The Naughan is reached by a magnificent circular staircase. Close to the mosque there are also some very old Buddhist caves, thought to be more than 1500 years old, cut into the hillside. The double-storey cave has six pillars with very fine carvings. There are other caves in Junagadh including some thought to date back to the time of Ashoka. The soft rock on which Junagadh is built encouraged the construction of caves and wells.

Maqbara

The mausoleums of the Nawabs of Junagadh are interesting and in the Durbar Hall and Sileh Khana of the Palace, weapons and armour from the Nawabs are displayed.

Other

Junagadh's zoo in the Sakar Bagh has Gir lions, should you be unable to visit the Gir Forest. The garden also has a fine museum. Junagadh has a number of other lovely gardens. Narsi Mehta, a Gujurati 'poet-saint', has a shrine in the city.

Ashoka Edicts

On the way to the Girnar Hill temples you pass a huge boulder on which the Emperor Ashoka inscribed 14 edicts around 250 BC. His inscription is in the Pali script. Later inscriptions were added in Sanskrit around 150 AD and 454 AD. The latter was made by Skandagupta, the last emperor of the Mauryas.

Girnar Hill

It's a 600 metre ascent, up 2000 stone steps, to the 1118 metre high summit of Girnar. Like Palitana the temple topped hill is of great significance to the Jains. The sacred tank of Damodar Kund marks the start of the climb to the temples. The path ascends through a wood to the marble temples near the summit. Five of them are Jain temples, including the largest and oldest of them — the 12th century temple of Neminath, the 22nd Jain Tirthankar. There is a large black image of Neminath in the central shrine and many smaller images around the temple. Nearby is the triple temple of Mallinath, the 19th Tirthankar, which was erected by two brothers in 1177. During festivals this temple is a favourite gathering place for sadhus. A great fair is held here during the Kartika Purnima festival in November or December. On top of the peak is the temple of Amba Mata, where newly weds are supposed to worship at the shrine of the Goddess in order to ensure a happy marriage.

Information

The tourist office is beside the Durbar Hall museum.

Places to Stay

Junagadh has railway retiring rooms and a number of rather basic hotels such as *Sharada Lodge* where there is a dormitory (Rs 4) as well as rooms from Rs 10. Other places include the *Jai Shri Guest House* and the *Tourist Guest House*. *Sharada Lodge*, which is only a couple of hundred metres from the railway station, offers big, filling meals.

Getting There

Bhavnagar is 269 km from Ahmedabad, trains take about 10 hours. There is a daily flight from Bombay to Keshod, 47 km from Junagadh. The flight takes one hour and 20 minutes and the fare is Rs 195.

AROUND JUNAGADH

Chorvad

On the coast, 70 km from Junagadh and just 20 km from Veraval, Chorvad is a popular beach resort. This was the site of the summer palace of the Junagadh Nawabs and it has now been converted into a guest house.

Somnath

The Temple of Somnath, at Somnath Patan which is near Veraval and about 80 km from Junagadh, has had an extremely chequered history. The earliest history of the temple fades into legend. It was said to have been originally built by Somraj, the Moon God himself, out of gold, only to be rebuilt by Ravana in silver, then by Krishna in wood, then by Bhimdev in stone. What is more certain is that a description of the temple by Al Biruni, an Arab traveller, was so glowing that it prompted a visit in 1024 by a most unwelcome tourist — Mahmud of Ghazni. At that time the temple was so wealthy that it had 300 musicians, 500 dancing girls and even 300 barbers simply to shave the heads of visiting pilgrims.

Mahmud of Ghazni, who was to gain quite a reputation for his raids on the riches of India from his Afghan kingdom, descended on Somnath and after a two day battle took the town and temple and after carting off its fabulous wealth destroyed it for good measure. He started a tradition of Moslems destroying the temple and Hindus rebuilding it for in the following centuries it was razed again in 1297, 1394 and finally in 1706 by Aurangzeb, that notorious Moghul spoilsport. It was rebuilt in 1169 after Mahmud's visit and again in 1325 and soon after 1394. But after the 1706 demolition it was not finally rebuilt until 1950.

The current temple was built to traditional patterns on the original site by the sea. The temple is one of the 12 most sacred Shiva shrines, or Jyotirlingas, in India. Remains of the old temple are in a museum. There's a simple dining hall in the temple compound, north of the main gate, where you can get lunch.

Other Somnath Sites

The town of Somnath Patan is entered by the Junagadh Gate from Veraval. This was the gate through which Mahmud finally broke through to take the town and the triple gate is very ancient. Close to the second gate is an old mosque dating from Mahmud's time. The Jami Masjid, reached through the town's picturesque bazaar, was constructed using parts of a Hindu temple and has interesting Bo tree carvings at the four corners. It is now a museum with a collection from many of the temples. About a km before the Junagadh Gate, coming from Veraval, is the finely carved Mai Puri which was once a Temple of the Sun. This Hindu temple was converted into a mosque during Mahmud's time and there are thousands of tombs and palias around it. Close by are two old tombs and on the shore is the Bhidiyo Pagoda which probably dates from the 14th century.

To the east of the town is the Bhalka Tirth where Lord Krishna was mistaken for a deer (he was sleeping in a deerskin) and wounded by an arrow. The legendary spot is at the confluence of three rivers. You get to it through the small

Sangam (confluence gate) which is also known simply as the Nana (small gate). North of this sacred spot is the Temple of the Sun or Suraj Mandir which Mahmud also had a go at knocking down. This very old temple probably dates from the same time as the original Somnath Temple. Around the walls are a frieze of lions with elephants' trunks. Back inside the small gate is a temple which Ahalya Bai of Indore built as a replacement for the Somnath Temple.

Veraval

Only a few km from Somnath this was once the major seaport for Mecca pilgrims before the rise of Surat. It still has some importance as a port.

Places to Stay Veraval has a *Tourist Bungalow*. You can get good vegetarian thalis for Rs 4 in the *Hotel Shri Nivas*, near the station.

Sasan Gir Forest

The last home of the Asian lion is 54 km from Junagadh via Keshod. There are less than 200 lions left. The sanctuary covers 1400 square km and the best time to visit this dry scrubland is between October and June. Apart from the lions there are also bear, antelope, hyenas, foxes and a number of species of deer. The deer include the largest Indian antelope, the nilgai, the graceful chinkara gazelle, the chousingha and the barking deer. The tourist office in Junagadh will have details about visiting the park — you need a jeep. You can wait in Sasan in the early morning for a group to form, a jeep will cost about Rs 100 and will carry up to eight people.

Places to Stay The State Forest Department has a *Guest House* and the ITDC operates a *Forest Lodge*.

Tulsi Shyam

In the Gir Forest, 165 km from Junagadh, there is a scenic hot spring together with a temple to Bhim and a holiday home.

JAMNAGAR (population 350,000)

The princely state of Jamnagar was ruled by the Jadeja Rajputs prior to independence. The city is built around a lake with an island in the middle reached by a bridge. The Lakhota Fort on this island is a museum with a good collection of sculptures and archaeological finds from surrounding villages — particularly Ghumli in the Bardo Hills to the south. Also on the island the Kotha Bastion was an old well from which water can be drawn by blowing into a small hole in the floor. Jamnagar has two local ports, Rosy and Bedi. The town also has a long history of pearl fishing and there is a local variety of tie dyeing.

Places to Stay

There are a number of hotels along Station Rd and also the *Lal Bungalow*.

Getting There

There are direct trains from Ahmedabad, 308 km away, via Rajkot, and from Mahsena. There is a daily flight from Bombay, taking one hour and five minutes and costing Rs 254.

DWARKA

On the extreme western tip of the Kathiawar Peninsula, Dwarka is one of the four holiest Hindu pilgrimage sites and is closely connected to the Krishna legend. It was here that Krishna set up his capital after his flight from Mathura. Dwarkanath, the name of the temple, is a title of Lord Krishna. The temple is only open to Hindus, but the exterior, with its tall five storey spire supported by 60 columns, is far more interesting than the interior. Archaeological excavations have revealed five earlier cities at the site, all now submerged. Dwarka is the site for an important festival at Janmashtami which falls in August or September.

Island of Bet

A little north of Dwarka you can ferry across from Okha to the island of Bet where Vishnu is said to have slain a demon. There are modern Krishna temples on the island. There are other important religious sites around Dwarka.

Places to Stay

Dwarka has railway retiring rooms, a rest house and a number of small hotels.

Getting There

Dwarka is 145 km from Jamnagar and connected by rail.

PORBANDAR

On the south coast, about mid-way between Veraval and Dwarka, the town is today chiefly noted as the birthplace of Mahatma Gandhi. As in so many places in India there is a collection of Gandhian memorabilia in the Kirti Mandir. In ancient times the city was known as Sudamapuri after Sudama, a compatriot of Krishna, and at one time there was a flourishing trade from here to the Persian Gulf and Africa.

Places to Stay

There is a modern *Tourist Bungalow* and a number of cheap hotels.

Getting There

Porbandar is on the rail line through to Dwarka and is also connected by a daily flight from Bombay which costs Rs 234.

RAJKOT (population 350,000)

This pleasant town was once the capital of the princely state of Saurashtra and also British government headquarters. Mahatma Gandhi spent the early years of his life here while his father was the chief minister, or *Diwan*, to the Rajah of Saurashtra. Gandhi's family home from that time, the Kaba Gandhi no Delo, now houses a permanent exhibition of Gandhi items. In the Jubilee Gardens the Watson Museum and Library has exhibits relating to Saurashtra's culture.

Wankaner

Situated about 50 km from Rajkot the Royal Palace of Wankaner is now, like so many Indian palaces, a hotel and holiday resort. The regal palace has a swimming pool, museum and game reserve, not to mention the Maharana's collection of vintage cars. From here those who can afford it can make excursions to the Little Rann of Kutch or to the palace and monuments of Halvad.

Wadhwan (Surendranagar)

On the route to Rajkot from Ahmedabad this town has the very old temple of Ranik Devi who became involved in a dispute between local rulers Sidh Raja (who planned to marry her) and Rao Khengar (who carried her off and did marry her). When Sidh Raja defeated Rao Khengar she chose sati over dishonour and Sidh Raja built the temple as a memorial to her.

Places to Stay

Better class hotels in Rajkot include the *Havmor Hotel*, the *Luxury Hotel* and the *Taj Hotel*. There are a large number of cheaper places plus railway retiring rooms.

Getting There

Rajkot is 216 km from Ahmedabad and accessible by road or rail. The daily flight from Bombay takes one hour 45 minutes and costs Rs 221.

KUTCH (KACHCHH)

The western-most part of Gujurat is virtually an island, indeed during the monsoon period from May it really is an island. The Gulf of Kutch divides Kutch from the Kathiawar Peninsula while to the north Kutch is separated from the Sind region of Pakistan by the Great Rann of Kutch. This low lying marsh area is virtually completely barren due to the salt in the soil, only on scattered 'islands' which rise above the salt level is there vegetation. During the dry season the Rann is a vast expanse of hard dried mud. Then with the start of the monsoon in May it is flooded by sea water, then flooded deeper again by the fresh water from rivers as they fill up. Kutch is also separated from the rest of Gujurat to the east by the Little Rann of Kutch.

The Gulf of Kutch is a breeding ground for flamingoes and pelicans during the winter. In the Little Rann of Kutch the rare Indian wild ass roams. Because of their isolation the people of Kutch have maintained their local customs and traditions.

BHUJ (population 50,000)

The major town of Kutch, Bhuj is an old walled city — until very recently the city gates were still locked each night

from dusk to dawn! The city is connected by road with the old port of Mandvi to the south-west and by road and rail to the new port of Kandala. It is intended that Kandala should substitute for Karachi as a port for this area. There is a boat service from Kandala to Navlakhi, which is on the Kathiwar Peninsula and connected to Morvi and Wankaner by rail. Gandidham, near Kandala, is a new town which was established to take refugees from the Sind, following partition. About 150 km north-east of Bhuj the remains of an Indus Valley Civilisation fortification have been discovered.

Places to Stay

There are some simple hotels like the *Mahalaxmi Guest House* near the Government Hospital or the *Panchayat Guest House*. Plus there is a *Circuit House*.

Getting There

Bhuj is 310 km from Ahmedabad and connected by road and rail. The railway line, via Gandhidham, terminates at Bhuj. The daily Indian Airlines flight from Bombay to Jamnagar continues on to Bhuj in another 25 minutes. Fare is Rs 299 from Bombay, Rs 65 from Jamnagar.

Madhya Pradesh

Population: 46 million
Area: 442,841 square km
Capital: Bhopal
Main language: Hindi

The large state of Madhya Pradesh is the geographical heartland of India. Most of the state is a high pleateau and in summer it can be very dry and hot. The size and geographical isolation of Madhya Pradesh, historically known as Malwa, kept it relatively immune from outside invaders but virtually all the phases of Indian history have left their mark on the state. There are still many pre-Aryan Gond and Bhil tribal people in the state but Madhya Pradesh is overwhelmingly Indo-Aryan with the majority of the people speaking Hindi and following Hinduism.

The state's history goes right back to the time of Ashoka, the great Buddhist emperor whose Mauryan empire was powerful in Malwa. At Sanchi you can see the Buddhist centre founded by Ashoka, the most important reminder of Ashoka in India today. The Mauryans were followed by the Sungas and the Sungas by the Guptas before the Huns swept across the state. Around a thousand years ago the Parmaras ruled in south-west Madhya Pradesh — they're chiefly remembered for Raja Bhoj who gave his name to the city of Bhopal and also ruled over Indore and Mandu. Between 950 and 1050 AD the Chandellas constructed the fantastic series of temples at Khajuraho, in the north-east of the state. Today Khajuraho is one of India's major attractions. Between the 12th and 16th century the region saw continuing struggles between Hindu and Moslem rulers or invaders. Often the fortified city of Mandu in the southwest was the scene for these battles but finally the power of the Moghuls overcame Hindu resistance and controlled the region, only to fall to the rise of the Marathas who, in turn, were to fall to the advance of British power.

Two of Madhya Pradesh's attractions are remote and isolated — Khajuraho is off to the north-east, a long way from anywhere and most easily visited by travelling between Agra and Varanasi. Jabalpur, with its marble rocks, is in the south-east of the state and can be reached if you are travelling between the west of India and Calcutta or Orissa on the east coast. Most of the state's other attractions are on or close to main Delhi-Bombay rail line. From Agra, just outside the state to the north, you can head south through Gwalior, with its magnificent fort, Sanchi, Bhopal, Ujjain, Indore and Mandu. From there you can head east to Gujurat or south to the Ajanta and Ellora caves in Maharashtra.

GWALIOR (population 450,000)

In the extreme north-west of Madhya Pradesh, only a few hours from Agra by train or road, Gwalior is famous for its very old and very large fort. Within the fort walls there are a number of interesting temples and ruined palaces. The dramatic colourful history of the great fort certainly goes back over a thousand years.

Gwalior's legendary beginning stems from a meeting between Suraj Sen and the hermit Gwalipa, who lived on the hilltop where the fort stands. The hermit cured Suraj Sen of leprosy with a drink of water from the Suraj Kund, which still remains in the fort. Then he gave him a new name, Suhan Pal, and said his descendants would remain in power so long as they kept the name Pal. His next 83 descendants did just that but number 84 changed his name to Tej Karan and, you guessed it, goodbye kingdom.

What is more certain is that in 1398 the Tomar dynasty came to power in Gwalior and over the next several centuries Gwalior fort was a scene of continual intrigue and clashes with neighbouring powers. Man Singh, who came to power in 1486, was the greatest of these Tomar rulers but in 1516, after earlier repelling an assault by Sikander Lodi of Delhi in 1505, the fort was besieged by Ibrahim Lodi. The siege had no sooner started than Man Singh died but his son held out for a year before finally capitulating. Later the Moghuls, under Babur, took the fort and held it, despite an assault by Man Singh's grandson during the time of Akbar, until the Mahrattas took it in 1754.

For the next 50 years the fort changed hands on several occasions including being taken twice by the British. It finally passed into the hands of the Scindias although behind the scenes the British retained control. At the time of the Indian Mutiny in 1857 the Maharaja remained loyal to the British but his troops didn't and in mid-1858 the fort was the scene for some of the final, and most dramatic, events of the mutiny. It was near here that the British finally defeated Tantia Topi and it was in the final assault on the fort that the Rani of Jhansi was killed. See Jhansi for more details on this heroine of the mutiny. There is a memorial to her in Gwalior.

Information & Orientation

The Tourist Office is located in the Tourist Bungalow, about a half km west of the railway station. Old Gwalior town is off to the north of the fort which, topping the long hill to the north of the newer part of town totally dominates the area. The newer town is known as Lashkar and stands to the south-west of the fort. The railway station and the modern town is to the south-east. There are regular tempos running along the main route from the railway station to Lashkar.

Fort

You can approach the fort from the south-west or the north-east. The north-east path, starting from the Archaeological Museum, follows a wide, winding slope to the doors of the Man Singh Palace. The south-west entrance is a long gradual ascent by road, passing cliff face Jain sculptures on the climb. The climb up to the fort can be hot, sweaty work in the hot season. A taxi or autorickshaw up the south-west road is probably the easiest way in, you can then walk down from the palace to the museum when you've looked around the fort. Note that there are no refreshments available at the fort at all. Come prepared in the summer.

The fort hill rises 100 metres to less than 200 metres. The fort walls, which continue around almost the entire hilltop, are 10 metres high and impossingly solid. Beneath the walls the hill

face drops sheer away to the plains. On a clear day the view from the fort walls is superb, the crowded streets of the older part of the town, known as Lashkar, is off to the south-west while the more spacious part of the town lies to the south-east. Old Gwalior itself clings to the northern and north-eastern end of the fort hill. The view extends far out over the surrounding plains.

There are a number of things to see in and around the fort although most of the enclosed area is simply open space and fields. Entry to the fort costs 20p.

Archaeological Museum

The museum is within the Gujari Mahal palace, at the start of the north-east ascent to the fort. The palace was built in the 15th century by Man Singh for his favourite queen Mrignayani. The building is now rather deteriorated but the museum has a collection of Hindu and Jain sculptures and copies of the Bagh Caves fescoes. The museum is open 10 am to 5 pm daily, closed on Mondays, admission is just 20p.

North-East Entrance

There are a whole series of gates as you ascend the path to the Man Singh palace. At one time the path had steps in it but it has now been smoothed into one long ascent though still more suitable for feet than wheels. The first of the six gates is the Alamgiri Gate, dating from 1660. It was named after Aurangzeb who took the title of Governor of Alamgiri in this region. The second gate

dates from the same period as the Gujari Mahal and is known as the Badalgarh, after Badal Singh, Man Singh's uncle, or as the Hindola Gate after a swing or *hindol* which used to stand here. The third gate, the Bansur or archer's gate, has disappeared.

The interesting fourth gate was built in the 1400s and named after the elephant headed god Ganesh. There is a small pigeon house or Kabutar Khana here and a small four-pillared Hindu temple to the hermit Gwalipa, after whom the fort and town was named. Next you pass a Vishnu shrine dating from 876 AD known as Chatarbhujmandir, shrine of the four-armed. A tomb near here is that of a nobleman killed in an assault on this gate in 1518. From here a series of steps lead to rock cut Jain sculptures at the north-east of the fort. They are not of the same size, quality and importance as the sculptures on the south-west side. There are other Hindu sculptures along this same face.

The Hathiya Paur, or Elephant Gate, forms the entrance to the palace. Within the palace was the final gate, the Hawa Gate, but this has also been removed.

Man Singh Palace

The palace, or Man Mandir, which forms the entrance to the fort is a delightfully whimsical building, also known as the Chit Mandir, or Painted Palace, because of the tiled and painted decorations of ducks, elephants and peacocks. Painted blue, with hints of green and gold, it still looks very good today. The palace was built by Man Singh between 1486

1	Railway Station	9	Wengier's Restaurant
2	Bus Station	10	Man Mandir & Gujri Mahal
3	Indian Airlines		Museum
4	Tourist Office & Tourist Bungalow	11	Teli Ka Mandir
5	GPO	12	Tansen & Muhammad Gaus Tombs
6	Usha Kiran Hotel	13	Moti Mahal
7	Gujri Mahal Hotel	14	Palace Museum
8	Kwality Restaurant	15	Jayaji Chowk

and 1516 and repaired in 1881. The palace has four storeys, two of them underground and all of them now deserted. The subterranean ones are cool even in the summer heat and were used as prison cells during the Moghul period. The east face of the fort, with its six towers topped by domed cupolas, stands over the fort entrance path.

Other Palaces

There are a number of other palaces clustered within the fort walls at the northern end. None of them are as interesting or as well preserved as the Man Singh Palace. The Karan Palace or Kirti Mandir is a long, narrow, two storey palace on the western side. At the northern end are the Jahangiri and Shah Jahan Palaces with a very large and deep tank. The Jauhar Tank, north-west of the palaces, was named after the *jauhar*, or ritual Rajput suicide, that took place here in 1232.

Sasbahu Temples

The 'mother-in-law' and 'daughter-in-law' temples stand close to the eastern wall about mid-way along that side of the fort. The two temples are similar in style and date from the 9th to 11th centuries. The larger temple has an ornately carved base and figures of Vishnu over the entrances. Four huge pillars carry the heavy roof.

Teli-ka-mandir

On the opposite side of the fort, beyond the Suraj Kund tank, this temple probably dates from the 9th century and has a peculiar plan and design. The roof is Dravidian while the decorations, the whole temple is covered with sculptures, is Indo-Aryan. A Garuda tops the 10 metre high doorway. This is the highest structure in the fort.

South-West Entrance

The long ascent on the south-west side climbs up through a ravine to the fort gate. Along the rock faces flanking this road are a large number of Jain sculptures, some of impressively large size. Originally cut into the cliff faces in the mid-1400s they were mutilated by the forces of Babur in 1527 but were later repaired. The images are in five main groups and are numbered. In the Arwahi group image 20 is a 17 metre high standing image of Adinath while 22 is a 10 metre high seated figure of Nemnath, the 22nd Jain Tirthankar. The south-eastern group is the most important and covers nearly a km of the cliff face with more than 20 images.

Jai Vilas Palace

Located in the 'new town', which actually dates from 1809, this was the palace of the Scindia family. Although the current Maharaja still lives in the palace a large part of it is used as a museum which is open daily, except Mondays, from 10 am to 5 pm, admission Rs 3. It's full of the erratic sort of items Hollywood Maharajas are supposed to collect — like Belgian cut glass furniture, including a rocking chair. Or what looks like half the tiger population of India, all shot, stuffed and moth-eaten. Then there's a little room full of erotica including a life-size marble statue of Leda having her way with a swan. But the piece-de-resistance is a model railway that carried brandy and cigars around the dining table after dinner. Note that it's a long walk from the palace entrance around the part still in use to the museum section. If you go there by auto-rickshaw get it to drop you off at the museum, not at the palace entrance.

The palace is in Lashkar, which took its name 'camp' from the camp which Daulat Rao Scindia set up here in 1809 when he took control of Scindia. The Moti Mahal Palace is also in Lashkar and there is another museum.

Old Town

The old town of Gwailor lies to the north and north-east of the fort hill.

The 1661 Jami Masjid mosque is a fine old building constructed of sandstone quarried from the fort hill. Muhammad Ghaus, a Moslem saint who played a key role in Babur's acquisition of the fort, has his fine, large tomb on the eastern side of the town. It has hexagonal towers at its four corners and a dome which was once covered with glazed blue tiles. It's a very good example of early Moghul architecture. Close to this large tomb is the smaller Tomb of Tansen, a singer much admired by Akbar. Chewing the leaves of the tamarind tree near his grave is supposed to do wonders for your voice.

Places to Stay

There's nothing much close to the railway station but only a minute or so walk from there (turn left) there's the very (very) basic *Hotel Ashok* with accommodation at Rs 6 per person. Straight across the road there's the rather better, but at Rs 25/30 for singles/doubles rather more expensive, *Hotel India*. Both are rather noisy but there are plenty of eating places around. The station has *Railway Retiring Rooms*.

About a half km from the station, it's possible to walk there or get there by auto-rickshaw for Rs 1.50 or Rs 2, is the *Tourist Bungalow* (tel 22491). It's comfortable and has reasonably well kept rooms with attached bathrooms at Rs 30/40 for singles/doubles. It's also possible to camp in the garden here and the food is good and reasonably priced. It's a popular place for foreign visitors.

None of Gwalior's accommodation is concentrated in one area — there's nothing much around the bus station in Lashkar either. *Hotel Gujri Mahal* (tel 23492-93) on High Court Lane has singles/doubles as low as Rs 18/25 although there are others at much higher prices (Rs 60 and up with air-con). Quite reasonable rooms and quite a pleasant hotel. Gwalior's top end hotel is the *Usha Kiran Palace Hotel* (tel 22049 & 23453) at Jayendragunj, Lashkar. It's right behind the Jai Vilas Palace. The 32 rooms are all air-con or air-cooled and cost Rs 110 single, 150 double.

There's the usual selection of places to eat including a *Kwality* and a *Wengier's Restaurant*, both between the station and Lashkar. The Kwality has air-conditioning of Arctic intensity.

Getting There

Gwalior is on the main Delhi-Bombay rail line, 317 km from Delhi, 118 km from Agra and 1225 km from Bombay. From Delhi the express or mail trains take about six hours to Gwalior and the fare is about Rs 77 in first class, Rs 18 in second class. It's only two hours between Agra and Gwalior and the fares are about Rs 39 in first class, Rs 8.50 in second class.

There are also regular bus services from Gwalior to Delhi, Agra, Ujjain, Indore, Bhopal, Jabalpur and Khajuraho as well as to nearby centres like Shivpuri.

There's a daily direct flight from Delhi costing Rs 156. There are also daily connections from Bhopal (Rs 189), Indore (Rs 273) and Bombay (Rs 534).

Getting Around

Taxis, rickshaws, auto-rickshaws and tempos. Auto-rickshaw drivers in Gwalior will not use their meters — arrange the fare before you depart. Tempos run regular services around the city, from the railway station to Bada, the main square in Lashkar, is 75p.

AROUND GWALIOR

The old summer capital of Shivpuri is 117 km south-west of Gwalior or 51 km east of Jhansi. The road runs through a national park where you sometimes see animals on the road.

The *Chinkara Motel* (tel 297) in Shivpuri has singles/doubles at Rs 30/40. Near Shivpuri there's a pleasant lake with gardens around the perimeter. The road from Gwalior passes through Narwar with a large old fort. Between Gwalior and Agra, actually on a finger of Rajasthan that separates Madhya Pradesh and Uttar Pradesh at this point, is Dholpur, near where Aurangzeb's sons fought a pitched battle to determine who would succeed him as emperor of the rapidly declining Moghul empire. The Shergarh fort in the old Dholpur state is very old but now in ruins. Near Bari is the Khanpur Mahal, a pavilioned palace built for Shah Jahan but never occupied.

To the east of the railway line, 61 km south of Gwalior towards Jhansi, a large group of white Jain temples are visible scattered along a hill. They're one of those strange, dream-like appar-

itions that so often seem to simply materialise in India. Sonagir is the nearest railway station. Only 26 km north of Jhansi is Datia with the now deserted seven-storey palace of Raja Birsingh Deo. The town is surrounded by a stone wall and the palace is to the west of the town.

CHANDERA

At the time of Mandu's greatest power this was an important place as the many ruined palaces, sarais, mosques and tombs, all in a Pathan style similar to Mandu, indicate. The Koshak Mahal is a ruined Moslem palace still maintained. Today the town is chiefly known for its gold brocades and saris. Chandera is 33 km west of Lalitpur which in turn is 90 km south of Jhansi, on the main railway line.

JHANSI (population 225,000)

Situated 101 km south of Gwalior, Jhansi is actually in Uttar Pradesh — a finger of that state extends into Madhya Pradesh, but for convenience we'll include it here. Although Jhansi has played a colourful role in Indian history most visitors to the town today go there simply because it's a convenient jumping off point for Khajuraho. This is the closest point the Delhi-Bombay rail line runs to Khajuraho and there are regular buses.

Orchha, only 11 km south of Jhansi, was once the capital of a powerful state in this area. Bir Singh Deo ruled from Orchha between 1605 and 1627 and built the Jhansi fort. A favourite of the Moghul Prince Salim he feuded with Akbar and in 1602 narrowly escaped the emperor's displeasure; his kingdom was all but ruined by Akbar's forces. Then in 1605 Prince Salim became the Emperor Jahangir and for the next 22 years Bir Singh was a powerful figure.

In 1627 Shah Jahan became emperor, Bir Singh once again found himself out of favour and his attempt to revolt was put down by 13 year old Aurangzeb.

In the 18th century Jhansi rose to power, eclipsing Orchha, but in 1803 the British East India Company got a foot in the door and gradually assumed control over the state. The last of a string of none too competent rajas died without a son in 1853 and the British, who had recently passed a neat little law allowing them to take over any princely state under their patronage when the ruler died without a male heir, pensioned the Rani off and took full control. The Rani of Jhansi, who wanted to rule in her own right, was unhappy about this enforced retirement and when, four years later, the Indian Mutiny burst into flame she was in the forefront of the rebellion at Jhansi. The British contingent in Jhansi were all massacred but next year the rebel forces were still quarrelling amongst themselves and the British retook Jhansi. The Rani fled to Gwalior and in a valiant last stand she rode out against the British, disguised as a man, and was killed. She has since become a heroine of the Indian independence movement, a sort of Joan of Arc of central India.

The Jhansi fort, now much modernised, still offers excellent views from its ramparts. The British ceded the fort to the Maharaja of Scindia in 1858 then exchanged it for Gwalior in 1866.

Orchha
The former capital of this region is now just a village but the old fort still stands and contains Bir Singh Deo's fine palace and another palace built for, but never used by, Jahangir. The fort is on an island in the Bekwa River.

Places to Stay
There are dorm beds in the *Railway Retiring Rooms* and a handful of low price dives. Turn left out of the station and head straight a few hundred metres to half a km. The *Central Hotel* and *Hotel Sipri* are both close to the junction and cost Rs 15 a double. *Hotel Ashok* is more expensive but no better.

SANCHI
Beside the main railway line, 68 km north of Bhopal, a hill rises from the plain. It's topped by some of the oldest and most interesting Buddhist structures in India. Although this site had no direct connection with the life of Buddha himself it was the great Emperor Ashoka who built the first stupas here in the third century BC and a great number of stupas and other religious structures were added over the succeeding centuries. Then, with the decline of Buddhism, the site decayed and was eventually completely forgotten. In 1818 a British officer rediscovered the site but in the years that followed amateur archaeologists and greedy treasure hunters did immense damage to Sanchi before a proper restoration was first commenced in 1881. Finally, between 1912 and 1919, the structures were carefully repaired and restored to their present condition by Sir John Marshall.

Information & Orientation
Sanchi itself is little more than a tiny village at the foot of the hill. At the base of the hill, where you pay admission to enter the site, there is a small museum. You can get a copy of the guidebook *Sanchi*, published by the Archaeological Survey of India here.

The Great Stupa
Stupa 1, as it is listed on the site, is the main structure on the hill. Originally constructed by Ashoka in the third century BC it was later enlarged and the original brick stupa enclosed within a stone one. In its present form it stands 16 metres high and 37 metres in diameter. A railing encircles the stupa and there are four entrances through magnificently carved gateways or *toranas*. These toranas are the finest works of art at Sanchi and amongst the finest examples of Buddhist art in India.

Toranas
The four gateways were erected around 35 BC and had all fallen down at the time of the stupa's restoration. The scenes carved onto the pillars and their triple architraves are mainly tales from the *jatakas* — the episodes of the Budha's various lives. At this stage in Buddhist art the Buddha was never represented directly. His presence was always alluded to through symbols such as the Bo tree, the wheel of law or his footprint. Even a stupa is itself a symbol of the Buddha. Go round the stupa

clockwise, as one should around all Buddhist monuments:

Northern Gateway The north gateway, topped by an unfortunately broken whell of law, is the best preserved of the gateways. It shows many scenes from the Buddha's life both in his last incarnation and in earlier lives. Scenes include a monkey offering a bowl of honey to the Buddha, whose presence is indicated by a Bo tree. In another panel he ascends a road into the air (again represented by a Bo tree) in the 'miracle of Sravasti'. This is just one of several miraculous feats he performs on the north gateway — all of which leave his spectators stunned. Elephants facing in four directions support the architraves above the columns while horses with riders and more elephants fill the gaps between the architraves.

Eastern Gateway This gateway includes scenes of the Buddha's entry to nirvana on a pillar. Across the front of the middle architrave is the 'great departure', where the Buddha (symbolized by a riderless horse) renounces the sensual life and sets out to find enlightenment. Maya's dream, of an elephant standing on the moon, which she had when she conceived the Buddha, is also shown on one of the columns. The figure of a *yakshi* maiden, hanging out from one of the architraves, is one of the best known images of Sanchi.

Southern Gateway The oldest of the gateways this includes scenes of the Buddha's birth and also events from Ashoka's life as a Buddhist. As on the western gateway the tale of the Chhadenta Jataka features on this gateway.

Western Gateway The western gateway, with the architraves supported by dwarves, has some of the most interesting scenes. The rear face of one of the pillars shows the Buddha undergoing the temptation of Mara while demons flee and angels cheer that he manages to resist. Mara also tempts

Sanchi

A Monastery 47
B Monastery 45
C Ashoka Pillar
D Building 43

on the back of the lowest architrave. The top front architrave shows the Buddha in seven different incarnations but since he could not, at that time, be represented directly he appears three times as a stupa and four times as a tree. His six incarnations prior to the seventh, Gautama Buddha, are known as the Manushi Buddhas. The colourful events of the Chhaddanta Jataka are related on the front face of the bottom architrave. In this tale the Buddha, in a lower incarnation, took the form of a six-tusked elephant but one of his two wives became jealous and managed to re-incarnate as a queen and then arranged to have the six tusked elephant hunted and killed. But the sight of his tusks, sawn off by the hunter, was sufficient for the queen to die of remorse! Pot-bellied dwarves support the architraves on this gateway.

Pillars

Scattered around the site are a number of pillars or the remains of pillars. The most important is pillar 10 which was erected by Ashoka and stands close to the south entrance to the great stupa. Only the base of this beautifully proportioned and executed shaft now stands but the fine capital can be seen in the museum. The three back-to-back lions which once topped the column are an excellent example of the Graeco-Buddhist art of that era at its finest. They now form the state emblem of India and can be seen on every bank note. Pillars 25 and 35, both dating from the 5th century AD, are not as fine as the earlier Ashoka pillar. Pillar 35, also broken, stands close to the north gateway of the great stupa and again the capital figure is in the museum.

Other Stupas

There are many other stupas on the hill, some of them tiny votive stupas less than a metre high. They date from the 3rd century BC to the 12th century AD. Eight of the stupas were built by Ashoka but only three of the Ashoka stupas remain, including the great stupa. Stupa 2, one of the most interesting of the lesser stupas, is half way down the hill to the east. If you come up from the town by the main route you can

walk back down via stupa 2. There are no gateways to this stupa but the 'medallions' which decorate the surrounding wall are of great interest. Their design and execution is almost childlike but full of energy and imagination. Flowers, animals and people, some of them mythological creatures, are found all around the stupa.

Stupa 3 stands north-east of the main stupa and is similar in design, though smaller in size, to the great stupa itself. It has only one gateway and is thought to have been constructed soon after the completion of the great stupa. Almost totally destroyed, stupa 4 stands right behind stupa 3. Between stupa 1, the great stupa, and stupa 3 is stupa 5 and it is unusual in that it once had an image of the Buddha, now displayed in the museum. Stupa 3 once contained relics of two important disciples of the Buddha. They were removed and taken to London in 1853 but returned to Sanchi in 1953. Stupa 2, down the hill, also contained relics of important teachers of Buddhism but it is thought this lower spot was chosen for their enshrinement as the top of the hill was reserved for shrines to the Buddha and his direct disciples.

Temples

Immediately south of stupa 1 is stupa 18, a *chaitya* hall which in style is remarkably similar to the classical Greek columned buildings. It dates from around the 7th century AD but traces of earlier, wooden buildings have been discovered beneath it. Beside this temple is the small temple 17 which is also Greek like in style. The large temple 40, slightly south-east of these two temples, dates in part right back to the Ashokan period. Temple 6 stands between 40 and 18. It is known as the Gupta Temple and dates back to the 4th century AD. The flat roofed structure is made of stone slabs. It too shows a Greek influence probably stemming from the use of

Bactrian craftsmen. This temple is interesting in that it shows the style of Indian temple, where a porch leads to the central shrine, which later developed into classical Hindu temples at Khajuraho and in Orissa.

Monasteries

The earliest monasteries on the site were made of wood and have long since disappeared. The usual plan is of a central courtyard surrounded by monastic cells. Monasteries 47 and 45 stand on the higher, eastern edge of the hilltop. They date from the later period of building at Sanchi and show the strong Hindu elements in their design during this transition period from Buddhism to Hinduism. There is a good view of the village of Sanchi and away to Bhilsa (Vidisha) from this side of the hill. Monastery 51 is part way down the hill on the western side toward stupa 2.

Other buildings

The modern vihara (monastery) on the hill was constructed to house the returned relics from stupa 3. The design is a poor shadow of the former artistry of Sanchi. Close to monastery 51 is the 'great bowl' in which food and offerings were placed for distribution to the monks. It was carved out of a huge boulder. The Sanchi guidebook describes all these buildings, and many others, in much greater detail.

Places to Stay

Best value for money in Sanchi is probably (and surprisingly) the *Railway Retiring Rooms*. There are just two of them at Rs 16 double or Rs 8 single. They're big, spacious, spotlessly clean (in fact the whole Sanchi station is most

un-Indian like — clean, prim and proper). Crowning touch is the toilets though — you've got a western and Asian toilet side by side! Almost beside the station is the *Buddhist Guest House* which is rather more spartan — doubles Rs 15, dorm beds at Rs 5, supposedly you should make reservations in advance but in practise you can just drop in.

Continue on to the main road and turn right 250 metres to the *ITDC Traveller's Lodge* (tel 23). Singles here cost Rs 25, doubles Rs 40 (Rs 25 extra for air-con) and the rooms are neither as nice as the railway's or anywhere near as well kept. Nice lounge though. If you crossed the main road towards the hill you'd come to the Gothic looking *Rest House* on the left just before the museum (doubles Rs 8.25 but only two of them and mainly for government people) or the very pleasant looking *Circuit House* (tel 22) on the right (Rs 20 double and again usually unavailable).

Foodwise you've got a choice of the *Travellers Lodge* where the food is both terribly bland and very overpriced or the cluster of food stalls on the main road — most of them remarkably insanitary looking.

Getting There

Sanchi is on the main Delhi-Bombay railway line only 68 km north of Bhopal. Note that certain mail and express trains do not stop at Sanchi. First class passengers who have travelled a minimum distance to Sanchi can request that the train be halted for them. It is necessary to arrange this in advance. There are also buses from Bhopal to Sanchi, the two hour trip costs Rs 5. You can get everywhere in Sanchi on foot.

AROUND SANCHI

In the immediate vicinity of Sanchi there are a number of other Buddhist sites although none are of the scale or

in the state of preservation of Sanchi itself. They include Sonari, 10 km south-west of Sanchi where there are eight stupas, two of them quite important. At Satdhara, west of Sanchi on the bank of the Beas River, there are two stupas, one 30 metres in diameter and the other seven metres in diameter. At Bhojpur (Pipaliya), 11 km southeast of Sanchi, no less than 37 stupas were discovered, the largest 20 metres in diameter. Another eight km southeast is Andher where there are three small, but well preserved, stupas. These stupas around Sanchi were all discovered in 1851, after the discovery of Sanchi itself. Other places of interest around Sanchi include:

Vidisha (Bhilsa or Besnagar)

Vidisha was an important town in Ashoka's time, his wife came from here. Today the city is known as Besnagar and Bhilsa railway station has an important collection of antiquities discovered in the area. The Khamb Baba pillar is one of the more interesting attractions. It was erected by Heliodorus, a Greek ambassador to the city from Taxila (now in Pakistan). The pillar celebrates his conversion to Hinduism and is dedicated to Vishnu. Also in the town is the Bija Mandal, a mosque built from the remains of Hindu temples.

Udayigiri

The Gupta caves here date from 320 to 606 AD, two of them are Jain, the other 18 are Hindu. In cave 5 there is a superb image of Vishnu in his boar incarnation. Cave 7 was cut out for King Chandragupta II's personal use. The caves are seven km west of Vidisha.

Raisen

On the road to Bhopal, 23 km south of Sanchi, the huge and colourful hilltop fort has temples, cannons, three palaces, 40 wells and a large tank. This Malwa fort was built around 1200 AD but was

later dependant to Mandu. Raisen declared its independence at one time but was conquered by Bahadur Shah.

Gyaraspur

There are tanks, temples and a fort at this town, 51 km north-east of Sanchi. The town's name is derived from the big fair which used to be held here in the 11th month, Gyaras.

Udaypur

Reached through Basoda and Gyaraspur, Udaypur is 90 km north of Sanchi. The large Neelkantheswara Temple is thought to have been built in 1059 AD. It's profusely and very finely carved with four prominent decorated bands around the shikara. The temple is aligned so that the first rays of the morning sun shine on the Shiva lingam in the sanctum. It's a particularly fine example of Indo-Aryan architecture and is reached via the railway station at Bareth, seven km away.

BHOPAL (population 425,000)

The capital of Madhya Pradesh takes its name from its legendary 11th century founder Raja Bhoj. He is supposed to have created the lakes around which the city is built, by constructing a dam or *pal*. Hence Bho-pal. The present city was laid out by the Afghan chief Dost Mohamed Khan. Dost Mohamed had been in charge of Bhopal during Aurangzeb's reign but took advantage of the confusion following his death in 1707 to carve out his own small kingdom.

Information & Orientation

The Tourist Office is at 5 Hamidia Rd (tel 3400) quite close to the railway station. It's open from 11 am to 5.30 pm daily. The bus station is a little further down the same road. The older part of town is north of the twin lakes while the newer part, where you'll also find the youth hostel, is to the south of the lakes. The GPO is near Hamidia Hospital.

Taj-ul-Masjid

Commenced by Shah Jahan Begum, but never really completed, the Taj-ul-Masjid is one of the largest mosques in India if not the largest. It's a huge pink mosque with two massive white-domed minarets and three white domes over the main building.

Other Mosques

The Jama Masjid was built in 1837 by Qudsia Begum and is surrounded by the bazaar. It has very squat, short minarets. The Moti Masjid was built by Qudsia Begum's daughter, Sikander Jahan Begum, in 1860. Similar in style to the Jama Masjid in Delhi it is a smaller mosque with two dark red minarets crowned by golden spikes.

The Lakes

The larger Upper Lake covers six square km and a bridge separates it from the Lower Lake. You can rent boats to get out on the lakes which are very picturesque when they reflect lights from houses around the lake at night.

Other

From the Shamla Hill or the Idgah Hill you get a very fine view over the city and the lakes. The minarets of the city's mosques can be seen, towering over the lesser buildings, from far away. On the Arera Hill, south of the Lower Lake, there's a modern Lakshmi Narayan Temple and a temple museum. It's open from 8 am to 12 noon and from 2 to 6 pm daily, admission is free. There's also an Archaeological Museum near Tagore Bhavan — open 10 am to 5 pm daily, admission free. There are parks and gardens around the Lower Lake.

Tours

The State Tourism Development Corporation has a number of tours in and around Bhopal. Each Thursday there are city tours for Rs 9 which depart at 8 am and 1.30 pm, returning at 12.30 pm and 5 pm respectively. On Wednesdays and Fridays there is a Rs 20 all-day tour to Sanchi and Udayigiri. It departs at 8.15 am and returns at 5 pm. Tour buses depart to Kerwan Dam every hour from 9 am to 4 pm on Sundays and Mondays. One way is Rs 2, double that for return. On Saturdays buses also depart hourly, for the same price, to Islamnagar. Bookings can be made through the Tourist Office on Hamidia Rd.

Places to Stay

There are a lot of hotels along Hamidia Rd which runs between the railway station and the bus station and on which the tourist office is located. If you come out the front of the railway station you'll have to get an auto-rickshaw down along the line and over the railway lines on a flyover. If you

Bhopal

Airport
Delhi
Agra

Delhi

Indore
Ujjain

Sultania Road

Hamidia Rd.

Railway Station

Hamidia Rd.

G.P.O.

Sanchi

Upper Lake

Lower Lake

Lakshmi
Narayan
Temple

Shamla
Hill

Youth
Hostel

Arera Hill

Bhadbhda Rd.

T. T. Nagar

Bhadbhda
Falls

Key:-
① Imperial Sabra Hotel
② Taj-ul-Masjid
③ Jama Masjid
④ Bus Station
⑤ Central Library
⑥ Moti Masjid
⑦ Rajdoot Hotel
⑧ Manohar's & Neelam's Hotels
⑨ Tourist Office
⑩ Hotel Gulshan
⑪ Ranjit Hotel
⑫ Ransom's Hotel
⑬ Samrat & Meghdoot Hotels
⑭ Grand Hotel
⑮ Museum
⑯ Indian Airlines

cross the other way there's a footbridge which brings you out right on the Hamidia Rd corner. Hotels along Hamidia Rd include the older, basic, but reasonable *Grand Hotel* (tel 4070) with singles at Rs 10 to 15 and doubles at Rs 20 to 40, depending on facilities. The *Hotel Ranjit* (tel 3641) is also on Hamidia Rd and has singles/doubles at Rs 15/25. Similar prices at the adjacent *Gulshan Lodge*.

Still on Hamidia Rd the *Hotel Samrat* is newish and in not bad condition — Rs 20/30 for singles/doubles. Ditto for the *Hotel Meghdoot.* The *Rajdoot Hotel* (tel 2797) is also new but rather grubby. Singles range from Rs 25 to Rs 40, doubles from Rs 40 to over Rs 100 with air-con. There are plenty of other places along this popular hotel road including Bhopal's number one location, *Hotel Ramsons International* (tel 2298, 2299) with air-con and non air-con rooms starting from around Rs 75 and running up to Rs 250 or more. Other more expensive hotels in Bhopal include the *Pagoda* (tel 3949) still on Hamidia Rd and the *Imperial Sabre*, out of town in the old palace grounds.

Bhopal has *Railway Retiring Rooms* at the station with air-con rooms from Rs 40, non air-con from Rs 15 and dorm beds at Rs 8. The *Youth Hostel* (tel 63671) is in North TT Nagar, to the south of the lakes. It costs about Rs 3 for an auto-rickshaw there from the station. Dorm beds cost Rs 8.

There are a lot of places to eat along Hamidia Rd of course. *Neelam's* and *Manohar's* are both vegetarian places,

side by side. Good fruit juice drinks in *Manohar's*. The *Ranjit Hotel* has a good air-con restaurant and it's open late at night. There's also a restaurant, though not so good, in the *Rajdoot.*

Bhopal Warning

As in many reasonably large Indian towns which do not, however, get many tourists, it can be difficult to change travellers' cheques. At the best of times changing TCs in India is laborious and time consuming. When you have to search out the city head office of a bank before you can start into the paperwork it's especially bad. A good reason for changing money as infrequently as possible.

Getting There

Bhopal is on the main Delhi-Bombay railway line. It's 705 km from Delhi, takes 11 to 13 hours and costs about Rs 142 in first class, Rs 35 in second. From Bombay it's 837 km and takes 13 to 16 hours. The fare is about Rs 160 in first class, Rs 40 in second. Sanchi is only 68 km north of Bhopal but note the warning in the Sanchi section on non-stop trains.

There are regular buses to Sanchi from Bhopal. They leave every couple of hours, take two hours to get there and the fare is Rs 5.

Bhopal is on the Delhi-Gwalior-Bhopal-Indore-Bombay air route. The fares are Rs 345 to Bombay, Rs 189 to Gwalior, Rs 98 to Indore and Rs 306 to Delhi.

AROUND BHOPAL

Neori, only six km from Bhopal, has an 11th century Shiva temple and a popular picnic spot. Islampur, 11 km out, was built by Dost Mohamed Khan and has a hilltop palace and garden. It's on the Berasia road. At Ashapuri, six km north of Bhopal, there are ruined

temples and Jain palaces with statues scattered on the ground. Chiklod, 45 km out, has a palace in a peaceful sylvan setting.

Bhojpur

Raja Bhoj built not only the dam at

Bhopal but also a dam here, which created the largest lake in Asia. Hoshang Shah, the ruler of Mandu, destroyed it. A massive, but never completed, Shiva temple dating from the 11th century overlooks the lake. Bhojpur is 28 km from Bhopal.

Ginnorgarh Fort
This hilltop fort is 61 km from Bhopal

and reached its peak in the 13th century during the reign of Udayavarman. It's famous for its parrots.

Bhimbetka
Neolithic caves and cave paintings discovered in this village, 40 km from Bhopal, are one of the earliest traces of man in India.

UJJAIN (population 225,000)
Only 80 km from Indore, on the right bank of the River Sipra, Ujjain is a very holy city for Hindus. It is also the site for the triennial Kumbh Mela, which comes to Ujjain every 12 years — next time in 1992.

The city has a long and distinguished history. It was an important city in the kingdom ruled by Ashoka's father, when it was known as Avanti. Later it was so attractive to Chandragupta II (380-414 AD), one of the Gupta kings, that for long periods he ruled from here rather than his actual capital, Pataliputra. His court supported the 'nine gems' of Hindu literature including the important poet Kalidasa.

Later Ujjain became a centre for much turmoil and although it was, for a time, capital of the Malwa region it passed between the Rajputs and Moghuls before eventually falling to the Scindias of Gwalior.

Temples
The Mahakala Temple, later restored by the Scindias, was destroyed by Altamish of Delhi in 1235. An ancient gateway, known as the Chaubis Khanba Ghaj, is said to date from the original temple. It stands near the palace of Maharaja Scindia. The riverside temples and ghats are west of here. Other temples include the small Bridh Kaleshwar, south of the Mahakala. The marble spired Gopal Mandir was built by Jai Singh of Jaipur but is so buried in the

bazaar that it's easy to miss. The Temple of Nine Planets is on the Indore road where two other rivers join the Sipra.

Other
Out of the city, which was once bounded by a stone wall, to the south-west, is the Jantar Mantar — another of those strange observatories constructed by

mongoose
mongoose

Maharajah Jai Singh. This one is in poor condition and not as impressive as the Jantar Mantar of Jaipur or New Delhi. Eight km north of the town is the water palace of the Mandu Sultans. Known as Kaliadah it stands on an island in the Sipra River. River water is diverted over stone screens in the palace and the bridge to the island uses carvings from the sun temple which once stood on the island.

Places to Stay
The *Ujjain Motel* (tel 1862) has singles/doubles at Rs 30/40. There are also *Railway Retiring Rooms* and a variety of hotels.

INDORE (population 600,000)
Indore is not of itself of great interest but it does make a good jumping off point for visiting Mandu. It's an affluent looking town, a major textile producing centre, with plenty of new houses and flats. The rivers Khan and Sarasvati run through the town. From 1733 the town was ruled by the Holkar dynasty who were firm supporters of the British even at the time of the mutiny.

Information & Orientation
The older part of town is on the western side, the newer part on the east. The railway line forms a rough north-south dividing line while Mahatma Gandhi Rd bisects the town in an east-west direction. The railway and bus stations are quite close together but separated by a complicated flyover system. The Tourist Office (tel 38888), from where tours are operated to Mandu, is in the Sarwate bus station. Curiously there seem to be as many pigs congregating in the bus and train stations as the ever-present cows. Rupayana, by the Central Hotel, is a reasonably good bookshop.

Palaces
In the old part of town the multi-storey gateway of the Rajwada or 'old palace' looks out on to the main square in the crowded streets of the Kajuri Bazaar. It's now given over to government offices while the 'new palace' has become a hospital. The bazaar streets are crowded and picturesque with deep verandahs on to the streets. The Manik Bagh, to the south of the city, and the Lal Bagh, to the south-west, also have palaces.

Kanch Mandir
On Sunday St (Jawahar Rd), close to the Rajwada, is the Kanch Mandir or Seth Hukanchand Temple. This Jain temple is very plain externally but inside is completely mirrored with pictures of sinners being tortured in the after-life as light relief.

Museum
Near the GPO, the museum has a car park which was a 'battlefield in the Independence War of 1857'. It specialises in sculptures and coins excavated in the Malwa region. In particular there are over 700 pieces from Mandsaur. It has the biggest collection of antiquities in Madhya Pradesh. Admission is free, it's closed on Mondays.

1	Railway Station	6	Central Hotel
2	Bus Station	7	Indian Airlines
3	GPO	8	Hotel Samrat
4	Kanch Mandir	9	Ashoka & Janata Hotel
5	Museum		

Indore

Chattris

The chattris or memorial tombs of the region's former rulers are now neglected and forgotten. They stand in the Chattri Bagh on the banks of the river Khan. The cenotaph of Malhar Rao Holkar I, founder of the Holkar dynasty, is the most impressive.

Tours

The ITDC have a number of conducted tours from Indore. From Wednesday to Sunday there is a Mandu tour. On Monday the tour goes to Omkareshwar and on Tuesday to Ujjain. The tours all start at 8.30 am from the bus station and cost Rs 25.

Places to Stay

The railway station and bus station are only a few minutes walk apart and there's a reasonable selection of places directly opposite the bus station on Nasia Rd. There are *Retiring Rooms* in the bus station at Rs 10/15 for singles/doubles. The *Janta Hotel*, across from the bus station, (tel 37695 & 36691) is OK — fairly clean, fans in the rooms, singles/doubles at Rs 9/13 or Rs 17/25 with their own bathroom. Flanking it on one side is the *Standard Lodge* (tel 37370 & 36889) with singles from around Rs 10 to Rs 20, doubles from Rs 14 to Rs 25. On the other side is the newish *Hotel Ashoka* (tel 37391-95) which is rather more expensive at Rs 29/39 for singles/doubles. Pleasant, clean, well kept — the front rooms are a little noisy, due to the bus station. *Hotel Neelam* at 33/2 Chhoti Gwaltoli (tel 37161 & 37274) is also close to the railway and bus stations — singles/doubles from Rs 12/18 (no bath) to Rs 18/23 (with bath).

A little further away from the bus/train centres on Mahatma Gandhi Rd there are a number of more expensive places to choose from. The *Central Hotel* in the Rampurawala Building at number 27 (tel 32131 & 32041) is a little old-fashioned and has big, fairly well kept rooms. Prices start from Rs 25/35 for fan cooled singles/doubles, up through Rs 55/80 and Rs 65/100 for air cooled and air-con rooms. If you cross the railway tracks on M G Rd you'll find the *Hotel Sheba* (tel 7720 & 7750) at 562, right by the statue of the Mahatma. Prices start from Rs 20/30 and head up with air-con. A bit further down there is the *Hotel Samrat* (tel 30758-59) at 18/5 M G Rd with slightly higher prices. These latter two hotels are both quite new — of the Indian 'rapidly deteriorating as soon as it's completed' variety. Indore's top hotel, the *Suhag Hotel* (tel 36580-89, 33270-79), is four km out of the city on the Bombay-Agra road towards Dewas Rd. Rooms start from Rs 50/80 for non air-con singles/doubles and go up to over Rs 200 for a de-luxe air-con double.

Places to Eat

There are a number of good places to to eat close to the bus stand. The *Janta* and *Standard Restaurants*, in the hotels of the same name, are both good value. The former has a surprisingly long list of Indian beer varieties, cold. The *Volga Restaurant*, near the Mahatma Gandhi statue on M G Rd, has good vegetarian food and aggressive air-conditioning.

Getting There

Indore is not on the main broad gauge line between Delhi and Bombay. That runs north of Indore through Ujjain. There is, however, a broad gauge spur that runs down to Indore from Ujjain. The 80 km trip takes about 2½ to three hours and costs Rs 29 first class, Rs 5.50 in second class. There is a daily express starting and terminating in Indore which runs through Ujjain to Bhopal and then east to Jabalpur and Bilaspur. There is also a metre gauge line through Indore. Services run on this line from Ajmer and Chittorgarh, north of Indore in Rajasthan, south-east to Khandwa, Nizamabad and Secunderabad.

Buses run from Indore to Ujjain (Rs 4), Bagh (about the same), Mandu (8.30 am, 12.30 and 3.30 pm for Rs 6), Bhopal (hourly for Rs 13). Getting down to the Ajanta and Ellora caves and Aurangabad in Maharashtra can be rather complicated. There is only one straight through bus a day, otherwise you may have to make a whole series of changes at Khandwa, Burhanpur, Bhusawal or Jalgaon and the trip may take up to 14 hours.

Indian Airlines have a daily flight from Bombay to Indore (one hour 50 minutes, Rs 260) and between Delhi and Indore although on some days this may involve a flight change at Bhopal. To Bhopal the fare is Rs 98, to Delhi Rs 384.

Getting Around
Indore's railway station and the Sarwata bus stand are close together but separated by a complicated flyover system. Not surprisingly a large number of gaps have appeared in the fences by the railway lines and most people just march straight across the line between the stations. Lots of taxis, auto-rickshaws, rickshaws and tempos in Indore.

AROUND INDORE
Omkareshwar
This island in the Narmada River was said to be the site of two of India's 12 great Shiva temples when Mahmud of Ghazni marched to Somnath to destroy the temple there in 1024. The Temple of Omkar was on the island and that of Manileshwar on the south bank of the river. Today the temples on the island and the nearby river banks have all been damaged by Moslems or time but there are still some very fine buildings to be seen. The island temples are all dedicated to Shiva but on the river banks are temples to Vishnu and Jain temples.

Getting There Omkareshwar Road is on the railway line 60 km from Khandwa. Omkareshwar is 10 km from here. From Indore it is 80 km to Omkareshwar. There is a day tour from Indore to Omkareshwar every Monday at a cost of Rs 25.

Maheshwar
The chattri of Ahalya Bai, who died in 1795, is located here. She was the widow of Malhar Rao Holkar's son (see Indore) and after his death she ruled with great ability. She also has a cenotaph in the Chattri Bagh in Indore. Maheshwar is 100 km from Indore on the banks of the Narmada River.

Dhar
Founded by Raja Bhoj, the legendary founder of Bhopal and Mandu also, this was the capital of Malwa until Mandu rose to power. There are good views from the ramparts of Dhar's well preserved fort. Dhar also has the large stone Bhojashala mosque with ancient sanskrit inscriptions and the adjoining tomb of the Moslem saint Kamal Maula.

MANDU
The extensive, and now mainly deserted, hilltop fort of Mandu is one of the most interesting sights in central India. There is accommodation actually in Mandu or you can make a day-trip from Indore if your time is short. Mandu is situated on an isolated outcrop which is separated from the tableland to the north by a deep and wide valley over which a natural causeway runs to the main city

Mandu Fort

Scale

Key:-
1. Champa Baoli
2. Hindola Mahal
3. Jahaz Mahal
4. Gada Shah's Palace

Alamgir Gate
Indore
Bhangi Gate
Suraj Talao
Tourist Bungalow
Ram Mandir
Ashrafi Mahal
Hushang's Tomb
Jami Masjid
Munja Talao
Rampol Gate
Darya Khan's Tomb
Hathi Mahal
Baz Bahadur's Palace
Rewa Kund
Rupmati's Palace
Bhagwania Gate
Sagar Talao
Nil Kanth
Songarh
N

gate. To the south of Mandu the land drops steeply away to the plain far below and the view is superb. Deep ravines cut into the sides of the 20 square km plateau which the fort occupies.

Mandu, known as the 'city of joy', has had a chequered and varied history. Founded as a fortress and retreat in the 10th century by Raja Bhoj (see Bhopal) it was conquered by the Moslem rulers of Delhi in 1304 but when the Mongols invaded and took Delhi in 1401 the Afghan Dilawar Khan, governor of Malwa, set up his own little kingdom and Mandu embarked on its golden age. Even after it was added to the Moghul empire by Akbar Mandu it retained a considerable degree of independence until the declining Moghuls lost control of it to the Marathas. The capital of Malwa was then shifted back to Dhar and Mandu became a ghost town. For a ghost town it's a remarkably grandiose and impressive place and worth a day's inspection at the very least. Mandu has one of the best collections of Afghan architecture to be seen in India.

Although Dilawar Khan first established Mandu as an independent kingdom it was his son, Hoshang Shah, who shifted the capital from Dhar to Mandu and raised it to its greatest splendour. Warlike as he was, Hoshang's rule, from 1405, was marked by the construction of the Delhi Gate, the Jami Masjid, his own fine tomb and the extensive and complex fortifications.

His son ruled for only a year before being poisoned by Mahmud Shah who became king himself and ruled for 33 years during which Mandu was in frequent and often bitter dispute with neighbouring powers. There are few architectural remains of his reign for his most imposing structures, such as his own tomb, were poorly designed and built and soon collapsed. Nevertheless his constant war-making raised Mandu to great importance and prosperity.

In 1469 his son, Ghiyas-ud-Din, ascended the throne and spent the next 31 years devoting himself to women and song — if not wine, for he was reputed to be teetotal. His son, Nasir-ud-Din, became so fed up with waiting for over-indulgence to finish off his father that he poisoned him in 1500, when he was 80 years old. He lived only another 10 years before dying, some say, of guilt. His son Mahmud had an unhappy reign during which his underlings, like Gada Shah and Darya Khan, often had more influence than he did. Finally, in 1526, Bahadur Shah of Gujarat conquered Mandu.

In 1534 Humayun, the Moghul, defeated Bahadur Shah but as soon as Humayun turned his back an officer of the former dynasty took over. Several more changes of fortune eventually led to Baz Bahadur taking power in 1554 but his chief pursuits were not conquest or building, like his predecessors, but music. In 1561 he fled from Mandu rather than face Akbar's advancing troops and Mandu's period of independence ended. Although the Moghuls maintained the fort for a time and even added some new, minor, buildings its period of grandeur was over.

Information & Orientation

The buildings of Mandu can be divided into three groups. When you enter through the Delhi Gate at the north a road branches off to the west almost immediately. This leads to the group of buildings known as the Royal Enclave. If you continued straight on from the entrance you'd pass the Tourist Bungalow and come to the tiny village which is all that Mandu is today. The buildings here are known as the village group. Continuing on beyond here you'll eventually reach the Rewa Kund group at the extreme south of the fort. You can get a copy of the Archaeological Survey of India's excellent guidebook *Mandu* from the Taveli

Mahal in the Royal Enclave. There are many other buildings in Mandu apart from those described below.

Royal Enclave — Jahaz Mahal

The 'Ship Palace' is probably the most famous building in Mandu, it really is ship-like being far longer (110 metres) than it is wide (15 metres) and the illusion is completed by the two lakes that flank it to the east and west. It was built by Ghiyas-ud-Din, son of Mahmud Shah. Ghiyas had become thoroughly fed up with his father's warring ways and decided to dedicate himself to more pleasurable pursuits. The Jahaz Mahal is his magnificent harem. At the northern end of the 'ship' is a beautifully tiered bath where one can easily imagine the ladies of the harem lolling around seductively.

Hindola Mahal

Just north of Ghiyas' stately pleasure dome this church-like hall is known as the 'swing palace' because the inward slope of the walls is supposed to create the impression that the walls are swaying. 'Supposed' to anyway. A wide sloping ramp in the northern end of the building is said to be for the ruler to be conveyed upstairs by elephant. The building is massively constructed, quite strong enough to handle the odd elephant.

Champa Baoli

To the west of the first two Royal Enclave buildings is this interesting building on the north shore of the lake. Its subterranean levels featured cool wells and baths and it was obviously a popular hot weather retreat. There are a number of other buildings in the enclave including the 'house and shop' of Gada Shah and the 1405 Mosque of Dilawar Khan, one of the earliest Moslem buildings in Mandu. Just south of the Jahaz Mahal is the Taveli Mahal which is used as a rest house.

Village Group — Jami Masjid

The huge 1454 mosque dominates the village of Mandu. It is claimed to be the finest and largest example of Afghan architecture in India. Construction of the mosque was commenced by Hoshang Shah who patterned it on the great mosque in Damascus, Syria. The mosque features an 80 metre square courtyard.

Hoshang's Tomb

Immediately behind the mosque is the imposing marble tomb of Hoshang who died in 1435. The tomb is entered through a domed porch and the interior is lit by stone 'jali' screens — typical of the clear Hindu influence on the fine design of this tomb. You enter the tomb through a double arch and the squat central dome is surrounded by four smaller domes. It is said that Shah Jahan sent his architects to Mandu to study this tomb before they embarked upon the design of the Taj Mahal. To one side of the tomb enclosure is a long, low colonnade with its width divided into three by rows of pillars. Behind is a long, narrow hall with a typically Moslem barrel-vaulted ceiling. This was intended as a shelter for pilgrim's visiting Hoshang's tomb.

Ashrafi-Mahal

The ruin of this building stands in front of the Jami Masjid, directly across the road from it. Originally built as a madrasa (religious college) it was later extended by its builder, Mahmud Shah, to become his tomb. But the design was simply too pretentious for its builders' abilities and it later collapsed. The seven-storey, circular tower of victory which Mahmud Shah erected has also fallen. A great stairway still leads up to the entrance to the empty shell of the building.

Rewa Kund — Palace of Baz Bahadur

It is about three km south from the village group, past the large Sagar

Talao tank, to the Rewa Kund group. Baz Bahadur was the last independent ruler of Mandu. When he fell to Akbar and the Moghuls, Mandu became a mere shadow of its former glory. His palace, constructed around 1509, is beside the Rewa Kund and there was a water-lift at the northern end of the tank to supply water to the palace. The palace is a curious mix of Rajasthani and Moghul styles and was actually built well before Baz Bahadur came to power.

Rupmati's Pavilion

At the very edge of the fort, perched on the hillside over the plains below, is the pavilion of Rupmati. The Malwa legends relate that she was a beautiful Hindu singer and that Baz Bahadur persuaded her to leave her home on the plains by building her this pavilion. From its terraces and domed pavilions Rupmati could gaze down on the Narmada River, winding across the plains far below. It's a romantic building, the perfect setting for a fairytale romance — but one with an unhappy ending. Akbar, it is said, was prompted to conquer Mandu partly due to Rupmati's beauty. And when Akbar marched on the fort Baz Bahadur fled, leaving Rupmati to poison herself.

Darya Khan's Tomb & Hathi Mahal

To the east of the road, between the Rewa Kund and the village, are these two buildings. The Hathi Mahal or 'elephant palace' is so named because the pillars supporting the dome are of massive proportions — like elephant legs. Nearby is the tomb of Darya Khan which was once decorated with intricate patterns of mosaic tiles.

Nilkanth Palace

Situated at the end of one of the ravines which cuts into the fort this palace is actually below the level of the hilltop and reached by a flight of steps down the hillside. At one time this was a Shiva shrine as the name, the god with the blue throat, suggests. Under the Moghuls it became a pleasant water palace with a typical Moghul water cascade running down the middle. It was a favourite place for the Emperor Jahangir but today it has once again become a Shiva temple, and a favourite playground for monkeys. Although it is of no great architectural merit it's a very pretty and pleasant place.

Places to Stay

There is an *Archaeological Rest House* with accommodation at Rs 12 per person. It's situated by the Jahaz Mahal in the Royal Enclave. Or on the main road into the fort to the village group there's a *Travellers' Lodge* at Rs 25 a single, Rs 40 a double and the *Tourist Bungalow* (tel 35) at Rs 15 a double. Rooms at the Tourist Bungalow can also be booked through the Tourist Office in Indore. There are a number of small eating places in the village and a dharamsala (less than Rs 5) near the bus stop, but it's not very good value.

Getting There

There are buses from Bhopal, Mhow, Ujjain, Dhar and Indore to Mandu. From Indore buses depart at 8.30 am, 12.30 and 3.30 pm and the trip costs Rs 6. It's 115 km from Indore to Mandu. There are tours from Indore to Mandu on most days of the week, departing at 8.30 am they cost Rs 25.

BAGH CAVES

The Bagh Caves are seven km from the village of Bagh and three km off the main road. Bagh is about 50 km west of Mandu, on the road between Indore and Baroda in Gujrat. The caves date from 400 to 700 AD and are Buddhist but are all in very bad shape. Cave-ins, smoke and water damage have reduced them to such a poor condition that restoration work is barely worthwhile. Compared to the caves of Ajanta or Ellora the Bagh Caves are hardly worth the not inconsiderable effort of getting

to them. In the Archaeological Museum in Gwalior you can see reproductions of the wall paintings from Cave 4, known as Rang Mahal or the Painted Hall, when they were in much better shape than today. There is a *PWD Dak Bungalow* at the caves.

KHAJURAHO

The temples of Khajuraho are one of India's major attractions — close behind the Taj and up there with Varanasi, Jaipur and Delhi. The temples, of course, are superb examples of Indo-Aryan architecture but it's the decorations with which the temples are so liberally embellished that has made Khajuraho so famous. Around the temples are bands of sculptures of exceedingly fine and artistic stone work. The sculptors have shown many aspects of Indian life a thousand years ago — gods and goddesses, warriors and musicians, animals real and mythological. But two elements appear over and over again and in greater detail than anything else — women and sex. Stone figures of 'apsaras' or 'celestial maidens' appear on every temple. They pout and pose for all the world like Playboy models posing for the camera. In between are the 'mithuna' couples — couples, on some of the temples even larger groups, running through a whole Kama Sutra of positions and possibilities. Some obviously require amazing athletic contortions, some just look like good fun!

These temples were built during the Chandella period, a dynasty which survived for five centuries before falling to the onslaught of Islam. Khajuraho's temples almost all date from one century long burst of creative genius. These magnificent structures were almost all built between 950 and 1050 AD. Almost as intriguing as the sheer beauty and size of the temples themselves is the question of why and how they were built here. Khajuraho is simply a long way

from anywhere and was probably just as far off the beaten track a thousand years ago as it is today. There is nothing of great interest or beauty to recommend Khajuraho as a building site, there is no great population centre here and during the hot season Khajuraho is very hot, very dry, very dusty and very uncomfortable. Having chosen such a strange site how did the Chandellas manage to recruit the labour to turn their awesome dreams into stone? To built so many temples of such monumental size in just 100 years must have required a huge amount of manpower. Whatever their reasons we can be thankful they built Khajuraho where they did because its very remoteness must have helped to preserve it from the desecration Moslem invaders were only too ready to inflict on 'idolatrous' temples elsewhere in India.

Information & Orientation

The modern village of Khajuraho is a cluster of hotels, restaurants, shops and stalls around the bus station. A little north of this there are three government run hotels and by the bus stand there is also the museum, a mosque, the tourist office (tel 47) and the post office. The temples are in three groups. Right by this modern part of Khajuraho is the western group, most of the temples in this group are in a well kept enclosure, and it includes the largest and most important temples at Khajuraho. A km or so east of the bus stand is the old village of Khajuraho and around the village are the temples of the eastern group.

Finally there are the two southern group temples, further to the south. Apart from everything else Khajuraho is a delightful place to lie around in, restful, interesting and easygoing. Small images of the gods can be bought from the shop in Khajuraho — plus lots of post cards.

Terminology

The Khajuraho temples follow a fairly consistent design pattern and it's pretty well unique to Khajuraho. Understanding the architectural conventions here and some of the terms used to describe it will help you enjoy the temples more. Basically the temples all follow a five part or three part plan.

PLAN OF
LAKSHMANA TEMPLE

sikhara

maha-
mandapa
pradakshina
ardha-
mandapa
antarala
mandapa
garbha-
griha

You enter the temples through an entrance porch known as the *ardha-mandapa*. Behind this is the hall or *mandapa*. This leads into the main hall or *mahamandapa*, supported with pillars and with a corridor around it. A vestibule or *antarala* then leads into the *garbha-griha*, the inner-sanctum where the

image of the god to which the temple is dedicated is displayed. An enclosed corridor, the *pradakshina*, runs around this sanctum. The simpler three part temples delete part 2 (the *mandapa*) and part 5 (the *pradakshina*) but otherwise follow the same plan as the five part temples.

Externally the temples consist of successive waves of higher and higher towers culminating in the soaring *sikhara* which tops the sanctum. While the lower towers, over the mandapa or mahamandapa, may be pyramid shaped the *sikhara* is taller and curvilinear. The ornate, even baroque design of all these vertical elements is balanced by an equally ornate horizontal element from the bands of sculptures that run right around the temples. Although the sculptures are so superbly developed in their own right they are also a carefully integrated part of the overall design — not some tacked on afterthought. The interiors of the temples are as ornate as the exteriors. The whole temple sits upon a high terrace known as the *adisthana*. Unlike temples in most other parts of India there is no enclosing wall but the temples often had four smaller shrines at the corners of the terrace — these have often disappeared today. The finely carved entrance gate into the temple is a *torana*. The lesser towers around the main sikhara are known as *urusringas*.

The temples are almost all aligned east-west with the entrance facing east. Some of the earliest temples were made of granite or granite and sandstone but all the temples from the classic period of Khajuraho's history are completely made of sandstone. At this time there was no mortar so all the blocks are simply fitted together. The sculptures and statues play such an important part in the total design that many have their own terminology:

apsaras — heavenly nymphs, the beautiful dancing women who adorn the temples.

salabhanjikas — women figures with trees which together act as supporting brackets in the inner chambers of the temple. Apsaras also perform this bracket function.

surasundaris — when a surasundari is dancing she is an apsara. Otherwise they attend to the gods and goddess by carrying flowers, water, ornaments, mirrors or other offerings. They also engage in everyday activities like washing their hair, applying make-up, taking a thorn out of their foot, fondling themselves, playing with pets or babies, writing letters, playing musical instruments or simply posing seductively.

nayikas — it's really impossible to tell a nayikas from a surasundari since the only difference is that the surasundari is supposed to be a heavenly creature while a nayika is human.

mithuna — Khajuraho's most famous images, the sensuously carved erotic figures which adorn so many of the temples. They're reputed to have been shocking people from Victorian archaeologists to blue-rinse tourists but no one is really certain about their purpose. Some say they represent the sexual side of the path to final deliverance others that they are simply another part of life and that the sculptors were trying to include all of life in the temples. Whatever the reason they're certainly an important part of what makes Khajuraho so interesting.

sardulas — a mythical beast, part lion part some other animal or even man. Sardulas, usually carrying an armed man on their back, can be seen on many of the temples. They all look like lions but the faces are often different. They may be demons or *asuras*.

Western Group

The western group of temples is the most conveniently situated to the tourist part of Khajuraho and also has the most interesting temples. Most of them are contained within a fenced in enclosure which is kept as a very well maintained park. The enclosure is open from sunrise to sunset and your 50p admission covers you for multiple entries for one day. It also permits entry to the archaeological museum across the road so don't lose your ticket. Admission is free on Fridays. The enclosure temples are described below in a clockwise direction.

Lakshmana Temple

The large Lakshmana Temple is dedicated to Vishnu although in design it is similar to the Kandariya Mahadev and Vishvanath temples. It is one of the earliest of the western enclosure temples, dating from around 930 to 950 AD, but also one of the best preserved since it has not only the full five part floor plan but also still retains its four subsidiary shrines. Around the temple are two, rather than the usual three, bands of sculptures and the lower one has some fine figures of *apsaras* and some erotic scenes. On the subsidiary shrine at the south-west corner you can make out an architect working with his˙ students — it is thought this may be the temple's designer, including himself in the grand plan. Right around the base of the temple there is a continuous frieze with scenes of battles, hunting and processions. The first metre or two of the frieze consists of a highly energetic orgy including one gentleman proving that a horse can be man's best friend while a stunned group of women look aside in shock.

Lakshmi & Varah Temples

Facing the large Lakshmana Temple are these two small shrines. The Varah Temple, dedicated to Vishnu's boar incarnation or Varah Avatar, actually faces the Matangesvara Temple which is outside the enclosure. Inside this small, open shrine is a huge, solid and intricately carved figure of the boar.

Kandariya Mahadev

The first of the temples on a common base at the back of the western enclosure is the one temple to see in Khajuraho above all others. The Kandariya Mahadev is not only the largest of the temples it is also artistically and architecturally the most perfect. Built between 1025 and 1050 it represents Chandela art at its most finely developed phase. Although the four subsidiary shrines which once stood around the main temple have long disappeared the central shrine is in superb condition and shows the typical five part design of Khajuraho temples.

The main spire soars 31 metres high and the temple is lavishly carved. The English archaeologist Cunningham counted 226 statues inside the temple and a further 646 outside — 872 in total with most of them nearly a metre in height. The statues are carved around the temple in three bands and include gods, goddesses, beautiful women, musicians and, of course, some of the famed erotic groups. The *mithuna* on the Kandariya Mahadev include some of the most energetic eroticism to be seen at Khajuraho. In the sexual olympics there would definitely be some gold medal winners here.

Mahadeva

This small, and mainly ruined, temple stands on the same base as the Kandariya Mahadev and the Devi Jagadamba. Although it is so small and insignificant in comparison to its mighty neighbours it houses one of Khajuraho's best sculptures — a fine figure of a person (man or woman, observers have been unable to decide) caressing a lion.

Devi Jagadamba

The third temple on the common platform is slightly older than the Kandariya Mahadev and of a simpler, three-part design. The temple was probably originally dedicated to Vishnu but later changed to Parvati and then Kali. Some students believe it may still be a Parvati temple and that the Kali image (or Jagadamba) is actually an image of Parvati, painted black. The sculptures around the temple are again in three bands. Many of the two lower band images are of Vishnu with *sharduls* in the inner recesses. But on the third and uppermost band the *mithuna* again come out to play and some feel that this is Khajuraho's most erotic temple.

Chitragupta

The fourth temple at the back of the western enclosure does not share the common platform with the other three. Similar in design to the Devi Jagadamba, this temple is probably slightly later and is unique, at Khajuraho, in being dedicated to Surya, the Sun God. The temple has obviously been much restored and is not in such good condition as other temples. Nevertheless it has some very fine sculptures including processions, dancing girls, elephant fights and hunting scenes. In the inner sanctum Surya can be seen driving his chariot and seven horses while on the central niche in the south facade you can see an 11-headed statue of Vishnu. The central head is that of Vishnu himself, the 10 others are of his incarnations.

Parvati

Continuing around the enclosure you come to the Parvati temple on your right. The name is probably incorrect since this small, and not so interesting, temple was originally dedicated to Vishnu and now has an image of Ganga riding on the back of a crocodile.

Vishvanath Temple & Nandi

Believed to have been built in 1002 this temple also has the complete five-part design of the larger Kandariya Mahadev temple but also has two of its four sub-

Khajuraho

Key:-
1 Lakshmi Temple
2 Varah Temple
3 Matangesvara Temple
4 Lakshmana Temple

Rajnagar(5km)
Raneh Falls (19 km)

Tourist Bungalow

Rahil Janta Hotel

Khajuraho Hotel

Chitragupta
Devi Jagdambe
Mahadeva
Kandariya Mahadev

Nandi
Vishvanath
Parvati

Tourist Office

Mosque

Gupta Lodge
New Bharat Lodge

Bus Station

Archeological Museum

Brahma Temple

Chausath Yogini Temple

Vamana Temple

Javari Temple

Khajuraho Village

Ghantai Temple

Adinath Temple
Parsvanath Temple
Shanti Nath Temple

Hotel Chandela

Hotel Temple

Airport (5km)

Duladeo Temple

Khodar River

sidiary shrines still standing. That it is a Shiva shrine is made very clear by the large image of his vehicle, the bull Nandi, which faces the temple from the other end of the common platform. Steps lead up to this high terrace, flanked by lions on the northern side and elephants on the southern side. The sculptures around the temple include the usual Khajuraho scenes but the sculptures of women are particularly notable here.

They write letters, fondle a baby, play music and, perhaps more so than any other temple, simply languish around in provocative poses.

Matangesvara Temple
Standing next to the Lakshmana Temple this temple is not within the fenced enclosure because it is still in everyday use, unlike all the other old Khajuraho temples. It is one of the older temples

at Khajuraho, dating from around 900 to 925 AD. The temple is rather simpler in floor plan than the later, more highly developed temples and does not have the same profusion of carvings. Inside the shrine is a highly polished 2.5 metre high lingam.

Chausath Yogini

Standing beyond the tank, some distance from the other western group temples, this ruined temple is probably the oldest at Khajuraho, dating from 900 AD or earlier. It is also the only temple constructed entirely of granite and the only one not to be aligned east-west. Chausath means 64 — the temple once had 64 cells for figures of the 64 yoginis who attended the goddess Kali. A 65th cell sheltered Kali herself. A further half km west is the Lalguan Mahadev Temple, a small ruined shrine dedicated to Shiva and constructed of granite and sandstone.

Archaeological Museum

Close to the western enclosure, across the road from the post office, the museum has a fine collection of statues and sculptures rescued from around Khajuraho. It's quite small and definitely worth a visit. The museum is open from 9 am to 5 pm daily and the western enclosure entrance fee also includes the museum. Opposite the museum, is the Archaeological Survey of India's compound beside the Matangesvara Temple, there are many more rescued sculptures — but it's off limits.

Eastern Group

The eastern group of temples can actually be subdivided into two groups. The first is the walled enclosure which contains an interesting group of Jain temples. The other four temples are scattered through the small village of Khajuraho. The easiest way to see these temples is to take a rickshaw out to the Jain enclosure and then walk back

to your hotel through Khajuraho village. Alternatively you can visit all these temples en route to the southern group.

Parsvanath Temple

The largest of the Jain temples in the walled enclosure is also one of the finest temples at Khajuraho. Although it does not approach the western enclosure temples in size, or attempt to compete in the sexual activity stakes, it is notable for the exceptional skill and precision of its construction and for the beauty of its sculptures. Some of the best known figures at Khajuraho can be seen here including the classic figures of a woman removing a thorn from her foot and another of a woman applying eye make-up. Although it was originally dedicated to Adinath an image of Parsvanath was substituted about a century ago and the temple takes its name from this newer image.

Adinatha

Adjacent to the Parsvanath Temple the smaller Adinatha has been partially restored over the centuries. It has fine carvings on its three bands of sculptures and, like the Parsvanath, is very similar to the Hindu temples of Khajuraho. Only the Jain image in the inner sanctum indicates that it is Jain rather than Hindu.

Santinatha

This temple is a relatively modern one built about a century ago but it contains many components from older temples around Khajuraho and a fine collection of Jain sculpture. The Jain compound also contains a small museum.

Ghantai Temple

Walking back from the eastern Jain temple group towards Khajuraho village you come to this small ruined temple. Only the pillared shell of this Jain temple remains but it is interesting for the delicate columns with their bell and chain decoration and for the figure of a Jain goddess astride a Garuda which marks the entrance.

Javari Temple

You walk right through the village, a typical small Indian settlement, to this temple. Dating from around 1075 to 1100 AD it is dedicated to Vishnu and is a particularly fine example of Khajuraho architecture on a small scale. The exterior has more of Khajuraho's delightful women.

Vamana Temple

About 200 metres north this temple is dedicated to Vamana, the dwarf incarnation of Vishnu. Slightly older than the Javari Temple, the Vamana Temple stands out in a field all by itself. It's notable for the relatively simple design of its shikara. The bands of sculpture around the temple are, as usual, very fine with numerous 'celestial maidens' adopting numerous interesting poses.

Brahma Temple

Turning back towards the modern village you pass this granite and sandstone temple, one of the oldest at Khajuraho. It was actually dedicated to Vishnu and the definition of it as a Brahma temple is incorrect. Taking the road directly from the modern village to the Jain enclosure you pass a temple to Hanuman with a large image of the monkey god.

Southern Group

There are only two temples in the southern group, one of which is several km south of the river.

Duladeo Temple

A dirt track runs to this isolated temple, about a km south of the Jain enclosure. This is the latest temple at Khajuraho and experts say that at this time the skill of Khajuraho's temple builders has passed its peak and that the sculptures are more 'wooden' and 'stereotyped' than on the earlier temples. Nevertheless it's a fine and graceful temple with figures of women in a variety of pin-up poses and a number of *mithuna* couples.

Chaturbhuja Temple

South of the river, about three km from the village and quite a healthy hike down the dirt road that leads to it, this ruined temple has a fine large (three metre high) image of Vishnu.

Tours

There are a number of walking tours available around the western group of temples. The Archaeological Survey of India has a guided lecture tour twice daily except on Fridays and holidays — it's free. At 10 am and 3.30 pm (July to March) and 8 am and 4.30 pm (April to June) the Government of India Tourist Office has a two hour tour which costs Rs 2.

Places to Stay — Top End

The *Hotel Chandela* (tel 54) is south of the modern village, towards the airport. It's the number one hotel at Khajuraho and its rooms are all air-con, costing Rs 200/300 for singles/doubles. *Hotel Khajuraho* (tel 24), a short walk north of the modern village, is a little cheaper at Rs 140/200 for singles/doubles with air-con, Rs 90/160 without. Both have restaurants, reasonably good food at the Khajuraho.

Places to Stay — Bottom End

The *Rahil (Janata Hotel)* (tel 62) is fairly close to the Khajuraho Hotel. Run by the state government it is new, clean and comfortable and costs Rs 35 single, Rs 50 double. In the dormitory there are beds at Rs 6 each. In the nearby *Tourist Bungalow* (tel 64) the rooms are all four bedded and cost Rs 60. Both of these hotels have parking places so they're good for people with vehicles.

Near the bus station there are a number of cheap local hotels. Rooms in these hotels are all from around Rs 15 or Rs 20 and some of them are quite reasonable. Try the *New Bharat Lodge*, popular with travellers, or the *Jain Lodge* (tel 52).

Food in the *Hotel Rahill* is quite good, Rs 5 for a vegetarian dinner. Opposite the entrance to the western enclosure, *Raja's Cafe* is run by a Swiss woman. It's a popular gathering spot under the large shady tree in the restaurant's courtyard. *New Bharat Lodge* does good thalis and other food plus really good tea — if you're heartily sick of the usual over milky, over sweet tea in India.

Getting There
Getting to Khajuraho can be a major pain. Khajuraho is really on the way from nowhere to nowhere and is not near any railway station. Although many travellers slot Khajuraho in between Varanasi and Agra it involves a lot of travelling to cover not particularly great distances. If you can afford to fly, then do, you'd save a lot of time.

Flying Indian Airlines have a daily flight which operates Delhi-Agra-Khajuraho-Varanasi-Kathmandu then returns by the same route to Delhi. It's probably the most popular tourist flight in India and can often be booked solid for days by tour groups. Delhi-Khajuraho costs Rs 260, Agra-Khajuraho Rs 182 and Varanasi-Khajuraho Rs 182. If you're continuing on to Thailand after India see the introductory travel section about the bargain tickets to fly Delhi-Agra - Khajuraho - Varanasi - Kathmandu - Calcutta-Bangkok.

Train & Bus From the west there are

bus services from Agra (412 km), Gwalior (293 km) and Jhansi (192 km). Jhansi is the nearest approach to Khajuraho on the main Delhi-Bombay rail line and there are at least three buses a day on the Jhansi-Khajuraho route. This is the most popular route to Khajuraho by public bus but from Agra there is a daily Uttar Pradesh government bus which takes eight hours to make the trip via Gwalior and costs Rs 30.

There is no direct route to Varanasi from Khajuraho. Satna, 120 km from Khajuraho, is the nearest railhead for visitors from Varanasi, Calcutta or Bombay. It's on the Bombay-Allahabad line. From Varanasi it takes about nine hours to Satna on the Sarnath Express. Once there you walk up the road and to the left to the local bus station. A bus leaves around 3.30 or 4 pm for Khajuraho and costs about Rs 9. The trip takes about four hours if you get a straight through bus, longer if you have to change on the way. So an early morning departure from Varanasi should get you to Khajuraho by evening at an all up cost of about Rs 30. Satna has a motel with singles/doubles at Rs 30/40. In the opposite direction you could take a bus from Khajuraho then a train around midnight would get you to Varanasi early in the morning.

Getting Around
The airport bus into town costs Rs 5 but a taxi only costs Rs 10. The western temples are all for viewing on foot. To the eastern or southern group take a rickshaw. For Rs 1 you can get out to the Jain enclosure and walk back from there. Or for Rs 3 or 4 make a round trip to Duladeo. All the rickshaw wallahs have 'fixed rates' to any temple or group of temples you care to name but it's all for show.

JABALPUR (population 550,000)

Almost due south of Khajuraho and due east of Bhopal the large town of Jabalpur, the second largest town in the state, is principally famous today for the gorge of the Narmada River known as the Marble Rocks. A century ago Jabalpur was the centre for the long British effort to suppresss the practise of 'Thuggee'. The practitioners of this strange activity were known as 'Thugs', from which the word comes. They engaged in ritual murders, strangling their victims with a silken cord, in order to please the goddess Kali. In 1829 Colonel Sleeman was appointed to wipe out this bizarre activity and the 'School of Industry', where at one time suspected Thugs were interned, can still be seen in Jabalpur. Today it is used as a boys' reform school. It took the best part of 50 years to totally wipe out the Thugs. Today Jabalpur also has the Rani Durgavati Museum.

Marble Rocks

Known locally as Bhera Ghat the marble rocks are white limestone cliffs rising 30 metres above the water of the Narmada River. The gleaming rocks have a magical effect, especially by moonlight. If you wait for a group to form its costs Rs 2 to boat up the gorge. The water falls down the Dhuandhar or 'smoke cascade' at the top of the gorge and on the trip down the gorge you can see the Hathi-ka-paon or 'elephant's foot', a group of curiously shaped rocks, the ledge known as 'monkey's leap' and an inscription cut by Madho Rao Peshwa.

It's about 24 km to the marble rocks, you can take a bus, or, if you're feeling fit, cycle out and back in a day. The

road is fairly flat and there are plenty of stalls to stop at along the way. You can buy cheap marble carvings there.

Madan Mahal & Chausath Yogini Temple

This ancient Gond fortress is on the route to the marble rocks, perched on top of a huge boulder. The Gonds, who worshipped snakes, lived in this region even before the Aryans arrived and maintained their independence right up until the arrival of Akbar.

Above the lower end of the gorge a flight of over 100 stone steps leads to the Chausath Yogini or Madanpur Temple. The circular temple has damaged images of the 64 yoginis, or attendants of the goddess Durga.

Places to Stay

The *Raja Gokuldass Dharamsala*, near the railway station, is very good for just Rs 2 on the first day, Rs 1 for succeeding days in a private room. At the other end of the scale there's *Jackson's Hotel* (tel 21320) in Civil Lines. Singles/doubles costs from Rs 60/100. The Tourist Department's *Marble Rocks Inn* (tel 38) has just four rooms at Rs 35/50 for singles/doubles. There are a number of local hotels also. At the station there is a Tourist Office (tel 2211).

Getting There

There are buses to Jabalpur from Allahabad, Khajuraho, Varanasi, Bhopal and other main centre. Jabalpur is on the Bombay-Allahabad-Calcutta railway line. It's 1183 km from Calcutta, 369 km from Allahabad and 990 km from Bombay. Three times weekly there's a Bombay-Jabalpur-Raipur and return flight.

OTHER PLACES — East & South-East

Pachmarhi

At an altitude of 1100 metres this is Madhya Pradesh's hill station. It's near

Itarsi on the Bombay-Jabalpur-Allahabad railway line. There are fine views out over the surrounding red sandstone hills and some interesting walks to be made.

Places to Stay The Tourist Department has a variety of accommodation at Pachmarhi. The *Satpura Forest Lodge* (tel 97) has singles/doubles at Rs 50/70 while in the *Holiday Homes* (tel 99) there are rooms at Rs 10 and Rs 30. The more expensive Holiday Homes have cooking facilities.

Bandhavgarh National Park
In the Vindhyan Mountain Range in central Madhya Pradesh there is a wide variety of wildlife in this national park. Umaria, on the Katni-Bilaspur rail line, is the nearest railhead. It's also accessible from Satna on the Bombay-Allahabad rail line.

Places to Stay *White Tiger Forest Lodge* in the park has singles/doubles at Rs 40/60. Accommodation can be booked in advance in Bhopal or Jabalpur.

Mandla & Ramnagar
On the route to Nagpur in Maharashtra, 100 km south of Jabalpur, is the fort of Mandla which is situated in a loop of the Narmada River so that the river protects it on three sides and a ditch on the fourth. Built in the late 1600s the fort is now subsiding into the jungle although some of the towers still stand. About 15 km away is Ramnagar with a ruined three storey palace overlooking the Narmada. The palace, and then the fort, were both built by Gond kings, retreating south before the advance

of Moghul power. Near Mandla there is a stretch of the Narmada where many temples dot the riverbank.

Kanha National Park
There are rest houses and watchtowers in this park, 77 km from Mandla and 173 km from Jabalpur.

Places to Stay There are a variety of accommodation possibilities including the *Kisli Youth Hostel* with dorm beds at Rs 5 and *Forest Bungalows, Forest Lodges* and *Log Huts* at Rs 20/30 singles/doubles up to Rs 40/60.

Bilaspur & Raipur
There are larger towns in the east of the state on the Bombay-Calcutta railway line. Ratanpur, 25 km north of Bilaspur, was the capital of the old kingdom of Chattisgarh, the 'kingdom of 36 forts'.

OTHER PLACES — North-West
Indore/Ujjain-Chittorgarh
The railway line passes through Ratlam, capital of a former princely state whose ruler died in one of those tragically heroic Rajput battles against the might of the Moghuls. At Mandsaur, north of Ratlam, a number of interesting archaeological finds were made in a field three km from the town. Some others displayed in the museum at Indore. Two 14 metre high sandstone pillars are on the site, an inscription commemorates the victory of a Malwa king over the Huns in 528 AD. In the fort there are some fine pieces from the Gupta period.

Orissa

Population: 24 million
Area: 155,842 square km
Capital: Bhubaneswar
Main language: Oriya

The State of Orissa lies along the eastern seaboard of India, south of Bengal. The main attractions of Orissa are the temple towns of Puri and Bhubaneswar and the great Sun Temple at Konarak. These three sites make a convenient and compact little triangle and Bhubaneswar is on the main Calcutta-Madras railway route. The state is predominantly rural with fertile green plains along the coast rising up to the hills of the Eastern Ghats.

Orissa's hazy past comes into focus with the reign of Kalinga. In 260 BC he was defeated by Ashoka, the great Indian emperor, but the bloody battle left such a bitter taste with Ashoka that he converted to Buddhism and spread that gentle religion far and wide. Buddhism soon declined in Orissa, however, and Jainism held sway until Buddhism reasserted itself in the 2nd century AD. By the 7th century AD Hinduism had, in turn, supplanted Buddhism and Orissa's golden age was in full swing.

Under the Kesari and Ganga kings the Orissan culture flourished and countless temples from that classical period still stand today. The Orissans managed to defy the Moslem rulers in Delhi until the region finally fell to the Moghuls during the 16th century. Many of Bhubaneswar's temples were destroyed at that time. Today Orissa is tapping the hydro-electric potential of its many rivers and fledgling industries are being started but the state is still a region of green fields and small villages.

Temple Architecture

Orissan temples, whether it is the mighty Lingaraj in Bhubaneswar, the Jagannath in Puri, the Sun Temple at Konarak, or the many smaller temples all follow a similar pattern. Basically there are two structures — the *jagamohan*, or entrance porch, and the *deul*, where the image of the temple deity is kept and above which the temple tower rises. The design is complicated in larger temples by the addition of one or more entrace halls in front of the *jagamohan*. These are the *bhoga-mandapa* or 'hall of offering' and the *nata-mandir* or 'dancing hall'.

deul   jaga-mohana   nata-mandira

bhoga-mandapa

PLAN OF LINGARAJA TEMPLE

The whole structure may be enclosed by an outer wall and within the enclosure there may be other smaller subsidiary temples and shrines. The most notable aspect of the temple design is the soaring tower and the intricate carvings that cover every surface of the temple. These may be figures of gods, men and women, plants, trees, flowers, animals and every other aspect of every day life, but to many visitors it is the erotic carvings which create the greatest interest. They reach their artistic and explicit peak at Konarak where the close up detail is every bit as interesting as the temple's sheer size and imagination.

BHUBANESWAR (population 125,000)
The capital of Orissa is known as the temple town due to its many temples in the extravagant Orissan architectural style. At one time the Bindusagar tank had over 7000 temples around it. Today there are about 500 but most of these are just decayed fragments. Perhaps a dozen are of real interest including the great Lingaraj Temple, one of the most important temples in India. The Puri temples are in a variety of Orissan styles and date from the 8th to the 13th century AD.

Orientation
Bhubaneswar is a sprawling town divided into old and new parts — the railway line forms the approximate dividing line. The bus stop and the Indian Airlines office are both in the new town as are most of the hotels. The Tourist Bungalow (and tourist office) and the ITDC Ashoka Hotel are both across the tracks. Most of the temples are within reasonable walking distance of the Tourist Bungalow. The airport is very close to the centre.

Lingaraj Temple
The great temple of Bhubaneswar is off limits to all non-Hindus. Close to the wall, on the northern side, is a viewing platform originally erected for Lord Curzon during the days of the Raj. It's the best view you'll get of the temple and you really need binoculars to see anything. The temple is dedicated to Tribhuvaneswar or 'Lord of the Three Worlds', also known as Bhubaneswar. In its present form the temple dates from 1090 to 1104 AD although parts of it are over 400 years old. The granite block which represents Tribhuvaneswar is said to be bathed daily with water, milk and bhang (hashish). The temple compound is about 150 metres square and dominated by the 40 metre high temple tower. The ornately carved tower is intricately sculptured, from the viewing platform you can easily see the lions crushing elephants, said to be a representation of the re-emergence of Hinduism over Buddhism. More than 50 smaller temples and shrines crowd the enclosure. In the north-east corner a

smaller temple to Parvati is of particular interest.

Bindusagar

The 'Ocean Drop' tank is just north of the great temple and is said to contain water from every holy stream, pool and tank in India. Consequently when it comes to washing away sin this is the tank which washes whitest. There are a number of temples and shrines scattered around the tank, several of them with towers in imitation of the Lingaraj Temple's. In the centre of the tank is a water pavilion where, once a year, the Lingaraj Temple's deity is brought to be ritually bathed.

Siddharanya

Close to the main Bhubaneswar-Puri road, on the same side as the Lingaraj Temple, the 'Grove of the Perfect Beings' is a cluster of about 20 smaller temples, including some of the most important in Bhubaneswar. Right by the road the small, 11 metres high, Mukteswar Temple is finely detailed with some excellent carving but unfortunately much of it is defaced. The dwarves are particularly nice. The Mukteswar features an arched torana, a gateway showing clear Buddhist influence. Also by the road, across the path from the Mukteswar, the Kedareswar is one of the older temples at Bhubaneswar and has a small tank. Close to the Mukteswar is the Siddeswar Temple, an interesting

old temple with a fine standing Ganesh figure. If you follow the path from these temples towards the Lingaraj you soon come to the Prashurameswar on your right. It's the best preserved of the early (7th century AD) temples and has interesting bas reliefs of elephant and horse processions. All its fine carvings are vigorous and alive.

If you work up a thirst while temple hunting the shop beside the cinema near the junction has the coldest and cheapest soft drinks in town.

Raj Rani

Across the road and about a hundred metres to the right the Raj Rani stands alone in a green field. It's one of the latest of the Bhubaneswar Temples and particularly finely sited. Statues of nymphs, embracing couples, elephants and lions fill the niches and decorate the pillars.

Brahmeswar

About a km east of the main road the Brahmeswar Temple stands in a courtyard flanked by four smaller structures. It's notable for its very finely detailed sculptures, with an erotic element and some quite amusingly carved — such as the young lady with the surprised look on her face, no doubt due to her lover's hand in her pants! The temple dates from the 9th century. Close by are two other temples which are not of such great interest. The Bhaskareswar has an

Bhubaneswar

National Highway 5

Cuttack

Orissa Trunk Road

National Highway 5

24

Airport

Chatrapur
Madras

N

Bindu Sagar

Sisupal
Garh

Scale

0   1   2 km

Puri
Konarak

unusual 'stepped' design in order to accommodate an unusually large (three metre) lingam it once contained. The Megheswar is in a courtyard and its shrine entrance is topped by a figure. Beside it there is a tank.

Other Temples
Close to the Bindusagar Tank the Vaital has a double storey 'wagon roof', an influence from Buddhist cave architecture. The Lakshamaneswar is a very plain temple, dating from the 7th century it is one of the earliest specimens of Orissan architecture and acts as a gateway to the city.

Museum
The museum is opposite the Hotel Ashok Kalinga and has an interesting collection relating to Orissan history, culture and architecture and to the various Orissan tribes. The Tribal Research Bureau is also located here. The museum is open 10 am to 5 pm daily except Mondays.

Tours
During the season there are various tours operated from the Tourist Bungalow including a tour of temples and caves of Bhubaneswar for K10 or a Puri-Konarak tour for K25. The latter tour takes from 8 am to 6 pm.

Discrimination
Two of the main attractions in Puri and Bhubaneswar (the Temple of Jagganath and the Lingaraj Temple) are 'off limits' to foreigners (non-Hindus). Nowhere in the tourist office's Orissa brochures is this ban mentioned — should tourist attractions be promoted if the tourists are not allowed into them? Even more to the point should you pay for places you're banned from? At the Lingaraj Temple there'll be someone waiting for you near the viewing platform to ask for not one but two donations — one for upkeep of that temple you're not fit to enter and a second for 'upkeep' of the viewing platform; which has clearly had no upkeep at all since the British built it. You'll also be asked for a donation for viewing the Jagganath Temple from the Raghunandan Library. Fair enough, since it's a private building, but Rs 1 is quite enough. Just because all the names in the visitors' book have Rs 25 written after them doesn't mean for a moment that's what they've 'donated'!

Places to Stay — Top End
The conveniently situated *Hotel Ashok Kalinga* (tel 50745) and the *Prachi Resort* are Bhubaneswar's two top hotels. There's also the *State Guest House* but that's mainly for officials. The *Ashok Kalinga* is modern, centrally air-conditioned and situated just across from the museum. It also has a good restaurant and bar. Singles/doubles cost Rs 100/150. The *Prachi Resort* (tel 52521) at 6 Janpath is in the same price bracket.

Places to Stay — Bottom End
The popular *Panthanivas Tourist Bungalow*, (tel 50099) where you will also find the Tourist Office, is only a couple of hundred metres from the Hotel Ashok Kalinga and conveniently near to the many temples. Singles/doubles cost Rs 15/25 and there are also a couple of four-bedded rooms at Rs 30 which can also be used as dormitories at Rs 8 per bed. The state government run Tourist Bungalows are all similarly priced throughout Orissa and offer very similar standards. They're well kept, all rooms have attached bathrooms and there's also a reasonably priced restaurant. Food can get a little monotonous though.

Most other accommodation is in the new town part of Bhubaneswar. There are a lot of hotels; most of them of similar standard to the Tourist Bungalow or below. Two particularly good value hotels are the *Bhubaneswar Hotel* (tel 51977) near the railway station with singles/doubles at Rs 15/20, and also some more expensive air-con rooms. A big, well kept and clean place. Similar standards, but Rs 5 more expensive, at the centrally located *Rajmahal Hotel* (tel 52448) near the bus station and market. The nearby *Banaraswalla Hotel* (tel 50947) is cheaper at Rs 15 a double. There are plenty of other hotels in this central area.

The railway station has *retiring rooms* (tel 52233) as does the bus station — upstairs at Rs 20 a double. Out at the Udayagiri-Khandagiri hills there's a very run down building claiming to be the *Khandagiri Youth Hostel.*

Places to Eat

The *Tourist Bungalow* has a reasonably priced, if monotonous, dining hall. Amongst the eating places in town you could try the *South Indian Hotel*, close to the Rajmahal, for a tali. The *Ashok Kilinga* is an excellent place for an escape to air-con comfort and good food — say Rs 25 to Rs 40 per person for a complete meal.

Getting There

Rail Bhubaneswar is 469 km from Calcutta and 1222 km from Madras. Since it is on the main Calcutta-Madras railway line there are plenty of trains to Bhubaneswar as well as the trains terminating at Puri. The crack Coromandel Express departs Calcutta at 5.40 pm and arrives in Bhubaneswar just over six hours later, just before midnight. Other trains are rather slower, the Madras Mail leaves at 8 pm and takes 8½ hours. Other trains can take as long as 10 hours. Second class fare on a mail or express train is about Rs 23, first class is about Rs 87.

From Madras the Coromandel Express takes about 19 hours, the Madras Mail about 24 hours and other trains 30 or more hours. Fare from Madras is about Rs 50 in second class, Rs 190 in first class. Trains terminating in Puri take 1½ to two hours longer from Calcutta or Madras.

Five days a week there are trains from Delhi to Bhubaneswar and Puri. The once weekly Kalinga Express takes about 37 hours to Puri but other trains take closer to 48 hours. The fare is about Rs 70 second class, Rs 275 first class.

Air There are daily flights between Calcutta and Bhubaneswar. The one hour 25 minute flight costs Rs 202 and continues on to Visakhapatnam then returns. Three times a week there is a second flight from Calcutta which continues on to Varanasi (two hours 15 minutes, Rs 338) and then Delhi.

To Puri & Konarak There are frequent private buses from Bhubaneswar to Puri. The trip takes 1½ to two hours and costs Rs 3.50. See Konarak for Puri-Konarak information. If it is not possible to get a direct bus to Konarak any Puri bus will go through Pipli where the Konarak road branches off.

Getting Around

The Indian Airlines airport bus costs Rs 5 but only to the IA office. A taxi costs Rs 15 but you could also get a rickshaw for Rs 5, rather uphill from the town though. From the Tourist Bungalow a rickshaw to town or the Lingaraja Temple would be Rs 2 to Rs 3.

AROUND BHUBANESWAR

There are two interesting sites close to Bhubaneswar, both dating from the Buddhist period.

Udayagiri & Khandagiri Caves

About five km out of Bhubaneswar these two hills, flanking the road on each side, are riddled with caves. On the right of the road the Udayagiri, or Sunrise Hill has the most interesting caves, scattered at various levels up the hill. At the base of the hill, round to the right, is the two storey Rani ka Naur or Queen's Palace cave (1). All the caves are numbered. Both levels have eight entrances and the cave is extensively carved.

Return to the road via the Chota Hathi Gumpha (3) with carvings of elephants coming out from behind a tree. The Jaya Vijaya Cave (5) is again double storeyed and a bo-tree is carved in the central compartment. Back at the entrance ascend the hill to cave 9, the Swargapuri, and 14, the Hathi Gumpha or 'Elephant Cave'. The latter is quite plain but an inscription relates, in 117 lines, the exploits of its builder, King Kharaveli of Kalinga who ruled from 168 to 153 BC.

Circle round the hill to the right to the Ganesh Gumpha (10) which is almost directly above the Rani ka Naur. The carvings here tell the same tale as in that lower level cave but are better drawn. The cave is only single storey. Retrace your steps to cave 14 then on to the Pavana Gumpha 'Cave of Purification' and the small Sarpa Gumpha or 'Serpent Cave', the tiny door to which is surmounted by a three-headed cobra.

Only 15 or so metres from this is the Bagh Gumpha (12) or Tiger Cave, entered through the mouth of the beast. The hill is topped by the foundations of some long gone building. The oldest of these various caves date back to the 2nd century BC. Some are of Jain origin.

Across the road the Kandagiri hill is not so interesting apart from the fine view back over Bhubaneswar from its summit. You can see the airport, the tower of the Lingaraj Temple rising behind it, and further away the Dhauli Stupa. The steep path divides about a third of the way up the hill. The right path goes to the Ananta Cave (3) with carved figures of athletes, women, elephants and geese carrying flowers. The right path leads to a series of Jain temples. At the top of the hill is an 18th century Jain temple.

Around Bhubaneswar

Getting There There are only a few buses specifically to the caves but there are plenty going by the nearby road junction. It's 50p into town or by rickshaw you can get there for about Rs 5.

Dhauli Edicts
About eight km south of Bhubaneswar, to the right of the Puri road, King Ashoka carved his famous edicts into a rock five metres by three metres. The famous Buddhist emperor related the horrors he experienced in the Kalinga wars, which he won, and his subsequent conversion to Buddhism. These 13 inscriptions are still remarkably clear after over 2000 years and the site is also marked by a new Peace Pagoda.

Other
The only partly excavated ruins at Sisupal Garh are thought to be the

remains of an Ashokan city. At Nandankanan, 30 km from Bhubaneswar, there is a garden divided into a wildlife sanctuary, botanical garden and lake. You can rent boats on the lake.

PURI (population 75,000)

On the coast, 61 km from Bhubaneswar, Puri is one of the four holiest cities in India. The city revolves around the great Jagannath Temple and its famous Rath Yatra or Car Festival. It is thought that Puri was the hiding place for the Buddha tooth of Kandy before it was spirited away to Sri Lanka. There are similarities between the Rath Yatra and the annual Kandy procession.

Orientation

There is only one wide road in Puri, the Baradand or Grand Road which runs from the Jagannath Temple to the Gundicha Mandir. Buses stop along this road. Most of the hotels are along the seafront. The tourist office is in the Tourist Bungalow.

Jagannath Temple

The temple of Jagannath, 'Lord of the Universe', is not open to non-Hindus but amongst Hindus its considerable popularity is partially due to the lack of caste distinctions — all are welcome before Jagannath. Non-believers can look down into the temple from the roof of the Raghunandan Library, opposite the main entrance to the temple. You'll be asked for a donation.

The temple enclosure is nearly square, measuring almost 200 metres on each side. The walls of the enclosure are six metres high. Inside there is a second wall enclosing the actual temple. The conical tower of the temple is 58 metres high and is topped by the flag and wheel of Vishnu. It is visible from far out of Puri. The temple was built in its present form in 1198. In front of the main entrance is a beautiful pillar, topped by an image of the Garuda, which originally stood in front of the temple at Konarak.

The main entrance is known as the Lion Gate from the two stone lions guarding the entrance.

Balabhadra, Subhadra & Lord Jagannath

In the central Jagmohan, pilgrims to the temple can see the images of Lord Jagannath and his brother Balbhadra, and sister, Subhadra. Although non-believers are not, of course, able to see them, the many shop stalls along the road outside the temple all sell small wooden replicas. The curious images are carved from tree trunks, in a child like caricature of a human face. The brothers have arms but the smaller Subhadra does not. All three are garlanded and dressed for ceremonies and the various seasons. The temple employs 6000 men to perform the temple functions and the complicated rituals involved in caring for the gods. It has been estimated that in all 20,000 people are dependent on Jagannath and the God's immediate attendants are divided into 36 orders and 97 classes!

Rath Yatra or Car Festival

One of India's greatest annual events takes place in Puri each June or July when the fantastic festival of the cars sets forth from the Jagannath Temple.

It commemorates the journey of Krishna from Gokul to Mathura. The images of Jagannath, his brother and his sister are brought out from the temple and dragged in huge 'cars' known as *raths* down the wide Bradand to the Gundicha Mandir or 'Garden House' over a km away. The main car of Jagannath stands 14 metres high and over 10 metres square and rides on 16 wheels, each over two metres in diameter. It is from these collosal cars that our word 'juggernaut' is derived and in centuries past devotees were known to have thrown themselves beneath the wheels of the juggernaut in order to die in the God's sight. To haul the cars takes over 4000 professional car-pullers, all employees of the temple. Hundreds of thousands of pilgrims (and tourists) flock from all over India to witness this stupendous scene. The huge and unwieldly cars take an enormous effort to pull, are virtually impossible to turn and once moving are nearly unstoppable.

Once they reach the other end of the road the Gods take a week long summer break, then are loaded back onto the cars and trucked back to the Jagannath Temple, in a virtual repeat of the previous week's procession. Following the festival the cars are broken up and used to make religious relics. New cars are constructed each year. At intervals of eight, 11 or 19 years or combinations of those numbers, depending on various astrological occurrences, the gods themselves are also disposed of and new images made. In the last century and a half there have been new images in 1863, 1893, 1931, 1950, 1969 and 1977.

Gundicha Mandir
The Garden House, in which the images of the Gods reside for seven days each year, is also off-limits to non-believers. The walls enclose a garden in which the temple is built. Puri has a number of other temples but these too are forbidden to non-Hindus.

The Beach
Puri has a fine stretch of white sand in which Indian pilgrims bathe in their customary fully attired manner. Orissan fishermen wearing conical straw hats guide bathers out through the surf. You can hire your own lifeguard for Rs 3 a morning or afternoon!

Places to Stay
Almost all the accommodation in Puri is along the seafront. It's found in two distinct clumps. To the north there's the delightfully 'olde worlde' *South-East Railway Hotel* (tel 63) with air-con singles/doubles including all meals at Rs 135/230. Non air-con rooms start from Rs 100. It has a pleasant lounge, bar, dining hall and an immaculate stretch of lawn. Meals cost Rs 12 for breakfast, Rs 25 for lunch or dinner.

A little south there's the *Panthinivas Tourist Bungalow* (tel 131) with singles/doubles at Rs 15/25. Well kept, well located and, as usual, it has a dining hall and the local tourist office. Very close to it is the very neat, clean and tidy *Sea Side Inn*. It's small, friendly and breakfast and snacks are available. Doubles cost Rs 25 in this neat little hotel. Between here and the South-East Railway Hotel is the big, new *Youth Hostel* with dorm beds at Rs 5. There's also the more expensive *Mahodadhinivas Tourist Bungalow*.

The other hotels are almost all clustered together on the main bathing beach about a km south of this northern group. They're generally very basic, aimed at the Indian pilgrim trade and quote all inclusive tariffs only. Most cost Rs 20 to 25 per person with all meals. The *Puri Hotel* is slightly higher standard than the many others. There are also railway *retiring rooms* and a 'railway camping coach'.

Getting There
See Bhubaneswar for transport from there, Konarak for Puri-Konarak details.

Although there is a rail line from Bhubaneswar it is easier to go by bus. There are direct buses for Calcutta, the trip takes 13 to 15 hours.

Getting Around

A rickshaw from Puri bus stand to the hotels along the beach is around Rs 2. There are lots of rickshaws in Puri.

KONARAK

Situated on the coast, 64 km from Bhubaneswar and only about 30 km north of Puri there is, unfortunately, no direct route between Puri and Konarak. The site consists of little more than the mighty temple and a handful of shops, stalls and places to stay. The Temple of the Sun was constructed at some time in the 13th century but remarkably little in known about its early history. It is thought it was built by an Orissan king to celebrate a military victory. It has been in ruins for centuries but until the early 1900s it was simply an interesting ruin of impressive size.

Then in 1904 debris and sand was cleared from around the temple base and the sheer magnitude of its architect's imagination was revealed. The entire temple was conceived as a chariot for the Sun God, Surya. Around the base of the temple are 24 gigantic carved stone wheels, seven mighty horses haul at the temple and the whole immense structure is covered with carvings, sculptures, figures and bas reliefs. It is not known if the construction of the temple was ever actually completed. If the tower was completed it would have soared to 70 metres high and archaeologists wonder if the sandy foundations could have supported such a structure. Part of the tower was still standing in 1837 but by 1869 it had collapsed and today the interior of the temple has been filled in to support the ruins.

The main entrance, from the Tourist Bungalow side, is guarded by two stone lions, crushing elephants. Steps ascend to the main entrance, flanked by the straining horses. The entrance porch or *jagamohan* still stands but the *deul*, behind it, has collapsed. The three images of Surya, the Sun God, still stand and are designed to catch the sun at dawn, at noon and at sunset. Between the main steps up to the *jagamohan* and the enclosure entrance there is an intricately carved 'dancing hall' or *natamandir*. To the north are a group of elephants and to the south a group of rearing horses, trampling down men.

All around the base of the temple and up the walls and roof are a continuous procession of carvings. Many in erotic style for which Konarak, like Khajuraho, is so famous. These erotic images of entwined couples or solitary exhibitionists can be minute images on the spoke of a temple wheel or life size figures higher up the walls.

Outside the temple enclosure there is a museum (open 9 am to 5 pm) containing many sculptures and carvings found during the temple excavation. The sea is a couple of km from the temple, you can walk there or hire a bicycle rickshaw. The temple was once known as the Black Temple by sailors, in contrast to the whitewashed temples of Puri. It was said to contain a great mass of iron which would draw unwary ships in to the shore.

Places to Stay

The *Tourist Bungalow* (tel 21) is very close to the main entrance to the temple. As usual doubles are Rs 25, singles Rs 15 and it's well kept, pleasantly located and has a dining hall and the tourist office. Close to it is the basic *Santosh Restaurant*. Between the Tourist Bungalow and the bus halt is the small ITDC *Ashok Tourist Lodge* — rather more expensive at Rs 30/50 for singles/doubles. It also has dining facilities — breakfast Rs 8, lunch Rs 18, dinner Rs 19 but the meals are poor value. For emergencies there's the Inspection Bungalow and around the bus halt there's a collection of extremely basic little 'boarding & lodging' huts.

Getting There
Puri-Konarak There is no direct route along the coast, 30 odd km, between Puri and Konarak although a coast road is 'planned'. The regular route goes back towards Bhubaneswar to Pipli then doubles back to the coast — total distance 85 km. Several buses depart between 6.30 and 8 am from Puri and there are sometimes buses in the after-

noon too. It takes three hours, at least, more if the bus stops a lot. Fare is Rs 5. Konarak buses depart with reasonable regularity.
Konarak-Bhubaneswar There are also buses fairly regularly to Bhubaneswar including at least one express bus at 1.30 pm. Fare is Rs 3.50.

PIPLI
At the junction, where the Konarak road branches off from the Bhubaneswar-Puri road, this small village is notable for its applique craft. The colourful materials are used to make temple umbrellas and wall hangings.

CHILKA LAKE
South of Puri the Chilka Lake is dotted with islands and is noted for the many migratory birds which flock here each December-January. The shallow lake is

about 70 km in length and averages 15 km wide, it is separated from the sea only by a narrow sand bar. The railway line and the main road run along the inland edge of the lake. It is 130 km from Bhubaneswar to Rambha at the lake. There is another Ashokan rock edict at Jangada.

Places to Stay There are *Tourist Bungalows* at Rambha, at the southern end of the lake, and Barkul, six km north of the railway station of Balugaon and 32 km north of Rambha. The *Barkul Tourist Bungalow* is very small with just two rooms. At both locations singles/doubles cost Rs 15/25.

GOPALPUR-ON-SEA
This popular little beach resort is 18 km from Berhampur where there is a railway station. There are regular buses between Berhampur and Gopalpur. From here you can also make excursions to the hot springs at Taptapani, 45 km away.

Places to Stay At the top end there is the 21 room *Palm Beach Hotel* while at the other end of the scale there is a 16 bed *youth hostel* (Rs 5) and a selection of local hotels.

CUTTACK (population 200,000)
Only 35 km north of Bhubaneswar, this riverine city was the capital of Orissa until the new city was constructed at Bhubaneswar. Only a gateway and the moat remains of the 14th century Barabati Fort. The stone revetment on the Kathjuri River, which protects the city from seasonal floods, dates from the 11th century. Cuttack also has a museum.

Places to Stay There is the *Asian Hotel*, the *Cuttack Hotel* and a number of other small hotels but if you wish to visit Cuttack it is probably easier to stay in Bhubaneswar.

BALASORE & CHANDIPUR
Balasore is the first major town on the railway line from Calcutta in north Orissa. It was once an important trading centre with Dutch, Danish, English and French factories. It was, in 1634, the first British East India Company factory in Bengal. Remina, eight km away, has the Gopinath Temple, an important pilgrimage centre. Chandipur, 16 km away on the coast, is a beach resort where the beach retreats six km at low tide! There are buses twice a day from Balasore.

Places to Stay There are a few small hotels in Balasore such as the *Hotel Sagarika* or *DK Lodging*. In Chandipur there is a *Tourist Bungalow*.

OTHER PLACES
In the north of Orissa, about 200 km inland from the coast, Khiching was once an ancient capital and has a number of interesting temples and temple ruins and a small museum. Further inland is the important industrial city of Rourkela with a major steel plant. North-east of Cuttack, about 100 km from Bhubaneswar, there are Buddhist relics and ruins at the three hilltop complexes of Ratnagiri, Lalitgiri and Udayagiri. The Ratnagiri site has the most interesting ruins. At Lalitgiri craftsmen make replicas of stone sculptures. In the extreme west of the state the twin villages of Ranipur-Jharial are 30 km from Titlagarh and are noted for the extensive collection of temples on an outcrop of rock. They include a circular 64-yogini temple, similar to the one at Khajuraho. Harishankar, near Bolangir in the west, has a number of temples and a waterfall. The Similipal National Park is in the north-east of the state near Khiching. The Ushakothi Wild Life Sanctuary is in the north-west. In the south-west of the state is the Gupteswar Cave, this is the region of the Bonda tribespeople. A little north-west of Cuttack is the Shiva temple of Kapilas.

THINGS TO BUY

Orissa handicrafts include the applique work of Pipli and the filigree jewellery of Cuttack. In Sambalpur tie-dye fabrics are produced and there are a variety of Orissan handloom fabrics. At Puri you can buy strange little wood carved replicas of Lord Jagannath and his brother and sister. At Balasore lacquered children's toys are manufactured.

Tribal People

Orissa has no less than 62 distinct tribal groups, aboriginal people who date from prior to the Aryan invasion of India. They live mainly in the hilly area of central Orissa. Amongst the better known tribes are the Kondh's who still practise colourful ceremonies, although animal sacrifices have now been substituted for the human ones which the British took so much trouble to stop — particularly around Russellkonda (Bhanjanagar). The Bondas are known as the 'naked people' and are renowned for their wild ways and the dormitories where young men and women are encouraged to meet for night-time fun and frolics. Other major tribes are the Juangs, the Santals, the Parajas, the colourful and primitive Godabas and the Koyas.

Entry Prohibited

One clear contrast to the general Indian mood of tolerance is the way westerners are not allowed into Hindu temples. This chiefly applies to the temples in Orissa, in Varanasi and in some temples in the south. It's in complete contrast to Jain and Buddhist temples or to Moslem mosques where you are almost always allowed to wander at will. There is nothing much, you can do about it although these regulations have been much relaxed over the years and there are today far fewer places where an outright ban applies. An irritation is that in many cases the national or state tourist boards expound at length about the glories of these temples and never mention even in the smallest print that if you're a westerner you will not be allowed inside.

WHY KILL FOR FOOD
BE VEGETARIAN

Bombay

Population: 7 million
Main language: Marathi

Bombay is capital of Maharashtra

Bombay is the economic powerhouse of India. It's the fastest moving, most affluent, most industrialised city in India. It also has India's busiest airport for international arrivals and departures and India's busiest port, handling nearly 50% of India's total foreign trade. It's the stronghold of free enterprise in India, a major manufacturing centre for everything from cars and bicycles to pharmaceuticals and petrochemicals. It's the centre for India's important textile industry. Bombay is the financial centre of India, an important base for overseas companies and Nariman Point is rapidly becoming a mini-Manhattan with India's tallest buildings. Yet once upon a time is was nothing more than a group of low-lying, swampy and malarial mud flats and was passed on to the British by its Portuguese occupiers as a wedding dowry!

When the Portuguese arrived on the scene Bombay consisted of seven islands whose only occupants were simple fisherfolk known as Kolis. In 1534 the seven islands from Colaba in the south to Mahim in the north were ceded to Portugal by the Sultan of Gujurat in the Treaty of Bassein. The Portuguese did little with them and in 1661 the major island of the group, Mumbadevi, was part of the wedding dowry when Catherine of Braganza married England's Charles II in 1661. In 1665 the British took possession of all seven islands and in 1668 the British government leased them to the East India Company for an annual £10 in gold.

Soon after the British takeover Bombay started to develop as an important trading port. One of the first signs of this was the arrival of the Parsis who first settled in Bombay in 1670 and built their first Tower of Silence in 1675. In 1687 the Presidency of the East India Company was transferred from Surat to Bombay and by 1708 it had become the trading headquarters for the whole west coast of India. Although Bombay grew steadily for the next century it was around the middle of the 1800s that Bombay's most dynamic development took place. The first railway was laid out of Bombay in 1854 and one of the effects of the Mutiny of 1857 was to further improve the city's image as a 'safe' place, far from the insurrections of the north. Then the American Civil War provided Bombay's young cotton and textile industries with an enormous boost as supplies of cotton from the US dried up. In 1862 a major land reclamation project joined the original seven islands into a single land mass and a year later the governor, Sir Bartle Frere, dismantled the old fort walls and thus sparked off a major building boom.

During this century Bombay has further extended its position as the major commercial, industrial, financial and trading centre of India. It's an active, alive city, full of interest in its own right and yet also an ideal gateway to the states around it.

Orientation

Bombay is an island, connected by bridges with the mainland. At one time it was actually a number of islands and low swampy areas indicate where these divisions once were. The principal part of the city is concentrated at the southern end of the island and the northern end is comparatively lightly populated. The airport, Santa Cruz, is 26 km to the north. There are three main railway stations in the city centre. Churchgate and Victoria Terminus are conveniently central but Bombay Central is some distance further out.

Orientation in Bombay is relatively simple. The southern promontory is Colaba Causeway and the northern end of this promontory is known as Colaba. Most of the cheap hotels and restaurants together with a number of Bombay's top notch establishments are located here. Bombay's two main landmarks — the Gateway of India and the Taj Mahal Hotel — are at Colaba. Directly north of Colaba is the area known as Bombay Fort since the old fort was once here. Most of the impressive buildings from Bombay's golden period during the last 40 years of the last century are located here together with the GPO, offices, banks, the Tourist Office and the two main railway stations. To the west of the fort is Back Bay around which sweeps Marine Drive. The southern end of this drive is marked by Nariman Point. This is the modern business centre of Bombay with more international class hotels, skyscrapers, airline offices (including Indian Airlines and Air India) and banks. The other end of the drive is Malabar Hill, a classy residential area.

Information

The Government of India Tourist Office is at 123 Maharshi Karve Rd, Churchgate (tel 293144) directly across from the Churchgate Station. It's open from 8 am to 7 pm, Mondays to Saturdays and 8 am to 12.30 pm on second Saturdays and holidays. It's closed on Sundays. They also have a counter at the airport and in the Taj Inter-Continental Hotel. The main office has a comprehensive leaflet and brochure collection and can be quite helpful. There is also a Maharashtra Tourism Development Corporation Office (tel 296241) at CDO Hutments, Madame Cama Rd. They also operate city and suburban tours of Bombay.

The GPO, with its efficient poste restante service, is an imposing big building on Nagar Chowk near the Victoria Terminus Station. The American Express office is on Dadabhoy Naoroji Rd (tel 269421). Indian Airlines (tel 258911) share the large Air India Building on Nariman Point with Air India. The airport buses depart from here and there are a number of shops and fast money changers in the building. Nalanda bookshop in the Taj Hotel is excellent. There is also a good pharmacy here.

Airlines Offices Some of the airlines flying through Bombay include:

Air India	Air India Building, Nariman Point (tel 259380)
British Airways	Vulcan's Building, Nariman Rd (tel 294071)
East African Airways	199 Churchgate (tel 297492)
Japan Air Lines	Air India Building, Nariman Point (tel 297 492)
Kuwait Airways	86 Vir Nariman Rd (tel 298351)
PIA	Hotel Oberoi-Towers, Nariman Point (tel 253817)
Pan American	Taj Mahal Hotel, Apollo Bunder (tel 255459)
Qantas	Vulcan Building, Nariman Rd (tel 294071)
Swissair	90 Vir Nariman Rd (tel 293535)

444 Bombay

Consulates Due to Bombay's importance as a business centre many countries maintain consulates or embassies in Bombay as well as in the capital, New Delhi. They include:

Germany (West)	10th floor, Hoechst House, Nariman Point (tel 296023)
Netherlands	16 M Karve Rd (tel 296840)
UK	2nd floor, Mercantile Bank Building, Mahatma Gandhi Rd (tel 259981)
USA	Lincoln House, Bhulabhai Desai Rd (tel 363611)

Movies

Quickly, which is the biggest film producing city and country in the world? Hollywood and the USA? Wrong twice, Bombay and India! The Indians turn out 500 to 600 full length feature films a year and of these nearly half get made in Bombay. Calcutta makes some arty, intellectual films; Madras some family comedies or musicals but for extravagance, action dramas, the 'starcast' A features it's Bombay all the way.

A visit to the film studios in Bombay is easy to arrange — just tell the tourist office you'd like to see a film being made and they'll fix it all up for you. It's a real education, as we found when we turned up at Famous Film Studios. For a start the film production company and the studios are totally separate. Bombay has about 12 studios and far more film makers. When they want to make a film they simply hire the studio by the day. Nor are Indian films made one-at-a-time as in the west. A big star could be involved in a number of films simultaneously — shooting a day on one, a week on another, a morning on a third. This involves phenomenal scheduling and also means that Indian films generally take a long time to make.

A glance at Indian film posters or film magazines gives you the impression that Indian movie actors are a band of escapees from weight watchers. Well there's no glamour in being thin in India. Every beggar on the street is skinny; it's the well padded look which appeals. It's amsuing to see how this works on western films shown in India — familiar European and American film stars become remarkably rotund when they're repainted for the Indian posters.

Our image of these chubby, smug actors was quickly shattered when we were asked into the dressing room to meet the star of the film we went to see. He was friendly, very open about the problems involved in making films in India — and not a kilo overweight! Life for a lot of Indians is not all that much fun and illiteracy is still widespread. Bombay film-makers are not trying to produce something for a sophisticated and intellectual audience. It's pure, straightforward, down-to-earth entertainment. Escapism and nothing more.

Indian films are always a bit of everything — drama, action, suspense, music, dancing, romance — all mixed together into one extravagant blend. They've even got a name for them — 'masala films', since masala is the all-purpose word for spices, something you add to make it tasty.

Within their commercial constraints Indian moviemakers often do a surprisingly good job, particularly the cameramen and technicians who manage to produce reasonable standard film from hopelessly outdated equipment. Apart from the restrictions on importing new equipment a large slice of the proceeds goes to the Indian government. Film admission prices may be only 3, 4 or 5 Rs but the government gulps down about 75% of that figure. To make an Indian movie and make money out of it you really have to know what you're about.

Tony & Maureen Wheeler

Gateway of India

In the days when most visitors came to India by sea and when Bombay was India's principal port this was indeed the 'gateway' to India. Today it's merely Bombay's principal landmark. The gateway was conceived following the visit of King George V to India in 1911 and officially opened in 1924.

Architecturally it is a conventional Arch of Triumph with elements in its design derived from the Moslem styles of 16th century Gujurat. It is built of yellow basalt and stands on the Apollo Bunder, a popular Bombay meeting place in the evenings. The Taj Mahal Inter-Continental Hotel overlooks the Apollo Bunder and launches run from here across to Elephanta Island. Close to the gateway are statues of the Maratha leader Shivaji astride his horse and of Swami Vivekananda.

Colaba Causeway

The streets behind the Taj Mahal Hotel are the travellers' centre of Bombay. Here you will find most of the cheap hotels and restaurants. Colaba Causeway, now renamed Shahid Bhagat Singh Rd, extends down to the end of the Colaba promontory, the southern end of Bombay Island. Sassoon Dock is always interesting to visit around dawn when the fishing boats come in and unload their catch in a colourful scene of intense activity. There's an old lighthouse at the end of the promontory although the actual lighthouse used today is further south still on a rocky island.

St John's Church

The Afghan Church was built in 1847 and is dedicated to the soldiers who fell in the Sind campaign of 1838 and the First Afghan War of 1843.

Prince of Wales Museum

Beside the Wellingdon Circle, close to the Colaba Causeway hotel enclave, the Prince of Wales Museum was built to commemorate King George V's first visit to India in 1905, while he was still Prince of Wales. The first part of this interesting museum was opened in 1914. It was designed in the Indo-Saracenic style and has sections for art, art & paintings, archaeology and natural history. Amongst the more interesting items are a very fine collection of miniature paintings, images and bas reliefs from the Elephanta Caves, Buddha images and models of the Parsi Towers of Silence. The museum is open from 10 am to 6.30 pm March-June, 6 pm July-September and 5.30 pm October to February. It is closed on Mondays and entry is Rs 0.75, except on Tuesdays when it is free.

Jehangir Art Gallery

Within the compound of the museum stands Bombay's principle art gallery. There are often special exhibitions of modern Indian art here.

University & High Court

Along K B Patel Marg, overlooking Cross Maidan, there are a number of imposing public buildings erected during Bombay's period of great growth under the British. The University is in Gothic 14th-15th century style and dominated by the 80 metre high Rajabai Tower. This impressive clock tower rises above the university library and if you can obtain permission to ascend it there is a fine view from the top. Statues of Justice and Mercy top the huge High Court building beyond the university. It was built in Early English style and completed in 1878.

Flora Fountain

This is the business centre of Bombay, around which many of the major banks and business offices are centred. Now officially renamed Hutatma Chowk it was named after Sir Bartle Frere, who was Governor of Bombay from 1862 to 1867, during the time Bombay experienced its most dramatic growth due to the worldwide cotton shortage caused by the American Civil War. Close to the fountain is the Cathedral of St Thomas which was begun by Gerald Aungier in 1672 and finally formally opened in 1718. There are a number of interesting memorials

Bombay

inside the cathedral which has had a number of additions and alterations over the years.

Horniman Circle
Several interesting old Bombay buildings stand close to Horniman Circle. If you're walking from the GPO back to Colaba sometime it's worth pausing to have a glance at some of these buildings. The old Mint was completed in 1829 and has an Ionic facade. It was built on land reclaimed in 1823 and adjoins the Town Hall. Behind the Town Hall stands the remains of the old Bombay Castle. Opened in 1833 the Town Hall still houses the library of the Royal Asiatic Society. Ascend the imposing steps at the front of the Town Hall and have a short wander inside. There are statues of a number of the government officials and wealthy benefactors of Bombay's golden period including Sir Bartle Frere and Sir Jamsetjee Jeejeebhoy. Continuing you pass the Old Customs House which was built in 1720. The old Bombay dockyards stand behind the building.

Marine Drive
Now officially renamed Netaji Subhash Rd, Marine Drive is built on land reclaimed in 1920. It runs along the shoreline of Back Bay, starting at Nariman Point and sweeping around by Chowpatty Beach and up to Malabar Hill. The road is backed with high residential buildings and this is one of Bombay's most popular promenades.

Taraporewella Aquarium
Constructed in 1951 the aquarium, on Marine Drive, is one of the best in India and has both freshwater and saltwater fish. It's open from 11 am to 8 pm, closed Mondays, and admission is Rs 0.50. Also along Marine Drive, before the aquarium, are a series of cricket pitches where in summer there always seem to be games underway.

Chowpatty Beach
Bombay's famous beach attracts few bathers and even fewer sunbathers — neither activity has much of a following in India and in any case the water is none too healthy. Chowpatty has plenty of other activities though. It's one of those typical Indian slices of life where anything and everything can happen and does. Sandcastle sculptors make elaborate figures in the sand, contortionists go through equally elaborate contortions and family groups stroll around. In between there are kiosks selling Bombay's popular snack, bhelpuri, and kulfi ice cream. Chowpatty Beach is also the scene for the annual Ganesh Chaturthi festival in which large images of the elephant headed god are immersed in the sea.

Mani Bhuvan
At 19 Laburnum Rd, near August Kranti Maidan, is the building where Mahatma Gandhi stayed on his visits to Bombay between 1917 and 1934. Today it has a pictorial exhibit of incidents's in Gandhi's life and contains a library of books by or about the Mahatma. It is open from 9.30 am to 6 pm.

Malabar Hill
At the end of Back Bay, Marine Drive climbs up to Malabar Hill. This is an expensive residential area for not only is it a little cooler than the sea-level parts of the city but there are also fine views over Back Bay and Chowpatty Beach to the town. At the end of the promontory is Raj Bhavan, the old British government headquarters. Close to this is the temple of Walkeswar, the 'sand lord', an important Hindu pilgrimage site. According to the Ramayana, Rama rested here on his way from Ayodya to Lanka to rescue Sita. He constructed a lingam of sand at the site. The temple is about a thousand years old.

Jain Temple

This marble temple was built in 1904 and is dedicated to the first Jain Tirthankar, Adinath. It's typical of modern Jain temples in its gaudy, mirrored style. The walls are decorated with pictures of incidents in the lives of the Tirthankars.

Hanging Gardens

On top of Malabar Hill these gardens were laid out in 1881 and are correctly known as the Pherozeshah Mehta Gardens. They take their name from the fact that they are built on top of a series of reservoirs that supply water to Bombay. The formally laid out gardens have a notable collection of hedges cut into the shape of animals and there are good views over the city from here.

Kamala Nehru Park

Directly across the road from the Hanging Gardens this park offers more superb views over Bombay. It was laid out in 1952 and was named after Nehru's wife. For children there is a large nursery rhyme 'old lady's shoe'.

Towers of Silence

Beside the Hanging Garden, but carefully shielded from viewers, are the Parsis' Towers of Silence. The Parsis hold fire, earth and water as sacred and thus will not cremate or bury their dead. Instead the bodies are laid out within the towers to be picked clean by vultures. Elaborate precautions are taken to keep ghoulish sightseers from observing the towers, despite which a Time-Life book on Bombay provided a bird's eye view of one of the towers. The Parsis power in Bombay is sufficiently strong that the book was black ink censored. Tour guides like to tell you that the reason the Hanging Garden reservoirs were covered over was that the vultures had an unpleasant habit of dropping the odd bit in the water supply.

Mahalaxmi Temple

Descending from Malabar Hill and continuing around the coastline you come to the Mahalaxmi Temple which is the oldest in Bombay and, appropriately for this city of business and money, dedicated to the goddess of wealth. The images of the goddess and her two sisters were said to have been found in the sea. Near here is the Mahalaxmi Racecourse, said to be the finest in India, where horse races are held each Sunday from November to March. The road along the seashore by the racecourse was once known as the Hornby Vellard and was constructed in the 18th century to reclaim the swampland on which the course is now constructed.

Haji Ali's Tomb

This tomb and mosque are devoted to a Moslem saint who was drowned here. The buildings are reached by a long causeway which can only be crossed at low tide. A scene of typical Indian ingenuity and resourcefulness takes place along this pathway. Hundreds of beggars line the length of the causeway waiting for the regular stream of pilgrims. At the start of the causeway are a small group of moneychangers who, for a few paise commission, will change a one rupee coin into 100 one paise coins. Thus a pilgrim can do his soul the maximum amount of good for the minimum expenditure. No doubt at the ebb tide the mendicants can change their handfuls of one paise coins into something a little more manageable thus giving the moneychangers their small change for the next low tide and, no doubt, providing them with another commission rake off.

Victoria Gardens

These gardens, which contain Bombay's zoo and the Victoria & Albert Museum, have been renamed the Veermata Jijabai Bhonsle Udyan. The museum has some interesting exhibits relating to old Bombay. Just outside the museum building there is the large stone elephant which was removed from Elephanta Island in 1864 and from which the island got its name. The museum is open from 10.30 am to 5.30 pm and admission is Rs 0.10. The zoo is open sunrise to sunset and admission is also Rs 0.10.

Other

The Nehru Planetarium is on Dr Annie Besant Rd at Worli near the Haji Ali Tomb. There are shows in English at 3 and 6 pm daily and also at 12 noon on Saturdays and Sundays. The planetarium is closed on Mondays, admission is Rs 5. Falkland St is the centre for Bombay's notorious red light district known as 'the cages'. The ladies stand behind metal barred doors, hence the name. A 130 bus from the museum passes through this interesting area.

Tours

There are a wide variety of tours in Bombay but they tend to be more expensive than in most Indian cities. Daily city tours are operated by the ITDC and the Maharashtra Tourist Development Council. The ITDC tours can be booked at the Tourist Office and leave from there at 10 am and from the Taj Mahal Hotel at 10.15. The tour covers the main city sights, finishes at 2 pm and costs Rs 20. It does not operate on Mondays. The MTDC tour costs Rs 25, lasts from 9 am to 1 pm and also does not operate on Mondays.

In the afternoons there are MTDC tours from 2.30 to 6.30 pm for Rs 18. Again the tours are daily except Mondays. There are also privately operated tours leaving the Tourist Office at 2.15 pm and the Taj Mahal Hotel at 2.30. The tour finishes at 6.30 pm and costs Rs 25. The tour operates daily including Mondays.

There are also a variety of suburban tours which basically go to the Aarey Milk Colony, Kanheri Caves and Juhu Beach. The Sanghi Travels tour departs the Tourist Office at 8.45 am and the Taj Mahal Hotel at 9 am. The tour returns at 1.30 pm and costs Rs 40. On Sundays and holidays the MTDC have a tour which leaves at 11.45 am and returns at 7.30 pm. Cost is Rs 28. There is also a Sunday tour in a normal public transport bus (all other tours are in air-con buses). This leaves the Gateway of India at 8.45 am and the Tourist Office at 9 am and returns at 5.30 pm. Cost is Rs 12 but there is no guide.

Launch services and tours to Elephanta leave regularly from Apollo Bunder and can be booked at the kiosk there. The round trip takes four hours. The ITDC and the MTDC have some tours further afield such as a Friday to Monday tour to Aurangabad and the Ajanta and Ellora Caves. Check at the Tourist Office for details.

Places to Stay

Bombay suffers from an acute room shortage so accommodation is not only hard to find it's expensive when you find it. This applies particularly in the low price bracket where you can pay high prices for low standards. The answer is to book well ahead or, if you're in the low price bracket, arrive early in the morning. If all else fails visit the Tourist Office since they usually seem to be able to find something for you.

Places to Stay — Top End

Bombay has the hotel reputed to be the best in India. It's certainly a place with an air of glamour about it and since most of Bombay's cheap hotels cluster right behind it, and it has a comfortable air-conditioned lounge, and one of the best bookshops in Bombay, you'll also find a fair number of backpackers around it too! The *Taj Mahal Hotel* is an elegant turn-of-the-century building on Apollo Bunder near the

Gateway of India. More recently a multi-storey modern hotel, the *Taj Inter-Continental* (tel 243366), has been added to it so you have basically two hotels in one. There are 650 rooms, all the usual amenities and singles/doubles cost Rs 500/600.

Round at Nariman Point on Marine Drive the *Hotel Oberoi-Towers* (tel 234343) is a new hotel with 450 rooms. Singles/doubles cost Rs 500/600. Situated rather out of the way at 90 Cuffe Parade, about half-way down Colaba Causeway, the *Hotel President* (tel 219141) is also part of the Taj Group of hotels. Singles/doubles range from Rs 375/450.

At *Hotel Fariyas* (tel 215911) singles/doubles are Rs 250/300. It's at 25 Off Arthur Bunder Rd in Colaba. *Hotel Bombay International* at 29 Marine Drive (tel 240060) is another smaller and slightly cheaper hotel with singles/doubles at Rs 200/300. The *Ritz Hotel* (tel 295061) is at 5 Jamshedji Tata Rd and has singles/doubles at Rs 285/335. The *Ambassador Hotel* (tel 291131) at Churchgate Extension has singles/doubles at Rs 150/200.

Places to Stay — Middle
Many of the middle bracket hotels are also located in the Colaba area — along with the Taj and most of the cheapies. Three popular ones can be found along Garden Rd. The *Ascot Hotel* (tel 240020) at number 38 is a reasonable sort of place with air-con singles/doubles at Rs 160/200. It's good value in this bracket by Bombay standards. A few doors down the *Godwin Hotel* (tel 241226 & 241290) at 41 is almost identically priced and of similar standard. The *Garden Hotel*, a couple of doors down again, is about Rs 10 cheaper but, like the real cheapies, these places all tend to be permanently full.

At 24 Mereweather Rd, on the corner of Ormiston Rd, the *Hotel Diplomat* (tel 231661) is marginally more expensive at Rs 170/210. It's directly behind the Taj Hotel. Away from Colaba you could try the *Sea Green Hotel* at 145 Marine Drive (tel 296107 & 296153) where air-con rooms run Rs 130/170 for singles/doubles or a bit cheaper without air-con. There are many other hotels in this bracket — like the *Sea Green South* (tel 295360) also on Marine Drive or the *Astoria* (tel 299171) at 4 Jamshedji Tata Rd or the *West End Hotel* (tel 299121) at 45 Marine Drive.

A little cheaper, and back in Colaba, there are a few places that bridge the bottom to middle brackets. The *Strand Hotel* (tel 241624) is on Apollo Bunder and has air-con singles/doubles at Rs 100/140, a bit cheaper without air-con. *Cowies Guest House* on Walton Rd is similarly priced but not so special. Finally the *Celeste Hotel* (tel 215898), opposite the entrance to Sassoon Docks on Colaba Causeway, has air-con singles/doubles for Rs 80/150 including breakfast.

Places to Stay — Bottom End
Bombay's accommodation shortage is most painful at the bottom end. The only real answer is to be there when people leave in the morning and sit in the hotel office until a room becomes free. If Bombay is your arrival point in India you do have the small advantage that most international flights into Bombay tend to arrive in the early morning. If you arrive at a less convenient hour and simply cannot find a thing, first of all try the Tourist Office who can often suggest something. If that fails you can hand your fate over to the Colaba hotel touts. They're usually young kids who know just where the last room is left — you may end up in some windowless, miserable cubicle at an inflated price but next morning you

Colaba Causeway

1 Hotel Fariyas	15 Sun Rise Restaurant
2 Hotel Ascot	16 Carlton Hotel
3 Godwin Hotel	17 Laxmi Vilas
4 Garden Hotel	18 Leopold Restaurant
5 Cowie's Guest House	19 Apollo Restaurant
6 Shelley's Guest House	20 Olympic Coffee House
7 Strand Hotel	21 Delhi Durbar
8 Sea Palace Hotel	22 Majestic Dining Hall
9 Whalley's Guest House	23 YWCA International Guest House
10 Pure Drinks	24 Cafe Mondegar
11 Ananda Punjabi	25 Regal Cinema
12 Dipti's Pure Drinks	26 Nanking Restaurant
13 Salvation Army Red Shield Hostel	27 Ali Baba Restaurant
14 Rex & Stiffles Hotels	28 Mandarin Restaurant

can start out early to find a better home.

The cheap hotels are mainly concentrated in the Colaba area, directly behind that useful landmark, the Taj Mahal Inter-Continental. Best known are the *Rex* and the *Stiffles* at 8 Ormiston Rd. The Rex is on floors 3 and 4, the Stiffles on 1 and 2. Rooms start

from around Rs 30 for airless little cubicles and run up through reasonable doubles (if they were cleaner) at Rs 60, with bathroom at Rs 70, to air-con rooms at Rs 100 or more. The management are sour, the countless uniformed lackeys lounging around the stairs do nothing for the cleanliness of the place and frankly it's grubby and you should beware of bed bugs. But for Bombay it's reasonable value. The Rex is probably better then the Stiffles.

Curiously they both have a steady Arab clientele (complete with harems!); it appears that citizens of the oil states who can't quite run to Paris and London opt for Bombay and if they can't afford the Taj, well the Rex and Stiffles will have to do. It's said they particularly like Bombay in the monsoon — all that rain. They spend a lot of time squatting on the pavement outside, haggling over saucepans with local merchants.

Across the road, on the corner of Mereweather Rd (at 30), is the *Salvation Army Red Shield Hostel*. A dorm bed is Rs 25 and a double Rs 65 including rather bland and tasteless meals. To get in you must be waiting at the door at 9 am, no earlier, no later. They are not too keen on real freaks here and couples must be married. Bombay seems to be the final home for all those legendary hippie-junkies and the hostel wants no part of them.

The *Carlton Hotel* at 12 Mereweather Rd is around Rs 50 or 60 for a double with breakfast. None too special but nothing around here is. Bombay is not a good introduction to Indian hotels, things improve as soon as you leave.

There are a number of Ys in Bombay. The *YWCA International Guest House* (tel 230445, 235161) is at 18 Madame Cama Rd, just round from the Prince of Wales Museum. Singles/doubles with air-con cost Rs 60/100, a non air-con double is Rs 90. Good value for Bombay but you must book (and pay for two nights) well ahead. There is a *YMCA International Guest House* (tel 891191, 377573) at Club Back Rd, Central. Singles/doubles cost Rs 70/100 or Rs 65/90 without air-con. This includes breakfast but there is an additional Rs 20 temporary membership charge.

Elsewhere in Bombay you could try the *Welcome Hotel* near the GPO where you might get a single for less than Rs 30. There are other small hotels scattered around Churchgate and Fort, near the stations. *City Lodge*, opposite the Victoria Terminus main gate (tel 260029, 265515), is Rs 40 a double for example. The *Lawerence Hotel* (tel 243618), 3rd floor, Ashok Kumar House, Dubhash Rd in the city centre is clean and reportedly pretty good. A Rs 70 double includes a breakfast of toast, bananas, boiled eggs and tea. It's behind the museum. There are *Railway Retiring Rooms* at both Victoria Terminus (tel 268041) at Rs 10 a bed and at Bombay Central (tel 37729) at Rs 20 a bed.

Places to Stay — Airport & Juhu

There are quite a few hotels at Juhu beach, which is only six km from the airport, and at the airport itself. They're mainly more expensive places although Juhu also has some cheaper accommodation if you want to escape from the city. The *Centaur Hotel* (tel 535431) is right at the airport and singles/doubles in this large, circular hotel cost Rs 400/450. The *Hotel Airport Plaza* (tel 579476) is at 70C Nehru Rd, Vile Parle, only half a km from the airport. It's a smaller hotel with singles/doubles at Rs 220/270.

At Juhu the *Holiday Inn* (tel 579417, 579481) is on Juhu Turner Royal Lane and costs Rs 400/450. At 37 Juhu Beach the *Hotel Horizon* is similarly priced as is the *Sun-n-Sand Hotel* at 39 Juhu Beach. There are quite a few hotels bridging the gap from these top end places to the bottom end ones. The *South End Hotel* (tel 537421) at 11 Juhu Tara Rd is Rs 50/80 or Rs 25 more with air-con. The air-con *Sea Side Hotel* (tel 562170, 561972) at 39/2 Juhu Beach is marginally more expensive. There's even a Krishna Consciousness hotel, the *Iskcon* (tel 566860) with singles/doubles at Rs 80/100 or Rs 30 more with air-con. More expensive again at Rs 150/200 is *Hotel King's* (tel 579141-3) at 5 Juhu Tara Rd or the *Riviera Hotel* (tel 568122) near the Horizon Hotel with rooms at Rs 250/300.

Down at the bottom end there are places like the *Sea View Hotel* (popular for people with vehicles) at Rs 50 a double, right on the beach. Or the *Purnima Guest House* (tel 541215) with singles/doubles at Rs 40/60.

Places to Eat — Top End

The accommodation shortage certainly doesn't spill over into restaurants. Bombay probably has the best selection of restaurants of any major Indian city. As in other cities a meal in a better class restaurant can be one of India's bargains. A foray into the more expensive places is a worthwhile investment even for the backpackers.

The Taj Mahal has a whole range of restaurants and snack bars including the *Sea Lounge*, a good place for a snack or beer overlooking the waterfront. The *Shamiana* has light meals, the *Rendez-vous* on the rooftop caters for western tastes but the *Tanjore* is probably the best place for a splash-out meal — traditional Indian food (most dishes Rs 20 to 40) accompanied by sitar music and classical Indian dancing. The thought of a Rs 30 thali will probably bring a smile to the face of backpackers though!

There are a string of restaurants along K Dubash Marg, just across from the Jehangir Art Gallery and Prince of Wales Museum. Close to the junction with Mahatma Gandhi Rd the *Khyber Restaurant* has a varied menu with particularly good tandoori dishes and kebabs. Try the chicken tikka kebab. Most dishes are around Rs 10 to 20. A complete meal including dessert (and they offer 'leeches & cream' as a possibility!) will probably come to about Rs 35 to 40 per person. A bit further along there's the similarly priced *Copper*

Chimney — not so extensive a menu though. In between you'll find the *Chinese Home* with good Chinese food.

The *Delhi Durbar* on Falkland St is reputed to have excellent curries but you're advised to take a taxi there. There's a second *Copper Chimney* branch at Worli. The *Kabab Corner* in the Hotel Natraj on Marine Drive is also good. There's a second *Delhi Durbar* too, on Colaba Causeway (Shahid Bhagat Singh Rd) near Wellingdon Circle with a similar menu to the Khyber at slightly lower prices. There are branches of *Kwality* at Colaba, Worli and Kemps Corner. Good ice cream desserts.

Bombay has a particularly good selection of Chinese restaurants and some say the *Nanking* on Shivaji Marg in Colaba has the best Chinese food in India. Most dishes are in the Rs 7 to 12 bracket. Directly across the road the *Mandarin* is marginally more expensive.

Places to Eat — Bottom End

There are plenty of places to eat around Colaba. *Dipti's Pure Drinks*, near the Rex and Stiffles, is popular for its fruit juices (a bit expensive at Rs 2.50 to 4), fruit salads and ice cream (Rs 4). The high prices don't put people off this tiny establishment. On the corner of Mereweather and Ormiston Rd the *Sun Rise Restaurant* is a local meeting place for travellers although the food is really pretty bad.

Round the corner on Nawroji Furounji Rd *Laxmi Vilas* has excellent vegetarian thalis for Rs 3.50. On Wodehouse Rd (alias Shahid Bhagat Singh Rd alias Colaba Causeway) the *Ananda Punjabi* is more expensive but tasty, say Rs 30 for two. The *Leopold Restaurant* is a good place for breakfast — eggs & toast, etc, good 'tray tea'. It's also good for a cold beer. The *Cafe Mondegar* is a pleasant coffee bar place. Across the road the *Majestic Dining*

Hall is a big vegetarian plate-meal specialist. The *Samovar* in the Jehangir Art Gallery is a good place for a cold drink or a quick snack.

Colaba is renowned for fine prawns and seafood. You can get fish & chips in a few places, including right beside the Marine Drive aquarium! Bhelpuri is a Bombay speciality — a tasty snack of crisp noodles, spiced vegetables and other mysterious ingredients for a rupee or less. It's available from stalls all over town but particularly on Chowpatty Beach.

Daba Lunches

Mr Bombay Business-Wallah sets off from home, boards his train or bus and heads into the city every morning — just like his office worker counterpart in Australia, England or America. Just like many of his overseas office-wallah brothers he'd like to take his lunch with him and eat in the office. But an Indian lunch isn't as simple as a couple of sandwiches and an apple. A cut lunch could never satisfy an Indian — there has to be curry and rice and parathas and spices and a lot of things that take a lot of time to prepare and would hardly slip into a brown paper bag in the briefcase.

Naturally there's a supremely complex, yet smoothly working, Indian solution to this little problem — it's called the daba lunch system. After he's left for work his wife (or more likely the cook or bearer) sets to and fixes his lunch. When it's all prepared it's packed into a metal bucket about 15 cm in diameter and about 30 cm high. On the lid there's a mysterious colour coded notation. The container is then carried down to a street corner pick up point where it meets up with lots of other little lunch buckets and heads towards their city office destination. From the pick up point they're conveyed to the nearest train station where they're transported to the appropriate city station.

In the city they're broken down to their separate destinations and between 11 and 12 in the morning thousands up on thousands of individually coded lunches pour out of Victoria Terminus, Churchgate, Bombay Central and other stations. On the heads of porters, carried in carts, slung from long poles, tied on bicycle handlebars those lunch buckets then scatter out across the city. Most of the daba-wallahs involved in this long chain of events will be illiterate but by some miracle of Indian efficiency when Mr Business-Wallah opens his office door at lunchtime there will be his lunch by the door. Every day, without fail, they never lose a lunch.

Getting There

Air There is a very extensive network of flights operating into and out of Bombay's Dabolim airport. Delhi-Bombay there are several flights daily. Some examples of fares include Ahmedabad Rs 315, Aurangabad Rs 225, Bangalore Rs 590, Calcutta Rs 1065, Cochin Rs 735, Dabolim (Goa) Rs 305, Delhi Rs 780, Madras Rs 740.

Rail Two railway systems operate out of Bombay. Central Railways handles services to the east and south plus a few trains to the north. The booking office (tel 264321) is at Victoria Terminus, sometimes referred to as Bori Bunder. It's open from 9 am to 1 pm and 2 to 4.30 pm. Western Railways have services to the north from Churchgate and Central stations. Bookings in 1st class are made at Churchgate (tel 291952) between 9 am and 4 pm. Bookings in 2nd class are made at Central (tel 395757) between 9 am and 4 pm.

Note that there are four Central trains that do not depart from either Central or Churchgate but from Dadar Station which is further north of Central. These trains are the Amritsar Express, the Varanasi Express, the Dadar-Nagpur Express and the Dadar-Madras Express. The latter is the fastest train to Madras.

From Bombay it is 28 hours to Delhi and the fare is about Rs 270 in 1st class, Rs 64 in 2nd. Bombay-Calcutta is a lengthy 1968 km trip taking 36 hours and costing Rs 320 in 1st class, Rs 77 in 2nd class. Bombay-Madras is 1279 km and takes from 26 hours at a cost of Rs 229 in 1st class, Rs 56 in 2nd.

Bus Long distance buses depart from the State Transport Terminal opposite Bombay Central Station. The state bus companies of Maharashtra, Gujurat, Karnataka and Madhya Pradesh all have offices here and bookings can be made (tel 374272 or 376622) between 8 am and 11 pm. Some travel times and costs include:

Aurangabad	11 hours	Rs 30
		Rs 40*
Bangalore	25 hours	Rs 70
Indore	16 hours	Rs 40
		Rs 60*
Surat	9 hours	Rs 20
Hyderabad	16 hours	Rs 52
Ganeshpuri	3 hours	Rs 6
Mahabaleshwar	8 hours	Rs 20
Mangalore	25 hours	Rs 68
Nasik	5 hours	Rs 12
		Rs 15*
Baroda	10 hours	Rs 42
Panaji (Goa)	17 hours	Rs 42
		Rs 58*
Pune (Poona)	5 hours	Rs 11

*de-luxe buses

Boat See Goa for more details on the popular Bombay-Goa ferry, a very pleasant alternative to taking a bus or train. Departures are every day except Tuesday but the service is suspended during the monsoon between June and September. Cabins cost Rs 120, 135 and 160. Upper deck-class is Rs 52.50, lower deck-class is Rs 33.

Getting Around

Airport There is an airport bus service which runs from the Indian Airlines/ Air India terminal at Nariman Point. It also picks up and drops off at the Taj Mahal Hotel, very convenient for all the Colaba cheap hotels. The fare is Rs 9. A taxi from the airport would cost about Rs 35 to 40 to Colaba; Rs 30 to Churchgate or only Rs 15 to nearby Juhu Beach. You can also get to the airport by taking a train from Churchgate or Central to Santa Cruz or Vile Parle from where it is only a short bus or taxi ride to the airport. Some real shoestringers have even been known to walk it. Don't consider this route during the rush hours particularly if you're carrying anything more than a toothbrush.

Taxis Bombay has a large fleet of metered taxis — as usual the meters are way out of date and drivers carry a fare conversion card.

Buses Bombay has probably the best public transport system of any major Indian city. There are lots of well kept double decker buses with fares ranging from Rs 0.20. They tend to be crowded, especially during rush hours and Bombay's pickpockets are notoriously adept. Take care. The buses are operated by BEST (Bombay Electric Supply & Transport) and they have separate route maps for their extensive city and suburban services. From the Victoria Terminus Railway Station take a 1, 6 Ltd, 7 Ltd, 103 or 124 to 'Electric House' which is a useful landmark in Colaba. From Bombay Central take a 70 or a 124. Ltd means 'Limited stops'.

Trains Bombay has an extensive suburban system operated by electric trains. It's virtually the only place in India where it's worth taking trains for city travel. If you arrive in Bombay at Bombay Central Station your ticket will take you on a local train on to the more convenient Churchgate station.

Things to Buy

Bombay has a number of intriguing markets. Chor Bazaar is Bombay's thieves' market. It's off Grant Rd (Maulana Shaukatali Rd) and here you'll find a phenomenal collection of 'antiques', jewellery, wood items, leather and general bric-a-brac. Mutton St has a particularly interesting collection of shops for miscellaneous 'junk'. Shops are generally open from 10 am but are closed on Fridays.

Crawford Market, officially renamed Mahatma Phule Market, is the centre for flowers, fruit, vegetables, meat and fish in Bombay. This is the place to look for Bombay's two famous fish — the pomfret and the 'Bombay duck'. The market building was constructed in 1867 and it's one of the most colourful and photogenic places in Bombay. Near here is Javeri Bazaar, the jewellery centre off Mumbadevi Rd. There is some fantastic stuff here, especially silver belts and old statues and charms. Near there is the brass bazaar on Kalbadevi Rd.

There are all sorts of places selling handicrafts, artifacts, antiques and art around the Colaba area. Shops in the Taj Hotel specialise in high quality — and high prices. Check the Jehangir Gallery by the Prince of Wales Museum too.

AROUND BOMBAY
Elephanta Island

The island of Elephanta is about 10 km north-east from Apollo Bunder and is Bombay's major tourist attraction due to the four rock-cut temples on the island. They are thought to have been cut out between 450 and 750 AD and at that time the island was known as Gharapuri, the 'fortress city'. When the Portuguese arrived they renamed it Elephanta from the large stone elephant near the landing place. This figure collapsed in 1814 and the remaining pieces were removed to the Victoria Gardens in Bombay in 1864 and reassembled in 1912.

Unfortunately the Portuguese took their traditional disdain for other religions to its usual lengths at Elephanta and did considerable damage to the sculptures. Although some people feel that Elephanta is not as impressive as the rock-cut temples of Ellora the size, beauty and power of the sculptures is unexcelled.

The caves are reached by a stairway up the hillside from the landing place. There is one main cave with a number of large sculptured panels, all relating to Shiva, and a separate lingam shrine. The most interesting of the panels includes one of Trimurti or the three-headed Shiva where he also takes the role of Brahma, the creator, and Vishnu, the preserver. In other panels Shiva appears as Arddhanariswar where he unites both sexes in one body, one side of the sculpture is male, one side female. There are figures of Shiva and his wife Parvati and of their marriage. In another panel Shiva dances the Tandava, the dance that shakes the world. Parvati and their son, Ganesh, look on a little astonished. One of the best panels is that of Ravana shaking Kailasa. The demon king of Lanka decided to carry Shiva and his companions off by the simple expedient of removing their Himalayan home, the mountain Kailasa. Parvati became a little panic stricken at his energetic attempts to jerk the mountain free but Shiva calmly pushed the mountain back down with one toe, trapping Ravana beneath it for ten thousand years.

Launches leave regularly from Apollo Bunder by the Gateway of India. They cost from Rs 7 to Rs 15, more with air-con. The more expensive trips also include a guide. A good guide, and there are some excellent ones, can considerably increase your enjoyment and understanding — even, as one tubby little gentleman with glasses does, show just how Shiva danced the Tandava. During the monsoon there are no boats to the island since the water is too rough.

Around Bombay

Juhu

Close to Bombay's international airport, Santa Cruz, Juhu is 18 km north of the city centre. It's the nearest beach to the city and has quite a collection of upper notch hotels but it's no place for a pleasant swim. On weekdays it is fairly quiet but on weekends there are donkeys, camels, dancing monkeys, acro-bats and every other type of Indian beach entertainment. From Santa Cruz station you can get there on a 182, 231 or 253 bus.

Aarey Milk Colony

Fresh milk, something of a rarity in cow-infested India, is produced at this model milk production centre. It's not-able also for its hilltop viewpoint with a fine view over the island.

Krishnagiri Upavan National Park

Reached via the Borivli station the Kan-heri Caves and the lakes which act as reservoirs for much of Bombay's water supply are in the national park. At the entrance to the park there's a huge out-door movie lot, including a fort front-age, partly constructed from old oil drums. Also near the park entrance is, believe it or not, a Lion Safari Park. Open from 9 am to 5 pm, daily except Mondays (Tuesdays if Monday is a public holiday), a half hour trip through the park in a 'safari vehicle' costs Rs 4. The lakes are Vihar, Tulsi and Powari.

Kanheri Caves

Within the national park, about 42 km from Bombay, there are 109 caves along the side of a rocky ravine. The caves are Buddhist and date from around the 2nd to 9th century AD. Although there are so many of them most are little more than holes in the rock and only a hand-ful are of real interest. The most import-ant is cave 3, the 'Great Chaitya Cave' which has a long colonnade of pillars around the dagoba in the back of the cave. Further up the ravine there are some good views right out to the sea.

Kanheri can be visited on the regular suburban tours or you can take a train to Borivli station and then a taxi the 10 km or so to the caves. On Sundays and holidays there is a bus service from the station to the caves. Entrance to the caves is Rs 0.50.

Other Beaches

Bombay's best known beach, Juhu, is too close to the city and not sanitary enough for a pleasant swim but there are more remote beaches on the island. Marve and Manori beaches are near to each other, about 40 km out of the city. You can get to them via the station at Malad, 32 km out. Marve is a stretch of unspoilt and lightly populated beach. There's an interesting fishing village and an old Portuguese church nearby. You have got a short ferry ride to take to get to Manorvi and then a km and a bit walk to the beach.

Other beaches around Bombay include Madh, 45 km out and also reached via Malad. Versova is 29 km from the city, reached via Andheri station. Getting to Uran involves a 74 km trip, the last 10 km by sea. Launches leave from the New Ferry Wharf.

Montpezir & Jogeshvari Caves

There are a small number of Hindu caves, one of which was converted into a Portuguese church, at Montpezir, near Borivli. The Jogeshvari Caves are near the Andheri station.

Bassein

Just across the river which separates the mainland from Bombay island is Bassein, a Portuguese fortified city from 1534 to 1739. The Portuguese took Bassein at the same time as Daman, further north in Gujarat. They built a fort containing a city of such pomp and splendour that it came to be known as the 'Court of the North'. Only the Hidalgos or aristocracy were permitted to live within the fort walls and by the end of the 17th century there were 300 Portuguese and 400 Indian-Christian families here, with a cathedral, five convents and 13 churches.

Then in 1739 the Marathas besieged the city and the Portuguese surrendered after three months of appalling losses. Today the city walls are still standing and there are the ruins of some of the churches and the Cathedral of St Joseph. Bassein is 11 km from the Bassein Road (Vasai Road in Marathi) railway station. Sopara, near Bassein Road, is thought to be the Biblical Ophir. About an hour by bus from the station are the Vajreshwari hot springs.

Chaul

South of Bombay this was another Portuguese settlement although not as important as Bassein. They took it in 1522 and lost it to the Marathas at the same time as Bassein. There are a few remains and old ruined churches within the Portuguese fortifications. Looking across to the Portuguese fort from the other side of the river is the hill top Moslem Korlai Fort. Ferries run to Revas from the New Ferry Wharf, a 1½ hour trip. From there you've got a 30 km bus trip to Chaul. It's possible to continue on from here by road to Mahabaleshwar or to join the Bombay-Pune road.

Maharashtra

Population: 56 million
Area: 307,762 square km
Capital: Bombay
Main language: Marathi

The state of Maharashtra is one of the largest in India both in terms of population and area. Its booming capital, Bombay, makes it not only one of the most important states economically but also a major arrival point for overseas visitors. From Bombay you can head off into India in a number of directions but most travellers will either be heading south through Pune (Poona), with its famous ashram, to Goa or north-east to the amazing cave temples of Ajanta and Ellora. Most of the state stands on the high Deccan pleateau and historically this was the main centre for the Maratha empire which defied the Moghuls for so long and under the fearless rule of Shivaji carved out a large part of central India as their own domain.

Cave Architecture

The rock cut caves in Maharashtra all have several distinct design elements. All the Buddhist caves, which are generally the older ones, are either chaityas (temples) or viharas (monasteries). Chaityas are usually deep and narrow with a stupa at the end of the cave. There may be a row of columns down both sides of the cave and around the stupa.

The viharas are usually not as deep and narrow as the chaitya caves. These caves were usually intended as living and sleeping quarters for the monks and often have rows of cells along both sides of the cave. In the back there is a small shrine room, often containing an image of the Buddha. At Ajanta the cliff face the caves are cut into is very steep

and there is often a small verandah or entrance porch in front of the main cave. At Ellora the rock face is more sloping and the verandah or porch element often evolves into a separate courtyard.

The cave temples reach their peak of complexity and design in the Hindu caves at Ellora, in particular the magnificent Kailasa temple. Here they are hardly caves any longer for the whole enclosure is open to the sky. In design they are much like other temples of that era — except that instead of being built up from the bottom they were cut down from the top. They are an imitation of conventional architecture of that period.

The caves are notable for their sculptures and paintings but the famous Ajanta 'frescoes' are not, technically speaking, frescoes at all. A fresco is a painting done on a wet surface where the colour is absorbed into the surface. The Ajanta paintings are more correctly tempera since they were painted on a dry surface. The rough hewn rock walls were coated with a cm thick layer of clay and cow-dung mixed with rice husks. A final coat of lime was then applied to produce the finished surface on which the artist painted. The final surface was then polished to produce a high gloss.

MATHERAN

The nearest hill station to Bombay, Matheran is 171 km from the city via Neral on the Bombay-Pune railway line. The name means 'jungle topped' or 'wooded head' which is just what it is — an undulating hill top, cloaked in shady trees. It's the abundance of shade as much as the 700 to 800 metre altitude which makes Matheran a slightly cooler place than Bombay. Matheran became a popular hill station during the days of the Raj, Hugh Malet is credited with its discovery in 1850.

Getting to Matheran is half the fun; from Neral you take a tiny, narrow gauge toy train up the 21 km route to the hill. It's a choice of train or walk, there are no motor vehicles in Matheran and the trekking route is an 11 km long climb. The train twists, turns and winds on its steep, two hour ascent. Food and drink vendors cling to the outside and at one point you pass through 'one kiss tunnel'.

On the top Matheran sprawls north-south along the hill top. There are many km of walking tracks leading to the viewpoints that ring the station. At many of the points the ground drops sheer to the plains, far, far below. On a clear day the view can be fantastic and even in the hazy air of the pre-monsoon dry season the eerie views of surrounding hills are very fine. From Porcupine, Monkey or Hart Points on the north-west of the hill you can see the lights of Bombay on a clear night. Porcupine is also a good place for catching the sunset but Panorama Point, at the extreme north, is said to have the finest views. The western side, from Porcupine to Louisa Point, is known as Cathedral Rocks and Neral can be seen far below, straddling the Central Railway line. At the south, near One Tree Hill, a trail down to the valley below is known as Shivaji's Ladder, since the Maratha leader is said to have used it.

Places to Stay

Most of the more expensive places provide boarding and lodging only — you must take all your meals at the guest houses. These include the *Lord's Central House* (tel 28) (also called just Central Hotel) and the *Regal Hotel* with costs around Rs 80 to 100 per person. At *Brightlands* (tel 44) per person cost is Rs 70. Somewhat cheaper — but still quite comfortable — are the *Alexander Guest House* (tel 51) at Rs 35 per person (somewhat more with air-con) or the *Silvan Guest House* (tel 74) at Rs 50. The latter also has room-only accommodation at Rs 20 per person. All these places have their own attached bathrooms and small verandahs with chairs and tables.

Moving down a notch you could try *Laxmi Hotel* with double rooms at Rs 25, still with your own bathroom. *Khan's Cosmopolitan Hotel* (tel 40) is very close to the centre but rather primitive, Rs 10 to Rs 15. For the real economisers there is dormitory accommodation at the *Holiday Camp* (the train stops at the camp, a km or two before Matheran) or at *Maneklal Terrace*, two km south of the railway station. At the latter a mat on the floor, plus all meals, costs Rs 9 per day.

Away from the hotels and guest houses there are a string of snack style eating places in the town centre. Good fruit juices at the *Kwality Fruit Juice House*. Matheran is famed for its honey and for chikki — a toffee like confectionery made of gur sugar and nuts. Chikki is sold at many shops in Matheran. There are many monkeys in Matheran, watch out for them if you buy bananas in the market!

Getting There & Around

From Bombay the Pune expresses or the Karjat local trains will take you to Neral from where the toy train runs up to Matheran. It's about two hours from Bombay to Neral and two hours again

up to Matheran. The Matheran train generally connects with the Pune expresses. Fare from Bombay is Rs 12 in 2nd class, Rs 55 in 1st — the Matheran toy train has pink curtains on the 1st class carriage!

Trains depart from Matheran for Neral at 6 am, 12.45 and 2.35 pm. There's a Rs 4 'capitation tax' on each arrival at Matheran, you pay it as you leave the station. During the monsoon the Neral-Matheran train service is suspended. In Matheran itself the only transport is rickshaws — one man pulls, two push (or hold it back on the descents). If your gear is too heavy to carry very far, and you're staying a long way from the station, you may want to use one to get your bags to the hotel. Ponies can also be hired for riding on the many trails that wind around Matheran.

KARLA & BHAJA CAVES

Situated 126 km south-east of Bombay on the main rail line to Pune, Lonavla is the place from which to visit the Karla and Bhaja caves. Lonavla doesn't have much of great interest to attract you however and the Government Holiday Camp, near the Malvali railway station, is actually closer to both caves. The Karla Cave is about 12 km from Lonavla, about a km off the main road. The Bhaja caves are a bit further off the road, you can also reach them by rail from Lonavla.

Karla Cave

It's a steep climb over 100 metres up the hillside to the Karla Cave. The cave is Hinayana Buddhist and was completed around 80 BC. It's one of the best preserved cave temples of its type in India and also dates from the time when this style of temple was at its height in terms of design purity. The Karla Cave is comparatively little known and untouristed compared to the caves of Ajanta and Ellora principally because it is just one cave all by itself, compared to the multitude of caves at the other sites.

A beautifully carved 'Sun Window' filters the light in towards the small stupa at the inner end of the deep, narrow cave. Unfortunately an ugly little modern temple has been erected just outside the cave entrance. Inside the pillars are topped by figures of two kneeling elephants with two seated figures with their arms over each other on the elephants. Generally the figures are male and female but sometimes they are of two women. The roof of the cave is ribbed with teak beams which are said to be original; at Ajanta and Ellora the wooden beams that may once have been there are now all gone. On the sides of the vestibule there are carved elephant heads which once had real ivory tusks.

Other carvings can also be seen along the sides. A pillar topped by four back-to-back lions, an image usually associated with Ashoka, stands outside the cave. It may be older than the cave itself.

There are some small monastery or vihara caves at Karla, further round the hillside. Some of these have been converted into Hindu shrines.

Bhaja Caves

It's a fairly rough route from the main road to the 18 Bhaja Caves. They're in a rather lusher, green setting than the dry hillside with the Karla Cave. The caves are though to date from around 200 BC and cave 12, a chaitya cave similar in style to the Karla Cave, is the most important. South of this is a strange group of 14 stupas, five inside and nine outside the cave. The last cave on the south side has some fine sculptures including the famous 'dancing couple'.

Karla Caves

Other

Further along the line, six km south-east of Kamshet station, are the Bedsa Caves. They are probably newer than the better executed Karla Cave. At one time the roof of the main cave was probably painted. There are a number of old forts in the vicinity including the hill-top Lohagen Fort, six km from Malvali, which was taken twice by Shivaji, and lost again on each occasion. Above the Bhaja caves is the Visapur Fort. Khandala, before Lonavla, is picturesquely situated overlooking a ravine. In the wet season there is a fine waterfall near the head of the ravine.

Tours

There's a daily tour to Lonavla and Khandala at 4.30 pm, it departs from the Holiday Camp for Rs 8 and from the Lonavla Railway Station for Rs 6. The Tourist Office at the Lonavla station is pretty useless.

Places to Stay — Lonavla

Lonavla is a compact town and there are several reasonable places close to the railway and bus stations. If you walk straight out of the station, turn left at the roundabout, you'll soon find the

Adarsh Hotel (tel 353) right beside the bus station. Very basic doubles at Rs 20, better at Rs 30 and lux ones at Rs 60. Along the main Bombay-Pune road there are some more basic lodges. If you continue a little beyond the roundabout, then turn right, you reach the *Hotel Gir Kunj* (tel 529) in a few minutes walk. Pleasant doubles at Rs

Lonavla

50. Right across the road from it is the rather drab *Janata Hotel* (tel 689) with Rs 25 doubles and right behind the Giri Kunj is the *Hotel Dinesh* (tel 561) at Rs 30 and Rs 40.

There are a number of eating places along the Bombay-Pune road through Lonavla and others across the railway tracks in the main parts of this small town.

Places to Stay — Khandala
Khandala is the station before Lonavla and can be used as an alternative jumping off point for the caves. The *Hotel Mount View* (tel 746) on Khandala Rd is reasonably cheap. The *Khandala Hotel* (tel 239) and *Hotel on the Rocks* (tel 690) are at the luxurious end of Khandala's scale.

Places to Stay — Karla
The most convenient location for a cave visit is the government operated *Holiday Camp* (tel 30) just off the Bombay-Pune road near the caves. There are two types of accommodation blocks at Rs 15 and Rs 20 per day plus a couple of dormitories. From the Holiday Camp you can get to both the Karla and Bhaja caves relatively easily but during the monsoon you can't get to the camp from the Malvali railway station because a river blocks the way. At that time you must leave the train at Lonavla and bus to the camp. Food is available at the camp — Rs 4 for a vegetarian thali.

Getting There
Buses and trains operate to Lonavla from Bombay or Pune. By train Bombay-Lonavla is two to three hours and 126 km. Pune-Lonavla is two hours and 64 km.

Getting Around
From Lonavla it's Rs 1 by bus to the Karla Cave and they depart every three hours. About Rs 15 for an auto-rickshaw one-way, a bit over twice that for a return trip via the Bhaja caves since the access road is rather bad. By rail to Bhaja you get down at Malvali then walk to Bhajagaon and on to the caves — hot and hard work.

PUNE (POONA) (population 950,000)
Shivaji, the great Maratha leader, was raised in Pune which was granted to his grandfather in 1599. Later it became the capital of the Peshwas but in 1817 went to the British, under whom it became the capital of the region during the monsoon. It has a rather more pleasant climate at that time than muggy Bombay. Although Pune has a number of points of interest and can be conveniently visited if you're heading from Bombay to Aurangabad (for Ajanta and Ellora) or to Goa, its major attraction to western visitors today is the Shree Rajneesh Ashram. The ashram has become so well known that it's even included on the city bus tour, where, in a superb reversal of roles, Indians flock to view westerners.

Information & Orientation
There's a Tourist Information Counter at the railway station where tours can be booked and some information is available. The Regional Tourist Office is in Central Buildings but is not of any great use. The city is at the confluence of the Mutha and Mula Rivers. The railway and bus stations are side by side and there are a number of hotels and restaurants and the Indian Airlines office in this same central area.

Rajneesh Ashram
Bhagwan Shree Rajneesh's Ashram is virtually the sole reason for Pune's large population of westerners. He's both one of the most popular of India's 'export gurus' and quite probably the most controversial. His followers are also

1	Poona Railway Station, State & Municipal Bus Terminals	8	Kasturba Samadhi (Aga Khan's Palace)
2	Shivajinagar Railway Station	9	Bund Gardens
3	Tourist Office (Central Buildings)	10	Rajneesh Ashram
4	Indian Airlines	11	Empress Gardens
5	GPO	12	Parvati Temple
6	City Post Office	13	Raja Kelkar Museum
7	Swargate State & Municipal Bus Terminal	14	Shanwarwada
		15	Panchaleshwar Temple

highly visible since every Rajneesh ashramite is always clad in orange from head to toe and wears a picture of their guru on a wooden bead chain around their neck.

The ashram is in Koregoan Park, a relatively spacious suburb of Pune, and at any one time there are three or four thousand followers in Pune. Only about 1000 actually live in the ashram though. The rest are scattered around Pune and come in by bicycle or other transport each day. Germans are the biggest single group of ashramites, in all 90% of his followers are westerners. The ashram is clean, neat and modern with neat little touches, like signs suggesting that you 'don't waste time queueing for mail, rent your own mailbox'.

Rajneesh's approach to the guru business has caused controversy from the start. His ashram is a curious blend of Indian mysticism and Californian pop-psychology. You don't just meditate at the ashram — you do 'dynamic meditation'. Hyped up tales of tantric sexual rites have also fuelled the controversy and tabloid papers in the west are always happy to run a headline with 'Sex Guru' in it. Whatever the pros and cons of the ashram, his followers all seen pretty convinced of his abilities. Despite their conspicuous garb they're not too communicative a group, however.

Raja Kelkar Museum
This interesting museum is one of Pune's real delights. The exhibits are the personal collection of Shri Dinkar Kelkar, a smiling old man in a white dhoti whom visitors will often see wandering around the building. There's actually far more to his zany collection than there is actually on show. The museum building is simply too small and exhibits have to be rotated. Amongst the items you might see are Peshwa and other miniatures, a coat of armour made of fish scales, a bizarre collection of musical instruments, carved doors and windows, hookah pipes, strange locks, oil lamps and a superb collection of betel nut cutters. The museum is housed in a quaint purple, red and green Rajasthani-style building.

Shanwarwada Palace
In a section of the town where narrow and winding streets form a maze stands the imposing fortress like Shanwarwada Palace. Built in 1736 the massive walls enclosed the palace of the Peshwa rulers — until it was burnt down in 1827. Inside today there is a pleasant garden and little signs proclaiming which rooms used to stand there. The palace is entered through sturdy doors studded with spikes in order to dissuade enemy elephants from leaning too heavily against the entrance! In a nearby street the Peshwa rulers used to execute offenders by trampling them with elephants.

Temples & Gardens
The Empress Gardens, with fine tropical trees and a small zoo nearby, has a moated Ganesh temple in the middle. The Bund Gardens, on the banks of the river, are a popular place for an evening stroll. The bridge here crosses the river to Yeravda and the Aga Khan's Palace. The Parvati Temple is on the outskirts of the town on a hilltop. There's a good view from the top, and the last Peshwa ruler is said to have watched his troops defeated by the British at Kirkee from up here. The rock cut Panchaleshwar Temple, a small 8th century temple similar in style to the much grander rock temples of Ellora, is fairly central. The 150 metre long Wellesley Bridge crosses the Mutha River to Sangam, the promontory of land where the Mutha and Mula join. It dates from 1875. There's a fine equestrian statue of Shivaji near the Panchaleshwar Temple.

Aga Khan's Palace

Across the river in Yeravda is the fine palace of the Aga Khan. At one time Mahatma Gandhi and other leaders of the movement for Indian independence were interned here and today it is maintained as another memorial to Gandhi. Kasturba Gandhi, the Mahatma's wife, died here while in internment and her memorial tomb stands in the palace grounds.

Tours

There are two tours daily from the railway station in Pune — the morning tour departs at 8 am, the afternoon tour at 3 pm and they last 3½ hours. The tours cost Rs 10 and go to all the main sights in Pune.

Places to Stay — Bottom End

The Shree Rajneesh orange folk tend to stack the hotels in Pune — leaving the casual visitor with a choice only of poor value (or simply poor) places. You may have to ask around a bit before finding a place to stay and even then it may well be overpriced. There is the usual collection of grubby, drab and/or dismal places close to the railway station. *Green Hotel* in Wilson Garden is reasonable at Rs 25 double. Next door the *Samrat* is similarly priced, across the road the *Central Lodge* is cheaper at Rs 17 a double and next door again the *Alankar Hotel* (tel 20670) is rather better at Rs 35 a double. Wilson Gardens start directly opposite the railway station, beside the *National Hotel* which is Rs 30 a double. All of these places are quite likely to be full up.

There are quite a few others in the immediate vicinity if you draw a blank at all of the above — but some are of extremely poor quality, quite uninhabitable. If you follow the road in front of the station to the left you'll soon come to Connaught Rd. The Indian Airlines office is here, at the bigger, flashier Amir Hotel. Down a little from the Amir is the *Gulmohr* and then the *Shalimar* (tel 20290-91) at 12A Connaught Rd. The latter is clean enough but very rundown, drab grey, dismal and poorly cared for. It's indicative of the accommodation squeeze in Pune that it should cost Rs 50 a double.

There are *Railway Retiring Rooms* at the station — dorm beds at Rs 8 each or rooms at Rs 12 a head. *Hotel Saras*, (tel 44 8499) run by the state tourist office, is actually built into the Nehru Stadium, about a Rs 4 auto-rickshaw ride from the railway station but very close to the Swargate Bus Station. Singles/doubles cost Rs 33/44 and it's quite pleasant. Other cheaper hotels include the *Ellora Hotel* (tel 40714) at 2156 Sadashiv with rooms from Rs 15 to 25 per person. The *Metro* at 14 Connaught Rd (tel 24145) runs from Rs 20/25 for singles/doubles.

Places to Stay — Top End

Very close to the railway station the *Hotel Amir* (tel 27371) is at 50 Connaught Rd. This is one of the best places in Pune with air-con rooms at Rs 125/175 and non air-con at Rs 80/100. It has the usual mod cons, a vegetarian restaurant and a good (and fairly reasonably priced) snack bar if you're in need of something non-Indian.

The *Blue Diamond* (tel 27334, 28735) is in Koregoan Park, very handy for the ashram. Rooms here are from Rs 250/350 for air-con singles/doubles and again it's all mod cons including a swimming pool, restaurants and coffee bar.

Places to Eat

The food scene is much better in Pune. The Amir and Blue Diamond have more expensive restaurants but there are several good cheap places right in front of the station to the left. *Neelam Restaurant* is pleasant and the *Hotel Madhura* (only a very small sign in English but it's in the big Hotel Metro building) has excellent thalis from Rs 3 to Rs 4, good lassi and super-cool drinks. A couple of doors further down there's the *Savera Restaurant*, also with good food.

Getting There
Pune is 192 km from Bombay and the trains take four or five hours and cost around Rs 52 in first class, Rs 12 in second. There are daily air-con buses between Bombay and Pune for Rs 33 and you can also get taxis between the two cities for Rs 47 per seat. Bus fares from Pune include Mahabaleshwar Rs 9, Panjim (Goa) Rs 33, Aurangabad (via Ahmednagar) Rs 15. Pune-Aurangabad takes about six hours. From Pune they operate from the Pune taxi stand in front of the railway station.

Pune has three bus stations:

Railway Bus Stand — points south including Goa — Belgaum, Panjim, Kolhapur, Mahabaleshwar, Ratnagiri,

Panchgani, Satara and Sholapur.

Shivaji Nagar Bus Stand — points north and north-east — Ahmednagar, Amravati, Aurangabad, Belgaum, Dehu, Jalgaon, Lonavla, Murud, Nanded, Nasik.

Swargate Bus Stand — Baneshwar, Bhorgar, Daund, Khodakwasla, Morgaon, Purandar, Saswad, Shivapur and Sinhagad.

There is a daily flight Bombay-Pune which costs Rs 85.

Getting Around
Lots of taxis and auto-rickshaws — from the railway station to the Swargate Bus Stand or the Saras Hotel costs about Rs 3 to Rs 4, to Shivaji Nagar Bus is about Rs 3. Pune is packed with bicycles and lots of places rent bicycles out — they obviously view every westerner as a Rajneesh follower because at first they always quote you a monthly rate!

AROUND PUNE
Simhagad, the 'lion fort', is 25 km south-west of Pune and was the scene of another of Shivaji's daring exploits. The fortress stands on top of a sheer sided hill at 1270 metres altitude. In 1670 Shivaji's general Tanaji Malusre led a force of men who scaled the steep hillside in the dark and defeated the unprepared forces of Bijapur. Legends

about this dramatic attack relate that the Maratha forces used trained lizards to carry ropes up the hillside. Tanaji died in the assault and there are monuments at the spot where he died and also at the place where he lost his left hand before his death. Purandar is another old fortress, it's 27 km south-east of Pune, further by road.

MAHABALESHWAR
This popular hill station was the summer capital of the Bombay presidency during the days of the Raj. At an altitude of 1372 metres Mahabaleshwar has pleasant walks, good lookouts (the sea, 30 km away, is visible on a clear day) and the area has interesting historical connections with Shivaji. Mahabaleshwar was founded in 1828 by Sir John Malcolm.

Elphinstone Point, Babington Point, Bombay Point, Kate's Point and a number of other lookouts around the wooded plateau offer fine views over the plains below. Arthur's Seat, 12 km out, looks over the coastal strip between the ghats and the sea known as the Konkan, a sheer drop of 600 metres. There are pleasant waterfalls such as Chinaman's Waterfall (2½ km out), Dhobi Waterfall (3 km) and Lingmala

Waterfalls (6 km). Venna Lake, within Mahabaleshwar, has boating and fishing facilities. In the village of Old Mahabaleshwar there are three old temples. The Krishnabai or Panchganga ('Five Streams') Temple is said to contain five streams including the Krishna River.

Pratapgarh Fort

Built in 1656 this fort is about 24 km, and 500 steps, from Mahabaleshwar. It's connected with one of the more notable feats in Shivaji's dramatic life. Outnumbered by the forces of Bijapur, Shivaji arranged to meet with the opposing General Afzal Khan. Neither would carry any weapon or wear armour but neither, it was to turn out, could be trusted. When they met Afzal Khan pulled out a dagger and stabbed Shivaji but the Maratha leader had worn a shirt of mail under his white robe and concealed in his left hand was a deadly set of 'tiger claws'. This nasty weapon consisted of a series of rings to which long, sharpened, metal claws were attached. Shivaji drove these claws into Khan and disemboweled him. Today a tomb marks where their encounter took place and a tower was erected over the Khan's head. There is a statue of Shivaji in the ruined fort. There is another Shivaji fort at Raigarh, 80 km from Mahabaleshwar.

Places to Stay

There are a lot of hotels at Mahabaleshwar. More expensive hotels, with tariffs over Rs 100, include the *Race View Hotel* (tel 238-76), *Dina Hotel* (tel 246) and the *Fredrick Hotel* (tel 240). Other hotels go down to less than Rs 20. The *Ripon Hotel* (tel 257) is Rs 40, the *Bharat Hotel* (tel 233) is around Rs 25. There is also a state government operated *Holiday Camp* (tel 318) with rooms from Rs 15 to 30. Reservations can be made through the Maharashtra Tourism Development Corporation at Express Towers, Nariman Point, Bombay (tel

234522-482). There are tourist information centres at the bus stand (tel 271) and at the Holiday Camp (tel 318).

Getting There

Pune is the normal departure point for Mahabaleshwar. Pune is also the nearest railhead. It's 120 km from Pune, via Panchgani which is 19 km before Mahabaleshwar. From Pune the ordinary bus fare is Rs 9, there are also state transport de-luxe buses and taxis. From Bombay it's 286 km via Pune or 259 km via Mahad.

PANCHGANI

'Five Hills' is just 19 km from Mahabaleshwar and, at 1334 metres, just 38 metres lower. It's a popular hill station but overshadowed by better known Mahabaleshwar. On the way up to Panchgani you pass through Wai, a site which featured in the Mahabharata.

Places to Stay

As in Mahabaleshwar there are a variety of hotels from the Rs 100 plus *Amir Hotel* (tel 211, 346) on down. Here too there is a *Holiday Camp* with rooms from Rs 20 to Rs 30.

SATARA

On the main road from Pune to Belgaum and then Goa, but 15 km off the railway line from Satara Road, this town houses a number of relics of the Mahratha leader Shivaji. Situated near the new palace a building contains his sword, the coat he wore when he met Afzal Khan and the Waghnakh or 'tiger's claws' with which he killed him. The Shivaji Maharaj Museum is opposite the bus station. The Fort of Wasota stands on the south of the town — it has had a colourful and bloody history including being captured from the Mahrathas in 1699 by the forces of Aurangzeb only to be recaptured in 1705 by means of a

Brahmin who befriended the fort's defenders then let in a band of Mahrathas.

OTHER PLACES IN THE SOUTH

Kolhapur, with a population of nearly 300,000, was once the capital of an important Mahratha state. The old palace contains some interesting items including a collection of swords. One of Kolhapur's maharajas died in Florence, Italy, and was cremated on the banks of the Arno where his chhatri (cenotaph) now stands. Ratnagiri, on the coast 130 km west, was the place where Thibaw, the last Burmese king, was interned by the British from 1886 until his death in 1916. Panhala and Pawangarh are interesting hill stations — at Panhala there is a fort with a long and interesting history, it was originally the stronghold of Raja Bhoj II in 1192. The Pawala Caves are near here with a couple of Buddhist cave temples.

AHMEDNAGAR (population 130,000)

On the road between Pune (82 km away) and Aurangabad, Ahmednagar has had a colourful history. It was here that the Emperor Aurangzeb died in 1707, aged 97. The town's imposing fort was erected in 1550 and at one time Nehru was imprisoned here by the British.

NASIK (population 200,000)

This interesting little town with its picturesque bathing ghats makes a good stopover on the way from Bombay to Aurangabad. The town is actually about eight km north-west of the station, which is 187 km from Bombay. Nasik stands on the Godavari River, one of the holiest rivers of the Deccan. Like Ujjain this is the site for the triennial Kumbh Mela which comes here every 12 years. The riverbanks are lined with steps above which stand temples and shrines. Although there are no particularly notable temples in Nasik the Sundar Narayan Temple, to the west of the city, is worth seeing.

Other points of interest in Nasik include the Sita Gupha cave from which Sita was supposed to have been carried off to the island of Lanka by the evil king Ravan, according to the Ramayana. Near the cave, in its grove of large banyan trees, is the fine house of the Panchavati family. Also near here is the temple of Kala Rama or 'black Rama', in a 96-arched enclosure. The Kapaleswar temple is upstream and is said to be the oldest in the town.

Kumbh Mela

Aeons ago the gods and demons, who were constantly at odds, fought a great battle for a kumbh or pitcher, drinking the contents of which would ensure immortality. They had combined forces to raise the pitcher from the bottom of the ocean but once safely in their hands Vishnu grabbed it and ran. After a struggle lasting 12 days the gods eventually defeated the demons and drank the nectar — it's a favourite scene in illustrations of Hindu mythology. During the fight for the pitcher's possession four drops of nectar spilt on the earth — at Allahabad, Hardwar, Nasik and Ujjain. Thus each holds its own Kumbh Mela over a 12 year (for a god's day is a human's year) span — the mela span — the mela is held each three years, rotating between the four cities.

Pandu Lena

About eight km south-west of Nasik, close to the Bombay road, are these 21 Hinayana Buddhist caves. They date from around the 1st century BC to the 2nd AD. The most interesting caves are 3, 10 and 18. Cave 3 is a large vihara with some interesting sculptures. Cave 10 is also a vihara and almost identical in design to cave 3 although it is much older and finer in its details. It is thought to be nearly as old as the Karla Cave. Cave 18 is a chaitya cave and thought to date from the same time as the Karla Cave. It too is well sculptured and its elaborate facade is particularly noteworthy. Cave 20 is another large vihara but the other caves are not of great interest.

Trimbak

The source of the Godavari River is here, 33 km from Nasik. From its source high on a steep hill the river virtually dribbles into a bathing tank reputed to perform the usual washing duties upon one's sins. From this tiny flow the Godavari eventually flows right down to the Bay of Bengal, clear across India.

AURANGABAD (population 175,000)

It's easy to think of Aurangabad simply as a place to stay when visiting the cave temples of Ajanta and Ellora. In fact Aurangabad has a number of attractions in its own right and could easily stand on its own were it not so overshadowed by the famous caves. The city is named after Aurangzeb but earlier in its history it was known as Khadke.

Information & Orientation

The railway station, tourist office and a variety of cheaper hotels and restaurants are clustered at the south of the town. There's a fairly open gap from here to the more crowded and older part of the town to the north, where you'll also find the bus station. The more expensive hotels are between the old town and the railway station or on the road out to the airport. There is a state Tourist Office in the Holiday Camp (tel 4713) while just around the corner on Station Rd there's a Government of India Tourist Office (tel 4817).

Bibi-ka-Maqbara

This poor man's Taj was built in 1679 by Aurangzeb's son for Rabia-ud-Darani, Aurangzeb's wife. It's a poor imitation of the Taj both in design (somehow it simply looks awkward and uncomfortable compared to the sophisticated balance of the Taj) and execution (where the Taj has gleaming marble this tomb has flaking paint). Nevertheless it's an interesting building and the only

example of Moghul architecture on the Deccan plateau. It stands to the north of the city and on the main gate an inscription reveals precisely how many rupees it cost to build.

Panchakki

The water mill takes its name from the mill which was used to grind grain for pilgrims. In 1624 a Sufi saint, a spiritual guide to Aurangzeb, was buried here and the pleasant garden with its series of fish-filled tanks serves as his memorial. It's a cool, relaxing and serene place. Note the vaults which support the second tank.

Aurangabad Caves

Although they're easily forgotten, standing as they do in the shadow of the Ajanta and Ellora caves, there are also a group of caves in Aurangabad. They're a couple of km north of the Bibi-ka-Maqbara and were built around the 6th or 7th century AD. They consist of nine caves, five in the western group and four in the eastern group, which are about a km distant, and are all Buddhist. There are actually some other caves further east but these are little more than natural caves.

Except for cave 4 all the caves are *viharas* (monasteries) rather than *chaityas* (temples). Cave 3 is square and supported by 12 highly ornate columns and has an interesting series of sculptures depicting scenes from one of the jatakas. Cave 6 is fairly intact and the sculptures

Aurangabad

Key:-
1. Central Bus Station
2. Tourist Office
3. Rama & Ajanta Ambassador Hotels
4. Aurangabad Hotel & Indian Airlines
5. Youth Hostel
6. Kathiawad Hotel
7. Tourist Home
8. Hotel Natraj
9. Municipal Travellers Bungalow
10. Panchakki
11. Holiday Camp

Aurangabad Caves (1½ km)

Bibi-ka-Maqbara

Ajanta (103k)
Jalgaon (160k)

Ghati Rd.

G.P.O.

Safara Road

Begumpura Rd.

Juna Bazar Chowk

Purnima Lodge

Greens Hotel

Ashoka Hotel

Jaina Road

Ellora (29 km)

Station Road

Adalat Rd.

Airport
Jalna (60km)

Hotel Nandavan

Railway Station

Paithan (50 km)

of women are notable for their exotic hairdos and ornamentation. There is a large Buddha figure here. Cave 7 is the most interesting of the Aurangabad caves. As in the other Aurangabad caves the figures and sculptures are particularly interesting — the figures of women, scantily clad but ornately bejewelled, are very well done. A huge figure of a Bodhisattva (near-Buddha) prays for deliverance from eight fears which are illustrated as fire, the sword of the enemy, chains, shipwreck, lions, snakes, mad elephants and death, represented as a demon.

Tours

There are a variety of tours from Aurangabad to the Ajanta and Ellora caves and the sights of Aurangabad. The Maharashtra Tourist Development Corporation (MTDC) and the ITDC both operate a daily tour to the Ajanta Caves for Rs 30 and to the Ellora Caves for Rs 16. They start from the Holiday Camp and the Government of India Tourist Office respectively but also pick up from the major hotels. The Ellora tour includes Daulatabad and the attractions in Aurangabad itself (but not the Aurangabad Caves) so it saves a lot of travelling and waiting time compared to doing it yourself. On the other hand it's quite a distance to the Ajanta Caves and many people prefer to stay near the caves rather than day-trip from Aurangabad. If you're thoroughly fed up with local buses it's worth enquiring about taking the tour bus to or from the caves — much faster than the stop-start-stop-start local bus service. As well as the MTDC and ITDC tours the state transport system also runs daily tours which start from the railway station. At Rs 8 for Ellora and Rs 18 for Ajanta they are much cheaper than the other tours and from all reports they're quite OK.

Places to Stay — Top End

There are two new 'international standard' hotels situated a couple of km out of the town towards the airport. The *Hotel Rama International* (tel 8241) has all mod-cons from air-con, restaurants, swimming pool to tennis courts and costs Rs 275/350 for singles/doubles. The *Ajanta Ambassador* (tel 8211) is virtually beside it in Chikalthana and is similarly equipped. Singles/doubles here cost Rs 250/325.

The *Aurangabad Ashoka* (tel 2921) is more centrally located on Dr Rajendra Prasad Marg and costs Rs 125/175 for air-con singles/doubles or Rs 80/140 for rooms without air-con. Along Station Rd, towards the railway station and cluster of cheaper hotels, is the *Nandavan* (tel 3571) with singles/doubles at Rs 60/100 and the *Printravel* (tel 2707) at Rs 75/160.

Places to Stay — Bottom End

Most of Aurangabad's cheaper hotels are close to the railway station. The notable exception is the excellent *Youth Hostel* which is midway between the railway station and the main part of town. Dorm beds cost Rs 5 (Rs 1 less for YHA members and is spotlessly clean, has hot and cold water; breakfast and evening meals are available.

A hundred metres or so from the station is the *Government Holiday Camp* where you'll also find the state government tourist office. There are several wings in this large accommodation complex with doubles from Rs 21 to Rs 30. Rooms have mosquito nets and bathrooms and they're excellent value.

There are lots of other possibilites around. On the other road out from the station there's the *Kathiawad Hotel* with doubles at Rs 15 and a helpful manager. The *Tourist Home* is Rs 20 a double with your own bathroom — fair to reasonable. The *Hotel Natraj* costs Rs 30 but is not so special. Back round the corner towards the Holiday Camp you'll find the *Hotel Ashok* or *Ashok*

Lodging which is dirt cheap — Rs 10 a double and with standards to match the price. Or the *Arnanda Lodge* with doubles at Rs 15 (without bath), Rs 20 (with).

There are also a string of places to eat along this stretch of road. The *Hotel Guru* has good food including breakfast cornflakes. The Holiday Camp has a dining hall which serves the usual state government menu — when it's open.

Getting There
The cave groups at Ajanta and Ellora are off the railway lines and are usually approached from either Aurangabad (Ellora 30 km, Ajanta 106 km) or from Jalgaon (Ajanta 59 km). Jalgaon is on the main broad gauge line from Bombay to Allahabad which requires a change to metre gauge line at Manmad. On the other hand Aurangabad is the access point from Pune (by road) or Hyderabad (by rail). Plus it has the airport. There's a daily flight connection Bombay-Aurangabad - Udaipur - Jaipur - Delhi — another popular tourist route flight. Bombay-Aurangabad costs Rs 163, Delhi-Aurangabad is Rs 488.

Jalgaon is 420 km from Bombay, the trip takes about eight hours by rail and

costs about Rs 95 in first class, Rs 22 in second. From Jalgaon there are frequent buses to Ajanta and Aurangabad. By rail direct to Aurangabad you change train at Manmad, 261 km from Bombay for the 113 km trip to Aurangabad. Travelling time is about eight hours, plus the time changing trains and the cost is around Rs 90 in first class, Rs 20 in second. From Hyderabad (Secunderabad), which is on the same line as Manmad, it's 510 km, takes 12 hours and costs about Rs 107 in first class, Rs 26 in second class.

Getting to the Caves
Aurangabad is a good base for visiting either cave. Unless you're planning on doing a day tour from Aurangabad to Ajanta you'll probably find it more convenient to actually stay at Ajanta though. Bus fares from Aurangabad are Rs 3 to Ellora (every half hour), Rs 8 to Ajanta, Rs 11 to Jalgaon, Ajanta-Jalgaon is Rs 5. Most of the Ajanta accommodation is actually at Fardapur, about five km from the caves — Rs 1 or so by the reasonably frequent buses. You can negotiate round trip rates to the caves by taxi — say Rs 120 for Ellora, Rs 350 for Ajanta.

AURANGABAD TO ELLORA
Daulatabad
Situated between Aurangabad and the Ellora Caves is the magnificent hilltop fortress of Daulatabad. The fort is surrounded by five km of sturdy wall while the central bastion tops a two hundred metre high hill. In the 14th century the slightly nutty Muhammed Tughlaq, Sultan of Delhi, conceived the crazy plan of not only building himself a new capital but marching the entire population of Delhi 1100 km south to populate it. His unhappy subjects proceeded to drop dead like flies on this forced march and 17 years later he turned round and marched them all

back to Delhi. The fort remained.

It's worth making the climb to the top for the superb views over the surrounding country. Along the way you'll pass through a complicated series of defences including multiple doorways so that elephants could not charge them and spike studded doors, just in case they did. A magnificent tower of victory, the Chand Minar, soars 60 metres high. It was built in 1435 and the Qutb Minar in Delhi, five metres higher, is the only loftier victory tower in India. On the other side of the entrance path is a mosque built from the remains of a Jain temple.

Higher up is the blue tiled Chini

Around Aurangabad

Purna River

Bhusawal

Viramgaon

Jalgaon

Erandol

Dhulia

Parola

Jamner

Lohara

Pahur

Bhodgaon

Pachora

Fardapur

Ajanta Caves

Ajanta Village

Malegaon

Chalisgaon

Bhamarwadi Village

Kannad

Shillod

Pithalkara Caves

Manmad

Ellora Caves

Verul Village

Phulambri

Yeola

Khuldabad

Vijapur

Daulatabad

Aurangabad

Kopargaon

Jalna

Godavari River

Gangapur

Poona
Ahmednagar

Poona

Hyderabad

Nagpur

Bombay

Mahal palace where the last king of of Golconda was imprisoned for 13 years until his death. Finally you climb the central fort to a huge six metre cannon, cast from five different metals and with Aurangzeb's name engraved upon it. The final ascent to the top goes through a pitch black spiralling tunnel down which the forts defenders could hurl burning coals at any invaders. Of course, your guide may tell you, the fort was once successfully conquered despite these elaborate precautions — by the simple expedient of bribing the guard at the gate.

The hill the fort stands on was originally known as Devagiri, the 'hill of the gods' but Muhamad Tughlaq renamed it Daulatabad, the 'city of fortune'.

Rauza
Also known as Khuldabad, the 'heavenly abode', this walled town is only three km from Ellora. This is the Karbala or holy shrine of Deccan Moslems and a number of historical figures are buried here including Aurangzeb, the last great Moghul emperor. Aurangzeb built the battlemented wall around the town

which was once an important centre although today it is little more than a sleepy village. The emperor's final resting place is a simple affair of bare earth in a courtyard of the Alamgir Dargah in the centre of the city. Aurangzeb's pious austerity extended even to his own tomb for he stipulated that his mausoleum should be paid for with money he earned himself by copying out the Koran. Within the building there is also supposed to be a robe worn by the Prophet Mohammed, it is only shown to the faithful once each year. Another shrine across the road from the Alamgir Dargah is said to contain hairs of the Prophet's beard and also lumps of silver from a tree of solid silver which miraculously grew here after a saint's death.

Guidebooks

At many places in India there are excellent locally produced guidebooks which you can buy very cheaply at the sites and which will help to give you a deeper appreciation of what you are seeing. The caves of Ajanta and Allora are no exception and both *Aurangabad, Daulatabad, Ellora &Ajanta* by Professor Dr S Siddiqui and *Ajanta, Ellora & Aurangabad Caves − an Appreciation* by T V Pathy are worthwhile investments. The former has good black and white pictures which help in the identification of the actual sculpture or painting being described. The latter guide has more examples of the delightful way Indians have with English. The author describes a statue as being of a 'semi-nude dryad with a slender waist, pouting lips and abundant mammalian equipment......'. What a fine way of saying she had big boobs.

ELLORA CAVES

The caves of Ellora are about 30 km from Aurangabad. Whereas the Ajanta caves are noted for their paintings, here it is the sculpture which is remarkable. Chronologically the Ellora caves start where the Ajanta caves finish — it's thought that the builders of Ajanta moved to Ellora when they suddenly ceased construction of their earlier site. But the Ellora caves are not all Buddhist like those of Ajanta. Here the earliest caves are Buddhist but during this time Buddhism in India was in a period of decline and a later series of Hindu, then Jain cave temples were added.

In all there are 34 caves at Ellora: 12 Buddhist, 17 Hindu and five Jain. Although the temples are numbered consecutively, from one at the southern end to 34 at the northern end, and although the various religious groups do not overlap, the caves are not arranged chronologically. It is thought that construction of the Hindu caves commenced before the Buddhist caves were all completed, for example. Roughly the Buddhist caves are thought to date from around 600 to 800 AD, the Hindu caves to around 900 AD, while the Jain caves were not commenced until about 800 AD and were completed by 1000 AD. The caves are cut into a hillside running north-south. The hill slopes down rather than drops steeply as at Ajanta. Therefore many of the caves have elaborate entrance halls to the main shrines. From south to north the caves cover about two km.

Buddhist Caves

Apart from cave 10 all the Buddhist caves are *viharas* (monasteries) rather than *chaityas* (temples). They are not as architecturally ambitious as the Hindu caves although 11 and 12 show signs of attempting to compete with the complex Hindu designs. The Buddist caves chart the period of Buddhism's division and decline in India.

Caves 1 to 4 These caves are all vihara caves and cave 2, with its ornate pillars and figures of the Buddha is quite interesting. Caves 3 and 4 are earlier, simpler and less well preserved.

Cave 5 This is the biggest vihara cave here and the rows of stone benches indicate it may have been an assembly or dining hall.

Caves 6 to 8 In cave 6 there is a large seated Buddha in the shrine room but this ornate vihara also has a standing figure thought to be either the Hindu goddess of learning, Saraswati, or her Buddhist equivalent, Mahamayuri. Caves 7 and 8 are not so interesting.

Cave 10 The Viswakarma or Carpenter's Cave is the only chaitya cave in the Buddhist group. It takes its name from the ribs carved into the roof, in imitation of wooden beams. The temple is entered by steps to a courtyard followed by further steps to the main temple. A finely carved horseshoe window lets light into the cave and a huge seated Buddha figure is in front of the nine metre high stupa.

Cave 11 The Do Thal, 'two storey', cave is also entered by a courtyard. Curiously it actually has three storeys but the third was not discovered until 1876. Construction of the middle floor was never completed.

Cave 12 The Tin Thal, 'three storey' cave also has three storeys and is entered through a courtyard. There is a very large seated Buddha and a number of other figures in the cave and the walls are carved with relief pictures, just like in the Hindu caves.

Hindu Caves

The Hindu caves are the most dramatic and impressive of the Ellora cave temples. In size, design and energy they are in a totally different league to the Buddhist or Jain caves. If calm contemplation described the Buddhist caves then dynamic energy is the description for the Hindu caves. The sheer size of the Kailasa Temple (cave 16) is overwhelming. It covers twice the area of the Parthenon in Athens and is one and a half times as high. Remember that this whole, gigantic structure was cut out of solid rock! It has been estimated that carving out the Kailasa entailed removing 200,000 tons of rock! All these temples were cut from the top down so that it was never necessary to use any scaffolding — their builders started with the roof and moved down to the floor. It's worth contemplating the skill and planning that must have gone into such a process — there was no way of adding a panel or a pillar if things didn't work out quite as expected.

Cave 14 The first Hindu cave, cave 13, is not impressive but cave 14, the Rava Kakhai, sets the scene for the other Hindu caves. Like all the others it is dedicated to Shiva and it is Lord Shiva who appears in many of the carvings around the cave. You can see Shiva dancing the *tandava*, a victory dance over the demon Mahisa, or playing chess with his wife Parvati, or defeating the buffalo demon. Parvati also appears in the form of Durga while Vishnu also makes several appearances including one as Varaha, his boar incarnation. The seven 'mother goddesses' can also be seen and Ravana makes yet another attempt to shake Kailasa.

Cave 15 The Das Avatara cave is one of the finest at Ellora and the two storey temple is reached by a long flight of steps. Inside there is a modern image of Shiva's mount, the bull Nandi. Many of the familiar scenes involving Shiva can be again found here but you can also see Vishnu resting on a five-hooded serpent or rescuing an elephant from a crocodile. Vishnu also appears as the man-lion Narsimha while Shiva emerges from his symbolic lingam and in another panel he marries Parvati.

Cave 16 The mighty Kailasa Temple is the central attraction at Ellora. Here Indian rock cut temple architecture reaches its peak. Kailasa is, of course, Shiva's Himalayan home and the Kailasa

Temple is a representation of that mountain. The temple consists of a huge courtyard, 81 metres long by 47 metres and 33 metres high at the back. In the centre the main temple rises up and is connected to the outer enclosure by a bridge. Around the enclosure are galleries while towards the front are two large stone elephants with two massive stone 'flagstaffs' flanking the Nandi pavilion which faces the main shrine. As in the previous two caves there are a variety of dramatic and finely carved panels, the most impressive being the image of Ravana shaking Kailasa. In the *Ramayana* the demon king Ravana flaunted his strength by lifting up Shiva's mountain home. Unimpressed Lord Shiva simply put his foot down on the top and pressed the mountain and the upstart Ravana back into place. Vishnu also appears along one gallery as Rarsimha once again — in this legend he defeats a demon who could not be killed by man or beast by the simple expedient of becoming a man-lion, neither man nor beast.

Other Caves The other Hindu caves pall beside the majesty of the Kailasa but several of them are worth at least some study. Cave 21, known as the Ramesvara, has a number of interesting interpretations of scenes also depicted in the earlier temples. Shiva once again marries Parvati and plays dice with her, and the goddesses Ganga and Yamuna once again appear. The figure of Ganga, standing on her crocodile or *makara*, is particularly notable. The very large Cave 29, the Dumar Lena, is similar in design to the Elephanta Cave at Bombay. It is thought to be a transitionary model as the designers moved from the simpler hollowed out caves towards the fully developed temples exemplified by the Kailasa.

Jain Caves
The Jain caves mark the final phase of Ellora. They do not have the drama and

high-voltage energy of the best Hindu temples nor are they as ambitious in size but they balance this with their exceptional detail work. There are only five Jain temples and they are several hundred metres north of the last Hindu temple.

Cave 30 The Chota Kailasa or 'little Kailasa' is a poor imitation of the great Kailasa Temple and was never completed. It stands by itself some distance from the other Jain temples which are all clustered closely together.

Cave 32 The Indra Sabha or 'Assembly Hall of Indra' is the finest of the Jain temples. The ground floor plan is similar to the Kailasa but upstairs, reached by a stairway, is as ornate and richly decorated as downstairs is plain. There are images of the Jain *tirthankars* Parasnath and Gomatesvara, the latter surrounded by vegetation and wildlife. Inside the shrine is a seated figure of Mahavira, the 24th and last *tirthankar* and founder of the Jain religion. Traces of paintings can still be seen on the roof of the temple.

Cave 31 is really an extension of 32.

Cave 33, the Jagannath Sabha, is similar in plan to 32 and has some particularly well preserved sculptures. The final temple, the small cave 34, also has interesting sculptures. On the hilltop over the Jain temples a five metre high image of Parasnath looks down over Ellora. An enclosure was built around it a couple of hundred years ago.

Grishneshwar

Close to the Ellora Caves in the village of Verul this 18th century Shiva temple is one of the 12 Shiva *jyotorlingas* in India.

Places to Stay

Although most people stay in Aurangabad there is some accommodation available right at the caves. The relatively expensive *Hotel Kailasa* has singles/doubles at Rs 28/44 — all rooms with attached bath and it's very close to the caves. There is also a restaurant attached to the hotel and it's cheaper than the other government restaurant here — intended for tour groups.

AJANTA CAVES

The caves of Ajanta pre-date those of Ellora so if you want to see the caves in chronological order you should visit here first. Although the Ellora caves are easily visited using Aurangabad as a base it's much easier to stay near the Ajanta caves rather than make a day trip to them. Unlike the Ellora caves, which are Buddhist, Hindu and Jain, the Ajanta caves are all Buddhist and, whereas at Ellora the caves are masterpieces of sculpture, at Ajanta it's the magnificent paintings for which the caves are famous.

The caves, after their abandonment with the move to Ellora and the decline of Buddhism, were gradually forgotten and their rediscovery was dramatic. In 1819 a British hunting party stumbled

upon the caves and their remote beauty was soon unveiled. Their isolation had contributed to the fine state of preservation in which some of the paintings remain to this day. The caves are cut into the steep face of a deep rock gorge. There are 29 caves in a curve of the gorge and there is a good viewpoint from across the ravine. The caves date from around 200 BC to 650 AD. They do not follow the chronological order that the Ellora caves generally do; here the oldest caves are mainly in the middle and the newer ones to each end.

The cave paintings initially suffered some deterioration after their rediscovery and some heavy handed restoration also caused damage. Between 1920 and 1922 two Italian art experts conducted a meticulous restoration process and the

Ajanta Caves

paintings have been carefully preserved since that time. Many of the caves are quite dark and without a light the paintings are hard to see — it's worth paying for a lighting ticket which will ensure the cave guards turn the lights on for you. Or you could try tagging along with a tour party although normally the doors are shut after each party enters a cave.

Five of the caves are *chaityas* or temples while the other 24 are *viharas* or monasteries. Caves 8, 9, 10, 12 and 13 are the older Hinayana caves while the others are Mahayana. In the simpler, more austere Hinayana school the Buddha was never represented directly — his presence was always alluded to by a symbol such as the footprint or wheel of law. The Ajanta paintings are not, strictly speaking, frescoes but tempera paintings — a difference purely of technique. Although the Ajanta paintings are particularly notable there are also many interesting sculptures here.

Cave 1 This vihara cave is one of the most recent and also most fully developed of the Ajanta caves. A verandah at the front leads to a large square hall with elaborate carvings and paintings and a huge Buddha statue. Cave 1 is notable both for its sculpture and its paintings. Amongst the interesting sculptures is one of four deer sharing a common head. There are many paintings of women, some remarkably similar to the paintings at Sigiriya in Sri Lanka. Notable paintings include those of the 'black princess' and the 'dying princess'. Other paintings include scenes of the jatakas (events from the Buddha's previous lives) and portraits of the Bodhisattvas (near-Buddhas), Padmapani (holding a lotus flower) and Vajrapani.

Cave 2 Also a more recent vihara cave, this one also has a number of important paintings although some of them are unfortunately damaged. As well as murals on the walls there are paintings on the ceiling. Scenes include a number of jatakas and events connected with the Buddha's birth including his mother's dream of the six-tusked elephant which heralded the Buddha's conception.

Cave 4 This is the largest vihara cave at Ajanta and is supported by 28 pillars.

Although it was never completed the cave has some fine sculptures including scenes of people fleeing from the 'eight great dangers' to the protection of the Buddha's disciple Avalokitesvara. One of the great dangers is an angry looking elephant in pursuit of a man and woman. Caves 3, 5 and 8 were never completed.

Cave 6 This is the only two-storey cave at Ajanta but parts of the lower storey have collapsed. Inside there is a seated figure of the Buddha with an intricately carved door to the shrine. Upstairs the hall is surrounded by cells with fine paintings on the doorways.

Cave 7 This cave is of unusual design in that the verandah does not lead into a hall with cells down the sides and a shrine room at the rear. Here there are porches before the verandah which leads directly on to the four cells and the elaborately sculptured shrine. Cave 8 is used solely for the generating equipment which lights the caves.

Cave 9 This is a chaitya cave and one of the earliest at Ajanta. Although it dates from the Hinayana period there are two Buddha figures flanking the entrance door which were probably later, Mahayana, additions. Similarly the paintings inside, which are not in excellent condition, show signs of being refurbished at some time in the past. Columns run down both sides of the cave and around the three metre high dagoba at the far end. At the front there is a horseshoe shaped window above the entrance and the vaulted roof has traces of wooden ribs.

Cave 10 is thought to be the oldest cave and was also the cave first spotted by the British soldiers who rediscovered Ajanta. It is also the largest chaitya cave and is similar in design to cave 9. The facade of the cave has collapsed and the paintings inside are rather damaged, in some case by graffitists soon after the caves' rediscovery. Caves 11, 12 and 13 are not of great interest — they are all relatively early, either Hinayana or

from the early years of the Mahayana period. Cave 14 is an incompleted vihara, standing above cave 13. Cave 13 is also an early Mahayana vihara.

Cave 16 Some of Ajanta's finest paintings can be seen in this, one of the later vihara caves. It is thought that cave 16 may have been the original entrance to the entire complex and there is a very fine view of the river from the front of the cave. Best known of the paintings here is the 'dying princess'. Sundari, wife of Buddha's half-brother Nanda, is said to have expired at the hard news that her husband was renouncing the material life (and her) in order to become a monk. This is one of the

far out!

Electric spotlight in the darkened caves

Tour guide & freak • AJANTA CAVES •
MARVELLING AT THE NATURAL WONDERS...

finest paintings at Ajanta. Nanda features in several other paintings including his conversion by Buddha.

Cave 17 This is the cave with the finest paintings at Ajanta. Not only are they in the best condition they are also the greatest in number and variety. They include beautiful women flying overhead on the roof while carved dwarfs support the pillars. A popular scene shows a woman, surrounded by attendants, applying make-up. In another there is a royal procession while in another a couple engage in a little private love making. The Buddha returns from his enlightenment to his own home to beg from his wife and astonished son in another panel. A detailed panel tells the story of Prince Simhala's expedition to Ceylon. With his 500 companions he is shipwrecked on an island where ogresses appear as beautiful women, only to seize and devour their victims. Simhala escapes on a flying horse and returns to conquer the island.

Cave 19 The facade of this chaitya cave is remarkably detailed and includes an impressive horseshoe shaped window as its dominant feature. There are two very fine standing Buddha figures flanking the entrance. Inside this excellent specimen of a chaitya cave there is a tall dagoba with a figure of the Buddha on the front. There are some fine sculptures and paintings in this cave but one of the most important is outside the cave to the west where there is an image of the Naga king with seven cobra hoods arrayed around his head and his wife, topped by a single cobra, seated beside him.

Caves 20 through 25 are either incomplete or not of great interest although cave 24 would have been the largest vihara at Ajanta if finished. You can see how the caves were constructed from this example — long galleries were cut into the rock and then broken across to each other.

Cave 26 The fourth chaitya cave's facade has fallen and almost all trace of its paintings have disappeared. Nevertheless there are some very fine sculptures remaining. On the left wall there is a huge figure of the 'reclining Buddha', lying back as he prepares to enter Nirvana. Other scenes include a lengthy depiction of the Buddha's temptation by Mara. In one scene Mara attacks the Buddha with demons, then his beautiful daughters tempt him with more sensual delights. The Buddha's resistance is too strong however and the final scene shows a glum and dejected looking Mara having failed to deflect the Buddha from the straight and narrow.

Cave 27 is virtually a vihara connected to the cave 26 chaitya. Caves 28 and 29 are higher up the cliff face and relatively hard to get to.

Places to Stay

There is a good, but with only two rooms, *Forestry Rest House* right by the caves. Most people stay at Fardapur, five km from the caves. The caves are a couple of km off the main road from Aurangabad to Jalgaon and Fardapur is a little further down the main road towards Jalgaon. There are regular buses to the Ajanta caves, costing 65p. At Fardapur there is an excellent *Holiday Camp* run by the state government. Rooms along the pleasant verandah cost Rs 18 a double, Rs 10 for a single, cheaper in the June to September off-season. All rooms have attached bathrooms and there is a restaurant at one end. You can also get simple food from the stalls along the road through Fardapur. The small village of Fardapur, set back from the road, is worth wandering around.

NAGPUR (population 950,000)

Situated on the River Nag, from which the town takes its name, Nagpur is the orange growing capital of India. This was once the capital of the central province but was later incorporated into Maharashtra. Long ago it was a centre for the aboriginal Gond tribes who remained in power until the early 18th century. Many Gonds still live in this region. Later it went through a series of changes before eventually falling to the British. About 40 km north-east of Nagpur is Ramtek with a number of picturesque 600 year old temples surmounting the 'Hill of Rama'. In summer this is one of the hottest places in India.

Wardha & Sevagram

About 80 km south-west of Nagpur, near Wardha station, is Sevagram, the 'Village of Service', where Gandhi established his ashram in 1933. For the 15 years from then until India achieved independence this was in some ways the alternative capital of India. The Centre of Science for Villages (Magan Sangrahalaya) is a museum intended to explain and develop Gandhi's ideals of village level economics. The huts of his ashram are still preserved in Sevagram and at Mahadev Bhawan, beside the Sevagram hospital, there is a photo exhibit of events in the Mahatma's life. Only three km from Sevagram is the ashram of Vinoba Bhave, Gandhi's follower who walked throughout India persuading rich landlords to hand over tracts of land for redistribution to the landless and poor.

Sometimes the frustrations of trying to do things in India soar far beyond the merely annoying into the realms of grand comedy. I wanted to phone a friend at his office, my hotel room had a phone, but no phone directory. I contacted the hotel operator and asked her to get me A F Fergusson. Twenty minutes passed and I called her back, directory enquiries had been unable to get the number she would now look it up in the directory herself. After another half hour had passed I realised that this was one of those cases of being unable to do it but not wanting to lose face by telling you. I went down to the front desk and asked for a phone directory. We haven't got one. Nor has the girl at the switchboard. Nor has the manager. But you have one in your room. No I don't. Yes you do. I go upstairs again, search the room, look under the bed. No directory. Back downstairs to report there is definitely no directory, how about getting me one. OK. Time passes, is there anywhere else I can find a directory I finally ask. The restaurant upstairs they suggest. Meanwhile the lift operator has disappeared and the steps, of course, are locked. Eventually I get to the restaurant where my request for a phone directory is met with a table and, ten minutes later, a menu. No a p-h-o-n-e d-i-r-e-c-t-o-r-y please! Not even a drink? No. Eventually a phone directory is found. It's in Hindi. Someone comes to my rescue but although it's easy to look up Kumara or Ashoka or Akbar in a Hindi directory A F Fergusson proves difficult. Others also come to the rescue and long discussions develop on how to trans-literate F or FER. Eventually they give in and I trek back to the front desk and suggest that if they cannot find me a phone directory perhaps they could change my room to a room with a phone directory. This amazing suggestion works, one of the half dozen lackeys who are always hanging around hotel front desks in India is despatched to another room and promptly returns with a phone directory. Ten seconds later I've looked the number up. Total time to make one call about an hour and a half. I could have walked the km or two to his office in ten minutes.

Tony Wheeler

Goa

Population*: 9 million
Area*: 3813 square km
Main languages: Marathi, Konkan
& Gujurati

*including Daman & Diu

The small former Portuguese enclave of Goa is still one of India's most touristically important places. It combines old Portuguese architecture with a Portuguese flavour to the lifestyle which somehow manages to exist even 20 years after India took Goa over. Most important, to many travellers, there are the superb beaches and the 'travellers' scene' which so many of them offer. Officially Goa is governed together with two other Portuguese coastal enclaves, Daman and Diu, which were taken over at the same time. The latter two are both in the state of Gujurat and are covered in the Gujurat section of this book.

Goa has a long history stretching back to the 3rd century BC when it formed part of the Mauryan Empire. It was later ruled by the Satavahanas of Kolhapur at the beginning of the Christian era and eventually passed to the Chalukyas of Badami who controlled it from 580-750 AD. Over the next few centuries it was ruled successively by the Shilharas, the Kadambas and the Chalukyas of Kalyani. The Kadambas are credited with constructing the first settlement on the site of Old Goa in the middle of the 11th century when it was called Thorlem Gorem. Goa fell to the Moslems for the first time in 1312 but they were forced to evacuate it in 1370 by Harihara I of the Vijayanagar Empire whose capital was at Hampi in Karnataka state. The Vijayanagar rulers held on to Goa for nearly 100 years and during this time its harbours were important as places where Arabian horses were landed on their way to Hampi to

strengthen the Vijayanagar cavalry. In 1469, however, Goa was reconquered, this time by the Bahmani Sultans of Gulbarga. When this dynasty broke up the area passed to the Adil Shahis of Bijapur who made Goa Velha their second capital. The present Secretariat building in Panjim is the former palace of Adil Shah, later taken over by the Portuguese Viceroys as their official residence.

The Portuguese arrived in Goa in 1510 under the command of Afonso de Albuquerque after having been unable to secure a base on the Malabar coast further south due to opposition from the Zamorin of Calicut and stiff competition from the Turks who, at that time, controlled the trade routes across the Indian Ocean. Blessed as it was by natural harbours and wide rivers, Goa was the ideal base for the seafaring Portuguese bent on their quest for control of the spice route from the east and the spread of Christianity. For a while, their control was limited to a small area around Old Goa but by the middle of the 16th century they had expanded to include the provinces of Bardez and Salcete.

Goa reached its present size in the 18th century as a result of further annexations, first in 1763 when the provinces of Ponda, Sanguem, Quepem and Canacona were added and later in 1788 when Pednem, Bicholim and Satari were added. The Marathas nearly vanquished the Portuguese in the late 18th century and there was a brief occupation by the British during the time of the Napoleonic Wars in Europe. It was not until 1961, when India ejected the Portuguese in a near bloodless operation, that the Portuguese finally disappeared from the sub-continent. The other enclaves of Daman and Diu were also taken over at the same time. Despite the 20 intervening years of Indian rule Goa still maintains its distinctively Portuguese flavour and easy going ways.

Goan Food

Although food in Goa is much like anywhere else in India there are a number of local specialities including the popular pork vindaloo. Other local pork specialities include the Goan sausage *chourisso*, and the pig's liver dish known as *sarpotel*. Seafood of all types is, of course, plentiful and fresh in Goa. There are the usual travellers' menu items at the beach restaurants. Although the ready availability of alcohol is a contrast to some other parts of India the Goans also brew their local feni spirits, made from coconut or cashews.

PANJIM (PANAJI)

Panjim is one of India's smallest and pleasantest state capitals. Situated on the south bank of the wide Mandovi River, it became the capital of Goa in 1843 though the Portuguese Viceroys had shifted their residence from the outskirts of Old Goa to the former palace of Adil Shah at Panjim as early as 1759. The town has preserved its Portuguese heritage remarkably well and parts of it still consist of narrow winding streets, old houses with overhanging balconies, red-tiled roofs and numerous small bars and cafes. Signs in Portuguese over shops, cafes and administrative buildings are still visible in many places. People are friendly and the atmosphere is easy-going. The main attraction for travellers is, of course, Old Goa, nine km east of Panjim and the former capital founded by Afonso de Albuquerque in 1510. Nevertheless, Panjim, apart from the services and facilities which it offers, is well worth a visit for its own sake.

Panjim's main attraction is the narrow winding streets, small cafes and bars and the occasional old stone buildings dating from the 16th and 17th centuries. Its 'sights' as such are few but among those worth visiting are the old *Church of the Immaculate Conception* built on the hillside at one end of the Municipal Gardens and the *Mahalaxmi Temple*. If you're staying in Panjim rather than on the beaches of Goa, then the nearest beach to Panjim is at Miramar, three km along the road to Dona Paula.

Information & Orientation

The town has a wide range of hotels, many excellent restaurants, old churches and monuments and is well served by transport facilities connecting it to the rest of India. It not only has its own State Tourist Office but also tourist offices for the states of Karnataka and Andhra Pradesh and an Indian Railways Out-Booking Office (the rail head is at Vasco da Gama on the other side of the Zuari River). The airport is at Dabolim near Vasco.

The Tourist Office, located on Rua Afonso de Albuquerque, is pretty chaotic and they have precious little literature and no street plans of Goan towns so it's hardly worth visiting. Part of this office, however, is the South Central Railway Out-Agency Booking

Office which is very useful if you're staying north of Panjim and want to book a sleeper in 2nd class on a train. Note that they only have a quota on 2nd class sleepers. If you want 1st class you will have to go either to Vasco or Margao stations to book it. Naturally, you can also book 2nd class at either of these stations as well. The office is open daily except Sundays from 10 am to 12.30 pm and from 2.30 pm to 5 pm. On public holidays it's open only between 9.30 am and 12.30 pm.

There are also Tourist Offices for Andhra Pradesh (Rua de Ourem); Karnataka (in the office building which dominates the eastern side of the Municipal Gardens), and Maharashtra (on the ground floor of the Tourist Hostel). Unlike the Goan Tourist Office, these offices have a good selection of literature.

The Poste Restante at the GPO is pretty efficient. They give you the whole pile to sort through yourself and will willingly check other pigeon holes if expected letters are not arriving.

Indian Airlines is at Dempo Building, D Bandodkar Marg, on the river front (tel 3822). Air India are located in the same building (tel 3081). Indian Airlines operates buses to Dabolim airport in time for flights, the fare is Rs 10. There is also an agent of Indian Airlines next to the Safari Hotel opposite the Municipal Park.

Undoubtedly the best travel agents in Panjim are MGM International Travels opposite the GPO (First Floor) — tel 2150. Reliable, honest, efficient and very friendly service. If these people can give you a discount, they'll do it. Unlike many other travel agents in Goa who generate business by advertising what appear to be rock-bottom prices and then when it comes to paying for the ticket and there's no time to go anywhere else slap you for 'service charges' and the like — (which can be quite considerable!) — these people will tell you how much a ticket is on your first visit. And that's exactly how much you end up paying. They have a branch office at Calangute beach. Highly recommended.

Tax Clearance Certificates only concern you if you've stayed in India more than 90 days and are about to leave. Most travel agents will fix it up for you but will charge you Rs 50-100 for the privilige which is ridiculous since, if you do it yourself, it will cost Rs 10. The best person to get the affidavit from is Vasco da Silva Ferreira, a solicitor who has an office on the first floor next to the New Punjab Restaurant opposite the Municipal Park. The Taxation Department is located in the Shanta Building at the end of 18th June Rd.

Booksellers include Furtado Enterprises, Tourist Hostel; Sarmalkar Book Depot, near Mahalaxmi Temple; Singbal Book Depot, near Church of the Immaculate Conception (tel 2693). Music stores include Pedro Fernandes & Cia, near GPO; New Music Art, near Govind Building; Paiva Music Centre, General Bernard Guedes Rd.

The dreaded weed — ganja is readily available (it's usually from Kerala) and costs Rs 10-12 per tola (about 10 gm). Travellers who've come from Kashmir or the Kulu valley will offer you resin for Rs 40-50 per tola. The quality of the latter varies. Test before buying.

Tours

Tours of Goa are offered both by the Tourist Office, Afonso de Albuquerque Rd, and by Radhakrishna Tours and Travels, Mascarenhas Building. The tours offered by the Tourist Office are considerably cheaper than those offered by Radhakrishna Tours and Travels but the latter's buses are definitely more luxurious. On the other hand, it's unlikely that any of the tours on offer other than the ones round the temples and churches of Goa and the excursion to

Key:-

① Secretariat (Adil Shah's Palace)
② G.P.O.
③ Tourist Office, Railway Booking Office ✦ Goa Lodge
④ Karnataka Tourist Office
⑤ Andhra Pradesh Tourist Office
⑥ Indian Airlines (Dempo Building)
Ⓜ Market
Ⓜ Mahalakshmi Temple
Ⓜ M.G.M. Travel Agents
⑩ Hotel Sona

⑪ Tourist Hostel
⑫ Republica ✦ Palace Hotels
⑬ Vistar Hotel ✦ Fatima Guest House
⑮ Aroma ✦ Safari Hotels
⑯ Hotel Mandovi
⑰ Neptune Hotel
⑱ Rajesh Lodge
⑲ Gujerat Lodge
⑲ Sunrise Lodge
⑳ Hotel Samrat

㉑ Solmar Hotel ✦ Youth Hostel ✦ El Gazelle Restaurant
㉒ Shalimar ✦ Taj Mahal Restaurants
㉓ Shere Punjab Rest.
㉔ New Punjab Restaurant
㉕ Cappuccina Cafe
㉖ Goa Tourist Lodge

Mapusa Calangute Aguada

Old Goa Ponda

Mandovi Bridge

Panaji Bus Station

Ourem Road

Bombay Steamer Jetty

Agassaim
Margao / Vasco / Airport
via ferry

Church of Immaculate Conception

Mandovi River

Presunguat Rd.

Dr. Dada Vaidya Rd.

Albuquerque

June Road

18th Road

Dr. Berkar

Govt.

Alfonso

Pestana Road

Dr. Dada Vaidya Road

Panaji

Dona Paula Marmagoa (via ferry)

Bondla forest would be of interest to travellers. The main reason for this is that they attempt to pack too much into a short day so you end up seeing very little. Another relates to the motivation for visiting the beaches. (It may amuse you to know that Anjuna beach is described in the tour leaflets as, 'Popularly known for Hippies gathering'). Nude and scantily-clad hippies seem to hold an enduring fascination for middle-class Indians but it's unlikely you'll find the supposed spectacle particularly rivetting.

The tours which might interest you run by Radhakrishna Tours & Travels are 'South Goa Special' — this tour includes visits to Old Goa, the temples of Shri Mangesh (near Ponda), Shri Mahalasa (at Mardol), Shri Ramnath (at Kaulem) and Shri Shantadurga (also at Kaulem), Margao, Vasco da Gama and Marmagoa Harbour. The tour costs Rs 25 in 'Super Luxury Coach' and Rs 20 in 'Semi-Luxury Coach'. It starts at 9.30 am from Panaji and ends there at 6.30 pm. 'Bondla Forest' — this is an excursion to the national park at Bondla. The tour costs Rs 18. It departs daily at 9.30 am and ends at 1 pm.

Of the tours organised by the Tourist Office the following may be of interest: 'Tour No 2' — this tour includes visits to the same places as the 'South Goa Special' above but costs only Rs 9. Tour begins at 2.30 pm and ends at 7 pm. 'Tour No 5' — is an excursion to the national park at Bondla. It costs Rs 11, departs at 9.30 am and returns at 5 pm (Sundays only).

Places to Stay

Whenever there is a religious festival in Goa — especially the festival of St Francis Xavier (several days on either side of 3rd December) — it can be difficult to find accommodation in Panjim even in the small inexpensive lodges. Also there is a law which demands presentation of your passport when checking into a hotel (probably as a means of keeping tabs on people whose visas have run out though it's obviously of limited efficiency). Some hotels are strict about this requirement; others don't care. Note there is no accommodation available at Old Goa.

Places to Stay – Top End

Hotel Fidalgo, 18th June Rd (tel 3023/ 3025) is probably the pleasantest of the top range hotels. Rooms here cost Rs 150 a single and Rs 200 a double including air-conditioning. The hotel has all the facilities you would expect of a hotel of this nature. *Mayfair Hotel*, Dr Dada Vaidya Rd, near the Mahalaxmi Temple is another very pleasant top range hotel where rooms cost Rs 70 a single and Rs 85 a double for air-con and Rs 40 a single and Rs 55 a double for non air-con. Recommended. *Aroma Hotel*, Cunha Rivara Rd, facing the Municipal Gardens (tel 3519) is a very pleasant hotel and one which is excellent value. Rooms here cost Rs 40 a single and Rs 60 a double (Rs 55 for single occupancy). Note they have only *one* single room in the entire hotel! Rooms are not air-conditioned but all the rooms have attached bathrooms which are tiled and spotless although hot water isn't available all day (as claimed). Friendly, honest staff and an excellent location. There's no attached restaurant but you can have breakfast delivered to your room if required. Highly recommended and popular.

Hotel Mandovi, Bandodkar Marg (tel 2286) is a popular top range hotel but housed in an ugly building. Rooms here cost Rs 90 a single and Rs 170 a double plus 10% tax. All rooms are air-conditioned. There is an excellent bookshop on the ground floor which also sells foreign magazines and newspapers. *Hotel Sona*, Rua de Ourem (tel 3582). Rooms here cost Rs 40 a single and Rs 60 a double for non air-con rooms with attached bathrooms and Rs

60 a single and Rs 90 a double for air-con rooms with attached bathrooms. All rates are plus 10% tax. It's not a very pleasant building but often full.

Places to Stay — Middle
Tourist Hostel (tel 2303) this is the bargain among the mid-range hotels. The only trouble is, it's often booked solid for up to eight weeks in advance! It's clean, cheap, semi-western in style and there's a whole complex of shops on the ground floor selling photographic supplies, postcards, souvenirs as well as the Maharashtra State Tourist Office. Rooms here cost Rs 20 a single and Rs 30 a double both with attached bathrooms. There is a restaurant on the first floor.

Safari Hotel, Cunha Rivara Rd facing the Municipal Gardens is a pleasant, Portuguese-style old hotel where rooms cost Rs 15 a single and Rs 25 a double with common bathroom and Rs 35 a double with own bathroom. There is also a dormitory for Rs 6 a night. Friendly staff and very popular. *Hotel Republica*, Jose Falcao Rd at the back of the Secretariat (tel 2638), is an old place with fine views over Panjim harbour where rooms cost Rs 12 a single and Rs 25 a double both with common bathrooms, popular and often full.

Hotel Palace is located next door to the Republica. Rooms here cost Rs 5-20 a single (the latter with own bathroom), Rs 15-20 a double with common bathroom and Rs 30 a double with own bathroom. This is a good place *if* you can get one of the rooms overlooking the street with a balcony. The other rooms are really grim — windowless cubicles with hardboard partitions topped with chuck wire. Friendly staff. *Glemar Lodge*, Rebelo Building, D Antao de Noronha Rd, round the corner from the Aroma Hotel on the Municipal Gardens is Rs 15/25 with common bath but the rooms are dingy although it's secure and the staff are friendly. *Central*

Lodge, behind the post office, is clean and quiet at Rs 20 a double, Rs 32 with bath. *Fatima Guest House* is a small rooming house round the corner from the Vistar Hotel. Rooms are Rs 10/20 for singles/doubles without bath or Rs 30 for a double with bath. It's often full.

Note that other than the Tourist Hotel and the Safari Hotel there's not a lot of choice in mid-range hotels in Panjim indeed most of the above would be better classed as budget hotels except that their prices don't reflect this.

Places to Stay — Bottom End
Most of the budget hotels in Panim are very definitely at the dim and dusty end of 'basic' though in most cases you wouldn't suspect this judging from the prices they charge. The majority of them are located in the narrow streets around the back of the GPO and include the *La Vista Lodge*, *Anand Ashram Boarding*, *Goa Tourist Lodge*, *Deluxe Lodge*, *Daluz Hotel* and the *Bharat Lodge*. The only one which can really be recommended is the *Goa Tourist Lodge* where rooms cost Rs 15 a double for rooms on the top floor and Rs 20 a double for any of the others on the lower floors. None of the rooms have their own bathrooms but they're pleasant and have fans. The beds were filthy but the management assured me they provide a clean sheet. Another possibility if there are three of you is the *Hotel Venite* which is more a quiet bar and cafe rather than a hotel but they do have two triple rooms which cost Rs 20 with common bathroom. Very friendly management.

There are one or two others including the *Goa Lodge* on Rua Afonso de Albuquerque, very close to the Tourist Office, where rooms cost Rs 20 a double with common bathroom. They also have a dormitory. The only trouble with this place is that the manager is an imbecile. In addition to the above there is the *Kiran Boarding & Lodging* opposite the Bombay Steamer jetty and the *Indira Niwas Lodging* and the *New Gujerat Lodge* next to the Market. You might also like to try the *Gujerat Lodge* and *Rajesh Lodge* both on 18th June Rd but they're often full.

If you don't mind staying some way out of Panjim there is the *Youth Hostel* at Miramar Beach (tel 2433), three km from Panjim. Dormitory accommodation is available here for Rs 5 a night. There are no eating facilities nearby, apart from the Solomar Hotel which has good food at reasonable prices.

Places to Eat

There are two very good restaurants which are very popular with travellers. *Cappuccina Restaurant*, located on the eastern side of the Municipal Park is an excellent place with a varied menu which includes fish, shellfish, mutton, chicken, beef, pork, biriyanis, veges and ice-cream. Their coffee isn't up to much but they have a wide selection of beers, wines and spirits though alcoholic drinks are only served between 9 am and 3 pm and between 6 pm and 11 pm. Most dishes average Rs 5-8 in price though they also have lobster for Rs 30-35. Food is well presented but the helpings tend to be small. If you go there a second time without having left a tip the first time you'll be met with indifferent service. You can meet other travellers here at almost any time of day.

New Punjab Restaurant, located on the opposite side of the Municipal Gardens from the Cappuccina, serves excellent Punjabi food and is cheap. Tandoori specialities are naturally more expensive (average Rs 20-30). The restaurant is open between 12 noon and 3 pm and again between 7 pm and 11 pm. Closed on Saturdays.

One place which ought to be popular with travellers but which no-one I met had ever heard of is the *Hotel Venite*

in the narrow streets behind the GPO (see map for location). This is a beautiful old place on the first floor with polished wood floor and balconies overlooking the street and bags full of atmosphere. There's rarely ever anyone in here but they have an extensive menu and it's a great place to sit and have a drink. It's friendly and even has a sound system. *Shanbag Cafe* on the Municipal Square has good thali for Rs 3 and good tea. *Jesmal Cafe*, round the corner from the Cappuccina, has excellent milkshakes (particularly mango). Good thalis at the *Tourist Hostel* for Rs 4.50.

Other good restaurants if you're looking for a minor splurge are the *Shere Punjab Restaurant* on 18th June Rd and the *Shalimar* and *Taj Mahal Restaurants* situated next to each other on Afonso de Albuquerque Road. The former is a non-vegetarian restaurant and the latter a vegetarian restaurant. All three restaurants have prices similar to those of the New Punjab Restaurant. If you're looking for a night out rather than just a meal then take a taxi to the *El Gazelle Restaurant* at Miramar but be prepared to spend some money! It's an elegant Portuguese restaurant set in a flower-drenched garden.

Getting There

Flights The airport is at Dabolim near Vasco da Gama. Indian Airlines runs special buses from their office in the Dempo Building, Panjim, to the airport. The buses cost Rs 10 per person. There are daily flights to Bombay which cost Rs 277 and take 45 minutes. You must book well in advance especially during the high season as the flight is often booked solid for up to two weeks in advance.

Goa-Bombay Steamer   Departs daily except Wednesday for Bombay at 10 am and arrives the next morning at 8 am. The service is suspended during the monsoon season and sometimes when the weather is very rough. This is one of the pleasantest ways of getting to Bombay and highly recommended by many travellers. The service is operated by Mogul Lines and their agents in Goa are V S Dempo & Co (tel 3842) who have their office opposite the steamer jetty in Panjim. The fares for the boat are Rs 160 for Deluxe 'A' Class, Rs 135 for Deluxe 'B' Class, Rs 120 for 1st Class, Rs 52.50 for Upper Deck and Rs 33 for Lower Deck. No concessions are available for students (except Indian nationals who are entitled to a 50% reduction). It's quite a pleasant trip on Upper Deck but if you want anything vaguely like comfort and space then avoid Lower Deck. The office is open for advance booking from 3 pm to 5.30 pm and for current booking between 7.30 am to 12.30 pm and 2.30 pm to 5.30 pm.

Long Distance Buses
To Bombay There are several private companies which offer luxury buses along this route. They have offices in Margao, Panjim and Mapusa. In Margao there is an office on the corner of the street opposite the top side of the Secretariat building. In Panjim there is an office next door to the Hotel Vistar. In Mapusa the office is located opposite the taxi stand. The air-con luxury buses cost Rs 74 and generally depart in the afternoons taking about 16½ hours. Advance booking is recommended as they're heavily subscribed.

Other long-distance buses include Karnataka State Transport Buses. The booking office is on the waterfront very close to the Bombay Steamer Jetty and is open from 8 am to 9 am, 9.45 am to 10.45 am and 3 pm to 5 pm. Buses can be booked up to three days in advance. Some useful buses include to Bangalore daily at 2.15 pm. Costs Rs 45 (Super Deluxe Bus). To Belgaum departs at 7.30 am and 11 am on alternate days. To Hubli daily at 9.30 am.

Maharashtra State Transport Corporation has a booking office next to the Karnataka State Transport Corporation booking office and is open daily between 9 am and 12 noon and 1 pm to 3 pm. Some useful buses include Bombay daily at 3.30 pm (luxury bus), 5.15 pm (ordinary bus), 5.45 pm (ordinary bus) and 6 pm (luxury bus). The luxury buses cost Rs 53.55 and the ordinary buses Rs 38.90. To Malwan daily at 10 am. To Poona daily at 7.30 am. To Ratnagiri daily at 12.30 pm. To Sawantwadi daily at 8 am, 9 am, 2 pm and 6.30 pm. To Vengurla (via Tulas) daily at 11.45 am.

Trains
The railhead in Goa is at Vasco da Gama (it actually continues on to Marmagoa but very few of the main trains start from there). To get to Vasco from Panjim you can either go via the Dona Paula ferry or the Agassaim-Cortalim ferry. For details of the buses and ferries see under the 'Getting Around' section. The other main station in Goa is at Margao. Seats and sleepers on the trains can be booked at Vasco, Margao or at the South Central Out-Agency Booking Office (part of the Tourist Office) in Panjim. If you're staying north of Panjim and planning on leaving by train, this Out-Agency office saves you the trouble of having to go to Vasco.

The timings of the trains from Vasco and Margao are as follows:

from Vasco da Gama

description	departure time	
Vasco-Londa Passenger	7	am
Vasco-Miraj Passenger	11.25	am
Vasco-Miraj 'Gomantak Express'	9.25	pm

from Margao

description	departure time	
Kolamb-Marmagoa Passenger	7.30	am
Miraj-Vasco 'Gomantak Express'	8.10	am
Kolamb-Vasco Passenger	11.10	am
Miraj-Vasco Passenger	4.30	pm

Londa-Vasco Passenger	7.35 pm
Vasco-Londa Passenger	8.12 am
Vasco-Miraj Passenger	12.40 pm
Vasco-Miraj 'Gomantak Express'	10.23 pm

There are other local trains which ply between Kolamb (another Goan town further up the line) and Marmagoa but they're of little interest to travellers.

How to get to Bombay, New Delhi & Bangalore.

1. Vasco-Bangalore

station	train numbers				
	296	297	205	205	
	202	208	238	204	
Vasco	7 am	11.15 am	9.25 pm	9.25 pm	depart
Margao	8.07 am	12.13 pm	10.08 pm	10.08 pm	arrive
	8.12 am	12.40 pm	10.23 pm	10.23 pm	depart
Londa	12.50 pm	4.40 pm	2.15 am	2.15 am	arrive
	Change to	Change to	Change to	Change to	
	202	208	238	204	
	1.25 am	6.22 pm	2.35 am	10.14 am	depart
Hubli	5 pm	8.25 pm	5.05 am	12.15 pm	arrive
			Change to		
			204		
	5.25 pm	8.50 pm	12.30 pm	12.30 pm	depart
Bangalore	6.20 am	7.45 am	10.05 pm	10.05 pm	arrive
journey					
time	23½ hr	20½ hr	25 hr	25 hr	

The train numbers correspond to the following trains:

296 — Vasco-Londa Passenger; 297 — Vasco-Miraj 'Mandovi Express; 205 — Vasco-Miraj 'Gomantak Express'; 202 — Miraj-Bangalore Mail; 204 — Miraj-Bangalore 'Mahalaxmi Express'; 208 — Miraj-Bangalore 'Karnataka Express'; 238 — Miraj-Hubli Express.

2. Vasco-New Delhi

Using train Nos 205 (Vasco-Miraj

'Gomantak Express'), 308 (Miraj-Bombay 'Konya Express'), 177 (Poona-Jammu 'Tawi Jheelam Express'). Total journey time is 46½ hours. The route is as follows: Depart Vasco at 9.25 pm; Arrive Margao at 10.08 pm. Depart at 10.23 pm; Arrive Londa at 2.15 am. Depart at 2.45 am; Arrive Belgaum at 3.55 am. Depart at 4.15 am; Arrive Miraj at 8.20 am. Change to 308. Depart at 9.10 am; Arrive Poona at 4.10 pm. Change to 177. Depart at 4.50 pm; Arrive New Delhi 8 pm the next day.

3. Vasco-Bombay

Station	Train Numbers				
	296	297	297	205	
	201	308	312	308	
Vasco	7 am	11.25 am	11.25 am	9.25 pm	depart
Margao	8.07 am	12.30 pm	12.30 pm	10.08 pm	arrive
	8.12 am	12.40 pm	12.40 pm	10.23 pm	depart
Londa	12.50 pm	4.40 pm	4.40 pm	2.15 am	arrive
	2.40 pm	5 pm	5 pm	2.45 am	depart
Belgaum	4.05 pm	6.25 pm	6.25 pm	4.15 am	arrive
	4.20 pm	6.33 pm	6.33 pm	4.15 am	depart

Miraj	9.15 pm	9.40 pm	9.40 pm	8.20 am	arrive
	Change to	Change to	Change to	Change to	
	304	304	312	308	
	10.40 pm	10.40 pm	11.55 pm	9.10 am	depart
Poona	3.40 am	3.40 am	7.10 am	4.10 pm	arrive
	4 am	4 am	7.35 am	4.55 pm	depart
Bombay VT	8.10 am	8.10 am	12.25 pm	9.30 pm	arrive
Journey					
Time	25 hrs	21 hrs	25 hrs	24 hrs	

As an alternative to taking the 304 from Miraj (in column one) you can also take the 312.

The train numbers correspond to the following trains:
296 — Vasco-Londa Passenger; 297 — Vasco-Miraj 'Mandovi Express'; 205 — Vasco-Miraj 'Gomantak Express'; 201 — Bangalore-Miraj Mail; 304 — Kolharpur-Bombay VT 'Mahalaxmi Express'; 308 — Miraj-Bombay VT 'Konya Express'; 312 — Miraj-Bombay VT 'Sahyadri Express'.

You can book 2nd Class sleeping berths on any of these routes at the South Central Out-Agency Booking Office in Panjim. You cannot book 1st Class here. This must be booked either at Vasco or Margao, where you can also book 2nd Class. The Out-Agency office is open daily except Sundays from 10 am to 12.30 pm and from 2.30 pm to 5 pm. On public holidays it's open from 9.30 am to 12.30 pm only.

Getting Around

Local Ferries One of the joys of travelling around Goa are the ferries across the many rivers in this small state. Almost without exception they are combined passenger/car ferries. The main ferries are:

Dona Paula-Marmagoa which runs between September and May only. There are regular crossings but they are somewhat infrequent and at certain times of the day you could find yourself waiting about two hours for a ferry. The crossing takes 30-45 minutes and costs

Rs 0.90. Buses wait on either side for the arrival of boats. This is a passenger ferry only.

Agassaim-Cortalim has ferries in either direction every 10 minutes or so between 5.30 am and 12 midnight. The crossing takes a few minutes and costs Rs 0.40. Cycles and scooters cost Rs 0.45 and cars cost Rs 3.75. Buses wait on either side for the arrival of ferries. A bridge is being constructed across the river at this point which, when completed, will make the ferries rebundant.

Old Goa-Piedade — ferries every 30 minutes between 7.15 am and 9 pm.

Other ferries include: Aldona-Corjuem; Colvale-Macasana; Pomburpa-Chorao; Ribander-Chorao; Siolim-Chopdem, and St Estevam-Tonca. There are also launches from the central jetty in Panjim to Aldona (once daily), Britona (twice daily), Naroa (twice daily) and Verem.

Buses If you've done much travelling by bus in Karnataka, Kerala or Tamil Nadu for instance then you're in for a pleasant surprise in Goa. Most of the buses here are privately owned and therefore pretty good as far as maintenance and standards of comfort go. There's not the same mad scramble for seats as there is in other states and people will make room for you instead of trying to squeeze you out. There is no timetable of buses but services to most places in Goa are frequent. The conductors of the buses holler out their destinations and buses go when approximately full. Some of the more popular routes you're likely to use include:

Panjim-Vasco da Gama/Marmagoa There are two ways of getting there. You can either go via the ferry from Dona Paula to Marmagoa or via the ferry between Agassaim to Cortalim. Unless you know there will be a ferry waiting at Dona Paula on arrival of the bus then the route via Agassaim and Cortalim is the quicker of the two. Via Dona Paula-Marmagoa (ferry, Rs 0.90, 30-45 minutes), Agassaim-Cortalim is as follows: Panjim-Agassaim (bus, Rs 1.20-1.50, 30-45 minutes), Agassaim-Cortalim ferry, Rs 0.40, 10 minutes), Cortalim-Vasco da Gama (bus, Rs 0.80, 15-20 minutes). If you're heading for the Youth Hostel at Miramar, take the Dona Paula bus from Panjim.

Panjim-Margao Again, there are two ways of getting there. You can either go via Agassaim and Cortalim or via Ponda. The buses via Ponda are known as 'direct' but in fact they take at least an hour longer to get there and you still have to get down and walk across the Bailey bridge at Borim (the bridge won't take the weight of a fully-laden bus). Going via Agassaim it's possible to get to Margao in 1½ hours). Panjim-Agassaim (bus, Rs 1.20-1.50, 30-45 minutes), Agassaim-Cortalim (ferry, Rs 0.40, 10 minutes), Cortalim-Margao (bus, Rs 1.20-1.50, 30-45 minutes).

Panjim-Old Goa To get here you can either take one of the frequent buses which go just to Old Goa or take any bus going to Ponda. The journey costs Rs 0.75 and takes 20-30 minutes.

Panjim-Calangute/Baga Beach The journey takes 30-45 minutes and costs Rs 1.10. Buses go first to Calangute and then on to Baga before turning round. Frequent service.

Panjim-Mapusa Buses cost Rs 0.90 and take about 25 minutes. Frequent service. There are also three buses daily direct to Chapora Village which go via Mapusa. Note that Mapusa is pronounced 'Mapsa' and this is what the conductors shout.

Bicycles It's quite easy to hire bicycles (Rs 4-5) at most of the major Goan towns or beaches. You can also hire motorcycles (if you've ever wanted to try a Rajdoot) from around Rs 50 or Rs 60.

OLD GOA (Goa Velha)

Even before the arrival of the Portuguese, Old Goa was a thriving and prosperous city and the second capital of the Adil Shahi dynasty of Bijapur. At that time it was surrounded by fort walls, towers and a moat and containing many temples, mosques and the large palace of Adil Shah. Today, nothing of these former structures remain except a fragment of the gateway to the palace. All the structures which remain there date from the Portuguese period.

Under the Portuguese the city grew rapidly in size and splendour eventually coming to rival Lisbon itself, despite an epidemic in 1543 which wiped out a large part of the population. Many huge churches, monasteries and convents were erected by the various religious orders which came to Goa under royal mandates, the Franciscans being the first to arrive. Old Goa's splendour was short-lived, however, as by the end of the 16th century Portuguese supremacy on the seas had been replaced by that of the British, Dutch and French. The city's decline was accelerated by the activities of the Inquisition and a devastating epidemic which struck the population in 1635 and indeed had not the Portuguese been in treaty relations with the British it is probable that Goa would either have passed to the Dutch or been absorbed into British India. Nevertheless, the city muddled on into the early 19th century as the administrative capital of Portugal's eastern empire (Goa, Daman and Diu in India; Timor in Indonesia, and Macau in China) but, following the transfer of the seat of power to Panjim in 1843 and repressive religious orders in 1835, the city was deserted. Today it's a small village surrounded by the huge churches and convents which were built during its heyday and which attract visitors from many parts of the world. Some of them remain in active use though others have become museums maintained by the Archaeological Survey of India — a maintenance very necessary since unless the lime plaster which protects the laterite structure is renewed frequently then the monsoons soon reduce such buildings to ruin.

Information

The Archaeological Survey of India publish an excellent booklet about the monuments at Old Goa which is well worth buying for background material and further detail. It's entitled, *Old Goa* by S Rajagopalan (New Delhi 1975). The booklet costs Rs 3.25 and can be bought from the Archaeological Museum at Old Goa.

Se Cathedral

The largest of the churches at Old Goa, the Se Cathedral was begun in 1562 during the reign of King Dom Sebastiao (1557-78) and substantially completed by 1619 though the altars were not finished until 1652. The Cathedral was built for the Dominicans and paid for by the Royal Treasury out of the proceeds of the sale of the Crown's property. Architecturally, the building is Portuguese-Gothic in style with a Tuscan exterior and Corinthian interior. There were originally two towers, one on either side of the facade, but the one on the southern side collapsed in 1776. The existing tower houses a famous bell, one of the largest in Goa and often referred to as the 'Golden Bell' on account of its rich sound. The main altar is dedicated to St Catherine of Alexandria and old paintings on either side of it

depict scenes from her life and martyrdom.

The Convent & Church of St Francis of Assisi

This is probably one of the most interesting buildings at Old Goa. It contains gilded, carved woodwork, old murals depicting scenes from the life of St Francis and a floor made up substantially of carved gravestones complete with family coats of arms dating back to the early 1500s. The origins of this church date back to the humble beginnings made by eight Franciscan friars who arrived here in 1517 and constructed a small chapel consisting of three altars and a choir. This was later pulled down and the present building constructed on the same spot in 1661.

The Convent at the back of this church is now the Archaeological Museum which is well worth a visit. It houses many portraits of the Portuguese Viceroys — most of them inexpertly touched-up — fragments of sculpture from Hindu temple sites in Goa which show Chalukyan and Hoysala influences, stone Vetal images from the animist cult which flourished in this part of India centuries ago, and a model of a Portuguese caravelle minus the rigging (surely someone someone could get it together to do the rigging?!). Entry to the Museum is free.

The Professed House & Basilica of Bom Jesus

The Basilica of Bom Jesus is famous throughout the Roman Catholic world since it contains the tomb and mortal remains of St Francis Xavier who, in 1541, was given the task of spreading Christianity among the subjects of the Portuguese colonies in the east. A former pupil of St Ignatius Loyala, the founder of the Jesuit Order, St Francis Xavier's missionary voyages in the east became a legend and, considering the state of communications at the time, are nothing short of miraculous.

Arriving in Goa in 1542, St Francis Xavier spent the next few years spreading the Christian faith along the Malabar and Coromandel coasts until news reached him that Christianity had begun to make inroads in the Molucca Islands (now part of Indonesia). Wishing to make sure that the converts properly comprehended their new faith he set out on a voyage to those islands, returning to Goa in 1548. He stayed in Goa only a short time, however, and soon embarked on a voyage to Japan where he sought permission to teach Christianity from the King of Yamaguchi. Though permission was granted, Francis made little headway due to the opposition of the Bonzes and so, disappointed, he boarded a ship bound for Goa but got off at Sancian Island just off the coast of China. There he fell ill and died in December 1552 at the age of 46.

His body was buried on Sancian but subsequently taken to Malacca and placed in the Church of Our Lady of the Mount there. Four months later Francis' successor had the grave opened in order to pay his respects but, finding that the body was still fresh and life-like, had it sent to Goa in 1554. It was first kept in St Paul's College but transferred to the Professed House in 1613. After canonisation the body was removed to the Basilica of Bom Jesus. The body is exposed to public view once every 10 years (next time is 1984) on the anniversary of St Francis' death; but is no longer whole having been through some weird and wonderful mutilations at the hands of relic seekers, both lay and ecclesiastical. While in Malacca, the body was kept in a grave too small which resulted in the neck being broken. One of the toes was bitten off in 1554 by a Portuguese woman who wanted a relic of the Saint. In 1615 part of the right hand was cut off and sent to Rome where it is venerated in the Church of Gesu and in 1619 the remaining part

of the hand was removed and sent to the Jesuits in Japan. Portions of the intestines have been removed from time to time and distributed to various places.

Apart from the ten year cycle of Expositions, there is a festival held in Old Goa every year on the anniversary of the Saint's death (3rd December) at which time the normally sleepy little village becomes a mad-house of pot and pan stalls, food and beer tents, trinket sellers, balloons, firecrackers, buses from all over Goa and even further afield, and thousands of pilgrims many of whom doss down in the cloisters of the Basilica. When Mass is said there isn't a square cm of space left in the church. It's like a sardine tin!

Apart from the richly gilded altars, the interior of the church is remarkable for its simplicity and is the only one which is not plastered on the outside. It was commenced in 1594 and completed in 1605. The point of interest inside the church is, of course, the tomb of St Francis, the construction of which was underwritten by the Duke of Tuscany and executed by the Florentine sculptor, Giovanni Batista Foggini. It took 10 years to build and was completed in 1698. The remains of the body are housed in a silver casket which at one time was covered in jewels and on on the walls surrounding it are murals depicting scenes from the Saint's journeys including one of his death on Sancian Island.

The Professed House next door to the Basilica is a two-storied laterite building covered with lime plaster which was completed in 1585 despite much opposition to the Jesuits. Part of the building was burnt down in 1663 but rebuilt in 1783.

Church of St Cajetan
Modelled on the original design of St Peter's Church in Rome, the Church of St Cajetan was built by Italian friars of the Order of Theatines who were

sent by Pope Urban III to preach Christianity in the Kingdom of Golconda (near Hyderabad). The friars were not permitted to work in Golconda and so settled down at Goa in 1640. The construction of the church was begun in 1655. Historically, it's of much less interest than the other churches.

Ruins of the Church of St Augustine
All that is left of this church is the enormous 46 metre high tower which served as a belfry and formed part of the facade of the church. What little is left of the other parts of the church is choked with creepers and weeds and access is difficult. The church was constructed in 1602 by Augustinian friars who arrived in Goa in 1587. It was abandoned in 1835 as a result of repressive policies followed by the Portuguese Government which resulted in the eviction of many religious orders from Goa. The church fell into neglect and the vault collapsed in 1842. Many years later in 1931 the facade and half the tower fell down, followed by more parts in 1938.

The Church & Convent of St Monica
This huge, three-storied laterite building was commenced in 1606 and completed in 1627 only to be burnt down nine years later. Reconstruction started the following year and it's from this time that the buildings date. Once known as the Royal Monastery, on account of the royal patronage which it enjoyed, the building is now used by the Mater dei Institute as a nunnery which was inaugurated in 1964. Visitors are not allowed inside.

Other monuments of minor interest at Old Goa are the *Viceroy's Arch*, the *Gate of Adil Shah's Palace*, *Royal Chapel of St Anthony*, the *Church of St John of God*, the *Chapel of St Catherine*, the ruins of the *Church of the Carmelites*, and the *Church of Our Lady of the Mount*.

Getting There
You need the best part of a day to wander around the churches and other monuments of Old Goa. There are frequent buses to Old Goa from the Bus Stand at Panjim but as all the buses from Panjim to Ponda also pass through Old Goa you can use these buses too. Buses take 20-30 minutes and cost Rs 0.75. Whenever there is a festival at Old Goa (such as the Festival of St Francis Xavier at the end of November/beginning of December) boats ply between Panjim (from the Bombay Steamer Jetty) and Old Goa. This is a very pleasant way of getting there. It costs Rs 2 and takes about 45 minutes.

MARGAO (MADGAON)
The capital of Salcete province, Margao is the main population centre of southern Goa and a pleasant provincial town which still displays many reminders of its Portuguese past. In itself it's not of great interest to travellers though the old Margao church is well worth a visit and the covered market definitely the best of its kind in the whole of Goa. Its importance is as a service and transport centre for people staying at Colva beach. If you're planning on staying at Colva you must first head for Margao which is connected to the rest of Goa and to the neighbouring states by bus, train and taxi.

If you're coming to Margao from outside Goa, note that the last bus to Colva beach leaves at 8 pm. After that you will either have to hire a taxi (or motorbike) to get to Colva or stay overnight in Margao.

Information & Orientation
The Tourist Office is housed in the

Key:
1. Bus Stand
2. Buss to Colva
3. Tourist Office
4. General Post Office
5. Poste Restante
6. State Bank of India
7. Hotel Metropole
8. Mobai Hotel
9. Goa Woodlands
10. Centaur Lodging & Paradise Bar & Restaurant
11. Milan Kamat Hotel
12. Vishranti Lodge & Sangam Boarding
13. Hotel Sankit
14. Marliz
15. Kandeal Restaurant & Bar
16. Hotel Prasad
17. Covered Market
18. Other Market

Margao

Railway Station

Colva via Benaulim

Gua E de Loiola

Sernton Rd

One Way Traffic

Margao Church

Margaa Church

Ponda
Agassaim
Panjim
Colva

Secretariat building on the bottom side of the Municipal Gardens. The staff are friendly and helpful though, like elsewhere in India, they're limited in what they can offer because of lack of funds. They do have maps of Margao and Panjim (which you cannot get at the Tourist Office in Panjim).

Note that the Post Restante is not located in the GPO on the top side of the Municipal Gardens but in a seperate office about 300 metres from the GPO — see the map of Margao for its location.

The covered market here is the best in Goa and a fascinating place to wander through even if you don't want to buy anything. If you'll be staying around at Colva for some time and renting a house, the other, smaller market behind the Secretariat building is excellent for pots, pans and other kitchen equipment which you might need. The taxi stand is located behind the Secretariat building. Rau Raje Deshprabhu, Old Market is an Indian Airlines Agent.

Places to Stay — Top End

Mabai Hotel (tel 3653-4-5-7), on the top side of the Municipal Gardens, is definitely the best of the top range hotels in Margao and very convenient for all the services. Rooms here cost Rs 75 a single and Rs 115 a double with air-con or Rs 45 a single and Rs 75 a double without air-con plus 10% service charges. All the rooms are large and airy, pleasantly decorated and have their own bathrooms with hot and cold running water, telephone and piped muzak. There's a restaurant, bar and roof garden (latter closed during the monsoon season). The staff is friendly and credit cards are accepted.

Hotel Metropole, Avenida Concessao (tel 3169/3405) is an ugly building and a little way out of town. This hotel has no single rooms and doubles cost Rs 100 for non air-con (Rs 75 for single occupancy) and Rs 135 for air-con (Rs 100 for single occupancy). During the monsoon season the rates are 50% less.

Places to Stay — Bottom End

Goa Woodlands Hotel, Minguel Loyala Furtado Rd (tel 3121). Rooms here cost Rs 20-30 a single and Rs 30-40 a double for non air-con. Rooms with air-conditioning cost Rs 50 a single and Rs 60 a double. The hotel is located on a quiet street and it's convenient for all services. *Milan Kamat Hotel*, just off Station Rd, costs Rs 14 a single and Rs 18 a double both with attached bathrooms. There is a vegetarian cafe downstairs which sells good cheap meals. *Centaur Lodging*, opposite the Milan Kamat Hotel, has no single rooms and doubles cost Rs 16 with common bathroom. The staff is friendly. *Sankit Hotel*, opposite the railway station, has rooms for Rs 10 a single and Rs 20 a double with common bathrooms and Rs 30 a double with own bathroom.

There are few budget-type hotels available in Margao but if you have to stay in Margao then you could find a cheap room at either the *Vishranti Lodge* or the *Sangam Boarding* located up the side street about 200 metres from the Sankit Hotel. Another convenient, though definitely very basic, budget hotel is the *Dil Khush Restaurant & Lodging* on Station Rd just beyond the Milan Kamat Hotel coming from the station.

Places to Eat

Hotel restaurants aside, the best restaurant in Margao is the *Kandeel* (or Icandeel — the orange and black sign at the entrance is indistinct, it could be a 'k' but it could also be 'ic'). Here they serve superb Goan-style food and the staff are extremely friendly. If you want a good meal, come here. I would suggest you try their Goan fish, masala chicken and rice which comes complete with chappati, papadum, salad and pickles. They also have ice-cold beers. The restaurant is partially air-conditioned.

La Marina Cafe, a few metres from the Colva bus stand, is also a very reasonable restaurant but although they have an extensive menu there are very few items available except in the evenings. Prices average Rs 3-5 per dish. There is a bakery next door. If you're looking for a vegetarian restaurant, the *Hotel Prasad*, opposite the covered market, serves typical South Indian vegetarian meals. It's cheap and popular with local people.

For snacks and breakfasts, the *Marliz* on the top side of the Municipal Gardens is an extremely popular cafe and has been for many, many years. It's always crowded — and for very good reason as its snacks are excellent. They include sandwiches, vegetarian and non-vegetarian pasties, cakes and coffee. You can eat well here for Rs 2-3.

Getting Around

To Colva Beach Buses run to Colva on an approximately hourly basis and go via Benaulim. The first bus from Margao leaves at about 7.30 am and the last at 8 pm. The fare is Rs 0.40 and the journey takes 20-25 minutes. If you'd prefer a taxi these cost Rs 1.50 per person — they usually take six people though sometimes more. There are a few drivers who demand Rs 6 even when the taxi is shared but fortunately they're an objectionable exception. Obviously, if you want a taxi to yourself this will cost Rs 6 (minimum).

An alternative to taxis are the motorbikes which you can pick up on the road outside the bus stand. This is the quickest way of getting to the beach and costs Rs 4-5. They have no objection to taking people with rucksacks.

To Panjim There are two ways of getting by bus from Margao to Panjim. The so-called 'direct' bus goes via Ponda and although it doesn't involve crossing any rivers by ferry you still have to get off at the Bailey bridge and walk across as the bridge isn't strong enough to take the weight of a fully laden bus. Going via this route takes 2½ hours and costs

Rs 2.80 which makes it the longest but the cheapest route. The fastest way to get there is to take a bus from Margao to Cortalim on the Zuari River (frequent buses which take 30-45 minutes and cost Rs 1.20-1.50 depending on which bus you catch); a ferry across the Zuari River from Cortalim to Agassaim (ferries every 10 minutes which cost Rs 0.40 and take 10 minutes), and then another bus from Agassaim to Panjim (frequent buses which take 30-45 minutes and cost Rs 1.20-1.50 depending on which bus you get). Going this way it's possible to get to Panjim in 1¾ hours. It's also the most interesting route not just for the sake of the ferry ride but because the buses go through several villages which have old white-washed churches and monasteries. At present a bridge is being constructed between Cortalim and Agassaim which, when completed, will make the ferry redundant. In a way, this is a great pity since one of the attractions of travelling around Goa is the many ferry crossings. As an alternative to the buses, you could take a taxi from Margao to Panjim. This will cost Rs 100 including the ferry charges. The drivers are willing to hang around in Panjim for a few hours if you have any business to do there. If you can find five or six people who all want to go there on a certain day this is a relatively cheap, fast and comfortable way of getting there.

Other buses You can find buses to most towns in Goa from the bus stand in Margao. There is no timetable as such as the buses are all privately owned and go when full but they are frequent. You'll rarely have to wait more than a few minutes for a bus, if at all.

Trains Since most travellers who come to Goa arrive by rail (the other main route is via the steamer from Bombay) trains are dealt with under the Panjim section.

MAPUSA

Mapusa (pronounced locally as 'Mapsa')
is the main centre of population in the
northern provinces of Goa and the main
town for supplies if you are staying
either at Anjuna or Chapora. If you're
staying at Calangute or Baga then you
have a choice of Panjim or Mapusa as a
service centre. In itself, there's nothing
to see in Mapusa though the Friday
market is perhaps worth a visit. You
may, however, need to stay here overnight if you're catching a bus to Bombay
the following day.

Places to Stay

Mapusa's best hotel is the *Hotel Bardez*.
Rooms here cost Rs 25 a single and
Rs 35 a double both with attached bath-
rooms. They also have suites for Rs 55.
If you're looking for something cheaper
there's very little choice. The only two
which can be recommended are the
Sanman Boarding a few metres from the
Bardez and the *Janji Shankar Lodge*.
Here you'll get a room for Rs 10 a single
and Rs 15-20 a double.

Places to Eat

The *Imperial Bar & Restaurant* serves
good non-vegetarian food which averages
Rs 2-4 for egg dishes and Rs 5-7 for
meat dishes. It's clean, easy-going,
popular with local people and they have
cold beers.

Getting Around

Buses As at Panjim, there's no schedule
as such but services are frequent. Buses
to Anjuna and Chapora can be very

crowded — mostly with westerners staying on the beaches. Mapusa-Panjim takes
about 25 minutes and costs Rs 0.90.
There are also buses to Calangute,
Anjuna and Chapora as well as to other
population centres in northern Goa.

As an alternative to the buses you
can take either a taxi or a motorbike to
where you want to go. A motorbike to
Anjuna will cost Rs 5-6 and takes about
15 minutes (taxis ask for considerable
more).

THE BEACHES

Goa is justifiably famous for its beaches
and westerners have been flocking to
them since the early '60s. They occasionally suffer from a bad press both in
the western and Indian media because
of the real or imagined nefarious activities of a small minority of visitors. If you
were to believe these outrageously exag-
gerated and one-sided reports you might
be tempted to give the beaches a miss
thinking that they're dens of iniquity.
Don't, because Goan beaches are still
magnificent and most people find them

extremely difficult to leave.

The only problem is deciding which one to head for. Calangute became almost a travellers' cliche in the '60s and early '70s and tourist literature is fond of referring to it as the 'Queen' of Goa's beaches but it isn't the best or the most beautiful. It certainly isn't the most serene and has been somewhat over-developed in the last few years. Baga, a little further north, is far superior. The vast majority of travellers these days head for either Anjuna or Chapora. At any one time there will be thousands of travellers staying here, many of them on a long-term basis in rented houses scattered among the coconut plantations which reach right up to the beach. Other than the Vagator Beach Resort complex, there are no hotels as such at Chappora and only two or three semi-permanently full ones at Anjuna but finding accommodation is no problem. Simply ask around in the cafes. On the other hand, if you want to rent a whole house you'll have to talk in terms of renting on at least a monthly basis —

often longer. Naturally, with a floating population of several thousand you won't find any deserted beaches but you will find plenty of action and despite the numbers both places have retained their charm. This isn't Kuta beach!

If any beach deserves the title of 'Queen' it is Colva. This beach is without equal in India. It's nothing short of paradise. 40 km of uninterrupted white sand beach fringed with coconut palms along the whole of its length and a warm, calm sea. It's very laid-back and there are rarely more than 50-100 travellers here at any one time. Go a little way in either direction from Colva village and you'll find the nearest thing to a deserted beach. For accommodation you have the choice of either an instant roof in a hotel or a restaurant/hotel or renting a house on a long-term basis.

The other main beaches at Aguada and Bagmalo are largely for the jet-set and sport 5-star hotels and the like. Few travellers go there.

COLVA

Colva is a touch of Paradise. With its seemingly endless beach of soft, clean, white sand, gentle, warm sea and sway-ing palms right up to the beach's edge it has no equal. Ten years ago Colva had two cottages available for rent and one cafe (Vincy's). Most people stayed on the beach itself or in palm-leaf humpies which they either took over from de-parting travellers or constructed them-selves. The beach was deserted except for the fishermen, who pulled their catch in by hand each morning, and the very occasional evening bus-load of middle-class Indian tourists who came to gawp at the hippies and wet their toe-nails in the surf. It has changed but it's still the best! The small area around Vincy's has been developed — but not over-developed — and now sports a few

hotels, restaurants and trinket stalls. Many of the fishermen have acquired motorised trawlers which stand anchored in a line off-shore but fishermen further along the beach still fish from rowed boats and pull their catch in by hand. This flotilla of trawlers is just beginning to pollute the beach but in the immed-iate vicinity of the developed area only. Colva offers the nearest thing you'll find in India to a deserted beach. Go two km in either direction from the village and, for most of the day, you'll have the beach all to yourself. Day-trippers don't walk this far so if you're tired of wear-ing clothes, take them off. Everyone does. If you want something even more laid-back than Colva, go to Benaulim.

As with the other beaches on Goa and at Kovalam in Kerala, the best deal for accommodation if you're thinking

Colva Beach

Map labels:
Margao
Colva Village
Post Office
Bank of Baroda
School
General store
Chai shops
Tourist Nest & Zodiac Rest.
Margao
Benaulim Village
Lactancia Rest.
Sukhsagar Hotel
Silver Sands Cottages
White Sands Hotel
Tourist Cottages
Mare Sol Hotel
Viney Bar
L'Amour Beach Resort
Fishermens' Cottages
Sunset Restaurant
Cafe
Hawaii Restaurant
Chai shop
Bar Pedro
INDIAN OCEAN

of staying for a while is to rent a room or a whole house — if you're alone or too small a group just ask around in the cafes and you'll soon have enough people. If you won't be staying that long or you're not sure then there's plenty of instant accommodation available in the shape of hotels, rooms rented out by restaurants and fishermen's cottages.

Note that because of the trouble in Iran and Afghanistan and the war between Iran and Iraq, business on most beaches in Goa is down by about 50% on previous years. This has prompted a propaganda war among the hoteliers and restauranteurs so you'll be told in Panjim and Calangute that Colva is 'very commercialised these days' and 'the beaches stink of drying fish'. You can dismiss the 'commercialisation': Calangute is much more commercialised. As far as the fish go, it's true that the fishermen use parts of the beach to dry their fish but then these people are part of the attraction of this beach and, anyway, they use only a small area. Don't let this silliness deter you. It's still a corner of paradise!

Information & Orientation

The nearest Post Office is in Colva village. Letters can be sent Post Restante to here. There is a branch of the Bank of Baroda in Colva village (housed in the old white-washed church there).

Places to Stay

The best deal is to rent a house, the going rate for a house varies from Rs 150-400 a month depending on the size and location and it's payable in advance. Between November and March it's unlikely that you'll find the house you want on the first day of arrival. Generally, you'll have to hang around for a few days until you've made some friends, made a few enquiries and had a look around. Avoid jumping at the first place you're offered unless it's what you want. The main areas are back from the beach up to Colva village on either side of the roads and at Benaulim. Remember that depending on where a house is located you might have to walk 10-20 minutes to the beach through the paddy fields. There are very few houses or rooms available for long-term rent on the beach itself.

For a short-term stay the following places are available: *Fishermen's Cottages* are located just before the Sunset Restaurant (Linda's Cottages). This is the cheapest deal available and has facilities which are the equal of any other budget accommodation right on the beach. There are only two rooms available and they cost Rs 10 a day. *Sunset Restaurant* (Linda's Cottages) is the next best deal at Rs 20 a double (Rs 15 if occupied by a single person). There are six double rooms available. They're roomy, simple, clean, secure and some have table fans. Agnel, the manager, is very friendly and does his level best in a very demanding situation (the restaurant is full much of the time because it serves excellent food and has a good sound system). Highly recommended (but, please, please, Agnel, try to find some time to fix those 'toilets' properly!).

Tourist Cottages are located next to the White Sands Hotel. Good, clean, simple rooms facing the sea. They cost Rs 25 a single (two rooms available) and Rs 35 a double (four rooms available).

White Sands Hotel is a Tourist Development Corporation undertaking, this hotel consists largely of whitewashed, self-contained cottages with verandahs and attached bathrooms. For what they offer they're very pleasant

and good value at Rs 45 a single and Rs 55 a double. If you want air-con rooms these cost Rs 90 a double. Attached restaurant and bar which serves good food at much the same prices as anywhere else. *Sukhsagar Beach Resort* is not a particularly attractive place and I didn't meet anyone who was staying here. Rooms cost Rs 55-65 a single or double for non air-con and Rs 80-90 a single or double for air-con.

In addition to the above there are several (unnamed) cottages for rent between the Vincy Bar and the uncompleted Silver Sands Hotel where rooms cost Rs 30 a single and Rs 40 a double. There's also the *Mare Sol Hotel* at the back of the Vincy Bar and the small cafe beyond the Sunset Restaurant which usually has one or two rooms.

Further south at Benaulim the best deal is *L'Amour Beach Resort* where rooms cost Rs 20 a double with attached bathroom. The rooms are spacious, clean, have verandahs and are aligned to catch the sea breezes. The manager, Joao Manuel Pereira, is very friendly. There are also a few rooms in the main building above the restaurant for Rs 25 a double with attached bathroom. Good restaurant attached, highly recommended. In addition to the L'Amour there is another building just opposite which contains rooms for rent but there's rarely anyone there — enquire at the Bar Pedro just in front of the L' Amour.

Want to sleep on the beach? No problem. Two km on either side of the main Colva area you'll have the beach all to yourself.

Places to Eat

It's in the nature of beach life that everyone has their own favourite restaurant so what suits one person won't necessarily attract another. Give the following a try: *Sunset Restaurant* is not the cheapest but probably the best. Their sea food is excellent, carefully presented and very popular though they prepare other dishes as well. Fish steak, salad and chips costs Rs 9; fish fry and salad (a smaller dish) costs Rs 2.50. Their several varieties of pancakes and lassis are also very popular. *Cold* beers cost Rs 6 a bottle and most nights they manage to keep up with demand for this (that's a lot of cold beers when two Australians and a Yorkshireman combine to see the night off, together with everyone else's demands!). They won't bring it to you if it's not cold. Both the manager, Agnel, and the rest of the staff — especially Anthony and 'Baba Baksheesh' (the old fisherman) — are very friendly and their sense of humour stays intact at all times of the day and night despite the fact that they work more or less non stop from 6 am till 11 pm with no holidays. That's a heavy work load for only Rs 160 a month! There's an excellent sound system here and, if Swiss Bruno is still there, a good selection of tapes. It's the best cafe from which to watch the sunset.

The small cafe further up the beach (north) from the Sunset also serves good food at slightly lower prices but it takes longer to arrive. Nevertheless, it makes a pleasant change of venue. They too have a sound system but their tape selection is limited. The *White Sands Hotel Restaurant* serves food of a similar quality and price to the Sunset but the atmosphere isn't as free and easy as the Sunset. *Vincy Bar & Restaurant* is the oldest establishment at Colva beach. Ten years ago it was just a house and verandah. Now they've expanded into the area in front of the house. They serve good food, expertly presented at similar prices to the Sunset. If you want a minor splurge come here. The staff think the sun shines out of their butts

but it doesn't and you may well find yourself surrounded by better-heeled customers radiating plastic smiles. It's about time the 'Under New Management' sign went up.

Lactancia Restaurant serves a similar range of sea food as the Sunset and at more or less the same prices. It's very popular with travellers and the staff are very friendly. The *Hawaii Restaurant*, right on the beach, is mainly a juice bar and popular with day-trippers. Often full of middle-class Indians and their spoiled brats. If you want Indian food as opposed to sea food there are a few chai shops at the road junction just before Colva village which serve snacks and a few basic restaurants at Benaulim village.

The *Bar Pedro* at Benaulim, located right next to the beach, is very popular with travellers. They serve mainly sea food though they offer other dishes as well. The manager will cook anything to order if you give him advance warning. The *L'Amour Beach Resort* also has a restaurant offering sea food but it doesn't have any atmosphere and you can't see the sea.

Getting There

Buses run to Margao via Benaulim village approximately hourly and take about 25 minutes. The fare is Rs 0.40. The first bus from Colva to Margao leaves at 7.30 am. The last bus back to Colva from Margao leaves at 8 pm.

A shared taxi from Colva to Margao costs Rs 1.50. These taxis take about six people though they sometimes pack in more! The occasional taxi driver will demand Rs 6 to take you to Margao even when it's shared. Wait for the next one. A motorbike from Colva to Margao costs Rs 4-5 but they're the quickest way of getting there.

VASCO DA GAMA

Close to Marmagoa Harbour and Dabolim Airport, Vasco da Gama is the terminus of the railway line to Goa — apart from a few local trains which continue to the harbour. If you arrive by train you can get down at Margao, near Colva Beach, but if you arrive by air it is possible to arrive in Goa too late to get much further than Vasco da Gama. There are a number of hotels in this not very exciting town.

CALANGUTE & BAGA

Until very recently, Calangute was the beach which all self-respecting hippies headed for, especially around Christmas when all psychedelic hell broke loose and the beach was littered with more budding rock stars than most people have hot dinners. If you enjoyed taking part in those mass pujas with their endless half-baked discussions about 'when the revolution comes' and 'the vibes, man' then this was just the ticket. You could frolic around with not a stitch on being ever so cool and liberated and totally disregard the feelings of the local inhabitants. You could get totally out of your head every minute of the night and day on every conceivable variety of ganja from Timor to Tenochtitlan, exhibit the most bizarre behaviour, babble an endless stream of drivel and bore everybody shitless. Naturally, John Lennon or The Who were always about to turn up and give a free concert. Ah, Woodstock! Where did you go!

Calangute's heyday as the Mecca of all expatriate hippies has passed and the place has settled down to the more bourgeois pursuits of selling handicrafts, jewellery and woven fabrics to the tourists. It no longer provides the Indian press with a permanent shock-horror story about decadent, drug-crazed fiends and naked bodies which were supposed to be rotting the moral

Places to Stay

The *Hotel Rebelo* (tel 2620), Vadem has singles from as little as Rs 20 to air-con doubles at Rs 80. *Lapaz Hotel* (tel 2121), Swatentrya Path is rather more expensive with air-con singles/doubles around Rs 75/150 and non air-con rooms at Rs 45/75. The *Hotel Zuari* (tel 2127) is similarly priced. There are a number of cheaper local hotels.

fibre of Indian youth. Indeed, it isn't that popular anymore — except with middle-class Indian holidaymakers. There are those who will continue to swear by it though it's difficult to fathom why since it's one of the least attractive of the beaches. Unlike at Colva, Anjuna and Chapora, there are hardly any swaying palms to grace the shoreline, much of the sand is contaminated with red soil and the beach drops pretty rapidly into the sea. It's also become quite expensive. Still its fame lingers on.

Baga, about two km north, is far superior and still a pleasant place to stay despite its proximity to Calangute. It still clings to its charm, the beach is much better and it still remains fairly laid-back. If you're thinking of staying at Calangute, try Baga first.

Information & Orientation

The Tourist Office is located next to the Bank of Baroda. You can change travellers cheques or cash at either the Bank of Baroda next to the Tourist Office or the State Bank of India a little further towards Calangute village. The Bank of Baroda is fast and there's no fuss.

MGM, the travel agents which we highly recommended in the section on Panjim, have a branch here opposite the Tourist Office. Space Travels also have a

branch office at the back of the Sea View Restaurant.

There are many stalls all the way from the cross-roads to the beach selling genuine and repro Tibetan and Rajasthani crafts. Most of it is very well made and some of it stunningly beautiful. It isn't cheap! There are also a number of impromptu stalls in the street below the Sea View Restaurant which sell some interesting jewellery, bangles and other ethnic trinkets (usually Tibetan, Kashmiri and Indian tribal in origin) at reasonable prices. Bargaining is obligatory.

Places to Stay

Unless you're thinking of renting a house there are the following places to stay: *Tourist Dormitory & Annapurna Restaurant* offers what is perhaps the cheapest accommodation in Calangute. A bed in the dormitory here costs Rs 8 (eight-bed dormitories). If the place is full the manager will direct you to a house across the street where they have two double rooms at Rs 20 a room. The *Tourist Hotel* is located on the beach front. This ugly and uncompromising building dominates the beach at this point. Rooms here cost Rs 20-25 a single and Rs 30-35 a double. There is an attached bar and restaurant.

Meena's Lodge is a small hotel with limited accommodation but it's pleasant. Rooms here cost Rs 30 a single and Rs 35 a double both with common bathroom. The rooms have fans. *Souza Lobo Restaurant* has several attractive rooms constructed out of bamboo matting which cost Rs 30 a double (there are no singles). The rooms are clean, have table fans, plenty of mosquitoes and common bathrooms but the place has a superb location right on the beach. Good restaurant attached. *Calangute Beach Guest House* is a modern, western-style hotel which looks a lot more expensive than it is. Rooms here cost Rs 20 a single and Rs 35 a double.

They're clean and secure and there's an attached restaurant which serves breakfasts to order and dinners if ordered in advance.

Quite why *Concha Hotel* is so outrageously priced is a mystery since it's nothing special. Rooms here cost Rs 65 a single and Rs 88 a double with attached bathrooms. The manager is at great pains to remind you that the price includes morning and evening tea or coffee. So it ought to at those prices! There are several other cheap places available among the palms at the back of the Concha and Calangute Beach Guest House.

Further along the beach towards Baga you'll find *Celestine's Place*, the best bargain between Calangute and Baga. It has beautiful, spacious rooms with their own bathroom, toilet and fan in a separate block from the main house and clean as a new pin. The rooms cost Rs 40 a double. The owners are very friendly people and are at pains to make you welcome. *Sea View Cottages* are in a beautiful location facing the sea. Rooms here cost Rs 60 a double. The nearest restaurant is the Richdavy. *Ancora Beach Resort Cottages* and located at the back of the Richdavy Restaurant. Rooms here cost Rs 40 a single and Rs 80 a double including own bathroom and fans.

At Baga Beach there is the *Cavala Motel*, located well back from the beach on the road between Baga and Calangute. A very modern, clean place where rooms cost Rs 75 a double including own bathroom and fan. This is one of the few places in India where I've seen the electrical hot showers so common in South America. If you use these showers make sure they're properly earthed! The motel has an attached restaurant.

Hotel Baia do Sol is a modern, top end hotel where rooms cost Rs 93 a double in the main building and Rs 110 a double in the self-contained cottages. All rooms have their own bathroom with hot and cold running water. There is a restaurant attached. *Hotel Riverside* is located well back from the beach by the river. It's a very pleasant place where rooms cost Rs 60 a double with attached bathroom.

Places to Eat

There are any number of small restaurants serving both Indian food and sea food all the way from Calangute village to the beach especially around the bus stand and a whole collection of them on the beach at Baga. *Sea View Restaurant* has reasonably good food but the helpings are small so if you're hungry you'll end up having to buy two meals. Fish, chips and salad costs Rs 4.50. There's a sound system with a good collection of rock music tapes.

Souza Lobo Restaurant is much the same as the above as far as food is concerned but the setting is far superior. A perfect place to watch the sunset or relax in the afternoons. *Richdavy Restaurant* is located half way between Calangute and Baga and is popular with travellers. Good food at reasonable prices and the management are very friendly. There's a free notice board here where you can leave messages or for sale notices.

ANJUNA

If you want to know where everyone went when Calangute had been filmed, recorded, reported and talked about into the sand then this is the beach to head for. It's one of the world's wierdest and most wonderful collections of overlanders, monks, defiant ex-hippies, gentle lunatics, 'orange' people, artists, craftspeople, seers, searchers and peripatetic expatriates who normally wouldn't be seen out of the organic con-

Getting There

There are frequent bus services to Baga, Mapusa and Panjim throughout the day. The bus to Panjim takes about 30 minutes and costs Rs 1.20.

The old adage that 'many hands make light works' certainly gets its comeuppance in India. Every job has at least twice as many people doing it as necessary and inevitably the result is it takes twice as long. Indian hotel employees always seem to be scurrying around cleaning things up but as often as not that simply means sweeping everything under the bed.

AGUADA

South of Calangute, near the mouth of the Mandovi River, Aguada is Goa's jet set beach. Its chief attraction is the 16th century Portuguese Aguada Fort in which the hotel is built.

Places to Stay

Fort Aguada Beach Resort (tel 3404) is built within the ramparts of the old fort and has rooms or individual cottages with prices from around Rs 300/400 for singles/doubles. The resort has a swimming pool, tennis courts, shops, boats and canoes to rent, or bicycles.

fines of their health-food emporia in San Francisco or London.

There's no point in trying to define what Anjuna is or what it's like since it's many different things to many different people. The only way to find out is to stay here for a while and make some friends. Full moon is a particularly good time to be here when there's usually a mass party with psychedelics freely available. Unlike Calangute, the place has retained its charm. Nude bathing is de rigeur with the added satisfaction that you're unlikely to attract the voyeuristic attentions of any but the most intrepid Indian holidaymaker.

Information & Orientation

There is a post office here to which you can have mail sent post restante but there is no bank.

Places to Stay

It isn't easy to find a place to stay between November and March. Most of the available houses are rented on a long-term basis, often six months to a year, by people who come back here again and again. There are only two or three hotels which are located near the junction where the road from Chapora meets the road to the beach but they're more or less permanently full. If you want to stay here you may initially have to make do with a very primitive shack or even sleep outside a restaurant, leaving your gear with the owner until

you've made some friends or had a good scout around for a house. It's not a beach to head for if you're expecting immediate comforts in the shape of a hotel. This beach is definitely for people with plenty of initiative. If you're only planning on staying a few days then it's not really worth coming here.

Places to Eat

As far as food and drink go, there are any number of restaurants and cafes strung out along the road to the beach and all along the beach front. Which one you choose as your favourite will depend largely on what sort of person you are and who you meet though one of the best for sea food (but not the most popular) is the *Rose Garden Restaurant*. The prices here are higher than elsewhere but the food is excellent and size of the helpings impressive. Fish steak, chips and salad — beautifully presented — costs Rs 6-7. They also have cold beers.

Getting There
There are buses every one to two hours to Chapora and Mapusa and plenty of motorcycles available. The latter cost Rs 5 to 6 to Mapusa and take about 15 minutes. The buses can be very crowded at certain times of the day.

CHAPORA

This is one of the most beautiful, interesting and unspoilt areas of Goa and a good deal more attractive than Anjuna either for a short or a long stay. Much of the inhabited area nestles under a canopy of dense coconut palms and the village is dominated by a rocky hill on top of which sits an old Portuguese fort. The fort is fairly well preserved and worth a visit and the views from its ramparts are excellent. Secluded, sandy coves are to be found all the way around the northern side of this rocky outcrop though the main beaches all face west towards the Indian Ocean.

It shares with Anjuna the distinction of being the most popular beach in Goa and at any one time there will be thousands of westerners staying here, many of them, as at Anjuna, on a long-term basis. Indeed there is probably one westerner to every Goan in Chapora village itself. If this sounds a little bit too much like a ghetto you can rest assured that it doesn't feel that way. Local people remain friendly and surprisingly unaffected by it all and since the houses which are available for rent are scattered over quite a large area and there are many beaches and coves to choose from it's rare to see more than a hundred travellers together in one place. The only exception to this is on a weekend at the Music Room when there's usually an open party with live electric music, food and handicraft stalls, a beer tent and other goodies. It's the nearest thing you'll get in India to the sort of action you're accustomed to back home. It's well worth going along to one of these Saturday night rages. You can't fail to like Chapora and you're going to find it very difficult to leave when you've stayed here for a little while.

Places to Stay
Other than the *Vagator Beach Resort*, an Indian version of the Club Med and which at Rs 80 a single and Rs 120 a double is definitely for the jet-set or the unimaginative, there are no hotels anywhere at Chapora but finding a place to stay is no problem. Simply ask around in the restaurants or on the beaches. Since many people rent houses on a long-term basis — often six months or a year — it's unlikely you'll find one until you've made a few friends or had a good look around. Be prepared, in the first place, to stay with a family or rent a room in someone's house though immediate accommodation is usually available at Dr Lobo's house for Rs 10 a room. They're a very friendly family and will do their best to make you welcome. Another place to try for immediate accommodation is *Papa's Restaurant* on the other side of the road from the church at the bottom of the dirt track from Dr Lobo's house — that's if you're not offered accommodation as you get off the bus in Chapora village. Wherever you decide to live, make sure you have a torch (flashlight) handy. This isn't a commercialised holiday resort and there are no street lamps. Finding you way along the paths through the coconut palms late at night when there's no full moon is a devil of a job without a light until you're familiar with the layout! As at the other beaches, houses for rent cost between Rs 150-400 a month depending on their size and location.

Places to Eat

For food, there are any number of restaurants all the way up the main street of Chapora village, opposite the church, at the back of the Vagator Beach Resort and along the beach south of the road which leads to Vagator. Many of them are really pleasant and serve good sea food and it's hard to recommend one as opposed to another except *Lobo's* (not to be confused with Dr Lobo's house in the village). Here you'll get the best sea food in Goa expertly presented. No-one else quite makes it up to their standard. King prawns, salad and chips will cost you Rs 7; fish a little less. They have cold beers too. It's a superb little restaurant and very friendly but if you want to be sure of getting a meal there turn up early. The place is well known for its excellent food and seating is limited. They're closed on Sundays. Forget about the two 'restaurants' at the end of the tarmac road to Vagator — they're a waste of time. If you'd like a drink in the nearest equivalent to a pub, try the *Goa Pub* which is part of the Music Room set-up.

Getting There

There are frequent buses to Mapusa throughout the day and three direct buses to Panjim daily (via Anjuna and Mapusa). The bus stand is near the road junction in Chapora village. There are also motorcycles here which will take you to Mapusa or Anjuna.

OTHER ATTRACTIONS IN GOA
Bondla Wildlife Sactuary

Located up in the foothills of the Western Ghats, Bondla is being promoted by the Department of Tourism and is a good place to see sambar and wild boar among other things. It's the smallest of the Goan Wildlife Sanctuaries but the only one at present which has accommodation for those wishing to stay more than a day. The larger sanctuaries are Molem Wildlife Sanctuary and Cotigao Wildlife Sanctuaries. You can get to Bondla under your own steam by bus via Ponda or go on one of the tourist bus trips organised by either Radhakrishna Tours and Travels or the Tourist Department. A trip with the latter is preferable since, although they only go on Sundays, the tour lasts from 9.30 am to 5 pm and costs only Rs 11. The Radhakrishna tours go daily but last only from 9.30 am to 1 pm and cost Rs 18.

Accommodation is available at Bondla at the *Tourist Cottages* where rooms cost Rs 10 a single and Rs 15 a double from October to May and Rs 6 a single and Rs 10 a double between June and September. There is also dormitory accommodation available for Rs 3 a bed.

Temples

When the Portuguese arrived in Goa they destroyed every Hindu temple and Moslem mosque they could lay hands on, so temples in Goa are generally back from the coast and comparatively new. Despite their earnest attempts to spread Roman Catholicism only 38% of Goans today are Christian. Most of the Hindu temples of interest are close to Ponda, on the inland route between Panaji and Margao. The Shiva temple of Shri Mangesh is at Priol-Ponda Taluka, about 22 km from Panaji. The small temple with its white tower, a local landmark, is situated on top of a small hill. Only a km further down the road is Shri Mahalsa, a Vishnu temple.

In Ponda itself there are three temples and the Safe Masjid. This mosque was built in 1560 and for some reason the Portuguese neglected to knock it down. Shri Ramnath and Shri Mahalakshmi face each other across the road and nearby is the Shri Shantadurga temple.

Dedicated to Shantadurga, the goddess of peace, it has a strange, almost pagoda like, tower in the temple compound.

Forts

There are quite a number of old Portuguese forts dotted around Goa, most of them on the coast. Most of them are in a reasonable state of preservation and are worth a visit if you have the time. The one at Chapora is particularly recommended. Only one of them has been converted into hotel accommodation. This is the one at Terekhol on the coast at the extreme northern tip of Goa. Rooms here cost Rs 10 a single and Rs 15 a double between October and May and Rs 6 a single and Rs 10 a double between June and September. Dormitory accommodation is also available for Rs 5 a bed in the high season and Rs 3 a bed in the low season.

Festivals

The Christian festivals in Goa take place on the following dates:

6 January	Feast of Three Kings at Reis Magos, Cansaulim and Chandor.
2 February	Feast of Our Lady of Candelaria at Pomburpa.
February/ March	Carnival.
Mon after 5th Sun in Lent	Procession of the Franciscan Order at Old Goa.
1st Sun after Easter	Feast of Jesus of Nazareth at Siridao.
16 days after Easter	Feast of Our Lady of Miracles at Mapusa.
24 August	Festival of Novidades.
1st fortnight of October	Fama de Menino Jesus at Colva.
3rd Wed of November	Feast of Our Lady of Rosary.
3 December	Feast of St Francis Xavier at Old Goa.
8 December	Feast of Our Lady of Immaculate Conception at Panjim and Margao.
25 December	Christmas.

Karnataka

Population: 32 million
Area: 191,773 square km
Capital: Bangalore
Main language: Kannada

The state of Karnataka, formerly known as Mysore, is one of the more easy-going Indian states. It's a state of strong contrasts with the modern, industrialised city of Bangalore at one extreme and the expanses of rural farming areas at the other. Karnataka also boasts some of the most interesting historic architecture in India and a varied and tumultuous history.

It was to Sravanabelagola in Karnataka that Chandragupta Maurya, India's first great emperor, retreated after he had renounced worldly ways and embraced Jainism. Later the mighty statue of Gomateshvara was erected at Sravanabelagola and it celebrated its 1000th anniversary in 1981. At Badami, in the north of the state, the Chalukyans built some of the earliest Hindu temples in India, 1500 years ago. All later south Indian temple architecture stems from the Chalukyan designs at Badami and the Pallavas at Kanchipuram and Mahabalipuram in Tamil Nadu. Other important Indian dynasties, such as the Cholas and the Gangas, have also played their part in Karnataka's history, but it was the Hoysalas, who ruled between the 11th and 14th centuries, who left the most vivid evidence of their presence. The beautiful Hoysala temples at Somnathpur, Belur and Halebid are gems of Indian architecture with intricate and detailed sculptures rivalling anything to be found at Khajuraho or Konorak.

In 1327 Hindu Halebid fell to the Moslem army of Mohammed bin Tughlaq and in the succeeding centuries Karnataka was held by first the followrs of one religion, then the other. Founded in 1336, the Hindu kingdom of Vijayanagar, with its capital at Hampi, is one of the least visited and thus most surprising of India's ruined kingdoms. Vijayanagar reached its peak in the early 1500s but in 1565 it fell to the Deccan Sultans and Bijapur became the most important city of the region. Today Bijapur is just a small city surrounded by an imposing wall and packed with an amazing collection of mosques and other reminders of its glorious past.

Finally Hyder Ali took control in 1761 and the seat of power moved back south to Srirangapatna near Mysore. His son, Tipu Sultan, with help from the French, further extended his father's kingdom and put the British in their place on more than one occasion before finally being defeated and killed in 1799.

The British installed a Hindu ruler when they brought the region under their control and a series of enlightened and progressive rulers held power right through to independence. The Maharaja at that time was so popular that he became the first governor of the state.

BANGALORE (population 2,500,000)
Though a modern, bustling city which is fast expanding into an important industrial centre, Bangalore remains one of India's pleasantest. The central area of the city is studded with beautifully laid out parks and gardens, wide tree-lined avenues, imposing buildings and lively bazaars. Situated 1000 metres above sea level and with a very pleasant climate it's the city to which people from all over India and from abroad have gone to look for work, business opportunities and higher education. As you might expect from a city of this nature the pace of life, like the intellectual and political climate, is brisk and hardly a day goes by without some new controversy boiling over across the front pages of its daily newspapers or into the streets. Now the capital of Karnataka State, Bangalore was founded by Kempegowda in the early 16th century and became an important fortress city under Hyder Ali and Tipu Sultan two centuries later though there are few remains from this period except for the Lalbagh Botanical Gardens. Bangalore is an excellent place to come if you're looking for a wide range of hotels, restaurants, films and other cultural activities otherwise its much-vanted 'attractions' are definitely over-rated. Bangalore means 'the town of beans'.

Information & Orientation

Life in Bangalore revolves around Kempegowda Circle and in the narrow, busy streets of Gandhi Nagar and Chickpet adjacent to the bus and railway stations. Here are located the main shopping areas, restaurants, cinemas, bookshops and many of the mid-range hotels. It's a very popular area at lunchtimes and in the evenings when the crowds spill over onto the roads and long queues form outside the cinemas. Further over to the west of Cubbon Park along Mahatma Gandhi Rd are situated the more expensive hotels and restaurants, travel agents, airline offices and tourist information centres. The budget hotel area lies south of the railway station along Cottonpet Bhashyam Rd and around the City Market on Sri Narsimharaja Rd. This is the old part of the city consisting of narrow, winding streets, an endless variety of small cottage industry services and manufacturing concerns, old temples, bullock carts and tea shops. Most government offices and museums are to be found either in or around Cubbon Park while Bangalore's few remaining historical relics are all located south of the City Market — some of them a considerable way to the south.

Useful Addressses

There are tourist information offices at 52 Shrungar Shopping Centre, M G Rd (tel 579139); Ground Floor, Public Utility Buildings, M G Rd (tel 52377) 10/4 Kasturba Rd (tel 578753/578901) and at 19 St Marks Rd. There are also tourist information kiosks at the airport and at the City Railway Station. Obviously, with so many different tourist offices, there's a considerable amount of unnecessary duplication and stretching of resources so that one office will offer you one booklet while another will offer you a different one but they won't both stock the same booklets. This is Indian bureaucracy at its most absurd. Anywhere else in the world it would be called 'work creation'. And as though this weren't sufficient there's yet another office at Badami House, Narsimharaja Square (tel 74711) which deals with reservations for the various tours operated by the Karnataka State Tourism Development Corporation!

The Railway Enquiry Offices are at the City Railway Station, (tel 74173/74174) and the Cantonment Railway Station, (tel 27000). For the KSRTC Bus Station Enquiry Office (tel 73377). Indian Airlines, City Office, CBAB Buildings, K G Rd, (tel 79431) or at the airport, (tel 52236). Air India, Unity

Buildings, J C Rd (tel 77222/76396). Thomas Cook & Sons, M G Rd, Bangalore I (tel 51729).

Vidhana Soudha

This is Bangalore's — and indeed one of India's — most spectacular buildings. Built of granite in the neo-Dravidian style of architecture and located at the northern end of Cubbon Park it houses both the Secretariat and the State Legislature. The cabinet room is famous for its massive door made of pure sandalwood. The building is floodlit on Sunday evenings and on public holidays. Visitors are allowed only after 5.30 pm and prior permission must be obtained to view the interior. For this contact the Under Secretary (Protocol), Department of Personnel & Administrative Reforms, Vidhana Soudha (tel 79401).

Cubbon Park

One of the main 'lungs' of the city, this beautiful shady park full of flowering trees covers an area of 120 hectares and was laid out in 1864. In it are to be found the red Gothic building which houses the Public Library, the High Court, the Government Museum and the Technological and Industrial Museum. The Government Museum, one of the oldest in India, was established in 1886 and houses sections on geology, art,

numismatics and relics from Mohnenjo-daro (one of the cradles of Indian civilisation, dating back 5000 years). Admission costs 20p and the museum is open daily except Wednesdays and public holidays from 8 am to 5 pm. The Technological and Industrial Museum, also on Kasturba Rd adjacent to the Government Museum, is open daily except Mondays and public holidays between 10 am and 5 pm. Admission costs 20p. Its theme is the application of science and technology to industry and human welfare.

Lalbagh Botanical Gardens

Again, a beautiful and popular park located in the southern suburbs of Bangalore. It covers an area of 96 hectares and was laid out in the 18th century by Hyder Ali and his son Tipu Sultan. It contains many centuries-old trees (most of them labelled), lakes, lotus ponds, flower beds, a deer park and one of the largest collections of rare tropical and sub-tropical plants in India. Refreshments are available at several places within the park.

The Fort

Located on Krishnarajendra Rd close to the City Market this was originally a mud-brick structure built in 1537 by Kempegowda. It was later rebuilt in

1	City Railway Station	7	The Fort
2	Central Bus Station	8	Tipu Sultan's Palace
3	Vidhana Soudha	9	Bull Temple
4	GPO	10	Sudha Lodge
5	Government Museum & Technological Museum	11	Kaveri Arts & Crafts Emporium
6	City Market	12	Cantonment Railway Station

Top End hotels & restaurants (Mahatma Gandhi Rd)

Bottom End hotels (City Market)

Mid Range hotels & restaurants (Kempegowda Circle & Gandhi Nagar)

Bangalore

Nandi Hills
Bellary

Margosa Rd.
Sampige Rd.
Bellary Rd.
Jayamahal Rd.
Borebank Rd.
St John's Rd.

Seshadripuram Rd.
Shankey's Rd.
Palace Rd.
Millers Rd.
Cunningham Rd.
Queen's Rd.
Broadway
Timmiah Rd.
Cavalry Rd.

Old Butts Road
Chandni Chowk Rd.
Ulsoor Lake

Race Course Rd.
Hospital Road
Cubbon Road
Dickenson Rd.

Race Course
Seshadri Rd.
Palace Rd.
Post Office Rd.
③ ④
Cubbon
M. Gandhi Rd.

① ②
Subahdar Rd.
Kempegowda Rd.
District Office Rd.
Nrupathunga Rd.
Park
⑤
Grant Road
Lavelle Road
St. Marks Rd.
Residency Rd.
Brigade Rd.
⑪
Madras

⑩
Balpet Rd.
Chickpet Rd.
Avenue Rd.
Kasturba Rd.

Cottonpet Bhashyam Rd.
Nagarthpet Rd.
Richmond Rd.
Airport

⑥
S. J. Park Rd.
Narasimharaja Rd.
Langford Road

⑦
Jagajeevanraj Rd.

Albert Victor Rd.
Lalbagh Rd.
Kengal Hanumanthaih Rd.

Puttannachetty Rd.
⑧
Hardinge Rd.

Shankarmutt Rd.
Jayachamaraja Rd.
Lalbagh Fort Rd.

Bull Temple Rd.
Vani Vilas Rd.

B. P. Wadia Rd.
Lal Bagh

⑨
Nagasandra Rd.
Kanakapura Rd.
Rashtreeya Vidyalaya Rd.
South End Road
Hosur Rd.
Hosur Rd.
Hosur

0   Scale   1   2 Km

stone in the 18th century by Hyder Ali and Tipu Sultan but much of it was destroyed during the wars with the British and you would be missing little if you left it out of your itinerary. It is supposed to be open daily from 8 am but this isn't always the case.

Tipu Sultan's Summer Palace

Situated on Albert Victor Rd near the junction with Krishnarajendra Rd this palace was begun by Tipu Sultan's father, Hyder Ali, and completed by Tipu in 1791. It resembles the Daria Daulat Bagh at Srirangapatna near Mysore City but has been sadly neglected and is falling into disrepair. You may well find the temple next to it of far greater interest. The palace is open daily from 6 am to 6 pm. Admission is free.

The Bull Temple

Situated on Bugle Hill at the end of Bull Temple Rd, this is one of Bangalore's oldest temples. Built by Kempegowda in the Dravidian style, it contains a huge monolith of Nandi similar to the one on Chamundi Hill at Mysore. Non-Hindus are allowed to enter and the priests are friendly. You will be offered jasmine flowers and expected to leave a small donation.

Other

The remains of the four watch towers built by Kempegowda are worth a visit if you're in the vicinity of the Bull Temple. They are situated about 400 metres to the west of the temple. Ulsoor Lake to the east of the Cubbon Park has boating facilities and a swimming pool.

Tours

The Karnataka State Tourism Development Corporation offer the following tours:
Bangalore City Daily except Sundays from the City Railway Station. The tour starts at 9 am and ends at 7 pm and includes visits to Tipu's Palace, Bull Temple, Lalbagh Botanical Gardens, Ulsoor Lake, Government Soap Factory, Vidhana Soudha, Cubbon Park, Government Museum, Technology Museum and Art Gallery. The tour costs Rs 20.
Srirangapatna, Mysore City & Brindavan Gardens Daily tours beginning at 7.15 am and returning at 10.45 pm. The tour includes visits to the Ranganathaswamy Temple, the Fort, Gumbaz and Daria Daulat Bagh at Srirangapatna and St Philomena's Cathedral, Chamundi Hill, the Palace, Art Gallery and Kaveri Arts and Crafts Emporium at Mysore. The tour costs Rs 40.
Belur, Halebid & Sravanabelagola On Fridays and Sundays only (except during the monsoon season). Depart from the City Railway Station at 7.15 am and return at 10 pm. The tour costs Rs 50.

These tours can be booked at any of the following places:
KSTDC, 10/4 Kasturba Road, Queens Circle, Bangalore I (tel 578753/578901).
KSTDC Booking Counter, Badami House, opposite Corporation Office, Bangalore (tel 74711).
KSTDC Information Counter, Public Utility Building, M G Road, Bangalore I (tel 52377).
KSTDC Tourist Information Counter, City Railway Station, Bangalore 2. (tel 70068).

Places to Stay — Top End

The *ITDC Hotel Ashok* (tel 79411) at Kumara Krupa, High Grounds is close to central Bangalore and has all mod-cons from tennis courts, shops and a swimming pool to full air-conditioning. Singles/doubles cost from Rs 175/250. The *Bangalore International* (tel 26011) is at 2A-B Crescent Rd, High Grounds and is rather smaller than the large Hotel Ashok. Singles/doubles here are available with air-con from Rs 110/150 or without from Rs 80/120.

The *West End* (tel 29281) is on Race Course Rd, High Grounds and is again fully air-con with singles/doubles from Rs 200/250. The *Woodlands Hotel* (tel 74114) is at 5 Sampangi Tank Rd and is of similar size, but lower standards and price, to the 183 room Hotel Ashok. Air-con singles/doubles cost from Rs 60/100, non air-con rooms start from Rs 40/60. Other more expensive hotels in Bangalore include:

Shilton (tel 54471), St Mark's Rd — singles/doubles Rs 40/80 non air-con, Rs 75/120 air-con.

Rama (tel 53381), Levelle Rd — singles/doubles Rs 80/100 non air-con, Rs 100/120 air-con.

Nilgiris Nest (tel 577501), 11 Bridgade Rd — singles/doubles Rs 40/60 non air-con, Rs 60/80 air-con.

Kwality (tel 52334), 40/1 Bridgade Rd — singles/doubles Rs 50/70 non air-con, Rs 70/100 air-con.

East-West (tel 53265), Residency Rd — singles/doubles Rs 100/160 non air-con, Rs 120/200 air-con.

Harsha (tel 74071), Shivajinagar — singles/doubles Rs 75/100 non air-con, Rs 100/130 air-con.

Cauvery Continental (tel 29358), 11-37 Cunningham Rd — singles/doubles Rs 50/80 non air-con, Rs 80/120 air-con.

Barton Court (tel 043571), Mahatma Gandhi Rd — singles/doubles Rs 100/140 non air-con, Rs 150/180 air-con.

Places to Stay — Middle

Hotel Swagash, 75 Hospital Rd, Balepet Cross. Singles/doubles cost Rs 30/50 plus Rs 15 if you have an extra person in a room. The charges include hot and cold running water and laundry facilities. Air-conditioned rooms are also available. *Hotel Mahaveen*, on the corner of Cottonpet Bhashyam Rd overlooking the Central Bus Station. Singles/doubles cost Rs 20/35. All rooms have own

bathroom, hot water, fan and clean sheets. *Hotel Hindustan*, Gandhi Nagar just off Kempegowda Circle has singles/doubles for Rs 15/30 all with attached bath, fan and clean sheets. This is a huge hotel and you'd be very unlucky to find it full.

Hotel Volga, opposite the Hindustan has singles/doubles from Rs 14/28-30 including attached bath, clean sheets and fan. Air-conditioned double rooms are also available from Rs 35. *Hotel Sumath*, S C Rd, 100 metres from Kempegowda Circle, singles/doubles cost Rs 18/30 including attached bath, fan and clean sheets. *Hotel Kamadhenu* (tel 54451) at Trinity Circle on Mahatma Gandhi Rd is a large place and also quite good value, singles/doubles cost Rs 30/40 without air-con, Rs 75 for an air-con double.

Places to Stay — Bottom End

Sudha Lodge, Cottonpet Bhashyam Rd has singles/doubles/triples for Rs 12/18/24. Most of the rooms have attached bathrooms with hot water available between 6.30 and 10 am. All the rooms have fans. It's clean, there's room service and the management are friendly — I even took the keys for a spare room late one night to put up a 'leg-less' (ie inebriated) Brahmin who had insisted on buying a bottle of rum and coming back to my room to polish it off. There were no problems in the morning. Nice people, definitely the best of the cheapies. *Hotel Tourist*, Race Course Rd near the junction with Subahdar Rd. Singles/doubles cost Rs 8/16.

Other cheapies are located around the City Market on Sri Narsimharaja Rd. They include the Hotels: *Bilal, Rainbow, Delhi Bhavan, Chandra Vihar, Nataraj* and *Isaquia*. If you want to get there on foot from either the railway station or the bus station, go down Cottonpet Bhashyam Rd as far as Kengeri Police Station (on the right hand side) and then turn left. This is Police Rd though there are no signs to tell you this. Continue down Police Rd for several hundred metres and you will find yourself outside City Market. It's 10-15 minutes' walk from the railway station. *Nanda Hotel* in Ghandi Nagar is Rs 20 a double and has a good restaurant.

There are two YMCAs (on Nrupatunga Rd (tel 24848) and on Infantry Rd, the latter being the cheaper of the two) but they seem to be permanently full with students from the various educational institutes so it's almost impossible to get a room there.

Places to Eat

In the Gandhi Nagar and Chickpet areas of Bangalore it's impossible to walk more than a few metres without coming across a restaurant. There are literally thousands. The only trouble is that most of them offer just the standard South India fare of dosa, idli, rice and vegetables and coffee but they are clean and extremely cheap — a masala dosa and coffee costs on average Rs 1.75. If you'd like something more substantial than this there are several *Kamat Hotels* (for example, on S C Rd and on Sri Narsimharaja Rd) where you can get a good 'plate meal' (thali) for Rs 3 consisting of three different curry sauces, fried vegetables, curd, pickles, three puris and rice. These cafes are always good value. If you'd like more choice, an excellent place is the *Hotel Blue Star* opposite the Tribhuvan Cinema in Gandhi Nagar at the back of Kempegowda Circle. They have an extensive menu (both vegetarian and non-vegetarian) which includes curried dishes, omelettes, chicken, fish (and chips!), tandoori. Chicken moghlai, nan, salad, lassi and tea cost Rs 11.50.

Getting There

Flights Indian Airlines operate the flights from Bangalore to Madras (twice daily) Rs 156; to Bombay (twice daily) Rs 436; to New Delhi (daily) Rs 806;

to Calcutta via Hyderabad (daily except Sunday); to Mangalore (daily) Rs 169; to Cochin via Coimbatore (daily) Rs 195; to Coimbatore (daily) Rs 130.

Trains Bangalore is connected by direct daily express trains with all the main cities in southern and central India and with New Delhi but, as elsewhere in India where there is more than one express per day, you should be careful to choose the right train if speed is your priority as journey times vary considerably from one express to the next. Naturally, the fastest night express trains are often booked out days in advance so your choice may be limited. Also note that no Tourist Quota is available for sleeping berths at Bangalore Station. They do have a VIP Quota but they are very reluctant to release these to tourists. If you're stuck it's worth a try — contact the Station Superintendant on Platform 1.

There is a twice weekly express from New Delhi which takes 38 hours to make the 2491 km trip. The Karnataka-Kerala Express costs Rs 375 in 1st class, Rs 91 in 2nd class. Bombay-Bangalore is 1211 km and the fare is Rs 219 in 1st class, Rs 54 in 2nd. The trains go via Pune and Belgaum and take from 24 hours. There are a number of direct trains between Madras and Bangalore each day. The fast Brindavan Express and the Bangalore Mail and Express take just over seven hours at a fare of Rs 83 in 1st class, Rs 19 in 2nd. To Secunderabad (Hyderabad) takes about 19 hours with fares around Rs 135 in 1st class, Rs 32.50 in 2nd. Bangalore-Mysore is only three hours with fares of Rs 40 in 1st class, Rs 8.20 in 2nd. To Trivandrum takes about 20 hours on the Island Express with fares of Rs 180 in 1st class, Rs 44 in 2nd class.

Buses Bangalore has a well-organised central bus station for all long-distance buses. It's situated directly in front of the City Railway Station. Some of the more important routes include to

Belgaum, three buses daily, first at 6.15 am; last at 9 pm. To Bellary, two buses daily at 3 pm and 9 pm. To Bijapur, three buses daily all of them in the evening, last at 8 pm. To Bombay, two buses daily at 8 am and 7 pm.

To Cochin/Ernakulum, two buses daily at 5 am and 7 am. To Hospet, one bus daily at 8.30 am. To Hubli, two buses daily at 1 pm and 11.15 pm. To Madras, two buses daily via Vellore at 7 am and 10 pm. One bus daily via Chittoor at 2 pm. To Mangalore, nine buses daily, first at 7.45 am; last at 11 pm. To Mysore, approximately 75 buses daily between 5.40 am and 9.20 pm. To Ootacamund, two buses daily at 6.30 am and 8 am.

In addition to the state buses detailed above there are many other private bus companies clustered around the road which circles the bus station. They cover similar routes but operate more luxurious (and therefore more expensive) buses, usually of the '36-seater super de luxe' type. For example, the South India Tourist Service (Hotel Pavana Building, near the City Railway Station) goes to Cochin (Rs 55); Belgaum (Rs 40); Bombay (Rs 110); Hyderabad (Rs 60); Madras (Rs 32); Mangalore (Rs 35); Tirupati (Rs 25) and Udipi (Rs 40). All the above depart at 9 am.

Things to Buy
The Kaveri Arts and Crafts Emporium, 23 Mahatma Gandhi Road (tel 51418), like its sister establishment at Mysore, stocks a huge range of superb handcrafted tables, carvings (many of them in sandalwood), ivory ware, jewellery, ceramics, carpets and agarbathis. Few things are cheap as such but this emporium stocks some of the best craft work in India.

AROUND BANGALORE
Nandi Hills
This popular hill station is 68 km from Bangalore and was a popular summer retreat even in Tipu Sultan's days. Tipu's drop, a 600 metre high cliff face, provides a good view over the surrounding country. There are two ancient temples here and cheap accommodation available through the Horticulture Department in Bangalore (tel 602231).

Kolar Gold Fields
The mines here, 100 km east of Bangalore, are the major gold producers for India and are said to have the deepest mine shafts in the world, reaching over 3000 metres below the surface. Visits to the mine can be arranged.

MYSORE (population 400,000)
Sandalwood City! Everywhere you go in this beautiful city you'll find yourself enveloped with the lingering aromas of sandalwood, jasmine, rose, musk, frangipani and a hundred others. Whenever you smell them again, you'll be reminded of this place. It's one of the major centres of incense manufacture in India and scores of small, family-owned agarbathi factories are scattered all over town, their products exported all over the world. Every one of those incense sticks is hand-made — usually by women and children — and a good worker can turn out at least 10,000 a day! They are made with thin slivers of bamboo, dyed red or green at one end, onto which is rolled a sandalwood putty base. The sticks are then dipped into small piles of powdered perfume and laid out to harden in the shade. You can see them being made if you visit the Government Sandalwood Oil Factory or enquire at

Mysore City

any of the small firms you come across.

Mysore is also a craft centre and there are numerous shops selling an incredible range of ivory, sandalwood, rosewood and teak carvings and furniture. Probably the most stunning display of these can be seen at the Kaveri Arts and Crafts Emporium in the centre of town. Their rosewood tables and elephants intricately inlaid with ivory and other woods are perhaps the best you will see anywhere in the world. Hardly anyone comes here and leaves empty-handed. It's impossible to visit the post office without seeing at least two or three travellers going through the motions of sending a package back home!

As if this were not enough, there are plenty of other reasons why you would not want to miss Mysore. Until independence, the city was the seat of the Maharajas of Mysore, a princely state covering much of present day Karnataka, and their walled Indo-Saracenic palace in the centre of the city draws visitors from all over the world. Its silhouette in many ways typifies what you would expect of Indian architecture. The ex-ruler still lives here (though the palace is open to visitors) and during the 10-day festival of Dussehra, during the first and second week of October each year, he leads one of India's most colourful processions. Richly caparisoned elephants, liveried retainers, cavalry, the gaudy and flower-bedecked images of

deities make their way through the streets to the sound of jazz bands, brass bands and the inevitable clouds of incense. It's an extravaganza you shouldn't miss if you're anywhere in the area at this time of year.

Just south of the city lies Chamundi Hill, 1062 metres above sea level, on top of which stands a typical south Indian temple with a seven-storied gopuram visible from far away. The hill can be climbed by a flight of 1000 steps or you can drive up there along the winding road with its many switchbacks. Two-thirds of the way up the hill is the famous Nandi (Shiva's Bull), a huge monolithic image always garlanded with flowers and a pilgrimage spot for Hindus.

Outside of the city to the northwest lie the extensive ruins of the former capital of Mysore, the fortress city of Srirangapatnam, built by Hyder Ali and Tipu Sultan on an island in mid-Cauvery. Tipu Sultan fought the last of his battles with the British here in the closing years of the 18th century. But probably the biggest attraction outside the city is the temple of Somnathpur. Built by the Hoysala kings (11th to 13th centuries), it is surely one of the wonders of the world with its perfectly proportioned ground plan and its unbelievable sculptural exuberance depicting stories from the Ramayana, Mahabharata and Bhagavata epics.

Mysore is a travellers' Mecca and it's

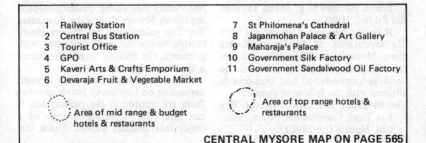

1	Railway Station	7	St Philomena's Cathedral
2	Central Bus Station	8	Jaganmohan Palace & Art Gallery
3	Tourist Office	9	Maharaja's Palace
4	GPO	10	Government Silk Factory
5	Kaveri Arts & Crafts Emporium	11	Government Sandalwood Oil Factory
6	Devaraja Fruit & Vegetable Market		

Area of mid range & budget hotels & restaurants

Area of top range hotels & restaurants

CENTRAL MYSORE MAP ON PAGE 565

easy to see why. Apart from the attractions mentioned above, it's a friendly, easy-going city with plenty of shady trees, well-maintained public buildings, clean streets, a good climate and yet small enough not to overwhelm (you can walk from one end to the other in 20 minutes).

Information & Orientation

The railway station and bus station are located conveniently close to the centre of the city and only a few minutes walk from all the main hotels and restaurants. The main shopping street is Sayaji Rao Rd which runs from New Statue Square on the north side of the Maharaja's Palace, across Irwin Rd to the north of the city. The budget hotels are mostly located along Dhanvantri Rd and around Gandhi Square. The mid-range and top-range hotels are clustered together in the area south of Government House and north-east of the Palace with one or two exceptions in the centre.

Useful Addresses & Services

There are three tourist offices. The Tourist Reception Centre, Old Exhibition Building, Irwin Rd (tel 23251) has no literature available. The Tourist Bureau, Kaveri Arts & Crafts Emporium, Sayaji Rao Rd is absolutely hopeless — unless they've replaced the no-nothing woman who was running it. The State Tourism Development Corporation is at 2 Jhansi Lakshmi Bai Rd (tel 23652).

Indian Airlines is at Jhansi Lakshmi Bai Rd (tel 21486).

If you're planning a visit to the wildlife sanctuaries of Bandipur (80 km from Mysore) or Nagarhole (93 km from Mysore) then it's advisable to book accommodation and transport in advance with the following people:

For Bandipur the Field Director, Project Tiger, Government House, Nazirbad, Mysore (tel 20901).

For Nagarhole: Assistant Conservator of Forests, Wildlife Preservation, Chamarajendra Circle, Vanivilas Rd, Mysore (tel 21159). At present there are two travellers' bungalows at Nagarhole — Kaveri and Gangothri. They both cost Rs 25 a double but Kaveri is the better of the two. There's also dormitory accommodation available. Contact the range officer there, Mr Chinappa, if you want to go for a ride in their safari van (24 km ride for Rs 5 per person. If you have your own van the entrance fee is Rs 14). No elephant rides are available at present.

Two very good bookshops in Mysore are the Geetha Book House, New Statue Square (at the bottom of Sayaji Rao Rd) and the Ashok Book Centre, Dhanvantri Rd (near the junction with Sayaji Rao Rd). Both have plenty of English-language paperbacks and Penguin books.

Maharaja's Palace

The beautiful profile of this walled, Indo-Saracenic palace, the seat of the Maharaja's of Mysore, dominates the city's skyline. It was built in 1911-12 at a cost of Rs 4.2 million to replace the former palace which was burnt down. Internally it reminds one of an Afghani waistcoat — an extravaganza of stained glass, mirrors, gilt and gaudy colours. But there are some beautiful carved wooden doors and mosaic floors as well as a whole series of mediocre, though historically interesting, paintings depicting life in Mysore during the Edwardian Raj. The palace even has its own Hindu temple inside the walls complete with gopuram. On Sunday nights the palace is spectacularly illuminated.

It's certainly worth a visit though, depending on how many tourist coaches there are outside in the parking lot, it can rival the departure lounge of a major international airport. Check this out before you go in! Entry is from the south gate only and the palace is open daily from 10.30 am to 5.30 pm. Tickets cost Rs 2 and you must leave your shoes at the shoe deposit (there's a 10p charge for this). Booklets about the palace are on sale inside. Outside in the parking lot there's a permanent gaggle of snakeskin sellers and postcard vendors. The postcards are abysmal; the snakeskins better but you have to haggle for at least 20 minutes before the price gets reasonable.

Chamundi Hill

You can spend a very pleasant half day walking up the 1000 steps to the top of this hill where the temple to Sri Chamundeswari stands. It's a fairly strenuous climb but there are plenty of trees on the way up. The views over the surrounding countryside and Mysore City, even from half way up, are superb. Two-thirds of the way up you come across the famous Nandi (Shiva's bull) carved out of solid rock and at five metres high perhaps the largest in India. It's always garlanded in flowers and constantly visited by bevies of pilgrims offering prasad to the priest in attendance there. Sri Chamundeswari temple on the summit is a huge structure with a seven-storied gopuram 40 metres high. Visiting hours (non-Hindus are allowed inside) are 9 am to 12 noon and 5 pm to 9 pm. The priests are quite enthusiastic to show you around. If you don't walk up the hill or, having walked up, you don't want to walk back down again, there are buses approximately every half hour from the central bus station. The terminus on the hill is about 300 metres from the temple. Demand for buses can be very heavy on Sundays (I've seen 500 people waiting for a bus!). Refreshments, snacks and south Indian plate meals are available at cafes around the temple. Note that local guide books and tourist literature will tell you that the summit is 13 km from the city. This refers to the road only. Going via the steps it's about four km.

Devaraja Fruit & Vegetable Market

This market stretches almost the whole length of Sayaji Rd from Dhanvantri Rd to New Statue Square and is one of the most colourful in India. Well worth a visit and, if you have a camera, excellent subject material for photographs.

Kaveri Arts & Crafts Emporium

Even if you're not going to buy anything this place is worth a visit — more details under 'What to Buy'.

Other

The **Government Sandalwood Oil Factory**, where sandalwood oil is distilled and incense sticks are made, used to be a really interesting place to visit but these days they tend to rush you round and quickly shepherd you into the sales office. Visiting hours are 9 am to 11 am and 2 pm to 4 pm daily except Sundays. Excellent sandalwood oil is on sale here at Rs 25 per 25 gm bottle. They also have some good incense.

The **Government Silk Weaving Factory**, where pure silk saris are made, is also worth a visit. Hours are 7.30 am to 11.30 am and 12.30 pm to 4.30 pm daily except Sundays.

Other places worth a visit in town are the **Sri Chamarajendra Art Gallery** housed in the Jaganmohan Palace. Not only does it display paintings, particularly by Ravi Varma, but also handicrafts, historical objects of interest and rare musical instruments. Visiting hours are 8 am to 5 pm daily. Entrance costs Rs 1. **St Philomena's Cathedral** is of interest if you want to see what the Christians got up to here in the last century. One of the largest churches in India built in the neo-Gothic style.

Tours

There are a number of tours available

from Mysore which include:

Mysore City, Somnathpur, Srirangapatnam, Brindavan Gardens, Rangana-
thittu Bird Sanctuary (latter only
in season). Daily tour starting at
7.30 am and finishing at 8.30 pm.
Costs Rs 22. Frankly, this tour
attempts to do too much in one day
but if you're in a hurry . . . . .

Belur, Halebid and Sravanabelagola —
the other two Hoysala temples and
the Jain pilgrimage centre where
the immense statue of Lord Gomateshvara stands. Tours on Fridays
and Sundays between December and
April starting at 7.30 am and finishing at 9 pm. Costs Rs 35.

Ootacamund — the hill station in the
Nilgiris. Daily tours in season starting
at 7 am and finishing at 9 pm. Costs
Rs 40.

You can book these tours at any of the
following places:

Mysore Tourist Centre, 2 Jhansi Lakshmi
Bai Rd.

Tourist Office, Kaveri Arts & Crafts
Emporium, Sayaji Rao Rd.

Tourist Office, opposite Shalimar Hotel
round the corner from the New
Gayathri Bhavan Hotel, Dhanvantri
Rd.

Many other places especially around
Gandhi Square.

Places to Stay — Top End

Being a major tourist centre, Mysore
has quite a number of western-style
hotels, the majority of them with air-
conditioning and attached restaurants
and bars. They include: *Hotel Highway*,
New Bannimantap Extension-7 (tel
21117), just off Sayaji Rao Rd in the
northern suburbs. Rooms here cost Rs
80 a single and Rs 120 a double. Their
restaurant serves excellent food. *Hotel
Aashirwad*, 3 Nazarbad Rd, Mysore-10
(tel 23210). Rooms here cost Rs 50-
70 a double. Convenient for the centre
of town. *Hotel Lalitha Mahal Palace*, T

Narsipur Rd (tel 23650). One of the
chain of ITDC hotels. Rooms here cost
Rs 100 a single and Rs 125 a double. If
you'd like to stay on top of Chamundi
Hill there is the *Hotel Rajendravilas Imperial* (tel 22050) with rooms at Rs 130
a single and Rs 170 a double.

Places to Stay — Middle

Hotel Anugraha, Sayaji Rao Rd, opposite
the central market (tel 20581) is very
conveniently located in the centre of
town. This attractive new building has
very pleasant rooms, is well maintained
and the staff are helpful and friendly.
Rooms cost Rs 25 a single and Rs 40 a
double both with attached bathroom.
Clean sheets are provided.

Hotel Srikanth, Gandhi Square (tel
22951) is very similar to the Anugraha
but with the added attraction of a rooftop restaurant and bar from where you
can see the Maharaja's Palace. Rooms
cost Rs 25 a single and Rs 40 a double
both with attached bathroom. Clean
sheets are provided. *Hotel Ritz*, Purniah
Park, close to the north end of the
Maharaja's Palace (tel 22668) has rooms
at Rs 25 a single and Rs 40 a double
both with attached bathrooms and clean
sheets.

Places to Stay — Bottom End

Virtually all the budget hotels are
located either along Dhanvantri Rd or
around Gandhi Square. There are literally scores of them but some of the
best are: *New Gayathri Bhavan*,
Dhanvantri Rd (tel 21224) where rooms
cost Rs 15 a single and Rs 30 a double
both with attached bathroom, fan,
clean sheet and pillow case. (If they try
to give you room 20 tell them you want
a different one — it's incredibly small!).
The rooms are secure and the staff is
pleasant. There's vaguely hot water in
the mornings and sometimes in the
evenings. 'Meals' cafe downstairs.

Agarwal Lodge, Dhanvantri Rd (tel
22730) has rooms for Rs 15 a single and

Rs 35 a double both with attached bathroom. Same quality and facilities as the Gayathri. *Hotel Indra Bhavan*, Dhanvantri Rd (tel 23933) has rooms for Rs 20 a single and Rs 35 a double both with attached bathroom. 'Meals' cafe on the ground floor. *Hotel Durbar*, Gandhi Square, is probably the best of the budget hotels on Gandhi Square. Rooms here cost Rs 12 a single with common bathroom and Rs 30 a double with attached bathroom. Cafe downstairs and a roof garden restaurant where you can eat in the evening.

Outside Mysore City there is accommodation available at Somnathpur, Srirangapatnam and the Brindavan Gardens. See 'Around Mysore'.

Places to Eat

There are any number of reasonably good 'meals' restaurants where you can get standard south Indian vegetarian food for between Rs 2.50-3. They include *New Gayathri Bhavan* and *Hotel Indra Bhavan* (Dhanvantri Rd); *Bombay Indra Bhavan* and *Indra Cafe* (Sayaji Rao Rd), and the *Hotel Durbar* (Gandhi Square). You may occasionally find one or another of these closed due to a strike by the employees (the workers in these cafes earn a mere Rs 95-100 per month!).

If you're looking for something other than the standard fare try the *Punjabi Restaurant Bombay Juice Centre*, Dhanvantri Rd near the junction with Sayaji Roa Rd. They serve Punjabi vegetarian and non-vegetarian dishes, fruit juices and milk shakes (the latter are somewhat expensive at Rs 4). A vegetarian meal here, including fresh lime juice and coffee, will cost you about Rs 10. A non-vegetarian meal (eg mutton or chicken) will cost about Rs 15 including drinks, and tandoori specialities will set you back Rs 25-35 including drinks. The food is excellent and well cooked and the place is popular with travellers.

Shilpashtri Restaurant & Bar, Gandhi Square, is located on the first floor above a liquor store, it includes an open-air rooftop section which is popular with travellers in the evenings. Excellent food and somewhat cheaper than the Punjabi Restaurant. They also serve the coldest beers in Mysore (UB Export costs Rs 9.50 a bottle). Friendly staff, if you go there, say hello to Raju who's worked there for 11 years.

Kwality Restaurant, Dhanvantri Rd, serve both vegetarian and non-vegetarian food as well as 'Chinese' and tandoori specialities but their vegetarian dishes all taste the same regardless of what they are and the waiters have an annoying habit of obviously hovering around for a tip when the bill comes. You can eat here for Rs 10-12 (three vegetarian dishes plus nan or chappatis). They also serve spirits and beers. In the evenings it can be really noisy as it fills up with Indian families whose kids kick up an incredible racket. *Gun House Imperial* is located close to the south-east corner of the Maharaja's Palace at the start of the Ooty road. This is a fairly select lunch and night spot with electric music in the evenings.

Getting Around

Local buses which you may find useful include I and IA (to Sandalwood Oil Factory) and 4 and 5 (to Silk Weaving Factory). For buses to Chamundi Hill go to the Suburban Bus Stand at the eastern end of Gandhi Square. They run approximately every 30 minutes. There are plenty of auto-rickshaws if you prefer this form of transport (Sayaji Rd to the Sandalwood Oil Factory will cost Rs 3-4). The drivers use the meters.

To Somnathpur First get a bus from the Suburban Bus Stand (Gandhi Square) to the village of Tirarasipura (tell the conductor you want to go to Somnathpur). This part of the journey costs Rs 2.75. At Tirarasipura take another bus to Somnathpur. You'll have no trouble locating this bus as all the local kids and the bus conductors will make sure you know when it arrives. These buses are frequent and this part of the journey costs Rs 0.75. You can either return to Mysore via the same route or go to Srirangapatnam. There is a direct bus from Somnathpur to Srirangapatnam at 1.10 pm. If you want to go before or after this first take a bus from Somnathpur to Bannur (Rs 0.75) and then another bus from there to Srirangapatnam (Rs 2.50). The buses from Bannur to Srirangapatnam can get incredibly crowded. The bus I was on had 202 people on board and I ended up with a child on my knee and two pails of milk in each hand!

To Srirangapatnam There are plenty of buses all day and night from the Central Bus Stand. Some go only as far as Srirangapatnam; other pass through on their way to somewhere else. The fare is Rs 1.30. There's no problem getting back to Mysore along the same route. As an alternative to the bus it's also possible to get there by taking the Bangalore passenger train from Mysore station. If you want to visit Somnathpur from Srirangapatnam use the route indicated above under 'Somnathpur' in the reverse direction.

Getting There
Long-Distance Buses All these buses leave from the Central Bus Station.

To Arsikere, 14 times daily from Platform 4. First bus at 6.30 am and the last at 11.30 pm. (You can use Arsikere as a base from which to visit Belur, Halebid and Sravanabelagola though Hassan is the more usual base). To Bandipur, three buses daily at 6.30 am, 2.30 pm and 3.15 pm. To Bangalore, non-stop buses every 20-30 minutes from 5.40 am to 9.20 pm. Ordinary stopping service every 30 minutes throughout the day starting at 6 am. To Bellary, one

bus daily at 9 pm from Platform 4. (This is the bus to take if you want to visit the Vijayanagar ruins at Hampi direct from Mysore).

To Calicut, six buses daily from Platform 3. First bus at 6 am and the last at 6.30 pm. To Cannanore, two buses daily at 10.45 am and 11.15 am from Platform 3. To Chikmagalur, seven buses daily. First bus at 6 am and the last at 4 pm. (This bus goes via Belur). To Coimbatore, three buses daily at 7.15 am, 3 pm and 3.20 pm from Platform 3. To Hassan, 15 buses daily from Platform 8. First bus at 5.30 am and the last at 9.30 pm. (Hassan is the usual base from which to visit Belur, Halebid and Sravanabelagola). There are other buses to Hassan from Platform 4 (six times daily) and Platform 6 (once daily). To Ernakulam, two buses daily at 8.30 am and 10.30 am from Platform 3. The buses go via Calicut. To Mangalore, 11 buses daily from Platform 7. First bus at 6 am and the last at 10.40 pm. To Nagarhole, two buses daily at 6.30 am and 1.30 pm. To Ootacamund, seven buses daily from Platform 3. First bus at 6.15 am and the last at 3 pm. (You can use these buses to get to the wildlife sanctuaries of Bandipur and Mudumalai). To Sravanabelagola, five buses daily. First bus at 7.30 am and the last at 3.45 pm. To Udipi, three buses daily at 8.30 am, 12 noon and 9 pm.

Trains
To Bangalore There are six express trains to Bangalore (140 km away) daily: Chamundi Express (6.15 am); Tipu Express (8 am); Bangalore Express (10.35 am); Nandi Express (2.20 pm); Bangalore Mail (5.45 pm); Kaveri Express (8.30 pm). In addition there are two passenger trains to Bangalore at 8.15 am and 10.55 pm and a passenger train to Maddur at 6.40 pm. These last three can be used to get to Srirangapatnam.
To Arsikere There are three passenger trains daily to Arsikere via Hassan at

7.10 am, 2.15 pm and 4.50 pm. If you're planning on visiting the Hoysala temples of Belur and Halebid and the Jain centre of Sravanabelagola and you're going to use Hassan as a base, these are the trains to take. To Hassan the journey takes 4½ hours and costs Rs 5.60.

To Chamarajanagar There are five passenger trains to Nanjangud daily and three passenger trains to Chamarajanagar daily but they're of little use to travellers since if you were heading for Bandipur it would be more convenient to take a bus.

If you're heading for Bombay but don't want to go through Bangalore the quickest route is to take the 4.50 pm Arsikere Passenger which has one coach going all the way to Miraj arriving there at 1.15 pm the next day. From Miraj there is an express train to Bombay the same day at 3.10 pm arriving in Bombay at 6 am the next morning.

The enquiry office at Mysore station is very good and rarely has more than two or three people in it.

Things to Buy

Mysore is famous for carved sandalwood and ivory articles, inlay works, silk saris and incense (agarbathi). The best place to see the whole range of what is available is the Kaveri Arts and Crafts Emporium on Sayaji Rao Rd. It's open daily except Thursdays from 10 am to 2 pm and 3.30 pm to 7.30 pm (Sundays from 10 am to 2 pm). They won't take credit cards but they will take foreign currency or travellers cheques and will arrange packing and export of anything except ivory for you (government regulations stipulate that ivory has to be carried personally). They do a very good job of packing things up. Few of the larger things are cheap by Indian standards (eg the smallest of the inlaid tables cost about US$100) but the place is worth a visit even if you're not going to buy anything. There are many other craft shops along Dhanvantri Rd with similar prices. Some of them specialise in ivory chess sets but a 10 cm set can cost you anywhere between US$1000-1500! The best bargains are the carved sandalwood images of Indian deities. They retain their scent for years. There are always a number of street hawkers outside the Kaveri Emporium. They sometimes have some interesting and cheap bangles, rings and old coins.

AROUND MYSORE
Srirangapatnam

16 km from Mysore on the Bangalore road stands the ruins of Hyder Ali and Tipu Sultan's capital from which they ruled much of southern India during the 18th century before being finally defeated by the British, allied with local disgruntled leaders and with the help of a traitor, in 1799. Tipu's defeat marked the real beginning of British territorial expansion in southern India. There isn't a great deal left of Srirangapatnam as the British did a good job of demolishing the place but the extensive ramparts and battlements and some of the gates still stand and the dungeon where Tipu held prisoner a number of British officers has been preserved. Inside the walls there's also a mosque and the Sri Ranganathaswamy temple, a popular place of pilgrimage with Hindus.

Across the other side of the road from Srirangapatnam stands the Daria Daulat Bagh, Tipu's summer palace, and the Gumbaz, Tipu's mausoleum. These are perhaps the most interesting part of a visit to Srirangapatnam. The Daria Daulat Bagh stands in well-maintained ornamental gardens and is now a

Mysore District

museum which houses some of Tipu's belongings as well as many ink drawings of him and his family and 'artists' impressions' of the last battle, executed by employees of the British East India Company. All around the internal walls of the ground floor are paintings depicting Tipu's campaigns against the British with French mercenary assistance. Ten years ago this summer palace was graced with ornamented leather awnings to keep out the sun but this has now dis-

appeared and it's obvious that maintenance of the building has been seriously neglected — a pity when they see fit to look after the garden so well. The Daria Daulat Bagh is open daily until 5 pm and costs Rs 0.50 entrance.

Places to Stay Contact the Assistant Engineer, PWD, Srirangapatnam for accommodation at the *Travellers Bungalow*, close to the Sri Ranganathaswamy temple.

Getting There There are scores of buses everyday in either direction from the central bus station in Mysore. The fare is Rs 1.30.

Somnathpur

45 km east of Mysore stands the Sri Channakeshara temple at Somnathpur, built around 1260 AD during the heyday of the Hoysala kings. It's one of the most beautiful and interesting buildings in the world. The walls of the star-shaped temple are literally covered with superb sculptures in stone depicting various scenes from the Ramayana, Mahabharata, Bhagavata and the life and times of the Hoysala kings. No two friezes are alike. If you like this place then don't miss the other Hoysala temples at Belur and Halebid, north of Mysore. The temple is open daily between 9 am and 5 pm and entry costs Rs 0.50. There is no fee for cameras.

A booklet, *The Hoysalas* by P K Mishra is on sale at the temple for Rs 6. As Indian booklets on these places go, it's pretty good and worth buying. For details on how to get to Somnathpur by public transport see the 'Getting Around' section.

Places to Stay Just outside the temple compound is a KSTDC *Tourist Home & Restaurant*. The rooms, rarely full, are excellent value with attached bathrooms, carpeted floors, curtains on the windows, clean sheets, pleasantly decorated and just Rs 25 for a double. You won't get a cleaner, more pleasant room anywhere at this price. The restaurant serves excellent food — a large omelette, onions and green chillis for only Rs 2, cheap tea and coffee too.

Bandipur Wildlife Sanctuary

80 km south of Mysore on the Mysore-Ootacamund road, this wildlife sanctuary is part of a larger national park which also includes the neighbouring wildlife sanctuaries of Mudumalai in Tamil Nadu and Wynad in Kerala. The sanctuary is noted for its herds of bison, spotted deer, elephant, sambar, tiger and leopard. The Forestry Department has jeeps and trucks available for hire and, as in Mudumalai, you can go on safari on elephant-back. Boats are also available for use on the river. Motorised transport and accommodation in the sanctuary must be booked in advance if you want to be sure of them. For reservations contact Field Director, Project Tiger, Government House Complex, Mysore (tel 20901). The best time to go is between October and May.

Ranganathittu Bird Sanctuary

One of three islands in the Cauvery River three km from Srirangapatnam. If you're interested in birds this is a good place to visit at any time of year though best between June and September. Access is by a motorable road open all year. Boats are available for use on the river but there are no accommodation facilities.

Brindavan Gardens

These ornamental gardens are laid out below the Krishnarajasagar dam across the Cauvery River, 19 km from Mysore. They're popular with middle-class Indians who come here for picnics and are pleasant enough but probably not worth a special trip to see. Entry costs Rs 0.50 plus Rs 4 if you have a camera. One of the tours operated by KSTDC will bring you here.

Places to Stay There are three places to stay at the gardens. The *Hotel Krishnarajasagar* (tel Mysore 20681) is an expensive western-style hotel with air-conditioning, restaurant and so on. Singles cost from Rs 120 to 180, doubles from Rs 180 to 300. The KSTDC *Tourist Home* is similar to the one at Somnathpur and doubles with attached bathroom cost Rs 25. Finally there's a

Travellers' Bungalow for which reservations are made with the Executive Engineer, Krishnarajasagar.

Shivasamudram

India's first hydro-electric power station was built here at the Cauvery River falls in 1902. Shivasamudram is 80 km east of Mysore, beyond Somnathpur. The twin falls known as Gaganachukki and Bharchukki drop nearly 100 metres in a series of cascades.

THE HOYSALA TEMPLES & THE JAIN PILGRIMAGE CENTRE
Belur & Halebid

The temples at Belur and Halebid along with that at Somnathpur, east of Mysore, are the cream of what remains of one of the most artistically exuberant periods of Hindu cultural development. These temples are superb and, as far as their sculptural decoration goes, even rival the temples of Khajuraho and Konarak. They also rival the best of Gothic art to be found anywhere in Europe. Amazing though they all are, the wealth of sculptural detail found on the Hoysaleswara temple at Halebid makes it easily the most outstanding example of Hoysala art. Every cm of the outside walls of this temple and much of the interior is covered with an endless variety of Hindu deities, sages, stylised animals and birds and friezes depicting the life and times of the Hoysala rulers. No two are alike. Scenes from war, hunting, agriculture, music, dancing and some very sensual material explicitly portraying the apres-temple activities of the dancing girls are all represented here, together with a huge Nandi (Shiva's bull) and a monolithic Jain statue of Lord Gomateshvara.

The Hoysala temples are squat and low, more human in scale than the soaring temples found elsewhere in India. What they lack in size they make up in the sheer intricate detail of their sculptures. They were carved from a soap stone which is relatively soft and easily cut when first quarried, but with age and exposure gradually hardens. The Hosaleswara Temple at Halebid was constructed about 10 years after the temple at Belur but despite 80 years labour it was never finally completed. There is also a smaller temple, the Kedareswara, at Halebid.

At Belur the Channekeshava Temple is the only one at the three Hoysala sites which is still used as a functioning temple. Non-Hindus are allowed inside. In design it is very similar to the others but here much of the decoration has gone into the internal supporting pillars and lintels and larger, but still very delicately carved, images of deities and guardian beast. As at Halebid the external walls are covered in friezes. The other, lesser, Hoysala temples here are the Channigaraya and the Viranarayana.

The Hoysalas, who ruled this part of the Deccan between the 11th and 13th centuries, had their origins in the hill tribes of the Western Ghats and were for a long time feudatories of the Chalukyas. They did not become fully independent until about 1190 AD though they first rose to prominence under their leader Tinayaditya (1047-78 AD) who took advantage of the waning power of the Gangas and Rashtrakutas. Under Bittiga (1110-52 AD), better known by his later name of Vishnuvardhana, they began to take off on a course of their own and it was during his reign that the temples of Belur and Halebid were built.

The times were one of great religious upheaval with the Jain faith being predominant due to the patronage of the Chalukyas and the Gangas and although tolerance of other sects was usually practised, religious persecution was not unknown. Bittiga's predecessors and he himself in his earlier years was a devout Jain who encouraged one of his generals, Gangaraja, to restore the Jain temples destroyed by the Shaivite Chola invaders from the south-east. Later in his reign he came under the influence of the famous saint, Ramanuja, who converted him to faith in Vishnu. As a result of this conversion he adopted the name of Vishnuvardhana and devoted himself to erecting temples honouring his new creed but continued to show tolerance for other religious sects. Indeed there are records of him making grants to Shaivite and Jain temples and of his making a pilgrimage to Sravanabelagola even after his conversion. Vishnuvardhana's conversion was one of the main factors which led to a decline of Jainism but it was not the only one. Corruption among the priesthood and the public defeat of the Jain texts by Ramanuja also undermined its influence but it was by no means extinguished and at least one of Vishnuvardhana's wives and a daughter continued to practice that faith. Later Hoysala rulers also continued to patronise the religion. This normally easy co-existence between Shaivites, Vaishnavites and Jainas explains why you will find images of all these various sects' gods, their consorts and associated companions in Hoysala temples.

The early temples of this dynasty naturally closely followed the style of those of their Chalukyan overlords but by Bittiga's time they had developed a distinctive style of their own. Typically, it is a relatively small star-shaped structure set on a platform to give it some height and in which most of the attention is devoted to sculptural embellishment. It's quickly apparent from a study of these sculptures that the arts of music and dancing reached a high point in grace and perfection during their time. As with Kathakali dancing in Kerala, this was used to express religious fervour, the joy of a victory in

battle or simply for domestic pleasure but there the similarity ends since it's obvious these were times of a relatively high degree of sexual freedom and prominent female participation in public affairs. Most books written by Indians which describe these temples and the ones at Khajuraho bend over backwards to play down the sensuality of these sculptures. Quite why they're so embarrassed about them is hard to fathom. Perhaps it just reflects the repressed attitudes of the average urban Indian today regarding all matters physical. Of course a century ago our Victorian ancestors were also slightly shocked by some Indian temples!

Both temples are open every day. Entry to Belur costs Rs 0.50 plus a 10p tip for the shoe minder. There is no charge for photography. A spotlight is available inside to enable you to see the sculptural work (it's quite dark otherwise) but if it's not already turned on then you'll be charged Rs 2 for the privilege. Entry to Halebid is free though, as at Belur, it's customary to tip the shoe minder 10p. This temple is now maintained by the Archaeological Survey of India and there is a small museum adjacent to the temple though it's of little interest after you've seen the latter. It does, however, sell excellent postcards of the temple and the one at Belur for Rs 0.50 each. The attendant who works here will attempt to waylay you before you get to the museum and sell you the same postcards for Rs 1 each. Where else but India?!

Places to Stay

Though Halebid was once the capital city of the Hoysala rulers it is now little more than a rural village. Belur is just a small town. Accommodation facilities are available in both places. At Halebid there are KSTDC *Tourist Cottages* adjoining the temple where rooms cost Rs 16 a single and Rs 20 a double with attached bathrooms and clean sheets.

It's a very pleasant place to stay and there are catering facilities. There is nowhere to stay in the village. Note that there is a sign in the centre of the village which indicates the temple as being 1.6 km away. Someone obviously can't measure since it's only 500 metres.

At Belur there are KSTDC *Tourist Cottages* 200 metres from the temple at the same price as the Halebid Cottages but they have no catering facilities (there are plenty of small cafes in the town). In addition to these there is a *Travellers' Bungalow* and two fairly basic hotels, the *New Hotel Gayatri* and the *Tourist Hotel.* Both have attached restaurants and are two minutes' walk from the bus stand.

Though it's obviously possible to stay in either place — and this would be a good idea if you wanted to spend a day at each temple — most people use Hassan as a base. Arsikere is another possibility. We cover accommodation and transport facilities at both of these places later in this section.

Sravanabelagola

One of the oldest and most important Jain pilgrimage centres in India and site of the huge statue of Lord Bahubali (Gomateshvara) which, at 17 metres high and carved out of a single piece of rock, is said to be the world's tallest monolithic statue. It stands on top of the rocky hill known as Indragiri, below which the small town of Sravanabelagola nestles, and is visible even at a distance of 25 km. Its simplicity is in complete contrast to the complexity of the sculptural work at the temples of Belur and Halebid.

Sravanabelagola has a long historical pedigree going back to the 3rd century BC when Chandra Gupta Maurya came here with his guru, Bhagwan Bhadrabahu Swami, after renouncing his kingdom. In the course of time Bhadrabahu's disciples spread his teachings all over the region and thus firmly established Jainism in the south. The religion found powerful patrons in the Gangas who ruled the southern part of what is now Karnataka between the 4th and 10th centuries and it was during this time that Jainism reached the zenith of its influence. Indeed it was during the reign of the Ganga king Rachamalla that the statue of Lord Bahubali was created. It was commissioned by a military commander in the service of Rachamalla and executed by the sculptor Aristanemi in 981 AD.

Legend has it that Bahubali was the youngest son of the Jain Emperor, Adi Thirthankara Vrishabha Deva, who ruled over a kingdom in northern India and later became the first Jain saint. When Vrishabha Deva renounced his kingdom and retired to the forest to perform penance, a bitter struggle for succession broke out among his two sons, Bahubali and Bharatha. The battle culminated in a duel between the two brothers in which Bahubali emerged the victor but in his moment of triumph he realised the futility of worldly success, gave his kingdom and all his worldly possessions to Bharatha, and retired to the forest to begin a 1000-year penance.

The statue is the subject of the spectacular Mahamastakabhisheka ceremony which takes place once every 12-14 years when the small town of Sravanabelagola (population 5000) becomes a Mecca for thousands of pilgrims and tourists from all over India and abroad. The 1981 festival coincided with the 1000th anniverserary of the erection of the statue and because of this attracted over one million people!! Seven satellite towns had to be constructed to accommodate the extra people and transport was diverted from all over the state! The climax of the Mahamastakabhisheka involves the annointing of Lord Bahubali's head with thousands of potfuls of coconut milk, yoghurt, ghee, bananas, jaggery, dates, almonds, poppy seeds, milk, gold coins, saffron and sandalwood from the top of a scaffolding erected for the purpose. There must be a lot of work for cleaners after this event!

At times other than this, Sravanabelagola reverts to a quiet little country town which is a very pleasant place to stay for a few days. The people are friendly, the pace is unhurried and the place is full of cosy little chai shops.

In addition to the statue of Lord Bahubali — which to get to you have to climb up 614 steps carved out of the sheer rock face of Indragiri Hill — there are several very interesting Jain *bastis* (temples) and *mathas* (monasteries) both in the town and on Chandragiri Hill, the smaller of the two hills between which Sravanabelagola nestles. Two of these — the Bhandari Basti and the Akkana Basti — are in the Hoysala style and a third — the Chandragupta Basti — is believed to have been built by the Emperor Ashoka the Great. They're all well worth a visit.

Information

There is a tourist office in Sravanabelagola a few metres to the left of the entrance to Indragiri Hill. The staff are friendly and helpful and have a good selection of leaflets. Postcards of the statue of Lord Bahubali are on sale here for Rs 1. You can leave your belongings safely in the tourist office while you climb up the hill. There's no charge for this but note that they're closed between 1 pm and 2.15 pm.

Places to Stay

There are only two hotels as such in the town and they are usually full and not at all cheap considering the standard of accommodation they offer. There is a *Tourist Bungalow* at the foot of Indragiri Hill but this too is often full so if you want to stay here for a few days it's best to ask around in the chai shops for a room. There are plenty of people willing to put up travellers for a few rupees or even for nothing. Accommodation is usually a floor, or a bed if you're lucky. The alternative to this is to stay at one of the pilgrims' rest houses all of which are two to three km from the town itself. A room in one of these costs Rs 6. As was pointed out in the section on Belur and Halebid, most people use Hassan as a base.

Getting There

Belur and Halebid are only 16 km apart and can be seen in one day using public transport and starting from Hassan around 9 am. On returning to Hassan there's still time to catch the 6.30 pm bus to Sravanabelagola or a bus to Mysore, Bangalore or Arsikere. It is *not* possible to see Belur, Halebid *and* Sravanabelagola all in one day using public transport. If you don't have a lot of time at your disposal and want to see them all in one day then the best thing to do is to go on one of the tours organised by the KSTDC in Mysore City.

HASSAN

Hassan is probably the most convenient base from which to explore Belur, Halebid and Sravanabelagola. In itself it has little of interest and so will be treated entirely in terms of its accommodation and transport facilities.

Information

The Tourist Office is friendly and helpful and with a good selection of leaflets on places of interest in the area. If you want to stay at the KSTDC Tourist Cottages at either Belur or Halebid book them in advance here.

Places to Stay

Although there are quite a few hotels in Hassan many of them appear to be semi-permanently full. An early check-in is advisable. The alternative is to check with the Tourist Office about the state of the booking at the KSTDC *Tourist Cottages* at Belur and Halebid and, if there's room, to go there.

Hotel Ashok is the best hotel in town and one of the chain of ITDC hotels you will find all over India. Rooms here cost Rs 60 a single and Rs 85 a double both with attached bathroom, clean sheets, etc. There is a restaurant attached.

At the other end of the scale *Hotel Dwaraka* is a very popular hotel which fills up rapidly. Rooms here cost Rs 7 a single and Rs 14 a double with common bathroom and Rs 10 a single and Rs 18 a double with attached bathroom. You're very unlikely to get a room here later in the day. The *Sathyaprakash Hotel* (above the Shanbag Cafe) next door is of a very similar quality. *Prashanth Tourist Home* is a very pleasant little place where rooms cost Rs 9 a single and Rs 16 a double both with attached bathroom. Another popular hotel which fills up rapidly. Watch the steps on the way down to the street — they're hazardous!

Hotel Madhu Nivas is the place to come if you can't find a room at the hotels above. Here rooms cost Rs 9 a single and Rs 15 a double with attached

bathroom. Mosquito nets are provided but clean sheets are not. The upstairs rooms are by far the best and are light and airy. The downstairs rooms are a fair imitation of the Black Hole of Calcutta. All the same, although they may look like they harbour every nasty creepy-crawly under the sun, there are no bugs. There's a passable 'meals' cafe in the basement but it's better to eat at the Shanbag. Other hotels you could try include *Sri Lakshmi Prasanna*, *Hassan Hotel*, *Ilhanes Hotel* and, as a last resort, the *Ashoka Lodge* (this latter is about as basic as you can get).

Places to Eat

Undoubtedly the best place to eat is the *Shanbag Cafe* next to the bus stand. For Rs 2.60 you'll get one of the best set meals in India — a huge plate of rice, chappatis, masala sauces, pickles, curd and as much mixed vegetable as you can eat. They also serve excellent masala dosa and coffee. The cleanest place in town. You can also get a vegetarian set meal in the *Madhu Nivas Hotel* for Rs 2.50 but it's not anywhere near as good. For non-vegetarian food, a good place is the *Three Star Lodge* (mutton curry Rs 3; chappatis Rs 2; onions and lime Rs 1). This is the only place which is open until late — the manager says he stays open until 1.30 am. It's popular with Indian students and young men late at night, friendly staff and good teas. If you want to suck on a beer there are several bars but you won't find a *cold* beer anywhere. A lukewarm beer will cost you between Rs 7.50 and 9 depending on where you go.

Getting Around

Trains Hassan to Mysore (passenger train), departures at 6.30 am, 9.14 am and 4.50 pm. The journey takes 4½ hours and costs Rs 5.60. Hassan to Arsikere (passenger train), departures at 11.30 am, 6.30 pm and 9.35 pm.

Note there are no express trains. The station at Hassan is about two km from the centre of town so if you want a choice of hotels when you get there, hire an auto-rickshaw.

Buses If you're planning on visiting Belur and Halebid in one day, there's no need to return to Hassan after you've seen one of the places as there are buses in either direction between Belur and Halebid.

To Belur there are 18 buses daily. First bus at 6.15 am and the last at 8.30 pm. The journey takes 1½ hours and costs Rs 2.90. Ignore the claim on the timetable about some of the buses being 'express', it's a figment of the imagination.

From Belur there are frequent buses to Halebid. Ask at the bus stand in Belur but once the bus arrives don't hang about. There is always a mad rush. This bus takes about half an hour and costs Rs 0.90.

To Halebid there are nine buses daily. First bus at 7.30 am and the last bus at 7 pm. The journey takes two hours and costs 2.10 (it's a dirt-track most of the way hence the two-hour journey).

If you went to Belur in the morning and Halebid in the early afternoon, there's a bus back to Hassan from Halebid at about 3.30 pm. Just hang

A man pummeling a slice of melon rind with implements of torture. To what end I cannot say, but he could 'do' 300 an hour

around in the centre of the village — several chai shops.

To Sravanabelagola there are three buses daily at 5.30 am, 9 am and 6.30 pm. It costs Rs 4 going there and Rs 3.60 on the way back. They must reckon that having made the effort you deserve a bonus. The journey takes 1½ hours. Going back to Hassan, there is a bus at 3.30 pm. If you miss the direct buses back to Hassan take a bus (frequent) to Channarayapatna. There are plenty of buses from there to Hassan until late. There is also a direct bus from Sravanabelagola to Mysore at 1 pm (among others).

To Arsikere buses depart many times daily though the exact times are hard to acertain as the bus schedule is entirely in Kanada. The journey takes about 1¼ hours along a good road and costs Rs 3.10.

In addition to the above there are at least 20 buses daily to Mysore and the same number to Bangalore.

ARSIKERE

Like Hassan, this is a convenient base from which to explore the temples of Belur and Halebid and the Jain centre of Sravanabelagola but, unlike Hassan, it has a Hoysala temple of its own. Unfortunately, much of the temple has been defaced and vandalised and many contemporary structures have been added so it's no longer very representative. Arsikere is also a railway junction where express trains to Bangalore and Bombay (via Miraj) can be taken.

Places to Stay

Fairly basic accommodation only is available in Arsikere. The *Tourist Lodge* is on B H Rd, one minute from the bus stand and about five minutes from the station and is probably the best of the hotels in Arsikere. Rooms here cost Rs 7 a single and Rs 12 a double with attached bathroom, fan and clean top cover on the bed. Possessions left in the rooms are secure. The rooms are pleasantly decorated and the bathrooms are clean though decorated with amusing graffiti from aspiring Indian romantic poets who seem to have read too much Shelley. Coffee is brought round at about 7 am. Friendly management though they seem perplexed at the sight of a westerner in this backwater.

New Gayitri Lodge, B H Rd directly in front of you as you come to the end of the road leading from the station, has rooms for Rs 5 a single and Rs 10 a double. It's not as pleasant as the Tourist Lodge. *Janatha Hotel* is next door to the Gayitri Lodge and the same price,

pretty basic. *Sri Raghavendra Lodge* is the first building on the left after leaving the railway station. A quiet pleasant place which costs the same as the Gayitri and has a vegetarian cafe downstairs.

Places to Eat

Prasanna Hotel is probably the best of the vegetarian places. They serve standard 'meals' and tiffin. Masala dosa and two coffees cost Rs 2.50. *Rathin Hotel* is next door to the Prasanna. Their 'meals' are OK but they won't give you extra vegetables — a very unusual occurrence in southern India. *Hotel Majestic* is a Muslim non-vegetarian cafe which serves food at very reasonable prices. Open late — at least until 11.30 pm — for food and tea.

Getting There

Rail There is no sleeping accommodation quota on the Bangalore-Miraj Mail at Arsikere. Arsikere-Bangalore is about Rs 45 in 1st class, Rs 10 in 2nd. If you're heading for Mysore there are several passenger trains daily. If you're trying to get from Arsikere to Hospet (for the Vijayanagar ruins at Hampi), take the passenger trains as far as Harihar and then a bus from there. The bus station at Harihar is just opposite the railway station.

Bus The bus schedule here is entirely in Kanada which is bad new if you've just mastered the rudiments of Tamil or Hindi (or Malayalam or Telugu or . . . . .) but there are plenty of buses. Just ask. People here are very friendly!

COORG & THE SOUTH-WEST

Until 1956, when it was included in Karnataka, Coorg was a mini-state in its own right. A mountainous area, Coorg is in the south-west of Karnataka, bordering with Kerala.

Mercara (population 25,000)

The small town of Mercara is the capital of Coorg and stands 124 km west of Mysore. There is a fort here which has played an important part in Karnataka's tumultous history and also the Omareswara Temple. This region, where the western ghats start to tumble down towards the sea, is green, scenic and fertile and an important coffee growing area. The view from the Raja's Seat is wonderful.

Places to Stay Mercara is a very pleasant hill station and a double room at the *Tourist Home* costs Rs 20.

Nagarhole
This 18 square km wildlife sanctuary is in the south-east of Coorg. Elephant rides are available in the early morning and the best time to visit the sanctuary is from October to May. Accommodation can be booked in Mysore, see 'Useful Addresses' under Mysore.

Mangalore (population 250,000)
The west coast railway line through Kerala crosses the border into Karnataka and terminates at this port. At one time Mangalore was a port of great importance and was the major seaport and shipbuilding centre of Hyder Ali's kingdom. Even today it is a major centre for the export of coffee and cashew nuts. The Sultan's Battery, the old lighthouse and nearby St Aloysius College Chapel are all worth seeing. There's a good view from Kadri Hill and temples such as Shri Yogeshwar Math are nearby. There may still be a shipping service which makes its way, with many stops, along the coast between Mangalore and Bombay.

Places to Stay *Nirmal Lodge*, near the bus stand, has single rooms at Rs 10. The government *Tourist Home* at Kadri

Hills, about three km away and just opposite the All India Radio Station, has rooms at Rs 10/15 for singles/doubles and also a Rs 4 dorm. At the other end of the scale there's the *Motimahal Luxury Hotel* (tel 25611) on Falnir Rd and the *Summer Sands Beach Resort* (tel 53) at Ullal, five km from Mangalore. Good vegetarian meals are served upstairs at the *Taj Mahal Restaurant* near the bus stand for Rs 3.

Near Mangalore
If you liked Sravanabelagola and would like to visit other famous Jain pilgrimage centres there are several of them fairly close to Mangalore.

Dharmastala Situated a little south of the Mangalore-Belur road, about half way between the two, there are a number of Jain bastis including the famous Manjunatha temple. There is also a 14 metre high statue of Lord Bahubali which was erected in 1973.

Venur Midway between Mangalore and Dharmastala, 41 km from the latter, there are eight bastis here and the ruins of a Mahadeva temple. An 11 metre high statue of Lord Bahubali stands on the south bank of the Gurupur River, where it was installed in 1604.

Mudbidri There are 18 bastis, the oldest of which is the Chandranatha Temple with its 1000 richly carved pillars, at this site 22 km from Venur.

Karkala A further 31 km north of Mudbidri there are several important temples and a 13 metre high statue of Lord Bahubali which was completed in 1432.

JOG FALLS
Near the coast, 348 km north-west of Mysore at the terminus of the Birur railway line, the Jog falls are the highest falls in India. The Shiravati River drops

260 metres in four distinctly separate falls known as the Rani, the Rocket, the Raja and the Roarer. During the dry season the falls can be very disappointing and during the wet they may be

totally obscured by mist. The best time to see them is just after the monsoon finishes.

Places to Stay *Hotel Woodlands* (tel 22) or the Karnataka Government *Youth* *Hostel* which has dormitory accommodation. There is also an electricity board *Guest House* and a Power Corporation *Guest House* since there is a major hydro-electric power plant nearby.

UP THE COAST

There are a number of good beaches and interesting small ports along the coast from Mangalore to Goa. Ullal beach is only five km from Mangalore itself.

Udipi Further up the coast from Mangalore is Udipi, where the 13th century Shri Krishna temple is located. There's also a *Tourist Bungalow* here.

Malpe Only five km from Udipi, Malpe has a good beach, swimming and fishing.

Marvanthe There's another good beach here, nine km from Coondapur.

Gokarna This is an important pilgrimage place due to the Mahabaleshwara Temple.

Karwar Only a short distance south of Goa, 56 km north of Gokarna, Karwar has excellent beaches. You can make trips up the Kali River from Karwar and there's an *Inspection Bungalow* (tel 305) for accommodation. Between 1638 and 1752 there was an English factory involved in the pepper trade at Karwar.

Inland from Karwar Near Yallapur on the Hubli-Karwar road are the Magod Falls (*Tourist Home* nearby) and the Lal Guli Falls.

OTHER PLACES IN CENTRAL KARNATAKA

Chitradurga

On the Bangalore-Hampi road Chitradurga has a famous fort of the Naik Pallegars (chieftains) of the 17th and 18th centuries.

Harihar

On the Bangalore-Hubli railway line, Harihar has a Hoysala temple dating from 1223. Shri Harihareswara was later added to in 1268 by Soma, who built Somnathpur near Mysore. The image in the temple is of Harihar, half-Shiva, half-Vishnu. There is a *Travellers Bungalow* here.

Gadag

There are a number of interesting temples in this cotton growing town south of Badami. The Shiva temple of Trimbakeswar (or Trikuteswar) the 'Lord of the Three Peaks' is elaborately carved and in the back of the enclosure is the Temple of Saraswati with a porch supported by extremely elegant pillars.

Lakkandi

Only 13 km south-east of Gadag, Lakkandi also has a number of interesting temples including the fine Kashi Vishwanath Temple, the Nandeswar Temple and the partially ruined, but very finely carved, Iswara Temple. Near the latter temple, which is thought to have been built by the architect and sculptor of Halebid, is a fine baoli or well. Beyond this is a temple to Manikeswar, another name for Krishna.

HAMPI – THE VIJAYANAGAR RUINS

Hampi (Vijayanagar) was once the capital of the largest Hindu empire in Indian history. Founded by the Telugu princes, Harihara and Bukka, in 1336 it reached the height of its power under Krishnadevaraya (1509-29) when it controlled the whole of the peninsula

Hampi Ruins (Vijayanagar)

Narahari Brindavana

Purandaradasara Mandapa

Vishnu Temple
Vittala Temple

Old Stone Bridge

King's Balance

Rama Temple

Talarigattu Gate

Tungabhadra River

Canal

Virupaksha Temple
Hemokuta Temple

Hampi Bazar

Sule Bazar

Achyutaraya Temple

Siva Temple

Kampli

Krishna Temple
Narasinha Colossus

Vishnu Temple

Chandikeswara Temple

Hanuman Temple

Malyavanta Raghunatha Temple

Lotus Mahal & Watch Tower

Underground Temple

Elephant Stables

Ganesha Temple

Hampi Power House

Hazara Rama Temple

Palace area

Mint

Queen's Bath

Siva Temple

Bhima's Gate

Domed Gate

Virabhadra Temple

P.W.D. Bungalow

Museum

Basavanna Temple

Kamalapura Village

Pattabhirama Temple

Hospet

Nagareswara Temple

Scale

0   1   2 km

south of the Krishna and Tungabhadra Rivers except for a string of commercial principalities along the Malabar coast. Comparable to Delhi in the 14th century, the city covered an area of 33 square km, was surrounded by seven concentric lines of fortification and was reputed to have had a population of about half a million. It maintained a mercenary army of over one million according to the Persian Ambassador, Abdul Razak, which included Moslem

mounted archers to defend itself from the Moslem states to the north.

Its wealth was based on control of the spice trade to the south and the cotton industry of the south-east and its busy bazaars, described by such European travellers as Nunez and Paes, were centres of international commerce. The religion was a hybrid of current Hinduism with the gods Vishnu and Shiva being lavishly worshipped in the orthodox manner though, as in the Hoysala kingdom, Jainism was also prominent. Brahmins were privileged, sati (the burning of widows on the funeral pyre of their husband) was widely practised and temple prostitution common. Brahmini inscriptions which have been discovered on the site date the first settlement here back to the 1st century AD and suggest that there was a Buddhist centre nearby.

The empire çame to a sudden end in 1565 after the disastrous battle of Talikota when the city was ransacked by the confederacy of Deccan Sultans (Bidar, Bijapur, Golkonda, Ahmadnagar and Berar) thus opening up southern India for conquest by the Moslems.

Hampi is set in a strange and beautiful landscape — hill country strewn with enormous rounded boulders — with the Tungabhadra River running through the centre of it. It has a certain magic quality to it and the ruins are superb though scattered over quite a large area. It is possible to see all the main sites in one day on foot if you start early but a hired bicycle would make life a lot easier. Signposting on the site is somewhat inadequate and a lot of the land between the ruins is planted out with sugar cane and other crops. All the same, even where the trail is indistinct there are plenty of cattle and goat tracks so you can't really get lost. Probably the most interesting sites are the Vittala Temple with its famous stone chariot, musical pillars and incredible sculptural work; the Purandara Dasara Mandapa (the riverside temple) with the ruined stone bridge nearby which used to span the Tungabhadra River; the Sule and Hampi Bazaars (the latter partially occupied by squatters — a surreal sight!); Achutaraya Temple; the Palace area with its Dasara Platform, Lotus Mahal, Elephant Stables and Watchtower; the Hazarama Temple, and the Queen's Bath.

Information & Orientation
There are no booklets for sale about Hampi or the Vijayanagar Empire anywhere at Hampi or Hospet. The only thing that's available is a very vague coloured sketch map of the ruins which costs Rs 0.50. There are good maps of the area (put up by the Archaeological Survey of India) in Hampi Bazaar, next to the Lotus Mahal in the Palace area and outside the Archaeology Office at Kamalapuram.

Hampi is 13 km from Hospet, the town which most people use as a base. There are two main points of entry to the ruins — Hampi Bazaar and Kamalapuram — and buses run to these two points from Hospet frequently. As an alternative to the buses you could hire a bicycle in Hospet. Having access to the latter would definitely make the going easier since there is no transport between the various sites. If you're walking, expect to cover at least seven km just to see the main sites. It is possible to see most of the ruins in a day though two days would allow a more leisurely pace.

Places to Stay
If you'd prefer to stay near the ruins rather than in Hospet there are two possibilities. The most convenient place is the PWD *Inspection Bungalow* at Kamalapuram opposite the Archaeological Office. It's a pleasant little place and you can stay here for Rs 4 in the dormitory. A chowkidar is available to cook meals. There's rarely anyone staying here but if you want to make sure check with the Assistant Engineer, PWD No 2 Division, Hospet (tel 8754). The other place is the *Hampi Power Station Guest House*, three km from Kamalapuram. Again, the chances are that you'll get in without prior reservation but if you want to make sure contact Superintending Engineer, HES,

Tungabhadra Board, Tungabhadra Dam, Hospet (tel 8272). There are also plenty of suitable places where you could camp among the ruins. There are a number of simple cafes in Kamalapuram where you could get a meal. Elsewhere there is a *Government Tourist Canteen* between the Hazarama Temple and the Palace site which has a *very* limited menu

(onion omelettes for Rs 2.50. Bread also available) and ice-cold beers for Rs 11. There is also a simple cafe in Hampi Bazaar and a chai shop next to the Varaha Temple near Sule Bazaar — a very friendly little place. Fruit sellers usually hang around between the King's Balance and the Vittala Temple.

HOSPET

Most people who come to see the Vijayanagar ruins at Hampi use Hospet as a base. It's a fairly typical Karnataka country town with dusty roads, plenty of bullock carts, bicycles and dilapidated buses with an unobtrusive industrial area near the Tungabhadra Dam. For much of the year it's not a particularly interesting place in itself but, because it has a large Moslem population, it comes alive during the festival of Moharam. If you're here at this time don't miss the firewalkers who walk barefoot across the red-hot embers of a bonfire that's been going all day and night. Virtually the whole town turns out to watch or take part and excitement gets to fever pitch around midnight. The preliminaries which go on all day appear to be a bewildering hybrid of Moslem and Hindu ritual and quite unlike any other festival I've ever seen in the Moslem world. It's well worth staying up half the night to witness.

Information

Tourist Information Office, Station Rd. Friendly people with a good selection of information. Their duplicated handout on Hospet, Hampi and Tungabhadra is pretty comprehensive but the map of the Vijayanagar ruins on the back page is a joke.

Places to Stay

Malligi Tourist Home, off Hampi Rd (tel 8377). Definitely the pleasantest hotel in town and, for the price, a bargain. Rooms cost Rs 10 a single, Rs 20 a double, Rs 25 a triple and Rs 30 a four-bed room all with attached bathrooms, clean sheets, fan and mosquito nets. The rooms are pleasantly decorated, there's running hot water between 6 am and 10 am and the management are very friendly. They also have two air-con rooms for Rs 40 a double. There is a vegetarian cafe attached which serves excellent meals (rice, puris (6), papadum

(3), masala sauces (2), vegetables (2), curd and two coffees came to Rs 4.50. A bargain).

Hotel Sandarshan, Station Rd (tel 8574) has rooms for Rs 8 a single and Rs 16-18 a double both with attached bathroom. It's convenient for the railway station and bus station but the rooms are not as pleasant as the Malligi. Vegetarian restaurant attached. *Hotel Mayura*, Gandhi Chowk, opposite the GPO (tel 8418) has rooms at Rs 5 a single with common bathroom, Rs 8 a single and Rs 14 a double both with attached bathrooms. There is a vegetarian restaurant downstairs.

Lokare Lodge, Station Rd (tel 8447) is a pleasant lodge but somewhat overpriced at Rs 6-8 a single with common bathroom, Rs 12 a single and Rs 20 a double with attached bathrooms. *MRK Lodge*, opposite the Old Bus Stand (tel 8780) cost Rs 5 a single and Rs 10 a double with attached bathrooms but there's no hot water and the management won't fetch you a bucketful even if you offer to pay. Fairly basic rooms with indifferent decor but there are good views from the roof. *Shanbag Hotel*, New Bus Stand, costs Rs 7 a single with common bathroom and Rs 12 a double with attached bathroom. There is also a dormitory for Rs 3 a bed.

In addition to the above there are the *Railway Retiring Rooms* (Rs 8 a double), *Pampa Lodge*, Station Rd (Rs 8 a single and Rs 14 a double with attached bath), *Janatha Lodge* (Rs 4 a single and Rs 8 a double with common bath) and the *Naga Lodge*, down a side street off Main Bazaar (Rs 6 a single and Rs 15 a double, latter with attached bath).

Remember that if you want to stay near the ruins at Hampi there are two possibilities for accommodation at Kamalapuram — see introductory section. There is also the *Tourist Home* near the Tungabhadra Dam.

Railway
Station

Canal

Vijayanagar Canal

Hotel Sandarshan

Station Road

Bellary Road

Canal

Tourist
Office

Malligi
Tourist
Home

New
Bus Stand
Shanbag
Lodge

Prabhu
Hotel

Tungabhadra
Dam

Nagarjuna
Restaurant

Lokare Hotel
Pampa Lodge

Sunder Lodge
Hotel Mayura

Post Office

Vegetable Market

Old
Bus Stand

Pai Hotel

Woodlands Hotel
Hotel Apsara

MRK Lodge

Naga
Lodge

Sathyasaibaba
Lodge

Tungabhadra
Dam

Main Bazaar

Harpanahalli
Harihar

Old Muddar Road

Hospet

Hampi
Kamalapur
Bellary

Places to Eat

For vegetarian set meals you can't beat those at the restaurant in the *Malligi Tourist Home* (restaurant open to non-residents). Another restaurant where you can get very good vegetarian set meals is the *Pai Hotel* near the MRK Lodge. For non-vegetarian food try the *Nagarjuna Bar & Restaurant* at the junction of Gandhi Chowk and Station Rd. This latter also sells ice-cold beer for Rs 8.50. If you like *plenty* of ginger in your food, try the *Prabhu Hotel*, Hampi Rd (not to be confused with the restaurant at the Malligi which has the same name).

Getting There

Trains The railway station in Hospet is a long walk (about 15 minutes) from the centre of town. Rickshaws quote Rs 1-2. The station has a healthy quota allotted them for express trains between Hubli and Bangalore and they are rarely booked up more than one day in advance.

If you're heading for Bijapur after Hospet note that there are no direct buses. You can get there by rail by taking any of the trains going west and changing at Gadag. The journey from Gadag to Bijapur (via Badami) by rail is very slow but there's usually plenty of entertainment en route in the form of buskers! If you're heading for Badami take the same route. This latter journey by rail takes four hours and costs Rs 9.15 (2nd Class).

Buses To Badami there is one bus daily at 7 am, it's quicker than the train. To Bangalore there are eight express buses daily, first bus at 6.30 am and the last at 11.45 pm. There is also a 'Tourist Bus' to Bangalore daily at 8.15 pm which is bookable from the agent next door but one to the MRK Lodge. This bus costs Rs 28.

To Bellary there are buses approximately every hour from 6.45 am until 8 pm. To Davangere there are six buses daily, first bus at 5 am and the last at 3.35 pm. To Hubli, two buses daily at 2.15 am and 4.45 pm. To Hyderabad, one express bus daily at 1.30 pm. To Karwar, one bus daily at 9 am. To Shimoga, three buses daily at 6.15 am, 12.45 pm and 3.15 pm. The last two are expresses.

Getting Around

To Hampi Frequent buses from Platform 10 at the New Bus Stand. Costs Rs 1.30 and takes 20-30 minutes. The terminus is at Hampi Bazaar but you can also get down at Kamalapuram and walk into the ruins from there (in which case the bus fare is Rs 0.90). Taxis from Kamalapuram to Hospet cost Rs 1 per person and go when full (they take four or five people).

To Tungabhadra Dam Frequent buses from Platform 12 at the New Bus Stand. (The buses have 'TB Dam' on the front). Costs Rs 0.40 and takes 15 minutes. If you find yourself waiting a long time for a bus back to Hospet from the dam, walk down to the junction at the bottom. There are more frequent buses to and from there.

Tungabhadra Dam

If you've ever spent any time browsing through Indian tourist literature you'll know that the Indians love their dams and will go into the most breathless eulogies to put them on the tourist map and project their unsurpassed potential as 'picnic spots'. Possibly it comes from living in a country where famine was always just around the corner when there were were no facilities to compensate for a failed monsoon. Whatever the reason Tungabhadra gets the same treatment but if you've seen dams before now this one isn't going to radically alter your appreciation of them. If you've already visited Hampi and have time to spare then it's worth a visit as there's very little else of note to see in

Hospet.

The literature makes the dubious claim that it's the largest masonry dam in the world. It is 2421 metres long and 49 metres high and has created a lake some 370 square km in surface area. It was begun in 1945 and completed in 1953 at a cost of over Rs 1,080,000,000. It's used to generate electricity and to irrigate Bellary and Raichur in Karnataka and Cuddapa and Kurnool districts in Andhra Pradesh.

Places to Stay

Naturally, a *Tourist Home* has been built below the dam where tourists are encouraged to stay but it's very inconvenient for anything other than the dam. Rooms here cost Rs 10 a single, Rs 18 a double and Rs 25 a triple all with attached bathroom. There's also a multistar western-style hotel, the *Vaikunta Guest House*, overlooking the dam on the hill top. There are frequent buses to the dam from the bus station in Hospet.

THE CHALUKYAN CAVES & TEMPLES — BADAMI, PATTADAKAL & AIHOLE

Set in beautiful countryside amongst red sandstone hills, rock-hewn 'tanks' (artificial lakes) and peaceful farmlands these three small rural villages were once the capital cities of the Chalukyan Empire which ruled much of the central Deccan between the 4th and 8th centuries AD. Here you can see some of the earliest and finest Dravidian temples and rock-cut caves whose forms and sculptural work provided inspiration for the later Hindu empires which rose and fell in the southern part of the peninsula before the arrival of the Moslems. Though principally promoters of the Vedic culture, the Chalukyans were tolerant of all sects and elements of Shaivism, Vaishnavism, Jainism and even Buddhism can be found in many of their temples and especially in the rock-cut caves at Badami.

At Aihole, the capital between the 4th and 7th centuries, can be seen Hindu temple architecture in its embryonic stage from the earliest Ladkhan Temple to the later and more complex structures like the Kunligudi and Durgigudi Temples. The Durgigudi is particularly interesting and probably unique in India being circular in shape and surmounted by a primitive gopuram — those structures which typify the temples throughout Tamil Nadu. There are over 70 structures in and around this village which stand witness to the vigourous experimentation in temple architecture undertaken by the Chalukyans. Most are in a good state of preservation.

Badami, magnificently nestled in a canyon and the later capital from about 540 until 757 AD when the Chalukyans were overthrown by the Rashtrakutas, is famous for its rock-cut temples. Cut into the cliff-face of the red sandstone hill and overlooking the picturesque tank of Agastyatirtha (itself constructed in the 5th century), these caves display the full range of religious sects which have grown up on Indian soil. There are five caves altogether, four of them artificial and one natural, all connected by flights of steps. Of the rock-cut temples, two are dedicated to Vishnu, one to Shiva and the fourth is a Jain temple. The natural cave is a Buddhist temple. Fragments of a fresco in the upper Vaishnavite temple show that the art of painting had reached a similar stage of perfection as sculpture and it's probably that most of the images in these caves were painted at the time of their creation.

The caves are only one of the many things to be seen at Badami. All over the sides and tops of the hills which enclose the tank on three sides are temples and fortifications, carvings and inscriptions dating not just from the Chalukyan period but from other times when its value as a fortress site has been appreciated. After it fell to the Rashtra-kutas, Badami was occupied successively by the Chalukyans of Kalyan (a seperate branch of the Western Chalukyas), the Kalachuryas, the Yadavas of Devagiri, the Viyanagar Empire, the Adil Shahi kings of Bijapur and the Marathas. All these various rulers have left their mark at Badami and there's even a Pallava inscription dating back to 642 AD when their king Narasimhavarman briefly overwhelmed the Chalukyans and occupied Badami for 13 years before being driven out again. Of these other monuments, some of the most beautiful are the two groups of lake-side temples (known as the Bhutanatha temples). Reflected in the water of the tank they're a most enchanting sight and have the simplicity and freshness found also in the very early Pallava temples at Mahaballipuram south of Madras. The Archaeological Museum on the north side of the tank is also well worth a visit It houses some superb examples of sculpture collected locally and some remarkable images of a fertility cult which flourished in the area — the Lajja-Gauri images.

Pattadakal reached the height of its glory during the 7th and 8th centuries when most of the temples here were built. It was not only the second capital of the Badami Chalukyas but the place where all coronations took place. The most important monument here, the Lokeshwari or Virupaksha Temple, is a huge structure whose sculptures narrate episodes from the Hindu epics, the Ramayana and Mahabharata, as well as throwing a lot of light on the social life of the early Chalukyans. The other main temple, the Mallikarjuna Temple, has sculptures which tell a different story — this time from the Bhagavata, the story of Lord Krishna. The old Jain temple with its two stone elephants about one kilometre from the centre is also worth visiting.

Information & Orientation

Badami, Pattadakal and Aihole are located fairly close to each other and can be visited from a single base which can either be Badami or Aihole or, if you're concerned to have a better class of accommodation, from Bagalkot. There are no accommodation facilities at Pattadakal. Both Badami and Bagalkot are on the railway line which runs from Gadag to Bijapur. Service buses connect Badami, Pattadakal and Aihole but you deserve a medal for tenacity and endurance if you can locate the right bus.

Badami railway station is five km from the village itself and a tonga from outside the station will cost you Rs 2 to 2.50. The locals pay 60p but you need brown skin, black hair, brown eyes and fluency in Kannada to get it for that! There are also service buses which run between the station and village approximately hourly. It takes a whole day to see the cave temples, ruins and fortifications at Badami. You could see Pattadakal and Aihole on the following day if you start out as early as possible.

It's convenient and pleasant to hire a bicycle to explore these places but bear in mind that the round trip will involve cycling about 100 km. If you're not up to this then you'll need two days. The bicycle shop opposite the tonga stand on the main road in Badami hires bicycles for Rs 4 a day plus a deposit. I was asked for Rs 300 deposit but managed to persuade them that my student card was a passport and left that.

There are no charges for visiting the monuments or the Archaeology Museum but the attendants at the cave temples won't allow flash photography. The so called Archaeological Office on the main road in Badami has a painted sketch map of the Badami-Pattadakal-Aihole area on the wall but nothing else. It appears that the staff (when they're actually around) are paid simply to

Bhutanatha Temples (II)

Bhutanatha Temples (I)

Archeology Museum

Agastyatirtha Tank

Cave Temples

Malagitti Shivalaya Temple

Mosque

Cave Temples

Malagitti Shivalaya Tippu Sultan's Treasury

Railway Sta.

Pattadakal Aihole

Archeological Office

Sri Mahakuteshwar Lodge

Bus Stand

Tonga Stand

Post Office

Badami

Tourist Bungalow

'oversee' the attendants who loaf about at the cave temples and museum. They have no information at all.

At the first cave temple you can buy a copy of *The Cave Temples of Badami* by A M Annigeri for Rs 4. If you'd like more detail about them or about the other monuments at Badami then it's worth buying though it's written in typically verbose Indian English and peppered with nonsense like, 'This shows dwarfs dancing in different poses . . . . . Some of them have interesting hair-styles . . . . . They are also engaged in different activities

. . . . . Visitors forget themselves at the sight of these delightful dwarfs', and, 'These dwarfs are very amusing and create laughter . . . . . These arrest the attention of the visitors.'

Badami

Badami is a small town and, off the main street, full of narrow, winding lanes, old houses, the occasional Chalukyan ruin and tiny squares. It's a pleasant place and people are friendly but the street kids can be incredibly persistent in hassling you for pens and money. They'll follow you down the streets in packs chanting 'Ta, ta!', 'Ta, ta!' or 'One pen!', 'One pen!' Of course you get this elsewhere in India. In most places in fact, but it's the persistence they do it with here that's surprising yet if you meet another traveller here you'll be lucky. Very few come this way.

Places to Stay
There are only two places to stay in Badami (many places are called Something or Other Boarding but, in fact, they have no rooms to let). *KSTDC Tourist Bungalow & PWD Inspection Bungalow* are located about a half km from the centre of town and is undoubtedly the best place to stay. Rooms here cost Rs 10 a single and Rs 20 a double both with attached bathroom. If you're travelling alone and all the single rooms are taken there are no price concessions for a singly occupied double room (as there is in most other places).

Sri Mahakuteshwar Lodge is located next to the bus stand and run by a reincarnation of The Mekon (Dan Dare fans). Rooms cost Rs 5 a single with common bathroom, Rs 10 a single and Rs 20 a double with attached 'bathroom'. The downstairs rooms are a determined attempt to recreate the Black Hole of Calcutta but all the rooms have been painted in the most ugly and depressing combination of colours I've seen anywhere in India. Mosquito nets are provided but since they don't reach the mattress are useless. The locks they provide are a joke (by this time of course you will have acquired one of your own in which case possessions left in the rooms are secure).

There is also a *Travellers Bungalow* close to the railway station but it's very inconvenient for anything other than the trains.

Places to Eat
Probably the best place to eat is the *Hotel Sanman*, next to the Sri Mahak-

uteshwar Lodge. A la carte vegetarian and non-vegetarian meals, cold beers (Rs 10 a bottle), other alcoholic drinks and loud music from current Indian films which the proprietor is loathe to turn down. There are plenty of small cafes especially around the tonga stand on the main road but most of them serve only tiffin. If you want a vegetarian set meal go to either *Sri Veera Bhadreshwar Boarding* or *Sri Raghuvendra Bhavan*. Both these stand opposite one another at the tonga stand and serve meals for Rs 2.50. One of the friendliest tiffin places is the *Udaya Vilas* on the main road.

Getting Around
To Pattadakal & Aihole If you can locate the service bus which will take you to either Pattadakal or Aihole at the bus stand in Badami then you deserve a medal for tenacity and endurance. Either that or you speak fluent Kannada. Every enquiry will produce a different response. In theory you take the Iikal buses of which there are nine daily. The first bus at 8 am and the last at 7.30 pm.

Other buses To Bijapur there is one bus daily at 7 am. To Bagalkot, 13 buses daily, first bus at 7.30 am and the last bus at 7.45 pm. To Hospet, one bus daily at 11 am. To Hubli, four buses daily at 7.30 am, 10 am, 1 pm and 5.15 pm. To Bangalore, two buses daily at 5.30 pm and 7.30 pm. To Gadag, five buses daily, first bus at 7.30 am and the last at 4.50 pm.

Trains All the trains from Badami station are passenger trains. There are no express trains. On the other hand, although the trains are slow, the journeys I made on this line were the liveliest I came across in India. Virtually the whole of the way from Gadag to Bijapur buskers board the train and entertain the passengers. Some of them are excellent, particularly the two women (very unusual to see this in India) who sing Kannada folk songs in harmony to the accompaniment of a harmonium. Judging by the way people delved into their pockets for small change and quietly sang along with them they must have been singing some very popular songs.

The schedule of the trains is as follows:
Hubli-Sholapur, daily at 1.04 am, 10.38 am and 3.18 pm. Sholapur-Hubli, daily at 2.33 am, 11.08 am and 4 pm. Gadag-Sholapur, daily at 5.14 am. Sholapur-Gadag, daily at 9.43 pm. Bijapur-Hubli, daily at 7.32 am. Hubli-Bijapur, daily at 7.22 pm.

If you're heading for Bijapur you can take either the trains for Bijapur or Sholapur. Similarly, if heading for Gadag, you can take either the trains for Gadag or Hubli. The journey from Badami to Bijapur takes 3½ hours and costs Rs 5.55.

Aihole

If you'd like to stay at Aihole accommodation is available at the *KSTDC Tourist Bungalow.* Rooms here cost Rs 10 a single and Rs 20 a double both with attached bathroom. It's of a similar standard to the Tourist Bungalow at Badami.

Service buses connect Aihole with Bagalkot and Badami (latter via Pattadakal). The nearest railway stations are at Bagalkot (46 km) and Badami (51 km).

BIJAPUR (population 120,000)

Bijapur is the Agra of the south, full of ruined and still intact gems of 15th to 17th century Moslem architecture — mosques, mausoleums, palaces and fortifications — and, like Agra, it has its world famous mausoleum, the Golgumbaz. This enormous structure with its vast hemispherical dome, said to be the world's second largest, dominates the landscape for miles around and was built during the reign of Mohammed Adil Shah (1626-1656). The austere grace of the monuments in this city is in complete contrast to the sculptural extravaganza of the Chalukyan and Hoysala temples further south. The Ibrahim Roza mausoleum, in particular, is one of the most beautiful and finely proportioned Islamic monuments anywhere in the world.

Bijapur was the capital of the Adil Shahi kings (1489-1686), one of the five splinter states formed when the Bahmini Moslem kingdom broke up in 1482. The others formed at roughly the same time were Bidar, Golkonda, Ahmednagar and Berar. Like Bijapur, all these places have their own collection of monuments dating from this period though the ones at Bijapur are definitely more numerous and generally in a better state of preservation. The rulers of these states spent their days fighting each other and the Hindus further south with any spare resources being used to build palaces and tombs for themselves and to pay for entertainers at their courts. They did, however, occasionally act in consort and it was a confederacy of these states which in 1565 overthrew the Hindu Vijayanagar Empire at the battle of Talikota, thus eclipsing Hindu rule in the south.

Bijapur is well worth a visit. It's a pleasant garden city, still strongly Moslem in character, and small enough not to be overwhelming. You will need at least two days to see the monuments in a fairly leisurely manner since they are spread out right across the city.

Information & Orientation

The Tourist Office is attached to the KSTDC Tourist Home. They have sketch maps of the city for Rs 0.60

Bijapur

and verbose leaflets which don't tell you a great deal, take up lots of paper and cost Rs 1.20. If you want a guide book to the city, pick up a copy of *Tourist Guide to Bijapur* by H Padmaraj, on sale at many stationers and bookshops for Rs 1.50.

The best place to change money is at the State Bank of India in the public offices in the Citadel. They have the current exchange rates and are fast. Avoid the banks in the old part of the city on the north side of Gandhi Rd (especially the Canara Bank). They'll keep you waiting all morning, tell you a lot of unadulterated garbage and then offer you a rate well below par.

Golgumbaz

The most famous and the largest though not the most beautiful monument in Bijapur, the Golgumbaz is a simple building whose four walls enclose a majestic hall 1704 square metres in area and are buttressed by octagonal seven-storied towers at each of the corners. This basic structure is capped by an enormous dome which is said to be the world's second largest (St Paul's in the Vatican City, Rome, has the largest). All the way around the base of the dome at the top of the hall is a three metre wide gallery known as the 'whispering gallery' since the acoustics here are such that any sound made is repeated 10 times over (some guide books claim it's repeated 12 times over). Fortunately you won't have chance to get embroiled in that controversy as the 'whispering

gallery' is permanently full of kids running amok up there and screaming at the top of their voices. Bedlam gallery would be a more appropriate name. Access to the gallery is via a narrow but, for most of the way, well-lit staircase up the left-hand tower. There's a notice on the wall just before you enter the gallery from outside the dome. It says, 'Silence please'. The views over Bijapur from the base of the dome are superb. You can see virtually every other monument and almost the whole of the city walls from here.

The Golgumbaz is the mausoleum of Mohammed Adil Shah (1626-56), two of his favourite wives, Rambha and Arusbib, one of his daughters and a grandson. Their caskets stand on a raised platform in the centre of the hall though their actual graves are in the crypt, accessible by a flight of steps under the western doorway.

Entrance costs Rs 0.50 except on Sundays when it's free. Shoes have to be left at the entrance.

Ibrahim Roza

Constructed at the height of Bijapur's prosperity by Ibrahim Adil Shah II (1580-1626) for his queen Taj-Sultana, the Ibrahim Roza is one of the most beautiful Islamic buildings you will see anywhere in the world. Unlike the Golgumbaz, which is impressive only for its immensity, here the emphasis is on elegance and delicacy. Its minarets, which rise 24 metres from the ground, are said to have inspired those of the

Taj Mahal. It's also one of the few monuments in Bijapur with substantial stone filigree and other sculpturally decorative work.

Buried here are Ibrahim Adil Shah, his queen, Taj-Sultana, his daughter, two sons, and his mother, Haji Badi Sahiba. There is no entrance charge but shoes should be left on the steps up to the platform on which the mausoleum stands.

Jami-e-Masjid
This is another finely proportioned building with graceful arches, a fine dome and a large inner courtyard containing fountains and a reservoir. It's quite a large monument covering an area of 10,800 square metres and has space for 2250 worshippers. Spaces for them are marked out in black on the polished floor of the mosque. There's very little ornamentation here, the whole concept being one of simplicity. The flat roof is accessible by several flights of stairs. This mosque was constructed by Ali Adil Shah I (1557-80) who was also responsible for erecting the fortified city walls, Gagan Mahal and installing a public water system. There is no charge for entry here.

Asar Mahal
Standing to the east of the citadel, the Asar Mahal was built by Mohammed Adil Shah in about 1646 to serve as a Hall of Justice. The rooms on the upper storey are profusely decorated with fresco paintings, many of them using foliage and flower motifs but some portraying male and female figures in various poses. These latter have all been defaced. The building was also used to house two hairs from the Prophet's beard. The front of the building is graced with a square tank still fed by conduits from Begum Tank.

The Citadel
Located in the centre of the city and

surrounded by its own fortified wall and wide moat, this once contained the palaces, pleasure gardens and Durbar Hall of the Adil Shahi kings. Unfortunately, most of them are now in ruin but some superb fragments remain and it's well worth spending some time wandering around this area. Of the most important fragments, the Gagan Mahal probably gives the best impression of the scale on which things were built here. This monument was built by Ali Adil Shah I around 1561 to serve the double purpose of a royal residence and a Durbar Hall. Essentially it's an enormous hall which was left completely open to the north so that an audience outside the hall would have a full and unobstructive view of the proceedings on the raised platform inside. The hall was flanked by small chambers used to house the families of the royal household. Through suspended screens which enclosed the projecting balconies overhanging the Durbar on all sides, the ladies of the harem were able to witness the proceedings down below. Most of this has now been destroyed but the immense arch which spanned the whole front of the Durbar still stands.

Nearby, the Sat Manzil, Muhammed Adil Shah's seven-storied palace, is now substantially in ruin and the remaining parts of it are used for public offices but just across the road from this stands one of the most delicate pieces of architecture in Bijapur. This is the Jala Manzil or Jala Mandir, a water pavilion no doubt intended as a cool and pleasant place to relax in the days when it was surrounded by secluded courts and gardens within the palace precincts. Opposite the Citadel on the other side of Station Road are the graceful arches of Bara Kaman, the ruined mausoleum of Ali Roza, which is also worth visiting.

Malik-e-Maidan
This huge cannon must be one of the

largest mediaeval guns ever made. It measures over four metres long and almost 1.5 metres in diameter and is estimated to weigh 55 tons! It was cast by Mohammad-bin-Hasan Rumi, a Turkish officer in the service of the king of Ahmednagar, in 1549 from an alloy of copper, iron and tin. It was brought to Bijapur as a trophy of war and set up here with the help of 10 elephants, 400 oxen and hundreds of men. Its outer surface is polished dark green and adorned with inscriptions in Persian and Arabic, one of them attributed to the Moghul Emperor Aurangzeb saying that he subdued this gun whose name means Monarch of the Plains.

Upli Buruj

This watch tower, 24 metres high and located on high ground near the western walls of the city, was built by Hyder Khan, a general in the service of Ali Adil Shah I and of Ibrahim II, in about 1584. The tower can be climbed by a flight of steps which winds around the outside of the building. The top commands a good view of the city and is well furnished with guns, powder chambers and water cisterns. The guns are much longer than the Malik-e-Maidan (nine metres and 8.5 metres respectively) but of much narrower bore — only 29 cm.

Other

There are a number of other monuments worth visiting in Bijapur, the most important of them being the Anand Mahal and the Mecca Masjid, both in the Citadel, and the Mehtar Mahal. This much-photographed latter building is typical of the architecture of Bijapur and has been richly decorated with sculptural work. It serves as an ornamental gateway leading to a small mosque.

Places to Stay

ITDC Travellers Lodge, Station Rd. The literature will have you believe this is the best place to stay in Bijapur. It's certainly the most expensive but as the *KSTDC Tourist Home* just across the road offers a similar quality of accommodation at a fraction of the cost, it's far from the best bargain. Rooms here cost Rs 35 a single and Rs 55 a double both with attached bathroom. They also have a few air-con rooms for Rs 20 a day extra. The building is pleasantly situated in well-maintained flower gardens and has an attached restaurant and bar. Note that the price list for the latter at the entrance is 'out of date' (and has been for quite some time).

KSTDC Tourist Home, located at the entrance to the Citadel just off Station Rd. This is the best deal you'll come across in Bijapur. Rooms cost Rs 10 a single and Rs 18 a double both with attached bathrooms — spotless, tiled and with constant hot water — clean sheets, carpeted rooms, fan, mosquito nets, very friendly staff and a quiet pleasant courtyard ablaze with bougainvillea. There's room service (tea and coffee is remarkably expensive!) and meals can be provided if ordered in advance except breakfast which can be made immediately. Building extensions are in progress and they will soon have a restaurant and bar. The Tourist Office is attached to this hotel.

Hotel Midland, Station Rd, cost Rs 5 a single with common bathroom, Rs 7 a single with own shower but common toilet, Rs 9 a single and Rs 16 a double both with own bathroom and toilet. There is a good vegetarian restaurant downstairs. *Hotel Tourist*, Gandhi Rd (a continuation of Station Rd) cost Rs 10 a single, Rs 15 a double and Rs 20 a four-bedded room, all with attached bathrooms. There is a good 'meals' cafe downstairs but it's not actually part of the hotel.

Mysore Lodge, Station Rd, is next door to the Hotel Midland. If you want basic accommodation, come here. Rooms cost Rs 5 a single and Rs 8 a double with common bathroom, Rs 12 a double with attached bathroom. Extra people can accupy any of the rooms for Rs 2 per person extra. It's a no-frills hotel.

Places to Eat
Good vegetarian set meals can be found in the restaurant attached to the *Hotel Tourist* (lunch and dinner for Rs 2.60. Excellent curd!). There are plenty of other such places along Gandhi Rd. If you're looking for an excellent non-vegetarian meal try the restaurant about two doors up from the Hotel Tourist. Popular with local middle-class people. The *KSTDC Tourist Home* offers breakfasts (omelette and toast) for Rs 2.50 but beware of their pots of tea which cost a staggering Rs 3 (unheard of anywhere else). Even the ITDC *Travellers Lodge* will serve you a pot of tea for Rs 2 and put it in a delightful pewter tea service!).

Getting Around
The most convenient forms of local transport are the auto-rickshaw and the tonga (horse-drawn cart). From the railway station to the Tourist Home will cost Rs 2-2.50 (local people pay Rs 0.60). From the Tourist Home to Ibrahim Roza will cost about Rs 3.50 per person in a tonga (these take four or five people). Haggling is a must.

Getting There
Trains Bijapur station has a healthy quota of sleeping berths allotted to it on all the main trains which pass through Sholapur and Gadag. These are rarely taken up more than one day in advance. Note that the line from Bijapur to Gadag though slow is one of the most entertaining rides you will find in India.

It's the permanent pitch of at least three lots of buskers.

Bijapur to Hubli takes nine hours (it's usually late) and costs Rs 10.15 in 2nd Class. If you're getting on at Sholapur the quotas available at Bijapur are:
Sholapur-Bombay (10 UP), 10 berths; Golgumbaz Express, four berths; Minar Express (Secunderabad-Bombay), four berths; Minar Express (Bombay-Secunderabad), two seats.

Getting on at Gadag the Vijayanagar Express (Bangalore-Hubli), 12 berths; Karnatak Express (Miraj-Bangalore), two berths.

Buses The main bus lines operating from Bijapur on to Aurangabad, two buses daily at 6.15 am and 6.30 pm. To Badami, two buses daily, both at 4 pm (one goes via Kerur). To Bagalkot, six buses daily, first bus at 9 am and the last at 10 pm. Use this as an alternative way of getting to Badami, Aihole and Pattadakal.

To Bangalore, two buses daily at 4 pm and 6 pm. To Belgaum, seven buses daily, first bus at 12.45 am and the last at 11.45 pm. To Bellary, one daily express bus at 7.45 am. Use this bus to get to Hospet and the Vijayanagar ruins at Hampi as there are no direct buses from Bijapur to Hospet.

To Bidar one bus daily at 12.55 am. To Bombay, one bus daily at 8 am. To Gadag, one bus daily at 10 am. To Hubli six buses daily via Jamkhandi. First bus at 2.30 am and the last at 9.30 pm. There is also a luxury bus once daily via Belgaum at 4.30 pm. To Miraj, one bus daily at 4.30 pm. To Poona, three buses daily at 11 am, 3 pm and 5 pm. To Sholapur, eight buses daily, first bus at 2.45 am and the last at 5.30 pm.

HUBLI
Hubli is important to the traveller principally as a major railway junction on the routes from Bombay to Bangalore, Goa, and north Karnataka. Other than this it's an industrial city and there's

precious little to see. We include it since you may have to spend the night here on your way somewhere else. All the main services — hotels, restaurants, etc — are situated conveniently close to the railway station.

Places to Stay

Hotel Ajanta, Jaichamarajanagar (tel 2216), located a short distance off the main street and visible from the railway station. It's a huge place and you'll always be able to find accommodation here. Rooms cost Rs 13 a single and Rs 25 a double both with their own bathroom, fan, clean sheets, etc. The rooms are pleasantly decorated, provided with mosquito nets, there is room service and the staff are friendly. On the ground floor there is a 'meals' cafe (meals cost Rs 2.60). Highly recommended.

Modern Lodge is located on the main street before you get to the Ajanta. This is a typical one night stand hotel with basic facilities. Rooms here cost Rs 7 a single and Rs 14 a double both with attached bathroom and fan but you must provide your own sheets. There is a 'meals' cafe on the ground floor where meals cost Rs 2.50.

Further down the street from the Modern Lodge on the opposite side of the road is the *Udipi Hotel* which offers similar accommodation to the Modern Lodge. There is a meals cafe on the ground floor.

Places to Eat

Kamat Hotel is located close to the Modern Lodge. Fairly good plate meals are available here for Rs 2.50 at lunch time and in the early evening. During the rest of the day coffee and tiffin are available. *Bombay Restaurant* is next door to the Kamat. It offers plate meals

similar to the Kamat for Rs 2.50. There is a juice bar/ice cream parlour opposite the Kamat Hotel which is excellent.

Getting There

Hubli is a major rail junction on the Bombay-Bangalore route and for trains to Bijapur and Hospet. If you're heading for Goa (either Vasco da Gama or Margao) note that on the 237 Hubli-Miraj 'Link Express' there is one 2nd Class 3-tier sleeping coach and another combined 1st Class/2nd Class 2-tier sleeping coach attached to the train which goes all the way to Vasco, so avoiding the need to change at Londa.

At Londa these coaches are detached from the 237 and added to the 206 Miraj-Vasco Express at about 3.30 am. There's a quota of 20 berths in the 3-tier sleeper, six in the 2-tier sleeper plus four seats, and a quota for 1st Class at Hubli station. The full quota is rarely taken up even on the day of departure but booking closes at 4 pm. After that time you have to apply for reservations at the Ticket Collector's Office between 6.30 and 7.00 pm but don't count on getting a reservation at that time — Indians get preference unless you have a calling card and look presentable. There's also baksheesh flying around for these unbooked sleepers.

If you're setting out from Hubli early in the morning and heading for Goa, the best train to get is the 207 Bangalore-Miraj 'Karnataka Express' which gets into Londa in plenty of time to let you have breakfast there at the station (the restaurant at Londa station is very good) and then catch the Miraj-Vasco Express which leaves Londa at 11.45 am. This train arrives at Margao or Vasco in time for you to get to Colva beach or to Panjim respectively.

BELGAUM (population 250,000)
In the north-west corner of the state and on the Bombay-Pune-Goa bus and

rail route, Belgaum was a regional capital in the 12th and 13th centuries. It has an old oval-shaped stone fort, a mosque, the Masjid-i-Sata, dating from 1519 and two interesting Jain temples. One has an extremely intricate and complicated roof while the other has some fine carvings of musicians. A little north of Belgaum, and eight km off the railway line from Gokak Road, are the Gokak Falls where the Ghataprabha River takes a 52 metre drop.

THE NORTH-EAST
Bidar
This little visited town in the extreme north-east corner of the state was the capital of the Bahmani kingdom from 1428 and later of the Barid Shahi dynasty. It's a pleasant town with a splendid old 15th century fort containing the Ranjeenmahal, Chini Mahal and Turkish Mahal palaces. The impressive Khwaja Mahmud Gawan Madrasa and the tombs of the Bahmani and Barid kings are also worth seeing.

Places to Stay The *KSTDC Tourist Home* near the bus station costs Rs 10 single, Rs 14 double or you can try the *Sri Venkateshwara Lodge* on the main street. The adjoining *Kalpana Hotel* has good food.

Gulbarga (population 160,000)
This town was the Bahmani capital from 1347 until its transfer to Bidar in 1428. Later the kingdom broke up into a number of small kingdoms — Bijapur, Bidar, Berar, Ahmednagar and Golconda. The last of these, Golconda, finally fell to Aurangzeb in 1687. Gulbarga's old fort is in a much deteriorated state but has a number of interesting buildings inside. The Jami Masjid, inside the fort, is reputed to have been built by a Moorish architect during the late 14th or early 15th century in imitation of the great mosque in Cordova, Spain. The mosque is unique in India with a huge dome covering the whole area, four smaller ones at the corners and 75 smaller still all around. The fort itself has 15 towers. Gulbarga also has a number of imposing tombs of Bahmani kings, a shrine to an important Moslem saint and the temple of Sharana Basaveshwara. There are a number of hotels in the town and a *KSTDC Tourist Home*.

Raichur
The town of Raichur was part of the 13th century Kakatiyas kingdom, then part of the Bahmani kingdom, became the first capital of Bijapur when the Bahmani kingdom fragmented in 1489 and later came under the rule of Vijayanagar. The fort, with its impressive gate, has a citadel with a fine view from the top. Raichur has hotels, Inspection and Tourist Bungalows.

Indian hotels often have amazingly complicated switch panels with switches for fans, bells, lights in bathrooms, entrance ways, over the beds, mirrors and so on. Generally three quarters of them don't work since failed light bulbs are rarely replaced as long as there is at least one still working.

Why, when Indians are so keen on writing everything down in triplicate, will waiters never (at least initially) write orders down? Trying to remember everything inevitably results in at least one item failing to appear.

Key :-
A   New Gayathri Bhavan
B   Agarwal Lodge
C   Hotel Indra Bhavan
D   Hotel Anugraha
E   Dasaprakash & Modern Cafe
F   Hotel Durbar
G   Hotel Srikanth

Central Mysore

Railway Station

Sayaji Rao Rd.

Irwin Road

Hospitals

Dhanvantri Road

A H B C

Devaraja Market

Sadar   Patel
         Road

Ashoka Road

E F

D

Gandhi Square

K

N

G

H   Kwality Restaurant
J   Punjabi Restaurant &
    Ashok Book Centre
K   Shilpashtri Restaurant
L   Kaveri Arts & Crafts
    Emporium
M   Geetha Book Centre
N   Buses to Somnathpur

New
Statue
Circle

M

Bus Station

Palace

Andhra Pradesh

Population: 49 million
Area: 276,754 square km
Capital: Hyderabad
Main language: Telegu

The large state of Andhra Pradesh was created by combining the old princely State of Hyderabad with the Telegu speaking portions of the former State of Madras. Most of the state stands on the high Deccan plateau, sloping down to the low-lying coastal region to the east where the mighty Godavari and Krishna Rivers meet the Bay of Bengal in wide deltas.

Andhra Pradesh was once a major Buddhist centre and part of Ashoka's large empire until it broke apart. Traces of that early Buddhist influence can still be seen in several places. Later the Chalukyas held power in the 7th century but they in turn fell to the Chola kingdom of the south around the 10th century. In the 14th century Moslem power finally reached this far south and for centuries the region was an arena for Hindu-Moslem power struggles. Finally it was taken over by a general of the Moghul Emperor Aurangzeb in 1713. His successors, the Nizams of Hyderabad, ruled the state right down to independence.

The final Nizam of Hyderabad was reputed to be one of the richest men in the world but Andhra Pradesh itself is one of the poorest and least developed states in India. New dams and irrigation projects are improving the barren, scrubby land of the plateau but much of the state remains economically backward. There is not a great deal of interest in Andhra Pradesh apart from the capital, Hyderabad. Visitors with a keen interest in architecture or archaeology may wish to visit some of the excavations or old temple sites but otherwise Hyderabad is the only real attraction.

HYDERABAD (population 1,800,000)
Like Bijapur, further to the west in neighbouring Karnataka state, Hyderabad is an important centre of Islamic culture and offers central India's counterpart to the Moghul splendours of the northern cities of Delhi, Agra and Fatehpur Sikri. Consisting of the twin cities of Hyderabad and Secunderabad, it is the capital of Andhra Pradesh state and famous as the former seat of the Nizams of Hyderabad, the last of whom was one of the richest men in the world. Here, lively crowded bazaars surround huge and impressive Islamic monuments dating from the 16th and 17th centuries. The city — India's fifth largest — was founded in 1590 by Mohammed Quli, the fourth of the Qutab Shahi kings who ruled this part of the Deccan from 1512 until 1687 when the last of their line was defeated by the Moghul emperor Aurangzeb following suspension of the annual tribute due to their

nominal suzerain in Delhi. Before the founding of Hyderabad, the Qutab Shahi kings had ruled from the fortress city of Golconda, 11 km to the west. The extensive ruins of this fort, which has roots going back to the earlier Hindu kingdoms of the Yadavas and

Kakatiyas, together with the nearby tombs of the Qutab Shahi kings, are the principal attractions of any visit to Hyderabad.

Following Aurangzeb's death in 1707, Moghul control over this part of India rapidly waned and the viceroys who had been installed to look after the interests of the empire broke away and established their own independent state taking the title, first, of Subedar and, later, that of Nizam. These new rulers became embroiled in the rivalry between the French and British for control of India during the latter half of the 18th century as allies of the French but, after the defeat of the French and subsequent Maratha raids which seriously weakened their kingdom, they were forced to conclude a treaty with the British and relinquish the bulk of their power. When independence came to India in 1947, the Nizam toyed with the idea of declaring independence and went so far as to allow an Islamic extremist group to seize control. This however led to his downfall as the Indian government, mindful of Hyderabad's Hindu majority of around 85% and unwilling to see the creation of an independent and possibly hostile state in the centre of the Deccan, used the insurrection as an excuse to occupy Hyderabad in 1948 and force its accession to the Union.

This dusty city retains much of its 19th century atmosphere and is quite unlike any of the cities further south. Lovers of graffiti should make a point of visiting Osmania University where every available square inch of stone and brickwork is plastered with political slogans. Though this is fairly common in many Indian cities, nothing quite so extreme as this can be seen anywhere else.

Information & Orientation

The old city of Hyderabad itself lies on either side of the River Musi and south of the lake, Hussain Sagar, which effectively divides the twin cities of Hyderabad and Secunderabad. In this part are located most of the historical monuments, the bulk of the hotels and cafes used by travellers, the city bus depot, Salar Jang Museum and the zoo. Most of the budget hotels are situated

in the area known as Abids between the GPO and Hyderabad railway station. The more expensive hotels are, in general, clustered around the Secretariat building at the south end of Hussain Sagar. The ruins of Golconda Fort and the tombs of the Qutab Shahi kings lie about 11 km to the west of the city. The more recent city of Secunderabad is situated on the north side of Hussain Sagar and, if you are coming by train, you will get off at Secunderabad railway station (the main station). The YMCA, YWCA and the Youth Hostel are located here but few travellers stay in Secunderabad itself. To get to Hyderabad you will have to take a bus, autorickshaw or taxi (about 10 minutes' journey). Note that few trains pass through Hyderabad railway station.

Services & Useful Addresses

There are tourist information kiosks at both Secunderabad and Hyderabad railway stations but you'd be advised not to waste your time going there. They have no literature, no city maps and will even direct you to the former address of the main tourist office. Incredible that they could be so out of touch!

Other than these, there are two tourist offices, both of them on Himayatnagar, Hyderabad. Andhra Pradesh Travel & Tourism Development Corporation, 2nd Floor, Diamond House, Himayatnagar (tel 36252) stocks hardly any literature and seems to exist solely to promote their sight-seeing tours of Hyderabad and Nagarjunasagar. India Tourism Development Corporation, Lidcap Building, 3-6-150 Himayatnagar (tel 220730) are the people to go to if you're looking for literature on Hyderabad and the rest of Andhra Pradesh or a street plan of the city. They also promote their own tours of the city and to Nagarjunasagar.

Air India and Indian Airlines are both located in Saifabad near the

Secretariat building. The telephone numbers are 222747 and 36902/72910 respectively.

Charminar

Standing in the heart of the old walled city this huge triumphal arch was built by Mohammed Quli Qutab Shah in 1591 to commemorate the end of the plague in Hyderbad. It's surrounded on all sides by lively bazaars and the views from the top are superb. An image of this building graces every packet of 'Charminar' cigarettes which hoardings all over India assure you are the only brand which 'satisfy a man like you'. The monument is open every day and entry costs Rs 0.50. No guides are necessary.

Mecca Masjid

Situated next to the Charminar, this is one of the largest mosques in the world and is said to accommodate up to 10,000 worshippers. Construction began during the reign of Mohammed Quli Qutab Shah in 1614 but was not finished until 1687, by which time the Moghul Emperor Aurangzeb had annexed the Golconda kingdom. The colonnades and door arches are made out of single slabs of granite which history records were quarried 11 km away and dragged to the site by a team of 1400 bullocks! The minarets were originally planned to have been much higher than they are but the enormous cost of erecting the main part of the building apparently forced the ruler to settle for something less grand. It's definitely a very beautiful and impressive building but disfigured by huge awnings of chicken wire which have presumably been erected to stop birds nesting in the ceiling and liming the floor. Nevertheless, they still get in and the steel supports which have been carelessly cemented into the tiled and patterned floor to hold this netting is nothing short of vandalism.

To the left of the mosque is an enclosure containing the tombs of the Nizams.

Birla Mandir (Naubat Prahad) Temple

This stunningly beautiful modern Hindu temple, built out of white marble, graces the rocky hill which overlooks the south end of Hussain Sagar. It's a very popular Hindu pilgrimage centre but non-Hindus are allowed inside. There's no entry fee and the priests make no efforts to press you for contributions. There are excellent views over the city from the summit.

Salar Jang Museum

This is India's answer to the Victoria and Albert Museum in London. The collection was put together by Mir Yusaf Ali Khan (Salar Jang III), the Prime Minister of the Nizam. It contains 35,000 exhibits drawn from the four corners of the world including sculptures, wood carvings, religious objects, Persian miniature paintings, illuminated manuscripts, armour and weaponry, the swords, daggers and clothing of the Moghul emperors and of Tipu Sultan, and many other objects. All of this is housed in one of the ugliest buildings imaginable. Open daily except Fridays from 10 am to 5 pm. Entrance costs Rs 2 (Rs 1 if you have a student card). All bags and cameras have to be deposited in the luggage office in the entrance hall — there's no charge for this and it's secure. Refreshments are available inside. Avoid going there on Sundays as it's bedlam (seems half the population of Hyderabad are there on this day!).

Archaeological Museum

Situated in the public gardens between Nampally High Rd and the branch railway line which leads to Hyderabad railway station the museum has a small collection of archaeological finds from the area together with copies of the

Ajanta frescoes. It's supposed to be open daily except Mondays from 10.30 am to 5 pm but appears to be semi-permanently 'under construction'.

Golconda Fort & the Tombs of the Qutab Shahi Kings

To see the ruins of this extensive fort thoroughly or with any degree of ease you need to put aside at least half a day. The bus tours of Hyderabad organised by the Tourist Office bring you here for just one hour which is a ridiculously short period of time — sufficient only to quickly climb to the summit and, equally quickly, come back down again.

Though the bulk of the ruins date from the time of the Qutab Shahi kings (16th-17th centuries), the origins of the fort have been traced back to the earlier Hindu periods of Deccan history when the Yadavas and, later, the Kakatiyas ruled this area of India. In 1512, Sultan Quli Qutab Shah, a Turkoman adventurer from Persia who had risen to be Governor of Telangana under the Bahmani rulers, declared independence and made Golconda his capital. It remained the capital until 1590 when the court was moved to the new city of Hyderabad but subsequently came into its own again on two separate occasions in the 1600s when Moghul armies from Delhi were sent against the kingdom to enforce payment of tribute. Abul Hasan, the last of the Qutab Shahi kings, held out in the fort of Golconda against a Moghul army commanded by the emperor Aurangzeb for seven months before losing it by treachery in 1687. Following Aurangzeb's death, early in the next century, the viceroys whom he had installed to look after Moghul interests rapidly became sovereign princes (soon to be known as the Nizams). They chose Hyderabad as their capital and abandoned Golconda.

The citadel itself is built on a granite hill 120 metres high and surrounded by battlemented ramparts constructed of large blocks of masonry, some of them weighing several tons. The massive gates are studded with large pointed iron spikes intended to prevent elephants from battering them and further protected by a cordon wall to check direct attack. Outside of the citadel stands another battlemented rampart with a perimeter of 11 km. All of these walls are in an excellent state of preservation. Unfortunately, many of the structures inside the citadel — the palaces and harem of the Qutab Shahi kings, assembly halls, arsenal, stables and barracks — have suffered a great deal from past seiges and the ravages of time but enough remains to give a good impression of what the place must once have looked like. Restoration work is underway on the buildings around the Balahisar Gate (the main entrance) and even the wrought iron work is being replaced but it will be many years before this is anywhere near completion.

One of the most remarkable features of this fort is its system of acoustics whereby the sound of hands clapped in the Grand Portico can be heard in the Durbar Hall at the very top of the hill — a fact not lost on tour guides (or their charges) who do their utmost competing with each other to make as much noise as possible! There is also supposed to be a 'secret' underground tunnel leading from the Durbar Hall to one of the palaces at the foot of the hill but, predictably, you are not allowed to investigate this.

The tombs of the Qutab Shahi kings lie about a km north of the outer perimeter wall of Golconda. They are fairly small but graceful structures surrounded by landscaped gardens. A number of them display beautifully carved stonework. Entrance to these tombs cost 25p plus Rs 2 if you have a camera or Rs 10 (!!) if you have a movie camera. A small guide book, *Guide to Colconda Fort & Qutub Shahi Tombs*, is on sale at both the tombs and the fort.

Golconda Fort

Qutab Shahi Tombs

Suggested route

Bus Stand

Balahisar Gate

Well

Steps

Nagina Bagh

Grand Portico

Barracks

Mahakali Temple

Ibrahim Masjid

Ambar Khana

Ramdas Jail

Durbar Hall

Steps

Arsenal

Taramati Mosque

Tank

Camel Stables

Dad Mahal

Harem

Rani Mahal

Shahi Mahal

Langer Khana

How much you pay for it depends on your bargaining power but Rs 2 should be sufficient. It's worth getting hold of if you're going to spend the day here.

If you want to make your own way to the Fort, take service bus 142 or 119 from Nampally High Rd opposite Hyderabad railway station. These will take you to the main entrance at Balahisar Gate. Otherwise taxis are available — negotiate the cost before setting off.

Nehru Zoological Park

One of the largest in India, it is spread out over 120 hectares of landscaped gardens with the animals contained in large open enclosures. They don't look any less bored than animals in zoos anywhere else in the world but at least here an effort has been made which is more than can be said for most other zoos in India. The park is open from 9 am until 6 pm daily except Mondays and entry costs 50 paise. There's also a Lion Safari Park which you can go around in a mini-bus for Rs 1 and a toy train for children. It's a very popular park with local people.

Other

Tourist literature on Hyderabad raves on about various 'lovely picnic spots', such as the lake of Osmansagar (Gandipet) from which the city receives its water supply, but it's as well to take this with a pinch of salt. They're nothing special and a definite case of over-enthusiasm.

Tours

Andhra Pradesh Travel & Tourism Development Corporation, Diamond House, Himayatnagar, Hyderabad, offer a daily tour of the city which includes visits to Osmania University, Birla Mandir, Qutan Shahi Tombs, Golconda Fort, Gandipet, Salar Jang Museum, Charminar, Mecca Masjid and the Zoological Gardens. The tour starts at 8 am and ends at 6 pm and tickets cost Rs 20. You have to pay your own entrance fees to the Zoo, Museum and Qutab Shahi Tombs. The lunch stop is at Gandipet lake.

India Tourism Development Corporation, Lidcap Building, Himayatnagar, Hyderabad, also offer daily tours of the city visiting the same places as above but in a different sequence. The tour starts at 8 am and ends at 6.30 pm. Tickets cost Rs 25 by deluxe coach and Rs 30 by air-conditioned coach. The cost of the ticket includes entry fees.

Both the above tours suffer from the same disadvantage in that insufficient time is allotted for visiting Golconda Fort and the Tombs of the Qutab Shahi kings (60 minutes on the former and 70 minutes on the latter) and a lot of time is wasted on an inconsequential visit to Gandipet lake. If there is anything to choose between them, then the ITDC tour would be the better of the two since the lunch break is in Abids in the centre of Hyderabad where there is a choice of restaurants. At Gandipet there

1	Secunderabad Railway Station	8	Salar Jang Museum	
2	Kacheguda Railway Station	9	Charminar and Mecca Masjid	area of budget &
3	Bus Station	10	Public Gardens and	mid-range hotels
4	Hyderabad Railway Station		Archaeological Museum	around Abids &
5	GPO (Abids)	11	Hotel Nagarjuna	Nampally High Rd
6	Tourist Office (ITDC — Lidcap Building)	12	Hyd-Inn and Ritz Hotel	
7	Birla Mandir Temple	13	Tourist Home & Tourist Hotel	
		14	Youth Hostel	

is no choice and facilities are very limited.

Places to Stay — Top End

The *Ritz Hotel* (tel 33571) on Hill Fort Rd, Basheer Bagh, between Nampally High Rd and J Nehru Rd is one of Hyderabad's more expensive hotels. Rooms cost Rs 150/190 for singles/doubles and there are all the usual mod cons from air-conditioning to swimming pool and tennis courts. The much larger *Hotel Banjara* (tel 221616) is at Banjara Hills, overlooking the lake and 15 minutes from the railway terminal by car. Rooms here run from Rs 250/325 for singles/doubles and again there are all the usual facilities and luxuries. *Bluemoon Hotel* (tel 30136) on Rajbhavan Rd, Begumpet is rather more central and has singles/doubles from Rs 100/150.

Hyd-Inn, Lake Hill Rd, Basheer Bagh (tel 38481) is a smaller, more pleasant and friendlier hotel than the Ritz. Rooms cost Rs 60 a single, Rs 110 a double and suites Rs 150 plus 10% service charges. All rooms are air-conditioned and prices include breakfast. *Hotel Nagarjuna*, J Nehru Rd, Basheer Bagh (tel 37201). Rooms cost Rs 90 a single and Rs 130 a double for non air-con rooms and Rs 160 a double for an air-con room.

Places to Stay — Middle

Jaya International, Abids (tel 223444) is situated just off to the left on J Nehru Rd as you face the GPO. A very pleasant modern hotel where rooms cost Rs 35 a single and Rs 50 a double non air-con and Rs 50 a single and Rs 80 a double for air-con rooms. All rooms have their own attached bath.

Taj Mahal Hotel, King Kothi Rd, Hyderabad (tel 221167) is a popular hotel for those not on a tight budget. Rooms cost Rs 30 a single and Rs 70 a double for air-con rooms. All rooms have attached bath.

Sri Brindavan Hotel, Station Rd, Abids (tel 220820) is probably the best and cheapest of the mid-range hotels. Rooms cost Rs 28 a single and Rs 39 a double. All rooms have a fan and attached bath and are built around a quiet courtyard well off the road. Room service is available, the staff are friendly and a newspaper is pushed under your door every morning. There is an attached restaurant but they serve only dosa, idli and puri in addition to coffee. Baggage can be left securely at the reception if necessary.

Tourist Hotel, Kachiguda, Hyderabad (tel 44491) is situated close to Kachiguda railway station and so it's convenient if you're heading for Guntakal, Bangalore or Madras by rail but otherwise somewhat out of the way. Rooms cost Rs 13-14 a single and Rs 20-22 a double. All rooms have fans and attached bath.

Places to Stay — Bottom End

Other than the Youth Hostel, YMCA and YWCA, the best of these are located on Nampally High Rd opposite Hyderabad railway station. There are others around the Charminar in the old part of the city but they're very basic.

Super Lodge, Nampally High Rd is probably the best of the budget hotels as the rooms are located off the main road which is noisy any time after 7 am until late at night. A variety of rooms are available from Rs 8 a single for a room without a fan or bath; Rs 10 a single and Rs 15 a double for ground floor rooms with a fan but common bathroom; Rs 20 a double for upstairs room with fan and attached bathroom. If you want hot water this costs Rs 1 per bucket. The manager is friendly, speaks excellent English and there's an attached restaurant.

Royal Lodge, Nampally High Rd has rooms for Rs 17.50 a single and Rs 29 a double. There are a few air-con rooms for Rs 10 extra. Somewhat overpriced for what it offers — the rooms are quite dingy. Sri Brindavan Hotel would be a better bet if you are prepared to spend this amount of money.

The *Youth Hostel*, behind the Boat Club at the north eastern end of Hussain Sagar, Secunderabad, is recommended by quite a few travellers since it offers the cheapest dormitory-type accommodation. There are 51 beds and the cost is Rs 5 per night.

In addition to the above there are the *YMCA* (tel 57850) and *YWCA* but they are often semi-permanently full with students. Only Secunderabad railway station (tel 70144/5) has *Railway Retiring Rooms* but you would be lucky to get one since they have only one double room (Rs 16) and one dormitory (four beds at Rs 10 per bed).

Places to Eat

Most travellers eat in their respective hotels since there are few good restaurants, as such, in Hyderabad. Good cheap vegetarian meals can be found at any *Kamat Hotel* where the standard fare costs Rs 2.50. While there are several of these hotels around Hyderabad, the most convenient one if you're staying in Abids is opposite the Public Gardens which are located between Nampilly High Rd and the railway line to Hyderabad railway station. There are any number of cheap vegetarian cafes along Nampilly High Rd, Station Rd and around the GPO on J Nehru Rd.

Getting There

Air There are flight connections between Hyderabad and Delhi (Rs 840), Calcutta (Rs 890), Madras (Rs 385), Bangalore (Rs 375) and Bombay (Rs 500).

Train Note that the main railway station is at Secunderabad. Hyderabad Railway Station is only a branch line. On the other hand if you're heading south to Guntakal, Bangalore or Madras and staying in Abids you can board the train at Kacheguda station instead of going all the way up to Secunderabad. As elsewhere, the fastest night express trains are booked up days in advance so reserve your seat or sleeper as early as possible.

New Delhi-Secunderabad can take less than 24 hours on the Andhra Pradesh Express. It's a 1675 km trip costing Rs 285 in 1st class, Rs 68 in 2nd class. It's 6½ hours on the Golconda Express between Hyderabad and Vijayawada (this train does go from Hyderabad). The fare is Rs 84 in 1st class, Rs 19 in 2nd class. The quickest route from Calcutta is to take the Madras Mail from Howrah Station (daily) and change at Vijayawada. If you're coming from Nagpur, change at Kazipet — just west of Warangal.

Bombay-Secunderabad takes as little as 15 hours on the Minar Express, fares are Rs 155 in 1st, Rs 38 in 2nd. It's a 19 hour trip to Bangalore costing Rs 135 in 1st, Rs 27 in 2nd. The line from Secunderabad to Aurangabad is metre gauge — the 517 km trip takes 12 hours at a cost of Rs 108 in 1st class, Rs 26 in 2nd. The express continues through Aurangabad to Manmad on the Bombay-Delhi line via Bhopal and Agra. The Secunderabad-Ajmer line is also metre gauge, this route goes through Khandwa, Mhow, Indore, Ratlam and Chittorgarh. All the way to Ajmer it's a 1818 km trip taking 39 hours at a cost of Rs 300 in 1st class, Rs 38 in 2nd.

Getting Around

Local transport is available by service bus, auto-rickshaw and taxi. Getting onto any service bus, other than at the terminus, in Hyderabad is (as one traveller put it) 'like staging a banzai charge on Guadalcanal'. He wasn't exaggerating! Useful ones which you might be able to get onto include No 2 — Secunderabad Railway Station to Charminar & vice versa. No 7 — Secunderabad Railway Station to Afzalganj & vice versa. This is one to catch if you're heading for Abids as it goes down Tankbund Rd and J Nehru Rd via the GPO. Nos 119 or 142 — Nampilly High Rd (opposite Hyderabad Railway station) to Golconda Fort & vice versa.

Auto-rickshaws are the cheapest alternative during the day. Unlike in many other cities in India, the drivers appear to need no prompting about use of meter. Some sample fares are Secunderabad Railway Station to Himayatnagar: Rs 3.75-4. Abids to Charminar: Rs 3-3.50. Himayatnagar to Abids: Rs 2.75.

AROUND HYDERABAD

Nagarjunakonda & Nagarjunasagar

Nagarjunakonda, 150 km south-east of Hyderabad on the Krishna River, was once one of the largest and most important Buddhist centres in southern India spanning a period from the 2nd century BC until the 3rd century AD. In those days known as Vijayapur, it takes its present name from Nagarjuna, one of the most revered of Buddhist monks and founder of the Madhyamika school, who governed the sangha for nearly 60 years around the turn of the 2nd century AD. The school which he established attracted students from as far afield as Sri Lanka and China.

The site was discovered in 1926 and subsequent excavations, particularly in the '50s and '60s, have unearthed the remains of stupas, viharas, chiatyas and mandapas as well as some outstanding examples of white marble carvings and sculptures depicting the life of the Buddha. These have been moved to a museum on the site following a decision to create the Nagarjunasagar dam which will eventually submerge the whole of this area. The dam is one of the largest masonry constructions in the world and India claims that it will create the world's third largest artificial lake.

The Nagarjunakonda panels lack the more elaborate sculptural features of those found further down river at Amaravathi — 32 km north of Guntur — but are the best you will find in this part of India today. Amaravathi itself, once the capital of Andhra during the Buddhist period but now described in tourist literature as 'a squalid little village', contained over 20 monasteries with over 1000 monks and had a huge marble stupa unrivalled anywhere else in the world. Every cm of this stupa and the rail which surrounded it was richly carved and the whole decorated with lamps on festive occasions but before you rush off to see it you should know that it was largely destroyed at the end of the 18th century by local people in their quest for building material. Marble is excellent raw material for a lime-kiln. The fragments which remained were spirited off to the Madras Museum and the British Museum in London during the 19th century.

Places to Stay

Project House, Hill Colony, 18 rooms in all, costing Rs 6 a single and Rs 9 a double. *River View*, Right Bank, Nagarjunasagar has four double rooms at Rs 9 per room. *Lake View*, Nagarjunasagar

A Dhobi Ghats at Halebid (Ka)
B Temple Carvings on the Hoysala Temple at Halebid (Ka)
C Gol Gumbaz Mausoleum at Bijapur (Ka)

has two double rooms at Rs 15 per room. *Vijaya Vihar*, Hill Colony has eight air-con rooms at Rs 15 per room.

In addition to the above there are three cottages which cost Rs 20 per night. All the above are managed by Executive Engineer, R & B Division, Nagarjunasagar Dam, Hill Colony. There are also the following places managed by Andhra Pradesh Travel & Tourism Corporation, Hill Colony: *Tourist Annexe*, Hill Colony, eight double rooms at Rs 8 per room. *Youth Hostel*, Hill Colony, consisting of 12 rooms and two halls. Cost Rs 1 per night.

Getting There

Probably the easiest way to visit Nagarjunakonda and Nagarjunasagar is to take the tourist coach from Hyderabad organised by the India Tourism Development Corporation, Lidcap Building, 3-6-150 Himayatnagar, Hyderabad (tel 220730) on Sundays and public holidays. The tour costs Rs 55 in air-conditioned coach and Rs 50 in non-air-conditioned coach and includes visits to the Nagarjunakonda Museum, Pylon (an engraved granite monolith from the Buddhist period), Nagarjunasagar dam, and the working model of the dam.

If you'd prefer to make your own way there, regular buses connect Hyderabad, Vijayawada and Guntur with Nagarjunasagar. The nearest railway station is at Macherla — a branch line running west from Guntur and ending at Macherla. If coming from Hyderabad, head first for Guntur. There are regular buses from Macherla to Nagarjunasagar.

Local sight-seeing tours of Nagarjunakonda and Nagarjunasagar are organised by the Tourism Department, Project House, Hill Colony, Nagarjunasagar and cost Rs 5 per head.

If you're not part of one of the local tours or those organised from Hyderabad, launches to Nagarjunakonda Museum which is situated on an island in the lake, depart at 9.30 am and 1.30 pm. The fare is Rs 3.50 return.

WARANGAL (population 160,000)
Once the capital of the Kakatiya kingdom which ruled the greater part of present-day Andhra Pradesh from the latter half of the 12th century until the early 14th century when it was conquered by the Tughlaqs of Delhi. The Hindu Kakatiyas were great builders and patrons of the arts and it was during their reign that the Chalukyan style of temple architecture and decoration reached the pinnacle of its development. The most notable examples which remain today are the Thousand-Pillared Temple on the slopes of Hanamkonda hill (one shrine of which is still in use), the Bhadrakali Temple situated on a hillock between Warangal and Hanamkonda, and the Shambu Lingeswara or Swayambhu Temple (originally a Shiva temple). There is also the Ramappa Temple at Palampet, 77 km from Warangal, which represents a combination of the Chalukyan and the later Hoysala styles. It's hard to get to but reputed to be one of the finest examples

A Friezes on the Hoysala Temple at Somnathpur, near Mysore (Ka)
B Street Scene below the Charminar, Hyderabad (AP)

of Deccan architecture.

The other main attraction at Warangal is the mud-brick fort built by the Kakatiyas. These same rulers were also responsible for the first fort at Golconda — also constructed from mud-brick but later converted to masonry by the Qutab Shahi kings.

If you have an interest in the various streams of Hindu temple development and have either visited or intend to visit the early Chalukyan sites at Badami, Aihole and Pattadakal in neighbouring Karnataka state, then an outing to Warangal would be worthwhile.

Places to Stay

Accommodation facilities are modest and there are no western-style hotels. Most of the hotels and lodges are located on R N Tagore Rd and on Chowrasta. They include *Hotel Nataraj* (about a km from the railway station) and *Krishna Lodge* (both on R N Tagore

Rd), *Annapurna Lodge, Ganesh Lodge, Hotel Kohinoor, Ananda Lodge* and the *Venkatarama Lodge* (all on Chowrasta). There are plenty of vegetarian restaurants in town. Good non-vegetarian meals can be found either at the *Kohinoor Hotel* or at the *Kwality Restaurant* (part of the chain of Kwality Restaurants you will find all over India).

Getting There

Rail The daily Warangal Express connects Warangal with Hyderabad. It departs Secunderabad railway station at 6 pm and takes three hours. If you're coming from outside the state, Kazipet, a few km west of Warangal is the most convenient point to alight. Regular buses connect Kazipet with Warangal.

Road Regular buses connect Warangal with Hyderabad, Nizamabad and other major centres of population. Local buses connect Warangal with Kazipet and Hanumakonda.

SOUTH OF HYDERABAD

Kurnool (population 150,000)

Situated 240 km south of Hyderabad, Kurnool has fragments of its old fortress still standing and a number of mosques and mausoleums. The Mallikarjuna temple near here is an important Shiva shrine and a major pilgrimage centre.

Tadpatri

50 km south-east of the junction town of Gooty, there are the remains of two temples which date from around 1485 when they were built by the rulers of Vijayanagar. The riverbank Rameswaraswami temple was never completed but is more imposing than the Chintalarayaswami.

Tirupati

On top of the 'holy hill' of Tirumala,

about 13 km from the Tirupati railway station, is the very old Tirumala temple. The temple is entered through a thousand pillared hall from which steps lead to the temple with its early-Dravidian gopurams. The temple is one of the richest in the south of India and an important pilgrimage centre. Non-Hindus are not allowed into the inner temple although they are allowed to ascend the hill. Tirupati is in the extreme south of the state, on the railway line to Madras, and there are regular buses between Tirupati and Tirumala hill.

Kalahasti & Tiruttani

Kalahasti is another important pilgrimage centre, east of Tirupati. Almost on the border with Tamil Nadu, 60 km south of Tirupati, Tiruttani is another very old hill top temple.

EAST COAST

Although the main Calcutta-Madras railway line runs along the east coast of Andhra Pradesh few travellers stop south of Orissa. During the monsoon the extensive deltas of the Godavari and Krishna Rivers may flood forcing the Calcutta-Madras trains to take an alternative route further inland through Raipur, Nagpur and Hyderabad.

Waltair

About 16 km off the railway line from Waltair Junction, Waltair is a popular seaside resort. Simhachalam Hill, about 10 km north of Waltair, has an 11th century Vishnu temple in fine Orissan style.

Visakhapatnam (population 400,000)

Virtually adjoining Waltair, this town is one of the major ports on the east coast of India. It is connected by broad gauge railway line to Raipur and by Indian Airlines to Calcutta, Bhubaneshwar and Hyderabad.

Rajamundry (population 200,000)

A three km long railway and road bridge, the second longest in India, crosses the Godavari River at Rajamundry. This delta region of the Godavari is very flat but 100 km inland, where the Deccan

plateau drops away to the delta, the scenery is very fine. Yanam, on the coast near Rajamundry, is another portion of the former French enclave of Pondicherry.

Vijayawada (population 380,000)

On the banks of the equally mighty Krishna River, only 149 km south of Rajamundry and the Godavari River, Vijayawada is the junction for the railway line to Warangal and Hyderabad. Two thousand years ago this was an important Buddhist area and there are interesting excavations upstream at Amaravati (now much damaged) and Nagarjunakonda. See 'Around Hyderabad' for more information. To reach Amarati you have to continue south to Guntur then turn back north, a distance of about 65 km. Kondapalli, only 20 km from Vijayawada, is renowned for the wonderful small toys which have been made here for many years. Only a few km from Vijayawada, but across the river, are the ancient Hindu cave temples of Undavalil. There is also a museum in Vijayawada itself. Masulipatam, 80 km from Vijayawada on the coast, once had English, Dutch and French factories and was once the subject of violent dispute between the English and French.

Tolerance

For all the aggravations and annoyances India can throw in your path there's one factor which almost every visitor praises about the country and that is its tolerance. In part it's related to the Hindu religion — it makes no effort to go out and convert people, it already has so many gods that other people's gods are quite welcome to join the happy band. In India anything seems

to go down. If an Indian wants to leave his job, family and comfort to don a loincloth and wander the country as a sadhu that's considered quite normal. Similarly if western visitors want to dress up in '60s flower power gear and wander the country they're quite welcome. If they want to take all their clothes off and lie on the beach at Goa it's considered a bit strange but that's OK too. Basically anything goes.

Kerala

Population: 23 million
Area: 38,864 square km
Capital: Trivandrum
Main language: Malayalam

Kerala, the land of 'green magic', is a narrow, fertile coastal strip bordered by the Western Ghats on the south-west coast of India. These high mountains have sheltered Kerala from invaders from the rest of India but at the same time Kerala has a very long history of contact with the outside world. In Cochin there is still a small community, descendants of Jewish settlers who fled from Palestine 2000 years ago. Kerala has also had Christians for as long as Christianity has been in Europe! The Portuguese were more than a little surprised to find Christianity already established along the Malabar coast when they arrived here 500 years ago. And more than a little annoyed that these Christians had never heard of the Pope. Long before Vasco da Gama led the Portuguese to India the coast had been known to the Phoenicians who came in search of spices, sandalwood and ivory. Kerala was not only a spice centre in its own right but also a transshipment point from the Moluccas. The Biblical Ophir, visited by King Solomon, is also thought to be in Kerala at the site of the small village of Puvar, south of Trivandrum. The Arabs and Chinese also made their mark on Kerala and fishermen still use Chinese fishing nets to this day.

The present day state of Kerala was created in 1956 from Travancore, Cochin and Malabar, which was formerly part of Madras State. The people speak Malayalam which hundreds of years ago was derived from Tamil. In 1957 Kerala became the first place in the world to freely elect a communist government. Although the communists are currently in power they have not always held power since that initial election success. The princely state of Travancore had, however, carried out a far-sighted policy of land distribution over a century ago. Today Kerala has a more equitable distribution of land ownership than almost anywhere else in India and this has resulted in unusually intensive cultivation and a much more even distribution of income than is found elsewhere in India. Although Kerala, predominantly agricultural and with little industry, is far from top of the per capita income scale in India it has remarkably little real poverty. This distribution of wealth applies also to education and health. The literacy rate in Kerala is 60%, twice the all-India average, and is actually growing faster than the rest of India despite the already high literacy level. Similarly infant mortality in Kerala is relatively low and both these achievements have been made without spending a higher proportion of the state's income on education or health than other states.

For visitors Kerala offers one of the best beaches in India at Kovalam, a unique wild life sanctuary at Periyar, its intriguing blend of cultures and some unusual ways of getting around. Perhaps more than anywhere else in India getting there can be half the fun, particularly on the backwater trips along the coastal lagoons. Best of all Kerala has an easy going, laid back atmosphere quite unlike the bustle you find elsewhere in India.

Things to Buy
Kathakali dance masks, sandalwood carvings, rush mats, handloomed cottons and brass temple lamps and figurines. There are Kerala Cottage Industries Emporiums in Trivandrum and Cochin.

Religions in Kerala
Kerala has an amazing mixture of religions, 24% of the population today are Christians and Christianity has been longer established here than almost anywhere in the world. St Thomas the Apostle, 'doubting Thomas', is supposed to have landed on the Malabar coast in 52 AD near Cranganore and in that town there is a church, with carved Hindu-style columns, supposed to date from the 4th century AD. Further south there is the 9th century Syrian church of Vallia Palli. Kerala's Syrian Christians were here at least as early as 190 AD for a visitor at that time reports seeing a Hebrew copy of St Matthew here. Kerala's now disappearing Jewish population also made a very early appearance on the sub-continent. The 'black Jews' are supposed to have fled here in 587 BC when Nebuchadnezzar occupied Jerusalem. Their descendants have now intermarried with the Hindu population but there are still a small number of the later 'white Jews' in Cochin.

NORTH OF CALICUT
Mahe, 60 km north of Calicut, was a small French dependancy made over to India at the same time as Pondicherry. Today Mahe's main function is to

supply passing truck drivers with cheap Pondicherry beer. It's still part of the Union Territory of Pondicherry. Only eight km north of Mahe is Tellicherry with some interesting houses and a fine bazaar. The English factory established here in 1683, to purchase pepper and cardamom, was set up by the Surat Presidency and was the first permanent English factory on the Malabar coast.

The East India Company had a fort here in 1708. Directly east of here, in the Western Ghats, is Sultan's Battery, a fort built by Tipu Sultan. Cannanore, 88 km north of Calicut, was another port where Vasco da Gama dropped in. The Portuguese built their Fort St Angelo here in 1505 but it later passed to the Dutch and was eventually taken by the British.

CALICUT (Kozhikode) (population 360,000)

Vasco da Gama first landed in India at Calicut in 1498. He was the first European to reach India via the sea route around the southern cape of Africa and his arrival heralded the period of Portuguese supremacy in India. The history of Calicut after that time was certainly dramatic. The Portuguese attempted to conquer the town, a centre of Malabar power under the Zamorins or 'Lords of the Sea', but their attacks in 1509 and 1510 were both repulsed although in the latter assault the town was virtually destroyed.

In 1513 the Zamorins and Portuguese reached an agreement which permitted the Portuguese to build a factory here. The British followed in 1616 but in 1766 the Zamorins were defeated and a period of local turmoil followed with Tipu Sultan adding to the damage in 1789 when he laid the whole region

waste and destroyed the coconut, sandalwood and pepper tree plantations. In 1792 the British arrived and established their rule.

Despite its colourful past Calicut does not have a great deal to see. The word 'calico' is derived from Calicut.

Places to Stay

The *Alakpuri Guest House* (tel 73361-66) on Jail Rd has singles/doubles from Rs 25/35 without air-con or Rs 60/100 with air-con. Or there's the *Beach Hotel* (tel 73851-53) on Beach Rd with non air-con rooms from Rs 25/40 and air-con rooms from Rs 40/60. *Hotel Maharani* (tel 76161) is on Taluk Rd and has rooms from Rs 20 without air-con or from Rs 60 with air-con. There is also a good *Tourist Bungalow* here. *Hotel Imperial* has budget-type accommodation in pleasant rooms for Rs 10 a double with attached bathroom. Good vegetarian food is available.

TRICHUR

Situated 74 km north of Ernakulam, Trichur has the old temple of Vadakkunnathan (Hindus only), a museum and a zoo with a notable collection of snakes. In April-May of each year the Pooram festival is one of the biggest in the south with fireworks and colourful processions including brightly decorated

elephants. The Kerala Kala Mandalam at Cheruthuruthy, north of Trichur, is an important centre for training Kathakali dancers.

Places to Stay

Trichur has a comfortable *Tourist Bungalow* or *Jaya Lodge;* costs Rs 6/12 for singles/doubles.

COCHIN & ERNAKULAM

Cochin population	480,000
Ernakulam population	130,000

With its wealth of historical associations and beautiful setting on a cluster of islands and narrow peninsulas, Cochin is one of India's most interesting cities. It reflects the eclecticism of Kerala perfectly. Here you can see the oldest church in India, winding streets crammed with old houses constructed by the Portuguese 500 years ago, cantilevered Chinese fishing nets, a Jewish community with roots going back to 1000 AD and a 16th century synagogue, a palace built by the Portuguese and given to the Raja of Cochin which was later renovated by the Dutch and contains perhaps the most beautiful murals to be seen anywhere in India, a performance of the world-famous Kathakali dance-drama and many other things.

This unlikely pastiche of mediaeval Portugal, Holland and an English country village somehow grafted onto the tropical Malabar coast, which you find in the older parts of Fort Cochin and Mattancherry, contrasts wildly with the bright neon lights, dimly-lit seamen's bars and big hotels of mainland Ernakulam. A strange contrast perhaps but Port Cochin is one of India's largest ports. On any day of the year the misty silhouettes of huge merchant ships can be seen anchored in the ocean off the point of Fort Cochin waiting their turn for a berth in the docks of Ernakulam or Willingdon Island. This man-made island was created with material dredged up when the harbour was deepened. It also provides a site for the airport. As you might expect in a major port, there's a lot of wheeler-dealing going on so don't be too surprised if, when staying in Ernakulam, you get approached with offers for things which are not easy to acquire in India such as cameras, watches, tape recorders and the like.

Information & Orientation

Cochin consists of mainland Ernakulam, the islands of Willingdon, Bolgatty and Gundu in the harbour, Fort Cochin and Mattancherry on the southern peninsula and Vypeen Island north of Fort Cochin. All these seperate parts are connected by ferry. In addition there is a road and bridges connecting Ernakulam with Willingdon Island and the Fort Cochin/Mattancherry peninsula. The railway station, bus station, Tourist Reception Centre and the bulk of the hotels and cafes are located in Ernakulam. Mahatma Gandhi Rd is the locale of most of the top range hotels while the road connecting the railway station to Mahatma Gandhi Rd and Shanmughan Rd on the waterfront have most of the mid-range hotels. The budget hotels are situated mainly on Press Club Rd and Canon Rd off Broadway with a few just outside the railway station.

Almost all the historical sites are in Fort Cochin or Mattancherry but hotel and restaurant facilities here are very limited — there are only four budget-type hotels in this area. The GPO (including the Poste Restante) and Chinese fishing nets are also in Fort Cochin. On Willingdon Island is the airport and, at the tip of the island opposite Fort Cochin, the main Tourist Office and Cochin's top hotel, the Malabar. One of the best hotel bargains in Cochin, the Bolgatty Palace Hotel, a former palace built by the Dutch in 1744, is situated on Bolgatty Island. To get there first go to the Tourist Reception Centre outside the shopping precinct where Shanmughan Rd meets Broadway in Ernakulam. They operate a launch to the island, Vypeen Island is only of interest if you want to see the nearest surviving Portuguese fort which is situated on the northern end of the island at Pallipuram.

Cochin-Ernakulam District

Trichur

Bolghatty Is.

Ferry

Bus Sta.

Gundu Is.

Ernakulam

Vypeen

Ferries

Railway Sta.

Fort Cochin

Malabar Hotel

Ferry

Mattanchery

Willingdon Island

Arabian Sea

Airport

Alleppey

Useful Addresses

Tourist Reception Centre, Shanmughan Rd, Ernakulam (tel 33234). Friendly, helpful staff but not a lot of literature. They'll fix you up with accommodation at the Bolgatty Palace Hotel and with the conducted boat cruise around the harbour.

Tourist Office HQ: Attached to the Malabar Hotel on Willingdon Island.

This is the best tourist office in Southern India. Friendly, helpful and a whole range of leaflets and maps.

Indian Airlines: Situated on Broadway above the Bharat Coffee House.

Fort Cochin — St Francis Church

This is the oldest church constructed by Europeans on Indian soil. Vasco da Gama, first European to reach India by sailing around Africa, died in Cochin in 1524 and his tomb is here. It was built in 1503 by Portuguese Franciscan friars who accompanied the expedition led by Pedro Alvarez Gabral. The original structure was one of wood but the church was later rebuilt in stone around the middle of the 16th century — the earliest Portuguese inscription found in the church dates back to 1562. In 1663 it passed into the hands of the Protestant Dutch with their capture of Cochin and they later restored it in 1779. After the occupation of Cochin by the British in 1795 it became an Anglican church and is at present used by the Church of South India.

Although it's the earliest church constructed by Europeans in India Christianity has a much longer history on the Malabar coast. Tradition has it that St Thomas the Apostle landed here in AD 52 though there's no archaeological evidence to support this and the first documentary evidence of churches in Kerala comes from the accounts of a Byzantine monk who travelled here in the 6th century. By the middle of the 9th century the Christian communities were playing an important part in the trade and commerce of this area and there are records of substantial gifts of property to the Church of Teresa (no longer in existence) during the reign of Sthanu Ravi (844-85).

These earlier Christian communities were all Syrian Orthodox and, until the 16th century when the Portuguese put a stop to the practice in their efforts to enforce the supremacy of Rome, all the Keralan bishops were brought from Persia and Mesopotamia. This suppression of the Syrian Church was only partially successful, however, and even today there are many Syrian Orthodox churches to be found in Kerala.

Also in Fort Cochin is the much later Cathedral of Santa Cruz which is worth a visit.

Chinese Fishing Nets

Strung out along the tip of Fort Cochin opposite Vypeen Island, these cantilevered fishing nets were introduced by traders from the court of Kublai Khan. You can also see them along the backwaters between Cochin and Kottayam and between Alleppey and Quilon.

Mattancherry — Mattancherry Palace

The 'Dutch' Palace was built by the Portuguese in 1557 and presented to the Cochin Raja, Veera Kerala Varma (1537-61), as a gesture of goodwill (and probably as a means of securing trading priviledges). It was substantially renovated by the Dutch after 1663, hence its other name, the 'Dutch' Palace. It's a double-storied quadrangular building surrounding a central courtyard containing a Hindu temple. The central hall on the first floor was the Coronation Hall of the Rajas of Cochin and there is a display there of dresses, turbans and palanquins which once belonged to these rulers.

The most important aspect of this palace, however, is the astonishing murals in the bed-chambers and other rooms, depicting scenes from the Ramayana and Puranic legends connected with Shiva, Vishnu, Krishna, Kumara and Durga. These are without doubt some of the most beautiful and extensive you will see anywhere in India. You can pick up pamphlet after pamphlet of Indian tourist literature containing breathless eulogies of the murals at Ajanta and Ellora but never see a mention of these yet they are one of the wonders of India. It's worth coming to Cochin just to see these murals alone! There are similar murals at the Shiva temple in Ettumanur (a few km north of Kottayam).

The Palace is open daily between 9 am and 5 pm. Entrance is free but flash photography is prohibited (which effectively precludes photography al-

Key:-
1. Fort Cochin Bus Stand
2. Ferry to Vypeen
3. Ferry to Ernakulam
4. Ferry to Ernakulam
5. G.P.O.
6. St. Francis' Church
7. Santa Cruz Cathedral
8. P.W.D. Bungalow
9. X.L. Hotel
10. Elite Hotel
11. Port View Lodge
12. Mattancherry Palace (Dutch Palace)
13. Jewish Synagogue

Ferry

Chinese Fishing Nets

Dutch Cemetery Road

FORT COCHIN

Quiros St.

K B Jacob Road

COCHIN

K. B. Jacob Road

Palace Road

Hindu Temple

MATTANCHERRY

"Jewtown"

Ferry

together) which is a great pity since there are no books or postcards for sale here. There are three black and white photographs of the murals in the Archeological Survey of India's booklet, *Monuments of Kerala* by H Sarkar (1978, Rs 3.25). Other books where you will find them illustrated are, *Cochin Murals* by V R Chitra & T N Srinivasan (Cochin, 1940) and, *South Indian Paintings* by C Sivaramamurti (New Delhi, 1968).

The Jewish Synagogue

Built in 1567, this is the oldest synagogue in the Commonwealth. It was preceded by an earlier one at Kochangadi, built in 1344, which has since disappeared although a stone slab inscribed in Hebrew from this earlier building can be found on the inner surface of the wall which surrounds the present synagogue. The present building was smashed up by the Portuguese in 1662 and rebuilt two years later when the Dutch took over Cochin. It's an interesting little place with hand-painted, willow-pattern floor tiles (no two alike) brought from Canton, China, in the mid-18th century by Ezekial Rahabi who had trading interests in that city. He was also responsible for the erection of the clock tower which surmounts the building.

The synagogue is open daily from 10 am to 12 noon and from 3 pm until 5 pm except Saturdays and Jewish holidays. Entrance is free. The synagogue guardian is very friendly, keen to tell you about the history of the place and the Jewish community here, and to talk about what's happening in the rest of the world. He speaks fluent English.

This unexpected and isolated Jewish community has roots going back to the time of St Thomas the Apostle's voyage to India in AD 52. They had their first settlement at Cranganore, north of Cochin. Like the Syrian Orthodox Christians, they became involved in the

trade and commerce of Malabar coast and a number of copper plates inscribed in tiny ancient Hebrew script are preserved to this day in the synagogue recording the grant of the village of Anjuvannam (near Cranganore) and its revenue to the Jewish merchant, Joseph Rabban, by King Bhaskara Ravi Varman I (962-1020). You may view these plates if you ask the synagogue guardian for permission.

The concessions given by Ravi Varman I included permission to use a palanquin and parasol — in those days the prerogative of rulers — and so, in effect, gave sanction for the creation of a tiny Jewish kingdom. On Rabban's death his sons fought amongst each other for control of this 'kingdom' and this led to its break-up and the move to Mattancherry.

Quite a lot of research has been done on this community and one particularly interesting study which was done by an American professor of ethnomusicology found that the music of the Cochin Jews contained strong Babylonian influences and that their version of the Ten Commandments was almost identical with a Kurdish version housed in the Berlin Museum Archives. Naturally, there's also been a lot of local influence and many of the hymns are similar to ragas.

The area around the synagogue is known as Jewtown and is one of the centres of the spice trade in Cochin where scores of small firms huddle together in old dilapidated buildings and the air is filled with the pungent aromas of ginger, cardamom, cumin, turmeric and cloves. Many Jewish names are visible on business premises and houses but the community has diminished rapidly since Indian independence and now numbers only 45. Most of the young people have gone to Israel and few people under 50 years of age remain. When they die the community will probably go the same way and the synagogue be turned into a museum. As a mark of its decline, there has been no rabbi within living memory so all the elders are qualified to perform religious ceremonies and marriages. All the same, it's an interesting area and well worth a visit. There are many curio shops on the street leading up to the synagogue where you might pick up something interesting.

Ernakulam — Kathakali Dancing

This is India's most spectacular dance-drama and yet one which almost died out until renewed interest, particularly by westerners, recently gave it a new lease of life. The main centre is at Gurukulam Kathakali Yogam (director is P K Devan), off Chittoor Rd (tel 39471) which offers performances every evening at 7 pm for Rs 15. If you'd like to see the dancers putting on the make-up and costumes and hear an explanation of the symbolism of the dance-drama by the director, you must be there by 6.30 pm. Traditionally, performances are done in the open air of a temple courtyard or on the village green and continue into the early hours of the morning but since most visitors don't have the inclination to stay up all night, the centre here puts on an abridged version lasting 1½ hours.

The origins of the dance can be traced back to the first temples in Kerala over 2000 years ago when it started out as a way of educating the people in religious philosophy, ethics and the 'dharma'. It gradually developed 110 different arrangements, each lasting all night, based on stories from the Ramayana and Mahabharata with the performers trained from the age of five for a minimum of 20 years. Most of the dancers were drawn from families which had been attached to temples for several generations and who were responsible for providing the chanting, drumming and flower garlands for the deities as well as accompanying the

images of the gods carried on elephant-back during festivals.

It's more than just a form of dancing — more a specialised form of yoga incorporating elements of Ayurvedic medicine. To the accompaniment of traditional musical instruments — two drums and finger cymbals — each of the stories is told in stylised and ritualistic gestures, facial expressions and graceful body movements with the aid of vivid and exotic costumes. All the props and make-up are fashioned out of natural materials — powdered minerals and the sap of trees for the bright colours of the face; wigs made from the beaten bark of certain trees dyed with fruits and herbs; coconut oil for mixing up colours and burnt coconut oil for the black paint around the eyes; egg-plant flowers tucked under the eyelids to turn the whites of eyes deep red; the masks and crowns made from special varieties of wood. Even the drums are made strictly out of very old jackfruit trees alone which have been growing near temples and a river to ensure that the wood will have absorbed the vibrations of temple music for a long time. Many other Ayurvedic potions and remedies are an integral part of preparation for the dance-drama and even a specialised form of massage has been developed to keep the dancers' bodies and minds at the peak of perfection.

This particular dance company was built up over 100 years by Guru Gopala who only died in 1977 at the age of 100 and who was still dancing until he was 96. His son, Shivaram, himself now in his 60s, has taken over but spends most of his time in America. When Guru Paniker started to dance, the art form was almost extinct and it was largely through his efforts that it survived. His other son, P K Devan, has spent much of his life chronicling the art and explaining its principles and methods to visitors from outside India.

The troupe has performed in many places around the world including the USA, Canada, UK, Japan, Fiji and Australia. As a result of the upsurge of interest in Kathakali dancing, a similar dance form known as Kuchipudi has recently been revived in Andhra Pradesh.

Gundu Island

The smallest island in Cochin harbour is located close to Vypeen Island. There is a coir factory here — the only building on the island — where attractive door-mats are made out of the coconut fibre. You come across their mats all over Cochin. The only way to get there is on the boat tour organised by the Kerala Tourist Development Corporation.

Tours

The Kerala Tourist Development Corporation offers two conducted boat cruises daily around Cochin harbour and includes visits to Willingdon Island, Mattancherry Palace and the Jewish Synagogue at Mattancherry, Fort Cochin including St Francis Church, Gundu Island and Bolgatty Island. The first tour is 9 am-12.30 pm and the second tour is 2-5.30 pm. Cost of the tour is Rs 10 and the tour is very worthwhile.

For reservations contact either the Tourist Reception Centre, Shanmughan Road, Ernakulam (tel 33234) or the Manager, Bolgatty Palace Hotel, Bolgatty Island (tel 35003). The tour starts and finishes at the boat jetty in front of the Sealord Hotel, Shanmughan Road, Ernakulam. You can also board the boat at the Tourist Office Jetty, Willingdon Island, 20 minutes after the start of each tour from the Sealord boat jetty.

Places to Stay

If you want top-range hotels then you have a choice of Ernakulam and Willingdon Island. For mid-range hotels you have a choice of Ernakulam and Bol-

gatty Island. If you want a budget hotel then you have a choice of Ernakulam, Bolgatty Island and Fort Cochin.

Places to Stay — Top End

Cochin's best hotel is the *Malabar Hotel* (tel 6811) at the tip of Willingdon Island. It has all the conveniences you would expect of a hotel of this nature plus a superb location overlooking the harbour. Rooms cost Rs 120 a single and Rs 200 a double with attached bathroom and air-conditioning. Bar and restaurant attached and the Tourist Office HQ is part of the complex.

Other upper end hotels include the *Casino Hotel* (tel 6821) on Willingdon Island with singles/doubles from Rs 100/150, all rooms are air-conditioned. The *Grand Hotel* on Mahatma Gandhi Rd, Ernakulam is all air-con and costs from Rs 100/150 for singles/doubles. On the same road the *International Hotel* (tel 33911) has singles/doubles from Rs 60/80 without air-con, Rs 80/100 with air-con. On Shanmugham Rd in Ernakulam the *Sealord Hotel* (tel 32682) has singles/doubles from Rs 100/175, all with air-con.

If having to endure the expensive monotony and luxurious tedium of the international jet-set isn't your primary concern then the *Woodlands Hotel*, Mahatma Gandhi Rd, Ernakulam, would be a very acceptable alternative. Rooms here cost Rs 30 a single and Rs 50 a double with attached bathroom but without air-conditioning, or Rs 50 a single and Rs 70 a double with attached bathroom and air-conditioning. Other hotels within walking distance of the Woodlands which are of a similar quality and price range include the *Grand Hotel* and the *Anand Bhavan*, both on Mahatma Gandhi Rd.

Places to Stay — Middle

Undoubtedly the best of the mid-range hotels is the *Bolgatty Palace Hotel* on Bolgatty Island. Formerly a palace built

1	Tourist Bungalow	11	Hotel National & Indian Coffee House
2	Premier Tourist Home		
3	Central Lodge	12	Basoto Lodge
4	Hotel Sangeetha	13	Indian Airlines & Bharat Coffee House
5	Hotel Sea Lines & Durbar Lodge		
		14	Hakoba Hotel
6	Indian Coffee House	15	Dubai Hotel
7	Anand Bhavan	16	Blue Diamond Hotel
8	Geetha Lodge	17	YWCA
9	Woodlands	18	Kathakali Dancing Centre
10	Grand Hotel		

by the Dutch in 1744 and later a British Residency, it is now run by the Kerala Tourist Development Corporation as a hotel. It's set in 6 hectares of lush green lawns with a golf course, bar and restaurant. Rooms here are a bargain at Rs 23 a single and Rs 35 a double both with attached bathroom. For the ferry service to the island contact the Tourist Reception Centre, Shanmughan Road, Ernakulam, or ring the hotel itself — 35003. Ferries to the island run on a definite schedule but if you want to get there or leave there at any other time, rowing boats are available (price negotiable). If you'd like to stay there make sure the KTDC union isn't about to call a strike. Two days after I got there all the personnel connected with the Tourist Offices, the Bolgatty Palace Hotel and the ferry service to Bolgatty Island went on strike and everyone had to leave! It doesn't happen often.

Some other very pleasant mid-range hotels include the *Hotel Blue Diamond*, Br Market Road. Rooms here cost Rs 16 a single and Rs 35 a double plus 10% tax both with attached bathroom. Very good value and the staff are very friendly. *Hakoba Hotel*, Shanmughan Rd, is on the waterfront with excellent views over the harbour from the front rooms which cost Rs 30 a double with attached bathroom (or Rs 25 a double if occupied by a single person). It's secure, clean sheets are provided and there's even a lift! Attached bar and restaurant.

Hotel Sea Lines, half way between Mahatma Gandhi Rd and Chittoor Rd (see map), is a clean, pleasant place with friendly staff. Rooms cost Rs 14.75 a single and Rs 22-27 a double both with attached bathrooms. Restaurant downstairs. *Hotel Sea Shells*, Shanmughan Rd is very close to the Hakoba Hotel. Rooms here cost Rs 15 a single and Rs 30 a double both with attached bathrooms. Lively bar and cafe downstairs. *Ernakulam Tourist Bungalow*, on the right past the Premier Tourist Home as you come out of the railway station. Rooms cost Rs 12 a single and Rs 20 a double. There's a good restaurant and bar attached.

Places to Stay — Bottom End

If you'd prefer the sleepy, laid-back atmosphere of the old part of the city then head for Fort Cochin. If you want the beer, drugs and city action of an international port then stay in Ernakulam.

In Fort Cochin you have a choice of the following: *PWD Bungalow*, Dutch Cemetery Rd. The best value in budget accommodation in the whole of Cochin. Superb location looking out over the Indian Ocean. Rooms are a bargain at Rs 4 a single and Rs 8 a double with common bathrooms and toilets. Very popular with travellers but because of its price and location often full. Well worth trying to get in here. *XL Hotel* is on the same street as the GPO. Another hotel which is popular with

Ernakulam

travellers. Rooms cost Rs 7 a single with common bathroom and Rs 14 a double with attached bathroom. There is a cafe and bar downstairs.

Elite Hotel Very close to St Francis Church (see map). Rooms here cost Rs 5 a single and Rs 10 a double both with common bathroom and toilets. Like the XL Hotel it's an old building so expect the floorboards to creak. The non-vegetarian cafe on the ground floor is excellent value (egg biriyani, papadum and coffee for Rs 3.50) and popular with local young people and students. The *YWCA* is a few metres from the GPO overlooking the green in front of St Francis Church. It's a very small place and often full but worth enquiring about if you're in the area.

Port View Lodge is about half way between Fort Cochin and Mattancherry (see map). One of the very few places that can be classified as a budget hotel (there are a few incredibly decrepit doss-houses along this road). It's an old place with beautifully carved stairways and bannisters which has been allowed to go to seed but it still retains a lot of character and the views from the roof are excellent but I'd be reluctant to leave anything valuable 'locked up' in a room here (I can't substantiate that, it's just a feeling). Rooms cost Rs 8 a single for an ordinary room and Rs 12 a single for a room which looks like an Indian impression of an *Anthony & Cleopatra* film set. Common bathrooms and toilets. Recommended by those travellers who swear by BIT Information travel guides.

In Ernakulam probably the best budget hotel is the *Premier Tourist Home*, on the right hand side out of the railway station. Rooms cost Rs 10 a single and Rs 15 a double with attached bathroom. Clean sheets are provided, there are mosquito nets on the windows and the staff are friendly and helpful.

Other than this you could try the *Hotel National*, Canon Shed Rd (oppos-ite the main boat jetty). Rooms cost Rs 8 a single and Rs 15 a double with common bathrooms and toilets. The rooms are built around a pleasant, quiet courtyard and the place is popular with budget travellers. Very friendly management and a convenient place to stay. *Central Lodge* is just outside the railway station on the left hand side on the road connecting the station to Chittoor Rd. A plain concrete edifice with indifferent management and somewhat over-priced rooms at Rs 12 a single and Rs 15 a double with attached bathrooms. The *Basoto Lodge* on Press Club Rd is another conveniently located budget hotel with similar facilities and prices to the Hotel National.

The budget hotels indicated in the Fort Cochin area are the only hotels in that part of the city. There are a few hotels south of Mattancherry on the road which goes past the palace but they are well out of the way.

There's a lot of union activity going on in the hotel business in support of better wages so you may find that some of the above hotels are temporarily closed due to a strike. For instance, the employees at the Sealord Hotel on the waterfront in Ernakulam have been on strike now for over a year and have had pickets at the entrance throughout that time! Considering that there's no system of Social Security in India, you can't help but admire their determination. The pickets, who were very friendly and eager to talk, told me they used to earn Rs 120/month and had struck in support of a Rs 30/month increase — hardly an outrageous demand considering the prices which used to be charged for rooms there. Nevertheless, the management refused to budge. Give them a donation if you go past — they need it.

Places to Eat

Many hotels have their own restaurants but apart from these the following can be recommended. There are several *Indian Coffee Houses* but the most convenient ones are at the bottom of Canon Shed Rd opposite the main ferry jetties and at the junction of Mahatma Gandhi Rd with the road from the railway station. They offer very good, cheap semi-western and Indian food and excellent real coffee. Very popular with local people and always busy.

Hotel Dubai, Shanmughan Rd, is one of the best cafes in Ernakulam. Serves excellent non-vegetarian food in pleasant surroundings and it's spotlessly clean. Mutton curry, peas masala, three parathas, fresh lime juice and coffee for Rs 8.45. Service is quick. *Ranjim Vegetarian Restaurant* on Chittoor Rd is part of the Sangeetha Hotel. Excellent food and a varied menu with an air-conditioned room upstairs if you need it. *Bharat Coffee House*, Broadway, is located below the Indian Airlines office, it's similar to the Indian Coffee Houses. Good, cheap, Indian vegetarian food and excellent coffee.

In Fort Cochin the very popular *Elite Hotel*, near St Francis Church, is recommended for good non-vegetarian meals. One traveller reported in glowing terms that the *Golden Dragon Restaurant*, opposite the Park Hotel, was an experience not to be missed. Good Chinese food and excellent music and decor — 'quite alien to India' in fact.

There are many lively, dimly-lit bars along Mahatma Gandhi Rd and Shanmughan Rd in Ernakulam if you're looking for some light entertainment. Non-stop Abba music with the occasional Beatles' song thrown in for a little variety in most of them (half of Abba's income must come from India.) Beers are the same price in all the bars — Rs 9.45 a large bottle.

Getting There

Air Indian Airlines have daily flights from Cochin to Madras (Rs 465), Bombay (Rs 735), Trivandrum (Rs 150) and Coimbatore (Rs 135).

Rail Twice a week the Karnataka-Kerala runs from New Delhi to Ernakulam, the 2833 km trip takes 43 hours and costs Rs 412 in 1st class, Rs 101 in 2nd. On the other days of the week it runs from Hazrat Nizamuddin, just outside New Delhi and goes to Cochin but is considerably slower.

The 201 km trip to Trivandrum takes four to five hours at a cost of Rs 52 in 1st, Rs 12 in 2nd. Bangalore is a 629 km trip taking 14 hours and costing Rs 133 in 1st, Rs 33 in 2nd on the Island Express. It's 1841 km and 38 hours to Bombay and the Jayanti Janata Express only has 2nd class which costs Rs 73. This train continues on right down to Trivandrum.

The Malabar Express makes a daily run from Mangalore to Trivandrum right along the Kerala coast through Calicut, Trichur, Ernakulam, Cochin, Kottayam, Quilon to Trivandrum. Other trains also follow part of this coastal route. The Ernakulam-Kottayam daily service at 7 am and 5.30 pm and the Ernakulam-Quilon service at 11.30 am are local passenger trains which you might find useful.

Bus Buses depart from the central Bus Station in Ernakulam. To Alleppey there are one to three buses every hour. First bus at 5.45 am and the last at 10.55 pm. To Bangalore, daily at 5 and 7 am. To Calicut there are six buses daily. First bus at 5.15 am and the last at 7.35 pm. To Cannanore, four buses daily at 2 and 9.30 am, 3 pm and 10.30 pm. To Kottayam, nine buses daily, first at 7.45 am and the last at 9 pm. To Palghat, 10 buses daily. First bus at 1.30 am and the last at 7 pm. Costs Rs 10.50 and takes four hours. To Quilon, three buses daily at 9.40 am, 5.40 and 7.15 pm. To Trichur, one per hour between 6.25 and 10.10 am; three per hour between 11 am and 1 pm and one per hour between 1 and 6.55 pm (last). Takes 2½ hours. To Trivandrum, two to three times per hour throughout the night and day. The majority of these buses start from Ernakulam but others come from further north.

Getting Around
Ferries These are the main form of transport between the various parts of Cochin. If you're going to be making your own way around the sights of Cochin and Mattancherry (especially if you're staying in Ernakulam) then you need to think about the sequence you're going to do it in since there are no ferries or convenient bus connections between Fort Cochin and Mattancherry. Also, there are two Fort Cochin ferry jetties and they too are not connected with each other (it's a 10-15 minute walk between the two). In some ways it's easier to get to the main part of Fort Cochin from Ernakulam by taking the ferry to Vypeen and then another ferry from there to Fort Cochin. There are no ferry connections between Fort Cochin and Willingdon Island so if you want to do this you have to hire a row boat (costs Rs 2 per person).

If you're taking the ferry from Ernakulam to Fort Cochin note that the boarding arrangements are ridiculously chaotic. It's the typical Indian mass hysteria trip. You often have to scramble across three boats to get to the ferry you want and there are no indications as to which boat is going where. It's suggested you don't attempt this with a rucksack! It's only this ferry on which you get the chaos — all the others are well organised. It doesn't make sense of course, except perhaps in an Indian context.

Perumanoor-Willingdon Island 35 times daily in either direction. First ferry at 6 am and the last at 10 pm. Costs 15p and takes 10 minutes. Not a very useful ferry since the jetty on Willingdon Island is a long way from the Tourist Office and Malabar Hotel.

Ernakulam-Mattancherry Goes via Willingdon Island. This is the ferry to take if you want to go to the Tourist Office or to the Mattancherry Palace and the Jewish Synagogue. 29 times daily in either direction. From Ernakulam the first ferry is at 6.30 am and the last at 9.40 pm. From Mattancherry the first ferry is at 6 am and the last at 9 pm. Costs Rs 0.50 and takes 20 minutes.

Ernakulam-Fort Cochin 18 times daily in either direction. From Ernakulam the first ferry is at 6.30 am and the last at 8.40 pm. From Fort Cochin the first ferry is at 6.50 am and the last at 9 pm. Costs Rs 0.50 and takes 10-15 minutes.

Ernakulam-Vypeen Island 40 times daily in either direction. From Ernakulam the first ferry is at 5.30 am and the last at 10.30 pm. From Vypeen the first ferry is at 6 am and the last at 10 pm. Costs Rs 0.50 and takes 15 minutes.

Mattancherry-Willingdon Island Willindon Island is known as 'Terminus' on the timetable board at Mattancherry. Two ferries every hour (on the hour and the half hour as a rule). The first ferry is at 6 am and the last at 9 pm. Costs 30p and takes 5-10 minutes.

Fort Cochin-Vypeen Island Every 10 minutes approximately in either direction throughout the day and evening. Costs 20p and takes 3-4 minutes. There is also a drive on-drive off car ferry between these two points which operates 15 times daily in either direction.

Buses There are no convenient bus services between Fort Cochin and the Mattancherry Palace/Jewish Synagogue. Buses do run from Fort Cochin down K B Jacob Rd to South Mattancherry but it's a 15 minute walk back to the Palace from where you get off. If you're planning on walking between the two (a pleasant half an hour walk) you can go either along K B Jacob Rd and then Palace Rd or along the port-side road. It's probably best to take an auto-rickshaw but none of the drivers are willing to use the meter so expect to pay at least Rs 3 (they won't take you unless you agree to the price asked).

In Ernakulam, auto-rickshaws are the most convenient form of transport and drivers use the meters. The trip from the bus station to the Tourist Reception Centre, Shanmughan Rd costs about Rs 2.

AROUND COCHIN

High in the Western Ghats, 137 km inland from Cochin, Munnar is a cool retreat amongst the tea plantations. Kaladi is 48 km north-east of Cochin and was the birthplace of the 8th century philosopher and monotheist Shankaracharya. Cranganore is only 35 km north of Cochin by ferry but 77 km north by road. There's a Portuguese Fort and Hindu temples here plus the oldest mosque in India. St Thomas first set foot in India in 52 AD at nearby Kottapuram.

KOTTAYAM

There is a regular ferry service (more than 10 boats a day) through the lagoons from Alleppey to Kottayam. This was a centre for the Syrian Christians of Kerala and there are a number of their churches including Cheria Pallia and Valia Palli about five km north-west of the railway station. Today Kottayam is also a centre for Indian rubber production. Kottayam is a good base for visits to the Periyar Wild Life Sanctuary.

Places to Stay

The *Anjali Hotel* (tel 3661) on K K Rd has singles/doubles from Rs 40/60 with air-con. At the *Hotel Ambassador* (tel 3755, 3293-94) also on K K Rd prices are similar but there are also some slightly cheaper non air-con rooms. Kottayam also has a *Tourist Bungalow*.

PERIYAR WILD LIFE SANCTUARY

This unique wild life sanctuary is close to the border with Tamil Nadu. The 800 square km sanctuary is centred around an artificial lake and you view the wild life from launches which go along the convoluted waterways. There are bison, elephants and a few tigers which come down to the lakeside to drink. November to March is the best time to visit Periyar although those rare tigers are more likely to be seen during the dry season.

Places to Stay

There is a *Tourist Bungalow* in the middle of the lake and launches can be arranged from there. The *Aranya Niwas Hotel* is at Thekkady. *Periyar House* has doubles with bath for Rs 35.

Getting There

Thekkady is 270 km from Cochin and 144 km from Madurai. There are buses from Trivandrum, Quilon, Alleppey and Kottayam. It's a very pleasant drive up from Kottayam, bus leaves at 2.45 pm.

QUILON (population 140,000)

Buried amongst coco palms and cashew tree plantations on the edge of Ashtamudi Lake this small market town of old wooden houses with red-tiled roofs overhanging winding streets is perhaps the most typical of Keralan towns. If you're coming up from the south, it's also the gateway to the backwaters of Kerala. The trip by boat to Alleppey through these backwaters is a fascinating and unique experience not to be missed.

Quilon has roots going back centuries and its history is interwoven with the rivalries between the Portuguese, Dutch

Railway Station
Shencottah
Trivandrum
YMCA
Clock Tower
Hotel Mrishtanna
Travellers' Bungalow
Main Road
Sika Lodge
Post Office
Temple
Bank of India
Metro Hotel & Cafe
Chithira Lodge
Hotel Guru Prasad
Hotel de Orient
Parameswar Nagar
Hotel Sudarsan
Lakshmi Tourist Home
Fruit & Vegetable Market
Anzar Lodge
Alleppey
Bus Station
Boat Jetty
Quilon
Scale
0 1/2 1 km
Lake

and English for control of commodities grown in this part of the sub-continent and the trade routes across the Indian Ocean. Only 3 km from the centre of town at Thangasseri stand the ruins of a fort originally constructed by the Portuguese and later taken over by the Dutch. In Ashtamudi Lake stand many Chinese fishing nets of the type more usually associated with Cochin further north.

Information & Orientation

The transport facilities are located at opposite ends of the town, three km apart, so if you arrive by rail and want to get to the bus station or the boat jetty you will need to take an autorickshaw (costs approximately Rs 2.50). Other than the Tourist Bungalow (not to be confused with the Travellers' Bungalow) which is a long way from the centre of town (Rs 7 auto-rickshaw ride), most hotels are located in the central area of town between the Clock Tower and the Post Office. There is no Tourist Office in Quilon. The GPO is open until 8 pm from Monday to Saturday and until 6 pm on Sundays and public holidays.

What to See

Other than the ruins of the Portuguese/Dutch fort at Thangasseri, there are few 'sights' as such in Quilon. It's just a pleasant place to stroll around for a day or so and soak up the atmosphere of a Keralan market town. Most travellers come here to take the boat through the backwaters or, if coming from Alleppey, are en route to Trivandrum. As such it's an overnight stop.

Places to Stay

The most interesting place to stay is the *Tourist Bungalow* — a former British Residency converted to a hotel and run by the Kerala Tourist Development Corporation. The tourist literature is fond of telling you that 'Lord Curzon slept here'. It's a beautiful place overlooking the lake but rather a long way from town. Rooms cost Rs 11 per person but there are only eight rooms and although meals are available they're on the expensive side. Although it might seem a cheap place to stay you must add on the cost of getting there by auto-rickshaw (about Rs 7 one-way).

In the town itself there are the following: *Hotel Sudarsan*, Parameswar Nagar, between the Post Office and the boat jetty. A large place with its own courtyard and friendly staff. Rooms cost Rs 20 a single, Rs 25 a double if occupied by one person and Rs 30 a double if occupied by two people. All rooms have attached bath, it's clean and sheets are provided.

Sika Lodge/Hotel Apsara, is 100 metres from the bridge across the river. Rooms cost Rs 15 a single and Rs 20 a double with attached bathroom. An initial deposit of Rs 25 is payable — any excess is returned to you when you leave. It's clean, pleasant and quiet, there is room service and the staff are friendly. The restaurant on the ground floor serves typical South Indian food.

Hotel Mrishtanna, 50 metres from the Clock Tower, is a fairly modern place. They have no single rooms and doubles cost Rs 16 with attached bathroom. It's often full. There's a restaurant on the ground floor. The *Travellers' Bungalow* is on the far side of the bridge across the river. Rooms here cost Rs 13 a double with own bathroom. *Hotel de Orient* is mainly a flop-house and drinking spot for single men which is unfortunate since it's set in beautiful grounds. It's pretty scruffy and the cell-like rooms cost Rs 10 (singles only).

Places to Eat

Metro Hotel & Cafe, Main Rd, a good clean non-vegetarian cafe offering a choice of mutton, chicken and egg dishes. Egg biriyani, pickle, onion salad, coffee and a cold drink will cost Rs 6.50. *Hotel Guru Prasad*, Main St, opposite the Metro Hotel, is a vegetarian cafe which serves excellent food.

Mahalakshmi Lodge, opposite the bus station, serves standard South Indian vegetarian banana-leaf meals. Better than the Mysore Restaurant next door if you want to preserve your teeth as they don't appear to seive the rice from the grit at that place. Otherwise it's very similar. The *Hotel Apsara* also serves good South Indian meals.

Getting There

Rail Quilon is 156 km south of Cochin and takes three or four hours by train at a fare of Rs 44 in 1st, Rs 9.50 in 2nd. The Madras-Cochin service continues on to Quilon, as does the Bombay-Cochin and the Mangalore-Trivandrum coastal service. There are also trains between Quilon and Madras Egmore via Madurai (eight hours, Rs 119 in 1st, Rs 29 in 2nd). Passenger trains between Quilon and Trivandrum are very slow in comparison to the buses (they take about three hours) but are also very cheap. From Quilon they depart daily at 6.25 am and 5.45 and 8.15 pm.

Buses

Note that many of the buses from Quilon bus station do not originate from there but are en route from somewhere else. Along the most important routes they depart as follows:

Going South To Trivandrum at least 23 times daily. First bus at 3.10 am and last bus at 10.40 pm. The trip takes about two hours and costs Rs 5.80.

Going North To Alleppey there are six buses daily. First bus at 5.30 am and last bus at 6.30 pm. To Ernakulam there are 15 buses daily. First bus at 1 am and last bus at 11.10 pm.

Going East To Shencottah there are six buses daily. First bus at 6.15 am and last bus at 8 pm. There are plenty of other buses going further up the coast and to intermediate towns.

Boats — The Backwater Trip

This trip is one of the highlights of a

visit to Kerala and one which you will remember fondly for a long time. It takes you across shallow palm-fringed lakes studded with cantilevered Chinese fishing nets, along narrow shady canals where coir (coconut fibre), copra (dried coconut meat) and cashews are loaded onto dugouts, and calls at many small settlements along the way. It's interesting to see how people live on narrow spits of land only a few metres wide, water all around, yet still manage to keep cows, pigs, chickens and ducks and cultivate small vegetable gardens. On the more open stretches of canal you'll see dugouts with huge sails and prows carved into the shape of dragons. The sight of three or four of these sailing towards you in the late afternoon sun is one never to be forgotten. The boat crews are friendly and will allow you to sit on the roof if you exchange a little conversation with them. There are two 10 minute 'chai stops' along the way where snacks and tea can be bought so there's no point in bringing these along with you. Daily departures from Quilon are at 10 am and 8.30 pm. From Alleppey at 7.30 am and 10.30 pm. The trip takes approximately 8½ hours and costs only Rs 3 per person.

Other, shorter boat trips are possible from Quilon if, for some reason, you can't make the trip to Alleppey. They are Quilon-Kapapuzha daily at 9.30 am and 9.45 pm. Quilon-Guhanandapuram daily at 7.30 am, 11 am, 1.30 pm, 5.30 pm, 8 pm and 10.30 pm. It's not necessary to book any of the boat trips in advance. There's always plenty of room and no problems with rucksacks, etc.

VARKALA

Only 19 km south of Quilon, 55 km north of Trivandrum, Varkala is a seaside resort with a mineral water spring on the beach and the Janardhana Temple. Near here at Anjengo one of the earliest British East India Company trading posts was established in 1684.

ALLEPPEY (population 175,000)

Like Quilon, a pleasant, easy-going market town surrounded by coco-palm plantations and built around canals which service the coir industry of the backwaters. There's precious little to see in Alleppey and in fact when I got there a bunch of medical students at St George's Lodge said to me, 'Why have you come here? There's nothing in Alleppey!' While that may be true for most of the year there is one event which you should not miss if you're anywhere in the vicinity on the second Saturday of August. This is the snakeboat races which take place here for the Nehru Cup. On this day scores of long low-slung dug-outs with high decorated sterns and up to 100 rowers compete for the cup watched by thousands of spectators on the banks. It's the biggest event of the year.

The other reason you might pass through here on any other day of the year is, of course, to make the backwater trip to Quilon (or, if you're coming from that place, to stay here overnight before heading further north). For fuller details on this unforgettable trip, refer to the section on Quilon.

Information & Orientation

The bus station and boat jetty are located conveniently close to each other on the canal but are some distance from the main hotels so, if you have a lot of baggage, it's worth taking an auto-rickshaw. If you don't want to do this, St George's Lodging — Alleppey's best bargain in hotels — is a good 15 minutes walk from the boat jetty. There is no rail connection with Alleppey.

What to See

The Hindu temple, opposite the Indian Coffee House, is worth a look although, as a non-Hindu, you won't be allowed inside. It's a fine example of an elaborately carved wooden South Indian temple somewhat reminiscent of those in Nepal. Alleppey has a lengthy but filthy beach.

Places to Stay

St George's Lodging is magnificent value. It's spotlessly clean, pleasantly decorated, has curtained windows, provides clean sheets and the staff are very friendly. There's even a Gideon's Bible on the desk! (The only time I've ever come across one in India.) Rooms cost Rs 6 a single, Rs 12 a double and Rs 14 a triple. Double and triple rooms have attached bathrooms. Single rooms share clean common baths. There's nowhere else to compare with this in

Alleppey.

Dhanalekshmi Lodge is diagonally opposite the Hindu temple. An older building than St George's Lodging and not as well-maintained. Rooms cost Rs 6 a single with common bathroom and Rs 12 a double with attached bath. *Raja Tourist Home* is probably the next best after St George's. Rooms here cost Rs 6 a single and Rs 12 a double, both with attached bathroom.

There are several other budget hotels opposite the boat jetty such as *Krishna Bhavan* and *Mahalekshmi Lodge* but they look decidedly scruffy.

Outside of town, close to the beach is the *PWD Bungalow*. It's a very pleasant place to stay and cheap at Rs 5 per person but you must add the cost of getting there by auto-rickshaw or taxi. Also, there are no restaurants nearby and meals at the PWD are expensive. Nevertheless, it's recommended by many travellers and is near the beach.

Places to Eat

One of the pleasant places to eat is the *Indian Coffee House* opposite the Hindu temple. It serves cheap non-vegetarian food and is divided up into several rooms furnished with comfortable chairs and coir matting on the floor. The waiters display a touch of the Raj in their white uniforms, cummerbunds and frilly turbans. Some sample prices include plain omelette Rs 1.60; tomato omelette Rs 1.70; mutton curry Rs 2.25; mutton biriyani Rs 4.50; masala dosa Rs 0.85. They serve excellent real coffee — of course. The cafe is popular with students and the local intelligentsia.

The *Komala Hotel*, on the other side of the canal bridge, has been recommended as having 'the best food in South India' by one traveller. If you're looking for vegetarian plate meals (standard South Indian menu), there are a number of vegetarian cafes near the Raja Tourist Home.

Getting There

Buses The main express services north and south are as follows:

Going South To Quilon there are eight buses daily. First bus at 7.20 am and the last at 9.05 pm. To Trivandrum there are 29 buses daily. First bus at 12.50 am and the last at 11.10 pm.

Going North To Ernakulam there are 38 buses daily. First bus at 1.50 am and the last at 10.35 pm. Takes 1½-2 hours and costs Rs 5. Note that if you are heading for Fort Cochin as opposed to Ernakulam then you can get off this bus just before the bridge which connects Cochin and Willingdon Island (see the district map of Cochin and Ernakulam) and take a service bus or auto-rickshaw from there into either Mattancherry or Fort Cochin. This will save you a lot of messing about with ferries when you get to Ernakulam.

To Cannanore daily at 9.17 pm. To Calicut (Kozhikode) daily at 5.30 pm. To Palghat daily at 8.15 am, 10.05 am, 1.20 pm and 4 pm.

Boats

To Quilon (the backwater trip) The boats depart daily at 7.30 am and 10.30 pm. The trip takes about 8½ hours and costs Rs 3. For more details on this incredible trip refer to the Quilon section.
To Alleppey It's also possible to boat between Alleppey and Quilon but the boats only operate at night so the bus is better.

To Kottayam These boats cross Lake Vembanad, taking 2½ hours and cost Rs 1.50. There are 14 boats daily, the first at 5 am and the last at 9.30 pm.

TRIVANDRUM (population 460,000)
Strolling around this friendly, laid-back city built over seven luxuriously forested hills, it's hard to imagine this is a state

capital. The 'City of the Sacred Snake' is quite unlike any other state capital in India and has managed to retain the magic ambience that is so characteristic of Kerala in general. Low sky-line, red-tiled roofs, narrow winding lanes, intimate corner cafes, beaten-up municipal buses and necessary business accomplished in a friendly manner with a relatively high degree of efficiency.

At least, this is how it is when political tensions between the various factions haven't got to the stage where they spill out into violence on the streets. Political slogans, emblems and flags, especially those of the communist parties, dominate the urban landscape of Kerala. Luckily, even when there's violence, it rarely affects the traveller or tourist and is generally an indication that you'll be drawn into some very lively discussions in the cafes and restaurants.

On the other hand, there isn't a great deal to see in Trivandrum itself other than the museum, art gallery and zoological gardens. The famous Sri Padmanabhaswamy Temple, though a magnificent example of South Indian architecture, isn't an 'attraction' as such (though the tourist literature will have you believe otherwise) since it's not open to non-Hindus. The main reason people come to Trivandrum is to stay at Kovalam beach, 16 km south of the city and one of the finest in all India. You also might find yourself staying here for a day or so if you're planning on flying to Sri Lanka or to the Maldive Islands.

Information & Orientation
Trivandrum is spread out over quite a large area but most of the services and places of interest are located on, or very near to, Mahatma Gandhi Rd which is the main road running through the centre of the city from the zoological gardens to the Sri Padmanabhaswamy Temple. The long-distance bus terminal,

railway station and Tourist Reception Centre are all to be found within a few metres of each other as are many of the budget hotels though very few of the latter can be recommended as pleasant places to stay. The municipal bus stand is five minutes' walk from the railway station opposite Sri Padmanabhaswamy Temple. From here bus No 15 runs to Kovalam beach 25 times daily, the first at 6.20 am, the last at 9 pm, and takes approximately half an hour. (Even if you have to take the last bus to Kovalam there's no problem finding accommodation when you get there). The post office in Trivandrum is a good quarter hour walk from the railway station and for the museum, art gallery and zoological gardens you will need to take either an auto-rickshaw or taxi.

Useful Addresses
Tourist Reception Centre: Situated between the railway station and Mahatma Gandhi Rd (right hand side). Open daily. They have maps of Trivandrum but precious little else that isn't 20 years out of date. It's here that you book tours of Trivandrum City, Cape Cormorin and Thekkady Wildlife Sanctuary. The headquarters of the Kerala Tourist Development Corporation is located on the north-east side of the Secretariat building.

Tourindia, Mahatma Gandhi Rd (tel 4407). One of the best travel agents in Trivandrum. They arrange coach tours to all the main places of interest in Kerala such as Padmanabhapuram Palace, Tekkady Wildlife Sanctuary, Quilon, Alleppey and Cochin, as well as airline tickets. Friendly service.

Museum, Art Gallery & Zoological Gardens
These are all located in the same area in the park at the north end of the city. They are open daily except Mondays and Wednesday mornings between 8 am and 6 pm.

Museum Housed in an attractive building, it offers a good collection of bronzes, historical and contemporary ornaments, temple carts, ivory carvings and life-size figures of Kathakali dancers in full regalia.

Sri Chitra Art Gallery Here are displayed paintings of the Rajput, Mughal and Tanjore schools together with works from China, Tibet, Japan and Bali. In addition, there are many modern Indian paintings, especially those of Ravi Varma.

Zoological Gardens This is one of the best laid-out zoos in Asia set amongst woodland, lakes and well-maintained lawns. It includes a botanical garden where there are examples of almost every tropical tree.

Aquarium
Situated quite a distance from the city centre near the airport. It houses what you would expect of an aquarium plus many rare species of aquatic animal. Open daily except Mondays between 9.30 am and 6 pm.

Padmanabhapuram Palace
55 km south of Trivandrum on the way to Kanyakumari (Cape Cormorin), this was once the seat of the rulers of Travancore — a princely state during the days of the Raj which included a large part of present-day Kerala and the western littoral of Tamil Nadu. It's a stunningly beautiful and elaborately carved wooden palace with decorative murals inside. Well worth the effort to go and see. To get there you can either take a service bus from Trivandrum (or Kovalam beach) or go on one of the tours organised by the Kerala Tourist Development Corporation. Closed Mondays.

Tours
Trivandrum City Tour Daily except Mondays at 8 am. The tour costs Rs 15 per person and includes visits to Sri Padmanabhaswamy Temple (for Hindus only), museum, art gallery, aquarium and Kovalam beach.

Cape Cormorin Daily at 7 am. The tour costs Rs 25 and includes visits to Padmanabhapuram Palace and Cape Cormorin.

Thekkady Wildlife Sanctuary This tour to the wildlife sanctuary in the mountains of Kerala near the border with Tamil Nadu departs every Saturday at 6 am and returns the following day at 9 pm. The tour costs Rs 60. If you're staying at Kovalam, you will miss the last bus back from Trivandrum.

Places to Stay — Top End
If comfort, air-conditioning and the facilities and conveniences of a modern five-star hotel are your priorities (let alone its incomparable setting) then you would do yourself a disservice if you didn't head for the ITDC *Kovalam Beach Resort* at Kovalam Beach (quarter of an hour away by taxi). It's one of the best hotels in India — and comparatively cheap for what it offers. Details under the Kovalam Beach section which follows.

If needs dictate that you stay in Trivandrum itself then the *Hotel Pankaj*, Mahatma Gandhi Rd (tel 66557) would be a reasonably suitable alternative. It offers very comfortable, air-conditioned rooms, air-conditioned restaurant, rooftop coffee shop, 24-hour room service, room telephone, banking and travel facilities.

Also in Trivandrum there is the *Hotel Belair* (tel 3487, 3402-03) on Agricultural College Rd with singles/doubles from Rs 130/180. The *Mascot Hotel* (tel 60720) is similarly priced but also has cheaper rooms without air-con.

Places to Stay — Bottom End
Here again, if cost isn't your primary concern, then you'd be well advised to

head for Kovalam beach. Some good alternatives in Trivandrum itself include *Nalada Tourist Home*, Mahatma Gandhi Rd, between the railway bridge and the Municipal bus stand. A modern building which is clean, well-organised and has room service in the mornings and evenings. Rooms cost Rs 12 a single, Rs 20 a double and Rs 25 a triple all with attached bathroom.

International Tourist Home, Press Rd (United Bank of India Building), opposite the GPO. Rooms cost Rs 9 a single, Rs 15 a double and Rs 20 a triple, all with attached bathroom. It's pleasant, quiet, clean and the staff are friendly.

There are many cheapies along the road from the station to the junction with Mahatma Gandhi Rd but they're all in various stages of dilapidation, noisy and pretty basic. The nearest which isn't quite so off-putting is the *MGM Lodge* (Annexe) on the south side of the railway, one street east of Mahatma Gandhi Rd (visible from the railway bridge). They have no singles and doubles cost Rs 15 with attached bath. The next best is perhaps the *Devi Tourist Home*, Press Rd, opposite the GPO. Rooms cost Rs 7 a single, Rs 12 a double without attached bath and Rs 15 a double with attached bath. It's clean but, again, pretty basic. You'd be well advised to stay at Kovalam beach unless you have no choice.

Places to Eat

If you're looking for a better class of restaurant try the *Azad Restaurant*, on Mahatma Gandhi Rd between the railway bridge and the Sri Padmanabhaswamy Temple. Popular with office workers in the area. Or there's the *Capri Hotel*, on the opposite side of the road from the municipal bus stand. The restaurant is upstairs and is air-conditioned. On the ground floor there is a 'meals' cafe where standard South Indian plate meals are served for Rs 2.50.

A good low-priced non-vegetarian restaurant is the *Ceylon Restaurant* adjacent to the GPO. They serve meat, fish and egg curries as well as omelettes and other breakfast foods. Friendly people. The *JAS Hotel* (follow the signs from the railway station) has a lovely dining rooms complete with hovering waiters, full silver service and good food.

Getting There

Air Indian Airlines have daily flights to Cochin (Rs 150), Madras (Rs 435) and Bombay (Rs 840). There are flights on four days of the week to Colombo in Sri Lanka and twice a week to Male in the Maldive Islands. See the introductory Getting There section for more details. There are also direct flights to Abu Dhabi (once weekly), Dubhai (twice weekly) and Kuwait (once weekly).

Rail Although buses are much faster than the trains Kerala State Road Transport buses, like most others in southern India, make no concessions to comfort and the drivers are pretty reckless. If you'd like to keep your adrenalin levels down then the trains are a pleasant alternative so long as you're not going too far.

The trains through Trivandrum are the same as those right down the coast through Cochin/Ernakulam and Quilon. The same twice weekly Karnataka Kerala Express departs from New Delhi and arrives at Trivandrum 48 hours later. The 3054 km trip costs Rs 435 in 1st class, Rs 107 in 2nd class. Madras-Trivandrum is a 921 km trip costing Rs 146 in 1st class, Rs 40 in 2nd class. It takes 18 hours on the Trivandrum Mail.

The Mangalore-Trivandrum coastal route takes 11 hours from end to end on the Yercaud Express. Trivandrum-Quilon is just 65 km (Rs 24 in 1st, Rs 4.50 in 2nd), Trivandrum-Ernakulam is 201 km (Rs 52 in 1st, Rs 11.50 in 2nd) and Trivandrum-Calicut is 414 km (Rs 92 in 1st, Rs 17 in 2nd).

Trivandrum-Bangalore takes 19 hours on the Island Express. Fares for the 950 km trip are Rs 177 in 1st, Rs 43 in 2nd. From Bombay it's a lengthy 45 hours on the 2nd class only Jayanti Janata Express. The 2062 km trip costs Rs 79. To

Mettuppalaiyam (for Ooty) is a 14 hour trip involving changes of train at Shoranur and Coimbatore — not a bad trip though.

Some of the important departure times from Trivandrum Central include:

destination	departure times	comments
Bangalore	10.25 am	Rs 4.55
Bombay	8.35 am	Rs 79.90
Cannanore	9.15 pm	
Ernakulam	6.00 am	Rs 13.15
Kanyakumari (Cape Cormorin)	7.00 am & 2.50 pm	
Madras (Central)	12.00 noon	Rs 43.30
Mangalore	5.10 pm	Rs 32.00
Nagarcoil	5.50 pm	
New Delhi (K K Express)	2.40 pm (Mon & Thur only)	Rs 106.20
Quilon	6.45 am, 1.15 pm and 5.45	Rs 4.55 and takes 3 hours

Buses The following buses go via Quilon and Alleppey: Alleppey daily at 12.30 pm and 12 midnight; Calicut (Kozhikoda) daily at 2 pm; Ernakulam 15 times daily from 12.30 am to 11 pm; Palghat daily at 6 am, 9.30 am and 12 noon; Quilon seven times daily from 6.30 am to 8.25 pm.

The following buses go via Kottarakara and Kottayam: Kottayam 13 times daily from 1 am to 8 pm; Palghat daily at 8.30 am and 10 pm; Shencottah eight times daily from 5 am to 8.30 pm; Thekkady daily at 3.30 am and 8.45 am.

In addition there are buses to Kanyakumari (Cape Cormorin) five times daily from 4.30 am to 6.30 pm. Direct buses run from Kovalam beach to Kanyakumari at 6.45 and 9.50 am, 1.45 and 6.40 pm. One bus also departs daily to Ernakulam from Kovalam beach at 7.30 am.

Getting Around
For local transport around the city and to Kovalam beach there are municipal buses (very crowded), auto-rickshaws and taxis. For transport around the city itself auto-rickshaws are probably your best bet. The drivers need no prompting about using the meters and fares are cheap (eg from the railway station to the GPO costs approximately Rs 1.50).

For Kovalam beach, bus No 15 runs 25 times daily from the Fort Bus Depot. The first departs at 6.20 am and the last at 9 pm (don't pay too much attention to the timings posted at the bus stop!). The journey takes about half an hour. Note that the bus starts out ridiculously overcrowded but rapidly thins out. There are also three much less crowded buses daily from the bus depot by the railway station.

KOVALAM

This is undoubtedly one of the best beaches in India if not *the* best. It consists of a number of small, palm-fringed bays separated by rocky headlands, white sand, good surf, plenty of cheap

places to stay and a choice of excellent sea food restaurants many of which stand right at the edge of the beach. The fact that it's a fairly popular, though still low key, beach resort hasn't radically affected the life style of the local people. The fishermen here still row their dugouts out to sea and pull the nets in by hand. Rice, copra and bananas still form the backbone of the local economy. Unlike some of the beaches in Goa, with their thousands of semi-resident westerners and the facilities which cater to their needs, you don't get the impression that it's all somewhat artificial. Here it's much gentler and less intrusive. Kovalam just isn't that well-known among travellers on the 'Overland through Asia' route who concentrate mainly on the Northern India-Goa-Kathmandu circuit. As a result you tend to find a more interesting mix of travellers here and the atmosphere is more relaxed. When I was there I met a Rastafarian from

Jamaica, an Iranian stranded by the Iran-Iraq war, a Frenchman who'd just spent two months on the Maldive Islands, an American archaeologist and a travelling commune from England. One of the latter bunch went into Trivandrum one day and bought a bat, ball and wickets. Three of us set up on the sand and, though it seemed there was hardly anyone about, within minutes we were joined by five Australians, a dozen Indians and half a dozen other people of assorted nationalities!

If you come to this part of India, don't miss this place. It's very beautiful. And don't be put off by tourist literature which tends to rave on about the ultra-modern, 5-star ITDC Kovalam Beach Resort Hotel. You wouldn't

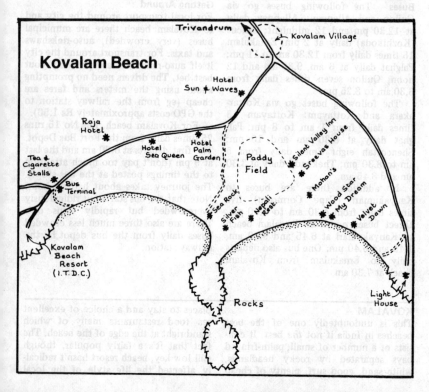

Kovalam Beach

know it was there unless you went up on top of the rocks at the northern end of the first bay. There are no trinket stalls lining the beach at Kovalam.

Having said all that, there should be a word of warning about the very strong rip (undertow) and cross-currents which you will encounter in the bays. Unless you're a very strong swimmer and have no doubts about getting out of a sticky situation, then don't get out of your depth. The sand on the bottom isn't uniformly even, so you need to approach it with caution until you know how it lies in any particular area. While I was there a young guy from Gujurat was drowned and the Iranian mentioned above had to be rescued and given artificial respiration. It nearly took me one day too. All the same, I'd go back there anytime. Many people turn up here intending to stay for a few days. Few see their intentions realised and most find it very difficult to leave.

Information & Orientation

The nearest Post Office is in Kovalam village. There is a bank which will change travellers' cheques without fuss or form-filling at the ITDC Kovalam Beach Resort. Suntan lotion, Nivea cream, pain-killers and other general store commodities can be bought from the chai stalls at the bus stop.

Note that the paths through the coco palms and around the back of the paddy field are difficult to negotiate at night without a full moon unless you're familiar with them. If you're not and want to try Silent Valley or Sreevas House for an evening meal go there before dark. This also ensures you eat before midnight at the former.

Places to Stay — Top End

The most luxurious place to stay is the ITDC *Kovalam Beach Resort* on the headland just above the bus terminal. It costs Rs 120-135 a single and Rs 180-200 a double plus 10% tax, complete with every facility you would expect including air-conditioning, swimming pool, bar, craft shop and boats for hire. It's a beautiful place and it's obvious that a lot of effort has been put into its design and construction. It has facilities for yoga and Ayurvedic massage, both of which are open to non-residents at a cost of Rs 15 per session. For an international 5-star hotel it's cheap. For Kovalam beach it's outrageously expensive. If you're planning on a night out as a non-resident and are thinking of going there for a drink, bear in mind that a beer will cost you Rs 20 which is over three times what it will cost you virtually anywhere else! There is a bank here which will change travellers' cheques with no fuss or form filling.

Raja Hotel is located 200 metres on the right before you get to the entrance to the ITDC Kovalam Beach Resort. Rooms here cost Rs 42 a double including attached bathroom. It's the next most expensive place to stay. There is an attached restaurant and bar which is very pleasant and puts on electric rock music most nights. Most of the music the bands play is American '60s stuff (with occasional earlier gems like *Blue Moon* creeping in) liberally mixed with Beatles' numbers. They're also fond of attempting live fade-outs which, of course, are disastrous but if you play guitar they'll let you jam with them. Beers here cost Rs 15 which, again, is twice what you'd pay anywhere else. Other hotels nearby which would be included in this bracket are *Hotel Palm Garden* and *Hotel Sea Queen* with similar prices.

Places to Stay — Bottom End

At the *Hotel Sun & Waves*, rooms cost Rs 20 a double with own bathroom. There is a restaurant and bar attached. The management are friendly and will fall over backwards to make you welcome. They need to. It's quite a long way from the beach. And considering what's available on, or very near to, the beach, a little overpriced.

Since most travellers here spend almost all the time on the beach or in the cafes there's little need for anything other than a place to sleep and lock up your belongings securely during the day. If you're planning on staying for more than just a few days (many people do regardless of previous intentions) then it's best to ask around for a house to rent — get a small group together if you're alone or a couple. There are a *few* really pleasant houses. Rents, of course, are by negotiation but generally work out cheaper than renting individual rooms. If you're only staying a few days or until you find a house, the following are examples of what is immediately available:

Silver Fish Restaurant is not really a restaurant at all (though they did have intentions of getting it together). Rooms here cost Rs 5 a double. The two back rooms have the nearest approximation to 'attached bath'. Very friendly and secure. No fans but electric light.

My Dream Restaurant where rooms cost Rs 5 a double with common bathroom and toilets. Friendly people who try hard to please.

Velvet Dawn Restaurant is very similar to the above.

Jeevan House is located next to the Wood Star Restaurant. Rooms cost Rs 7 a double with common bath and toilets.

Sreevas House is on the far side of the paddy field away from the beach. Rooms cost Rs 8 a double with attached bathroom. It has an attached restaurant and an extensive library. Popular with travellers who want something just slightly better than the cheapest. Very pleasant place but misses out on the sea breezes because of its location.

Sea Rock Restaurant Rooms here cost Rs 8 a double. The management aren't that friendly. In fact, they can be downright rude.

Mohan's Restaurant is 200 metres from the Wood Star Restaurant towards the paddy field. Sometimes has rooms to rent at around Rs 5 a double.

One or two other places are in the process of being built near the beach. It looks likely they'll be in the Rs 15-20 a double slot. Note that the prices quoted above can increase 'in season' which means anytime there are a lot of people chasing rooms or whenever someone doesn't take the trouble to talk it over. There are rarely more than 100 people on this beach at any one time. If you can't find a house to rent on the two main bays it's worth trying on the next bay south beyond the light-house.

Places to Eat

Just about all the cafes cater for that international palate — western breakfasts (porridge, omelettes, toast and jam, pancakes, etc), sea food (usually

A Backwater Trip from Allepey to Quilon (Ke)
B Statue of Gomateshvara, Sravanabelagola (Ka)
C Reading the book, Brihadeshwara Temple, Tanjore (TN)

fish with the occasional lobster) and French fries and a variety of fruit salads and custard-based sweets. In terms of quality there's little to choose between the cafes — they're all good. In terms of the size of helpings, waiting time, distractions in the meantime and lighting facilities there's quite a difference. The most popular ones include:

Wood Star Restaurant is on the beach and very popular with fairly quick service. Western rock music. Some sample prices are: fish (Rs 4.50), French fries (Rs 3), cheese omelette (Rs 2.50). Friendly staff.

My Dream Restaurant is next door to the Wood Star and also very popular. Western rock music (better selection than the Wood Star). Fairly quick service and similar prices to the Wood Star. Very friendly.

Velvet Dawn Restaurant is another popular restaurant with western music, fairly quick service and similar prices.

Silent Valley Inn is situated on the far side of the paddy field. There's no electricity here (though the wiring is in place) and the service is *very slow* — they have only one primus stove. On the other hand the food is good when it arrives and because there's no piped music people tend to come here to play guitar in the evenings so the atmosphere is completely different. You can watch the fire flies in the paddy field at night.

Mohan's Restaurant is between the Wood Star and the Silent Valley. No electricity and very slow service but the food is good. The fish helpings

are small in comparison to what you get in the other places. It's very relaxed and in the candle light looks like something out of a Breughel painting.

Sreevas House is similar to the Wood Star, My Dream and Velvet Dawn. Electricity and fairly fast service.

Sea Rock Restaurant is quite a boring place and shirty staff. Few people eat here.

In addition to the restaurants there are four or five local women who do the rounds of the beach every day except market day selling fruit and who begin to sound like commercial tv when you've been there a few days — 'Hello, Baba. Mango? Papaya? Banana? Pineapple? Coconut?' all delivered with a seductive glance and a smile. They can be really funny and are full of life. You have to bargain over the price of the fruit but once you've established what you consider to be a fair price for a particular size and variety of fruit, they'll generally agree to that on subsequent days. They rarely have any change but will bring it to you later and even help you eat the roasted peanuts which you bought earlier from the little girl who sells them. There are also young boys who try to sell exotic shells and two men who come round selling lunghis. Everyone appreciates a joke and time is no object.

Plenty of excellent ganja for sale and no problems smoking it. The average price is Rs 7 a tola (approximately 10 grams) for small quantities. It comes

A Meenakshi Temple, Madurai (TN)
B Tirikkalikundram (TN)
C The Rathas, Mahabalipuram (TN)

from the mountains around Thekkady. There are also people selling Kashmiri and Kulu Valley resin but it's naturally much more expensive (Rs 40-50 a tola) and variable in quality. Toddy (coconut beer) and feni (spirits made from coconut and cashew — the two varieties are quite different in taste) are available from shops in Kovalam village. Beers are available either at the more expensive hotels or at the shops in Kovalam village. Cigarettes are sold in most of the beach cafes except Silent Valley and Mohan's.

Getting There

The local bus to Trivandrum runs 25 times daily but the schedules are not too believable. The first bus is at 6.15 am and the last at 10 pm. The depot is right outside the Kovalam Beach Hotel.

There are also direct services to Ernakulam and Kanyakumari (Cape Cormorin) which are a good way of avoiding the crush at Trivandrum — see Trivandrum for details.

Tamil Nadu

Population: 46 million
Area: 130,069 square km
Capital: Madras
Main language: Tamil

The southern state of Tamil Nadu is the most 'Indian' part of India. The Aryans never brought their meat-eating influence to the extreme south so this is the true home of Indian vegetarianism. The early Moslem invaders and the later Moghuls never made more than a fleeting incursion into the region so Hindu architecture here is at its most vigorous and the Moslem architecture virtually non-existent. Even the British influence was a minor one, although Madras was their earliest real foothold on the subcontinent. There were a number of early Dravidian kingdoms in the south. The Pallavas, with their capital at Kanchipuram, were the earliest and they were superseded by the Cholas, centred at Tanjore. Further south the Pandyas ruled from Madurai while in the neighbouring region of Karnataka the Chalukyas were the main power.

Tamil Nadu is the home of Dravidian art and culture, characterised best by the amazingly ornate temples with their soaring towers known as gopurams. A trip through Tamil Nadu is very much a temple hop between places like Kanchipuram, Chidambaram, Tirichurippalli, Tanjore, Madurai and Rameswaram. There are also earlier temples in Tamil Nadu, particularly the ancient shrines of Mahabalipuram, and the state also has an important group of wildlife reserves, some fine beaches and a number of pleasant hill stations like the well known Ooty.

The people of Tamil Nadu, the Tamils, are familiar faces far from their home state. Many Tamils have im-

migrated to Singapore, Malaysia and Sri Lanka. Despite their reputation as hard workers Tamil Nadu is an easygoing, relaxed state. Things drift by here and even Madras, India's fourth largest city, is a laid back, unhurried and uncrowded place compared to the northern cities like Calcutta and Bombay.

For the traveller Tamil Nadu offers excellent value, particularly in accommodation. Prices are generally lower than they are further north and in addition standards are often higher. There are many modern low price hotels in Tamil Nadu. Food in Tamil Nadu is also good, you may get heartily sick of thalis while you're here but they are consistently good and consistently low priced. On the other hand Tamil Nadu has probably the strictest prohibition in India. You need a liquor permit to get a drink but note that your permit has a market value and that you will get plenty of offers to part with it.

Architecture

The Dravidian temples of the south, found principally in Tamil Nadu, are quite unlike the classic temple designs found further north. The central shrine is topped by a pryamidal tower of several storeys known as the *vimana*. One or more entrance porches, the *manda-*

Tamil Nadu

ANDHRA PRADESH

KARNATAKA

MADRAS

BANGALORE

Vellore

Kanchipuram

Chingleput

Mahaballipuram

Mysore

Pondicherry

Cuddalore

Salem

Ootacamund

Erode

Mettuppolayam

Tiruppur

Kumbakonam

Coimbatore

Karaikal

Tiruchirappalli

Tanjore

Nagapattinam

KERALA

Pudukkottai

Dindigul

Pt. Colimere

Kodaikanal

Madurai

Rajapalaiyam

Rameswarum

Talaimannar

Shencottah

Mannar

Quilon

Palayankottai

Tuticorin

TRIVANDRUM

SRI LANKA

Gulf of Mannar

Kanyakumari
(Cape Comorin)

pams, lead to this shrine. Around the central shrine there are a series of courts, enclosures, even tanks. Many of the larger temples have 'thousand-pillared halls' although rarely are there actually a thousand pillars. At Madurai there are 997, at the Sri Ranganathaswamy Temple in Trichy there are 940, at Tiruvarur there are only 807. The whole complex, which often covers an enormous area, is surrounded by a high wall with entrances through towering *gopurams*. These rectangular, pyramidal towers are the most notable element of Drav-

idian design. They are often 50 or more metres high, but size alone is not what makes them so interesting – they are generally completely covered with sculptures of gods, demons, mortals and animals. The towers positively teem with life, they're as crowded and busy as any Indian city street. Furthermore many of them are painted in such a technicolour fashion that the whole effect is like some sort of Hindu Disneyland. This is no recent innovation – like classical Greek statues they were all painted at one time.

MADRAS (population 3,500,000)

Madras is India's fourth largest city and capital of Tamil Nadu state but despite its size it is an example of how pleasant other Indian cities might be if they were not so overcrowded. Madrassis are not only zealous guardians of Tamil culture, which they regard as inherently superior to the hybridised cultures further north, but they also appear to know the meaning of relaxation and efficiency with regard to public services – a remarkable combination to be found only in isolated pockets elsewhere in India! Here it's possible to use public buses without undue discomfort and the urban commuter trains without a second thought. There are, it is true, slums and beggars as there are in other Indian cities, but they are far less obtrusive and smaller in number. The city also has the advantage of a long beach front on the Bay of Bengal which ensures a good supply of refreshing sea air and provides a popular place to relax in the evening.

Madras was the site of the first important settlement of the East India Company – founded in 1639 on land given by the Raja of Chandragiri, the last representative of the Vijayanagar rulers of Hampi. A small fort was built in the settlement in 1644 and a town which subsequently became known as Georgetown, in the area of Fort St George, arose north of it. The settle-

ment became independent of Batnam in Java in 1683 and was granted its first municipal charter in 1688 by James II. It thus has the oldest Municipal Corporation in India, a fact which Tamil Nadu state governors are only too keen to point out at every available opportunity.

During the rivalry between the British and French for supremacy in India during the 18th and early 19th centuries its fortunes waxed and waned, being briefly occupied by the French on one occasion, and the base from which Clive set out on his military expeditions during the Wars of the Carnatic. During the 19th century it was the seat of the Madras Presidency, one of the four divisions of British Imperial India.

Though it has long been important for textile manufacture, a great deal of industrial expansion has taken place in recent years and its concerns now include motor assembly plants, railway coach and truck works, engineering plants, cigarette factories, film studios and educational institutes.

Orientation & Information

The city may be conveniently divided into two parts. The older section of the city is west of the dock area and north of Poonamallee High Rd. In these narrow, busy streets and bazaars are the offices of shipping and forwarding agents, the bulk of the cheaper hotels and cafes, other large office buildings and the GPO and American Express. Its main focal point is Parry's Corner/Popham's Broadway which runs alongside the High Court Buildings. The official name of this road is Netaji Subhash Bose Rd but everyone knows it simply as Parry's Corner. Along this road are the municipal bus terminals and just off it, along Esplanade Rd, is the Tamil Nadu State Bus Stand and the Tiruvalluvar Bus Stand, the two long-distance bus terminals.

The other main part of the city is south of Poonamallee High Rd. Through it runs Madras' main road, Anna Salai which is still generally known as Mount Rd. Along it are situated most of the airline offices, theatres, banks, bookshops, craft centres, consulates, the tourist offices and the bulk of the top-range hotels and restaurants. It's the Janpat of Madras. Egmore and Central, Madras' two main railway stations, are close to Poonamallee High Rd. If you're arriving from anywhere other than Tamil Nadu or Kerala you'll come into Central Station. Egmore is the arrival point for most Tamil Nadu and Kerala trains apart from the principal Kerala expresses and the Nilgiri Express from Ootacamund.

The Indian Government Tourist Office (tel 86240 & 86249) is at 35 Anna Salai and is open daily except Sundays from 9 am to 6 pm. As tourist offices in India go this one on Mount Rd is good and the staff friendly and helpful. Leaflets and city maps are apparently in short supply, two people in front of me were offered maps without even requesting them whereas I was refused a copy until a calling card was produced. Indian officials fall over themselves over business cards, get some printed before you go!

Liquor permits are available free from the Tourist Office but you must present your passport which is then stamped. A bus 11 or 18 from Parry's Corner or Central Station will take you to the Tourist Office. There is also an information counter at the airport, open daily from 9 am to 9 pm.

The Automobile Association (tel 86121) is at 38A Anna Salai. Apart from route information the organisation has accommodation available for members of any foreign automobile association at Rs 15/25 for singles/doubles. They also have car parking facilities on the premises for between Rs 3 and 10.

American Express is at Binny Ltd, 7 Armenian St (PO Box 66), Madras 600001. This Amex office is unable to cash travellers' cheques, including their own. It's also suggested that if you lose or have your Amex cheques stolen you should have alternative sources of finance available if you report the loss here. Whilst I was there they told a German that he would have to wait six weeks for cheque replacement, despite the fact that he had reported the loss to the local police within 24 hours. So much for same-day replacement!

Other international banks include Bank of America (tel 82103) at 150B Anna Salai; First National City Bank (tel 810756) at 153 Anna Salai and Grindlay's Bank (tel 87474) at 36D Anna Salai. The State Bank of India has an airport office open from 6.30 am to 12 midnight on any day there is an international flight and to 8 pm on other days. Income tax clearance certificates are available from the Foreign Section, 121 Nungambakkam High Rd.

Consulates & High Commissions

Germany	Mico Building, 19 C-in-C Rd (tel 82125)
Japan	20 Nungambakkam Rd (te 88677)
Malaysia	110/1 Anna Salai (tel 443989)
Netherlands	150A Anna Salai (tel 86411)
Sri Lanka	3 Shafee Mohammed Rd, Rutland Gate (tel 85316)
UK	24 Anderson Rd (tel 83136)
USA	Gemini Circle, Anna Salai (tel 83041)

The British Council is still located in the Local Library Authority Building, 150A Anna Salai, where the British High Commission used to be located.

Shipping Agents

Binny & Co Ltd (tel 26894), 101/102 Armenian St

Indo-Malaysian Shipping Agency (tel 24525), 103 Armenian St

KPV Sheikh Mohammed Rowther & Co Ltd (tel 25756), 41 Linghi Chetty St

Note that Linghi Chetty St has been renumbered at least three times so the above company is often listed as being at 202 Linghi Chetty St.

Things to See

Without wishing to be off-putting, there isn't a great deal to see in Madras that isn't put well in the shade by the rest of the state. It's a very pleasant city in many ways but it's also something of a non-event. The main reason travellers come here is to transact business (mail, money, tickets, visas) or to make a long distance travel connection. But while you are here it's worth visiting the following places:

Fort St George & St Mary's Church

Built in 1653 by the British East India Company but much altered from its original design, the fort presently houses the Secretariat and the Legislative Assembly. The Fort Museum, open daily from 9 am to 5 pm, has a fascinating collection of memorabilia from the days of the East India Company and the British Raj, including a 'Clive's Corner'. Entrance to the museum is free. Nearby is the Banqueting Hall, built in 1802, around the walls of which hang many paintings of the Governors of Fort St George and other high officials of the British regime.

St Mary's Church was built in 1678-80, the first English church in India. There are reminders here of Robert Clive, who was married in this church in 1753, and of Elihu Yale, the early Governor of Madras who went on to found the famous university in the US. North of the fort is the old 1844 lighthouse and the 1892 High Court, with its lighthouse tower superseding the earlier one.

Government Museum & Art Gallery

Located on Pantheon Rd, near Egmore Station, the most interesting part of this museum is the archaeological section and the bronze gallery. The latter has some excellent examples of Chola bronze workmanship. The museum and gallery are open daily except Fridays and public holidays between 8 am and 5 pm. Entrance is free.

Kapaleeshwara Temple

Located off Kutchery Rd in the southern part of the city, this is an ancient Shiva temple with a typical Dravidian gopuram. It's worth a visit if your time is limited and you won't be visiting the more famous temple cities of Tamil Nadu. As with other functioning temples in this state, non-Hindus are only allowed into the outer courtyard.

San Thome Cathedral

Located near the Kapaleeshwara Temple at the southern end of South Beach Rd, near the sea front, this Roman Catholic church is said to house the remains of St Thomas the Apostle. It was originally built in 1504 but rebuilt in 1893.

Parathasarathy Temple

Located on Triplicane High Rd, the temple is dedicated to Lord Krishna. Built in the 8th century during the reign of the Pallavas it was subsequently renovated by the Vijayanagar kings in the 16th centrry.

The Marina & Aquarium

The sandy stretch of beach known as the Marina extends for 13 km, as far

south as the San Thome Cathedral. The aquarium is on the sea front near the junction of Pycroft's Rd and South Beach Rd and is open daily between 2 and 8 pm except on Sundays when it is open from 8 am. Entrance costs Rs 0.25.

Guindy Deer Park & Snake Park

Situated close to Raj Bhavan at Guindy on the southern outskirts of Madras, this is the only place in the world where it is still possible to see fairly large numbers of the fast-dwindling species of Indian antelope (black buck). It also has small numbers of spotted deer, civet cats, jackals, mongoose and various species of monkeys. The reptillium is open daily between 9 am and 6 pm and entrance costs Rs 0.50. Probably the best way of getting to Guindy is to take the urban commuter train from either Beach Railway Station, opposite the GPO, or from Egmore Station. There are also regular service buses from the centre of Madras (45 or 45B from Anna Square).

Tours

Tamil Nadu Tourist Development Corporation tours can be booked at their offices at 34 Anna Salai (tel 89581) or at 16 Commander-in-Chief Rd (C-in-C Rd).

City Sightseeing Tour Includes visits to Fort St George, Fort Museum, Museum & Art Gallery, Valluvar Kottam, Gandhi Mandapam, Snake Park, Kapaleeshwara Temple, San Thome Cathedral and Marina Beach. The daily tours cost Rs 20 and start at 2 pm, end at 6.30 pm.

Mahabalipuram A tour to the Pallavan antiquities and the famous shore temples at Mahabalipuram, 60 km south of Madras, operates daily. The Rs 30 tour starts at 7.15 am and ends at 1 pm.

Kanchipuram, Thirukkalikundram & Mahabalipuram Daily tours start at 7 am and end at 5.30 pm, the cost is Rs 35. This tour is only really for those in an inordinate hurry since to see either

Kanchipuram or Mahabalipuram properly requires a whole day for each.

Places to Stay

There are three main areas for hotels in Madras. The top-range hotels are mainly along Anna Salai (Mount Rd) and on the roads off this principal highway. Around Egmore Station plus along the section of Poonamallee High Rd between Egmore and Central Station are mid-range places interspersed with a few budget places. The cheaper hotels are in the old part of the city between Mint Rd, Netaji Subhash Bose Rd (Parry's Corner/Popham's Broadway) and North Beach Rd. Egmore Station is the most popular area for travellers these days but places like the YMCA and the Malaysia Lodge in the old city continue to be firm favourites.

Places to Stay — Top End

Hotel Taj Coromandel (tel 810441) at 17 Nungambakkam High Rd is probably Madras' most luxurious hotel with singles/doubles at Rs 200/300. The old-fashioned but elegant *Connemara Hotel* (tel 810051) on C-in-C Rd, just off Anna Salai near the Tourist Office, is still a firm favourite in this bracket. Singles/doubles cost Rs 150/225. There is an excellent bookshop in the hotel.

Welcom Hotel Chola (tel 82091) at 5 Cathedral Rd has singles/doubles at Rs 310/385. *Hotel Sudarsan International* (tel 812061), 53 Monteith Rd has singles/doubles from Rs 150/250. At 23A Edward Elliots Rd, *Hotel Savera* (tel 810031) costs Rs 175/225.

Places to Stay — Middle

Hotel Imperial (tel 845076) at 1A Gandhi Irwin Rd is opposite Egmore Station. The large complex of buildings surrounds a garden and courtyard and there's a restaurant, bar, night club-disco and bookshop. Rooms cost Rs 50/70 for singles/doubles, Rs 60/95 with air-con.

Hotel New Victoria (tel 843138) is at

1 Kennet Lane which runs between the Hotel Imperial and the Hotel Impala, opposite Egmore Station. Like the Imperial it is a large building and has a restaurant. Singles/doubles are Rs 45/75 or Rs 55/90 with air-con. Directly opposite the station is the somewhat older *Hotel Impala Continental*. The spacious rooms surround a courtyard and for the price it's the best of the mid-range hotels around Egmore — rooms cost Rs 22/34. All the rooms have fans and attached bathrooms and the staff are friendly in this popular hotel.

Chandra Lodge is again opposite Egmore Station and costs Rs 20/40 with attached bathroom. *Tourist Home* (tel 844079) is at 5 Gandhi Irwin Rd, opposite you-know-what. Rooms cost Rs 20/30 with bathroom and again it's popular with travellers. The *Tourist Hostel* at 38 Adyar Bridge Rd has rooms from Rs 14/22 and doubles with air-con for Rs 45. There's also a good vegetarian restaurant.

People's Lodge is round the corner of Gandhi Irwin Rd on the left hand side as you come out of the station. This very popular hotel is often full but it's a good place if you want to be near

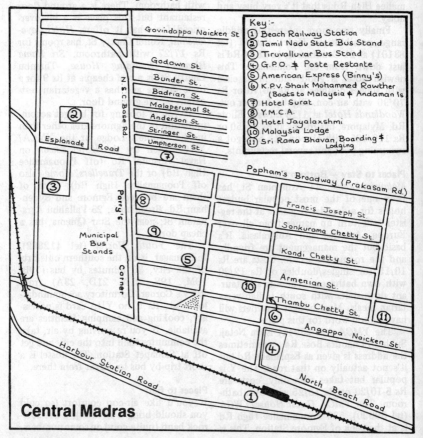

Key:-
1. Beach Railway Station
2. Tamil Nadu State Bus Stand
3. Tiruvalluvar Bus Stand
4. G.P.O. & Poste Restante
5. American Express (Binny's)
6. K.P.V. Shaik Mohammed Rawther (Boats to Malaysia & Andaman Is)
7. Hotel Surat
8. Y.M.C.A.
9. Hotel Jayalaxshmi
10. Malaysia Lodge
11. Sri Rama Bhavan Boarding & Lodging

Central Madras

Egmore and in a cheaper hotel. Rooms cost Rs 8 for bathless singles, Rs 20/35 for singles/doubles with bath. The *Palace Hotel* at 32 Egmore High Rd is Rs 25/35.

There are several other mid-range hotels along Poonamallee High Rd, including the *Hotel Blue Diamond* (tel 665540) at 498 Poonamallee High Rd with rooms at Rs 40/70, more with air-con. *Hotel Dasaprakash* (tel 661111) at 100 Poonamallee High Rd is Rs 25-35/45-60 for singles/doubles. Others are the *Hotel Devi* and the *Hotel Everest*. The only drawback to staying on Poonamallee High Rd is that it's very busy and noisy.

Finally two more interesting middle range possibilities: *Hotel Kanchi* (tel 83101) at 21 Commander-in-Chief Rd is just down from the Connemara. This newish hotel is good value in its class with singles/doubles at Rs 50/70 or Rs 70/90 with air-con. Slightly further out, *Woodlands Hotel* at 1/23 Edward Eliots Rd, Mylapore, has rooms at Rs 40/50 or Rs 110/125 with air-con. It's also got a swimming pool and several restaurants.

Places to Stay — Bottom End

Malaysia Lodge, 44 Armenian St, has been one of the most popular budget hotels for a decade. A glance at the register will turn up names from all over Europe, America and Australasia. It's basic but the management are friendly and the rooms are secure. Costs are Rs 10/15 for singles/doubles or Rs 12/20 with own bathroom. There is a restaurant downstairs with south Indian vegetarian meals. Most budget travellers will have a good word for this place.

The *YMCA* (tel 23941) is on Netaji Subhash Chandra Bose Rd — sometimes the address is given as Esplanade Rd but it's not actually on that road. The Y is popular but takes men only, costs are Rs 6-10/20 or Rs 15/25 with own bathroom. The *YMCA Guest House/YWCA* (tel 39920), 530 Poonamallee High Rd is at the back of Egmore Station. This is

another long term favourite especially for travellers with their own vehicles or with camping equipment. It's also the best budget choice if you want to stay in Egmore but can't get into the People's Lodge. A single costs Rs 16.50 plus Rs 2 membership charge. Camping is Rs 2 per person plus Rs 1 per tent. Parking costs Rs 3 per night. Men and women can stay here and there is an attached restaurant which serves western food.

Hotel Surat, Prakasam Rd (Popham's Broadway), is a modern concrete building with a friendly management and rooms at Rs 16/25 or Rs 21 for a single with bathroom. There is a ground floor restaurant but this place is a bit over-priced for what it offers. *Hotel Jayalakshmi*, Kondi Chetty St, has rooms for Rs 17/27 with bathroom. *Sri Rama Bhavan's Boarding House*, Thambu Chetty St, is a real cheapie at Rs 9 for a basic double and has a vegetarian restaurant on the ground floor.

If you're looking for budget accommodation in the Egmore area other than in the People's Lodge or the YMCA/YWCA then try the *Hotel Eswari* on Naval Hospital Rd (off Poonamallee High Rd) or the *Travellers' Home* (also off Poonamallee High Rd). Both of them are between Egmore and Sydenham Rd. *Broadlands*, 26 Vallabhu Agraharam St, near the Star Cinema, has a cheap dorm.

The *Youth Hostel* (tel 412882), Indiranagar, is on the southern outskirts of the city, 30 minutes by bus (19B, 19M, 19S, 21A, 21D, 23A) from Parry's Corner. Dormitory accommodation costs Rs 5, no YHA card is necessary, cooking and camping facilities are available. If you're arriving by air, take the commuter train into the city and get off at Saidapet Station. The hostel is a short trip by bus to Adyar from there.

Places to Eat

If you'd like air-con comfort (so cold you should bring a sweater), a live soft-rock band (quite good on some numbers, totally untogether on others) then try the *Hotel Imperial's* restaurant on Gandhi Irwin Rd, opposite Egmore Station. The menu is fairly extensive but the food is often indifferent despite the relatively high prices. The waiters also have an annoying habit of hanging around like hungry vultures to see if you're going to leave a tip. Count on around Rs 20 for a meal including tea or coffee. The permit bar is open until 10 pm and beers are Rs 10 a bottle.

Also opposite Egmore Station the *Impala*, at the junction of Kennet Lane and Gandhi Irwin Rd, is an excellent vegetarian and tiffin restaurant. It's popular with travellers and locals. Typical south Indian vegetarian meals are served at lunch and dinner or you could have a masala dosa and coffee for Rs 2. *Vega Vasanta Bhavan* is also good — tasty thalis and fine lassi.

In the Mount Rd area the *Buhari Hotel* at 3/17, is probably the best non-vegetarian restaurant. Excellent food, reasonable prices and again the air-con can be fierce. It's been popular with travellers for many years.

In the old part of town there are many vegetarian restaurants but few shine out. *Rama Krishna*, next door to the YMCA on Netaji Subhash Chandra Bose Rd (Parry's Corner), looks good but in fact it's overpriced, pretentious and the bureaucracy is astounding even by Indian standards. Your order passes from the person who takes your order, to a money taker, rubber stamper, order maker and finally to a waiter. And they call this self-service! *Madras Cafe*, off China Bazaar, two blocks from Popham's Broadway, has excellent Rs 5 thalis.

At *Madras Farm Agencies*, 23 Poonamallee High Rd, you can get a respectable glass of milk. It's on the left hand side of the road walking towards the YWCA from the main station.

Getting There

Air Madras is an international arrival point for India as well as an important domestic airport. There are flights from Singapore (Singapore Airlines and Air India), Penang (MAS) and Colombo (Air Lanka and Indian Airlines). There are frequent domestic connections between Madras and Bombay Rs 740, Calcutta Rs 930 and Delhi Rs 1100. Other Indian Airlines connections include Bangalore Rs 220, Cochin Rs 465, Coimbatore Rs 355, Hyderabad Rs 385, Madurai Rs 305, Nagpur Rs 605, Trichy Rs 225 and Trivandrum Rs 435.

Rail The rail journey to Delhi is 2188 km in length, taking from 40 hours and costing Rs 340 in 1st class, Rs 83 in 2nd. Calcutta is 1662 km away and takes from 33 hours at a cost of Rs 280 in 1st, Rs 68 in 2nd. Bombay trains take from 26 hours to cover the 1279 km at a cost of Rs 229 in 1st, Rs 56 in 2nd. The Bombay, Calcutta and Delhi trains all depart from Madras Central Station.

There are daily trains from Central to Ernakulam/Cochin — a 700 km trip taking 12 hours and costing Rs 142 in 1st, Rs 34 in 2nd. This train continues on to Quilon and Trivandrum. The daily Yercaud Express, also from Central, takes 10½ hours to make the 530 km trip to Mettuppalaiyam from where you continue by the rack train up to Ooty. Fares are Rs 110 in 1st, Rs 26 in 2nd.

Bangalore, 356 km away, is connected by frequent trains from Central. The fast Brindavan Express and Bangalore Mail take just seven hours at a fare of Rs 83 in 1st, Rs 19 in 2nd. Also from Central the daily Hyderabad Express whisks you to Hyderabad, a 794 km journey, in 16 hours for Rs 155 in 1st, Rs 38 in 2nd.

From Egmore there are a number of daily trains to Trichy — 337 km direct, eight hours, Rs 80 in 1st, Rs 18 in 2nd. They continue on to Madurai — 492 km, 11 hours, Rs 106 in 1st, Rs 25 in 2nd. Starting from Madras Beach Station on some days and Egmore Station on others, the Ganga Kaveri takes 18 hours to make the 666 km trip to Rameswarum at a fare of Rs 137 in 1st, Rs 33 in 2nd. There are also trains from Egmore to Pondicherry (a five hour trip costing Rs 52 in 1st, Rs 12 in 2nd), Chidambaram and Tanjore.

Apart from the two main railway stations there is also a Southern Railway Booking Office on Mount Rd (tel 85642) which is open 10 am to 6 pm but can only reserve 2nd class. If you want tourist quota sleeping berths it's best to check first with the Southern Railway booking office next to Central Station (tel 39101). The booking hours at Egmore and Central are 8.30 am to 1 pm and 1.30 to 4.30 pm for both classes.

Bus Both the Tamil Nadu State Transport and the privately run Tiruvalluvar Transport Corporation have their terminals off Esplanade Rd. The schedule at the State Transport depot is entirely in Tamil (as elsewhere in the state) except for the Mhabalipuram buses. This does not present any real difficulties since an army of young boys attach themselves to every foreigner who enters the terminal and for 10-20 paise (though, naturally, they try for more) find you your bus. Services to most large towns in the state are frequent. The Tiruvalluvar schedule is in English.

There are 11 daily State Transport buses (19A) to Mahabalipuram from 6.20 am to 8.15 pm. There are also 11 number 19C buses from 6 am to 8.30 pm and five number 68 buses from 9.30 am to 7.40 pm. The 2½ hour journey costs Rs 3.20 or 4.10 depending on whether the bus takes the shorter coast route or goes via Chingleput.

Tiruvalluvar buses include:

To Bangalore: five ordinary buses via Kanchipuram, Vellore, Ambur and Hosur from 7 am to 11 pm. Two aircon buses at 8.30 am and 8 pm via Kanchipuram and Chitoor.
To Coimbatore: five buses between 4 and 8.25 pm, the trip takes 12 hours.
To Madurai: two buses at 8.15 and

10.30 pm, they go via Trichy.
To Mysore: one bus at 9 am, the trip takes about nine hours.
To Nagarcoil: nine buses via Trichy and Madurai between 5.30 am and 11 pm. It's a 15 hour trip.
To Pondicherry: six buses between 6.30 am and 11.30 pm.
To Rameswarum: four buses at 9 am and 5.45, 7 and 7.45 pm.
To Tanjore: two buses at 6 am and 11 pm.
To Trichy: 10 buses from 4 am to 11.30 pm.
To Trivandrum: two buses at 4 pm (aircon) and 9 pm. The trip takes about 16 hours.

Boat The Shipping Corporation of India have two interesting services out of Madras. Their agents are K P V Shaikh Mohammed Rowther & Co, 202 Linghi Chetty St (tel 25756-7-8). Note that Linghi Chetty St has been renumbered several times and their address is sometimes quoted as 41. The services are:

To Andaman & Nicobar Islands: see the Andaman & Nicobar Islands section for details.
To Malaysia & Singapore: the usual route is Madras - Nagappattinam - Penang - Singapore - Port Kelang - Penang - Nagappattinam-Madras but some sailings also include Trincomalee in Sri Lanka.

The ship is the *mv Chidambaram* and the journey takes 4½ days to Penang and 6½ to Singapore including a one-day stop at Penang. Singapore passengers can disembark while the ship is in Penang. On the return journey Penang-Madras takes 3½ days. There is a sailing about every 21 days. Classes of accommodation range down from de-luxe — three cabins with attached sitting room, bathroom and a TV; A grade — 2-3 berth cabin with attached bathroom; B grade — similar to A; dormitory 1 — 4, 6 or 8 berth cabins, some with attached bathrooms others with shared facilities; dormitory 2 — 10-berth compartments with attached shower only; bunk — large compartments with shared bathroom and toilet facilities.

Bedding is not provided for bunk class passengers. There is a choice of Indian or western food for cabin class passengers, Indian only for dormitory and bunk class although there is a choice of vegetarian or non-vegetarian food which is served in a separate dining room. Westerners are not allowed in either dormitory 1 or bunk class. Fares include all surcharges and port taxes but there is an extra charge for staying on board in Penang if you are bound for Singapore. Student concessions are allowed only for nationals of Malaysia, India and Singapore. In rupees fares from Madras are:

class	to Penang	to Singapore
de-luxe	Rs 2580	Rs 2879
A grade	Rs 2189	Rs 2546
A grade	Rs 1915	Rs 2292
dormitory 1	Rs 1338	Rs 1515
dormitory 2	Rs 1201	Rs 1399
bunk	Rs 1101	Rs 1283

Getting Around

Airport The cheapest way of getting from the airport at Meenambakkam to the city is to walk to Ninambakkan railway station (about 10 minutes) and take a commuter train into the city. The train passes through Egmore Station and the last stop is Beach Station, opposite the GPO. There are frequent trains from 4 am to midnight. If you're heading for the Youth Hostel then get off the train at Saidapet Station and take a bus from there to Adyar.

Alternatively there is an airport bus for Rs 9 which stops at the major hotels and at Egmore Station and terminates at the Indian Airlines office on Mount Rd. A taxi will cost Rs 30 plus.

Bus If you're spending long in Madras and will be using city buses then a copy of *Madras City Tourist Guide* (Rs 2.50) will be useful as it contains a full list of all the city bus routes. Some of the more useful buses include:

9 & 10 — Parry's Corner to Central and Egmore Stations. Other buses which pass through Egmore include 4D, 16, 17, 17D, 17E, 22, 23A, 27, 27B, 27D, 29A, 29D, 38B, 40, 43 & 71A.

11A & 18 — Parry's Corner to Mount Rd (Anna Salai). Other buses which run along the city end of Mount Rd include 3A, 4G, 5A, 11D, 11E, 17A, 17C, 18, 18B, 18C, 18D, 18E, 19S, 23, 23B, 23C, 25, 25B, 27A, 27D, 36 & 36A.

27D — Mount Rd to Egmore Station.

VELLORE (population 150,000)

The only reason to come to Vellore, 145 km from Madras, is to see the 16th century Vijayanagar fort and the Jalakanteshwara Temple inside it. Both the moated fort and the temple are in an excellent state of preservation. Other than the fort and temple, Vellore is a fascinating semi-rural bazaar town full of bullock carts and street markets. It's a photographer's paradise.

The Fort

The fort, which is constructed out of granite blocks and has a moat supplied from a subterranean drain fed by a tank. It was built by Sinna Bommi Nayak, a vassal chieftan under the Vijayanagar kings Sada Sivaraja and Sriranga Maharaja, in the 16th century. It later became the fortress of Mortaza Ali, the brother-in-law of Chanda Sahib, who claimed the Arcot throne, and was taken by the Adilshahi Sultans of Bijapur in 1676. It then passed briefly into the hands of the Marathas until they in turn were displaced by Daud Khan of Delhi in 1760. The British were next to occupy the fort, following the fall of Srirangapatnam and the death of

Vellore

Moat

Jalakantesvara Temple

Fort

Moat

Palace Lodge

Hotel Arun

Lorry Park

Bus Station

Laxmi Lodge

Covered Market

Church

Santhi Lodge

Sekar Lodge

Venus Lodge

India Lodge

Temple

Venus Lodge Annexe

↑ Katpadi Railway Station

H. Safire

H. Best

H. Paradise

H. Sangeet

Triven Lodge

↓ Kanchipuram Madras

Tipu Sultan, and they used it as a prison for Tipu's sons and daughters. It's the Windsor Castle of southern India and is the only one of its kind in Tamil Nadu.

Jalakanteshwara Temple

The Jalakanteshwara Temple was constructed about the same time as the fort (around 1566) and is a gem of late Vijayanagar architecture. The stone carvings are superb and in an excellent state of preservation. You won't see Vijayanagar relics like this outside of Hampi. It's no longer a functioning Hindu temple so non-Hindus are allowed in every part of the building. It ceased to be used following the invasions by the Adil Shahis of Bijapur, the Marathas and the Carnatic Nawabs when it was occupied as a garrison and desecrated. It is now maintained by the Archaeological Survey of India as a museum. There is no charge for entry either to the fort or the temple. Both are open daily.

Places to Stay

Hotel Sangeet, about three minutes' walk from the bus stand, has singles/

doubles with attached bathrooms for Rs 10/20. There are a number of basic lodges around the bus stand, along the main bazaar street and near the Sangeet, all similar in quality and price. The *India Lodge*, opposite the clock tower (built for George V!) over the covered market, is perhaps one of the best with rooms with attached bathrooms for Rs 7/14 for singles/doubles. It's secure, the management are friendly, but don't bother asking them to wake you up if you have to get up early.

Downstairs there's a vegetarian restaurant with typical meals on a banana leaf for Rs 2.80. Other similar lodges include the *Laxmi Lodge*, *Venus Hotel*, *Palace Lodge*, *Sekar Lodge*, *Hotel Safire* and the *Triven Lodge*. If you want something really cheap, try the *Hotel Best*, opposite the hospitals.

Places to Eat
Hotel Paradise, opposite the hospitals, has good non-vegetarian food. Egg biriyani and coffee will cost Rs 4. There are any number of south Indian vegetarian places like the *Palace Cafe*. Good ice creams and ice-cold drinks are available from the *Simla Ice Cream Parlour* on the road opposite the fort entrance.

Getting There
Bus As elsewhere in Tamil Nadu there are the state buses and those run by the Tiruvalluvar Transport Corporation. The former are cheaper but the latter are generally faster and a good deal less degenerate.

There are 12 buses daily to Madras from 12.47 am to 6.30 pm. They go via Arcot, Kanchipuram and Poonamallee. There is also a non-stop air-con bus at 5 am daily but you must get a 'priority booking ticket' the day before and be at the depot at 4.30 am at the latest for this bus — at least in theory. The bus I was on was not only empty but stopped for a (very welcome) chai break at Kanchipuram. The buses cost Rs 7.20 and the journey takes about three hours.

There are five buses daily to Bangalore, departing at 2.25 and 10.25 am, 12.55, 4.25 and 10.25 pm. They go via Ambur, Thirupathur, Natrampalli and Krishnagiri and the fare is Rs 12.40 for the 5½ hour journey.

Rail The nearest railway station to Vellore is at Katpadi on the main Bangalore-Madras line. Buses wait for the arrival of trains outside the station. The fare into Vellore is Rs 0.35 and the journey takes 10-15 minutes. Katpadi to Bangalore costs Rs 13.50 in 2nd class and takes about five hours.

KANCHIPURAM (population 125,000)
Sometimes known as Siva Vishnu Kanchi, this is one of the seven sacred cities of India and was successively the capital of the Pallavas, Cholas and the Rajas of Vijayanagar. During Pallava times it was, on occasion, briefly occupied by the Chalukyas of Badami and the Rashtrakutas when the battle fortunes of the Pallava kings hit a low spot.

Kanchipuram is one of India's most spectacular temple cities and its many gopurams can be seen from miles away. Many of the temples are the work of the later Cholas and of the Vijayanagar kings. They're spread out all across the city and you'll need at least a whole day to see them. The best way to do this is to hire a bicycle for the day or to take on a rickshaw driver for the whole day (this should cost around Rs 10). There are no taxis or auto-rickshaws. You should have plenty of small change handy when visiting the temples to mollify various demands for baksheesh by 'temple watchmen', 'shoe watchers', 'guides' and assorted priests. As it's a famous temple city plenty of pilgrims and tourists come here and the army of hangers-on is legion. Almost to a man, the people who attach themselves to you as 'guides' are a complete waste of time and will bore you shitless. They'll hustle you round at the speed of light, fill your ears with nonsense and then demand you pay them up to Rs 10 for the unsolicited pain of their tedious company. Give them a miss!

Kanchi is also famous for its hand-woven silk fabrics. This industry has roots going back to the Pallava times when the weavers were employed to produce clothing and other fabrics for the kings.

Kailasanatha Temple

Dedicated to Shiva, this is one of the earliest temples and was built by the Pallava king, Rayasimha in the late 7th century though its front was added by the later king, Mahendra Varman III. It's the only one of the temples at Kanchi which hasn't been cluttered with more recent additions by the Cholas and Vijayanagar kings and so reflects the freshness and simplicity of early Dravidian architecture of which other examples can be seen at Mahaballipuram. A few fragments of the 8th century murals which used to grace the alcoves are still visible and a reminder of how magnificent the temple must have looked when it was first built.

Key:
① Kailasanathar Temple
② Ekambareshwara Temple
③ Kamakshiamman Temple
④ Vaikunthaperumal Temple
⑤ Varadarajaperumal Temple
⑥ Bus Stand & I.T.D.C. Travellers' Lodge
⑦ Post Office
⑧ Raja's Lodge
⑨ New Madras Cafe

Kanchipuram

If you have any interest in archaeology, the Archaeological Survey of India has an office opposite the temple and the staff are most willing to tell you more about the history of Kanchipuram.

Vaikuntaperumal Temple
Dedicated to Vishnu, this temple was built between 674-800 AD shortly after the Kailasanatha Temple by Parameshwara and Nandi Varman II. The cloisters inside the outer wall consisting of lion pillars represent the first phase in the evolution of the grand 1000-pillared halls of later temples.

Ekambareshwara Temple
Dedicated to Shiva, this is one of the largest temples in Kanchipuram and covers 9 hectares. Its huge gopuram, 59 metres high (192 ft), and massive outer stone wall were constructed by Krishna Devaraja of the Vijayanagar Empire in 1509 though construction was originally started by the Pallavas and later added to by the Cholas. Inside are five separate enclosures and a 1000-pillared hall. The name of the temple is said to be a modified form of Eka Amra Nathar — the Lord of the Mango Tree — and in one of the enclosures is a very old mango tree with four branches representing the four Vedas. The fruits of these four branches are said to have different tastes and there is a plaque nearby which claims that the tree is 3500 years old. Wishful thinking though this might be, it's revered as a manifestation of the god and is the only 'shrine' you'll be allowed to walk around as a non-Hindu and partake of the sacred ash (modest contributions gratefully accepted). You will not be allowed into the sanctum sanctorum as this is still a functioning Hindu temple. There's a temple elephant kept here which suffers from the worst boredom-induced eczema and running sores that I've seen anywhere in India.

This is undoubtedly the worst temple

for husslers and there's also a 'camera fee' of Rs 1 which goes towards the upkeep of the temple (the income from pilgrims and tourists tops Rs 200,000 annually!). A leaflet is on sale inside the temple entitled, *History of Sri Ekambaranathar Temple* which costs Rs 0.80. For a quick hit of esoteric nonsense and gobbledegook it's worth 80 paise!

Kamakshiamman Temple
Dedicated to the goddess Parvati, this imposing temple is the site of the annual car festival which falls on the 9th lunar day in February/March. When not in use the ornately-carved wooden car

is kept partially covered in corrugated iron half way up Gandhi Road.

Varadarajaperumal Temple

Like the Ekambareshwara Temple, this is another enormous monument with massive outer walls and a 1000-pillared hall. One of its most notable sculptural features is a huge chain carved out of a single piece of stone. The temple is dedicated to Vishnu and was built by the Vijayanagar kings. Entrance to this temple costs Rs 0.10 and there is a 'camera fee' of Rs 0.50.

The above are, of course, only the most famous of the Kanchipuram temples. There are many more both in the city and outside it. Walk in any direction and you will come across others.

Places to Stay

The *ITDC Travellers' Lodge* (tel 2561), 78 Kamakshi Amman, Sannathi St, is close to the bus stand, railway station and the Kamakshiamman Temple. Rooms cost Rs 25/40 for singles/ doubles or Rs 45/60 with air-conditioning. There is an attached restaurant and you can book in advance through the Tourist Office (tel 87621) in Madras.

Raja's Lodge, Nellukkara St, is also close to the bus stand and costs Rs 5-10

for singles, Rs 15-20 for doubles.The more expensive rooms have their own bathrooms. Other cheap lodges include the *Rama Lodge* (also on Nellukkara St) and the *Town Lodge*. There is also a *Municipal Rest House* (tel 2301) where rooms cost Rs 7.50/10.75, advance booking is advisable.

Places to Eat

There are many small vegetarian places in the vicinity of the bus stand where you can buy a typical plate meal for around Rs 2. If you're tired of thalis there's not much else but you could try the non-vegetarian *New Madras Cafe* or the *ITDC Travellers' Lodge*.

Getting There

Bus The timetable here, as elsewhere, is in Tamil but there is no problem about finding a bus in the direction you want to go. There are frequent services to Madras, Pondicherry, Vellore, Chingleput and so on. Direct buses to Madras (2½ to three hours) cost Rs 4.10 but going via Poonamallee, where you change, costs only Rs 3.20. To Mahabalipuram take a bus to Chingleput and then change.

Rail Trains run from Kanchipuram to Madras, Pondicherry and Madurai. There is also a branch line to Chingleput.

MAHABALIPURAM (Mamallapuram)

Mahabalipuram was the second capital and sea port of the Pallava kings of Kanchipuram, the first Tamil dynasty of any real consequence to emerge after the fall of the Gupta Empire, and is world famous for its shore temples. Though their origins are lost in the mists of legend they were at the height of their political power and artistic creativity between the 5th and 8th centuries AD during which time they established themselves as the arbiters and patrons of early Tamil culture. Most of the

temples and rock carvings here were completed during the reigns of Narasimha Varman I (630-668 AD) and Narasimha Varman II (700-728 AD) and are notable for the delightful freshness and simplicity of their folk-art origins in contrast to the more grandiose monuments left by the larger empires, such as the Cholas, which succeeded them. The shore temples in particular strike a very romantic theme and are some of the most photographed monuments in India.

The wealth of the Pallava kingdom

was based on the encouragement of agriculture as against pastoralism and thus the increased taxes and surplus produce which could be raised from this settled lifestyle. Their early kings were followers of the Jain religion but this came to an end when Mahendra Varman I (600-630 AD) was converted to Shaivism by the saint, Appar. This conversion was to have disastrous effects on the future of Jainism in Tamil Nadu and explains why the majority of the temples at Mahabalipuram (and Kanchipuram) are dedicated either to Shiva or Vishnu.

Today, Mahabalipuram is just a small but very pleasant and easy-going village consisting of essentially two streets standing at the foot of a low-lying, boulder-strewn hill where most of the temples and rock carvings are located. It's gradually becoming a travellers' haunt, though still in the formative stages, as people begin to rent houses and stay here for some time and cafes are set up catering to western tastes — usually sea food. After the noise, fumes, bustle and severely limited personal space of Madras and other large cities, Mahabalipuram is like coming to another planet. It's very relaxing and there is, of course, a superb beach which stretches for miles. There's nowhere else in southern India where you will find this combination of an excellent beach with cheap accommodation and good sea food available *and* the fascinating remains of an ancient Indian kingdom.

Information

There is a Tourist Office in Mahabalipuram though they only have a leaflet on the expensive tourist beach complexes further up the coast. Their main function seems to be the issuing of liquor permits to foreigners! They are open from 9.30 am to 1 pm and from 2 to 5 pm daily.

There is one bank in Mahabalipuram (Indian Overseas Bank) a few doors away from the Mamalla Bhavan where you can change travellers' cheques. The library near the Tourist Office here has a surprising little collection of English-language novels, history books, Hindu philosophy treatises, autobiographies of Gandhi and current India daily newspapers. An excellent little place if you need something to read.

Arjuna's Penance

This is one of the most interesting sights of Mahabalipuram. Here on the face of a huge rock, has been carved in relief the mythical story of the River Ganges issuing from its source high up in the Himalayas. The panel depicts animals, deities and other semi-divine creatures, fables from the Panchatantra, and Arjuna doing a penance to obtain a boon from Lord Shiva. It's one of the freshest, most realistic and unpretentious rock carvings to be seen anywhere in India.

Krishna Mandapam

One of the earliest rock-cut temples on whose walls is carved a pastoral scene depicting Lord Krishna lifting up the Govardhana mountain to protect his kinfolk from the wrath of Varuna, the god of rain.

Mandapams

In all there are eight mandapams (shallow, rock-cut halls) scattered over the main hill which are of interest for their internal figure sculptures. Two of the mandapams have been left unfinished.

Rathas

Here are the architectural prototypes of all the Dravidian temples with their imposing gopurams and vimanas, multi-pillared halls and sculptured walls which dominate the landscape of Tamil Nadu. The Rathas (literally temple chariots) are named after the Pandavas, the

heroes of the Mahabharata epic, and are full size models of different kinds of temples known to the Dravidian builders of the 7th century AD. With one exception, the Rathas depict structural types which recall the earlier architecture of the Buddhist temples and monasteries. Though they are popularly known as the 'Five Rathas' there are in fact eight of them altogether.

Shore Temples

These beautiful and romantic wind and sea ravaged temples are unique in India and one of its finest sights. They represent the final phase of Pallava art and were built in the late 7th century during the reign of Rajasimha. The two spires of these temples containing a shrine for Vishnu and one for Shiva were modelled after the Dharmaraja Ratha but with considerable modification. The temples are approached through paved forecourts whose weathered perimeter walls support long lines of bulls and whose entrances are guarded by mythical deities. Most of the detail of the carvings has, of course, disappeared over the centuries yet a remarkable amount remains especially inside the shrines themselves.

Places to Stay — Top End

There are a string of 'tourist complexes' along the beach two to three km north of the village. They're pleasantly luxurious beach places.

The *ITDC Temple Bay Beach Resort* (tel 51, two km) offers a range of air-con and non air-con cottages and rooms. Rooms in the main building cost Rs 110/150, all with air-con and bathrooms. The cottages, which are very pleasant and face the sea, cost Rs 65 or Rs 100 for ordinary or de-luxe cottages, with air-con they're Rs 90 or 160. You can also camp here for Rs 15 per night. In the May-June low season prices are discounted 20% but in the high season it's advisable to book in advance — con-

tact the Regional Manager, ITDC, 154 Mount Rd (Anna Salai), Madras 600002 (tel 89672). The complex includes a swimming pool, restaurant and bar — the latter two are open to non-residents but you need a liquor permit and beer is outrageously expensive at Rs 14 a bottle.

The *TTDC Tourist Cottages* (tel 35/36) are close to the Temple Bay resort and cost Rs 50/65 for singles/doubles or Rs 65/95 with air-con. *Silver Sands Beach Resort* (tel 28) is just a little further from the village and costs Rs 70/125 or Rs 140/195 with air-con. There are also some Rs 105 doubles which do not face the sea. Rates are lower in the April-September off season.

Golden Sands Beach Resort (tel 45, 2½ km) costs Rs 70/110 or Rs 90/130 with air-con. Again off season rates are offered, between 16 April and 14 August. *Ideal Beach Resort* (tel 40, three km) is the furthest from the village and costs Rs 35/50, Rs 55/75 with air-con. Low season here is May-July.

Places to Stay — Middle & Bottom

Mahabalipuram is a small village and cheaper accommodation is in limited supply. Depending on the season you may have little choice about where to stay for the first night or two. The other thing to bear in mind here is that very few of the hotel rooms face the sea and so they miss out on the cooling effects of the sea breezes. The top rooms in some of the smaller lodges can, as a result, become stifling by evening, even with the fan on.

Mamalla Bhavan (tel 31) is the most popular and so is often full. The rooms face the sea so they are cool, they have fans and their own bathrooms and cost Rs 15 for doubles — there are no singles. The management is very friendly and room service is looked after by the affable Raju who likes telling jokes and laughing all the time. Downstairs there is an excellent vegetarian restaurant with south Indian food on banana leaves for Rs 1.75 plus Rs 0.50 for curd.

Namalia Lodge is newly built and decorated but the rooms are small and do not face the sea so it can be hot as hell, even at night. Doubles cost Rs 10, with fan but shared toilets and showers which are reasonably clean. The management is friendly and there's a Rs 10 deposit if you haven't got your own lock for the door.

Royal Lodge costs Rs 18 for doubles with bathroom and fan but they're pretty dingy with windows high up on the wall. Clean and not too bad but rather over-priced. Other small lodges include the *Pallava Lodge*, *Chitra Lodge*, *Koteshwara Lodge*, *NCG Lodge* and the *Kamaran Lodge*.

If you want to stay longer it's possible to rent houses or rooms in houses on a monthly or weekly basis. Most of them are between the main street and the beach. Facilities are very basic so don't expect your own bathroom or even electricity but they are pleasant and rustic. Prices are variable and subject to negotiation but it's cheaper than renting a room in a lodge.

Places to Eat

At present there are only three restaurants serving western-style food — usually sea food. All of them have a sound system with a good selection of tapes except the Aromma Cafe which plays Tom Jones type Russian copies of current western rock music!

Rose Garden Restaurant is very tastefully done out in bamboo and run by very friendly people who share jokes and conversation with you all the time. If you want something they'll tell you where to get it or get it for you. The manager speaks French and English as well as Tamil. The food is superb and carefully presented — lobsters for Rs 25-35, grilled fish & French fries for Rs 10.50, prawns & mayonnaise for Rs 7.

They also have a range of vegetarian food at Rs 3-6 per dish, lassi from Rs 1.50 to 3.50 depending on what you want it mixed with, western breakfasts and other Indian food. It's very popular.

The Meeting Place, the other most popular restaurant, is run by a bunch of young guys from Thekkady in Kerala and is also very well done up. The atmosphere here is very laid-back and you're welcome to sit around if you don't actually want to eat. The food is excellent and similar in range and price to the Rose Garden. Again highly recommended.

The *Aromma Cafe*, next door, tries hard to match the other two but comes nowhere near. Apart from these sea food restaurants the *Mamalla Bhavan* is the best restaurant for typical thalis on a banana leaf. They cost Rs 1.75 plus Rs 0.50 for curd. It's clean, friendly and very popular, especially with Indian touring groups at certain times of the day. There are several other, more basic, vegetarian places.

Ganja (usually from Kerala) is available between Rs 7-10 per tola. If you want a beer the Temple Bay Beach Resort is the nearest place.

Getting There

Bus Buses 19A, 19C and 68 go to Madras. The 2½ hour journey costs Rs 3.35 and there are frequent departures. Direct buses leave for Pondicherry at 7.30 am and 6.30 pm. The 2½ hour journey costs Rs 5. Get there early if you want a seat. Every one to two hours a bus departs for Chingleput, the one hour journey costs Rs 1.60. This is the bus to take if you want to go to Tirukkalikundram.

It's theoretically possible to get to Pondicherry via Chingleput rather than taking the direct bus but you should resist the temptation. The buses all arrive full from Madras and most of them don't even stop. You'll be stuck there for hours. The Mahabalipuram

Tourist Office will tell you, with gay abandon, that it's possible and even give you bus numbers and arrival times at Chingleput but don't try it. If, however, you're a glutton for punishment the buses and times are 507 (9.30 am and 11 pm), 508 (6.30, 8.30, 11 am, 1.30, 7.30, 9, 10.30 and 11.30 pm), 583 (12.30, 7.30, 10 am, 3, 6.30, 10 and 12.30 pm). Don't do it!

Getting Around
Bicycles are available for hire in the village if you want to visit Tirukkalikundram or the Crocodile Farm.

Things to Buy
Mahabalipuram has revived the ancient crafts of the Pallava stone masons and sculptors and the town awakes every day to the sound of chisels chipping away at pieces of granite. There are several places where this is being done and there is some excellent work turned out. The yards here have contracts to supply images of deities and restoration pieces to many temples throughout India and Sri Lanka. Some of the smaller works are available for sale in the craft shops which line the road from the bus stand to the Rose Garden Restaurant. Also for sale in these shops are soapstone images of Hindu gods, wood carvings, jewellery and bangles made from sea shells and other similar products. This is one of the best places to buy soapstone work. Prices are very reasonable (although you must bargain) and there are few other places in southern India where you'll find such work.

OTHER PLACES AROUND MADRAS
Chingleput & Kovelong
Chingleput is on the Mahabalipuram-Madras road and has the ruins of an ancient Vijayanagar fort which had a chequered history during the British period. On the coast Kovelong is a fishing settlement with a fine beach.

Tirukkalikundram (Tirukazhukundram)
This pilgrimage centre, 14 km from Mahabalipuram, with its hill-top temple is famous as the place where two eagles come to be fed by a priest every day. Legend has it that they come from Varanasi (Benares). India, of course, is full of such legends. What most guide books ignore about this place, however, is the amazing temple complex with its enormous gopurams at the base of the hill. It's very impressive and seemingly little visited but well worth the effort. You can get here from Mahabalipuram either by bus or by bicycle.

Crocodile Farm
Located about 15 km from Mahabalipuram on the road to Madras, this farm is engaged in breeding crocodiles to augment their population in the wildlife sanctuaries of India. There are now only several hundred of these reptiles left. They welcome visitors and you can see all sizes from the newly hatched to the adults. The farm is signposted so you can't miss it. Probably the best way of getting there is by bicycle although you can take any Madras bus from Mahabalipuram.

Vedanthangal
This is one of India's major bird sanctuaries, 80 km from Madras. There's a Rest House and an observatory tower here. Peak time is immediately after the end of the rainy season when great numbers of aquatic birds flock here. Between 3 and 6 pm is the best time to see them.

Tiruvannamalai
Further south towards Pondicherry a 66 km detour inland from Tindivanam will bring you to this temple town. There are over 100 temples here but the Shiva-Parvati temple of Arunachaleswar is said

to be the largest in India. The main gopuram is 66 metres high and has 13 storeys and there is a 1000-pillared hall. The splendid old fortress of Gingee can be visited between here and Pondicherry.

Places to Stay You can stay at the *Park Hotel* or the *Modern Cafe* in Tiruvannamalai.

PONDICHERRY (population 400,000)

Formerly a French colony which was settled in the early part of the 18th century, Pondicherry became part of the Indian Union in the early '50s when the French voluntarily relinquished control. Together with the other former French enclaves of Karaikal (also in Tamil Nadu), Mahe (Kerala) and Yanam (Andhra Pradesh), it now forms the Union Territory of Pondicherry.

The tourist literature about this place will give you the impression that it's an enduring pocket of French culture on the Indian sub-continent but it's really nothing of the sort. The only visible French influence which remains are the red kepis and belts worn by the local police, the huge French Consulate-General which, together with the predictable Hotel de Ville, dominates the waterfront and a few streets around the central square which exude a Mediterranean ambience. Apart from that it's as Indian as anywhere else in India. It certainly doesn't compare with Goa's Portuguese or Darjeeling's English flavour. English is spoken everywhere, even the signs are in English or Tamil — not French. The name Pondicherry itself may soon disappear to be replaced by the older name, Puducherry, if a recent

state government resolution is put into effect.

The main reason people visit Pondicherry is to see the Sri Aurobindo Ashram and its off-shoot, Auroville, 10 km outside of town. The Ashram, founded by Sri Aurobindo in 1926, is one of the most popular in India with westerners and also one of the most affluent. Its spiritual tenets are based on a synthesis between yoga and modern science. After Aurobindo's death, spiritual authority passed to one of his devotees, a French woman known as 'The Mother', who herself died in 1973, age 97. Although the Ashram underwrites and promotes a lot of cultural and educational activities in Pondicherry it's very unpopular with local people since it owns virtually everything worth owing in the union territory but refuses to allow local participation in the running of the society.

Orientation

The town is constructed on a grid plan surrounded by a more or less circular boulevard so it's easy to find your way around. The Aurobindo Ashram, its offices, educational institutes and guest houses are all clustered around the streets between the waterfront and the

1	Government Square	11	Park Guest House
2	Bus Station		(Ashram accommodation)
3	State Bank of India	12	International Guest House
4	GPO		(Ashram accommodation)
5	Sri Aurobindo Ashram	13	Ellora Hotel
6	Ashram Beach Office & Auroville	14	Amala Lodge (main building)
	Information Centre	15	Amala Lodge (Annexe)
7	French Consulate-General	16	Geekay Lodge
8	French Institute	17	Market
9	Foreigners Registration Office	18	Aristo Hotel
10	Government Tourist Home,	19	Singapore Bar
	Tourist Information Office		
	and 'Youth Hostel'		

Pondicherry

drain to the left of the central Government Square. The French Consulate-General is also in this area. The streets in this part of town are very attractive and strongly reflect French influence.

Most of the hotels are to be found either along Rangapillai St which connects West Boulevard with the Government Tourist Home (the best of the mid-range) and the super-cheap Youth Hostel next door, which is part of the Tourist Information Centre. These are located on the southern edge of town close to the railway station. Auroville lies 10 km to the north-west of town. If you're planning on having a look around there, it's best to rent a bicycle for the day since everything is very spread out.

Note there's a good deal of Indianisation of street names taking place in Pondicherry so these may change slightly. For example, Rangapoulle has been changed to Rangapillai.

Information

The Tourist Information Centre, Uppalam Rd next door to the Government Tourist Home, has booklets about Pondicherry and street maps but the Ashram Beach Office has a better street map for Rs 1.

The Ashram Beach Office and Auroville Information Office, Goubert Avenue, has information about the Sri Aurobindo Ashram and Auroville. They have maps of Pondicherry, backed with one of Auroville which has a descriptive outline of the latter, cost is Rs 1. Handicrafts made at Auroville, such as incense, jewellery, hand-made paper, are sold here.

The Auroville Information & Reception Centre is part of the Promesse settlement on the main road to Madras, outside town. There's very little printed information about Auroville here — they mostly seem to sell books on and by Sri Aurobindo and The Mother. This is where you book accommodation in Auroville's International Guest House further up the road.

Sri Aurobindo Ashram

The main Ashram building is situated on Rue de la Marine and is surrounded by others which are all given over to the various educational and cultural activities of the Aurobindo Society. It's open every day and there are always people hanging around in the entrance lobby who will show you around if you're interested. The room where Aurobindo and the Mother used to meditate (Aurobindo's Samadhi) is open for viewing by appointment daily between 11.30 and 11.45 am only. Personally, I found its air of self-conscious other-worldliness somewhat contrived.

Opposite this building is the main educational centre where you can pick up a film, slide-show, play, or a lecture virtually every night of the week. These events are open to all and are very popular. Audiences are usually half-western and half-Indian. For most there's no entry charge but a donation is sometimes collected.

On the sea front is the Ashram Beach Office and Auroville Information Office. Here they have for sale books on and by Sri Aurobindo and The Mother, jewellery and hand-made paper. There's also a photographic exhibition of Auroville (which isn't that good) and information sheets with a map of Auroville and a short description of the place (cost Rs 1).

Auroville

The brainchild of The Mother and designed by the French architect Roger Anger, Auroville was meant to be 'an experiment in international living where men and women could live in peace and progressive harmony with each other above all creeds, politics and nationalities'. It took off at a ceremony on 28 February 1968 when the President of India and representatives of 121

countries came to pour the soil of their lands into an urn to symbolise universal oneness. For a time, idealism ran high. The project attracted many foreigners particularly from France, Germany, the UK, Holland and Mexico and money poured in from various state governments, the central Indian government and UNESCO. Construction of living quarters, schools, an enormous meditation hall (the Matri Mandir), dams, reafforestation, orchards and other agricultural projects were begun. The amount of energy and effort which went into Auroville in those days is obvious even now and the idealism with which the place kicked-off still surfaces in conversations with Aurovillians.

Unfortunately in 1973, the Mother, who was the undisputed spiritual and administrative head of the Sri Aurobindo Society and Auroville, died and a power struggle ensued for control of Auroville. In support of its case for control, the society quoted The Mother as having said that 'the township with all its property will belong to the Sri Aurobindo Society' but the Aurovillians countered this with another of her statements which was that 'Auroville belongs to nobody in particular, (it) belongs to humanity as a whole.'

The struggle soon developed into bitter acrimony with both sides trading accusations. On the one hand the Aurovillians accused the society of diverting and misusing funds meant for the project and of creating obstacles over the renewal of visas for the foreigners at Auroville. On the other hand, the society accused the Aurovillians of corrupting The Mother's concept by indulging in free sex and drugs. On two separate occasions, in August 1977 and again in April 1978, the cold war between the two erupted into violence and led to police intervention. Though the Aurovillians retained the sympathy of the Pondicherry administration, the odds were stacked against them since all funds for the project were channelled through the society. The society also had the benefit of powerful friends in the Indian Government — including three former Cabinet Ministers — who consistently sided with the Ashram. So, in order to demonstrate their hold over Auroville, the society began to hold up and delay funds for the project. This resulted in the abandonment of construction work, particularly on the Matri Mandir, and is why you will see so many moss-covered, half completed buildings when you visit Auroville.

The Aurovillians reacted to this takeover bid with admirable resourcefulness, pooling their assets to take care of the food and financial needs of the residents and setting up 'Auromitra', a friends-of-Auroville organisation to raise funds. Nevertheless, things got so serious in early 1976 that the Ambassadors of France, Germany and the USA were forced to step in with offers of help from their governments to prevent the residents from starving.

In the light of these conflicts the Indian government appointed a committee to look into the project and came up with the recommendations that the powers of the Aurobindo Society be transferred to a committee made up of representatives of the various interest groups including the Aurovillians and that there should be greater local participation. There was also an investigation of the financial affairs of the society which turned up some pretty unsavoury material regarding a grant of Rs 9.6 million which should have gone to Auroville. The committee's report was more or less shelved and events continued much as they had before until the news broke in November 1980 that the central government had decided to take over the running of the project. This has been greeted with cautious optimism by the Aurovillians.

At present, the project has 14 settlements and about 550 resident foreigners including children. The settlements include: *Promesse*, on the road to Madras, where the Auroville Information and Reception Centre is located; *Hope*, a 25 hectare farm with orchards set up as an experiment in organic farming; *Udavi*, where Aurovillians helping in the development of the nearby Tamil village of Edayanchavadi live; *Auroson's Home*, south of the Matri Mandir, which is involved with environmental research and the utilisation of natural sources of energy; *Dicipline*, an agricultural project; *Fertile, Two Banyans* and *Utility*, all of them engaged in tree planting and agriculture; *Fraternity*, a handicrafts community which works in close operation with local Tamil villagers, and *Aspiration*, at present the largest community, which is an educational, health care and village industry project. The huge Matri Mandir, designed to be the spiritual and physical centre of Auroville, is clearly visible from many points but its construction had to be abandoned when the Aurobindo Society cut off funds. Building will no-doubt be resumed when the central government has sorted out funds for the project. Just off to one side of the Matri Mandir is a very pleasant communal kitchen and dining hall where you can get a meal for a small donation and have a chance to talk to the residents.

The best way to visit Auroville is to rent a bicycle for the day through the hotel you're staying with in Pondicherry — average cost is Rs 3, no deposit necessary. The best places to enter are from the coast road at the village of Chinna Mudaliarchavadi and head towards Aspiration (don't worry about missing this turning: all the local people will point it out for you) or from the main road to Madras at the first turning on the right past Promesse (Auroville Information Centre). There's no chance

of you walking round Auroville in a day — it's too spread out.

Aquarium
Situated in the Botanical Gardens at the junction of West Boulevard and Lal Bahadhur St. It has some rare ornamental fish. Entrance costs Rs 0.10.

French Institute
Located on Dumas St it was established in 1955 primarily as a research centre for Indian culture. Its vegetation maps are universally acclaimed.

Tours
The Tourist Information Centre and Excursion Centre, Uppalam Rd (also known as Cuddalore Rd though the sign on the road is different again!) next to the Government Tourist Home, runs local sightseeing tours of Pondicherry and Auroville when there are at least 10 tourists wanting to go. They depart from the Government Tourist Home at 9 am and return at 6 pm. The tour costs Rs 5 and can be booked either at the Tourist Home (tel 694/958/968) or at the Directorate of Information, Publicity and Tourism, 19 Goubert Avenue (tel 398/278).

Places to Stay
Ellora Hotel (tel 2111), on Rangapillai St near the junction with Cathedral St, is the tallest building on the street and one of the ugliest. Doubles with attached bath cost Rs 80 or Rs 100 with aircon. The *Aristo Hotel* on Nehru St is similarly priced and the rooms are probably more attractive but neither of these two are good value compared to the *Government Tourist Home* (tel 694) on Uppalam Rd. A quiet, well-maintained place surrounded by lawns and gardens there are rooms for Rs 8/15 for singles/doubles or Rs 20/35 with aircon. All rooms have attached bathrooms and there is a canteen with standard

south Indian vegetarian food at normal prices. It's recommended.

There are two Sri Aurobindo Ashram Guest Houses: *International Guest House* (tel 2200), Gingy Salai St has rooms at Rs 10/15; *Park Guest House* (tel 2971) on Goubert Ave (also known as East Boulevard) costs Rs 10-25/20-50 and there is a canteen attached.

Many of Pondicherry's rock bottom hotels are very overpriced — perhaps it has something to do with the ashram's real estate folio? *Amala Lodge*, 144 Rangapillai St (this is the annexe, the main building is further down the street towards Government Square) is probably one of the best budget hotels. Rooms cost Rs 10/20 with bathroom, fan and clean (but holed) sheets. The place is slowly being improved so the bathrooms are new and clean while the rooms look pretty shabby. Still, it's bug-free, surprisingly secure (despite the flimsy door-fittings) and the friendly manager hires bikes for Rs 3 per day. *Shanti Guest House* is Rs 20 a double and popular with travellers.

Other cheapies include the *Municipal Travellers Bungalow* (tel 75), 6 rue Suffren, opposite the State Bank of India, with basic accommodation at Rs 5/10. The *Government Tourist Home* (tel 3045) on Indira Nagar, opposite the JIPMER Medical College, Pondicherry-6, is somewhat out of the way and has rooms at Rs 6/12 and an attached canteen.

The Tourist Information and Excursion Centre on Uppalam Rd, next door to the Government Tourist Home, is sometimes referred to as the *Youth Hostel*. You can get very basic dormitory accommodation for Rs 1 a night with a mat on the ground floor or Rs 2.50 for a two-tier bunk upstairs. There is supposed to be another hostel (part of the Indian YHA network) at Solaithandavankuppam, Muthailpet, Pondicherry-3 with 46 beds at Rs 4 a night.

Other budget places include the

Hotels Swagath and the *Palace*, both on Mahatma Gandhi Rd near the junction with Lal Bahadhur St and the *Hotel Emiraj*, 6 St Theresa St. The *Geekay Lodge* on West Boulevard is outrageously over-priced and the *RSK Lodge* on the same street is unbelievably filthy and also to be avoided.

Places to Eat

Hotel Aristo is probably the best restaurant in town. It has a 207-item menu with everything made to order so expect to have to wait at least 20 minutes before your food arrives. They put a lot of effort into the preparation and presentation of the food. Three of us ate really well there for Rs 35 which bought us a whole tableful of food including fresh lime and sodas and coffees. Popular with local people and tourists.

Hotel Bilal, West Boulevard opposite the junction with Rangapillai St, is a good, cheap, non-vegetarian cafe where a meal will cost you Rs 3. Outside of meal times they serve tiffin. *Hotel Dhanalakshmi*, Rangapillai St, is a good vegetarian restaurant.

Pondicherry (and Karaikal) are the only areas of Tamil Nadu where you can buy alcoholic beverages without a liquor permit (prohibition is in force in Tamil Nadu). Pondicherry is full of bars but most of them are seedy slums which make you feel like a social reprobate for liking a drink. One which isn't like this at all and has a very friendly manager who enjoys a conversation is the *Singapore Bar*, 48 Mission St, near the junction of Nehru St and Cathedral St. Haywards or Kingfisher beers cost Rs 5.50 to 6.25 a bottle depending on whether you want it 'cool' or definitely 'cold'. Other bars charge more than this for a 'cold' beer. They also stock a beer called 'Burton' which British-trained palates will appreciate.

Getting There

Train There is one direct train to

Madras each day (the Pondicherry Express) but, since the line to Pondicherry is a branch line, all other journeys by rail involve changing at Villupuram. There are several trains to Villupuram each day from Pondicherry. If you're heading south or coming from there, you can avoid having to back-track from Villupuram by going via Thiruppapuliyar Railway Station, a short Rs 1 bus journey from Pondi.

Bus The timetable at the bus station is entirely in Tamil though that's of little consequence since it's chaos anyway. Timetables in English are included in the booklet which the Tourist Office issues but they too are a figment of the imagination. The only way you find a bus here is by default, divine intervention or out of sheer desperation. Every enquiry produces a different response. If you're heading south, however, count yourself relatively lucky since there is one bolt-hole out of this silly situation and that is to take one of the frequent buses to Cuddalore, just down the coast (Rs 1.20, takes about an hour). The bus station here is much better organised and there's a greater choice of buses. If you're intent on braving the chaos at Pondicherry there are, in theory — and probably to a degree in practice, the following buses:

To Bangalore — TPTC bus at 7.30 am, ATC bus at 5.30 am, Sridhar/Bharathi bus at 10.30 am, cost is Rs 19.50.

To Kanchipuram — TPTC bus at 4 pm daily, costs Rs 5.50 and takes four hours.

To Madras — PTC buses 507, 508, 557 & 583 run 10 times daily, cost is Rs 8.50 and it takes 4¼ hours.

To Mahabalipuram — PTC bus twice daily at 8.30 am and 12.30 pm. These go via the direct route, cost Rs 5 and take 2½ hours.

To Nagapattinam — PTC bus 508 operates six times daily and costs Rs 8.50. There are also buses via Chidambaram and Karaikal: Lakshmi Transport (2.40 pm, Rs 6.25), JVS (5 pm, Rs 7.25), CRC Transport (4.50 am, Rs 7.50).

To Tanjore — buses at 2.52 and 11.52 am, via Chidambaram and Kumbakonam. Cost is Rs 9.20 and it takes 4½ to 5½ hours.

Good luck with the chaos!

TANJORE (Thanjavur)
(population 160,000)

Tanjore was the ancient capital of the Chola kings whose origins, like those of the Pallavas, Pandyas and Cheras with whom they shared the tip of the Indian peninsula, go back to the beginning of the Christian era. Power struggles between these groups were a constant feature of their early history with one or another gaining the ascendant from time to time. The Chola's turn for empire building came between 850 and 1270 AD and at the heights of their power they controlled the greater part of the Indian peninsula south of a line drawn between Bombay and Puri and included parts of Sri Lanka and even, for a while, the Srivijaya kingdom of the Malay peninsula and Sumatra.

Probably their greatest emperors were Raja Raja (985-1014 AD), who was responsible for building the Brihadeshwara Temple (Tanjore's main attraction), and his son Rajendra I (1012-1044 AD) whose navies competed with the Arabs for control of the trade routes across the Indian Ocean and who was responsible for bringing Srivijaya under Chola control. Most of the Chola emperors were generous patrons of the arts and it was during their rule that Dravidian culture reached the pinnacle of its development. The

Tanjore

Key:-
1. Mangalambika Lodge
2. Hotel Bilal
3. Tourist Bungalow (T.T.D.c)
4. Yagappa Lodge
5. Deen Lodge
6. Travellers' Lodge (I.T.D.c)
7. Arts & Crafts Emporium
8. Brihadeswara Temple, Fort & Sivaganga Tank

Scale

1 km

0   ½

temples, forts and palaces of Tanjore are all superb examples of this cultural explosion which had its roots in the early folk-art traditions originally developed by the Pallavas at Kanchipuram and Mahabalipuram. The wealth which underwrote all this seemingly endless construction came originally from the rich fertile rice growing area of the Cauvery River delta which, even today, is the rice bowl of southern India. It was later augmented by the profits which accrued from control of the lucrative trade between China and India, following Rajendra I conquest of Srivijaya.

But Tanjore wasn't the only place which was graced with Chola patronage and there are numerous other places, all within easy reach of Tanjore, with enormous Chola temples, the main ones being at Kumbakonam (45 km), Thiruvaiyyaru (13 km), Thirukandiyur (10 km) and Gangaikondacholapuram (71 km). There is also the enormous temple complex at Srirangam near Tiruchirappalli — probably India's largest — in which the Cholas had a hand. It's well worth putting aside several days to see Tanjore and its surrounding temple towns.

Orientation

Tanjore is dominated by the enormous gopurams of the Brihadeshwara Temple itself surrounded by fortified walls and a moat and located between the Grand Anicut Canal and the old town. The old town itself, consisting of winding streets and alleys and containing the vast labyrinthine ruins of the palace of the Naicks of Madurai, stands between the Grand Anicut Canal and the Vadavar River. It was at one time surrounded by a fortified wall and moat though most of this has now disappeared. Between the bus stand at the edge of the old city and the railway station runs Gandhiji Rd along which are located most of the hotels, a number of restaurants, the State Arts and Crafts Emporium and the GPO. Most of the other hotels are located at the back of the railway station on Trichy Rd. Although there is no Tourist Office the TNTDC Tourist Bungalow on Gandhiji Rd has good maps of Tamil Nadu showing all the main places of interest. If you're going to be spending any amount of time visiting the numerous temple cities of this state it's a good idea to get hold of a copy of this. The maps cost Rs 2.

Brihadeshwara Temple & Fort

Built by Raja Raja (985-1014 AD) this is the crowning glory of Chola temple architecture. It's a superb and fascinating monument which you could spend several days exploring and still not feel that you'd seen enough. The dome on top of the apex of the 63 metre (206 ft) high temple, which encloses an enormous Shiva lingam (Hindus only!), is a single piece of granite weighing an estimated 81 tons which was put in place by hauling it along an earthwork ramp six km long in a similar manner to which the Egyptian pyramids were built.

The gateway to the inner courtyard is guarded by a huge Nandi (Shiva's bull) also carved out of a single piece of rock. This Nandi is second only in size to India's largest at the Lepakshi Temple in Andhra Pradesh. The carved stonework of the temple, the gopurams and the adjoining structures is rich in detail and reflects not only Shaivite influences but also Vaishnavite and Buddhist themes. Recently discovered frescoes adorn much of the walls and ceilings of the inner courtyard surround. They have been dated to Chola times and were executed using the same techniques as were used in European fresco work.

Inside the inner courtyard off to the left is an Archaeological Museum which is well arranged and has some interesting exhibits as well as wall charts and maps detailing the history of the Chola empire. It's well worth a visit.

The temple and fort are open every day and there is no charge for entry but as the former is still a functioning Hindu temple non-Hindus are not allowed to enter the sanctum sanctorum. This is really no great loss.

The Palace, Art Gallery & Saraswati Mahal Library

This vast, labyrinthine building of huge corridors, spacious halls, observation towers and shady courtyards in the centre of the old town was built partly by the Naicks of Madurai around 1550 and partly by the Marathas. Some sections of it are now in ruins but a substantial amount remains intact. Housed in this building is the Art Gallery containing granite and bronze statues from the 9th-12th centuries and the Saraswati Mahal library established around 1700 AD. The library contains a collection of over 30,000 palm leaf and paper manuscripts in Indian and European languages.

All the above are open daily from 10 am to 5.30 pm except Wednesdays.

The Brihadeshwara Temple, though undoubtedly the most impressive and interesting, is only one of 74 other temples in Tanjore! Many of these may be seen by walking around the old town.

Places to Stay

Virtually all the hotels are either along Gandhiji Rd from the bus station to the railway station or at the back of the station on Trichy Rd. The *TTDC Tourist Bungalow* (tel 601) is an amazing place — it's a palace and, at the price, you won't find a better bargain in the state. Located on Gandhiji Rd it's spacious, spotless, very pleasantly decorated and the rooms have curtains, fan,

desk, wardrobe, comfortable bed with sheets and blankets (!) and your own bathroom with hot water in the mornings. The rooms surround a quiet and relaxing courtyard and there is prompt and very friendly room service. The staff bend over backwards to make you feel happy and comfortable. All this costs just Rs 30/45 for singles/doubles. There is an attached canteen on the ground floor but the food is nothing special and is relatively expensive. It's best to eat elsewhere, which is a pity since everything else is so good. The Tourist Bungalow is a Rs 2-3 rickshaw ride from the bus station or an easy five minute walk.

The *ITDC Travellers' Lodge* (tel 365) on Trichy Rd is another very pleasant place, set in its own gardens, but it is a long way from the sights and facilities. Rooms cost Rs 35/55 or Rs 70/120 with air-con. All rooms have attached bathrooms and there is a restaurant.

Yegappa Lodge is at the back of the railway station. Rooms with attached bathrooms cost Rs 10/17 and there is a restaurant on the ground floor. The *Deen Lodge*, round the corner on the opposite side of the road, is similar but smaller.

One of the best and cleanest of the budget hotels is *Hotel Bilal*, Gandhiji Rd. There are no singles but doubles with bathroom are Rs 8. A notice in the reception area says 'Families cannot stay here, except foreigners'. Quite why isn't clear. *Mangalambika Lodge*, Gandhiji Rd, is pretty basic and grubby. Rooms with attached 'bathroom' cost Rs 6/8. There is a vegetarian cafe downstairs which serves plate meals, tiffin and coffee.

Other budget hotels include *Sri Krishna Lodge* on South Rampart Rd (Rs 5/8), *Ajantha Lodge* on South Main St (Rs 5-6/8), *Sri Venkateshwara Lodge* on Gandhiji Rd (Rs 4-5/7 and a Rs 2 dormitory) and *Safire Lodge* on South Main St (Rs 5/8).

Places to Eat

There are plenty of simple vegetarian restaurants around the bus stand and along the beginning of Gandhiji Rd with plate meals for Rs 2-3. There is no decent vegetarian or non-vegetarian place for a minor splurge. The *TTDC Tourist Bungalow's* restaurant is nothing special and the presentation leaves a lot to be desired. In Tanjore it's thalis or nothing.

Getting There

Rail It's 8½ hours between Tanjore and Madras (Egmore) at a fare of Rs 82 in 1st class, Rs 19 in 2nd class. It only takes 1½ hours to Trichy at a cost of Rs 21 in 1st class, Rs 3.65 in 2nd. To Villupuram takes 4½ hours at a cost of Rs 52 in 1st, Rs 11.30 in 2nd. Tanjore to Madurai takes seven hours and costs Rs 56 in 1st class, Rs 12.50 in 2nd. To Coimbatore is Rs 71 in 1st, Rs 16 in 2nd.

Bus As usual the bus timetables are in Tamil but (also as usual) it's no real problem since conductors shout out their destinations and most people speak some English and will direct you to the right bus. Buses to most places within the state are frequent, the main destinations being Courtallim, Madras, Madurai, Nagarcoil, Palani, Shencottah, Trichy and Vellore.

Buses to Trichy depart approximately every 10 minutes from bay 11. The journey takes one hour and costs Rs 2.80. Buses to Kumbakonam, where there are more huge Chola temples, also depart approximately every 10 minutes. The trip takes one hour and costs Rs 2.

Things to Buy

Tanjore is famous for repousse and copper work inlaid with brass and silver. Bronze images are made at Samimalai, 72 km from Tanjore, by traditional craftsmen.

The best place to see the range of crafts made in and around Tanjore is the Poompuhar Handicrafts Emporium on Gandhiji Rd, just beyond the TNTDC Tourist Bungalow. They not only stock repousse and inlaid copper work but also excellent wood carvings taken from dismantled temple carts (the type which are drawn through the streets at festivals). These carvings are particularly cheap and it's well worth spending some time sorting through them as you won't find better examples at these prices anywhere else in the state. The emporium accepts international credit cards and can arrange packing and export of any items.

AROUND TANJORE

There are many smaller towns in the Tanjore area famous for their huge and impressive Chola temples.

Thirukandiyur (10 km)

The temples here are dedicated to Brahma Sirakandeshwara and Harsaba Vimochana Perumal and are noted for their fine sculptural work.

Thiruvaiyaru (13 km)

The famous temple here is dedicated to Shiva and known as Panchanatheshwara. Every January there is a music festival held here in honour of the saint Thiagaraja.

Thiruvarur

The Shiva temple at this town, between Tanjore and Nagapattinam, was gradually extended over the years. Its 1000-pillared hall actually has just 807 pillars!

Kumbakonam (36 km)

There are four enormous temples here of which the most important are Sarangapani, Kumbeshwara and Nageshwara. The largest of these is second only to the Meenakshi Temple at Madurai. The semi-erotic sculptural work is a feature of these temples. Once every 12 years a festival is held here at the Mahamaham tank. Thousands of devotees flock here as the waters of the Ganges are said to flow into the tank at that time! The next festival will take place in 1992. Of all the temple towns around Tanjore this is perhaps the best to visit if your time is limited. Unfortunately there are few places to stay except very basic lodges but excellent vegetarian meals are available at the *New Jayalakshmi Vilas.*

Gangakondacholapuram (71 km)

The gopurams of this enormous temple dominate the landscape for miles around. It was built by the Chola emperor Rajendra I in imitation of the style of the Brihadeshwara Temple at Tanjore, built by his father, and is dedicated to Shiva. There are many beautiful sculptures on the walls of the temple and its enclosures and a huge tank into which vessels containing the water of the River Ganges, brought by vassal kings to the court of the Cholas, were emptied.

Chidambaram

South of Pondicherry, towards Tanjore, is another of Tamil Nadu's gems of Dravidian architecture — the temple complex of Chidambaram with the great temple of Nataraja, the dancing Shiva. The complex is said to be the oldest in the south and covers 13 hectares. There are four gopurams, the north and south ones towering 49 metres high. Two of the gopurams are carved with the 108 classical postures of Nataraja, Shiva in his role as the cosmic dancer.

Other notable features of the temple include the 1000-pillared hall, the Nritta Sabha court which is carved out like a gigantic chariot, and the image of Nataraja himself in the central sanctum. There are other, lesser, temples in the complex including one to Parvati, Subrahmanya, Ganesh and a newer Vishnu temple. Chidambaram was a Chola capital from 907 to 1310 and the Nataraja temple was erected during the reign of Vira Chola Raja (927-997).

Places to Stay The *Tourist Bungalow* is good value at Rs 32 a double. There are a couple of other hotels around.

Getting There Buses to all the above places can be found at the bus stand in Tanjore and services are frequent.

TIRUCHIRAPPALLI (population 340,000)

Usually known by its shortened names of Trichy or Tiruchy, the city's most famous landmark is the Rock Fort Temple. This spectacular monument is perched on top of a massive outcrop of rock which rises abruptly from the plain and towers over the old city. There are a few other such outcrops on the way to Tanjore, one of which has a temple built on it, but none are as large or as tall as the one at Trichy. The Rock Fort Temple is reached by a seemingly endless, steep flight of steps cut into a tunnel through the rock and the views from the summit are magnificent.

The other landmark at Trichy is much less well-known which is surprising since it's probably the largest — and one of the most interesting — temple complexes in India. This is the Srirangam Temple built on an island in the middle of the River Cauvery which covers a staggering 250 hectares! It is surrounded by seven concentric walls and has 21 gopurams in all and as though this were not enough there is another huge temple complex nearby — the Sri Jambukeshwara Temple — which itself is surrounded by five concentric walls and has a total of seven gopurams. Both of these temples are visible from the summit of the Rock Fort Temple shrouded in coconut palms. Each one of these temples is worth spending at least a whole day exploring. Very few travellers seem to

THE DEVOTIONAL BELL AT SOME TEMPLES DOES NOT FAVOR THE DIMINUTIVE DEVOTEE...

find their way to Srirangam probably because of the fame of the other Tamil Nadu temples at Tanjore, Madurai and Rameswarum which is a pity since the temples at Trichy are fascinating and deserve far more recognition. Don't miss them!

Trichy itself has a long history going back to the centuries before the Christian era when it was a Chola citadel. In the first millenium AD it changed hands many times between the Pallavas and Pandyas until taken by the Cholas in the 10th century AD. When the Chola Empire finally decayed it passed into the hands of the Vijayanagar kings of Hampi and remained with them until they were defeated by the forces of the Deccan Sultans in 1565 AD. The town and fort as it stands today was built by the Nayaks of Madurai and it was one of the main centres around which the wars of the Carnatic were fought in the 18th century when the British and French were struggling for supremacy in India.

Other than the monuments, it's a pleasant place to stay with a good range of hotels and facilities and though spread out over a large area it has an excellent municipal bus system which doesn't demand the strength of an ox and the skin of an elephant to make use of.

Information & Orientation
Trichy is spread out over a considerable area and you will need transport to get from one part to another but most of the hotels, restaurants, the bus stand and railway station, the Tourist Office, airline offices and GPO are all located within two or three minutes' walk of each other in the so-called cantonment area. The Rock Fort Temple is situated several km north of this area near the banks of the River Cauvery. Further north still on an island in the Cauvery stand the temples at Srirangam. These latter lie on opposite sides of the main road to Madras and Salem. The Tourist Office is situated in the TTDC Tourist Bungalow directly opposite the bus stand but it has unusual opening hours (8.30 to 10 am and 5 to 8.30 pm).

The Tourist Office is attached to the TTDC Tourist Bungalow. It is open from 8.30 till 10 am and from 5 until 8.30 pm. They have a leaflet containing a good map of Trichy but a lot of the information on it is out of date. Both Indian Airlines and Air Lanka have their offices in the same building on Dindigul Rd. The telephone numbers are 23116 and 27951 respectively.

Rock Fort Temple
This monument which can be seen for miles around stands on top of a massive outcrop of rock, 83 metres high (273 ft) and is reached by climbing up 437 steps cut into a tunnel through the rock. It's a stiff climb but well worth it for the views from the top. Non-Hindus are not allowed into the

1	Rock Fort Temple	6	GPO
2	Teppakulam Tank	7	Selvam Lodge
3	Bus Stand (State Transport)	8	Guru Hotel & Vijay Lodge
4	Tourist Office & TTDC Tourist Bungalow	9	Hotel Anand
		10	Hotel Aristo
5	Tiruvalluvar Bus Stand	11	Hotel Sangam

sanctum sanctorum at the summit or into the Sri Thayumanaswamy Temple, dedicated to Shiva, half way up so a visit here tends to be a brief affair. It's open daily from 6 am until 8 pm and costs Rs 0.10 entrance fee plus an outrageous Rs 5 if you have a camera (the only photographically interesting vista is the one to the north over the temples at Srirangam). You must leave your shoes at the entrance. There are no guidebooks for sale. At the entrance you can amuse yourself by offering the temple elephant a coin which he takes in the tip of his trunk and passes it to his keeper. You're rewarded by a tap on the head with the elephant's trunk.

Apart from the climb up to the summit there are a few rock-cut cave temples nearby which are worth visiting. They date from the Pallavas (6th-7th centuries).

Srirangam — Sri Ranganathaswamy Temple

This superb temple complex is probably the largest in India. It's surrounded by seven concentric walls and has 21 gopurams in total. Many peoples have had a hand in its construction including the Cheras, Pandyas, Cholas, Hoysalas and the Vijayanagar kings though the bulk of it dates from the 14th to 17th centuries. It's very well preserved and has excellent carvings throughout with numerous shrines to various gods though the main temple is dedicated to Vishnu. Even the Moslems are said to have prayed here after the fall of the Vijayanagar empire. Non-Hindus are, of course, not allowed into the sanctum sanctorum but this is really no loss since the whole place is fascinating. Bazaars and Brahmins' houses fill the space between the outer four walls and you don't have to take your shoes off until you get to the fourth wall (it's customary to tip the shoe minder 10 paise on leaving). If you have a camera with you then you'll be charged

Rs 5 at this point. Opposite the shoe deposit is the 'Art Gallery' which is hardly worth a second thought but it's here that you buy Rs 0.50 tickets and go on top of the wall for a look over the complex. A guide will go with you to unlock the gates and make sure you don't take photographs of the golden gopuram. You can spend all day wandering around this complex with never a dull moment. The inner temple complex is open daily from 6.15 am to 1 pm and from 3.15 to 8.45 pm.

There is an annual car festival held here in the last week of December and the first week of January which draws pilgrims from all over India. If you're in the area at the time, make sure you see it.

There is a book for sale in certain shops within the temple complex which is called *Sri Ranga Kshetra Mahatmyam* by R Narasimhan Praveen which costs Rs 1.50. The intention of the author was probably to create a guidebook and collection of legends about the temple but it's full of the most prosaic Indian-English and incomprehensible nonsense you're likely to come across anywhere in India. For this reason alone it's worth buying. Some gems from it include:

'Pavithrotsava is conducted to the Lord for nine days from the Sukla-Paksha (bright fortnight) Ekadasi day. To the negligence committed during all these days in the year in the Pujas, remedy is being sought for otherwise Aparadakshanpana is being sought for.'

'Thondar-Adi — He is called as Vipra Narayana — He was born in a sacred place called Thirumadangudi. His Janma Nakashatra is Jyeshta in Margazhi month. He was living in Srirangam and engaged himself in presenting Thiru Thuzhai or Thulasi to Sri Tanganatha and garlands of beautiful and scented flowers were daily offered by him to the Lord. He has sung the famous Thirumalai, which is especially in devotion to Lord Sri

Ranganatha and no others. His another prabandha named Thiruppalli Yezhuchi is the most important part of the Thirumozhi group to wake up the Lord everyday. It is also spoken as Thirumalai Ariyar — Perumalai Ariyar — ie. Those who do not know Lord Sri Ranganatha. Sri Vanamal of Lord Vishnu took the avathar of this Tondar Adi Podi Alwar.'

Srirangam — Sri Jambukeshwara Temple
Located on the opposite side of the main Madras/Salem road from the Sri Ranganathaswamy Temple, this temple dedicated to Shiva has five concentric walls and seven gopurams. It's deity is a Shiva lingam which is submerged under water which comes from a spring in the sanctum sanctorum but non-Hindus are not allowed in this part of the temple. The complex was built about the same time as the Sri Ranganathaswamy Temple and is just as interesting as the latter. It's open daily between 6 am and 1 pm and between 4 and 9.30 pm.

Getting to any of the above monuments from the bus stand/railway station area is simplicity itself. Just take bus No 1 from either the railway station or the bus stand. The fare from the railway station to Srirangam is Rs 0.45. Buses are rarely full and the service runs approximately every five minutes.

Places to Stay
Sangam Hotel (tel 25202) on Collector's Office Rd is the best hotel in town and a very pleasant place. Rooms here cost Rs 65/90 for singles/doubles or Rs 45/65 without air-con. The hotel has the only bar in Trichy (permit holders only) but beers are a mite expensive at Rs 15 a bottle!

The *ITDC Travellers' Lodge* (tel 23498) on Race Course Rd is south of the railway station on the way to the airport. Rooms here are Rs 27.50/45 or Rs 37.50/60 with breakfast. The lodge is somewhat inconveniently situated.

Hotel Aristo (tel 26565), 2 Dindigul Rd, costs Rs 20/35 or Rs 45 for a de-luxe double, Rs 55 for an air-con double. There are also a few cottages which cost Rs 120-220.

The *TNTDC Tourist Bungalow* (tel 25383) is opposite the bus stand. All rooms have attached bathrooms and cost Rs 50/75 or Rs 20/30 without air-con. There is also an eight bed dormitory at Rs 5 per bed. It is nowhere near as palatial as the Tanjore TB. The Tourist Office is also in the Tourist Bungalow and there is a restaurant.

Hotel Anand (tel 26545), 1 Raquet Court Lane, is probably the most attractive of the mid-range hotels. Rooms here cost Rs 19/30 without air-con or Rs 60/75 with air-con. All rooms have their own bathrooms and there is a restaurant.

Opposite the bus stand at 13A Royal Rd *Guru Hotel* (tel 25327) is quite a pleasant place at Rs 12/20 for singles/doubles all with attached bathrooms. There are also de-luxe doubles at Rs 30, 35 and, with air-con, Rs 45. In the basement there is a vegetarian restaurant where you can get a good thali with curd for Rs 2.50. Just beyond the Guru is the slightly more expensive, but also pleasant, *Hotel Lakshmi.*

Sarada Lodge (tel 23216) on Royal Rd is diagonally opposite the Tourist Bungalow. Rooms cost Rs 15/25 or Rs 35 for a triple all with attached bathrooms. The hotel has its own restaurants but the staff are pretty hopeless. *Vijay Lodge* (tel 24311) is next to the Guru Hotel and costs Rs 13/20 with attached bathrooms. Again there's a restaurant — the pleasant outdoor *Uma Shankar Hotel.* Special dishes of the day are announced on a blackboard in the street.

There are a number of very cheap budget hotels along Junction Rd which stretches from the railway station to the bus stand. Although there's not a lot to choose between them the *Selvam Lodge* (tel 23114) has been the most popular with travellers for years. The rooms are very basic and cell-like and sheets are not provided. Costs are Rs 7/12 or Rs 18 for a double with attached bathroom. The lodge is secure and has a rooftop restaurant which is an excellent place to eat in the evenings. There is also a south Indian vegetarian restaurant on the ground floor and a dimly-lit, prison-like air-conditioned restaurant on the first floor.

Places to Eat
There are plenty of vegetarian meals cafes around the bus stand and along Junction Rd. One of the best is at the *Guru Hotel* and another good one is the rooftop of the *Selvam Lodge*, both mentioned above. If you're looking for something other than a thali then try the non-vegetarian restaurants at the *Vijay Lodge* and the *Hotel Anand*.

Getting There
Air Trichy has an airport and is connected with Madras and Colombo and Jaffna in Sri Lanka. There are daily flights to Madras for Rs 230. Indian Airlines and Air Lanka both fly to Colombo, Air Lanka also flies to Jaffna. If you're going to Sri Lanka it's worth considering the flights. The Rameswarum ferry is cheaper and you get the chance to see the magnificent temple but accommodation there is very tight. If you are heading for Rameswarum try to make advance bookings with the TNTDC Tourist Bungalow through a Tourist Office.

Getting There
Rail Trichy is on the main Madras-Madurai rail line. Some trains run directly from Madras (337 km, five to eight hours, Rs 80 in 1st, Rs 18 in 2nd) while others go via Chidambaram and Tanjore, 64 km further. The Ganga Kaveri, operating Madras-Rameswarum, also passes through Trichy. It's seven hours Trichy-Rameswarum.

From Trichy it's 155 km on to Madurai, taking 2½ to four hours at a cost of Rs 44 in 1st, Rs 9 in 2nd. There are many passenger trains as well as express services Trichy-Madurai but during the day you cannot reserve 2nd class seats so it's the usual battle for a space.

Bus Trichy has a state transport bus stand and a Tiruvalluvar bus stand only two minutes walk away. As usual the state bus stand timetables are only in Tamil. Express buses are distinguished from ordinary buses by the word 'Fast' (in English) on the direction indicator at the front. Services to most places are frequent and tickets are sold by the conductor as soon as the bus arrives. Just buy your ticket and hop on.

Trichy to Madurai takes about three hours and costs Rs 6.50. The 'Fast' bus only stops twice, one at Dindigul for chai. There is a service about every half hour, Tiruvalluvar bus company has the following (theoretical) schedule:

To Madras & Villupuram — hourly 5 am to 9 pm then up to six buses per hour from 10 pm to 5 am.

To Nagarcoil & Madurai — hourly 7 am to 12 midnight then up to five buses per hour from midnight to 6 am.

To Coimbatore — 15 buses spread fairly evenly throughout the day but with gaps between midnight and 5 am and between 9 and 11 pm.

Getting Tiruvalluvar buses in Trichy is a hopeless, complicated mess. Most buses are just 'passing through' from other places and tickets for the few empty seats are only sold by the conductor when the bus arrives. The scramble for tickets is far worse than on the state bus stand and there's no guarantee of success. On some routes 'priority tickets' are sold for Rs 0.50 which gives you priority for a ticket when the bus arrives. Getting hold of one of these, however, is an equally hopeless task as the ticket windows are hardly ever manned and when they are it's almost impossible to get their attention.

MADURAI (population 600,000)

This bustling city of over half a million people packed with pilgrims, beggars, businessmen, bullock carts and legions of under-employed rickshaw wallahs is one of southern India's oldest and has been a centre of learning and pilgrimage for centuries. Its main attraction is the famous Shree Meenakshi Temple in the heart of the old town, a riotously baroque example of Dravidian architecture whose gopurams are covered from top to bottom with a breathless profusion of multi-coloured images of gods, goddesses, animals and mythical figures. Nothing quite like it exists outside Disneyland! The temple seethes with activity from dawn till dusk and its many shrines attract pilgrims from all over India and tourists from all over the world. On any one day it's been estimated that there will be 10,000 people from outside the city here!

Depending on the time of day, you can bargain for bangles, spices or saris in the bazaar between the outer and inner walls of the temple, watch pilgrims bathing in the tanks, listen to temple music in front of the Meenakshi Amman shrine (which is relayed through the whole complex on a PA system), wander through the well-stocked museum or climb to the top of a gopuram. It's a city within a city and many travellers spend days wandering through its labyrinthine corridors and halls.

Madurai's history falls into roughly four periods beginning over 2000 years ago when it was the capital of the Pandyan kings and known to the 4th century BC Greeks via Megasthenes, their ambassador at the court of Chandragupta Maurya. In the 10th century AD it was taken by the Chola emperors and remained with them until the Pandyas briefly regained their independence in the 12th century only to lose it again in the 14th to the Moslem invaders under Malik Kafur, a general in the service of the Delhi Sultanate. Malik Kafur set up his own dynasty here which ruled for a while before being overthrown by the Hindu Vijayanagar kings of Hampi. After the fall of Vijayanagar in 1565, Madurai was taken over by the Nayaks who ruled from 1559 until 1781 AD. It was during the reign of Tirumalai Nayak (1623-55) that the bulk of the Meenakshi Temple was built.

Madurai passed into British hands in the shape of the East India Company who took over the revenues of the area after the wars of the Carnatic in 1781. In 1840, the company razed the fort which had previously surrounded the city and filled in the moat. Four broad streets — the Veli streets — were constructed on top of this fill and define the limits of the old city to this day.

This city is one huge, non-stop bazaar crammed full of shops, street markets, temples, pilgrims' choultries, hotels, restaurants and small industries. It's one of the south's liveliest cities yet small enough not to be overwhelming and it's very popular with travellers. You'll love it!

Orientation

The old town of Madurai is contained within the almost square enclosure marked out by the Veli streets (South Veli St, East Veli St, etc) on the south bank of the River Vaigai. Within this area are found almost all the main points of interest, the transport services, mid-range and budget hotels, restaurants, Tourist Office and GPO. Most of the hotels and restaurants used by travellers

Key:
① Meenakshi Temple
② Tirumalai Nayak Palace
③ Tourist Office
④ T.T.D.C. Tourist Bungalow
⑤ Radhakrishna Lodge
⑥ Hotel Apsara
⑦ New Raja Rest House
⑧ Hotel Senthosh
⑨ Santhanam Lodge
⑩ New College Hotel
⑪ Hotel Aiavai
Hotel International, Central Lodge, TM Lodge, GKS Rest House & Ruby Lodge

Madras

Tourist Bungalow

YWCA

Pandian Hotel

Circuit House

Gandhi Museum

Aiagar Koil Rd

Tamukkan Road

Gokale Road

Rajaji Park

Panangal Road

College Rd

Kodaikanal Road

Kadaikanal Road

P.T. Rajan Rd

Workshop Rd

Sandgal Rd

Town Hall Rd

Dindigul Rd

Kundram Rd

G.P.O.

West Veli St.

W. Masi St.

S. Market St.

South Veli St.

Railway Station

Bus Station

Madurai

River Vaigai

Siva Ganga Road

New Ramnad Road

Mariammam Theppakulam

Ramnad Road

Manal Road

Munichalai Rd.

Kesavan Rd.

Pasogam Rd.

P/O

E. Veli St.

East Market St.

Mahivadompokdr

Manjankara St.

E. Masi St.

N. Avani St.

S. Avani St.

S. Masi St.

S. Market St.

South Veli St.

North Veli St.

Vaki New St.

N. Masi St.

W. Avani Rd.

W. Masi St.

Chin maka dai St.

Airport

Bus Station

W. Veli St.

Railway Station

Trivandrum Tuticorin

are located west of the Meenakshi Temple between North Masi St and South Masi St but particularly along Town Hall Rd and West Masi St. The bus station, railway station and GPO are all located on West Veli St as is the Tourist Office which is close by the TTDC Tourist Bungalow near the junction with South Veli St.

Outside this area, on the north bank of the River Vaigai in the cantonment area, are the ITDC Tourist Lodge, YWCA, Circuit House, the Gandhi Museum and Madurai's best hotel, the Pandyan. The Mariammam Theppakulam tank and temple stand on the south bank of the Vaigai several km east of the old city.

Information

The Tourist Office, 180 West Veli St, is located close to the TTDC Tourist Bungalow. The staff here are friendly and helpful and maps of Madurai backed with some information about the city are available (free). There is also a branch office at Madurai Junction Station.

Shree Meenakshi Temple

The Meenakshi Temple attracts pilgrims from all over India in their thousands every day. Its enormous gopurams profusely covered with gaily coloured statues dominate the landscape for miles around and are visible from many of the rooftops in Madurai. It is named after the daughter of a Pandyan king who, legend has it, was born with three breasts. The king was told at the time of her birth that the extra breast would disappear when she met the man she was to marry and this duly happened when she met Lord Shiva on Mt Kailas. Shiva told her to return to Madurai and eight days later arrived there himself in the form of Lord Sundareshwara to marry her.

Though the present temple was designed in 1560 by Vishwanatha Nayak and substantially built during the reign of Tirumalai Nayak (1623-55 AD), it has a history going back 2000 years to the times when Madurai was the capital of the Pandya kings. It's a city within a city and bustles with life from dawn to dusk. Between the inner and outer walls on the east side is a bazaar with stalls selling everything from bangles to saris to coconuts. There's even a railway timetable posted on the wall near the Meenakshi shrine! Part of the temple complex has been converted into a museum — the Temple Art Gallery — which is well worth a visit and, although it's decidedly dilapidated these days and many labels are missing. It contains some beautiful stone and brass images, examples of ancient south Indian scripts, freizes and various attempts to explain the Hindu pantheon and the many legends associated with it. Entrance to the Art Gallery costs Rs 0.50 plus (officially) Rs 5 for a camera if you intend to use it though I wasn't even asked about mine.

You can climb to the top of the south facing gopuram by purchasing a Rs 0.50 ticket from the office on the left as you enter the temple. A guide takes you up there via many winding, grimy and gradually narrower and narrower stairways. If you suffer from vertigo this climb is not for you since you emerge on the very top of the gopuram and there are no restraining rails and very little else to hold on to but the views are excellent! On the way down the guide will hassle you for a 'tip'.

On most evenings between 6 and 7.30 pm and between 9 and 10 pm temple music is played outside the Meenakshi Amman shrine — mantras, fiddle, squeeze box, tabla and bells. It's well worth making it a point of going there to hear this as there are some excellent musicians among those who play.

The temple in general is open between 5 am and 12.30 pm and again between 4 and 10 pm. Photography is allowed inside only between 12.30 and 4 pm on payment of Rs 5. You can leave your shoes at any one of the four entrances where they will be looked after for Rs 0.10. Many of the priests inside are very friendly and will take the trouble to show you around and explain what's happening if you'd prefer that.

Thirumalai Naick Palace

About a km from the Meenakshi Temple (Rs 2 by rickshaw), this palace was built in 1636 by the ruler of the same name in the Indo-Saracenic style. Much of it has fallen into ruin and the pleasure gardens and surrounding defensive wall have disappeared but it was partially restored by Lord Napier, the Governor of Madras, in 1866-72 and further restoration work is in progress at present. Only the entrance gate and the main hall remain today but they're well worth a visit. The palace is open daily between 8 am and 5 pm and entrance costs Rs 0.40. There's no charge for photography.

Gandhi Museum

Housed in the old palace of the Rani Mangammal, this museum contains memorabilia of Mahatma Gandhi, a library and an exhibition of crafts produced by village industry concerns in South India. Part of the museum is also used for lectures and seminars. It's open daily between 10 am and 5.30 pm except Wednesdays.

Mariamman Teppakkulam Tank

This tank, several km east of the old city, covers an area almost equal to that of the Meenakshi Temple and is the site of the Teppam Festival (Float Festival) in January and February when images of Meenakshi and Lord Sundareshwara are mounted on floats and taken in procession to the tank. Here they are pulled back and forth across the water to the island temple in the centre of the tank. The festival attracts thousands of pilgrims from all over India. The tank was built in 1646 by Thirumalai Naick and is connected to the River Vaigai by underground channels.

Other

Besides the Meenakshi temple there are several other important temples worth visiting in Madurai all of them built in the typical late Dravidian style. Try the two along South Masi St between Kundram Rd and West Masi St. One of them has a temple elephant and the other offers some fine music in the evenings.

Places to Stay — Top & Middle

Madurai's best hotel is the *Pandyan Hotel* (tel 26671) on Alargarkoil Rd. Singles/doubles are Rs 85/120 with deluxe doubles at Rs 150 and 'luxury' doubles at Rs 275. There is a good restaurant which is open to non-residents.

The *TNTDC Tourist Bungalow* (tel 31435) on West Veli St is very near the bus stand. Rooms cost Rs 15/25-30 for singles doubles or Rs 40/60 with air-con. A four-bed room is Rs 50. Rooms have fans and attached bathrooms and this pleasant, well-maintained hotel has a restaurant which serves western and Indian dishes.

The *ITDC Travellers' Lodge* (the Madurai Ashok) (tel 23676) is on Alargarkoil Rd near the Pandyan Hotel. Rooms are Rs 35/50 or Rs 20 more with air-conditioning. The standards are similar to the TNTDC Tourist Bungalow but, like the Pandyan, it's an inconvenient bus or taxi ride out from the centre.

Hotel Apsara (tel 31444/5) at 137 West Masai St is very popular with travellers. Rooms with bathroom and fan cost Rs 25 a double. There are no singles and you have to pay a Rs 50 deposit at first but it's very clean and the staff are friendly. There's also an air-con permit bar and a restaurant but there may not be a sign outside so watch the numbers.

New College House (tel 24311), Town Hall Rd is a huge building in its own courtyard and is another popular place for travellers. Rooms with bath are Rs 15/30 and it's pretty clean although the walls may look grubby. The top floor has the best rooms, with excellent views of the Meenakshi Temple gopurams from the roof. There is also a vegetarian restaurant, bookshop and general store.

Hotel International (tel 31525 is on West Santhaipettai St which is also known as West Perumal Maistry St. It's opposite the New College House and is a very modern hotel but surprisingly cheap at Rs 25 a double with bath.

Hotel Alavai (tel 33151), 86 West Perumal Maistry St is excellent and clean with rooms at Rs 15/35 — all with fan and bathroom. *Hotel Senthosh* (tel 26692/3) at 7 Town Hall Rd costs Rs 13/20 or Rs 25 for a de-luxe double, all with own bathroom. *Santhanam Lodge*, Town Hall Rd is a modern hotel with rooms at Rs 14/18, again with own bathroom. There are several other mid-range hotels just off Town Hall Rd with similar standards including the *TM Lodge*, *GES Guest House* and the *Ruby Lodge* (good value at Rs 15 a double) all on West Perumal Maistry St.

Places to Stay — Bottom End

There are an endless number of cheap hotels and lodges in Madurai but appearances can be very deceptive and you should beware of making assumptions about the standards of the rooms based on the appearance of the reception area. The latter can look like the lobby of the Hilton while the rooms can be unredeemingly grim and filthy with hard beds, greasy sheets and slimy bathrooms. Luckily they're not all like this but if you find yourself in one that is, refuse to take the room or demand that it's cleaned out properly. It's a standard

demand in India so they'll be quite used to it. Most of the budget hotels are pilgrim flop houses.

Radhakrishna Lodge (tel 26910) is on Koodalalagarkoil St and is very popular with shoestring travellers although it's hard to see why as many of the rooms are filthy, air-less and dingy. The staff are friendly, however, and it has a quiet location. Doubles, with own bathroom, are Rs 9, singles Rs 6.

New Raja Rest House, off Dindigul Rd, is a huge building catering mainly to pilgrims. Rooms cost Rs 12/20 with their own 'bathroom' (a tap, bucket and toilet). It's overpriced for what it offers and pretty dirty into the bargain.

Places to Eat

There are many typical south Indian vegetarian restaurants all around the Meenakshi Temple, along Town Hall Rd, Dindigul Rd and West Masai St which serve thalis for Rs 2-3 and masala dosa and coffee for Rs 1.50-2. Some of the best are the restaurants at the junction of Dindigul Rd and West Masi St, the *New Arya Bhavan* on West Masi St (air-con) and another on Dindigul Rd about 200 metres from the junction with West Masi St. It only has a Tamil name (க ஓ ௱ க ௬ ∪) but serves the biggest masala dosa you'll get in Madurai.

For non-vegetarian food try the restaurant in the *Tourist Bungalow*, West Veli St, which has a variety of dishes including western breakfasts (toast and jam, omelettes, fried and scrambled eggs, etc). The *Indo-Ceylon Restaurant*, Town Hall Rd, very close to New College House, has vegetarian and non-vegetarian meals and excellent curd, as does the *Taj Restaurant*, Town Hall Rd. If you want really good non-vegetarian food then plan on a night out at the *Pandyan Hotel.*

Getting There

Air There are flights between Madurai and Madras for Rs 305 and Madurai and

Trivandrum for Rs 175.

Rail It's 492 km from Madras to Madurai and takes eight hours via Trichy, longer via Chidambaram and Tanjore. Fares are Rs 106 in 1st class, Rs 25 in 2nd. To Rameswarum it takes six hours to cover the 164 km. Fares are Rs 46 in 1st class, Rs 10 in 2nd.

If you're heading for Kerala then the best train to take is the morning Madras-Quilon Mail since the line goes through some spectacular mountain terrain and there are some superb gopurams to be seen at Srivilliputur (between Sivaksi and Rajapalaryam) and Sankarankovil. This train takes eight hours and costs Rs 67 in 1st class, Rs 15.50 in 2nd for the 268 km journey. It gets into Quilon in plenty of time for you to make it to Trivandrum or Kovalam Beach later in the afternoon.

Sleeping berths and seats can only be booked on the night trains out of Madurai. You cannot book a seat on a day train which does not start from Madurai but it's easy to get one from the compartment attendant when a train arrives. Many of the through trains are half-empty.

Bus The Central Bus Stand and the Tiruvalluvar Bus Stand are adjacent to each other on West Veli St. Their time-tables are entirely in Tamil but the actual buses sometimes have their destinations on in English. As elsewhere it is no problem to find a bus but if you'd like to plan ahead the tourist officer in the main Tourist Office on West Veli St knows many of the most important bus schedules. When the difficulties faced by non-Tamil speaking people were pointed out to him he held up his hands in despair and answered, 'this is a problem'.

Getting Around

Some useful local buses include 3 and 4 to the Gandhi Museum, 4 to the Mariammam Theppakkulam Tank, 5 to the Tiruparankundram rock-cut temple (eight km outside Madurai) and 44 to the Alagarkoil Vaishnavite shrine (21 km from Madurai).

Festivals

Madurai's principal festivals are:

Teppam Festival (Float Festival) This is a very popular festival which attracts pilgrims from all over India. The images of Shree Meenakshi and Lord Sundareshwara (Shiva) are mounted on floats and taken to the Mariammam Theppakkulam Tank where they are pulled back and forth across the waters of the tank for several days before being taken back to Madurai. The festival takes place between January and early February.

Chithirai Festival This festival takes place in late April/early May and celebrates the marriage of Shree Meenakshi to Lord Sundareshwara.

Avanimoola Festival Another popular festival which takes place in late August/early September. Temple cars are drawn round the streets of Madurai.

RAMESWARUM (population 11,000)

Rameswarum is the Benares of the south and a major pilgrimage centre both for Saivites and Vaishnavites. It's also the place from which the ferry to Talaimannar (Sri Lanka) departs except during November and December when it is normally suspended due to rough seas. The town's most famous monument is the Ramanathaswamy Temple which is a gem of late Dravidian architecture. Its most renowned features are the magnificent corridors lined with massive sculptured pillars which are noted for their elaborate design, style and rich carving. One of these corridors is an incredible 1220 metres (4000 ft) in length! — the longest in India.

Legend has it that Rama (of the Indian epic, the Ramayana) sanctified

Rameswarum

(map labels)
T.T.D.C. Tourist Bungalow
Ramamandram Guest House
Lakshmanar Theertham
Post Office
Bazar
Ramanathaswamy Temple
Devasthanam Cottage
Railway Station
Port Office
Jetty

(inset map labels)
Rameswarum Island
Palk Bay
Mandapam
Pamban
Rameswarum
Gulf of Mannar
Dhanushkodi

this place by worshipping Lord Shiva here after the battle of Sri Lanka. Rama sent his most devout disciple, Hanuman (the monkey god), to Mt Kailas to bring a lingam but the monkey god was delayed and as Shiva had to be worshipped at a certain time, Rama's wife, Sita, moulded one herself which subsequently became known as the Ramanatha. On Hanuman's return, Rama was forced to console the monkey god by having the lingam which he had brought from Mt Kailas installed near the Ramanatha and decreeing that the Hanuman lingam should have precedence over the Ramanatha.

The temple as it stands today was begun in the 12th century AD and added to by various rulers over the succeeding centuries. Its gopuram is 53.6 metres (176 ft) high.

Information & Orientation

Rameswarum is an island in the Gulf of Mannar which is connected to the mainland at Mandapam by rail only. Though a road bridge is being constructed it will be some time before it is completed and until then the only access to Rameswarum is by rail. It's a small town and most of the hotels, restaurants, the ferry jetty, railway station and post office are clustered around the Ramanathaswamy Temple. Note that it is often very difficult to find accommodation here especially if you arrive late in the day. If at all possible you should make an advance booking for the TNTDC Tourist Bungalow if you want to be sure of a reasonable place to stay for the night.

Things to See
The Ramanathaswamy Temple is, of course, Rameswarum's principal attraction and has already been described in the introduction. There is another famous temple at Dhanushkodi on the extreme tip of the island known as the Kothandaraswamy Temple. This temple was the only structure to survive the 1964 cyclone which washed the rest of the village away. Legend has it that Vibhishana, brother of Ravana, the kidnapper of Sita, surrendered to Rama at this spot. Dhanushkodi can be reached by road from Rameswarum.

Rameswarum's other attractions are its coral reefs and beaches fringed with swaying coconut palms and tamarind trees. From Gandhamathana Parvatham, a hillock to the north of Rameswarum and the highest point on the island, an excellent view over the whole island can be had.

Places to Stay
As mentioned above accommodation can be a real problem at Rameswarum and you should try to make advance bookings at the TTDC Tourist Bungalow if you want a reasonable place to stay. If you cannot do this then you must be prepared to take whatever is available. If you're really stuck there is a covered roof at the *Lakshmi Lodge*, near the temple, where you can sleep for Rs 3 a night.

The *TTDC Tourist Bungalow* (tel 77) is without doubt the best place to stay but is almost always full. The rooms are quite luxurious at Rs 45 a double with their own bathroom and balcony overlooking the sea. The food, on the other hand, is ghastly and you should eat elsewhere.

Nadar Mahajana Sangam Lodge, New St, is about 15 minutes' walk from the railway station. Rooms here cost Rs 10 a double with own bathroom. It's clean and quiet and the next best place after the Tourist Bungalow. *Alanka Tourist Home* is a new hotel near the temple entrance on the town side with doubles at Rs 20.

Railway Retiring Rooms at the station are Rs 6 for the two singles, Rs 10 for the three doubles and Rs 15 for the triple. There is also a 14 bed dormitory at Rs 2 per person. Other places to stay include the *Lakshmi Lodge, Meenakshi Lodge, Devasthanam Cottage, Vivekananda Illam, Rama Mandiram Guest House* and the *Tirupati Devasthanam Bungalow*. The prices of these places range from Rs 5-10 a single to Rs 15-20 a double.

Places to Eat
There are a number of vegetarian restaurants which serve typical south Indian thalis. They're all of a similar quality, none of them is outstandingly good and worth particular recommendation.

Getting There
There are trains from Madras and Madurai which arrive pre-dawn, ideal for the Sri Lanka ferry departures but the main mail-express train is the Ganga-Kaveri Express which arrives from Madras daily at 1.20 pm and departs for Madras at 1.50 pm.

Sri Lanka Ferry
See the introductory Getting There section for full details on the Rameswarum-Talaimannar ferry service.

KANYAKUMARI (Cape Cormorin)
Kanyakumari is the Land's End of India where the Indian Ocean, Arabian Sea and the Bay of Bengal meet. It's a famous pilgrimage place and one to which foreign visitors go to see the sunrises and sunsets. This is the only spot in India where it's possible to enjoy

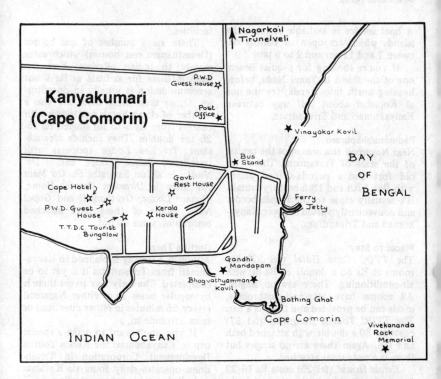

Kanyakumari
(Cape Comorin)

Nagarkoil
Tirunelveli

P.W.D
Guest House ☆

Post
Office ★

★ Vinayakar Kovil

BAY
OF
BENGAL

Bus
Stand ★

Govt.
Rest House

Cape Hotel ☆

P.W.D Guest ☆
House

Kerala
House ☆

T.T.D.C. Tourist
Bungalow

Ferry
Jetty

Gandhi
Mandapam ★

Bhagvathyamman ★
Kovil

Bathing Ghat ★

Cape Comorin

Vivekananda
Rock
Memorial ★

INDIAN OCEAN

the unique experience of seeing the sun set and the moon rise over the ocean simultaneously at full moon. There are some fine beaches here too and a 16th century Catholic church as well as an 18th century Dutch fort six km from the town. The main temple here is dedicated to the goddess Kanyakumari, an incarnation of Parvati, the wife of Shiva.

Information
There is a Tourist Office in the TNTDC Tourist Bungalow.

Kanyakumari Temple
Picturesquely located overlooking the shore, pilgrims from all over India come here to worship and to bathe at the Kumari Ghat. Legend has it that Parvati

in one of her incarnations as Devi Kanya did penance here to secure Shiva's hand in marriage but was unsuccessful and so vowed to remain a virgin (Kanya). The temple is open daily from 4.30 to 11.30 am and from 5.30 to 8.30 pm. Non-Hindus are not allowed into the inner sanctum.

Vivekananda Memorial
Located on two rocky islands which project from the sea about 200 metres from the shore line. The Indian philosopher, Swami Vivekananda came here in 1892 and sat on the rock meditating before setting out as one of India's most important religious crusaders. The mandapam which stands here in his memory was built in 1970 and employs architectural styles from all over India.

A boat service is available to reach the islands which are open to visitors between 7 and 11 am and 2 to 5 pm.

If you're looking for a quiet beach, one of the finest in Tamil Nadu, before heading north into Kerala, try the one at Kolachal about half way between Kanyakumari and Trivandrum.

Padmanabhapuram
Near Nagarcoil this was once the capital of the state of Travancore. There's an old fort and a pagoda-shaped palace with fine 17th and 18th century murals. It's actually close to the Kerala border and conveniently visited between Kanyakumari and Trivandrum.

Places to Stay
The *TTDC Cape Hotel* (tel 22) has rooms at Rs 35 a double or Rs 60 with air-conditioning. There are no singles. All rooms have attached bathrooms, meals can be provided and there is a bar. The *TTDC Tourist Bungalow* (tel 57) costs Rs 30 a double with attached bath and fan. Again there are no singles but there is a restaurant attached.

Kerala House (tel 29) costs Rs 16/22 for singles/doubles with attached bathroom and fan. There is a restaurant too. The *Government Rest House* (tel 26) is somewhat more basic than the above with rooms at Rs 6/19. There is one air-con room but no catering

facilities.

There are a number of rest houses (Devasthanam rest houses) which cater mainly to Indian pilgrims. You can sleep in these for as little as Rs 1 but accommodation is usually in dormitories. Other than these there are also a number of cheap hotels and lodges with charges from Rs 5-15 for singles, Rs 15-25 for doubles. They include *Meenakshmi*, *Tri Sea Lodge* (popular with travellers), *Palace Lodge* and *Dai Nivas* — all on Sannathi St. On Main Rd there is *Diraviam Tourist Home*, *Pioneer Lodge*, *Geethanjali* and *Gopal Nivas*. Some of these have attached bathrooms, some do not.

Getting There
Although a railway is planned to Kanyakumari from Trivandrum it is yet to be completed. The only way to get there is by regular buses from either Nagarcoil (every 25 minutes in either direction) or from Trivandrum.

If you don't want to make a special trip to Kanyakumari the Kerala Tourist Development Corporation in Trivandrum operates daily tours via Kovalam and Padmanabhapuram starting at 7 am and costing Rs 25. They are available from the Tourist Reception Centre near the railway station and bus stand in Trivandrum.

KODAIKANAL (population 16,500)
Of the three main hill stations of the south — Ootacamund, Kodaikanal and Yercaud — Kodaikanal is probably the most beautiful and certainly a lot quieter than Ooty. Located on the southern crest of the Palani Hills, 120 km from Madurai, amongst thickly wooded hillsides, waterfalls and rock outcrops it's the ideal place to escape from the heat of the plains below. Like Ooty, it has its own lake but the temperature — even in winter — never drops to the point where you need thick woollen clothing as you do in Ooty during winter and even sometimes during the monsoon.

The best time to visit Kodaikanal is in the months of April, May, June, September and October. The main rainy season is between November and December. The temperature ranges between 12 and 20°C in summer and between 8 and 18°C in winter.

Key:
1. Tourist Office ✦ Carlton Hotel
2. Paradise Lodge
3. Township New Rest House
4. Park View Rest House
5. Daisy Bank Rest House
6. Kamaraj Rest House
7. Munjikal Rest House
8. TTDC Tourist Bungalow
9. Hotel Jai

Kodaikanal

Information

The Tourist Office is located at the Township Office at the junction of Ghat Rd and Lake Rd. There is a branch of the State Bank of India in Kodaikanal which will change travellers' cheques.

Things to See

Like the other hill stations the main emphasis is on relaxation and light physical activities like walking, riding and boating. Boats are available for hire at the Boat Club on the lake. Some of the pleasantest walks include visits to Pillar Rocks (about seven km), Green Valley View (six km), Silver Cascade (eight km), Perumal Peak (20 km) and Bear Shola Falls (1.5 km).

The Flora and Fauna Museum, which is part of the Sacred Heart College at

Shembaganur near the town, is well worth a visit as is the orchidorium, also situated here. There is also an observatory which is open to the public daily during the months of March, April and June between 10 am and 12.30 pm and 7 to 9 pm. During the rest of the year it is open only on Fridays between 10 am and 12 noon.

If you go there this year (1981) be sure to ask if the Kurunji flower is blossoming. It does so only once every 12 years. The last time it blossomed was in 1969.

Places to Stay

The *TTDC Tourist Bungalow* (tel 481) on Fern Hill Rd costs Rs 35/65 for singles/doubles in the tourist season (16 April-15 June). In the low season prices drop to Rs 15/30. Cottages are available for Rs 65 in the high season, Rs 40 in the low. The Bungalow has an attached restaurant. The *Carlton Hotel* (tel 252) on Lake Rd costs Rs 50/90 including all meals.

There are many cheaper hotels clustered around the eastern end of the lake. They include the *Township Rest House* (Poet Thiagaraja Rd, tel 298), *Kamarajapuram Rest House, Daisy Bank Guest House, Park View Rest House* (tel 384), *Forest Department Tourist Bungalow, Hotel Jaya, Paradise Lodge* (tel 237) and the *Hotel Jai* (Lloyds Rd, tel 344).

Places to Eat

Both the *Tourist Bungalow* and the *Carlton Hotel* serve western, north Indian and south Indian food. For vegetarian south Indian dishes try the *Packiadeepam* at the bus stand and the *Shanmugavilas*. For non-vegetarian meals try the *Hotel Jai* and the *Hotel India*. The *Boat Club* also has a reasonable restaurant.

Getting There

The only way to get to Kodaikanal is by bus. Regular buses run to Kodaikanal from Madurai (125 km), Palani (64 km), Kodaikanal Road (80 km), Dindigul (105 km) and (during the tourist season only) from Coimbatore (175 km). The nearest railhead is at Kodaikanal Road which is connected to Madurai.

OOTACAMUND (Ooty)
(population 70,000)

Known as Udagamandalam in Tamil, this hill station in the Nilgiri mountains near the tri-junction of Tamil Nadu, Kerala and Karnataka was founded by the British in the early part of the 19th century to serve as the summer headquarters of the government of Madras. Before that time it was inhabited by the Todas, a tribal people, whose remnants still live in the area and whose animist shrines can still be seen at various places. Though it stands at a height of 2268 metres amongst some of the most spectacular mountains in southern India it's not, as you might expect it to be, similar to the Himalayas since it lacks the fascinating cultures which make those mountains so interesting. Indeed it's more a faded touch of the Raj and suffers from a bad case of over-enthusiasm on the part of the Indian tourist organisation. There's precious little to see here as such and not a great deal to do unless you're fond of long walks and boating on the weed-choked lake. The whole place has a run-down feeling about it and although this isn't unusual in India you are led to expect something special when really there isn't anything. The best part of Ootacamund is the journey there along a narrow, winding and very steep mountain road which passes first through luxuriant rain forest and then through tea plantations.

Having put the tourist literature into a more realistic perspective it should be said that Ooty is, nevertheless, a very pleasant and relaxing place and ideal as an escape from the heat of the lowlands. In winter and during the monsoon it can be quite cold, however, and you will need warm clothing. As far as general appearances go it's an unlikely combination of southern England and Australia with single storey stone cottages surrounded by twee fenced flower gardens scattered along leafy winding lanes and with tall eucalypt stands covering the otherwise barren hill tops. Since they were introduced back in the 19th century, the eucalypts have spawned a small oil-extraction industry in the area and bottles of eucalyptus oil can be bought in many shops in the town. The other main reminders of the British period are the stone churches and the huge boys' public school which sits in its own landscaped gardens at the bottom end

Ootacamund

Key:-
1. Railway Station & Hotel Gaylord
2. Bus Stand
3. Tourist Office
4. G.P.O. & Collector's Office
5. TTDC Tourist Bungalow
6. Nahar Tourist Home & Hotel Paradise
7. YWCA
8. Hotel Woodlands
9. Hotel Dasaprakash
10. P.W.D. Bungalow
11. Zodiac Room Restaurant
12. Tourist Cafe, rowing boats & horses
13. District Forest Officer

Mysore

Kotagiri

Mettupalayam Coimbatore Coonoor

of the lake. There's also the terraced and very English Botanical Gardens in which Government House stands on the lower slopes of Doddabetta, the highest peak in Tamil Nadu.

Ootacamund, although it quickly became the principal hill station in southern India during the Raj, was not the first in this area. As early as 1819 the British had begun to build houses at Kotagiri, 28 km from Ooty. This much smaller town still survives as a minor hill station and has a climate mid-way between that of Ooty and Coonoor.

Orientation
Ooty is spread out over a large area amongst rolling hills and valleys and connected by a complicated system of narrow, winding lanes and flights of steps through the main area of town containing the railway station, the bus stand, the bazaar, tourist office, restaurants and the GPO. Most of the hotels are located between the eastern end of the lake and the so-called Charing Cross (the junction of Coonoor Rd, Kelso Rd and Commercial Rd). Most of the top end and mid-range hotels are situated on the south side of the racecourse with the exception of the TNTDC Tourist Bungalow and the Nahar Tourist Home which, like the Tourist Office, are located around Charing Cross. The bulk of the budget hotels and cafes are scattered around the bazaar which stretches between Hospital Rd and Commercial Rd with a few others in the streets below Commercial Rd, east of the race course. There are other hotels strung out along High Level Rd and Avalanche Rd.

Information
The Tourist Office on Commercial Rd is opposite the Nahar Tourist Home. The only literature available here is a leaflet with a map of Ooty and details of the current hotel prices. The office is staffed by three idle layabouts who know nothing more than the leaflet they hand you.

Liquor permits are issued at the Taluk Office near the hospital. They can also be issued at the Tourist Office if the chief officer is in but he usually isn't in which case they'll send you to the Collector's Office next to the GPO which doesn't issue them any more (though of course there's still a notice on the door of the relevant office saying they do). Here there'll direct you to the Taluk Office — where else but India. Liquor permits can be sold for around Rs 100 outside the Co-operative Supermarket.

If you intend to visit Mudumalai it's wise to book accommodation in advance if you want to be sure of a bed for the night. This can be booked at the office of the District Forest Officer on Coonoor Rd.

What to See & Do
Ooty is a place for outdoor activities. Any number of long walks can be made, just head out in any direction you like. Some superb views over Ooty and the Nilgiris can be found. If you'd prefer to go on horseback, horses can be rented next to the boat house on the north side of the lake for about Rs 15 per hour. They can be delivered to your hotel for no extra charge. You can take them off on your own or hire one of the owners as a guide. Rowing boats and motor boats can be hired for use on the lake at the following hourly rates:

rowing boats	off-season	high-season
two-seaters	Rs 3	Rs 4.50
four-seaters	Rs 5	Rs 7.50
six-seaters	Rs 8	Rs 12
motor boats		
eight-seaters	Rs 15	Rs 25

The off-season is July-August and November-February, the high-season is March-June and September-October. The notice board which details these charges includes the gem of Indian-

English, 'Rowers are available for rowing capacity including rower's rowing cooly charges extra'. Work that one out! If you want to go out on the lake do it soon because water hyacinth has already claimed half the lake and will soon take over completely.

In the town itself the bazaar is worth a visit and you may come across some interesting crafts produced by the hill tribes in the area.

If you'd like a day or two's outing then take a bus to Kotagiri, a much smaller and quieter hill station about 28 km from Ooty. From this town you can visit Catherine Falls (eight km), Elk Falls (eight km) and Kodanad View Point (16 km). From the latter place there is a fine panoramic view over the eastern slope of the Nilgiris and onto the plains. There are a few basic lodges in Kotagiri such as the *Hotel Ram Vihar* where singles/doubles are Rs 10/18.

Tours
Kings Travel (tel 3137), c/o Nahar Tourist Home, Commercial Rd, offer two tours. The first covers Doddabetta Peak, Kotagiri, Kodanad View Point, Coonoor, Dolphin's Nose, Lamb's Rock and Sims Park. The tour runs from 8 am to 7 pm and costs Rs 50.

The other tour goes to Doddabetta Peak, the Botanical Gardens and Ooty Lake in the morning, then to the Mudumalai Wildlife Sanctuary in the afternoon. This tour runs from 9 am to 8 pm and costs Rs 50.

Charges include a vegetarian lunch, snacks, entrance fees, a guide and a group photograph (!). If you're hoping to see very much of Mudumalai then forget the second tour as you spend precisely 2¼ hours there.

Places to Stay
During the high season budget hotel prices may double or even triple. On the other hand the mid and top end places

may offer considerable reductions in the off-season.

Places to Stay — Top End
The *Palace Hotel* (tel 2170-2475), Fernhill costs Rs 85/105 in the high season but drops to Rs 65/80 in the low. Meals are available. *Hotel Savoy* (tel 2572-2463) costs Rs 130/220 for singles/doubles including all meals. Bed and breakfast only is Rs 45/90.

Hotel Brindavan (tel 2061-2-3) on Woodcock Rd, costs Rs 35/60-80 in the high season but drops to Rs 20/30-60 in the low. The *Hotel Fernhill Imperial* (tel 2055-2976) costs Rs 100/140 but drops to Rs 75/105 in the low season. They also have a number of cottages for Rs 125 to 225.

Places to Stay — Bottom End
The *TTDC Tourist Bungalow* (tel 2543-4) is on the hill above the Tourist Office. It's a reasonably pleasant and modern building although not up to the standard of other TTDC Tourist Bungalows. In the 15 April-15 June high season rooms cost Rs 50/90 but drop to Rs 30/50 in the low season. There is also a Rs 10 dormitory. The rooms are pleasantly furnished with table and chair, balcony, bathroom (hot water from 6 am to 9 am only). The radio doesn't work though and a heater in the room will cost an extra Rs 15. Vegetarian and non-vegetarian meals are available in the dining room on the top floor and there is a coffee bar and games room (table tennis). The staff are friendly and most of the rooms have excellent views over Ooty.

Hotel Dasaprakash (tel 2460-2680), on the hill south of the bus station, was once a grand building but has now gone to seed. Mouldy old moth-eaten photographs of the Maharaja of Mysore being shown around in better days attempt to recapture that old grandeur but it's no longer in that bracket. Rooms start at

Rs 25/50 and go on up to Rs 130 for de-luxe twin suites. There are also some Rs 35 doubles without attached bathrooms. There is a vegetarian restaurant.

On Commercial Rd opposite the Tourist Office the *Nahar Tourist Home* occupies a modern building. Singles/doubles, all with attached bathrooms and 24-hour hot water are Rs 30/50. The vegetarian restaurant downstairs is a bit expensive, Rs 7.20 for a thali with coffee.

The *YWCA* (tel 2218) on Anandagiri Ettines Rd takes both men and women and costs Rs 16 for a double with bathroom. It's quite luxurious — carpeted floors, spacious lounge upstairs with a log fire. Highly recommended.

Hotel Gaylord (tel 2378) is on the hill behind the railway station and costs Rs 15/25 or Rs 35 for a triple, Rs 60 for a de-luxe suite with four beds. There are also three-bed cottages for Rs 50. All the rooms have attached bathrooms and hot water but it's somewhat run down and dingy although it is very friendly. The attached restaurant purports to offer Punjabi, Bengali, Gujerati, continental and Chinese food if ordered in advance.

On South Lake Rd the *PWD Bungalow* is superbly located on the south shore of the lake and is one of the best mid-range places although accommodation is very limited. If it's early in the day then it's worth trying, otherwise you can make an advance reservation and stay elsewhere in the meantime. It's a good 15 minutes walk from the bus stand and railway station. On Ettines Rd *Hotel Nataraj* (tel 2772) costs Rs 25-35/60-75 in the high season, only Rs 15-25/25-40 in the low season.

Rock bottom places vary widely in quality and prices can increase dramatically in the high season. Do some shopping around, prices don't necessarily equate with quality — many of them are very dingy, some of them revoltingly filthy.

Sri K R Bhavan Boarding & Lodging costs Rs 6 for a double with common bathroom. It's small, friendly and has good food but you must provide your own bedding. *Green Lands Hotel* is another small cheapie with Rs 6 doubles.

On the second street on the left, off the road along the top side of the race course as you leave the bus stand or railway station, is the dirty, dingy doss house known as *Nataraja Lodge*. There is no hot water and singles/doubles cost an overpriced Rs 6/14 but it's an interesting place and the manager is a practising astrologer.

Places to Eat

Many hotels have their own restaurants which are open to non-residents but if you want a change you could try the *Hotel Paradise* on Commercial Rd. It's located diagonally opposite the cooperative supermarket and Tourist Office and has Punjabi and north Indian food of excellent quality and at reasonable prices. Ghobi (cauliflower & potato), curd, three chappatis and two coffees cost Rs 6.50.

Nahar Tourist Home has excellent, if slightly expensive, thalis in the ground floor restaurant. The Chinese *Zodiac Room* close to the GPO and State Bank has excellent meals for around Rs 7.

Getting There

Rail Like Darjeeling and Matheran, Ooty has its own miniature railway connecting it with the lowlands. The trains, with their quaint yellow and blue carriages, are not quite as small as the Darjeeling toy train but they're nowhere near as big as those on the main lines. The unique feature of this line is the toothed central rail which the locomotives lock into on the steeper slopes. Wellington, just above Coonoor, is a good place to watch the train climb one side of the valley, cross it by bridge and then double back to climb the opposite side. Like the journey up to Darjeeling by train, this is an excellent way of getting to Ooty and affords some spectacular views of the precipitous and eastern slopes of the rain-forest covered Nilgiris. Highly recommended!

The miniature railway starts at Mettupalayam, north of Coimbatore and goes via Coonoor to Ooty. The departures and arrivals at Mettupalayam connect with the Nilgiri Express which runs between Mettupalayam and Madras. If you're heading for Ooty, the Nilgiri Express departs Coimbatore at 6.35 am and arrives at Mettupalayam at 7.30 am. If you're coming from Ooty it departs Mettupalayam at 6 pm. The miniature trains depart Mettupalayam for Ooty at 8 am and Ooty at 11.20 am and 2 pm, the latter to connect with the Nilgiri Express. There are also trains from Ooty to Coonoor only at 7.30 am and 5.40 pm.

The 46 km journey takes about 4½ hours up to Ooty and about 3½ going down. Fares are Ooty-Coonoor Rs 18 in 1st, Rs 1.26 in 2nd; Ooty-Mettupalayam Rs 38.50 in 1st, Rs 3.20 in 2nd; Ooty-Coimbatore Rs 43.50 in 1st, Rs 9.45 in 2nd.

Bus – Local

To Kotagiri – hourly from 7.30 am to 6.30 pm, journey takes 1¼ hours and costs Rs 2.05.

To Coonoor – 11 buses from 7.20 am to 7 pm, journey takes one hour and costs Rs 1.35.

Bus – Long Distance

To Bangalore – daily at 6.30 and 10.30 am, the journey takes nine hours and costs Rs 16.05.

To Calicut – Eight buses from 5.30 am to 3.15 pm.

To Gudalur – five buses from 7.15 am to 7 pm.

To Gundulpet – buses at 8.30, 9.50, 10.50 am and 2.15 pm.

To Hassan – buses at 8 and 11.30 am, 2.30 and 5 pm.

To Mysore – buses at 8 and 9 am, 1.30 and 3.30 pm. The 5½ hour trip costs Rs 9.55. This is the bus to take if you're heading for the Mudumalai Wildlife Sanctuary under your own steam. Get off at Theppukady where the reception centre is located. The journey this far from Ooty takes about 2½ hours and costs Rs 5.95.

COIMBATORE (population 380,000)

Coimbatore is a large and busy city at the foot of the Nilgiri mountains, full of 'shirting & suiting' shops. Its only interest for travellers is as a way station to Ootacamund and the other Nilgiri hill stations.

Orientation

The bus station and railway station are a considerable distance from each other and both are well outside the centre of the city. You'll need an auto-rickshaw to get from one to the other. There are a number of mid-range and budget hotels clustered around the bus station – they are adequate for a night's stay.

Places to Stay

Hotel Sree Shakti, 11/148 Sastry Rd (tel 34225/34229) is a large modern hotel opposite the bus station. The rooms cost Rs 15/25 for singles/doubles and are pleasantly decorated, spotlessly clean and have attached bathrooms which smell strongly of bleach when you first arrive – a very rare and welcome indication of how well the place is maintained! The rooms have a fan, the staff are very friendly and room service is available.

Zakin Hotel, Sastry Rd, is a few doors up from Shakti and also opposite the bus station. Rooms here cost Rs 15/25 with attached bathrooms, Rs 10 for

Coimbatore

Key:-
① Railway Station
② Bus Station
③ Pallavan Bus Station
④ Hotels Sree Shakti & Zakin
⑤ Air India
⑥ G.P.O.

a bathless single. It's of a similar quality to the Shakti.

Places to Eat

The *Zakin Hotel* has an attached restaurant on the ground floor which serves excellent non-vegetarian food. A large meat and vegetable stuffed paratha, mutton curry with very tender meat and a coffee cost Rs 9. There are also a number of other vegetarian and non-vegetarian restaurants where you can get a good meal opposite the bus station along Sastri Rd. There's also a cheap cafe in the bus station itself.

Getting There

Air There are flights between Coimbatore and Cochin (Rs 135), Bangalore (Rs 185) and Madras (Rs 355).

Rail Coimbatore is a major rail junction and there are services to most major centres. The direct Karnataka Kerala Express operates twice a week from New Delhi and makes the 2627 km trip in 38 hours at a cost of Rs 390 in 1st, Rs 95 in 2nd. There are a number of daily trains between Madras (Central) and Coimbatore. The 494 km trip takes seven to nine hours and costs Rs 106 in 1st, Rs 25 in 2nd.

The daily trains to Madurai take from seven hours for the 229 km trip and costs Rs 58 in 1st, Rs 13 in 2nd. One of them goes on to Rameswarum, a 14 hour trip for 393 km at a cost of Rs 90 in 1st, Rs 20.50 in 2nd. Bangalore is 424 km away, the eight hour trip costs Rs 94 in 1st, Rs 22 in 2nd. Direct trains to Bombay take 33 hours for the 1635 km trip and cost Rs 280 in 1st, Rs 67 in 2nd.

Take the Nilgiri Express if you're heading for Ooty, it connects with the miniature railway at Mettupalayam.

Bus There's a huge and well organised bus station in Coimbatore. As elsewhere timetables are only in Tamil except for buses to Ooty and some interstate buses.

To Bangalore — buses at 6.30 and 8.30 am and 8 pm. There's also a Conti Travels air-con bus at 7 am.

To Guruvayur — buses at 4.40 and 10 am, 3.30 and 8 pm. The journey takes four hours.

To Kanya Kumari — buses at 5.30 am and 10.15 pm via Dindigul and Madurai.

To Madras — six buses from 5 pm to 11 pm. The first and last buses go via Vellore and Kanchipuram.

To Madurai — seven buses from 6 am to 11 pm, they go via Palani, Dindigul and Kodai Road.

To Mysore — daily at 6 am, takes 6½

hours.

To Naggapattinam — four buses from 5.30 am to 10.30 pm, they go via Trichy and Tanjore.

To Nagarcoil — six buses from 5 am to 8.30 pm via Dindigul and Madurai.

To Ootacamund — 26 buses from 5 am to 7.20 pm. The three hour journey costs Rs 6.40 and is one of the most spectacular bus journeys in southern India. Don't expect to get on the first bus which arrives because even in the off-season there will be a long queue for the buses. You generally can expect to get on the second or third bus to arrive after you join the queue.

To Palghat — one to four buses hourly from 4.45 am to 7.25 pm. The 1¼ hour journey costs Rs 3.40.

To Pondicherry — buses via Cuddalore at 9 am and 9.30 pm.

To Tanjore — buses via Trichy at 9.30 am and 7.30 pm.

To Trichy (Tiruchirappalli) — six buses from 6 am to 11 pm.

To Trichur — buses at 5.30 and 9 am, 12.45 and 5.15 pm. The journey takes 3¼ hours.

Getting Around

Useful buses around Coimbatore include bus 20 to the airport, bus 25 and 32A to the GPO and bus 1A, 7, 65 and 75 to Indian Airlines.

WILDLIFE SANCTUARIES IN TAMIL NADU

There are six wildlife sanctuaries in Tamil Nadu, three close to the east coast and the others in the richly forested mountains on the borders of Kerala and Karnataka. Mudumalai, at the foot of the Nilgiris in the extreme north-western tip of the state, is the largest and is contiguous with Bandipur Wildlife Sanctuary in Karnataka and Wynad Sanctuary in Kerala. The smallest is Guindy Deer Park within the metropolitan boundaries of Madras. All the sanctuaries except Guindy have accommodation and transport facilities and although it's possible to turn up at any of them without prior arrangements having been made it's advisable to book in advance. The reason for this is that rooms in sanctuary lodges and rest houses cannot be allocated to unan-

Andhra
Pradesh

Karnataka

Madras

Guindy

Vedanthangal

Pondicherry

Mudumalai
Ootacamund

Tiruchirappalli

Tanjore

Anamalai

Pt. Calimere

Madurai

Kerala

Mundanthurai
Tirunelveli

☆ Game Sanctuaries

nounced guests until very late in the afternoon when there's no further possibility of anyone with a booking arriving. There's also the question of arranging motorised transport to the more remote parts of the sanctuaries where you're far more likely to see animals which don't often venture too close to areas of human settlement or main roads. Some of the sanctuaries offer elephant rides through the forest and although these needn't be booked in advance and are great fun as far as they go you're unlikely to see many of the animals which live in these sanctuaries from the back of an elephant.

At present, most of the sanctuaries are geared to groups who arrive with their own transport and who have pre-booked at least a few days ahead. If you're alone and haven't booked then you could find that a lot of your time is taken up waiting for a group to arrive that you can attach yourself to. With-

out transport, too, your choice of accommodation is limited unless you can get a lift. It's time the Indian tourist organisation gave some thought to catering for visitors without their own transport and who can't, because of the way they travel, make bookings weeks in advance. All the same, don't let this put you off visiting at least one of the sanctuaries as it can be a very rewarding experience.

Mudumalai Wildlife Sanctuary

Located in the luxuriously forested foothills of the Nilgiris, Mudumalai is part of a much larger sanctuary which includes those of Bandipur and Wynad in neighbouring Karnataka and Kerala respectively. The main attractions here are the herds of spotted deer, gaur (Indian bison) and elephant, tiger, panther, wild pig, sloth and the otters and crocodiles which live in the River Moyar. It's possible to see all of these if you have made arrangements with the forest department for a vehicle to take you to the more remote parts of the sanctuary. Even around Theppukadu, where the Reception Centre is located, you will see spotted deer, elephant and wild pig and at night, if you're lucky, tiger. The Reception Centre has a board on which is kept a record of which animals were sighted and where. There's also a visitors' book which makes interesting reading especially the accounts of those who (perhaps foolishly) have gone out walking at night and met tigers!

The main service area in this sanctuary is the village of Theppukadu on the main road between Ootacamund and Mysore where the Wildlife Sanctuary Reception Centre, Sylvan Lodge, chai shops and elephant camp are. Any of the service buses which run between Ooty and Mysore will take you there. From Ooty it's a 2½ hour journey and costs Rs 5.95. It's advisable to book accommodation and transport in

Mudumalai Wildlife Sactuary

Main Roads
Metalled Tracks
Sanctuary Boundary
State Border
Elephant Migration Routes
Salt Licks
Water Holes

Bandipur Sanctuary (Karnataka)

Mysore

Moyar River

Kakkanhalla Check Post

Waterfalls

Masinagudi R.H. & Log House

Masinagudi Check Post & Range Office

Annai Katti R.H.

Sylvan Lodge

Thappakadu Reception Centre

Elephant Camp

Theppakodu R.

Range Office

Dormitory

Range Office

Abhayaranyan R.H.

Thorappolli Check Post

Wynad Sanctuary (Kerala)

Game Hut

Ooty

the sanctuary in advance either with the Forest Officer in Ooty on Coonoor Rd or at a Tamil Nadu Tourist Office. The scale of charges for the sanctuary is as follows:

Entrance fees:
  adults Rs 1, children Rs 0.50
  car Rs 5, jeep Rs 5, van Rs 7.50
  cameras Rs 2, movie cameras Rs 10
Hire charges for transport:
  jeep (up to six people): Rs 2/km
  van (up to eight people): Rs 3/km
  elephant rides (up to four people):
    Rs 20/elephant
Elephant rides are available between 6 and 10 am and again between 4 and 6 pm. If you're on your own there's no problem about finding space with another group. The elephants go crashing through the bush over a four to five km circuit and are great fun but you'll be lucky to see anything other than spotted deer, warthogs, buffalo and monkeys.

As far as places to stay are concerned, if you're relying on public transport then you'll have to stay either at Theppukadu or at Abhayaranyam which are both on the bus route. In any event, you first have to call at the Reception Centre where you have a booking or not. The following accommodation is available:

Abhayaranyam Rest House There are two suites here which cost Rs 5 for the first person and Rs 2.50 for each additional person. There is also a dormitory at the Range Office a short way from the Rest House for Rs 3 per person. Catering facilities are available.
Theppukadu Village The main place here is the *Sylvan Lodge* which has four suites at Rs 7.50 a single, Rs 11.25 a double and Rs 5 for each additional person. They also have a log house with three suites and a dormitory at Rs 3 per person. Meals are available here whether you are staying there or not

(good meals).

The Reception Centre has a dormitory attached to it with eight beds (four per room) which costs Rs 3 per person. There is an attached toilet and shower but no catering facilities. If you're staying here you can eat either at the two chai shops in the village or at the Sylvan Lodge. Baggage can be left safely at the Reception Centre whether you have a booking or not planning on staying for the night.
Masinagudi Village There are three possibilities here: *Masinagudi Rest House* which has three suites costing Rs 5 a single plus Rs 2.50 for each additional person, catering facilities are available. *Bamboo Banks Farm* (tel 22), accommodation here costs Rs 80 a single and Rs 135 a double with full board or Rs 40 a single and Rs 60 a double for bed and breakfast. *Mountania Rest House* (tel 37) where you can rent a de-luxe cottage with six beds for Rs 125 in the high season or Rs 100 in the low season; the same with three beds for Rs 75 in the high season and Rs 60 in the low season; the same again but with two beds for Rs 60 in the high season and Rs 50 in the low season. All the cottages have attached bathrooms. They also have a log cabin with 10 beds and common bathroom for Rs 8 per person in the high season and Rs 5 per person in the low season and a dormitory with 40 beds and four common bathrooms for Rs 10 per person in the high season and Rs 8 per person in the low season. Meals are available and the food is excellent. There is also a bar where you can get a drink without a liquor permit. Bookings can be made in advance at Safari Travels, opposite Union Church, Ooty (tel 3141).

Note that the Ooty-Mysore and Ooty-Hassan buses both stop at Theppukadu if there's anyone getting off or if they have spare seats. If not, they tend to drive straight through. If you're leaving the sanctuary then you have to make a determined effort to flag the bus down. On the other hand, it's relatively easy to have a word with people who arrive in their own transport and get yourself a lift back to either Ooty or Mysore or even to Masinagudi if you don't want to stay at Theppukadu for the night.

The best time to visit the sanctuary is between February and May though you can visit at any time of the year. Heavy rain is common in October and November.

Vedanthangal Water Birds Sanctuary
This is one of the most spectacular breeding grounds in India. Water fowl gather here for about six months of the year from October/November to March depending on the monsoons and peaks in December and January. At the height of the breeding season it's possible to see up to 30,000 birds at one time. The best time to visit is in the early morning or late afternoon. The best way to get there is via bus from Madras to Chingleput but you will have to hire transport to take you to the Forest Rest House. The only place to stay here is the *Forest Rest House* which has four suites at Rs 5 a single and Rs 7.50 a double plus Rs 4 for each additional person.

The main types of birds which come here to breed and nest include cormorants, egrets, herons, storks, ibises, spoonbills, grebes and pelicans. Many other species of migratory birds also visit the sanctuary.

Calimere Wildlife Sanctuary
Located on the east coast just south of the Pondicherry territory of Karaikal in Tanjore district, Point Calimere is noted for its congregation of black buck, spotted deer, wild pig and vast flocks of migratory waterfowl especially flamingoes. Every year in winter the tidal mud flats and marshes are covered with masses of birds — teals, shovellers, curlews, gulls, terns, plovers, sandpipers, shanks and herons. It's possible to see here up to 30,000 flamingoes at any one time. In the spring a different set of birds — the koels, mynas and barbets — are drawn here by the profusion of wild berries.

The best time to visit is between November and January. From April to June there is very little activity. The main rainy season is from October to December. You can get to Point Calimere either by rail on the Mayavaram-Thiruthuraipoondi section or by regular bus from either Tanjore or Mayavaram. A *Forest Rest House* is available with two suites which cost Rs 0.50 per person. Facilities are very basic and no meals are available.

Mundanthurai Tiger Sanctuary
One of the most recently created sanctuaries, Mundanthurai is located in the mountains near the border with Kerala. The nearest railway station is at Amabasamudram and there are regular buses from there to the sanctuary. As the name implies, this is principally a tiger sanctuary and the best time to visit is between January and September though you can visit at any time of year. The main rainy season is between October and December. Since you're most likely to see tigers in the very early morning or late evening you should stay here for the night. The Forest Department will arrange to take you around the sanctuary. Accommodation is in a *Forest Rest House* which has two suites costing Rs 2 a single, Rs 3 a double plus Rs 0.50 for each additional person. There is also a small charge for electricity.

Anamalai Wildlife Sanctuary
This is the third of the wildlife sanctuaries located in the mountains along the Tamil Nadu-Kerala border. Anamalai is south of Coimbatore and can be

reached either by regular bus from Coimbatore or by rail to Pollachi and then by bus to the sanctuary. The Reception Centre is located at Parambikulam dam. The major attractions at Anamalai are elephant, gaur, tiger, panther, spotted deer, wild boar, bear, porcupine and civet cats. The Nilgiri tahr, commonly known as ibex, can also be seen here. Transport through the sanctuary can be arranged by the Forest Department.

Accommodation is available at three places: *Forest Rest House* at Topslip, six suites are available here. *Varagaliar Rest House*, this is located deep inside the forest and offers basic accommodation but you must take your own provisions as there are no catering facilities. *Mount Stuart Rest House*, two suites are available here and meals can be provided. The sanctuary can be visited at any time of the year but the best

time of day to go is in the very early morning or late evening.

Guindy Deer Park

Located within the metropolitan boundaries of Madras city, this is the only place in the world where it is still possible to see fairly large numbers of the fast-dwindling species of Indian antelope (black buck). It also has small numbers of spotted deer, civet cats, jackal, mongoose and various species of monkey. There is also a reptillium within the park.

The Deer Park is adjacent to Raj Bhavan at Guindy and you can get there either by catching a commuter train from Beach Railway Station opposite the GPO or from Egmore Railway Station and getting off at Guindy Station. There are also regular service buses from Madras to Guindy.

Andaman & Nicobar Islands

Population: 130,000
Area: 8293 square km
Capital: Port Blair
Main languages: various tribal

In the middle of the Bay of Bengal half-way between India and Burma lies this string of over 300 richly-forested, tropical islands which reach almost to the tip of Sumatra. Ethnically, they are not a part of India and were, until fairly recently, peopled by several distinct tribes having different physiognomies and speaking different languages.

The tribes fall into three main groups. The Onges, concentrated mainly on Little Andaman, are a small, dark-complexioned tribe of hunters and gatherers who wear no clothes other than tassled genital decorations and are fond of colourful make-up. The Nicobaris, whose home is on Car Nicobar are a fair-complexioned people who have begun to adapt to contemporary Indian society. They live mainly on fish, coconuts and pigs and are organised into villages controlled by a village headman. The last group, the Shompens, are found on Great Nicobar. So far they have resisted integration into Indian society and tend to shy away from areas occupied by Indian immigrants from the mainland, prefering to lead their lives according to their own traditions.

The Indian Government is fond of eulogising its efforts to bring civilisation to these islands but, reading between the lines, it's obvious they regard these indigenous tribes as stone-age people and their attitude towards them is very condescending. In their efforts to develop the islands economically, the Indian government has completely disregarded the needs and land rights of the tribes and has encouraged massive immigration from the mainland — mainly of Tamils who were expelled from Sri Lanka — which has pushed population of these islands from 50,000 to 150,000 in just 15 years. It is little wonder that the islanders' culture is about to be swamped so, if you want to see anything of it, you will have to go there soon. This isn't as easy as you might imagine since not only is a permit required (in addition to any visa requirement for India as a whole) but there are numerous restrictions as to which parts you can visit on arrival.

The Andaman and Nicobar Islands were annexed by the Marathas from the mainland of India in the late 17th century. In the early 18th century they were the base of the Maratha admiral, Kanhoji Angre, whose navy harrassed British, Dutch and Portuguese merchant vessels at that time, frequently capturing them. Angre even managed to capture the British Governor of Bombay's yacht in 1713 and released it only after a ransom of powder and shot was delivered. Though attacked by the British and later by a combined British-Portuguese naval task force, Angre remained undefeated right up to his death in 1729.

The islands were finally annexed by

the British in the 19th century and used as a penal colony for Indian freedom fighters. The notorious 'cellular jail', one of the 'tourist attractions' of Port Blair, where many of the inmates were executed either judicially or clandestinely, was begun in the last decade of the 19th century and finished in 1908. During WW II the islands were occupied for a time by the Japanese but they were not welcomed as liberators and the local tribes took up guerrilla activities against them. When independence came to India they were incorporated into the Indian Union.

At present, a big effort is being made to develop the islands and vast tracts of forest have been cut down. There has been some replanting with 'economic' timber like teak but much of it has been turned over to rubber plantations. As for the climate, there is little seasonal variation. Continuous sea breezes keep the temperatures within the range 23-31°C but humidity stays around 80% all year. The south-west monsoons come to the islands between mid-May and October and the north-east monsoons between November and January. The best season to visit is between mid-November and mid-May.

Permits

All foreigners need a special permit before they can visit the Andaman and Nicobar Islands. You need to apply at least six weeks in advance of your proposed visit either to The Secretary, Government of India, Ministry of Home Affairs, New Delhi, India, or to your nearest Indian Embassy or Consulate. If you apply to the latter, they will forward your application on to New Delhi. Forms have to be filled in triplicate, three photos supplied and you must state the dates between which you want to be there. A two week stay is normally allowed. You need to think carefully about the dates you want to be there unless you're flying since the boats from Calcutta and Madras run on an *irregular* schedule.

What to See

For the sightseer, these islands don't

offer a great deal and probably the only reason you would come here would be to relax and/or visit the various tribes which live here. The Indian Tourist organisation run daily tours of the sights around Port Blair (the main settlement). These cost Rs 4.50 and include visits to the Cellular Jail, Chatham saw mills, the Anthropology Museum, the Fisheries Museum, Marina Park, Corbyn's Cove and the Cottage Industries Emporium.

Corbyn's Cove is the nearest beach to Port Blair (10 km) but is used by Air India package tours.

Places to Stay

Other than accommodation at Corbyn's Cove, South Andaman, all the available places to stay are controlled by various Indian Government departments (mostly the PWD and Forestry Departments) and the standard of accommodation is fairly basic. Charges for accommodation and meals at these latter places are standardised as follows:

Accommodation type	Sgl	Dbl
Dak Bungalows	Rs 20	Rs 20
Circuit Houses	Rs 15	Rs 20
Tourist Homes	Rs 10	Rs 20
Govt of India Guest Houses	Rs 10	Rs 20
Inspection Bungalows	Rs 10	Rs 20

Meals are available at the following charges:

meal	vegetarian	non-vegetarian
Breakfast	Rs 2	Rs 4
Lunch	Rs 5	Rs 8
Dinner	Rs 5	Rs 7

Government accommodation is available as follows:

South Andaman
Tourist Home, Haddo, Port Blair; *Tourist Home*, Corbyn's Cove, Port Blair; *Circuit House*, Haddo, Port Blair; *Government Guest House*, Haddo, Port Blair; *Dak Bungalow*, Haddo, Port Blair; *Inspection Bungalow*, Ferragunj;

Inspection Bungalow, Milletilak; *Guest House*, Hamfregunj; *Guest House*, Havelock Island; *Rest House*, Neil Island.

Other than the above there are the more expensive places catering largely to package tourists from the mainland;
Megapore Nest, Port Blair, rooms cost Rs 40 a single and Rs 80 a double for non air-con rooms and Rs 55 a single and Rs 110 a double for air-con rooms.
Nicobari Huts, Port Blair: These cost Rs 130 a double for non air-con and Rs 160 a double for air-con. There are no single rooms.
Centaur Beach Resort, Corbyn's Cove, Port Blair, rooms here cost Rs 200 a single and Rs 240 a double with air-con. This is the place that Air India uses for its package tours.

In addition to the above there are Rest Houses at Chidiatapu overlooking the sea on the southernmost tip of the island and the *Wright Myo Rest House* on the fringe of the forest. The Forestry Department also has a number of Rest Houses in the forest (contact the Forestry Department, Port Blair, for details of these).

Middle Andaman
Rest House, Betapur; *Rest House*, Kandamtala; *Rest House*, Rangat.

North Andaman
Rest House, Aerial Bay; *Rest House*, Diglipur; *Rest House*, Kadamtala; *Rest House*, Mayabunder; *Circuit House*, Mayabunder; *Rest House*, Parangara; *Rest House*, Tugapur.

Nicobars
Circuit House, Car Nicobar; *Inspection Bungalow*, Car Nicobar; *Guest House*, Kamorta Island.

Foreign exchange facilities are available at either the Cooperative Bank, near

Aberdeen Bazaar, Port Blair, or the State Bank of India, near the Deputy Commissioner's Office, Port Blair. The nearest hospital is Gobinda Ballabh Pant Hospital, Port Blair. Note that total prohibition is in force in these islands and alcoholic drinks are not available. It's definitely BYO.

Getting There

Flights Indian Airlines operate the following flights:

Calcutta-Port Blair: Depart Calcutta 6.20 am on Tuesdays and Fridays. Depart Port Blair 9 am Tuesdays and Fridays. The flight costs US$115 (one-way) and takes 2 hours.

Madras-Port Blair: Departs Madras Wednesdays and Sundays. Costs US$117 (one-way).

Boats The Shipping Corporation of India (13 Strand Rd, Calcutta 1) and their agents in Madras, K P V Sheikh Mohammed Rowther & Co (202 Linghi Chetty St, Madras 1 (tel 25756) operate three ships to the Andaman and Nicobar Islands every 15-20 days *but there is no regular schedule*. The disputes which occur in the shipping offices between intending Indian passengers (who do not require a permit) and the shipping clerks has to be seen to be believed! As a foreigner, your difficulties are compounded by the fact that you need a permit and that permit states the dates between which you are allowed to visit the islands. If these dates don't correspond with the departure and return of a ship then you might as well forget about going there — or fly — because the only way you can have the dates altered is to send your permit back to the Ministry of Home Affairs in New Delhi. Naturally this takes time and you cannot predict how much time it will take. Unfortunately, this isn't the only variable since tickets for the boats are issued only on the basis of the passenger list received at the ship-

ping offices from the authorities at Port Blair. It's necessary to make prior reservations with these people in Port Blair. For cabin class accommodation apply to Assistant Secretary, Chief Commissioner, Andaman and Nicobar Adminstration, Port Blair. For bunk accommodation apply to the Manager, Shipping Corporation of India, Port Blair. In your application you must state your name, father's name, address, nationality, purpose of visit, duration of stay, the approximate date you want to sail and the class of accommodation required.

If your luck holds out and/or you manage to ride out this ridiculously Kafkasque miasma then the prices of the various types of accommodation in the three ships are as follows:

	MV Harshavardhana	MV Andamans	SS Nancowry
deluxe cabins	Rs 558	Rs 513	Rs 558
A class cabins	Rs 513	Rs 500	Rs 500
B class cabins	Rs 389	Rs 488	Rs 389
C class cabins	Rs 355	—	Rs 100
air-con bunks	Rs 100	—	Rs 100
non air-con bunks	—	Rs 69	Rs 69

Note that the *SS Nancowry* is a passenger-cargo ship. Charges for food on board are Rs 8 a day in bunk class (Indian style) and Rs 28 a day in cabin class accommodation (choice of western or Indian style). The passage either from Calcutta or Madras takes two to three days. The ships stay in Port Blair for four days on average so if you don't have a lot of time at your disposal you could go there for just four days. The *MV Harshavardhana* is the quickest and most modern of the ships. There is a 50% reduction on the above fares for students (proof required).

Inter-Island Ferries

South Andaman Island There is a ferry around South Andaman Island three times daily at 6 am, 12.30 pm and 3 pm from the Fisheries Jetty, Port Blair, which calls at Bamboo Flat, Haddo Harbour, Dandus Point and Junglee Ghat.

Connections to the other islands Two ferries, the *Yerewa* and the *Onge* connect Port Blair with the other islands in the Andaman and Nicobar group on a once-weekly basis. Other small sea-going boats can be chartered from the Harbour Master, Port Blair (tel 528).

Glossary

Indian English is full of interesting little everyday expressions. Where as in New York you might get robbed by a mugger in India it will be a *dacoit* who relieves you of your goods. Politicians may employ strong arm heavies known in India as *goondas*. There are a whole string of Indian terms for strikes, lock outs and sit ins — Indians can have *hartals, bhands* and *gheraos* for example. And then there are all those Indian servants — children get looked after by *ayahs,* your house (and your *godown* if you have one) is guarded by a *chowkidar* (but they're reputed to be a lazy bunch much given to lying around on *charpois*), and when the toilet needs cleaning there is no way your *bearer* is going to do it, that requires calling in a *sweeper*.

Then there are all the religious terms, the numerous Hindu gods, their attendants, consorts, vehicles and symbols. The multiplicity of religions in India also provide a whole series of terms for temples, shrines, tombs or memorials. It's surprising also how many Indian terms have crept into everyday English usage. We can sit out on a *verandah,* wear *pyjamas* (or *dungarees* and *sandals* and they may well be *khaki*), *shampoo* our hair, visit the *jungle,* worry about protecting our *loot* — they're all Indian words.

The glossary that follows is just a sample of words you may come across during your Indian wanderings. See 'food' and 'religion' for lots more.

Acha — OK.

Acharya — revered teacher, originally a spiritual guide or perceptor.

Anikut — weir or dam.

Anna — one sixteenth of a rupee, now extinct but still used in market place conversation, ie eight annas is 50 paise, four annas is 25 paise.

Arrack — spirit drink made from coconut sap or rice wine.

Ashram — spiritual college come retreat.

Avalokitesvara — one of the Buddha's most important disciples.

Ayah — children's nurse.

Ayurvedic — Indian natural and herbal medicine.

Baba — religious master but also used in a more common manner.

Babu — lower level clerical worker.

Bagh — garden.

Bahadur — brave or chivalrous, honorofic title.

Baksheesh — tip, bribe or simply donation to a beggar.

Bandar — port or harbour.

Bandh — general strike.

Banian — T-shirt or under vest.

Baniya — money lender.

Banyan — Indian fig tree.

Baoli — well, particularly a steep well with landings and galleries.

Basti — Jain temple.

Bazaar — market area, a market town is called a bazaar.

Bearer — rather like a butler.

Beedis — small hand rolled cigars.

Begum — Moslem lady of high rank.

Betel — nut of the betel tree, chewed as a mild intoxicant.

Bhagvadgita — Krishna's lessons to Arjuna, part of the Mahabharata.

Bhang — lassi and charas mixture.

Bhisti — water carrier.

Bodhisattva — near Buddha, follower of Buddha.

Bo-tree — ficus religiosa, the tree under which the Buddha attained enlightenment.

Brahmin — highest Indian caste.

Bund — embankment or dyke.

Burka — one piece garment which totally covers Moslem women.

Cantonment — administrative and military area of a British raj era town.

Caste — what your station in life is.

Chaitya — Buddhist temple.

Chakra — focus of your spiritual power, disc like weapon of Vishnu.

Chalo, chalo, chalo — 'let's go, let's go, let's go' — what you yell as the bus leaves.

Chance List — the wait list on Indian Airline flights.

Chang — Tibetan rice beer.

Chaoultries — dharamsalas in the south.

Chappals — sandals.

Chappati — unleavened Indian bread.

Charas — ganga.

Charpoi — Indian rope bed.

Chat — general term for small snacks, papris etc.

Chatri — tomb or mausoleum.
Chauri — fly whisk.
Chela — pupil or follower, as George Harrison was to Ravi Shankar.
Chillum — pipe part of a hookah, commonly used to describe the small pipes for smoking ganga.
Chorten — Tibetan word for stupa.
Chowk — courtyard or market place.
Chowkidah — nightwatchman, often a cook as well.
Cong (I) — Congress Party (India) or Congress Party (Indira) depending on how cynical you are.
Country Liquor — locally produced liquor.
CPI — Communist Party of India.
CPI (M) — the Communisty Party of India (Marxist), it's the bigger, more powerful party and is currently in power in West Bengal (Calcutta).
Crore — 10 million.
Curd — yoghurt
Cutcherry — office or building for public business.

Dacoit — robber, particularly armed robber.
Dacoity — to suffer at the hands of a dacoit.
Dargah — shrine or place of burial of a Moslem saint.
Darshan — offering or audience with someone, usually a guru.
Darwaza — gateway or door.
Dhal — lentil soup, what most of India lives on.
Dharamsala — religious guest house.
Dharma — Buddhist teachings.
Dhobi — clothes washerman.
Dhopalta — scarf worn by Punjabi women.
Dhoti — like a longhi but the cloth is then pulled up between your legs.
Diwan — principal officer in a princely state, royal court or council.
Diwan-i-Am — Hall of Public Audience.
Diwan-i-Khas — Hall of Private Audience.
Dooli — cover litter or stretcher, you may still see elderly tourists being carried around some sights in a dooli.
Dravidian — ornate southern Indian architectural style, also southern Indian race.
Durbar — royal court, also used to describe a government.
Durga — same as Kali, terrible manifestation of Parvati.
Dwarpal — door keeper, sculpture beside the doorways to Hindu or Buddhist shrines.

Fakir — accurately a Moslem who has taken

a vow of poverty but also applied to Hindu ascetics such as sadhus.
Fenni — spirit drink made from cashews, found in Goa.
Firman — a royal order or grant.
Freaks — young westerners wandering India, the '60s live!

Gaddi — throne of a Hindu prince.
Ganesh — god of learning, elephant headed son of Shiva and Parvati, probably the most popular god in the whole Hindu pantheon.
Ganga — hashish.
Garuda — man-bird vehicle of Vishnu.
Ghari — horse carriage.
Ghat — steps or landing on a river, place where corpses are cremated.
Ghazal — Urdu songs, sad love themes.
Ghee — all purpose cooking oil.
Gherao — lock in, where the management locks the workers in!
Godown — wharehouse.
Gompa — Tibetan-Buddhist monastery.
Gonds — aboriginal Indian race, now mainly found in the jungles in central India.
Goonas — ruffians or toughs, political parties often have gangs of goondas.
Gopis — cow herd girls, Krishna was very fond of them.
Gopuram — soaring pyramidal gateway tower of a Dravidian temple.
Gurdwara — Sikh temple.
Guru — teacher or holy man.

Haji — a Moslem who has made the pilgrimage (haj) to Mecca.
Hanuman — monkey god.
Harijan — literally 'Children of God' but actually it still means simply the lowest caste, the untouchables.
Hartal — strike.
Haveli — traditional mansions with interior courtyards, particularly in Rajasthan and Gujurat.
Hookah — water pipe for smoking tobacco.
Howdah — framework for carrying people on an elephant's back.
Hypothecated — Indian equivalent of leased, you often see a small sign on a taxi or auto-rickshaw that the vehicle is 'hypothecated' to some bank or other.

Idgah — open enclosure to the west of a town where prayers are offered during the Moslem festival of Id.
Imam — Moslem leader.

Imambara — tomb of a Shi'ite Moslem holy man.

IMFL — Indian Made Foreign Liquor — beer or spirits produced in India.

Indra — king of the Vedic gods.

Jaggery — hard, brown sugar-like sweetener made from kitul palm sap.

Janata — people, thus the Janata Party is the People's Party.

Jauhor — ritual mass suicide by immolation, traditionally performed by Rajput women at times of military defeat to avoid being dishonoured by their captors.

Ji — honorific that can be added to the end of almost anything — thus Baba-ji.

Juggernauts — huge, extravagantly decorated temple 'cars' which are dragged through the streets during Hindu festivals.

Jumkahs — ear-rings.

Jyotorlinga — 12 holy Shiva shrines in India are known as the 12 Jyotorlingas.

Kachahri — see Cutchery.

Kadi — homespun cloth, Mahatma Gandhi spent much energy in encouraging people to spin their own Kadi cloth rather than buy imported English material.

Kali — Parvati's terrible side.

Karmachario — university term.

Kartikiya — God of war, Shiva's son.

Kata — Tibetan prayer shawl, traditionally given to a lama when one is brought into his presence.

Khan — Moslem honorific title.

Kibla — niche in the wall to which Moslems look when praying in order to face Mecca.

Kothi — residence, house or mansion.

Kotwali — police station.

Krishna — Vishnu's eighth incarnation, he's often coloured blue.

Kundalini — coiled serpent, the manifestation of Kali, the place at the base of your spine where your shakti resides.

Lakh — 100,000.

Lama — Tibetan-Buddhist priest or holy man.

Lassi — very refreshing yoghurt and iced water drink.

Lathi — baton, what Indian police hit you with if you get in the way of a lathi charge.

Laxmi (or Lakshmi) — Vishnu's consort, goddess of wealth, very popular in Bombay.

Lingam — phallic symbol, symbol of Shiva.

Lok — people.

Lok Dal — political party, one of the components of the Janata party.

Lok Sabha — lower house in the Indian parliament, comparable to the House of Representatives or House of Commons.

Longhi — loin cloth wrapped around your thighs.

Mahabharata — Vedic epics, the main Indian holy book.

Mahal — house or palace, queen.

Maharaja — Raja, Hindu king or prince.

Mahatma — literally 'great soul.'

Mahayana — large vehicle Buddhism.

Mahout — elephant rider/master.

Maidan — open place or square.

Mali — gardener.

Mandala — Tibetan geometrical and astrological representation of the world.

Mandir — temple.

Mandapam — pillared pavilion in front of a temple.

Mani stone — stone carved with the Tibetan-Buddhist chant 'Om Mani Padme Hum' — 'Hail to the jewel in the lotus'.

Mantra — prayer formula or chant.

Mara — Buddist god of death, has three eyes and holds the wheel of life.

Maratha (Mahratta) — war-like central Indian race which often controlled much of India and gave the Moghuls a lot of trouble.

Masjid — mosque, Jami Masjid is the Friday Mosque or main mosque.

Maund — now largely superseded unit of weight.

Math — monastery.

Mela — a fair.

Memsahib — European married lady, from 'madam-sahib', still more widely used than you'd think.

Mendi — ornate patterns painted on women's hands and feet for important festivals, particularly in Rajasthan.

Mihrab — see Kibla.

Moghul — golden period of Indian history from the emperor Babur to Aurangzeb, the last powerful Moghul ruler.

Monsoon — rainy period from around June to October, when it rains virtually every day.

Moorcha — mob march or protest march.

Mughal — same as Moghul.

Muezzin — one who calls Moslems to prayer from the minaret.

Mullah — Moslem priest.

Munshi — writer, secretary or teacher of languages.

Naga — snake or a person from Nagaland.

Nandi — bull, vehicle of Shiva and usually found at Shiva temples.

Narayan — an incarnation of Vishnu.

Narsimha (or Narsingh) — man-lion incarnation of Vishnu.

Nautch Girls — dancing girls, a nautch is a dance.

Nawab — nobleman or governor.

Naxalites — ultra-leftist political movement, started in northern part of West Bengal where it appeared as a rebellion against landlords by peasants. Characterised by extreme violence it originated in the village of Naxal but is now fairly subdued in West Bengal but still exists in Uttar Pradesh.

Nilakantha — form of Shiva with blue throat from swallowing poison that would have destroyed the world.

Nirvana — the ultimate aim of Buddhist existence, a state where one leaves the cycle of existence and does not have to suffer further rebirths.

Nizam — hereditary title of the rulers of Hyderabad.

Nullah — ditch or small stream.

Padyatra — 'foot journey', politicians do it to raise support at the village level.

Pagoda — Buddhist religious monument composed of a solid hemisphere containing relics of the Buddha — also known as a dagoba, stupa or chedi.

Palanquin — box like enclosure carried on poles on four men's shoulders, occupant sat inside on a seat.

Pali — the original language in which the Buddhist scriptures were recorded, scholars still look to the original Pali texts for the true interpretations.

Pan — betel nut plus the chewing additives.

Pandit — teacher or wiseman, often used in Kashmir where there are many Pandits, sometimes used deprecatingly to mean a bookworm.

Peepul — fig tree, especially a Bo tree.

Peon — lowest grade clerical worker.

Peshalsawari — (open class???)

Pice — a quarter of an anna.

Pinjrapol — animal hospital maintained by Jains.

Pooja — offering or prayers.

Pranayama — study of breath control.

Prasad — food offering, something you can eat.

Pukkah — proper, very much a Raj era term.

Punkah — cloth fan, swung by pulling a cord.

Puranas — the ancient Hindu scriptures.

Purdah — isolation in which Moslem women are kept.

Raga — somewhat equivalent to a piece, division or movement of western music.

Raj — rule or sovereignty but specifically applied to the period of British rule in India.

Raja — king.

Rajput — Hindu warrior caste, royal rulers of Rajasthan.

Ramayana — the story of Rama and Sita and their conflict with Ravana, one of the longest lasting of Indian legends and retold in various forms almost throughout South-East Asia.

Rani — wife of a princely ruler or a ruler in her own right.

Rath — temple chariot or car used in religious festivals.

Raths — rock cut Dravidian temples at Mahabalipuram.

Rickshaw — two wheeled vehicle in which one or two passengers are pulled. Only in Calcutta and one or two hill stations do the old man-powered rickshaws still exist. In towns they are now generally bicycle-rickshaws.

Rishis — great sages of old nowadays applied to any distinguished poet, philosopher or spiritual personality.

Sadhu — wandering holy man, generally Saivaites, generally laymen who have given everything up to seek religious salvation.

Sahib — 'lord', title applied to any gentlemen and most Europeans.

Saivaite (Shaivate) — follower of Lord Shiva .

Salwar blouse worn by Punjabi women.

Samadhi being interred alive, a popular yagna feat.

Sati — 'honourable woman', what a woman becomes if she throws herself on her husband's funeral pyre, although banned a century or so ago there are still occasional satis being performed.

Satsang — discourse by a swami.

Satyagraha — protest, involving a fast, in existence on truth and non-violence.

Sepoy — private in the infantry.

Serai — place for accommodation of travellers, specifically a caravanserai.

Shakti — spiritual energy, life force or strength.

Shikar — hunting expedition, now virtually extinct.

Shikara — gondola like boat used on Dal Lake in Kashmir.

Shirting — material shirts are made out of.

Sikhara — Hindu temple spire or temple.

Sirdar — leader or commander.

Sitar — Indian stringed instrument, very difficult to tune — which did not prevent it from becoming a '60s craze.

Sof — aniseed seeds, comes with the bill after a meal and you chew a pinch of it as a digestive.

Sonam — karma built up in successive reincarnations.

Sufi — ascetic Moslem mystic.

Suiting — material suits are made out of.

Swami — lower grade holy man.

Sweeper — lowest caste servant who performs the most menial of tasks.

Syce — groom.

Tabla — small drums, almost like bongo drums.

Tamil — people of south-east India.

Tank — artificial water storage lake.

Tanka — rectangular Tibetan painting on cloth.

Tantric Buddhism — Tibetan Buddhism with strong sexual and occult overtones.

Tatty — woven grass screen which is wetted and hung outside windows in the hot season, it provides a remarkably effective system of air-cooling.

Tempo — noisy three wheeler public transport vehicle.

Thali — traditional South Indian 'all you can eat' vegetarian meal, very widespread and an excellent, tasty meal — the name derives from the 'thali' plate the food is served on.

Theravada — small vehicle Buddhism.

Thirthayatara — sort of pilgrimage.

Thug — follower of thuggee, religious inspired ritual murderers in the last century.

Tiffin — snack, particularly around lunchtime.

Tirthankars — 24 Jain teachers.

Toddy — mildly alcoholic drink tapped from the palm tree.

Tonga — two wheeled horse or pony carriage.

Tope — grove of trees, usually mangoes.

Topi — sun hat much used by the British in the Raj era.

Torana — architrave over temple entrance.

Trimurti — three faced Shiva image.

Tripitaka — the 'three baskets', one of the classical Buddhist scriptures.

Untouchable — lowest caste for whom the most menial tasks are reserved, the name derives from the fact that higher caste risk defilement if they should touch one.

Upanishads — ancient Vedic scripts.

Vanaspati — cooking oil, edible oils.

Varuna — supreme Vedic god.

Vedas — ancient spiritual texts.

Vihar — monastery.

Vimana — principle part of a Hindu temple.

Wallah — person, can be added on to almost anything, thus dhobi-wallah (clothes washer), taxi-wallah (taxi driver).

Wazir — Prime Minister.

Yagna — religious self mortification, such as a snake-yagna where you sit in a cage full of snakes trying to break the Guinness Book of Records.

Yoni — vagina, female fertility symbol.

Zamindar — landowner.

Zenana — area of a high class Moslem household where the women are secluded.

Index

687

LONELY PLANET NEWSLETTER

We collect an enormous amount of information here at Lonely Planet. Apart from our research we also get a steady stream of letters from people out on the road — some of them are just one line on a postcard, others go on for pages. Plus we always have airmail to the ground for the latest on cheap airfares, new visa regulations, borders opening and closing. A lot of this information goes into our new editions or update supplements, in reprints. But we'd like to make better use of this information so starting in November '88 we're going to produce a quarterly newsletter packed full of the latest news from out on the road. It will appear in February, May, August and November of each year. If you'd like an airmailed copy of the most recent newsletter just send us A$1.50 (A$1 within Australia) or A$5 (A$4 in Australia) for a year's subscription.

LONELY PLANET NEWSLETTER

We collect an enormous amount of information here at Lonely Planet. Apart from our research we also get a steady stream of letters from people out on the road — some of them are just one line on a postcard, others go on for pages. Plus we always have an ear to the ground for the latest on cheap airfares, new visa regulations, borders opening and closing. A lot of this information goes into our new editions or 'update supplements' in reprints. But we'd like to make better use of this information so, starting in November '81 we're going to produce a quarterly newsletter packed full of the latest news from out on the road. It will appear in February, May, August and November of each year. If you'd like an airmailed copy of the most recent newsletter just send us A$1.50 (A$1 within Australia) or A$5 (A$4 in Australia) for a year's subscription.

The Authors

Geoff Crowther was born in Yorkshire, England and started his travelling days as a teenage hitch-hiker. Later, after many short trips around Europe, two years in Asia and Africa and short spells in the overgrown fishing village of Hull and on the bleak and beautiful Cumberland fells, Geoff got involved with the London underground information centre BIT. He helped put together their first, tatty, duplicated overland guides and was with them right through to the end. With Lonely Planet Geoff has researched and written *Africa on the Cheap* and *South America on a Shoestring* as well as this book for which he also drew the majority of the maps. Geoff now lives on an old banana plantation near the New South Wales/Queensland border in Australia. In late 1981 he's once more on the road researching an all new Lonely Planet guidebook.

Prakash A Raj was born in Nepal and later spent five years at university in Michigan, Nevada and Massachusetts in the USA. Following that he studied for a year in the Netherlands, travelled extensively in Europe and then returned to Nepal where he worked on the Kathmandu English language daily as a journalist and also for the Nepalese government's planning agency. For Lonely Planet Prakash researched and wrote *Kathmandu & the Kingdom of Nepal.* He has also written several other books about Nepal and his life there in both English and Nepali.

Tony Wheeler was born in England but spent most of his younger years overseas due to his father's occupation with British Airways. Those years included a lengthy spell in Pakistan, a shorter period in the West Indies and all his high school years in the USA. He returned to England to do a university degree in engineering, worked for a short time as an automotive design engineer, returned to university again to do an MBA then dropped out on the Asian trail with his wife Maureen. They've been travelling, writing and publishing travel guidebooks ever since. Tony has written seven of the Lonely Planet series including *South-East Asia on a Shoestring* and has also co-authored the Apa Insight Guides to Thailand and the Philippines. In late 1981 they will be on the road again, researching another new guide but this time accompanied by their daughter Tashi, who was born soon after they returned from their stint in India.

*   earlier editions were titled *Across
    Asia on the Cheap*
** available only in Australasia

Lonely Planet travel guides are available around the world. If you can't find them, ask
your bookshop to order them from one of the distributors listed below. For countries
not listed or if you would like a free copy of our latest booklist write to Lonely Planet
in Australia.

Australia —Lonely Planet Publications Pty Ltd, PO Box 88, South Yarra, Victoria 3141.
Canada — Milestone Publications, Box 6006, Victoria, British Columbia, V8P 5L4.
Hong Kong — The Book Society, GPO Box 7804, Hong Kong.
India — UBS Distributors, 5 Ansari Rd, New Delhi, 110002.
Japan — Intercontinental Marketing Corp, IPO Box 5056, Tokyo 100-31.
Malaysia — see Singapore
Nepal — see India
Netherlands — Nilsson & Lamm bv, Postbus 195, Pampuslaan 212, 1680 AD Weesp.
New Zealand — Caveman Press, PO Box 1458, Dunedin.
Papua New Guinea — Gordon & Gotch (PNG), PO Box 3395, Port Moresby.
Singapore — MPH Distributors (S) Pte Ltd, 71-77 Stamford Rd, Singapore 0617
Thailand — Chalermnit, 1-2 Erawan Arcade, Bangkok
UK — Roger Lascelles, 16 Holland Park Gardens, London, W14 8DY.
USA (West) — Bookpeople, 2940 Seventh St, Berkeley, CA 94710.
USA (East) — Hippocrene Books, 171 Madison Ave, New York, NY 10016.
West Germany — Buchvertrieb Gerda Schettler, Postfach 64, D-3415 Hattorf a H.